Masters
of the
Mystical Rose

MAREE MOORE

Joshua Books

joshuabooks.com

Joshua Books
P.O. Box 5149, Maroochydore BC
Queensland Australia 4558

All correspondence to the publisher
at the above address.

© Copyright Maree Moore
2005

All rights reserved.
This book may not be reproduced, wholly or in part,
or transmitted in any form whatsoever
without written permission, except by a reviewer
who may quote brief passages in a review.
All enquiries to the publisher.

ISBN 0 9751594 8 8

Category: Religious and Theology: History: Ancient Mysteries: Author

Joshua Books

joshuabooks.com

About the Author

Maree Moore was born in Perth, Western Australia.
From early childhood onwards, she accepted that some of the unusual experiences which occurred in her life (which the Irish call 'Fey' or 'Second Sight') were par for the course and attributed them to her Irish ancestral background.

After graduating from College, Maree worked for the Education Department and then travelled extensively throughout Asia and Europe, eventually working in London, Glasgow and Belfast in the United Kingdom. Always fascinated with history and mythology, (particularly Irish/Celtic mythology), her knowledge increased as she travelled.

Upon returning home to Australia in 1967, Maree joined Qantas, the Australian Airline company, where she worked as a Public Relations Officer and later as a travel consultant. Whilst working with Qantas, she met her future husband. After her marriage in 1970, Maree and her husband were transferred to Hong Kong where they lived for two years. Upon returning home to Australia, they raised a family of two children, a son and a daughter.

In the latter years, as the unusual experiences continued, with an unquenchable thirst for more knowledge, Maree decided to attend classes based on various forms of Christianity and esoteric spirituality, as most do when they seek the meaning of life. The result of such classes, plus a great deal of study brought her into contact with the 'Ascended Masters'.

After receiving her first visitation in 1993 by an 'invisible' person, dressed in a Knights Templar uniform, who identified himself as the 'Master of the Rose', and by a subsequent visitation by the Archangel Raphael, Maree realised that she was being chosen to put forth into the world more knowledge of their existence and of the role they play in assisting humanity evolve in the 'Divine Plan' for Earth's destiny.

With continual guidance by the Masters, Maree commenced her first book titled *The Masters of the Mystical Rose, A History of the Grail Family.*

In 2001, Maree was 'guided' to return to the United Kingdom, where she carried out further research in Ireland and Scotland. Upon her return home to Australia, she commenced the writing of *The Dove The Rose And The Sceptre, In Search of the Ark of the Covenant,* a sequel to the *Masters of the Mystical Rose, A History of the Grail Family.*

What others have said...

Congratulations on a wonderful text. You have presented the material in a rhythmic and very digestible fashion. I am proud that an Australian author should have taken so much time, care and attention with what I regard as a topic having a most profound impact on who we are today and how we got here. Great Bibliography! The laudation I am giving you is richly deserved.
Guy Perrin, New South Wales, Australia

One of the greatest books I own is 'The Masters of the Mystical Rose' by Maree Moore.
Don Samples, USA

Whilst I was in Glastonbury recently, I was in a book shop and the book 'Masters of the Mystical Rose - A History of the Grail Family' fairly flew off the book shelf and into my hands. As I excitedly began to browse, I was amazed to find quotes from my book 'St Germain - Twin Souls & Soulmates'. There was a down-pouring of quickening energy that I felt compelled to follow through by contacting you. Of course, I went ahead and purchased the book and then upon arriving back in Mt Shasta, there was your book again at the Golden Bough Bookshop! When reading your wonderful book, there was a great down-pouring of energy and the Presence of St Germain, Kuthumi and Anna. Thank you so much for all the historical research you put into 'The Masters of the Mystical Rose'.
Claire Heartsong, Author, Mt Shasta, USA

Your book is truly amazing. I couldn't put it down, I just wanted to keep learning more. Congratulations on all the time and effort you put into this great work.
Phyllis Williams, Toronto, Canada

I have just finished reading your book 'The Masters of the Mystical Rose' and thoroughly enjoyed it. Although Australian by birth, my ancestors are Celtic Scottish and a great deal of our family history is tied up in the myths and legends which you write of in your text. Your book has certainly triggered my interest in the whole subject and as a result, I have decided to take some long overdue leave next year and visit Scotland.
Jeff Logan, Lecturer, Curtin University of Western Australia

I wanted to drop you a line and express my appreciation of all the work that you put into 'The Masters of the Mystical Rose'. I don't believe the majority of people understood the Teachings of the Master Jesus - it all became too bogged down with religious fanaticism. Your book changed my life.
Ferdinand, Mareeba, Queensland, Australia

The wonderful script is fantastic, everything I have studied or come across, was placed into order and little gaps were filled. I have had some wonderful spiritual experiences myself so you can imagine my excitement to feel the connection to everything in the script of 'The Masters of the Mystical Rose'.
Bev, Sydney, New South Wales, Australia

I have to say that I was most impressed with your book - beautifully handled and researched.
Reviewer, Bantam Books, London, UK

I was in New Zealand recently for a Grail conference and whilst browsing through a book store in Auckland, I found your book 'The Masters of the Mystical Rose'. At the moment of writing to you, I am half way through it and really enjoying it. When I read your introduction about your experience with the beautiful scent of the roses, I could really relate to how you felt because I have had a similar experience myself.
Isabella, Perth, Western Australia

My wife and I just fell in love with the book, it is truly wonderful. This book is written in such a loving way and has a great energy about it. I was sorry when I had come to the end....I still wanted more. Although we purchased your book 'The Masters of the Mystical Rose' in the U.S.A. we also saw it at the Chalice Well Book Shop in Glastonbury, U.K. I have recommended it to all my spiritual friends and they love it. We can't wait until your next book, so hurry up and get writing!
Jim & Nancy Griffith, Detroit, Michigan, USA

Your book is absolutely fascinating and certainly proves a case for the Masters.
James Stewart McDonald, Lawyer, Perth, Western Australia

Your book is like an encyclopaedia, but upon reflection it is more a Handbook along Life's Way. I am also very impressed with the Bibliographies.
Joan Hamilton, New Zealand

I really enjoyed your book 'The Masters of the Mystical Rose'. I have been following St Germain and Kuthumi for a long time now, and your book has endless fascinating information. One beautiful work has us Celts and Druids. Thank you.
William Weekes, Santa Fe, New Mexico

I do enjoy your book immensely and find that I often re-read sections which really interest me.
Lynda Collier, New South Wales, Australia

My friends and I have devoured your book of 'The Masters of the Mystical Rose' and refer to it regularly with excitement.
C. Andrews, Sydney, New South Wales, Australia

A fascinating work so thoroughly researched.
Derek Rowlinson, Ulster Books, Northern Ireland

Your book is truly amazing and fascinating; my husband who is an editor was most impressed, especially with the Bibliographies which accented the amount of research undertaken.
V. Poole, Sydney, Canada

Congratulations on your book, may it prove to be a best-seller.
Edmund Harold, Author, Sydney, New South Wales, Australia

Your book is the perfect book for the individual seeking in-depth information, revelations and a wider appreciation of the spiritual journey itself.
Beryl, The Crystal Dolphin Book Shop, Mandurah, Western Australia

Your writing is very thorough and incredibly neatly woven as a beautiful tapestry should be.
Lesley Williams-Halverson, Author, Carina, Queensland

CONTENTS

"The spirits of truth and falsehood
Struggle within the heart of man;
Truth born out of the spring of Light,
Falsehood from the well of darkness.
And according as a man inherits truth
So will he avoid darkness."

(Essenes' Manual of Discipline)

"I am the Fountain of Light,
I am the Universe,
I am all Consciousness,
I am the Spirit of Light,
Deep unconditional and forever,
My Gift to the Light which is around me
is the spark of all life;
I carry it freely, generously;
In purity of the Soul"

(Prayer of the Cathars)

"Towards the close of each century,
there will be an outpouring of spirituality
during which time some one or more persons
have appeared in the world as advisers
at a critical time in history."

(Madame Helena Blavatsky)

"I am a servant of posterity; for these things require some ages for the ripening of them...always desiring with extreme fervency, to have that which has never yet been attempted, now not to be attempted in vain, to wit: to release man out of their necessities and miseries." (Francis Bacon - St Germain)

"The end which Bacon proposed for himself was the multiplying of human enjoyments and the mitigation of human sufferings. This was the object of his speculations, in every department of science...in natural philosophy, in legislation, in politics, in morals." (Macaulay)

Acknowledgements

**This book is dedicated to the Masters of the Great White Brotherhood,
'Masters of the Rose' - St Germain, Kuthumi, El Morya,
Madame Helena Blavatsky and Edgar Cayce.**

I would like to particularly thank my children Michael and Anna, my mother Kitty and Michael Hugh for their loving encouragement and unfailing support which they have given me throughout the duration of the compilation of this story. My gratitude also goes to my publisher, John Bannister, for his enthusiastic support.

Acknowledgement is given to all the authors of the books which have been important sources of information utilized in this story and as they are too numerous to mention individually, the ones from which the most information has been obtained, are specifically mentioned.

As a member of the Francis Bacon Research Trust, Warwick, U.K., I received a great deal of support from Peter Dawkins and his wife Sarah. I am indebted to Peter for his letters of encouragement, and for the assistance and permission that he gave me to utilize within my own book, quotations, from his own work. His numerous works, based upon his knowledge of Francis Bacon and his esoteric knowledge, have been of great inspiration to me and I hope it will be the same for others. Peter channels information from the 'Master R' (Master of the Rose, also known as the Master Ragoczy and as St Germain), who was once Sir Francis Bacon who wrote under the pseudonym of Shakespeare, the 'Spearer of the Truth'.

Peter is the author of *Arcadia, The Great Vision, Dedication To The Light, The Virgin Ideal, Francis Bacon, Herald of the New Age*, and numerous other books on the history of Francis Bacon. He is a world-wide recognised authority on the Baconian-Rosicrucian philosophies and Ancient Wisdom teachings, including especially the wisdom enshrined within the Shakespearian Plays. Peter has spent years deciphering the codes left behind for posterity in the works of Francis Bacon who wrote the Shakespearian plays and he is the Founder-Director of the Francis Bacon Research Trust. He is also a specialist in sacred architecture and a pioneer in the rediscovery of landscape temples, earth energies and the Western geomantic tradition and undertakes several tours each year at which time he gives lectures on these subjects.

Other wonderful recommended sources of information on the subject of Francis Bacon (St Germain) which have been utilized in this story, and to which grateful acknowledgement is given, are *Francis Bacon's Personal Life Story*, (1986) by the late Alfred Dodd to whom I pay tribute for the enormous effort he put into his research; Dr Raymond Bernard's *The Great Secret, Count Saint Germain* (1960); *Comte De St Germain* (1985) by Isabel Cooper-Oakley; *A Pioneer, In Memory Of*

Delia Bacon (1959) by Martin Pares, and *The Hidden Life In Freemasonry* (1926) by the late C.W. Leadbeater.

My gratitude also goes to Paul Broadhurst, Pendragon Press, Cornwall, U.K., author of *The Sun And The Serpent,* and *The Arthurian Mythos* for all the useful information that he has exchanged with me which helped to contribute towards many interesting subjects in this book, particularly on the subject of the Arthurian and Merlin legends and the history of Cornwall and Tintagel. Paul and his friend Hamish Miller, who has appeared in several British T.V. programmes, are authors whose speciality is researching and tracing the earth's sacred energies known in Britain as the Mary/Michael energy lines.

Sincere thanks also goes to the author of *The Occult Conspiracy*, (1987), Michael Howard from Wales, who assisted me with information and gave me permission to quote appropriate passages from his own impressive and thought-provoking book.

Grateful acknowledgement is given to Edmund Harold, author of *Second Sight,* for the assistance and permission that he gave me to use knowledge that he had obtained and utilised in his own books.

Sincere thanks to Simon Peter Fuller, author of *Rising Out of Chaos,* who contacted me on one of his visits to Western Australia and gave me permission to quote from his own work, and my thanks to Ross for providing me with information about the Cathars which he and Simon Peter Fuller collected on their inspirational and sentimental journey to the land of the Cathars in 1998.

My gratitude also goes to the author/historian William De Burgh, (whose family were originally of Norman descent and who were granted lands in Ireland during the reign of King John), of the Stirling Historical Library for the kind assistance he rendered me and for the useful information that he relayed to me regarding Sir James Stirling and Sir Joseph Banks. His knowledge of our local and Irish history was most informative, as was the book titled *Land Looking West* by local author, Malcolm Uren.

Thanks also to the Dublin Library, the library of the W.A. Theosophical Society, AMORC, and Adyar Bookshop in Sydney for their assistance in supplying me with the necessary books for research, which when ordered, arrived promptly.

Grateful acknowledgement is given to the following authors for useful information, which has been utilized from their books: Robert Graves, author/poet who wrote the remarkably detailed work titled *The White Goddess* (published in 1945) which was a most wonderful source of information, particularly on ancient mythology and Celtic mythology; Florence Marian McNeil, author of *Iona, The History of Saint Columba* (1920); John Allegro, author of *The Dead Sea Scrolls* (1956); Mary Ellen Carter who under the editorship of Hugh Lynn Cayce, wrote the book titled *Edgar Cayce On Prophecy*; Arnold J. Toynbee, author of *A Study of*

History Volumes 1, 2 and 3 (1934); William Foxwell Albright, author of *From The Stone Age To Christianity* (1957); Merrill F. Unger, author of *Archaeology And The Old Testament* (1954); Michael Baigent, Richard Leigh and Henry Lincoln, authors of *The Holy Blood And The Holy Grail* (1996) and *The Messianic Legacy* (1996); Peter Lemesurier, author of *The Armageddon Script* (1981); Christopher Knight and Robert Lomas, authors of *The Hiram Key* (1996) and *The Second Messiah* (1997); Dr Paul Brunton, author of *A Search In Secret Egypt* (1973); Michele Brown, BBC and ITV reporter for her book titled *Baby Name Book* (1985) which contains an amazing collation of the origin of historical names and historical facts throughout the centuries, and to Francis Hitching, author of *The World Atlas Of Mysteries* (1978).

My sincere thanks to all my friends who, with their encouragement, have greatly supported and assisted me including Kaye Kosonen, Anne Cox, Sharon Williams, Mandy Harrigan, Maggie Hamilton and her mother Joan, my cousins Lester, Jo and Pippy Moore and Jean McCarthy. Also sincere thanks to Joan and Teena who assisted me with French translations.

Finally, my sincere thanks to Graham for loaning me his family's nautical history books plus other useful information that he researched on my behalf.

PART ONE

PROLOGUE

Within the last five years since *The Masters of the Mystical Rose* was first published in 1999, a great deal of interest has been focused upon many of the subjects contained within the original edition, which are also retained and updated in this revised edition, along with new and fascinating additional topics.

In the first edition of *The Masters of the Mystical Rose*, it was revealed that the Master Kuthumi had once been John the Beloved Disciple, a close member of the *Family of the Holy Grail*, who wrote the Book of John and Revelation. The Master Kuthumi reincarnated in the 16th century as the Magus of the Elizabethan Renaissance, Sir John Dee who assisted Sir Francis Bacon (the Master St Germain), in the translation of what became known as the King James Authorized Version of the Bible - the Bible which is filled with codes, ciphers and *symbolism*. As Sir John Dee, he was the original 007. Sir John Dee belonged to the Order of Sion and he was the leader and Grand Master of the Rosicrucian (Order of the Rose-Cross) fraternity in England, prior to Sir Francis Bacon (St Germain) becoming its Grand Master.

During the 15th century of the Italian Renaissance, Kuthumi reincarnated as Leonardo da Vinci. As John the Beloved, he was the *First Master of the Grail* and as Leonardo da Vinci, he was appointed as the *Grand Master (Helmsman) of the Priory of Sion* (Jerusalem). In his incarnation as Leonardo da Vinci, Kuthumi chose his art work in order to convey his messages by utilizing intriguing and enigmatic *symbolism* within his paintings pertaining to *the Family of the Holy Grail*. These paintings are currently under close scrutiny and theories about them are numerous.

The cover of this book, *Masters of the Mystical Rose* was originally built up from the imagery of the Shroud of Turin. The authors, Christopher Knight and Robert Lomas, in their book titled *The Second Messiah*, believe the Second Messiah to have been the *Last Grand Master of the Knights Templar (who were the Guardians of the 'Grail')* namely Jacques de Molay.

Through carbon-dating tests, it has been proven that the Shroud of Turin dates back to only about six hundred years, and not two thousand years, when Christ, the Messiah, was crucified. This therefore places the Shroud of Turin in the same time period as Jacques de Molay, whom I believe to have been an incarnation of the Master Kuthumi for there is continuity in the pattern of his lives.

Jacques de Molay and the Knights Templar of France were arrested on Friday 13th October, 1307 upon the orders of King Philip the Fair. He was tortured and eventually crucified in the identical way to that of Christ. His tormentors even went so far as to have a crown of thorns placed upon his head. Molay did not die as a result of being crucified. After Molay was crucified, he survived and was wrapped in a white linen cloth, which is now claimed to be that of the Shroud of Turin. The actual death of Jacques de Molay occurred seven years later when he was burnt at the stake near the River Seine in Paris, on the 19ᵗʰ March, 1314.

Authors Lynn Picknett and Clive Prince, in their book titled *The Templar Revelation*, believe that the Shroud of Turin is a photographic image. They categorically state: "In brief, *the Turin Shroud is, among many other things, a five-hundred-year-old photograph of none other than Leonardo da Vinci.*" The authors believe that Leonardo da Vinci was a genius who faked the Shroud of Turin.

Whatever the truth may be, the mysterious Leonardo da Vinci who since the publication of Dan Brown's book titled *The Da Vinci Code*, has aroused world-wide interest. Could this be mere coincidence, or Divinely planned?

Readers of the *Masters of the Mystical Rose* are invited to learn of the 'Divinely-inspired' Leonardo da Vinci's past-lives and of the prominent roles which he, as the Master Kuthumi, being a *Master of the Mystical Rose*, has played throughout the history of the world.

Introduction

THE WHITE GODDESS

All saints revile her, and all sober men
Ruled by the God Apollo's golden mean -
In scorn of which we sailed to find her
In distant regions likeliest to hold her
Whom we desired above all things to know,
Sister of the mirage and echo.
The sap of spring in the young wood a-stir
Will celebrate with green the Mother,
And every song-bird shouts awhile for her;
But we are gifted, even in November
Rawest of Seasons, with so huge a sense
Of her nakedly worn magnificence
We forget cruelty and past betrayal,
Heedless of where the next bright bolt may fall.

(Robert Graves)

ADONAI (Lord)

And others came...Desires and Adorations,
Winged Persuasions and veiled Destinies,
Splendours, and Glooms, and glimmering Incarnations
Of hopes and fears, and twilight Phantasies.
He is made one with Nature: there is heard
His voice in all her music, from moan
Of Thunder, to the song of night's sweet bird;
He is a presence to be felt and known
In darkness and in light, from herb and stone,
Spreading itself where'er that Power may move
Which has withdrawn his being to its own;
Which wields the world with never-wearied love,
Sustains it from beneath, and kindles it above.

(Percy Shelley)

It was the year of 1993 on a beautiful Australian summer's evening as I sat in my garden. The leaves in the trees were still and the five wild ducks that had come for their nightly feed were swimming quietly in the pool nearby. Their reflections in the water were exquisite. All was quiet and serene, as I sat and listened to the sounds of silence. Quiet moments are heaven-sent and not to be taken for granted. No sounds of cars - of voices - or of telephones ringing. Even the birds had settled down for the night. I listened to the sounds of silence and, although I had heard the expression before, I had never fully realized exactly what it meant. It was so beautiful that I felt as if time had stopped still. Time - always time... "What's the time?" If only we had time...In time...our lives seem to be ruled by time!

Gazing into the stillness of the night, my thoughts wandered to a recent incredible experience when I had received a visitation twice in the one day from a very tall etheric figure robed in white with a hood over his head, his face hidden by shadow. The amazing illumination of 'Light' surrounding him was almost blinding. "Who are you?" I asked. He replied:

"With much love I come to speak to you today from the Realm of the God Life, to bring you greetings from your Holy One Our Father in Heaven and of the Light. We bow our heads in recognition of our connection to our Father and of the Light. What is written has been done so in the beginning. You do well. Your services are needed. You are being watched by the ancient Holy Ones who in time will teach you. Keep your intentions pure. Listen to the advice and you will keep contact within your spirit and with the greater spirit. You have commissioned yourself to do this at this time and all the assistance necessary for you will be given through those around you. Request as you do that you be given guidance and your whispers and if you are unsure, when you close your eyes to sleep, ask and your dreams will clarify for you."

"This is going to be far easier for you than you can imagine. You have some bless-ed people with you who will come in at the appropriate time. As you sweep away level after level, these ancients will come in and converse with you."

"I have come far to speak to you. You are in my charge and it is that I am pleasured to see you again so closely. Call my name in times of need and I will usher a command that you be administered to. I come from the Realms of the Angels on High and I bring you this word with much love. As I leave, I will say to you, my name is Raphael."

I did not know a great deal about Archangels - I did not understand anything of what was taking place. "Time," he had said, "In time the Ancient Holy Ones will teach you." Who were the Ancient Holy Ones? Where were they? What had I to do with them and them with me? Whom could I tell? Would I be believed? What did they want? When would they appear again? Who would teach me? How would they teach me? What was it they wanted to teach me? All these questions flowed through my mind. My thoughts were so loud in my head that the quietness no longer existed.

As I continued to ponder and stare across the pool, to my astonishment, I began to see the formation of an etheric regal-looking, beautifully-coloured peacock feather, which drifted backwards and forwards across the pool, as if seeking my attention. And then, the most elaborate, ornately woven huge white veil came down right in front of me. It remained there for several moments and then slowly lifted before my eyes, evaporating into the indigo-coloured sky. I held my breath in sheer amazement, wondering whatever would happen next.

Suddenly, I could smell the beautiful scent of roses, where there were none. It was the most exquisite scent that I have ever experienced. The nearest I could describe the scent would be to equate it with the lovely old fashioned English David Austen roses, but even that does not adequately describe the perfume, for I have smelt it many times since. I breathed in the scent deeply, hoping it would last forever! But what is forever? Time! Judging everything by time. Alas, the scent soon faded and I could no longer hold onto it. It was invisible and yet I wanted to grasp it and keep it forever.

As my eyes again searched into the darkness of the night sky, I saw a pink glow just in front of me and it began to take the form of a knight in a rose-red uniform. The face was indistinguishable and all I could make out was the tone of his skin, a beard and his incredible magnetic eyes looking into mine. The colour of his uniform was glorious - the jacket being a magnificent rose-red colour. Upon the collar, which was one of those old fashioned ones that stood up, not pointed, there was woven intricate gold embroidery. A blue mantle was draped over his shoulders and as he turned around, I could see an eight-pointed Maltese Cross embroidered on the back of the mantle. Beneath his red jacket were black trousers. As my eyes were again drawn to the brilliant colour of his jacket, I noticed that down the front of the jacket, where normally buttons would have been, were small Saltire-shaped gold crosses (X's). I stared at them in fascination, whilst all of the time thinking that all of this was totally unreal, until I heard a voice speaking to me telepathically. "Who are you?" I asked.

"I am your Master Teacher, I am the Master of the Rose", said he.

CHAPTER 1

The Masters of the Mystical Rose

"I have been teacher to all intelligences,
I have been fostered in the land of the Deity
I am able to instruct the whole Universe,
I shall be until the day of Judgement
Upon the face of the Earth"
(Taliesin/Merlin - St Germain)

"For like a Child sent with a fluttering Light
To feel his way along a gusty Night
Man walks the World: again and yet again
The Lamp shall be by Fits of Passion slain:
But shall not He who sent him from the Door
Relight the Lamp once more, and yet once more?"
(Attar)

How did civilization as we know it, begin? Who were the gods of ancient times and where did they come from? Was there a basis for all the mythological tales that we inherited from the Greeks, Romans and the Celts? Who were the Masters who helped to guide our planet's history? Did Atlantis and Lemuria really exist? Who was Noah? Who was the Teacher of Righteousness of whom the Essenes wrote about in the Dead Sea Scrolls? Did Merlin and Arthur really exist and if so, who were they? Where was Avalon? Was Tintagel the real birthplace of Arthur? Who was the mysterious Joseph of Arimathea? What was the importance of Glastonbury? What was the Grail? Who were the Fisher Kings? What was the importance of the Stone of Destiny and from whence did it originate? Why were the Celtic kings crowned upon it? What was the origin of the Knights Templar? Why did they adopt the emblem of the Rose-Cross? Who was the Bard who wrote under the name of *Taliesin*? Who really wrote the Shakespearian plays?

All these questions and more will be explored as this story unfolds.

In an endeavour to find some of the answers, my family and I journeyed overseas in 1996 to visit the places connected with the Grail legends and with the information I gathered from the interesting people with whom I became acquainted, some fascinating factors emerged, especially the Celtic connections relating to the Grail mysteries. The trail led us to Glastonbury, Stonehenge, Tintagel, St Michael's Mount, Land's End, Chester, Lincoln, and Ireland.

The story of the *Masters of the Mystical Rose* tells of the remarkable men and women of history who, through their many reincarnations, have helped to guide and shape our planet's destiny - the ultimate goal being to establish a peaceful and harmonious civilization on earth. They are known in the Eastern religions as Avatars and Ascended Masters.

Two Masters dominate this story, for there is a great deal of information now known about the roles that they have played in shaping our history. They are St Germain, and Kuthumi (mentioned in the Prologue), who are both Master Teachers. St Germain, who like Kuthumi, has had numerous incarnations, is known under various titles, such as the Master 'R' whom some refer to as the Master Ragoczy. However, the 'R' is also representative of him being known as a *Master of the Mystical Rose*.

There are various books now available discussing whom the Masters were and not all authors agree, for there are some conflicting statements. However, when dealing with the history of the past lives of the Masters, a particular pattern emerges - a synchronicity which allows us to presume their probable identities in certain time periods. This pattern takes into consideration their talents and ambitions of their past incarnations which they were to retain in future reincarnations.

For the purpose of this story, I have chosen to discuss the commonly accepted lives of the Masters and linked their lives with the appropriate historical periods - it also helps knowing that many of them chose to incarnate into the same time period in order to assist each other. And also, because the Masters have guided me throughout the writing of this story, they have given me names and places of their past incarnations in order for me to do the research necessary for the compilation of this book.

Of further aid in the assessment of their lives, is the fact that the Masters often had the same first names or surnames, or derivatives thereof and also reincarnated into places where they had lived or died before and into families of nobility, wherein they were in a position to have a great deal of influence upon society at large. However, not only did they reincarnate into influential families, they were also later recognised as saints because of the noble work which they had achieved. Finally, the lives they have lived is further assessed by the fact that they worked together to preserve the ancient Teachings of the '*Mystical Rose*' which is the subject of this story.

History is a combination of events that have been recorded about the people of the past and thus we are also dealing with human nature, "to err is human." History books have treated many famous people unkindly, often with a great deal of criticism, and, although this story is about the historical lives of certain Masters, they too were human - made mistakes - learnt from them and strove to achieve their best. The interesting factor of history is the motives, forces and influences that moulded the lives of the human race, particularly when eventually religion and politics were disastrously combined.

The Masters incarnated over and over again, seeking to perfect their own evolutionary path. They were human beings, just like us, living in the physical and evolving spiritually along the road to perfection which is the ultimate goal for all on this planet.

There were eras when the Masters incarnated as great leaders such as Alexander the Great, Charlemagne the Great, St Germanus, King David, and the Egyptian Pharaoh Tutmoses III, during which times they were forced to fight battles. Even some, who were later recognised as saints, participated in fighting battles. Many of the historical people mentioned in the *Masters of the Mystical Rose* were pharaohs, kings, queens, saints, martyrs, prophets, philosophers, inventors, and navigators who all contributed in a magnanimous way towards the development of our civilization.

Men, who were later to be recognised as saints, had lived lives in which they were forced to become embroiled in politics and religious opposition, dealing with the ambitious and the greedy who wished to be in 'control' of the world's population.

If we could place ourselves back in the medieval times and make comparisons with today's world of politics, power, violence, wars and corruption, we would find that not a great deal has changed as far as attitudes are concerned.

John the Beloved Disciple - Kuthumi

Kuthumi is a '*Master of the Mystical Rose*' who features prominently throughout this story. Kuthumi's symbolic representation is that of the *Eagle*. In his incarnation as John the Beloved Disciple, Kuthumi wrote the Book of Revelation about the 'Apocalypse' during the 1st century AD, whilst he was in exile on the island of Patmos. The *Eagle*, combined with clutching an olive branch in its right talon, was eventually to become the emblem of the Great Seal of the United States of America. This was designed by St Germain on one of his visits to America.

El Morya and The Rose Cross

The renowned authority upon the subject of the Order of the Rose Cross - the late Harvey Spencer Lewis (1883-1939) was the first Imperator and founder of the Ancient and Mystical Order Rosae Crucis (AMORC) in the United States of America.

Those initiated into the great Temples of ancient Egypt were known as the Great White Brotherhood. It is important to remember that the terminology of 'Great White Brotherhood' is not meant in any racial sense. They were given this title because they donned themselves in white-hooded robes when they were students in the Temples. The 'White' was equated with the 'Light' and symbolic of 'purity'. Following the same tradition, the Essenes and the Druidic priests of Celtic Britain also wore white robes.

In Spencer Lewis' book titled *The Mystical Life of Jesus*, we are informed that the origin of Baptism, the immersion into water and the use of water for purification in the rites and ceremonies of the Great White Brotherhood in Egypt, were first introduced by the Master of the Great White Brotherhood known as El Moira (Morya).

Spencer Lewis told of how El Moira, born at Lake Moeris in Egypt, in his first known incarnation, was educated and prepared for his great mission and established the principle of the law of 'baptism' as a spiritual step in the process of initiation. El Morya was also the prophet Elijah who, in a later reincarnation, became the one known as the Essenes' John the Baptist at which time he continued the ceremonial ancient Egyptian rites of purification by water.

El Morya was the famous Pharaoh Akhnaton (Amenhotep IV). His great great grandfather was Tutmoses III who was an incarnation of Kuthumi. According to Spencer Lewis, the Order of the Rose Cross dated back to 1489 BC, beginning with the Pharaoh Tutmoses III. Both Tutmoses III and Akhnaton delved in the ancient Mysteries. Such sacred Teachings taught in the Temples of Learning by the Egyptian priests could be traced even further back in time to Sumer and Atlantis.

In his incarnation as Pharaoh Akhnaton (Amenhotep IV) of Egypt, El Moira was the first to introduce the *symbology* of the Rose-Cross into the Sacred Mysteries known as the Arcana/Arkana - meaning 'secret'. He initiated and taught many of the Masters of the Great White Brotherhood, one of whom included Moses. During this era, St Germain had incarnated as Aaron, the brother of Moses and Moses is reputed to have been an earlier incarnation of the Master we know as Jesus.

The *Rose* mentioned in the title of this book, is a symbol of perfection and combined with the cross, was to become known as the Rose Croix - symbol of the Order of the Rose Cross (the Rosicrucians).

In the 12th century AD, during the reign of Richard the Lion Heart, the

Rose-Cross was to become the emblem of the Knights Templar and Britain's national emblem. It was St Germain who introduced the Order of the Rose Cross into Europe and America. He was responsible for the spreading of the Teachings of Arcana/Arkana during his incarnation as Sir Francis Bacon and was the Grand Master of the Freemasons.

These sacred Teachings had been preserved since the days of Atlantis and Lemuria where they had been taught in the Temples. St Germain was also the supreme Grandmaster of the Order of the Rose Cross in the 16th and 17th centuries.

Reincarnation and Energy

Man walks the World again and yet again (Attar)

Because this story is based upon the lives of the Masters, it is essentially written for those readers who are able to accept reincarnation - for those who are skeptical and unable to accept such a possibility, because of their religious beliefs, perhaps they may maintain an open mind. Once there were many references regarding the existence of reincarnation mentioned in the Biblical texts which were later removed by the Church of Rome. The exclusion of teaching of the pre-existence of the soul and reincarnation began back in circa 563 AD when the early Christian fathers held a council in Constantinople, under the orders of the Roman Emperor, Justinian, and decreed that all clear references to reincarnation be removed.

The pharaohs/kings of ancient Egypt believed in reincarnation. The Eastern religions such as Buddhism, also taught about reincarnation. Lao Tze, the Chinese philosopher c. 6th century BC, (an earlier incarnation of the Master Kuthumi) taught the Eastern religions about reincarnation and founded what is known as the Taoist religion. The word *'Tao'* means the 'way' or 'path'. Religious Taoism dealt with deities/gods, spirits, magic and soothsaying. The Master we know as Jesus also taught about reincarnation.

A majority of the past Masters were the great philosophers who expounded their esoteric philosophies upon the subject of reincarnation. All the Masters have a great love for humanity which, through philosophy, they have endeavoured to convey a love of the 'spiritual' aspect within human beings. These great people have included Aristotle (Kuthumi), Socrates (earlier incarnation of Jesus), Plato (St Germain), Hermes Trismegistus (Thrice Greatest), Pythagoras (Kuthumi) who gave us 'Mathematics' and Dante Alighieri who was famous for the *Divine Comedy* and was Grand Master of the Order of the Rose Cross during the 13th century.

Edgar Cayce (pronounced Cay-cee), the greatest prophet of the 20th century, wrote a great deal about reincarnation. In his book titled *Edgar Cayce, Modern Prophet* by Mary Ellen Carter, under the editorship of Edgar's son, Hugh Lynn

Cayce, Edgar described the soul/spirit as follows:

"Spirit, mind, and will are each a basic dimension of soul, each a distinct quality. Spirit is the life force. It is energy, the one and only energy in the universe. God is energy. When God created souls, this same energy, or spirit became a part of each soul. Each soul consists of the same life force as God and the rest of creation. Science recognizes today, four forms of energy: gravity, electromagnetism, and the strong and the weak atomic forces." Cayce taught that "all energy is of the same source. Atomic energy, solar energy, love, hatred etc., are different aspects of the same one energy. The first law of creation is that everything proceeds from the same one source, the same energy. That is the spirit."

In August, 1998, the Australian Broadcasting Commission in Western Australia presented a radio interview with Dr Paul Pearsall, regarding his book titled *The Heart's Code*. During the interview Dr Paul Pearsall told of how scientists are now coming to recognise the fact that reincarnation exists and he quoted many cases which have been investigated. One of particular interest was that of a nine year old child who told of how, in his past life he had been mauled by a shark and he described the teeth marks left upon his body. In his present life, the child has birthmarks upon his body which are shaped like the teeth-marks of a shark. The child told of his name from that particular past life and the details of his death. When such details were investigated, it was found that the person whom he named had, actually existed and met his death by a shark attack.

In John 3:3-12 we are told by Jesus about reincarnation (this version below is taken from the Good News Bible).

Jesus answered: *"I am telling you the truth: no one can see the kingdom of God unless he is born again."*

Nicodemus questions Jesus: "How can a grown man be born again?" "He certainly cannot enter his mother's womb and be born a second time!"

"I am telling you the truth" replied Jesus. *"No one can enter the Kingdom of God unless he is born of water and the Spirit."*

"A person is born physically of human parents but he is born spiritually of the Spirit."

"Do not be surprised because I tell you that you must all be born again."

"The wind blows wherever it wishes; you hear the sound it makes, but you do not know where it comes from or where it is going. It is like that with everyone who is born of the Spirit."

"How can that be?" asked Nicodemus.

Jesus answered: *"You are a great teacher in Israel, and you don't know this?"*

"I am telling you the truth: we speak of what we have seen and yet none of you is willing to accept our message."

"You do not believe me when I tell you about the things of this world; how will you ever believe me, then, when I tell you about the things of heaven?"

Joseph, Father of the Family of the Holy Grail
St Germain

Because this story is one of historical events, it should be remembered for easy clarification purposes, that there never was a year 'dot'. One BC is followed immediately by 1 AD in our present system of numbering, first introduced by Dionysius Exiguus in the 6th century AD.

Jesus was born during the era of King Herod, who died in 4 BC, and Jesus is believed to have been born about 7 BC. His father was Joseph, an incarnation of St Germain, the father of the Holy Grail Family. The relationship between St Germain and Kuthumi was a very close one during that era.

St Germain confirmed that as well as being Francis Bacon born into the Tudor royal family, he was once Joseph, the father of Jesus. In the book titled *St Germain - Twin Souls & Soulmates* channelled by Claire Heartsong, we are informed as follows:

St Germain: "I staged the death (of Francis Bacon) that still has some scratching their heads, and continued to work upon the European scene with a grand union, a grand vision to be in the footsteps of that One who was my son, the One you call Jesus."

Q: "As I understand it, you are saying that even during your youth as Francis Bacon you became aware of soul memory, including your life as Joseph?"

St Germain: "Indeed, not only my soul memory, beloved, but that which I had buried in a variety of different places, actual tangible records that I had laid up for a later time."

The Tudor Line

From information contained in Peter Dawkins' book titled *Arcadia* we learn the following important information:

"The Tudors formed the ancient royal line of British kings, with a genealogy carefully preserved and recorded by their bards. They trace their line of descent back to the famous King Arthur, with direct links (via the daughter of Joseph of Arimathea) with the Judaic royal line of David, and beyond even the later Celts to Hugh the Mighty (also known as Brut, or Brit), who led the original Trojan settlers to 'the White Land' (i.e. Albion) in the second millennium BC, and gave these islands their name of 'Britain' (meaning 'The Chosen Land')."

"This family provided the 'Crowned Princes (Cunos)' and 'High Kings' (Arviragus) of Ancient Britain, and carried with them the ancient initiatic knowledge. The High Kings, all of whom were elected from the 'blood royal' (i.e. the 'Tudor' blood line) and chosen for their strength, wisdom and initiatic powers, bore the hereditary title of 'Merlin' (Myrrdin), as they combined their office in the roles of both high priest and king."

Throughout this story, the life of Francis Bacon is discussed at length, however, it is important to reveal in this first chapter that he *was the* legitimate son of Queen Elizabeth I and Lord Robert Dudley. When the Queen realized that she was 'with child', Robert and she were married in secret and Francis was born in wedlock on the 22nd January, 1561. According to the renowned biographer of Francis Bacon, the late Alfred Dodd in his book titled *Francis Bacon's Personal Life Story*, the Queen and Lord Robert Dudley (later known as the Earl of Leicester) were married privately at the house of Lord Pembroke.

From Peter Dawkins' book titled *Arcadia* we learn that from the moment of Francis' birth, he was handed over to Lady Anne Bacon who was the Head Lady-in-waiting to Queen Elizabeth and also the wife of Sir Nicholas Bacon. The home of Lady Bacon and Sir Nicholas was York House which was next to Elizabeth's York Palace. Lady Bacon had recently lost her own baby and so she became the foster-mother of Francis. He loved her very much and he was always to maintain a wonderful relationship with her.

According to Alfred Dodd:

"The disclosure of his birth was concealed from the public because the disclosure would have affected the honour of the Queen. It became a State Secret. The Queen's marriage was also unknown, save to a mere handful of her advisers."

Peter Dawkins wrote: "There is little doubt that the Queen loved him (Robert Dudley) for she bore him two children." (Francis' younger brother, Robert, was born in 1566 and was adopted by Sir Walter Devereux and his wife Lettice).

According to Alfred Dodd:

"It was for the 'Virgin Queen' herself to decide whether or not Dudley should be openly recognized as the Queen's Consort and his progeny acknowledged as next in the 'Succession' to the English Throne. The 'Necessity of the Times' prevented her throughout her reign from declaring her marriage or the fruits of it. She was thus like Alexander the Great [incarnation of St Germain] and Julius Caesar, who left no legitimate Issue behind to succeed legally to the Throne, but nevertheless had 'Natural' Children of Royal Breed. This was Francis Bacon's own thought expressed *In Memoriam of Elizabeth* published by Dr Rawley in 1657."

Francis Bacon and the Golden Age of Enlightenment

St Germain

From the book titled *Francis Bacon Herald of the New Age* by Peter Dawkins, we learn the following pertinent information:

"Since the end of the Golden Age of Atlantis many aeons ago, a vision and hope for a new world-wide Golden Age of mankind has been nurtured by sages and saints. Not only was it seen in vision, but it was step by step prepared for down the ages by those who have understood something of the alchemical process and timing involved. As the cycle of avatars ('incarnations of divinity') have proceeded, so the world has moved nearer to the new Golden Age - or, as Francis Bacon put it, to a 'New Atlantis'."

"The work that the Master of the Rose accomplished under the *persona* of Francis Bacon was to 'herald' the Golden Age by designing and inaugurating the actual *method* by which the whole world would be taken through its final stages into the long-promised Golden Age of true enlightenment and brotherhood."

Besides being a renowned philosopher, Francis Bacon was also the greatest poet and dramatist of all time who wrote under the 'masked' name of William Shakespeare, the 'Shaker of the Truth'. Embodied within Francis Bacon's works, were the key exponents to the Ancient Wisdom (the Arcana) which according to Peter Dawkins, are as equally applicable today, as they were in Bacon's time.

It is interesting to note that Michael Drosnin relates in his book titled *The Bible Code*, the fact that many great people are referred to in the codes discovered in the Bible. One of these was Shakespeare and two of his plays are mentioned, namely *Hamlet* and *Macbeth*, both of which are based on historical events involving the Celtic race. However, *Hamlet* may be a play on words - as in 'little Ham' (Bacon) and *Macbeth* - 'son of Beth' = Elizabeth.

Peter Dawkins, in his book titled *The Great Vision*, goes to some lengths to explain Francis Bacon's (St Germain's) game of 'hide and seek'.

"A large part of Francis' fascinating and exciting life is only discoverable through a lot of hard work, and being able to piece together and interpret all the various clues, historical details and cipher records. Ciphers of all kinds, from pictorial to mathematical, play a substantial part in recording many of the key-experiences as well as some of the profoundest teachings in his life."

"Francis Bacon was an expert on cipher, and used many ciphers throughout his life-time in order to conceal from contemporaries and yet record for posterity the most intimate details of his life and those around him. He intended that posterity should discover the story and teachings, so he always left the necessary signposts and keys. However, it is a slippery path, testing one's capacities to be both open-minded, highly perceptive and also critical every step of the way."

"Both intuition and reason are required, which is what Francis Bacon purposely set out to teach and develop a high degree in mankind. The 'treasure hunt' to discover his real life and genius, and his work, comprises a universal education and an initiatory experience, developing the powers and the talents of each researcher stage by stage."

"The unravelling of the mystery requires, as Francis Bacon almost certainly intended, a group effort and a reasonably lengthy period of time in which to discover the truth step by step, a little at a time, to test it, to assimilate it, and to comprehend what it in fact means and what use it might possibly be to know that truth."

Peter Dawkins then relates that without the enormous amount of previous research done by others in the past, he wouldn't have been able to achieve as much as he has (which he still claims is a drop in the ocean, compared to what is still to be discovered) without their aid.

Such research requires many who are willing to share it with the rest of humanity which is what St Germain wishes.

The life of Francis Bacon was a most productive one, for apart from the numerous plays which he wrote under various pseudonyms, plus the works that he acknowledged as being his own under the name of Francis Bacon, as mentioned in a previous paragraph, he was extremely busily involved in founding lodges of the Order of the Rose Cross and the Freemasons, (of which the Order of the Rose Cross was an affiliation), throughout Britain, Europe and the United States of America.

There were those in the court of Queen Elizabeth, who knew the truth about his 'secret' birth. One of these was Robert Cecil who was Francis' sworn enemy who constantly plotted against him and endangered his life. Robert Cecil, and his father, William Cecil (Lord Burghley) were the right-hand men of Elizabeth I. Knowing the secret of Francis' parentage, they schemed against him and sowed doubts into the mind of Elizabeth about Francis wanting to usurp the throne of England.

Because the goal of Francis was to teach the world the 'Truth' during a time when all were in danger of having their heads lopped off if any hint of treason fell upon them, and because of the fact that Robert Cecil and others of the 'Cecil' Camp were constantly spying upon Francis, Francis cleverly wrote his works under 'masked' names.

Another of his sworn enemies was Sir Edward Coke who along with Lord Buckingham, schemed to have Francis defamed and persecuted. For a short time Francis was placed in the Tower of London during the reign of King James I of England (James VI of Scotland), but was later released and cleared of all the trumped up charges.

Francis Bacon - Shakespeare
St Germain

From the work titled *The Great Mystery Count Saint Germain* by Dr Raymond Bernard, we learn the following:

"Shakespeare was only one of the masks of the universal genius, Francis Bacon - prince of philosophers, prince of scientists, prince of political reformers, prince of poets and Prince of England. He had many other masks under which he inaugurated the Elizabethan Renaissance of literature in England, putting forth his prodigious literary productions in rapid succession under various names. Among these we find a host of plays, many of which were attributed to the pen of Shakespeare, whose authorship is unknown. Bacon chose the stage as a means of putting forth his message to humanity and to prepare the public mind for the democratic revolution which was his aim and the goal of the secret societies for political reform (Freemasonry and Rosicrucianism - the Order of the Rose Cross) which he founded."

Leonardo da Vinci (1452-1519), The Lion of Vinci
Kuthumi

During the Italian Renaissance period, prior to the Elizabethan Renaissance into which Francis Bacon was born, many great artists incarnated, who incorporated into their wonderful paintings secret symbols which only members of the Freemasons understood.

One of these great artists was Leonardo da Vinci, who, as mentioned in the Prologue, was an incarnation of the Master Kuthumi. Leonardo was born in Vinci, a village near Florence and was the illegitimate son of a Florentine notary and a peasant woman. In about 1469, the family settled in Florence and Leonardo was afforded the best opportunities of that time.

As a young man, Leonardo was extremely handsome and intelligent, physically strong, persuasive in conversation and a fine musician, to name but a few of his talents. Leonardo often amused people with his improvisations and delighted in designing theatre props, using his artistic abilities. From his early years, he studied engineering and seemed to have inherited a natural and profound knowledge in everything he endeavoured to partake of including the study of natural sciences.

At the home of Leonardo in Le Clos-Luce in Amboise, France, (which has been turned into a museum), are his original drawings showing designs of mechanical flying-machines, inventions and some of his sketches for his paintings.

Leonardo was also brilliant at mathematics, which comes as no surprise really, because he had once been Pythagoras, the *Father of Mathematics*. Consequently, he was not only a skilled engineer, but also a great architect and he was employed as an engineer to design and oversee the building of the canals in Florence. There was no limit to his talents - he was a genius!

He studied both sculpture and painting and in 1472, he entered the painters' guild of Florence at which time he was given a great deal of support by his patron, Lorenzo de Medici. Among his most famous paintings are the portrait of *St Jerome*, *Virgin on the Rocks*, and *The Baptism of Christ*.

His major work was the *Adoration of the Magi* which was quite significant given that the 'Magi' were the 'Wise Men' who visited the infant Jesus not long after his birth, bearing gifts of Gold, Frankincense and Myrrh.

Kuthumi was one of those 'three wise men' - the Magus known as Balthazar. His immediate incarnation after that was as John the Beloved Disciple, who was the brother of Jesus and thus they were both sons of St Germain in his incarnation as Joseph. Most of Leonardo's paintings were done in a religious fashion, for they needed to pass the judgement of the Church of Rome. However, Leonardo, as previously stated, managed to convey secret meanings by the utilization of symbolism within his paintings.

Kuthumi, in his incarnation as Leonardo da Vinci, was born just one year after Christopher Columbus (the 'Dove') - St Germain, and they worked together establishing 'secret societies' to protect the 'Greater Mysteries', the Arcana of the Freemasons and the Order of the Rose Cross. Assistance was also rendered to them by Lorenzo de Medici. One of the secret societies was known as the Priory of Sion (Jerusalem) and the Grand Master (known as the Helmsman) was Count Rene of Anjou, who was the titled king of Jerusalem. It was Rene who was to appoint Leonardo as the Grand Master of the Priory of Sion.

Sir John Dee

Kuthumi

In his next reincarnation after that of Leonardo da Vinci (died in 1519), Kuthumi was born eight years later into the Elizabethan period, as the great Magus of the Elizabethan Renaissance, Sir John Dee, and once again he assisted St Germain (who had reincarnated as Francis Bacon), particularly with the translation of the Bible from Greek into English. Dee was also a Grand Master of the Order of the Rose Cross and had a close association with Elizabeth I, being the Queen's astrologer. Kuthumi had also once been 'Arthur', crowned by Merlin - St Germain, as King of the Celts in the 6th century AD.

Portia, St Germain's twin soul, in the book titled *St Germain - Twin Souls &
Soulmates*, channelled by Claire Heartsong, informs us as follows:

"He [St Germain - Francis Bacon] followed the steps of a previous
embodiment that he had known as Merlin, one of the Merlins. *There was one with
him in the court who previously had walked with him as Arthur (King). There
were others as well who took re-embodiment to gather again* at the great Round
Table of consciousness that would draw down the heavens into the Earth and lift
up the humanity that had been asleep for so long ..." "So it was that this one, with
a number of other ones, was privy to many, many books and records of bygone
eras and they went on pilgrimages together."

According to Peter Dawkins' book titled *Arcadia*:

"Sir John Dee was born in 1527, was of Welsh descent and always claimed
that he was in fact related to the Tudors. His family tree indicated that his family
was of the greatest antiquity and highest respectability, and was traceable to Roderick
the Great, the ancient Prince of all Wales."

In Welsh, Tudor was spelt Tewdwr. The original Tewdwrs were descended
from the princes of South Wales, through the female line. According to Peter
Dawkins' book titled *The Great Vision* "Arthur (King) had been of direct lineage
of the earlier British Kings, and a direct descendant of Joseph of Arimathea's
daughter, Anna, who had married a Welsh prince of the royal Silurian line."

From Peter Dawkins' book titled *The Virgin Ideal* we are given more pertinent
information regarding the Tudors. "The Tudors were Welsh sovereigns of an ancient
royal lineage, recorded as being descended from the Trojan Aeneas (and thus related
closely to the Trojans and the Romans), who was himself descended from Judah,
eldest son of Jacob (called Israel) via Judah's second twin son, Zarah. Thus the
British nobility had a common ancestry with the Tribe of Judah and the House of
David, reinforced by inter-marriages, of which one marriage was particularly notable
- that of a Welsh prince with Joseph of Arimathea's daughter from which marriage
the Tudors were descended."

"The Tudors were very proud of this. They brought with them to England
their bards - their poet-historians - and the great history of the Celtic times, which
together with their initiations and their teachings, was married with the Renaissance
learning that was coming over from Italy and Spain via France. The two streams
came together during the Elizabethan period."

(Aeneas belonged to the Trojan Royal family. The great grandson of Aeneas
was Brutus who brought a party of Trojans to England and founded the city of
Troynovant, meaning 'new Troy' which later became known as the city of London.
Aeneas is considered to be the founder of the British people).

Sir John Dee received his Master of Arts Degree at Trinity College,

Cambridge in 1548 and graduated as a Doctor at Louvain in 1550.

Of significance was the brilliance of Dee's mind. It is a fact that Sir John Dee was the originator of what we today know as Scotland Yard. He was the original 007, who, like St Germain/Francis Bacon, was a master of ciphers and codes.

Queen Elizabeth granted Sir John Dee her personal protection, which was certainly needed in those times of religious bigotry, superstition and intolerance and Sir John Dee played a major role in the advancement of learning during the Renaissance period of the Elizabethan era.

The Magus of the Elizabethan Renaissance
Kuthumi

From information contained in Peter Dawkins' book titled *Arcadia*, we learn more about Sir John Dee:

"Dr John Dee was a master exponent of the art of symbolism, dissimulation and disguise. He was brilliant at geography, navigation, geometry, mathematics, numerology, mechanics, astrology, alchemy, Greek, Hebrew, Cabbala, Hermeticism and architecture. All in all, he was fitted to become a Renaissance Magus."

"Dee had a comprehensive library, but one of the most significant facts that we can perceive, from a study of Dee's literary collection and his known interest and work, is the major part that poetry, drama, architecture and occult mathematics played in the whole scheme. This cannot be stressed enough. Occult mathematics is really the scientific basis of the Cabbala, which links numbers (and hence geometry and numerology with language and culture), and with levels of consciousness of being. Every letter of the alphabet has its own numerical value, which is itself a rational expression of a particular idea, power and purpose."

"Moreover, all number is linked together in one comprehensive and geometric whole that is perfectly ordered and harmonious, just as all ideas are essentially organised parts of one Divine Idea. The same is true for the alphabet, whose letters properly (i.e. mathematically), ordered, make comprehensible words, and whose words form the language that expresses and communicates ideas. Not in vain was it said:

'In the beginning was the Word, and the Word was with God, and the Word was God.

The same was in the beginning with God.

All things were made by Him; and without Him was not anything made that was made.

In him was life; and the life was the light of men.

And the light shineth in the darkness; and the darkness comprehended it not.

There was a man sent forth from God; whose name was John [The 'Beloved' - Kuthumi]
The same came for a witness, to bear witness of the Light, that all men through him might believe.'"

"Dee, and those directly associated with him, used cryptographic methods in all that they published, and in their associated programme to usher in a Golden Age. Dee believed in the royal dignity and importance of the ancient Tudor line and promoted the importance of the British Isles in their world role. Undoubtedly, he also knew that the Renaissance period (from 1440-1620) corresponded with the zodiacal period of Virgo in the cycle of the Piscean Age, and that the Elizabethan period in world history was thus exceedingly important. His motto was 'Nothing is useful unless it is honest'."

"Dee had a mystical vision of Britain as the new leader in reuniting Christian Europe and re-establishing the new Golden Age of civilization for the benefit of the entire world. He was far from being the only proponent of them, but he became the principal *Magus* of the movement in the early Elizabethan England."

"The whole Tudor lineage, with its entourage, embodied this knowledge and purpose, guarded it and bore it from one generation to the next; and every so often the bloodline produced someone who could understand and interpret what it all meant better than others. (Looked at another way, all mankind shares in the same 'royal' blood, as descendants of Adam and Eve, the first 'son-daughter of God'), and also because of the continual and healthy intermixing of the blood-lines - the 'sharing of the Holy Grail'. But the real Holy Grail is a description of the sainted or illumined souls of all ages, who are pure vessels of love-light, and who together form the Communion of Saints or the Brotherhood of Light (The White Brotherhood). They are the true Grail line or family, who are in a real communion of love and consciousness with each other and all of life."

The House of Sion

From *Arcadia* by Peter Dawkins, we learn that "many of Sir John Dee's works were a *blueprint for modern Freemasonry*, which Francis Bacon and his group later formed; it was nothing new but a revival of something very ancient - for Freemasonry is said to be the oldest science and art. Dee was often at court where he enjoyed universal esteem, and likewise many courtiers were to be found at Dee's house at all times. Sir Francis Walsingham, Adrian Gilbert and Edward Dyer, for instance, constantly visited Dee, as did the rest of the group of scholar-poets that became known as the English Areopagus, together with the Syon (Sion) house group. Dee also received many visitors from abroad at his Mortlake home."

"Also at the heart of Dee's library was an almost complete collection of *prisci theologia*, which were clearly of the highest importance to him. The *prisci theologi* were divinely inspired pre-Christian authors, and included Hermes Trismegistus (also known as Mercurius), Zoroaster, Orpheus, Pythagoras, Plato, Philolaus and the other Greek philosophers. Their writings carried sublime truths, and demonstrated that the great truths were understood by sages of many cultures and epochs, and that the same truths underlie all religions. They showed, for instance, a handing on of the Wisdom Tradition from Ancient Egypt to the Greek philosophers as well as to Moses, and from thence into Christianity and the Renaissance. Considered together with other notable works, and with Dee's own writings, this collection points out Dee as being what might be called a 'religious Hermetist', which is precisely what Bacon's Great Instauration is founded upon."

The Great Instauration and the New Age

According to Peter Dawkins in his book titled *Francis Bacon Herald of the New Age*:

"The formation of Francis Bacon's scheme, the Great Instauration, was greatly influenced and helped by his foster-father, Sir Nicholas Bacon, Queen Elizabeth I's great statesman and Lord Keeper of the Great Seal, who carried on Sir Thomas More's [the Master El Morya's] secret work; by *Dr John Dee, the Elizabethan Magus* and leader (in England) of the 'Rosicrucian' fraternity before Bacon; by the Pleiades, the famous group of French Renaissance poet-philosophers led by Pierre de Ronsard, and by other members of the 'Family of Love' (one of the many names given to the fellowship of Rosicrucians in Europe before the name of 'Rosicrucian' was publicly applied)."

"All of these had laboured for similar purposes, which was to help bring about the gradual illumination of mankind and the restoration of a state of paradise on earth. But Bacon's vision and scheme went beyond even that of his peers and contemporaries, completing what they had prepared for, even drawing in and synthesizing the various Wisdom traditions, purifying all that needed a catharsis, and like an 'Orpheus', revitalizing the whole Mystery stream ready for the New Age."

"With the help of others, he actually put into practice a world-wide reformation of all arts and sciences, which themselves govern the actions of mankind and mould civilisation. For this reason, in some quarters the master soul who was Francis Bacon is known today as the Lord of Civilisation and Avatar of the Aquarian Age."

Higher Intelligence

The majority of earth's populations through the aeons have believed in some kind of supernatural Power or Powers that somehow governed the world of nature. In 1997, it was announced in the newspapers that an Israeli mathematician, (who presented proof in a major science journal), had endeavoured to prove that the Bible was full of codes containing past and future events. It was indicated that the Bible was coded in such a way that it could only be broken by the use of modern technology such as the advanced computers which we have at our disposal today. We can therefore assume that it could only have been written by a superhuman or 'super intelligence' - the understanding of which is beyond our present comprehension.

How else could the author who coded the Bible have known of the events which would happen over such a lengthy period *unless he was a most incredible prophet* with knowledge far beyond our own capacity to comprehend his abilities? In other words *it could only have been achieved by a Master of considerable importance who was brilliant at cryptics.*

The question arises, could this Master be the same one of whom the Essenes refer to in the *Dead Sea Scrolls* as the Teacher of Righteousness? The Essenes believed that their 'Teacher' reincarnated many times and that he was a prophet with amazing abilities, whose important job was to preserve the Sacred Arcana Teachings.

Modern scholars continue to argue over the true meanings in the Scrolls, but most agree that they were carefully prepared and placed in the jars so that they could be found at a designated time in the future. The *Teacher of Righteousness* (St Germain) who belonged to the Order of Zadok (meaning 'instructor'), may indeed have been the one who was responsible for these mysterious codes in the Bible, assisted by a close associate.

The Two Greatest Masterpieces of the English Language

It was St Germain in his incarnation as Sir Francis Bacon, who with the assistance of Sir John Dee (Kuthumi), translated the Bible in the 16th century during the reign of King James 1st of England (6th of Scotland) and it became known as the King James Authorized Version. The King James Version is otherwise known as the Protestant Bible and it is noteworthy that it differs from the Roman Catholic Bible.

From the book titled *The Great Secret, Count Saint Germain* by Dr Raymond

Bernard, A.B., M.A., Ph. D., we learn the following information:

"The King James translation of the Bible and the Shakespeare Plays - the two greatest masterpieces of the English language, which did so much to make this language what it is - were both the creations of Francis Bacon; and while his editorship of the Bible is easier to understand, his authorship of the Shakespeare Plays is generally not admitted."

"Yet both literary productions reveal themselves, by their unique superior excellence, to have had a common author. Smedley, in his *Mystery of Francis Bacon*, wrote that "It will eventually be proved that the whole scheme of the Authorized Version of the Bible was Francis Bacon's.""

"He was an ardent student of not only the Bible, but of the early manuscripts. St Augustine, St Jerome and writers of theological works were studied by him with industry. He left notations in many copies of the Bible and in scores of theological works. The translation must have been a work in which he took the deepest interest and only one writer of the period was capable of turning the phrases with the matchless style which is the great charm of the Shakespeare Plays."

Taliesin

"By Johannes [John] the Diviner [Beloved] I was called Merddin [Merlin]"

(Taliesin)

During the 6th century AD, the Bard/prophet, the greatest poet of his time, wrote under the pseudonym of *Taliesin* which in Welsh means 'radiant brow'. The radiance which emanated from him was the illumination of his powerful aura, truly the sign of a great Master.

Taliesin was a Master who had passed all the greater degrees of the Sacred Arcana Teachings which had been preserved since the days of Noah (St Germain) and the fall of Atlantis. Within *Taliesin's* poems are cryptic clues about his previous reincarnations and they were written in a series of riddles to be unravelled in a future time.

The *Mabinogion* is a mixed collection of poems which were finally collated in the 13th century in what became known as the *Red book of Hergest* which includes *The Book of Taliesin*. The *Mabinogion* is a relatively modern title given to the works by Lady Charlotte Guest who endeavoured to translate them in 1848.

There are eleven stories in the *Mabinogion* and they are considered to be amongst the finest of the Celtic genius - a masterpiece of medieval literature. The stories are about the Four Branches of a Celtic family of kings whose origins date back to the dawn of the Celtic world. Contained within the compilation is the story of *Culhwch and Olwen*, which was the earliest Arthurian tale.

Also included are the children of Llyr (Lear) who dominate the story. The same author who wrote under the pseudonym of Taliesin was to write his famous work *King Lear* under the pseudonym of 'Shakespeare' in the 16th century AD - one thousand years later. *'Hwch'* as in 'Culhwch' meant a 'boar' which was not only an animal revered by the Druids, but was also the emblem of the Bacon family into which Francis was adopted.

According to Robert Graves, in his book titled *The White Goddess* (published in 1945), the *Book of Taliesin* contains medleys or poems awaiting resurrection and the work that Robert achieved in translating the meanings was not offered as being in any sense, final, for he felt that there would be others in the future who may be able to offer more clues.

Robert Graves was a recognised authority on mythology and was himself a poet of renown. He stated that he did not believe in paranormal experiences, and yet it was interesting to read in the final chapter of his book that Robert mentions many mystical experiences and coincidences which occurred throughout the time he was compiling *The White Goddess*. He found these experiences to be 'superlatively unscientific'. It would also seem that Robert did not believe in reincarnation, so that when he translated the poems, it possibly did not occur to him that the poet, Taliesin, was telling of his previous incarnations.

It was the opinion of Robert Graves *that the poet who called himself Taliesin, Chief of Bards, was well versed in Latin, French, Welsh, English and the Irish classics - and in Greek and Hebrew literature too, and it became obvious as Robert endeavoured to translate the meanings of the poems, that whoever Taliesin was, he was hiding an ancient religious mystery - a blasphemous one from the Church of Rome's point of view - under the cloak of buffoonery; but he had not made this secret altogether impossible to guess. Robert states that the 6th century Taliesin spent much of his time during the last third of that century as a guest of various Celtic chiefs and princes to whom he wrote complimentary poems. And, furthermore, the author of the poems was a paganistic cleric with Irish connections!*

This is an important statement because as the story of the Masters of the Mystical Rose unfolds, so too, will the true identity of Taliesin be revealed. One of his cryptic verses (quoted under this heading) tells us that he was the *Merlin* of the 6th century AD and therefore we know that he was an incarnation of St Germain because we know that the 6th century Merlin who anointed Arthur as a Celtic King, was St Germain.

Yet, we have still to ascertain exactly who he really was during that era and also where the island of 'Avalon' was, the mystical island where Arthur was not only anointed as King but was taken there to be buried after his demise. This is a puzzle that has kept readers of the Merlin and Arthurian legends guessing for aeons.

It is most obvious that the poet/Bard *Taliesin* must have known that the person, who in the 6th century addressed him as *Merlin*, was a reincarnation of the person who had been John the Divine/Beloved in the 1st century AD. Both John the Beloved Disciple and King Arthur were incarnations of the Master Kuthumi.

Robert Graves states that all the strange poems in the *Book of Taliesin* medley read like nonsense, only because the texts have been *deliberately* confused, *doubtless as a precaution against them being denounced as 'heretical' by some Church officer.* He also states that the bard seemed to lament the relaxation or abandonment of the ancient custom of the court of the house of Tewdwr (afterwards called the English House of Tudor), where he frequently visited. It was no coincidence that St Germain, one thousand years later, was born as a prince into the English House of Tudor whose emblem was the Tudor *Rose.*

The highly flattering comments made by renowned authors about the works of Taliesin, show that he was a genius and the greatest of the bards during that era. In the 16th century, St Germain was again to prove his genius as the greatest bard of all time, when he wrote under the pseudonym of 'Shakespeare'.

Francis Bacon - Genius

From the work titled *The Great Secret - Count Saint Germain* by Dr Raymond Bernard, we learn the following pertinent information:

"Francis Bacon was undoubtedly the greatest genius that the modern world has ever known. Our indebtedness to this great benefactor of humanity cannot be overestimated."

"To him we owe all that differentiates the present scientific and democratic age from the medieval, monarchial one that preceded it."

"He not only prophesied the coming of most of our inventions - the steamboat, steam engine, airplane, submarine etc., in his *New Atlantis*, but in his *Novum Organum*, he gave mankind the inductive, experimental method of research by which modern science and invention became possible."

"All that we denote by the words 'progress' and 'civilization' today we owe to him. Macaulay writes:

'Ask a follower of Bacon what the new philosophy has effected for mankind, and his answer is ready - it has lengthened life; it has mitigated pain; it has extinguished diseases; it has increased fertility of the soil; it has given new security to the mariner; it has spanned rivers and estuaries with bridges of forms unknown to our fathers; it has guided the thunderbolt innocuously from heaven to earth; it has lighted up the night with the splendour of the day ['electricity']; it has extended the span of human vision; it has multiplied the power of the human muscle; it has accelerated motion; it has annihilated distance; it has enabled man to descend into the depths of the sea; to soar into the air, to penetrate securely into the noxious recesses of the earth; to traverse the land with cars that whirl along without horses, and the ocean with ships which sail against the wind.'"

"In short, Bacon ushered in the New Age: he brought the medieval age to a close and brought into being the modern age of science, which he intended for the benefit of humanity. Before his time, philosophy was an abstract quest for truth; it distained to be useful and preferred to be stationary. But Bacon's practical inductive philosophy turned human powers of perception and understanding the external nature, to the mastery of the forces of nature for the good of man."

"Bacon was not only the greatest figure in the history of modern philosophy and science, but he was also the greatest figure in English literature, for it was he who was the fountainhead of the Elizabethan Renaissance through his writings which appeared under the name of Shakespeare, and other pen names such as Christopher Marlowe, etc."

"Ignatius Donnelly comments:

'He tried to hurry up civilization. He sought to use the royal power to give the seventeenth century the blessings of the nineteenth. His heart thirsted for the good of mankind. He saw in his mind's eye things akin to the marvels of steam and electricity. He foresaw airships, submarines, life-preservers, the telephone, microphone, patent-rights, quarantine, the microscope; he anticipated Roemer's discovery of time being required for the propagation of light; Newton's theory of gravitation and Darwin's variation of the species. He was the founder of Freemasonry.'"

Dr Bernard continues: "No man ever lived upon earth who had nobler aims than Francis Bacon. He stands at the portal of the opening of civilization of modern times, a sublime figure - his heart full of love for mankind, his busy brain teeming with devices for the benefit of man; the most far-extending human work that ever set a foot on the planet. He said: 'I am a servant of posterity; for these things require some ages for the ripening of them.' Adding: 'always desiring with extreme fervency, to have that which has never yet been attempted, now not to be attempted in vain, to wit: to release man out of their necessities and miseries'."

"Macaulay said: 'The end which Bacon proposed for himself was the multiplying of human enjoyments and the mitigation of human sufferings. This was the object of his speculations, in every department of science...in natural philosophy, in legislation, in politics, in morals'."

Pallas Athena

It is pertinent at this point of time, to quote from information sent to me by Peter Dawkins:

"'Shakespeare', particularly when printed with a hyphen as 'Shakes-peare', is a clear indication of a symbolic pseudonym. It is the literal meaning of Pallas Athena, the Supreme Muse of Poetry and the Arts, who, together with her companion, Apollo, was represented as shaking her lance at the dragon of ignorance - a reference which Ben Johnson used in his tributary poem to the Author of the First Folio of Shakespeare plays."

'Pallas' was also a title of the goddess Athene represented in the painting *Pallas and the Centaur* by Botticelli. Athena was the patron of the arts and crafts and the personification of wisdom whom the Romans identified with Minerva. She is commonly shown in ancient art wearing a helmet and a spear, both of which were symbolical of 'Wisdom' and 'Truth'.

Within the Arthurian literature, is the story of Sir Gawain and the Green Knight, written by an anonymous author in the 14th century. In the tale, Gawain encounters a Knight and enquires his name.

In reply, he is informed that the Knight's name was Joseus (another name for Joseph) and that his lineage was that of Joseph of Arimathea. His uncle was 'King Fisherman' and his father was *King Pelles* which was a disguised name for *Pallas*, referring to the fact that his father was a teacher of the 'Ancient Wisdom' of Sophia, also known as 'Athena'. This relationship will be explained later on in our story.

Many of the names utilized in the Arthurian legends were actual people but their names were 'masked' in almost 'pun-like' fashion, most typically a play on words. Apart from the name Pelles for Pallas, another interesting one was Lancelot - lance is another name for a 'spear'. The majority of the characters mentioned within the Arthurian legends were related to each other.

Even the real Merlin's parents were called Eithne (Athena) and Pallas. They were a dynastic family whose lineage was that of the Fisher Kings of the Grail stories - descendants of the Royal House of Judah, the House of David, first established by St Germain when he anointed David as King of the House of Judah.

The name of Pallas was strongly connected with *Arcadia*, particularly during the era that St Germain incarnated as Francis Bacon in the 16th century. The helmet which Pallas Athena wore became an important symbol of Arcadia during the Renaissance period. It was also during that era that King James the First of England (6th of Scotland), bestowed upon Francis the title of Viscount Verulam, which was another name for a 'spear/lance'.

From Peter Dawkins' book titled *The Virgin Ideal*, we learn more about the symbology of Athena.

"ATHENA is normally spelt with an 'E; on the end of her name (Athene), but the initiates spelt it with an 'A' at the end - a Double 'A' (AA) - and, in many of the printed poetry, plays and writings produced by the Renaissance initiates, the call sign which they used was a 'Double A' symbol as a headpiece on a page, with one of the A's shaded, the other left light."

"The Double 'A' has, of course, a deeper significance than just being two letters of Athena's name. Every letter of the alphabet is actually a symbol, deriving from a spiritual form or archetype with a numerical value and spiritual meaning. Two equilateral triangles placed together in a certain way create what is known as the Seal of Solomon, the perfect plan underlying the structure of the Temple, which, when it is filled with light, becomes the Blazing Star of David or Christ Star, the Creator's Star."

"Symbols of Athena are:

(1)   *The olive tree, for oil from the olive tree was used to anoint kings and priests and represented qualities such as enlightenment, peace, concord and prosperity.*

(2)   *The owl for its wisdom-knowledge and ability to see and hunt in the dark and silence.*

(3)   *A spear, given to Athena by Zeus, representing power of enlightenment in the Soul realm.*

(4)   *A helmet of gold which is known as the helmet of invisibility as well as the helmet of salvation and illumination. Its gold quality represents the wonderful halo of Christ light which cannot be seen by those who are spiritually blind, and which bestows the protection of light and love upon the wearer. One of the early names that Francis gave to his initiate group was 'Knights of the Helmet', which refers to the golden helmet of Athena."*

Cryptics of Taliesin

In medieval texts, Taliesin is considered to be the chief of the Bards, par excellence. I have chosen some verses at random, taken from Robert Graves' book *The White Goddess*, in order to convey Taliesin's messages and where it is appropriate, I have utilized them for chapter headings. When reading them, it is important to bear in mind that it was actually St Germain who wrote them under the pen-name of Taliesin during his incarnation as 'Merlin', the 'Magus' - the 'Wise man' of the 6th century AD. In the following verses, we are able to ascertain some of the clues he left for us regarding his past lives:

"I have been in Asia with Noah in the Ark,
I was in Canaan when Absalom was slain,
I conveyed Awen (Divine Wisdom known as 'Sophia') to the level of the
vale of Hebron, (Hebron Valley)
I strengthened Moses through the waters of the Jordan,

In deciphering some of the cryptics by Taliesin/Merlin/St Germain, he was with 'Noah in the Ark' because he was Noah. (That St Germain was once the grand patriarch known as 'Noah' is confirmed in the book titled *St Germain - Earth's Birth Changes*, channelled by Azena Ramanda). Noah's symbol was that of the 'Dove of Peace' and it was not coincidence that in two of his other incarnations, his name translated into the word 'Dove'. The 'Ark' may be alluding to the fact that Noah rescued the Sacred Teachings of the Arcana/Arkana from the Temples of Atlantis just prior to the deluge and subsequent sinking of Atlantis.

'Absalom' was one of the sons of King David (Kuthumi). During that particular era, St Germain incarnated as the prophet, Samuel, who anointed David of Hebron as King of Jerusalem. In this same time period, El Morya incarnated as the wise King Solomon, son of David. Taliesin also tells us that in one of his past lives he conveyed 'Divine Wisdom', which is otherwise known as 'Sophia' or the 'Wisdom of Athena', through the Hebron Valley and this would also have been during the time that he was the prophet Samuel. The 'Divine Wisdom' was the 'Sacred Teachings', the *Arcana* (meaning 'mystery/secret' from *arca* - a chest).

In his incarnation as Aaron, the brother of Moses, St Germain assisted Moses across the Jordan River. (According to the Mark-Age School of Education, St Germain was once a spiritual leader in early Egyptian days known as Rama and Rama was once Aaron, brother of Moses). It was to Aaron and his sons that the Sacred Tablets of Moses were given for safekeeping. The 'Sons of Aaron' were to become the Essenian 'Sons of Zadok', of the Order of Melchizedek (whom Edgar Cayce confirmed was an earlier incarnation of the Master Jesus).

The Covenant and The Rose Cross

The Sacred Tablets given to Aaron (St Germain) for safekeeping became known as the Ark of the Covenant, which in a future century, were to be housed in the Holy of Holies in the Temple of Jerusalem built by King Solomon (El Morya) upon the instructions of his father, King David (Kuthumi). (The most probable location of the Ark of the Covenant is given in the sequel to this story, *The Dove, The Rose and The Sceptre, In Search of The Ark of the Covenant*).

From information contained in the *Encyclopedia Of Mystical & Paranormal Experiences* by Rosemary Ellen Guiley, we are informed as follows: "Lewis [Spencer] traced Freemasonry back to Solomon's [El Morya's] use of Rosicrucian Teachings to build the Temple. This early period culminated in the life of the Master Jesus Christ, whom Lewis claimed had been expected by the Essenes, the Rosicrucians of Palestine."

St Germain, The Master of the Age of Aquarius

"I am a wonder whose origin is not known,
I have been teacher to all intelligences,
I have been instructed in the land of the Deity,
I am able to instruct the whole Universe,
I shall be until the day of Judgement
Upon the face of the Earth
Is it not the wonder of this world that I cannot be discovered?"
(Taliesin/Merlin - St Germain)

St Germain is known as the Master for the New Age of Aquarius and is also known as the Master of the Violet Ray, the Seventh Ray, which signifies an era of completion of spiritual lessons on the physical plane, the goal being to live in Divine love and peace.

His teachings are about the 'Art of Discovery', 'seek and ye shall find'. It is a teaching method that St Germain loves, for it is his way of teaching us to discover the truth by means of a treasure trail or game of hide and seek, which appeals to the child in all of us, for there is no fun in being handed the truth on a platter - we need to seek it for ourselves by using our own discernment.

St Germain has left many clues for us to discover, just as he did when he wrote under the pseudonym of *Taliesin* in the 6th century AD and one of his tantalizing cryptic verses was: *"Is it not the wonder of this world that I cannot be discovered?"*

When translating the *Preiddeu Annwm* (The Spoils of Annwm) by Taliesin, Robert Graves correctly arrived at the conclusion that some of the verses refer to the era of Jesus as being the Sixth Age [Pisces], and that the Seventh Age [Aquarius] would be that of Taliesin.

In other words, St Germain, writing under the pseudonym of Taliesin, left us clues that he would be the Master of the Aquarian Age.

Cryptics in the Bible

It is important to remember that the Bible is full of Pythagorean numbers, and it is significant that the 'Father of Mathematics' was also an earlier incarnation of the Master Kuthumi, who in his reincarnation as John the Beloved Disciple, when he wrote the Book of Revelation, incorporated cryptics that no one has as yet, completely deciphered. The Gospel of John also has hidden meanings to unravel. In today's world, it is the 'mathematicians' who, with the aid of advanced computer technology, are able to break the codes in the Bible as was prophesied and planned. The author, Michael Taylor, in his book titled *The Master R, Lord of Our Civilisation*, questions where is the Master R now? Michael Drosnin, author of *The Bible Code* also questions as to where the person who inserted the Codes in the Bible is now? The answer is given in the verses by *Taliesin/Merlin* who was St Germain.

"I have been on the Galaxy at the throne of the Distributor [God];
I have been teacher to all intelligences;
I am able to instruct the whole Universe;
My original country is the region of the Summer Stars;
I know the name of the stars from the North to the South;"

St Germain is a Master teacher who dwells in the fifth dimension, or the etheric, the 'invisible realms', watching over us, guiding and protecting earth's destiny.

During the 19th century, Madame Helena Blavatsky, founder of the Theosophical Society, was taught by the Masters El Morya, St Germain, Kuthumi, and Djwhal Khul, whilst sojourning in Tibet. In her book titled *The Secret Doctrine*, Helena divulged information about the fifth and other dimensions that exist.

In his book titled *The Bible Code*, Michael Drosnin, who was skeptical about the existence of the fifth dimension, consulted renowned physicists who informed him that today, the majority of them now agree that the fifth dimension does indeed exist, but they are still unable to explain exactly how.

'Choices' and The 'Lord of Code'

Life is a matter of choices and, if at times we make the wrong choices, we 'reap what we sow'. This is sometimes referred to as 'Karma'. In the very ancient days of Egypt, it was called the Land of Karm/Khem and it is possible that this was the origin of the word 'karma'.

From the time of the fall of Lemuria and Atlantis, Noah (St Germain), the ancient land of Sumer occupied by the Sumerians, the Arkadians, the Pharaohs of Egypt, particularly Tutmoses III (Kuthumi) and his great great grandson Akhnaton (El Morya); Moses and his brother Aaron (St Germain); King David (Kuthumi) and his son Solomon (El Morya); the Essenes - Jesus, his brothers and sisters; their parents Mary and Joseph (St Germain); St John the Beloved (Kuthumi) and the other Disciples; the mysterious Joseph of Arimathea who took the *Grail* to Glastonbury; Celtic Saints; King Arthur (Kuthumi) and Merlin (St Germain), - *all* have played a major role in our civilization and *all* of these Masters desire that we choose to live in peace and save our beautiful planet.

The overall reality is that a higher intelligence than we mortals on planet earth exists, and in ancient times the higher intelligence were called 'gods' because they were the Master Race of civilization, once referred to as the 'Golden Giants' or the Elder Race. The ancient Egyptians, Greeks, Phoenicians, Sumerians, Romans and Druids worshipped the gods and goddesses of which mythology consists, and many of them did exist in those times.

With the coming of Christianity, the early Roman Church fathers attempted to bring the various religious cultures under the one umbrella, without taking into consideration the very ancient traditions or their origins.

Think of how many times wars have been and still are being fought over religion or the lack of toleration for each other's beliefs and traditions and, from the etheric - the fifth dimension, the Masters continue to watch over and warn us, particularly through the codes in the Bible.

The person of higher intelligence who inserted the codes in the Bible asks the question "will you choose to change?" He was referring to the prophecies and the fact that the planet earth has 'free will'. Prophecies are just about events that may happen - we can prevent them if we so choose, particularly if we heed the warnings that have been given to us.

From the *Romance of Taliesin*, one of the verses states:
"I shall be till the day of judgement
On the face of the earth"

This verse provides us with yet another clue that the Master St Germain is watching over us, and if we choose to heed the warnings of the ancient prophecies, we can alter the course of our history and not repeat the past history of Atlantis. The Atlanteans misused their advanced laser and crystal technology. This led them to cause total destruction and Atlantis sank. Those Atlanteans who were power-hungry and greedy, utilized 'fear' as a means of 'control' over the population. Thus, it could be said that in today's world, nothing has changed.

Edgar Cayce (pronounced Cay-cee) was born in March 1877 and died in January, 1945. He was known as the 'Sleeping Prophet', because during his lifetime, when in a trance-like state, he recorded over thirty thousand readings. Cayce revealed that he had lived a previous existence in Atlantis and that in one of his past lives he was known as Ra-Ta, a High Priest in Egypt 10,600 years ago.

(He also recorded that he had once been a ruler in Persia and a disciple of Jesus, Lucius [Luke] of Cyrene who was a member of the Essenes. The Evangelist, Luke, was known as the 'Beloved Physician'. Cayce believed that he had acquired his scientific and medical knowledge from a former life as an alchemist at Troy in the ancient days of Greece. He was a truly remarkable man, who for the duration of his life, without having any medical experience in his life as Edgar Cayce, was able to diagnose and cure hundreds of people, even through absent healing. Cayce also related that John the Beloved [Kuthumi], his brother James Zebedee were Essenes).

Edgar prophesied that he would reincarnate in the year 1998, just prior to the second millennium. During trance channellings, Cayce told of how the war-mongering inhabitants, who caused the destruction of Atlantis, continued to reincarnate with war still in their consciousness. The majority of people, who were born after World War II, are conscious of preventing any future wars.

From the study of history we know of man's successes, failures, triumphs and disasters, and it is has been said that "we learn from history that we do not learn from history."

Such a statement is indeed true of today's world. The evidence of the past is there for us to read about, however, few choose to change the course of history, when, at all stages, changes are possible by our freedom of 'choice', which was clearly the message left to us within the Biblical codes currently being deciphered, placed in the Bible by the person who identifies himself as the 'Lord of Code'.

In the book titled *Edgar Cayce, Modern Prophet*, we learn the following important information:

"Early in this century, Edgar Cayce began to prophesy the return of both types of Atlanteans in vast numbers. He warned that for every advance of science and material emancipation the Sons of the One God might bring with them, the Sons of Man could also bring corruption and chaos."

"'Atlantean souls are extremists; they know no middle ground,' Cayce stated uncompromisingly, adding that 'Atlanteans of every genre were to be found among the leaders of all the nations involved in the two World Wars. So as a rough standard of comparison, we can see Roosevelt and Churchill at the one end of the scale and Hitler and Stalin at the other.'"

"'Granting that reincarnation is fact', Edgar Cayce said elsewhere, 'and that souls once occupied such an environment as Atlantis, and that these are now entering the earth's sphere - if they made such alterations in the earth's affairs in their day as to bring destruction on themselves - can there be any wonder that they might make such changes in the affairs of peoples and individuals today?'"

WILL WE CHOOSE TO CHANGE THE PROPHECIES?

MASTERS DISCUSSED IN THIS CHAPTER

Noah - St Germain
Aaron, the brother of Moses - St Germain
Samuel the Prophet - St Germain
Alexander the Great - St Germain
Taliesin/Merlin - St Germain
St Germanus - St Germain
Charlemagne the Great - St Germain
Francis Bacon/Shakespeare - St Germain
King David - Kuthumi
Pharaoh Tutmoses III - Kuthumi
Chinese Philosopher, Lao Tze - Kuthumi
Greek Philosopher, Pythagoras - Kuthumi
Greek Philosopher, Aristotle - Kuthumi
John the Beloved Disciple - Kuthumi
King Arthur - Kuthumi
Leonardo da Vinci - Kuthumi
Sir John Dee - Kuthumi
Pharaoh Akhnaton - El Morya
King Solomon - El Morya
Elijah the Prophet - El Morya
John the Baptist - El Morya

NOTES AND RECOMMENDED READING

Robert Graves, *The White Goddess*, (Faber & Faber, U.K., 1961)

Alfred Dodd, *Francis Bacon's Personal Life Story*, (Rider & Company, U.K., 1986)

Peter Dawkins, *The Great Vision*, (Francis Bacon Research Trust, Warwick, U.K.)

Peter Dawkins, *Arcadia*, (Francis Bacon Research Trust, Warwick, U.K.)

Peter Dawkins, *The Virgin Ideal*, (Francis Bacon Research Trust, Warwick, U.K.)

Peter Dawkins, *Dedication to the Light*, (Francis Bacon Research Trust, Warwick, U.K.)

Peter Dawkins, *Francis Bacon Herald of the New Age*, (Francis Bacon Research Trust, Warwick, U.K. 1997)

Dr Raymond Bernard, A.B., M.A. Ph. D., *The Great Secret Count Saint Germain*, (U.S.A.)

Isabel Cooper-Oakley, *Comte De St Germain - The Secret of Kings*, (Theosophical Society Publishing House, London, U.K., 1985)

Azena Ramanda, *St Germain - Earth's Birth Changes*, (Triad Publications, Queensland, Australia, 1993)

Azena Ramanda and Claire Heartsong, *St Germain - Twin Souls & Soulmates*, (Triad Publications, Queensland, Australia 1994).

Michael Taylor, *The Master R. Lord Of Our Civilisation*, (Rawley Trust, Christchurch, New Zealand, 1997)

Mary Carter, *Edgar Cayce, Modern Day Prophet*, (Bonanza Books, U.S.A., 1970)

Joseph Weed, _Wisdom of the Mystic Masters_, (Parker Publishing Co. U.S.A., 1968)

Annie Bessant, _Ancient Wisdom_, (Theosophical Publishing House, U.S.A., 1994)

Spencer Lewis, _The Mystical Life of Jesus_, (AMORC, U.S.A., 1929, available through the Theosophical Society)

Spencer Lewis, _Rosicrucian Questions And Answers_, (AMORC, U.S.A. 1929, available through the Theosophical Society)

C.W. Leadbeater, _The Hidden Life in Freemasonry_, (Theosophical Publishing House, U.K., 1975)

Madame Helena Blavatsky, _The Secret Doctrine_, (Theosophical Publishing House, Quest Books, U.S.A. 1966)

Albert G. Mackey, _A History of Freemasonry Vol. 5_. (Masonic History Co. New York, U.S.A., 1898)

Dr Hiroshi Motoyama, _Karma & Reincarnation_, (Piatkus, London, U.K. 1992)

Charles W. Hedrick & Robert Hodgson Jnr., _Nag Hammadi Gnosticism And Early Christianity_, (Hendrickson Publishers, U.S.A., 1986)

John Allegro, _The Dead Sea Scrolls_, (Penguin Books, U.K., 1964)

George F. Jowett, _The Drama Of The Lost Disciples_, (Covenant Publishing Co. Ltd., U.K. 1980)

William Foxwell Albright, _From The Stone Age To Christianity_, (Doubleday Anchor, U.S.A. 1957)

Merrill F. Unger, _Archaeology And The Old Testament_, (Zondervan Publishing House, Michigan, U.S.A)

E.A. Wallis Budge, _Legends Of The Egyptian Gods_, (Dover Publications, U.S.A, 1994)

Paul Brunton, _A Search in Secret Egypt_, (Samuel Weiser, Inc., U.S.A., 1973)

Stephen Quirke, _Ancient Egyptian Religion_, (British Museum Press, U.K., 1992)

Arnold J. Toynbee, _A Study of History_, (Oxford University Press, London, U.K., 1934)

Roger Whiting, _Leonardo (da Vinci)_, (Barrie & Jenkins, London, 1992)

Daniel J. Boorstin, _The Discoverers, A History of Man's Search To Know His World And Himself_, (Random House, U.K., 1983)

Time Life Books, _Voyages of Discovery_, (Amsterdam, 1989)

Ian Wilson, _Holy Faces, Secret Places,_ (Corgi Books, U.K., 1992)

Elizabeth Hallam, _The Plantagenet Encyclopedia_, (Tiger Books International, U.K., 1996)

Elizabeth Hallam, _Chronicles of the Crusades_, (Weidenfeld and Nicholson, Ltd., London, U.K.)

T.H. White, _The Once And Future King_, (Collins, U.K. 1958)

T.H. White, _The Book of Merlin_, (Collins, U.K. 1978)

David Day, _The Quest For King Arthur_, (De Agostini Editions, U.K., 1995)

Geoffrey of Monmouth, _The History of the Kings of Britain_, (edited by Lewis Thorpe, Penguin, 1966)

Geoffrey of Monmouth, _The Vita Merlini_, (trans. J.J. Parry, University of Illinois, 1925)

Douglas Monroe, _The 21 Lessons of Merlyn_, (Llewellyn Publications, U.S.A., 1992)

John Mathews, _The Grail,_ (Thames & Hudson, U.K., 1994)

Jean Markale, _Merlin_, (Inner Traditions, Vermont, Canada, 1995)

Mike Dixon-Kennedy, _Celtic Myth & Legend_, (Blandford U.K., 1996)

Mike Dixon-Kennedy, _Arthurian Myth & Legend_, (Blandford U.K., 1995)

Andrew Sinclair, _The Discovery of the Grail_, (Century, London, U.K., 1998)

Paul Broadhurst and Hamish Miller, _The Sun And The Serpent_, (Pendragon Press, Cornwall, U.K. 1995)

Paul Broadhurst, _Tintagel and the Arthurian Mythos_, (Pendragon Press, Cornwall, U.K. 1995)

Janet & Colin Bord, _Mysterious Britain_, (Paladin, U.K., 1975)

Janet & Colin Bord, _Dictionary of Earth Mysteries_, (Thorsons, U.K., 1996)

Philip Carr-Gomm, _The Druid Renaissance_, (Thorsons, U.S.A, 1996)

John Michell, _The Earth Spirit_, (Thames & Hudson, U.K., 1975)

Robert K.G. Temple, _The Sirius Mystery_, (Destiny Books, Vermont, Canada, 1976)

Jose Arguelles, *The Mayan Factor*, (Bear & Co., Santa Fe, 1987)

Adrian Gilbert & Maurice M. Cotterell, *The Mayan Prophecies*, (Element, U.K. 1995)

J.C. Cooper, *An Illustrated Encyclopaedia Of Traditional Symbols*, (Thames & Hudson, U.K., 1979)

Emile Legouis, *A History of English Literature*, (J.M. Dent & Sons Ltd., U.K. 1945)

Boris Ford, *The Age of Shakespeare*, (Penguin Books, U.K. 1955)

Frank Kermode, John Hollander, *The Oxford Anthology of English Literature*, (Oxford University, U.K., 1973)

Edward Fitzgerald, *The Rubaiyat of Omar Khayyam*, (Collins, U.K., 1974)

Edmund Harold, *Second Sight*, (Grail Publications, Sydney, Australia, 1994)

Edmund Harold, *Master Your Own Vibration*, (Grail Publications, Sydney, Australia, 1986)

Gareth McDonnell, *Kuthumi - A Pebble In A Pond*, (G. McDonnell, Victoria, Australia, 1993)

Michael Drosnin, *The Bible Code*, (Weidenfeld & Nicholson, London, U.K. 1997)

Michael Howard, *The Occult Conspiracy*, (Ryder & Ryder, U.K. 1989)

Michael Baigent, Richard Leigh & Henry Lincoln, *The Holy Blood And The Holy Grail*, (Arrow Books, U.K., 1996)

Michael Baigent, & Richard Leigh, *The Temple And The Lodge*, (Corgi Books, U.K. 1996)

Michael Baigent, Richard Leigh & Henry Lincoln, *The Messianic Legacy*, (Arrow, U.K. 1996)

Peter Lemesurier, *The Armageddon Script*, (Element Books, U.K. 1981)

Lynn Picknett & Clive Prince, *The Templar Revelation*, (Corgi Books, U.K. 1997)

Christopher Knight & Robert Lomas, *The Hiram Key*, (Century, U.K., 1996)

Christopher Knight & Robert Lomas, *The Second Messiah*, (Century, U.K. 1997)

Rosemary Ellen Guiley, *Encyclopedia Of Mystical & Paranormal Experience*, (Grange Books, London, U.K., 1991)

Simon Peter Fuller, *Rising Out Of Chaos*, (Kima Global, South African, 1994)

F.L. Rawson, *Life Understood,* (The Crystal Press Ltd., U.K., 1920)

Dr Douglas Baker, B.A., M.R.C.S., L.R.C.P., F.Z.S., *The Jewel in the Lotus*, ('Little Elephant', Essendon, U.K., 1985)

CHAPTER 2

Lemuria & Atlantis

"I have been loquacious [talkative]
prior to being gifted with speech"

(Taliesin/Merlin/St Germain)

Edgar Cayce prophesied that not only would the secrets of the pyramids of Egypt be revealed by approximately the year 2,000 but also that Atlantis, which was once part of Lemuria, would be found.

Once there was a civilization known as the Elder race, and in mythology they were called the 'Golden Giants'. Many of the so-called mythological tales were in fact true and the gods and goddesses did exist. Within the Book of Genesis we have the story of the origin of man that is not only symbolical but parts of it are historical. According to Madame Helena Blavatsky, in her book titled *The Secret Doctrine*, the Lemurians built huge cities of rare earths and metals. The divine Dynasties such as the Egyptians, Chaldeans, Greeks etc., had gained their knowledge from the Master race which had once been part of Atlantis and Lemuria.

"The Aryan [Arian] nations could trace their descent through the Atlanteans from the more spiritual races of the Lemurians, in whom the 'Sons of Wisdom' had personally incarnated. Helped by Divine Intelligence which informed them, they built cities, and cultivated arts and sciences. The Lemurians were very large, the 'giants' whose physical beauty and strength reached their climax, in accordance with evolutionary law, toward the middle period of their fourth sub-race."

"The oldest remains of Cyclopean buildings were all the handiwork of the Lemurians and the stone relics found on the small piece of land called Easter Island by Captain Cook, are very much like the walls of Pachacamac or the Ruins of Tia-Huanuco in Peru."

We are all descendants from the lost continents of Lemuria and Atlantis which were actual civilizations some 33,000 years ago. Lemuria was at one time situated along the lower part of Australia and included New Zealand and Hawaii. We are informed by St Germain in the book titled *St Germain - Earth's Birth Changes* channelled by Azena Ramanda: "Australia is a grand island. It is indeed the participation of the outer rim of the ancient land called Lemuria." "Indeed, that which is Australia has a special place in my heart, but I love the others as well." With reference to New Zealand, St Germain informs us: "It is indeed a part of the Lemurian continent as well."

According to Madame Helena Blavatsky in her book titled *The Secret Doctrine*: "As a master says, why should not your geologists bear in mind that under the continents explored and fathomed by them...there may be hidden, deep in the fathomless, or rather unfathomed ocean beds, other and far older continents whose strata have never been geologically explored; and that they may some day upset entirely their present theories?"

"Why not admit that our present continents have, like Lemuria and Atlantis, been several times already submerged, and had the time to re-appear again and bear their new groups of mankind and civilizations..."

Lemuria

"It must be noted that Lemuria which served as the cradle of the Third Root-Race, not only embraced a vast area in the Pacific and Indian Oceans (such as Australia and New Zealand), but extended in the shape of a horse-shoe past Madagascar, round South Africa, through the Atlantic up to Norway."

"No more striking confirmation of our position could be given than the fact that the elevated ridge in the Atlantic basin, 9,000 feet in height, which runs for some two or three thousand miles southwards from a point near the British Isles, first slopes towards South America, then shifts at right angles to proceed in a south-easterly line toward the African coast. This ridge is a remnant of the Atlantic continent. The Atlantic portion of Lemuria was the geological basis of what is generally known as Atlantis."

"Lemuria was once a gigantic land. It covered the whole area of space from the foot of the Himalayas, which separated it from the inland sea rolling its waves over what is now Tibet, Mongolia, and the great Gobi desert."

"It stretched South across what is known to us as southern India, Ceylon [Sri Lanka] and Sumatra [Indonesia] then embracing on its way, as we go south, Madagascar on its right hand and Australia and Tasmania on its left, it ran down to within a few degrees of the Antarctic Circle, when from Australia, an inland region on the Mother Continent in those ages, it extended far into the Pacific Ocean."

[Note: Tasmania is a small island off the coast of Australia and is part of Australia].

It is noteworthy that according to the book titled *Voyages of Discovery*: "a theory of the Greek philosopher, Aristotle, was that somewhere in distant latitudes there existed *terra Australis incognita*, an unknown southern land." Aristotle was an incarnation of the Master Kuthumi.

Atlantis

Plato (St Germain) told of the existence of Atlantis in his works titled *Timaeus* and *Dialogues* around 335 BC. He wrote of a city that flourished beyond the Pillars of Hercules - the Straits of Gibraltar, in circa 9,000 BC. (During the Renaissance period in Florence in the 15th century AD and in England in the 16th century, the teachings of Plato were established in what became known as the Platonic Academies).

How did Atlantis and Lemuria obtain their names?

According to St Germain in the book titled *Earth's Birth Changes*, channelled by Azena Ramanda:

"A grand, grand master of life (from the Pleiades) emerged upon the plane and his name was Atlas. He was the one who chose to create peace and splendour and glorious exemplification of a light of God upon the plane. The father of Atlas' mate was called Muras and he went forth and developed a grand golden civilization called Lemuria."

Most of what we know about the mythology of Atlantis is from the philosopher, Plato, an incarnation of St Germain. According to mythology, it was believed that Atlas held up the world in order to prevent the sky from falling down.

In the Middle Ages it was believed that Atlas taught men astrology through his association with the sky and the stars. The sisters of Atlas were the Pleiades, one of which was named Maia, whom the Romans were later to worship as one of the nature goddesses. (The month of 'May' was named after her).

The god, Atlas, was one of the ten kings who ruled Atlantis, from which his name was derived and Atlantis was named in honour of him by the sea god Poseidon.

Atlas was considered to be a very wise ruler and his descendants continued to rule Atlantis in the same fashion. Each king had his own portion of land to govern and for aeons the people lived in peace and harmony in a glorious semi-tropical paradise, full of beautiful plants, flowers, animals and birds.

The Atlanteans built a wonderful advanced canal system so that everything flourished and later, after the 'Fall', they were to introduce this canal system into the ancient land of Sumer. No king had dominance over the other and the people were governed fairly.

Edgar Cayce recorded that the inhabitants of Atlantis communicated telepathically which is a further clue that Taliesin/Merlin/St Germain gave us in the quotation: *"I have been loquacious [talkative] prior to being gifted with speech."*

The Atlanteans could 'read' each other's minds and were able to tell a great deal about one another from having the ability to be able to see auras, and, because these consisted of a spectrum of colours, which had designated meanings, the inhabitants of Atlantis could tell whom to trust or if someone was not telling them the truth. For example, if someone was really angry, the aura would show 'red'- hence the saying 'seeing red'. Because of these abilities, speech was not developed as it was not necessary.

The Fall of Atlantis

The Elder race were rulers and priests who reigned upon the earth in a time when everything was shared. There was no greed, no materialism, and all lived in unity, peace and harmony - a true *Garden of Eden*.

Apart from the Bible and ancient Jewish records, many other cultures such as the Mayans, have recorded that these lands did exist and both the Lemurians and the Atlanteans were very skillfully developed nations.

As briefly mentioned in the previous chapter, eventually the Elder race became entrapped in enslavement of materialistic values and the final fall of Atlantis began, whereby they virtually destroyed their own continent by abusing their technological powers, especially with laser and crystal technology.

According to St Germain, the sinking of Atlantis was not an event that happened over night; it was a very gradual progression in which the ancient civilization gradually degenerated and perished in a series of cataclysms that destroyed large portions of their inhabited land-masses. An explosion of incredible force finally destroyed these continents, splitting them and sinking many areas that were once joined. The result was torrential rain and flooding - referred to in the Bible as the 'Noah' period.

As Noah, St Germain had served as a High Priest and prophet in one of the temples of Atlantis. He and the other highly initiated priests from the temples, the *Illumined Ones*, realized that their land was doomed and made preparations to depart, carrying with them their secret and sacred doctrines. When the fall of Atlantis occurred, the remnants of their civilizations scattered to various parts of the world, taking with them their cultural knowledge and skills.

Discovery of Atlantis

In January, 1998, the newspapers reported that there were plans by Russian scientists to search for the lost city of Atlantis 160km off Britain's Land's End. This perplexed the British team who were embarking on an identical search in Bolivia, South America!

Somewhere off the tip of Land's End, is said to lie beneath the sea, the legendary lost land of Lyonesse which, according to local Cornish legend, once lay between Cornwall and Brittany (France). Evidence of this exists in the Scilly Islands where hilltops of the Scillies are believed to be part of the sunken Lyonesse.

Russian explorers, who received permission from the British government, used geological evidence that there was once a fertile plain beyond the Isles of Scilly known as the Celtic Shelf and they believed it to be the City of Lions (Lyonesse) which once had one hundred and forty temples. The Russian scientists based their investigations on new and accurate translations of original Greek texts, particularly those of Plato [St Germain] who stated that Atlantis disappeared beneath the ocean in the 10th millennium BC.

The English explorers, through means of a satellite, detected a canal on the Bolivian-Peruvian high plain. According to a recent television programme on the History Channel (December, 2003), the explorers have discovered a series of numerous man-made canals and it will take many years and a great deal of finance to explore them and support their theory.

After the Great Flood

Throughout the period of the disintegration of Atlantis, once a glorious civilization, and in the ensuing aftermath, new races of humanity established themselves in many parts of the globe, the prophets holding onto their dreams of restoring peace and harmony in a universal Golden Age. After the Great Flood had subsided, it was Noah's dream that those survivors and their descendants would found a civilization that would have learnt its lessons from the past, and not self-destruct as had the civilizations of Lemuria and Atlantis. Noah (St Germain), the prophet was to be the grand patriarch of the new land, bringing the genealogy and technology of the Atlanteans and Lemurians into the new continents which were established as a result of the great flood.

One of the lineages from this ancient race of people, were to become known as the Celts who eventually settled in Gaul (France), Ireland, Scotland, Wales, and the west coast of Cornwall, whereby they became known as the Celtic Druids. Others were to settle in Greece, Rome, Israel, Africa, Europe, Peru and some became the people known as the Mayans.

The Mayans

A great master who taught the Mayan and Mexican civilizations was known as Quetzalcoatl whose name meant the Plumed or Feathered Serpent (of Wisdom). Quetzalcoatl was regarded as an Avatar and is credited with the sacred astrological calendar of ancient Mexico.

From the book titled *Fingerprints Of The Gods* by Graham Hancock, we learn of the description of Quetzalcoatl: "...a mysterious person...a white man with strong formation of body, broad forehead, large eyes, and a flowing beard. He was dressed in a long, white robe reaching to his feet. He condemned sacrifices, except of fruits and flowers, and was known as the god of peace. When addressed on the subject of war he is reported to have stopped up his ears with his fingers."

"He was a 'wise instructor' who came from across the sea in a boat that moved by itself without paddles. He also built houses and showed couples that they could live together as husband and wife; and since people often quarreled in those days, he taught them to live in peace. One of the other names by which he was known was Kukulkan and like Quetzalcoatl, when translated into English, both names meant Plumed Serpent."

Like Poseidon, Quetzalcoatl was equated with being a sea god, because he had arrived by sea and upon his departure, disappeared in or out to sea. It is considered that many of the so-called gods that appeared in the various countries to teach and instruct civilizations in advanced technology, especially the Mayans, were priests of Atlantis.

What has confounded historians is why the Mayas abandoned their major cities by 830 AD. The most amazing achievement that the Mayans left to humanity was the Mayan Calendar which predicted at various levels of time, exactly what would occur in the future. They even predicted the era of the birth of the great philosophers such as Pythagoras (Kuthumi), Socrates (earlier incarnation of Jesus), Plato (St Germain), Aristotle (Kuthumi), Lao Tzu (Kuthumi) in China and Buddha (reputedly earlier incarnation of Jesus) in India, the Celts spreading across Europe, the Coming of Jesus, and the Crusades. Simply amazing!

The Fifth Root Race

According to Madame Helena Blavatsky in her book titled *The Secret Doctrine*, the remnant tribe of Atlantis became known as the 'Fifth Root Race', the

Aryan (Arian) Race. Noah was the grand patriarch and progenitor of the descendants of that race and through the millenniums, taking in the eras of the kings (pharaohs) and queens of Egypt, through to the time of the Essenes, the Arians traditionally kept their blood-lineage pure by only marrying within their own tribe and according to the Rosicrucian authority, the late Spencer Lewis, Jesus was of pure Arian blood, as were his parents.

It will be remembered that Madame Blavatsky stated unequivocally that the Arian Race were descendants of Atlantis and had once been the Lemurians who were the 'spiritual' ones. Also, it was mentioned in the first chapter that Edgar Cayce prophesied that from his own time onwards, there would be the return of both types of Atlanteans in vast numbers, the ones who worked for the 'Light' - the 'spiritual ones', who work for the good of mankind versus the ones who work for the 'Dark' - the extremists who "know no middle ground."

In a future chapter, the Book of Enoch will be discussed. The back of the book mentions the writings of Madame Blavatsky stating that **the last advent and the destruction of the Anti-Christ - signify, *esoterically*, that some of the great adepts will return in the Seventh Race, when all Error will be made away with, and the advent of TRUTH will be heralded by the 'Sons of Light'.**

Therefore, it is not coincidental that St Germain is known as the Lord of the Seventh Ray for the Age of Aquarius - the Essenes were called the 'Sons of Light' whose instructor, the *Teacher of Righteousness*, was St Germain.

Reference was given in the previous chapter, to one of the poems of Taliesin, namely the *Preiddeu Annwm* (The Spoils of Annwm) and that Robert Graves correctly reached the conclusion that the era of Jesus referred to the Sixth Age (Pisces), **and that the Seventh Age (Aquarius) would be that of Taliesin [St Germain].**

The Theosophical Society

(Theo-God, Sophia = wisdom/knowledge)

Charles W. Leadbeater related that St Germain was one of the teachers of Madame Helena Blavatsky and that Helena, having been encouraged by the Masters, was the founder of the Theosophical Society. Leadbeater related that at that time, St Germain went by the name of Pere (Father) Joseph. This was the second known time that he was called Joseph - having been Joseph the Father of the Holy Grail Family in the first century AD.

According to Leadbeater, one of Leadbeater's principal teachers in a previous life had been the Master known as Djwhal Khul. Djwhal Khul had been the disciple and cousin of Jesus, known as John Mark, one of the Four Evangelists.

An author, who is a great source of information on the lives of the past

Masters and the Arcana Teachings, was Annie Bessant (1847-1933). Annie was also a member of the Theosophical Society and shared her leadership with Charles Leadbeater. She was described as a 'Diamond Soul' for she had many brilliant facets to her character.

Annie was a champion of human freedom, a philanthropist and author of more than three hundred books, guiding thousands of men and women all over the world in their spiritual quest. In her earlier days in England, Annie achieved remarkable results as a Free-thinker who supported noble causes including women's suffrage. One of her well known books is *The Ancient Wisdom*, first published in 1939. In this book, Annie adequately explains the subject of 'Reincarnation' and 'Karma'.

Isabel Cooper-Oakley, author of *Masonry and Medieval Mysticism* and *The Comte De St Germain*, was a friend of Madame Helena Blavatsky and was appointed by Annie Bessant as the International President of the Committee for Research into Mystic Traditions.

NOAH - ST GERMAIN, WAS THE GRAND PATRIACH FROM ATLANTIS

MASTERS DISCUSSED IN THIS CHAPTER
Noah - St Germain
Plato - St Germain
The Essenes' Teacher of Righteousness - St Germain
Taliesin - St Germain
Madame Helena Blavatsky
Edgar Cayce

NOTES AND RECOMMENDED READING

Mary Carter, *Edgar Cayce, Modern Day Prophet*, (Bonanza, U.S.A, 1970)
Madame Blavatsky, *The Secret Doctrine*, (Theosophical Publishing House, Quest Books U.S.A. 1966)
Richard Laurence, *The Book of Enoch The Prophet*, (Wizards Bookshelf, U.S.A, 1983)
Azena Ramanda, *St Germain - Earth's Birth Changes*, (Triad Publications, Queensland, Australia, 1993)
Graham Hancock, *Fingerprints Of The Gods*, (Mandarin Books, U.K. 1995)
Time-Life Books, *Voyages of Discovery*, (Amsterdam, 1989)
C. W. Leadbeater, *The Hidden Life in Freemasonry*, (Theosophical Publishing House, U.K. 1975)
Isabel-Cooper-Oakley, *Comte De St Germain*, (Theosophical Publishing House, U.K. 1985)
Jose Arguelles, *The Mayan Factor*, (Bear & Co., Santa Fe, New Mexico)
Spencer Lewis, *The Mystical Life of Jesus* (AMORC, U.S.A, 1929, available through the Theosophical Society)
Robert Graves, *The White Goddess*, (Faber & Faber, U.K. 1961)

CHAPTER 3

The Ancient Land of Sumer & the Arcadians

"I have been in Asia with Noah in the Ark"
"I have been the chief director of the work of the tower of Nimrod"
"I saw the destruction of Sodom and Gomorrah"
"I know the names of the stars from north to south"
(Taliesin/Merlin/St Germain)

"All things Begin and End in Albion's [Britain's] Ancient Druid Rocky Shore."
(William Blake)

From Atlantis, Noah and his descendants brought with them the advanced technology that was to be inherited by the people of the land of Sumer. Shinar was the land of 'Sumer' where these people became known as the Sumerians. They were also to become known as the Arians (Aryans) and the Arkadians/Arcadians.

According to Francis Hitching in the book titled *The World Atlas of Mysteries*, "a cuneiform text called *The Epic of Gilgamesh*, transcribed in the 7th century BC tells of a flood long ago that is identical, except for detail, with the Hebrew flood legend of Noah (in the Sumerian version, the preceding rains lasted only seven days and nights, compared with the Biblical forty)."

From the book titled *Fingerprints Of The Gods* by Graham Hancock we are informed as follows:

"There was a king, in ancient Sumer, who sought eternal life. His name was Gilgamesh. We know of his exploits because the myths and traditions of Mesopotamia, inscribed in cuneiform script upon tablets of baked clay, have survived. Many thousands of these tablets, some dating back to the beginning of the third millennium BC have been excavated from the sands of modern Iraq."

"They transmit a unique picture of a vanished culture and remind us that even in those days of lofty antiquity human beings preserved memories of times still more remote - times from which they were separated by the interval of a great and terrible deluge."

"The story that Gilgamesh brought back had been told to him by a certain Utnapishtim, a king who had ruled thousands of years earlier, who had survived the great flood, and who had been rewarded with the gift of immortality because he had preserved the seeds of humanity and of all living things. It was long, long ago, said Utnapishtim, when the gods dwelt on the earth: Anu, Lord of the firmament, Enlil, the enforcer of the divine decisions, Ishtar, goddess of war and love and Ea, Lord of the waters, man's natural friend and protector."

History tells us that the earliest known civilization on Earth was Sumer and it was this land of Sumer that the Golden Giants first inhabited. Sumerian records show that their ancestors came from a paradise called Dilmun. The Sumerians lived and worshipped their own gods, long before the Pharaoh Akhnaton (Amenhotep IV - El Morya) first introduced the idea of 'one God', one 'Deity' to the Egyptians.

The cities of Sumer, in the southern region of Mesopotamia, and many other ancient sites of cities have been discovered. In some of the ancient libraries and other repositories, there have been found more than ten thousand clay tablets inscribed with many historical events written in hieroglyphics. Historians and archaeologists have been able to ascertain much of the history of the Sumerians such as their religion, laws, education, science, philosophies, trade and commerce. It was the Sumerians who built the first city states and they seemed to have appeared suddenly with full knowledge of sciences, astrology, engineering skills and agricultural instruments.

There has always been a great deal of mystery surrounding the Sumerian civilization because no evidence of a gradual process of development has ever been discovered to substantiate their beginnings. They just seemed to have sprung into existence with skills such as using ox-drawn ploughs for their agriculture, a highly skilled system of irrigating their fields, and engineering feats such as hydrological works and sewerage systems.

The Sumerians were also highly skilled masons, astronomers, architects and musicians. Their temples were designed by their architects, built by their masons and incorporated into their temples were stones which were sacred to them.

They invented the art of writing and they are the ancestors of our own culture. Evidence has been discovered inscribed in stone, stating that their arts and skills were taught by 'god-men'. The Egyptians, Mayans and Chinese also claimed that their advanced knowledge was given to them by 'god-men'.

The Sumerians had knowledge of planting their crops according to the phases of the moon and the positions of the planets, knowing that phases of the moon influenced the germination of seed and thus the growth of their crops. They worshipped the sun and the moon, and believed in life after death (reincarnation) knowing that the 'soul' never dies - it is a part of infinity.

They were a very highly intellectually advanced race that was also skilled in medicine, especially with the use of plants and using their own herbs. It can be seen that their descendants such as the Egyptians, the Essenes and the Druids, inherited these skills and knowledge which has been subsequently preserved down through the ages.

The Sumerians lived in well-planned cities around which were farms of wheat and barley, orchards, vineyards and grazing cattle, which were fed from a very advanced system of irrigational canals. Al Falaj is the name of the ancient Arabic canal system operational by gravity flow which is still used today. The land of Sumer must have seemed like a true 'Garden of Eden'.

The Mysterious 'X' - 3000 BC

According to information contained in the book titled *The Message of the Masters* by Robert J. Scrutton:

"By 3,000 BC the Sumerians had developed numeration to a high science. Their Mathematicians used quadric and cubic equations to develop ideas in architecture, engineering and astronomy. The mysterious X beloved by modern mathematicians to denote unknown quantities, was also used to indicate the unknown...the subject was one of the 'Mysteries of the Initiate'..."

The 'X' is a symbol frequently represented in the Irish *Book of Kells* attributed to St Columba and written on the island of Iona which was then known as the Island of the Druids. The X was adopted as the emblem of the Celtic Scots and became known as the Saltire - the St Andrew's cross, representing a dividing shield into four compartments, symbolic of the four directions and the four elements of earth, fire, water and air.

The Origins of the Maltese Cross

According to Robert J. Scrutton:

"The priests and kings of Sumer and Babylon knew the mystery of Anu, the initiation of a new member into a craft guild was by no means a ritual without substance or practical meaning and they were vowed to secrecy. It was revealed to the members of the guilds that *Anu* was one and many, an abstract deity that informed and ruled the whole expanse of ethereal space. *His sign was a star, shaped like a Maltese Cross, a symbol of rotation.*"

The star became equated with the Star of David.

From *The Hidden Life In Freemasonry* by C.W. Leadbeater we learn the following pertinent information:

"The Blazing Star (six-pointed) is used as a symbol in Lodges, the sign of a Deity. In the old Jewish form of Masonry they used the word Y H V H (Yod He Vod He), standing for Jehovah. In Co-Masonic Lodges the usual form of the figure is a serpent curled round with its tail in its mouth, a symbol of eternity."

According to Leadbeater, "four tassels around the border of a mosaic pavement used in Masonry are symbolic of temperance, fortitude, prudence and justice; but they also stand for the four great orders of Devas (nature spirits) connected with the four elements, earth, water, air and fire. At the initiation of candidates in Co-Masonic Lodges, four Rulers of the elements are invoked and the consequences of that are very real and beneficial, little as many members of the fraternity may be aware of the fact." (The Maltese Cross, like the *Saltire* - St Andrew's Cross, is also divided into four compartments).

A most interesting factor is that apart from the 'dove' being a symbol of St Germain, his main one is the Maltese Cross and the Maltese Cross and St Andrew's Cross both feature in the Irish Book of Kells written on the island of Iona, whose name also means the 'Dove'.

Throughout Britain, particularly Tintagel (the legendary birth place of Arthur) where there was once a Celtic monastery established in the 6th century AD., and in regions of Scotland where Celtic monasteries were established, there are ancient carvings of the Maltese Cross.

Anu - Anna

Anu was derived from the sacred letters AN (from which the word 'heaven' is derived). In Celtic mythology, the Irish race trace their ancient lineage back to the tribe of the Tuatha de Danaan (a derivative of Anna/Anu), who called themselves the children of Anna/Anu - 'the children of the Light'.

When the Church of Rome made its presence felt in Ireland, it Christianized the worshipping of this ancient goddess into St Anna. However, as can be seen, her origins are far older than that.

The Romans called her Anna Peranna (Perennial Anna) whom they worshipped as the sacred goddess of the wells. The tradition of throwing coins into a well or fountain (as in the Trevi fountain in Rome) in order to make a wish and receive good fortune, originated from the worship of this ancient goddess and this was the origin of the saying 'Lady Luck'.

According to information contained in Robert Graves' book titled *The White Goddess*:

"The Sumerian goddess was sometimes called Anna-Nin which became abbreviated to Nana (a name which we sometimes use as an abbreviated form of grandmother)."

From information contained in Peter Dawkins' book titled *The Great Vision*, we learn the following pertinent information:

"In the Hebrew-Christian tradition, the God-name for the Divine Mind (or Heavenly Father) is *AN*, whilst that for the Divine Mother (or Earthly Mother) is *ANNA*. *AN* is sometimes spelt *ON*, and we derive our word ONE from this mystery name." (The Pythagorean X represents the number '10' which is symbolic of 'oneness').

"The *'A'* represents Divine BEING, the Absolute, the initial Desire-to-be from which all else proceeds. The 'N' is its inherent Wisdom and creative powers that can vibrate Matter into the infinite variety of forms that manifest the divine Being. The vibratory sound of 'A' provides, in its first sense, the gasp of wonder or credulous query, whilst in its last sense, it conveyed the amazed wonder of sudden revelation and comprehension. [An example of this is when we exclaim Ahhhh! and when a baby makes similar sounds before it learns the art of speech]."

" *AN* is the mystery name of the supreme Heavenly Father who is 'Heaven', the Divine Mind, and who is the 'heavenly' polarity of all existence, all being. *ANNA* is referred to in exoteric tradition as the Black Virgin or Earth Mother, the Dark Waters or Deep, barren and infertile, but who brings forth the White Virgin, the Virgin Mary. In Christian parable, Anna is the mother of the Virgin Mary. The 'blackness' of Anna refers to the state of darkness or unconsciousness, of divine Matter in its Absolute state. The 'virginity' of Anna refers to the pure or pristine condition of that Divine Matter."

The Fall of the Sumerians - c.2400 BC

As the Sumerians travelled westward round the Arabian Desert into Syria, the Persian Gulf and north-westward over the Taurus Range onto the eastern part of the Anatolian Plateau, they spread their cultural knowledge and skills. (The Anatolian Plateau was later to be called Cappadocia and was the place where St Germain reincarnated in the 1st century AD as Apollonius of Tyana). The people who settled in the northern part of Mesopotamia were known as the Arcadians (Arkadians), otherwise known as the Aryan race or Arians.

Eventually this peaceful paradise of Sumer, whose inhabitants formed the society known as 'Sumero-Akkadian', was invaded by Sargon of Agade. In circa 2400 BC, Sargon began a military campaign which finally conquered the land of Sumer, wherein he established the world's first known empire. Eventually, Sargon's empire was invaded by a barbaric race called the 'Guti' who destroyed the whole of

Sumer.

In 1843 AD, Paul Emile Botta commenced the excavation of Khorsabad, the ancient capital of Sargon of Assyria. According to Merrill F. Unger in his book titled *Archaeology And The Old Testament*, when Sargon's palace was recovered, the royal annals and other records of Sargon's reign showed him as being the best known of the Assyrian monarchs.

Phoenicians - the 'Master Race' - 2000 BC

"I know the names of the stars from north to south"
(Taliesin/Merlin/St Germain)

In 2000 BC, one group of Arians sailed from Europe to found Phoenicia at which point of time they became known as the Phoenicians who navigated by the stars. They were a very seaworthy race who navigated the waters of the Gulf, trading all over Europe, Mesopotamia, Persia, Africa, India and also *founded Troy and Athens.*

They also traded and formed colonies in Syria where they became known as the Hyksos. This is thought to have occurred in the 16th century BC. Their language was a mixture of Phoenician and Hebrew; the Hebrew (meaning 'wanderer') race had established themselves in the lands of Egypt and Israel. According to information contained in Peter Dawkins' book titled *Arcadia*:

"The Phoenicians were considered to be the 'Master Race' and in the historical sense, they were the 'Elect' because they were the remnants of Atlantis and Lemuria who wished to establish a 'Golden Civilization', one of peace and Utopia." ('Utopia' comes from the Greek words *Ou topos* - it is the root word for dreams of social and political perfection). The Arians/Arcadians have always been the 'Guardians' and many of them became the Celtic Druids, Archdruids and kings (such as Arthur) who preserved the ancient Teachings.

How 'Arcadia' Derived its Name

Further information contained in *Arcadia* informs us that: "Arcadia derives its name from Arcas, the son of Zeus and the beautiful Callisto. Callisto was given the form of a bear by Zeus, represented in the sky by *Ursa Major*, the Great Bear. When Arcas died, Zeus made him into a constellation and set him beside his mother. In Arcas we have *Ursa Minor*, the Little Bear. The first star of the seven stars of the Little Bear is the present North Pole Star, and it carries the name of Arcas. It signifies the crown 'jewel' of the world and its heavens."

The People of the 'Covenant'

"*Ursa Minor* was also known as *Phoenice*, or *Ursa Phoenicia*. The Arcadians were known as 'the Bear Race'; they were also (in their most ancient sense) the original Phoenicians. Furthermore, the stars of *Ursa Minor* were those principally used in all navigation by land as well as by sea, to direct the course of the traveller. Thus the Arcadian or Bear Race was known as the guides or pathfinders of mankind, leading and lighting the way like Mercury or Hermes. The 'Bear' is also known as an 'Ark' or 'Boat'; and the Arcadians were the 'People of the Ark' or the 'Arch Race' - 'the People of the Covenant'. As Phoenicians, they were renowned sailors and navigators, as well as teachers and healers."

Peter Dawkins further relates: "with all this in mind, we can begin to see the real significance of the Areopagus of English poets, the chief of who were the Dudleys or Tudors, and their symbolism of Arcadia intermixed with the symbolism of Britain. When we also come to realise that the Ancient British derived their ancestry from the Trojans [people of Troy], who came to the 'Fortunate Isles' from the Aegean (the 'Summerland' of the Trojan Empire, which once included Greece, Thracia and Asia Minor as a mountainous 'ring' around the Aegean Sea) in the 2nd millennium BC, we can begin to see the whole picture with far more meaning."

"Then add to this the fact that the Trojans claimed to be but another, later wave of settlers to Britain from the Aegean area, and were related as *Cymry* to the previous 'giant' inhabitants of Britain - the megalithic builders - who had been led from the Aegean to these 'Fortunate Isles' by Albion in about the 4th millennium BC. Finally, take into account that the Cymry relate, in the stories concerning their origins, that they originated from the 'Blessed Land' (later to be called the 'Fortunate Isles')..."

In the English language there are many derivatives of the Arcadian name, e.g. ark, Archangels, arcade, arches, archaic, archaeology, archbishop, academy and the word 'phone' is a derivative of 'Phoenicia'.

We also have the word 'phoenix' (like an eagle) which is the bird that 'rises from the ashes to regenerate its life'. The Egyptians and the Romans believed in the Phoenix and their legends told of how it would visit the temple of On at Heliopolis - the Temple of the Sun. They identified the Phoenix as one of the beasts of their calendar so that when the Sun had completed its revolution, the Sun-eagle was therefore returned to the nest for the inauguration of the new Phoenix Age.

The Constellations of the Dove and the Bear

Other important information is conveyed in Peter Dawkins' work titled *The Great Vision* which gives enlightenment to the meaning of King Arthur, sometimes referred to as the 'Bear' and, also given is an important explanation of the earth's wobble which people seem so concerned about:

"Because of the 'wobble' of the Earth's axis as it moves about the sun, although the general direction that the axis points in is constantly orientated towards the same portion of the celestial sphere, nevertheless the real poles of the Earth's celestial sphere appear to rotate about the imaginary fixed north and south poles."

"If there was no 'wobble', the position of the Earth's north pole in the celestial sphere would lie in the heart of *Draco*, the Dragon; but because of the 'wobble' the Earth's north pole tours around the Dragon 'heart' in a great circle which takes approximately 26,000 years."

"At present the North Pole is in a highly significant position, almost coinciding with the seventh star in the constellation, called (in Arabic) *Al Ruccaba*, 'the turned, or ridden upon' - the central star and hub of the zodiacal wheel (at present), and thus called (in Latin) *Polaris*."

"The Little Bear is not the original name for this constellation, although now its name (and that of its companion, the Great Bear) is built into the legends of Arthur the King, who is described as the mighty Bear. But the original name is more meaningful, being (in Hebrew) *Dohhver*, 'a fold' (of animals, but particularly sheep). The name, besides meaning 'sheepfold' which Jesus and others refer to, recorded in the Bible and elsewhere, also means 'rest' or 'security' - the place of peace into which the righteous are shepherded, where the Assembly of the Holy Ones takes place, and from whence the Saviours or 'Shepherds' of mankind come. But in Hebrew there is a similar sounding word, *Dohv*, meaning 'Bear', hence the confusion in the translation."

"Similarly, the confusion with the English word, Dove, which this constellation also represents symbolically: for in the seven stars of *Dohv* the Word is sounded and the Light is poured out upon the Earth to baptize, vitalize, guide, teach and illumine mankind. Arthur is derived from *Ar-Thor*, meaning 'the Word of Love' i.e. the Christ."

"This word is borne by and spoken in the holy Breath of God (i.e. Divine Love), which Breath is symbolised by the Dove but can in fact be seen as a (deliberate?) borrowing phonetically of *Dohv*, which essentially means the Place of Peace - which of course is the perfect abode of love, the 'sheepfold' of the Bible. The 'lambs of God' are they who come from this perfect place of Peace, of Love, being the divine love and its radiant wisdom to the world."

"In the East the seven stars of *Dohv* are called the Seven *Rishis* or Teachers, and represent the Seven Rays of the one White Light of Christ. It is significant that one of those seven stars or *Rishis* is the present Pole Star of our world."

"The 'North' is known as the Place or Seat of Government, and the 'Mount of Congregation' of the Lord is in the north, where the Assembly of the Holy Ones is to be found. The 'north wind' is the creative Breath of God: and *Hyperborea*, 'the land of the north wind', is the source from which the north wind comes."

"That source is the Heart of God; and this is the secret that is manifesting in the heavens, in *Dohv*. On earth, *Hyperborea* has a special relationship to the country of Britain, and thus Arthur is primarily the great king of Britain."

"Esoterically, Britain is the heart-abode of the incarnate *Dohv* and the principal home-land of the great teachers of humanity from the most ancient times. The history and destiny of Britain is connected with this, and this important (but esoteric) fact lies behind the works of Francis Bacon."

Abraham - c.1900 BC

"I saw the destruction of Sodom and Gomorrah"
(Taliesin/Merlin/St Germain)

According to a Biblical Chronology contained in the Good News Bible, it was in circa 1900 BC that the grand patriarch, Abraham, lived. Abraham was to become the progenitor of the twelve tribes of Israel. According to the antiquarian, Stukeley, Druidism was descended from Abraham whom Stukeley called the 'Father of all Druids'. (In later centuries, Pythagoras - Kuthumi, St Joseph of Arimathea, Mary Magdalene and the 'Bethany party' also belonged to the Order of the Druids).

In Genesis, chapter 19, we learn of the destruction of Sodom and Gomorrah, during the time of the patriarch, Abraham who according to some sources, is reputed to have been an incarnation of El Morya. However, considering that St Germain writing under the pseudonym of 'Taliesin' informs us that he was a witness to the destruction; it would appear that he was the patriarch, Abraham, which would make sense because he had once been the patriarch, Noah.

According to a recent documentary on the History Channel, archaeologists believe that the fire and brimstone mentioned in the Biblical description of the destruction of Sodom and Gomorrah, was asphalt otherwise known as 'bitumen'(tar) and that an earthquake caused the area to fall into the Dead Sea (once known as the Valley of Siddim). Genesis 14 mentions that the valley was full of tar pits.

During this same era, lived Melchizadek, who according to the Bible was the king of Salem and was also a priest. Melchizadek was on good terms with Abraham. (According to the late Edgar Cayce, Melchizadek was an earlier incarnation of Jesus).

After the demise of Abraham, his sons Isaac and Ishmael buried him in a field which Abraham had purchased from the Hittites.

Isaac did not marry until he was forty years of age. When he was sixty years of age, Isaac and his wife, Rebecca, had twin sons, one of whom they named Jacob. It was Jacob who later in life laid his head upon a stone pillow during which time he experienced a profound vision in which the Lord told him that his future descendants would be of the House of David. The Lord then re-named Jacob, 'Israel', and thus his descendants became known as the 'Israelites' - 'Children of Israel'.

This same sacred 'Stone Pillow' belonging to Jacob is the one reputed to have been eventually taken to the Royal Palace of Tara in Ireland where all the future High Kings of Ireland stood upon it in order to be crowned. It became known as the *Stone of Destiny*. In the 5th century AD, it was transferred to Albany (Scotland) where the future Celtic kings of the Scots continued the sacred tradition, and when being anointed as kings, as they stood upon the *Stone* at the time of their coronation, they recited their ancestry back to Noah (St Germain).

Jacob had twelve sons who became the ancestors of the twelve tribes of Israel. The most prominent of these sons was Joseph who became the adviser to the king (pharaoh) of Egypt who appointed him as governor.

Because St Germain was once the grand patriarch Noah, it is plausible to presume that he was also Jacob who experienced the vision upon the *Stone of Destiny*, for, in his incarnation as Samuel the Prophet, he anointed David (Kuthumi) as King, and thus began the House of David, the House of Judah, which was later to become the House of Tudor - the Royal House into which St Germain was born as Sir Francis Bacon in the 16th century AD. (The story of Jacob and his descendants - the Lost Tribes of Israel, is told in the sequel to the *Masters of The Mystical Rose*, titled *The Dove, The Rose and The Sceptre, In Search of the Ark of the Covenant*).

The Arian Race, the Origin of Maryanna And the Decline of the Hyksos 1580 BC

Some of the Arian race travelled to India whilst others made their way across Iran and Iraq into Syria and overran Egypt towards the beginning of the 17th century BC. The Hyksos, as the Egyptians called these warlords, ruled an empire embracing Egypt and Syria. In about 1580 BC, the Hyksos were expelled from Egypt by Ahmose I, of Thebes who thus became the founder of 'the new Empire'. (Ahmose I became the father of Amenhotep I, and these Egyptian pharaohs are discussed in the following chapter).

The rulers in Syria continued to be called by an Arian name which was

'Marianna' (also spelt Maryanna) and continued to worship their gods, one of whom was Mithra. *Ari*, as in Arian, means 'noble', as found in the name of *Arimathea* and in the name of the philosopher *Aristotle* (who was an incarnation of the Master Kuthumi). The Hyksos were considered to be a mixed multitude of Arians and Kharrians who had joined ranks on their way across South-West Asia.

It is of interest to note just how far back in time the names of Mari/Mary and Anna can be traced. In later centuries, the Essenes who were the original Arian race, continued to use these names.

Those familiar with the Biblical texts of the four Evangelists, will realise just how many Marys' there were and although there is no mention of the parents of Mary (the mother of Jesus and his brothers and sisters), it is known from ancient documents that her name was Anna and that she was a princess who was married to her first cousin, Joachim, who was a prince.

According to information contained in Robert Graves' book titled *The White Goddess*: "*An is Sumerian for 'Heaven' and the Goddess Athene was another Anna, namely Ath-enna*. 'Ma' is a shortening of the Sumerian Ana, 'mother', and Ma-ri means 'the fruitful mother' from rim, 'to bear a child'."

"Mari (another form of Mary) was the name of the goddess on whose account the Egyptians of 1000 BC called Cyprus 'Ay-mari'. Mari-enna is the fruitful mother of 'Heaven', alias Miriam, Marian, Marianna, but the basic word is Anna who to the Christian mystics, is known as the Lord's Grandmother." (In Celtic tradition, Anna was the water goddess and the Church of Rome 'Christianized' this goddess into St Anne. Similarly, the Church of Rome 'Christianized' St Bridget who was the Celtic fire goddess, Bride, and numerous others).

We learn from information contained in Merrill Unger's book titled *Archaeology And The Old Testament* that the 'Mari Letters' were discovered in 1935, prior to the Dead Sea Scrolls being discovered in 1947.

The Integration of the Khatti Tribe with the Babylonians 1173 BC

After the destruction of Sumeria, the Pharaoh Tutmoses III (an incarnation of Kuthumi), reigned for nearly fifty-four years and regained the former domain of the Sumeric Society by conquering Syria. Tutmoses III was a great teacher who belonged to the Great White Brotherhood in Egypt.

When the Arians established themselves in Cappadocia, the Arcadian language was used for local records and diplomatic correspondence and the literary independence of the new society in Cappadocia was thus developed from the Sumerians. One of the older cities was Khattusas (Boghazkoy/Boghazkeui) which held a position of prominence by the beginning of the 15th century BC.

'Khatti' is the original name of 'Hittite' which appears in the Old Testament.

It seems probable that the Khatti people were in later centuries to become known as the 'Cathars' or the Albigensians, the people of Alba, the people of the 'Light'. (The Cathars were virtually wiped out during the Albigensian Crusade, launched in 1208 AD upon the instructions of Pope Innocent III and their story will be discussed in a future chapter). Merrill F. Unger in his book titled *Archaeology And The Old Testament* informs us that Hittite monuments at Bogazkeui were discovered in 1906. Arcadian astrological and divinatory texts were also discovered at Bogazkeui.

According to William Foxwell Albright in his book titled *From The Stone Age To Christianity*:

"Excavations in many Late Bronze-Age sites of Palestine have shown a progressive thinning out and impoverishment of the population which suggest that Egyptian domination was very oppressive. The great edict of Haramis (Haremhab) repeatedly alludes to the corruption and rapacity of Egyptian officials and soldiers about 1340 BC. The external history of Western Asia in this age centred around the political relations of the central state, Mitanni, with its neighbours."

"From the campaigns of Tutmoses III [Kuthumi] in Syria to the time of Tutmoses IV, Egypt was almost continually engaged in war with Mitanni. At the end of this period, the Hittites awoke from their sleep of two centuries and began to exert increasing pressure on the Mitanni from the northwest. Naturally, therefore, the latter hastened to make peace with Egypt and for three successive reigns, Mitannian princesses married pharaohs." (Tutmoses III is discussed in the next chapter).

"About 1370 Suppiluliuma of Khatti conquered Mitanni, which he reduced to a tributary state, though it continued to exist for another century until its final subjugation by Shalmaneser I of Assyria (cir. 1264-1235 BC). From 1360 to after 1295 BC the Egyptian and Hittite empires were neighbours in Syria, the boundary between them standing roughly at the Eleutherus Valley on the coast and fluctuating to the interior."

"For the first fifty years (cir. 1360-1310 BC) each empire seems to have been too much occupied by internal affairs to interfere seriously in the affairs of its neighbour, and during much of this period the Hittites were kept busy by wars and rebellions in Asia Minor."

"The energetic kings of the Nineteenth Dynasty, Sethos I (1308-1290) and Ramesses II (1279-1212), resumed hostilities, which seem on the whole to have resulted unfavorably for Egypt, though the Hittites, were too much weakened by disorders in the north and west to take advantage of their victories. In the year 1270 a formal peace was made by the two antagonists, who seem to have kept it more or less faithfully until the final collapse of the Hittite Empire."

The destiny of the Hittite Society was decided by the history of the Khatti state. In the 14th century BC when 'the New Empire of Egypt' lost its grip upon its dominions in Syria, the King of Khatti (circa 1380-1346 BC) who was a contemporary of Akhnaton (El Morya), substituted Khatti for Egypt as the paramount Power in Northern Syria by a combination of fraud and force.

However, the King of Khatti left a fatal legacy to his successors in a series of destructive wars between Khatti and Egypt in which the Hittite Power suffered more severely. The two Powers eventually made peace in circa 1278 BC and in circa 1190 BC the Khatti Empire was brought down, at which time many of them migrated. By 1173 BC, the Kassite dynasty as such, ceased to exist; they integrated with the Babylonians.

The Descendants of Noah (St Germain)
"I have been the chief director of the work of the tower of Nimrod"
(Taliesin/Merlin/St Germain)

Traditionally, Nimrod (son of Cush) was one of the grandsons of Noah, however, he was also known as the hero/hunter who was the founder of the Assyrian-Babylonian Empire; Noah is reputed to have lived for over one hundred years. In the above quotation, we are told that in one of his previous incarnations (as Noah) St Germain assisted Nimrod, most probably in the founding of the Babylonian empire.

The youngest son of Noah, was Ham, and according to Merrill F. Unger in his book titled *Archaeology And The Old Testament*:

"Ham is regarded as the eponymous ancestor of the African peoples, as Japheth his brother is of the Indo-Europeans, and Shem of the Semites. In the Hamitic line is traced the rise of the earliest imperial world power, first under Nimrod in Babylonia and later in such seats of ancient empire as Asshur and Nineveh on the upper Tigris. Egypt too, founded by these people, very early became a centre of centralized authority."

According to Genesis 10 in the Bible, the sons of Ham (youngest son of Noah - St Germain) were Cush, Egypt, Libya, and Canaan.

King of Assyria and the Origin of 'Cymry' - The Celts

According to information contained in the book titled *The Drama Of The Lost Disciples* by George F. Jowett:

"In the British Museum can be seen the famous Black Obelisk of Shalmaneser II. This important relic bears reference to the captivity, and to all kings subject to the King of Assyria. Amongst these rulers... was Jehu, the 'son of Omri', king of

Israel. The obelisk is a series of twenty small reliefs with long inscriptions. The second relief depicts 'the son of Omri' on his knees, paying tribute in gold and silver in obeisance to the Assyrian ruler."

"In Keltic [Celtic] the word Kymri is still pronounced with the vowel sound, K'Omri, and easily became Kymri, from which Kimmerii, Kimmerians, Keltoi, Keltic and Cymri [Cymry] evolved. It is interesting to know that the Welsh are the only members of the Keltic race that retained throughout time to the present the original name of Kymri. Today it is usually spelt Cymri, and their ancient language Cymric."

According to Peter Dawkins in his book titled *Arcadia*:

"When the flood subsided....the Cymry settled in Aegaea (which was once an extensive land surrounded by a ring of mountains, until the Black Sea burst through the Bosporus and formed the Aegean Sea and its many islands); but where ever conditions became suitable, or when they were forced to, they made successive migrations back to their original homeland."

The Land of the Covenant

George F. Jowett writes:

"After the Kimmerians [also known as the Cimmerians] had settled in the Isles of the West, they were known to the rest of the world by another name. They became known as British."

"They believed in One Invisible God...they had no graven images, abhorring the sight of idols. They always worshipped in the open, facing east. They had a passionate belief in the immortality of life, to such an extent that both friend and foe claimed this belief made them fearless warriors, disdainful of death."

"The religious ritual that appeared to make the greatest impression on the foreign historians was their custom of carrying a replica of the Ark of the Covenant before them in all religious observances, as did their forefathers in old Judea. For centuries, as the Kymri passed through foreign lands in migratory waves on their march to the Isles of the West, the chroniclers noted that this custom was never omitted. It was this ritual that gave birth to their British surname."

"The name British is derived from the ancient Hebrew language, with which the old Cymric language was contemporaneous, formed from two words, 'B'rith' meaning 'covenant', and 'ish' meaning man or woman. Joined as one word the meaning is apparent: 'British' means a 'covenant man or woman'. The ancient word 'ain' attached to the word 'B'rith' signifies 'land', therefore the interpretation of the word 'Britain'...is 'Covenant Land'."

"Unknowingly, the ancients named the Keltoi rightly. They were, and still are, the original adherents of the Covenant Law."

The Celts - The Druids

"All things Begin and End in Albion's [Great Britain's] *Ancient Druid Rocky Shore"*
(William Blake)

According to George F. Jowett:

"It has already been pointed out how the ancient Kymry [Cymry] were bonded in the ancient patriarchal faith even before they arrived in Britain. Organized by Hu Gardarn (Hugh the Mighty) the faith took on the name of Druid, a word some claim derived from the Keltic word 'Dreus' meaning 'an oak', arising out of the custom of worshipping in the open within the famous oak groves of the island. A more likely derivation is from 'Druithin' - a 'Servant of the Truth'. The motto of the Druids was 'The Truth against the World'."

When Joseph of Arimathea arrived in Britain and founded the first Christian church at Glastonbury (one of the Avalons), his party were known as the Culdees derived from the word 'Ceile'De' meaning 'servant of the Lord'. Joseph and his disciples continued to spread the Celtic faith throughout Britain, the faith linked back to Abraham, who as previously mentioned, the antiquarian Stukeley claimed was "the Father of Druidism".

The great Learning centre founded at Iona, Scotland, by St Columba in the 6th century AD, consisted of a group who also called themselves the Culdees. The Culdees continued to exist by that name well into the middle ages until under persecution from the Church of Rome, they were forced to go underground, later emerging to be known as the *Gnostics*.

ABRAHAM WAS THE FATHER OF ALL DRUIDS
AND
CELTIC BRITAIN IS 'THE LAND OF THE COVENANT'

MASTERS DISCUSSED IN THIS CHAPTER
Grand patriarch Noah - St Germain
Grand patriarch Abraham - possibly St Germain
King Melchizadek of Salem - earlier incarnation of the Master Jesus
Prophet Samuel - St Germain
King David of the House of Judah - Kuthumi
Pharaoh Tutmoses III - Kuthumi
Pharaoh Akhnaton - El Morya
Joseph, Father of Jesus - St Germain
The 'Bard' Taliesin/Merlin - St Germain
The 'Bard' Sir Francis Bacon - St Germain

NOTES AND RECOMMENDED READING

Peter Dawkins, *The Great Vision*, (Francis Bacon Research Trust, Warwick, U.K.)

Peter Dawkins, *Arcadia,* (Francis Bacon Research Trust, Warwick, U.K.)

Robert J. Scrutton, *The Message Of The Masters*, (Neville Spearman, Jersey, U.K. 1982)

Graham Hancock, *The Fingerprints Of The Gods*, (Mandarin Books, U.K. 1995)

Francis Hitching, *The World Atlas of Mysteries*, (Pan Books, U.K. 1978)

Robert Graves, *The White Goddess*, (Faber & Faber, U.K. 1961)

Madame Blavatsky, *The Secret Doctrine*, (Theosophical Publishing House, Quest Books, U.S.A. 1966)

C. W. Leadbeater, *The Hidden Life in Freemasonry*, (Theosophical Publishing House, U.K. 1975)

Florence Marian McNeil, *Iona*, (Blackie & Sons, Glasgow, Scotland, 1920)

Arnold Toynbee, *A Study of History*, (Oxford University Press, U.K. 1934)

F.J. Dennett, *Europe, A History*, (Lineham & Shrimpton, Melbourne, Australia, 1961)

Daniel J. Boorstin, *The Discoverers*, (Random House, U.K., 1983)

George F. Jowett, *The Drama Of The Lost Disciples*, (Covenant Publishing Co. Ltd., U.K. 1980)

William Foxwell Albright, *From The Stone Age To Christianity*, (Doubleday Anchor, U.S.A. 1957)

Merrill F. Unger, *Archaeology And The Old Testament,* (Zondervan Publishing House, Michigan, U.S.A)

CHAPTER 4

𝕿𝖍𝖊 𝕰𝖌𝖞𝖕𝖙𝖎𝖆𝖓 𝕻𝖍𝖆𝖗𝖆𝖔𝖍𝖘 & 𝖙𝖍𝖊 𝕺𝖗𝖎𝖌𝖎𝖓 𝖔𝖋 𝖙𝖍𝖊 𝕽𝖔𝖘𝖊 𝕮𝖗𝖔𝖘𝖘

"For the mystical symbols are well known to us
who belong to the Brotherhood"
(Plutarch)

"What's in a name?
A Rose by any other name would smell just as sweet"
(Shakespeare - St Germain)

"Look to the blowing Rose about us 'Lo, Laughing', she says
'Into the world I blow...'"
(Rubaiyat of Omar Khayyam - Kuthumi)

"I strengthened Moses through the waters of the Jordan"
"I was in Canaan
When Absalom was slain"
I conveyed Awen (Divine Spirit of the Wisdom of 'Sophia')
To the level of the vale of Hebron."
(Taliesin/Merlin/St Germain)

The majority of the 'key' personages throughout history who are referred to as the Masters, belonged to what was known as the Great White Brotherhood and who, as mentioned in the first chapter, are also called by the title of the Ascended Masters. Throughout their numerous incarnations they eventually became highly evolved 'initiates' into the greater 'Sacred Mysteries' of creation, whereby they finally reached a level of mastership, one that could be termed the 'University of Life'.

Because of their close affiliation, they considered themselves as a fraternity (from 'Frater' meaning 'brother') of brothers and sisters, and although the term Brotherhood may seem rather male-orientated, there were many female High

Priestesses who were prominent members.

The Arcana was the basis of all the Grail Mysteries. It has also been previously explained that the Sacred Teachings into which the Masters were initiated were known as the *Arcana/Arkana*, which the Oxford dictionary defines as 'mystery' or 'secret' and it originates from the word *arca* meaning a 'chest', synonymous with the Ark of the Covenant. It has also been established that the word *Ark* could be traced back to Noah and the descendants of Atlantis who became known as the Arkadians/Arcadians

Masters of the Great White Brotherhood would choose to reincarnate to serve humanity at a crucial time in history when civilization had reached low ebb.

They reincarnated to assist humanity to 'blossom as the rose'. As the author Haroutiun Saraydarian so aptly put it in his book titled *Christ, The Avatar of Sacrificial Love*, "the great teachers appear at intervals, perform their duties then withdraw. When the need arises for further esoteric teachings to humanity the centres are reactivated or replaced by others."

Often the Masters are referred to as *Avatars* or the *Illumined Ones* who tread the path in the 'Light' and service to the Creator/God. The expression of the *Illumined Ones* meant that through their many years of study and initiations, they became very 'enlightened' as a result of the knowledge and wisdom which they gained. *Perfection is not bestowed; it is achieved.* The Masters taught the art of symbolism, the language of 'Divine Truths' whereby the Ancient Mysteries of the Arcana were protected from the profane. The adepts of the ancient Mystery Schools were 'wise Master Builders' with the vision to see, with the courage to do, and with the wisdom to remain silent.

The Egyptian pharaohs were regarded as divine gods and as Masters of the Great White Brotherhood they were God's representatives on earth. Tutmoses (also Thutmoses), which was a name given to several of the pharaohs, means 'Born of the god of Thoth'. (Thoth is discussed in Chapter 7).

It is noteworthy that the chronological dates for Egyptian pharaohs vary greatly. No-one knows the precise ones. Therefore, although I have given the dates specified by archaeologists, they could be out by some five hundred years. The ones that I am reasonably certain of, are those of the era of King Solomon, Akhnaton and Moses - the reason being that the Rosicrucian authority, the late Spencer Lewis supplied their dates in his book titled *Rosicrucian Answers And Questions*, and accordingly, the Rosicrucians have had the ancient Egyptian records passed down to them for posterity.

Ahmose I and Amenhotep I

The founder of the 18th Dynasty was Ahmose I. According to the historian, Manetho, Ahmose reigned for about twenty-six years; Spencer Lewis gives the dates of his reign from 1580-1557 BC.

In a previous chapter it was mentioned that some of the Arian race travelled to India whilst others made their way across Iran and Iraq into Syria and overran Egypt towards the beginning of the 17th century BC. The Hyksos, as the Egyptians called these warlords, ruled an empire embracing Egypt and Syria. In about 1580 BC, the Hyksos were expelled from Egypt by Ahmose I, of Thebes who thus became the founder of 'the new Empire'. (Ahmose I became the father of Amenhotep I).

After the death of Ahmose I (who expelled the Hyksos from Egypt), his son Amenhotep I, in common with his father, Seqenenre II, left few records. According to Spencer Lewis, Amenhotep I became a teacher in the 'Secret School' for three years.

Spencer Lewis quotes the Egyptologist Sir E.A. Wallis Budge discussing the 'Secret School' and the Ancient Mysteries:

"It is impossible to doubt that there were 'mysteries' in the Egyptian religion, and this being so, it is impossible to think that the highest order of the priests did not possess esoteric knowledge which they guarded with the greatest care. Each priesthood, if I read the evidence correctly, possessed a 'Gnosis', a 'superiority of knowledge', which they never did put into writing, and so were enabled to enlarge or diminish its scope as circumstances made necessary."

"It is therefore absurd to expect to find in Egyptian papyri descriptions of secrets which formed the esoteric knowledge of the priests. Among the 'secret wisdom' of the priests must be included the knowledge of which day was the shortest of the year, i.e. the day when OSIRIS [who will be discussed in a future chapter] died and the new sun began his course, and the day when SIRIUS would rise heliacally, and the true age of the moon, and the days when the great festivals of the year were to be celebrated."

According to Spencer Lewis:

"If the *secret wisdom* was imparted in any tangible form, it is to be found to exist in the symbolism of the Egyptians, namely, in such devices as were not an integral part of their language or common writing. In this manner, a symbol would exoterically depict to one mind one meaning and to another a far different significance. This is not merely a supposition, but a fact borne out by such a vast number of circumstances and indications, as to remove them from the realm of coincidence."

Tutmoses I, Reigned 1538 BC

Upon the demise of Amenhotep I, a middle-aged military leader, who was married to princess Ahmose, became Pharaoh Tutmoses I.

From information contained in the book titled *Rosicrucian Questions and Answers*, by Spencer Lewis, we are informed that Tutmoses I was crowned in January 1538 BC, succeeding Amenhotep I.

The duration of his reign is considered to have only been about six years. He was the leader of some brilliant military campaigns and was the first pharaoh to be buried in the Valley of the Kings at Thebes.

Tutmoses II c.1518 - c.1536 BC

We are informed by Merrill F. Unger in his book titled *Archaeology And The Old* Testament as follows:

"Since Thutmose I left no surviving legitimate [male] heir to the throne, his daughter Hatshepsut was in line for succession. But being prevented by her sex from succeeding as king, she possessed no more than the right to convey the crown by marriage to her husband and to secure the succession to her children." (Hatshepsut was the elder daughter of Tutmoses I and Queen Ahmose).

"To circumvent a dynastic dilemma and to prevent the loss of the crown to another family, Thutmose I was obliged to marry his daughter to her younger half-brother, a son by a lesser marriage, who took the throne as Thutmose II."

"But the legitimate marriage of Thutmose II, like that of his father, failed to supply a male heir to the throne. Again steps had to be taken to safeguard the survival of the dynasty (18th dynasty). Thutmose II, accordingly, named as his successor a young son by a minor wife [princess Mutnefert - sister of Tutmoses' Queen Ahmose]. Appointing the lad as co-regent and strengthening his claim to the throne by marrying him to his half-sister, Thutmose II's daughter by Hatshepsut, the young prince ascended the throne and was crowned as Thutmose III."

Tutmoses III (Kuthumi) c.1537 - d.1447 BC

Tutmoses (Thutmoses) III was a teacher of the secret school of the Great White Brotherhood. Queen Hatshepsut, his stepmother and aunt, refused to surrender her regency even after Tutmoses III became of age. Many years passed but eventually he did succeed to the throne.

According to Spencer Lewis' calculations, he would have been aged thirty-five years when he ascended the throne, which would have been about 1500 BC. The Egyptian Chronicles have Tutmoses III ruling 'about' 1504 BC so the dates are appropriately near enough. Tutmoses III, whose mother was named Isis, married princess Neferure, the daughter of Tutmoses II by Hatshepsut. (Neferure died before Tutmoses became Pharaoh of Egypt.).

Tutmoses III later married Hatshepsut-Mertyre who became his principal queen; there were other minor wives, as was common with Egyptian pharaohs. (Their son Amenhotep II became Tutmoses' heir. According to Spencer Lewis, Amenhotep II ruled from 1448 to 1420 BC. He was succeeded by his son Tutmoses IV, who ruled from 1420 to 1411 BC. Tutmoses IV was the father of Amenhotep IV who re-named himself Akhnaton).

The 'Mystical' Experience of Tutmoses III

The Rosicrucian authority, Spencer Lewis, informs us that "history relates a very strange occurrence in the life of Tutmoses III that is mystically important to us." A wonderful feast took place on the Spring equinox, "held in the Temple of Amen, one of the prevailing gods of the time, in the great Temple of what is now Karnak at Thebes, Egypt."

Tutmoses III (Thutmoses III) was present and the chief of priests known as the Kheri Hebs went amongst the gathered crowd as if seeking someone whilst at the same time carrying a little image symbolic of the god Amen. Finally he reached Tutmoses III.

"He placed at the feet of Thutmoses III the image of Amen which depicted, in the customs of the time that he, Thutmoses III, had been chosen instead of his brother to succeed the father upon the throne, and the great assemblage broke forth in acclamation."

"He had no knowledge that he was to be chosen to become Pharaoh, because by right of accession, his brother should have been. But when the image was placed at his feet, he was seen to stand up; however, according to Thutmoses III he felt 'raised' as though his feet hardly touched the ground, and as though he had ascended into the heavens, and there he tells us God duly appointed him to serve his people. In fact, he felt as though he had been divinely ordained because of the mystical experience, and it became not even necessary for him to journey to Heliopolis where the Sun Temple was located, as had been the custom, to be formally coronated."

According to Spencer Lewis:

"It was Tutmoses III who organized the present secret physical form followed by the present secret Brotherhood and outlined many of its rules and regulations."

At Karnak in Thebes, which then, was the great capital city, Tutmoses built a new temple. The temple was called the Festival Hall and it was decorated like and was called the 'Botanical Garden', with the walls covered in flora and fauna.

(In a later life, when Kuthumi incarnated in Lincoln, England, as Sir Joseph Banks in the 18th century, he was to retain the same love of botanical gardens, flora and fauna and was to make great contributions to the world as a result of his great love of nature. He was responsible for the founding of the famous Kew Gardens).

The Obelisk of Tutmoses III

According to an ancient prophecy, an Obelisk once erected in Egypt, upon the instructions of Tutmoses III, was destined to eventually be re-erected in the country where the Eagle spreads its wings and the Obelisk now stands in Central Park, New York, America.

(When Kuthumi reincarnated as John the Beloved - one of the four Evangelists, his symbol became the Eagle. The *Eagle*, combined with clutching an olive branch in its right talon, became the emblem of the Great Seal of the United States of America, and the person who instigated the designing of the Great Seal, was none other than St Germain. The olive branch was symbolic of peace but it was also symbolic of the dove that Noah, who, in the traditional story of the Ark and the Deluge, sent forth to search for dry land at which time the dove returned with an olive branch).

Tutmoses III has been recognised as the greatest pharaoh in Egyptian history. In Kuthumi's incarnation as Leonardo da Vinci, he has been recognised as the greatest artist of his time.

Tutmoses III (Kuthumi) 'Military Expert'

Kuthumi in his incarnation as Tutmoses III demonstrated his prowess on the battlefield, regaining lands that had been lost to Egypt during the long reign of Hatshepsut. It was an era in which Egypt was constantly contending with outbreaks of war and Tutmoses III needed a strong permanent army to protect the country from outside invaders. Interestingly, Tutmoses III's brilliant military achievements were comparable with those of King David.

According to Merrill F. Unger:

"The new monarch was one of the greatest foreign conquerors in Egyptian history. In numerous victorious campaigns in Syria-Palestine, he pushed the frontiers of Egypt into the Euphrates River. Lists of his conquests in Asia include many familiar Bible names such as Kadesh, Megiddo, Dothan, Damascus, Hamath,

Laish, Geba, Taanach, Carmel, Beth-Shemesh, Gath, Gerar, Ekron, Gezer and Bethshan." Accordingly the lists recorded at Karnak of his achievement, detail over 350 cities that fell to Egyptian might.

The American Egyptologist, James Henry Breasted called Tutmoses III the 'Napoleon of Egypt'.

The Capture of Jerusalem by King David (Kuthumi) 'Military Expert'

The story of King David, will be discussed further on in this chapter, however, it is relevant under this heading to tell a little about him.

David originally lived in the Hebron Valley, in the land of Canaan. The land of Canaan had been invaded back in c. 1210 by Joshua and Israel remained as a loose confederation of tribes until the reign of King David, at which time it became the united Israelite Kingdom. (After the death of King Solomon, David's son, the Israelite Kingdom split into two Kingdoms, Judah - the Southern Kingdom, and Israel, the Northern Kingdom).

Comparing the life of King David with that of Tutmoses III, who invaded Palestine, (Palestine was originally the land of Canaan), let us now ascertain the achievements of David as a military expert.

From Merrill F. Unger, we learn how David captured Jerusalem.

"As soon as he was chosen king over all the tribes, David set himself to the task of establishing the kingdom. One of his first and most important accomplishments was his conquest of the Jebusite stronghold at Jerusalem, which he made his new capital. Situated on a plateau of commanding height twenty-five hundred feet above the Mediterranean and thirty-eight hundred feet above the Dead Sea, the Jebusite fortress, scarped by natural rock for defense, with stout walls, gates and towers, was considered impregnable. So secure did the native Jebusite defenders consider themselves that they taunted David and the Israelite besiegers with the words: 'You will not come in here, but the blind and the lame will ward you off - this king David cannot come in here'."

"Although David's men evidently scaled the walls of Jerusalem (Israel) and did not gain entrance to the Jebusite fortress, as heretofore thought, by means of the city's underground water system, archeology has shown conclusively that the ancient citadel which David took called 'the stronghold of Zion' and subsequently the 'city of David', which the king built, were located on the eastern hill above the Gihon Fountain and not on the so-called western hill of Zion, separated by the Tyropoean Valley. This is clear from excavations and from the fact that the water supply determined the earliest settlement in Jerusalem."

"David's conquest of Jerusalem was an exceedingly important event, making possible the choice of the city as his capital. Moreover, he displayed great wisdom in his selection of the conquered city as the focal point of his new government. He realized its strategic importance and doubtless had it in mind as his new capital before conquering it."

"The city stood on the border of Judah and Israel and its neutral location tended to allay the jealousy between the northern and southern portions of his kingdom. Its liberation from the Canaanites opened the highway between Judah and the North, expedited commercial and social intercourse, and helped to further unite the kingdom."

Pharaoh Shishak (c. 945-924 BC) 'Military Expert'

The Egyptian Pharaoh, Shishak, lived during the same era as King David's son Solomon.

Merrill F. Unger informs us that that there is evidence supporting the fact that Shishak did journey to Israel.

According to Merrill, the Biblical Shishak was Sheshonq I (c.935-914 BC) of Egypt, founder of the Twenty-second Dynasty and Merrill states that "the Egyptian records do not give the date of Shishak's expedition and with the uncertain chronology of the early kings of the Davidic line scholars are not agreed on the precise date."

"His triumphal inscription at Karnak (ancient Thebes) gives a long list of his conquests, which include towns in all parts of Judah and extend to the coastal plain, across the Plain of Esdraelon into Gilead, showing that he invaded the Northern Kingdom as well, in spite of his previous friendship of Jeroboam (I Kings 11:40). A part of Shishak's stela has been excavated at Megiddo, proving that he actually did take and occupy this important city, as recounted in his Karnak inscription."

Megiddo was also the scene of Tutmoses III's victory and he initiated the practice of carving on the walls of the great Temple of Amun in Karnak (Upper Egypt), the names of the territories that he conquered. Shishak/Sheshonq was the last of Egyptian rulers to follow this custom.

Was Pharaoh Tutmoses III otherwise known as Pharaoh Shishak?

Some theorists believe that Tutmoses III was King David and that he was also the Pharaoh Shishak mentioned in the Bible who lived during the era of King Solomon, son of King David.

According to the Bible, David (Kuthumi) (c.1010- c.970 BC) ruled as King for forty years - ruling seven years in Hebron and thirty-three years in Jerusalem - the number thirty-three is symbolic of Freemasonry and Tutmoses III was a Master of the Great White Brotherhood who taught in Egypt. According to Rosicrucian records, he died in 1447 BC which puts the dates of Tutmoses III and King David out by approximately five hundred years.

If the dates are out by some five hundred years, then the question could be raised, did David spend the rest of the time ruling over Egypt as a Pharaoh?

Is it possible that Kuthumi was King David, Tutmoses III and the Pharaoh Shishak i.e. did he have three titles?

The common denominators are as follows:

1. King David was an incarnation of Kuthumi.
2. King David was a great military expert.
3. King David and Bathsheba's son became King Solomon (El Morya).
4. King Solomon married Pharaoh Shishak's daughter, Princess Aye.
5. Pharaoh Shishak is mentioned in the Bible as having invaded Jerusalem and he was a military leader of renown.
6. Pharaoh Tutmoses III was an incarnation of Kuthumi.
7. Pharaoh Tutmoses III was a great military expert.

It is not exactly known when Tutmoses III became Pharaoh of Egypt - by utilizing Spencer Lewis' information, the occurrence happened when he was thirty-five years of age making it about the year 1500 BC.

Merrill F. Unger dates Queen Hatshepsut (pronounced *hat cheap suit*) who ruled as co-regent for Tutmoses III, as 1504-1482 BC. According to Egyptian chronicles, the era of Tutmoses III was 1504-1450 BC which concurs with the Rosicrucian authority, the late Spencer Lewis who states in his book titled *Rosicrucian Answers And Questions* (1929) that Tutmoses III ruled from approximately 1500 BC until his demise in 1447 BC.

There are 'missing years' of the life of Tutmoses III. During the time that Queen Hatshepsut occupied his throne, he no doubt spent much of his time away from Egypt. From all accounts there was no love lost between them and so he probably stayed out of her way as much as possible.

Theorists also believe that Solomon was the architect and consort of Queen Hatshepsut, known as Senenmut, the royal Chief Steward. (This topic is discussed more fully in the following chapter).

According to Merrill F. Unger, excavations at Jerusalem and Palestine in general show how *"not a trace of the Solomonic temple nor of the palaces of the Davidic kings has remained."*

Mystery of the Burial Place of Tutmoses III (Kuthumi)
d. 1447 BC

According to Spencer Lewis, Tutmoses III ruled for nearly fifty-four years and when he died he was one week off being eighty-nine years of age. (According to the Bible, King David also lived to a ripe old age). Tutmoses III died on the 17th March, 1447 BC. Interestingly, this is the same date that we celebrate St Patrick's Day - and St Patrick was an incarnation of the Master Kuthumi.

When Tutmoses III died in 1447 BC, he was buried in tomb KV34 in the Valley of the Kings, which unfortunately by the time it was discovered in 1898 by Victor Loret, had been robbed and stripped of its former glory. The sarcophagus was there, but the body/mummy was missing.

Seventeen years previously, the mummy was discovered in the great royal cache at Deir el-Bahari. It is believed that it had been reburied there after Year 11 of the 22nd Dynasty of the Pharaoh Sheshonq I (945-924 BC -Shishak in the Bible), though the reasons why remain a mystery.

Accordingly, the mummy of Tutmoses III was identified by scraps of original wrappings which were still upon it - but the question could be raised, how did the archaeologists know what the original wrappings looked like considering the fact that there were no scraps of any kind found in the tomb discovered by Victor Loret in 1898? Was it really the mummy of Tutmoses III?

According to Merrill F. Unger, "the gold-masked body of Shishak was discovered in his intact burial chamber at Tanis (Egypt) in 1938-1939.

The Prophet Samuel (St Germain) c.1010 - c.970 BC
David King of Judah (Kuthumi)
"I was in Canaan
When Absalom was slain"
I conveyed Awen (Divine Spirit)
To the level of the vale of Hebron."
(Taliesin/Merlin/St Germain)

We are informed by Merrill F. Unger in his book titled *Archaeology And*

The Old Testament that "*Canaan* denotes the descendants of Ham [son of Noah - St Germain], (Gen.9:18, 22) who settled in the land later known as Palestine and from whom the country took its original name. Thus originally Hamitic, according to the Table of Nations, the Canaanites, settled in a tiny country that furnished a bridge between Egypt and the great Semitic empires that flourished on the Fertile Crescent."

Merrill F. Unger then relates how it was Moses who merged the Hebrews into a nation at Sinai, gave them a common faith and laid down for them their civil and ecclesiastical law, and it was David who was "the real founder of the Hebrew Monarchy. It was he who carried into effect the whole system, civil and ecclesiastical, which had been foreshadowed at Sinai."

St Germain, in his incarnation as the Zadok High Priest - the Prophet Samuel, anointed David, (Kuthumi), the son of Jesse, as King of Judah. The Lord promised David that Israel would always be ruled by his descendants.

Describing David, Unger relates as follows:

"David possessed a singularly gentle and winsome personality and showed a remarkable gift for attracting friends. This pre-eminent element in his character not only eventually won for him the kingship which was entirely unsought, but assured him the fullest success in it when once he was chosen in the high office."

"After he became king of Judah, similar tactics of patience and moderation in national affairs won for him the kingship over all Israel and in international affairs enabled him to carve out a substantial empire to bequeath to his son Solomon."

"This feat of empire building he was able to accomplish largely without resorting to wars that were waged for conquest. By simply fighting in defense of the Israelite nation when it was threatened by those who refused his overtures of friendship and who were jealous of his expanding power, he was able to extend his domains apart from actual military aggression."

"David's policy as king seems clearly to have been 'to be strong at home, but to live side by side with other nations as his allies'."

"Later Hebrew history looked back upon David as the ideal king, and regarded his reign, and that of his son Solomon, as the golden age of the Hebrew kingdom. In the esteem of the nation David was accorded a place only second to Moses himself."

John Dominic Crossan in his book titled *Jesus A Revolutionary Biography* makes the following interesting statement:

"...David [Kuthumi] was more than just a monarch from the past; he was, like Arthur [Kuthumi], the once and future king."

One of David's sons was Absalom. As briefly mentioned in the first chapter, this era was the incarnation to which the Bard Taliesin (St Germain) was alluding, for Absalom was slain in the Hebron valley, in the territory of Judah, where Samuel and David both resided.

According to Merrill F. Unger, Hebron was situated in the hill country of Judah some nineteen miles in a southwesterly direction from Jerusalem.

As Samuel the prophet, St Germain conveyed 'Divine Spirit' (the 'Wisdom' of Sophia also known as 'Athena') to David. It seems highly probable that St Germain, as Samuel the prophet, taught and initiated David into the Greater Mysteries of the Arkana/Arcana handed down from the days of Atlantis when St Germain had been the prophet, Noah.

How Jerusalem derived its Name

According to Robert Graves in his book titled *The White Goddess*, the ancient worshipping of the great goddess *Anna*, sometimes called *Anna Fearina*, the 'Queen of Spring' (the name of which was derived from the ancient Syrian/ Arian tribe of *Marianna/Maryanna*), had another title which was *Salmaona/Salmon*.

Salma became a 'divine' name in Palestine and Solomon; Salmon and Absalom, are variants of this name. Salma was the god to whom the hill of Jerusalem was originally dedicated. This place is mentioned in the Egyptian Tell Amarna Letters (1370BC) and in Assyrian monuments it is written as Ur-Salim which when translated is the 'City of the God Salim/Salem'.

Eventually, the hill upon which Jerusalem was built became known as *Zion*. *Ze* was a code name for the 'Sons of Light'. *ON* was the Temple in Heliopolis, Egypt, where the Masters of the Great White Brotherhood were taught. These Masters included Moses, King Solomon and Jesus. It can thus be seen how the Order of Sion/Zion obtained its name when it was established during the days of the Crusades and the Knights Templar.

ON was also the ancient name of Egypt and of Sumeria which means 'Light'.

The salmon (derived from the word Salma), was revered by the Druids; they had their own Salmon god who was associated with the sacred wells and in Celtic tradition the salmon was symbolic of wisdom. In mythology, 'Merlin' was able to change into a salmon.

David's son, King Solomon, carried out his promise to his father and built the Temple of Jerusalem in which to house the Sacred Tablets of the Covenant. Thus began the long saga of the House of David and the Temple of Jerusalem and it was in the Temple of Jerusalem that the Ancient Mysteries were taught.

These sacred Tablets had been given to Moses by the Lord, and were subsequently passed on to Aaron (St Germain) of the tribe of Levi, for safekeeping. In Chronicle I, 54, we learn that the Lord assigned descendants of Aaron, the territory of Hebron.

The Wise King Solomon (El Morya) c.970 - c.913 BC
"Solomon obtained in Babel's Tower,
All sciences of Asia's land."
(Taliesin/Merlin/St Germain)

From the book titled *The World Atlas of Mysteries* by Francis Hitching, we learn that "King Solomon 'exceeded all the kings of the earth for riches and wisdom'. He traded with spice merchants and kings of Arabia, importing gold, ivory, silver, precious stones, exotic flora and fauna. His Temple was a marvel of gold and brass, with immense carved statues on its ornate pillars. He was supported by a great navy and an army...truly the Golden age of Hebrew prosperity and power."

(According to the Bible, Solomon married the daughter of a Pharaoh who was powerful enough to sack the Philistine city of Geza and present it to Solomon as a dowry. According to Kings in the Bible, the king of Egypt who was Shishak had attacked Gezer and captured it, killing its inhabitants and setting fire to the city. Then he gave the city as a wedding present to his daughter when she married Solomon, and Solomon rebuilt it. Solomon also rebuilt Hazor and Megiddo. By marrying the Egyptian princess, Solomon made an alliance with the king of Egypt. Solomon brought her to live in Jerusalem and this was *prior* to the beginning of the building of the Temple).

"After Solomon's death, his Temple was sacked by a Pharaoh called Shishak, and the amassed treasures described in minute detail in the Bible were carried off to Egypt. Shishak, in the orthodox view, is Shoshenk I, a minor king who left a list of Palestinian cities and little else - no mention of Jerusalem, or conquest, or the Temple, or even one item of treasure."

And yet, according to archaeologist, Merrill F. Unger, "His triumphal inscription at Karnak (ancient Thebes) gives a long list of his conquests, which include towns *in all parts of Judah* and extend to the coastal plain, across the Plain of Esdraelon into Gilead, 'showing that he invaded the Northern Kingdom as well, in spite of his previous friendship of Jeroboam (I Kings 11:40)'. *A part of Shishak's stela has been excavated at Megiddo, proving that he actually did take and occupy this important city, as recounted in his Karnak inscription."*

Merrill F. Unger states that Shishak/Sheshonq "possessed considerable power, since he was able to claim and partially enforce authority over Palestine."

Solomon's Journey to Egypt - 999 BC

According to ancient Rosicrucian records, King Solomon journeyed to Egypt where he studied the Greater Mysteries at El Amarna. Spencer Lewis in his book titled *Rosicrucian Questions And Answers*, states that "about the year 1,000 BC, there came to Egypt a character whose name is recorded as Saloman but who was identified in later years with Solomon. He desired instruction in the higher Egyptian sciences and philosophy, and was directed to El Amarna with a letter of introduction from the *intendant* at Thebes. He reached El Armana on the 4th day of June, 999, under the name of Saloman, *the youthful leader.*" (This suggests that Solomon was very young at the time of his journey to Egypt).

Solomon in Egypt 952 BC, 980 BC

"The next word of him is as a resident at the *royal home* in Bubastis in the Delta where Shishak I had established himself. *This was in the year 952 BC and Saloman is referred to as an instructor [tutor] to the Pharaoh's son...in another place he is referred to as advisor in political matters...*"

"Whether he had been at this residence all the intervening years from 999 to 952 BC is not definitely established, but there is a record of his presence at Thebes in the year 980 when he visited some *games* in company with the *intendant* of Thebes, and a group of scholars with whom he seemed on the most intimate terms." (There were two cities named Thebes, one in Greece and the Egyptian one was situated on the southern banks of the Nile River).

"When Shishak I secured Thebes he appointed his son priest in the religion of Ammon, and gave his daughter, Aye, to Saloman to wed."

"Then within a year or so Saloman departed [from Egypt] for Palestine where he became a mighty power, and by a prearranged plan, permitted Shishak I to rule over his people. The history of Saloman or *Solomon* in Palestine is too well known to warrant any further comment except on one point."

"Five years after Saloman began his rule in Palestine he completed a Temple there in which to house a 'society' or brotherhood such as he had found at El Armana."

"An examination of the plans and cross-section views of the so-called Saloman's Temple shows it to be not only typically Egyptian in architecture and decoration, but copied after the mystic Temple at El Armana, even to the location of the Altar, with the exception that the side structures which made the original building a *cross* were eliminated in Saloman's plans."

This is very interesting from the point of view that El Morya, in his incarnation as Pharaoh Akhnaton established his city at El Armana. "He [Akhnaton] built a new capital at El Amarna in the plain of Hermopolis on a virgin site at the edge of the desert and abandoned Thebes because it was the *magnificent city of Ammon*." So, virtually, El Morya was copying his own original plan in his incarnation as King Solomon. The Temple plan was that of the Temple of Jerusalem in which the Ark of the Covenant was housed.

Akhnaton (Amenhotep IV) (El Morya) 1378 - 1350 BC

There were three known Masters of the Great White Brotherhood who reincarnated during this era, namely - St Germain who was Aaron (whose previous known incarnation was as the Prophet Samuel during the era of King David and King Solomon); the Master Jesus who was reputedly Moses, and El Morya.

El Morya was the pharaoh, Amenhotep IV, who became the ruler of Egypt in 1367 BC. He was the great great grandson of Tutmoses III (Kuthumi).

According to Spencer Lewis, in his book titled *Rosicrucian Questions and Answers*, Amenhotep IV was born on November 24th 1378 BC at the Royal Palace at Thebes, and his mother, Queen Tia, was of Arian birth. He began his reign at the tender age of eleven years old and during the course of his reign, changed his name from Amenhotep to Akhnaton. (He married the beautiful Nefertiti).

The Symbolism of The 'Rose'

The Rose is also synonymous with the *Lotus* blossom of India and Egypt, signifying the unfolding blossoms of spirituality. The symbolism of the Rose with the Cross was introduced by the Egyptian Pharaoh Akhnaton (Amenhotep IV) (El Morya).

According to the Rosicrucian authority, Spencer Lewis: "At the time of his crowning he took the title 'Amenhotep, King, *Living in Truth*.' He began a sweeping reformation throughout Egypt in the fifth year of his reign. His decree prohibited any other form of worship except the living God. He then changed his own name so that it would not be inconsistent with his reform: Amenhotep meant 'Ammon is satisfied'; this he altered to Akhnaton meaning 'pious to Aton' or 'Glory to Aton'."

"At El Amarna he also built a large Temple for the Brotherhood, in 'the form of a cross' and a large number of houses for his Council."

"Akhnaton (Amenhotep IV) not only built his Temple in the form of a cross, but he added the cross and the rose as symbols and further adopted the Crux

Ansata [one of the earliest forms of a cross, it is oval resting on a tau cross, or letter T - as a symbol of life] in a special coloring, as the symbol to be worn by all teachers (Masters). In fact, the last year of his life was spent in evolving a wonderful system of symbols used to this day, to express every phase and meaning of the Rosicrucian sciences, arts, and philosophies and while some of these have become known to the uninitiated through the researches of Egyptologists, many remain secret and all are understandable only to the initiated."

"That the Rosy Cross became the true esoteric symbol of not only the Rosicrucians, but of the inner circle of the Essenes, the Templars and the Militia Crucifera Evangelic is due to the fact that all of these organizations were, and still are, channels for the work of the Great White Brotherhood. The secret ritual of the Templars contains many allusions to the significance of the Rosy Cross..."

The *Rose* is *the* symbol of perfection, equated with the 'heart' and unconditional love. It is not coincidence that 'hearts' are always depicted in a rose-colour (which represents 'love') and that red roses are given as a celebration of 'love', particularly on Valentine's Day.

Annie Bessant in her book titled *The Ancient Wisdom* when writing about the auric field which is able to be seen by clairvoyants, states: "Love, according to its quality, will set up forms more or less beautiful in colour and design, all shades of crimson to the most exquisite and soft hues of rose, like the palest blushes of the sunset or the dawn..."

Many today, are drawn to collecting or wearing pink rose-quartz crystals which energize the emotions of love which come from the heart. The heart is the centre where emotion is experienced.

Moses

There are various theories about the time period of Moses. Ancient Rosicrucian records which have been preserved relate that Moses was born in the same time period as Akhnaton and there were no slaves during that era. According to Merrill F. Unger in his book titled *Archeology And The Old Testament*, archeologists are not certain of the exact date of the 'Exodus' but place it at 'about' 1441 BC. Akhnaton died in 1350 BC, so given the ninety-one years difference between 1441 BC and 1350 BC, the time period fits with Akhnaton's reign.

According to Spencer Lewis, it was Akhnaton who gave assistance to Moses and his brother Aaron to lead the 'Chosen' people to Palestine. (This of course, makes a great deal of sense because as previously stated, the Masters of the Great White Brotherhood incarnated during the same important time periods in order to assist one another).

We are all familiar with the story of Moses in the bulrushes and how the Pharaoh's daughter raised him to be a prince. But the fact that he was named Moses is surely a clue that he really was, by virtue of his royal birth, a Tutmoses.

Traditionally, Moses is supposed to have lived during the era of Ramesses I (Menpehtyre, 1293-1291 BC) and his son Seti I. However, according to Egyptian history, Ramesses was two hundred years after the reign of Tutmoses and at least one hundred years after Akhnaton. Reputedly, it was Ramesses and his son Seti who held the slaves captive during their massive building campaign.

Historically, Ramesses I, was not of royal blood, for he was previously a vizier to the Pharaoh Horemheb and when Horemheb failed to produce an heir, he bestowed the line of succession to Ramesses. Ramesses only ruled for two years at which time Seti I succeeded him and ruled for thirteen years.

Seti I married Tuya and they named their daughter Tia. Their son was named after his grandfather Ramesses I and Ramesses II became one of Egypt's powerful Pharaohs, who endeavoured to restore the past glories of the earlier 18th Dynasty Pharaohs, Tutmoses III (Kuthumi) and Akhnaton (El Morya). He lived to about ninety-two years of age.

It was during Seti's reign that tremendous building projects were undertaken and he worshipped the god Osiris dedicating a temple to Osiris, Isis, Horus Ptah and Amun-Ra. Seti I was buried in the Valley of the Kings and his tomb, which was discovered in 1817, is considered to be the finest in the Valley.

According to Wallace E. Budge in his book titled *Legends of The Egyptian Gods*, the Legend of the Destruction of Mankind is written in hieroglyphs and is found on the four walls of a small chamber in the tomb of Seti I.

Francis Hitching in the book titled *The World Atlas of Mysteries* informs us as follows:

"The era of the Exodus is generally considered to have been during the reign of Ramesses II (1290-1224 BC) who was a powerful and prosperous Pharaoh whom it is hard to imagine giving way to a rebel slave leader. *In the hieroglyphic texts describing his rule, there is no mention of Moses, of the Plagues, of the Israelites fleeing or the Egyptians attempting to return them to Egypt, nor of the inevitable social upheavals that must have accompanied their departure.*"

"Alternatively, it is suggested that the Exodus took place during the reign of his successor, Merneptah - in many ways an even more unlikely choice - since the stele commemorating his exploits tell of famous victories over the Israelites on their own territory..."

Francis Hitching also relates that "tiles of Ramesses III discovered in one of his palaces show Greek letters on the reverse side, which proves that a revised chronology is needed, because Ramesses is usually dated to a time four centuries before the time the Greek alphabet was invented." (At the time that Ramesses III ruled, whose chief Queen was also called Isis, the Greek Trojan War took place and the fall of the Mycenaean empire).

In Spencer Lewis' book titled *The Mystical Life of Jesus*, we are informed as follows:

"It was while Akhnaton was Pharaoh that the children of Israel dwelt in Egypt and the leaders of those tribes became initiates of the Great White Brotherhood, and it was at this time that Moses, as one of the initiates, became acquainted with the fundamentals of the religion which he afterward modified to present to those who followed him out of Egypt into Palestine. It was also Akhnaton that Moses made his appeal to for aid in taking the tribes of Israel out of Egypt, and it was through the aid thus given by Akhnaton and by the Great White Brotherhood in secrecy that the tribes of Israel evaded the heathen priesthood and had a safe journey."

Moses and Aaron (St Germain), Akhnaton's Nephews

Considering the fact that these pharaohs during this time period were called Tutmoses, it would seem rather obvious that the Biblical Moses was a son of the same royal lineage, born to a princess who was the sister of a pharaoh who could only have been Akhnaton, because, according to ancient Rosicrucian records, Akhnaton taught and initiated Moses.

Moses would have been a nephew of Akhnaton as would Aaron (St Germain), and their sister Miriam (a variant of Mary), would have been Akhnaton's niece. In the Biblical story of Moses, he was raised by the Pharaoh's sister in the palace and he could have become the king of Egypt. According to the Bible, the father of Moses was Amram of the House of Levi. The descendants of the House of Levi were to become the Essenes and priests of the Sanhedrin in Jerusalem and this will be elaborated upon further in our story.

Aaron (St Germain), the brother of Moses, had four sons, Nadab, Abihu, Eleazar and Ithamar (Chronicles I: 6). One of the descendants of Eleazar was Azariah, who served in the Temple which King Solomon built. In St Germain's life as Joseph, the Father of the Holy Grail Family, he was again to name one of his sons 'Eleazar'.

Moses and the Cabbala

The name of Moses in Hebrew means 'Law giver'. According to Manetho, (who was a High Priest at the temple of Heliopolis -The Temple of the Sun), Moses was educated and initiated at Heliopolis, at which time he became a High Priest of the Great White Brotherhood and his sister, Miriam, became a High Priestess. Moses established a branch of the Egyptian Brotherhood from which the Essenes descended.

Also, according to Manetho, the Sacred Tablets that were given to Moses upon the Mountain of Sinai were a 'veiled' account of Egyptian initiations. (Moses gave the Sacred Tablets to his brother Aaron - St Germain for safekeeping and they formed part of the Cabbala which was handed down to the Essenes).

The Cabbala is an esoteric teaching centred on a system of symbols which reflect the mystery of God and the Universe; the keys to the Cabbala lie hidden in the Holy Scriptures.

The 'Chosen' People and the Exodus

"Moses obtained
In great necessity
The aid of three dominical rods."
[Dominical is derived from 'dominus' - lord]
"I strengthened Moses through the waters of the Jordan"
(Taliesin/Merlin/St Germain)

The great 'Divine' plan of this era, to be carried out by the Masters of the Great White Brotherhood, was to lead the 'Chosen' people of the twelve tribes of 'Israel', back to the land of their ancestors. In the verse by Taliesin/Merlin/St Germain: *"I strengthened Moses through the waters of the Jordan"*, (which was briefly mentioned in the first chapter), the author of *The White Goddess*, Robert Graves, could not decide whether the answer was Aaron or Hur who helped Moses, because they both assisted Moses and Robert came to the conclusion that it was 'Hur'. However, it was Aaron because Aaron was St Germain.

The 'Chosen Tribe' were descendants of Jacob whom the Lord re-named 'Israel', and thus they became the 'Children of Israel' subsequently called the 'Israelites'. From the book titled *The Virgin Ideal* by Peter Dawkins, we learn that the word *"Israel* is actually Egyptian in origin - IS-RA-EL, and it refers to the Brotherhood of Light. It was after the 'Exodus' that many of the 'Chosen' people's descendants became the Essenes and some journeyed to Britain and Ireland and became the Celtic Druids. *The Essenes were the 'Chosen' tribe mentioned in the Bible for the word 'Essene' comes from the Greek word 'essaios' meaning 'mystic' or 'secret' and the Egyptian symbols of 'light' and 'truth' were represented in the word 'chosen' which translated into Greek, becomes 'Essen'.*

Thus far, we are able to see the pattern of continuity emerging. St Germain was the grand patriarch, Noah, and in all probability, he was Jacob whom the Lord re-named 'Israel' who subsequently incarnated as Aaron, guiding his people across the Jordan to the 'Promised Land'.

After the death of Aaron, he was succeeded by his sons and only those related to Aaron by blood could serve as a High Priest. This same tradition continued right down to the era of the Essenes in Jerusalem. It is recorded in the Dead Sea Scrolls that the Essenes' Teacher of Righteousness would be a reincarnation of ben Aaron, meaning a descendant or reincarnation of Aaron (St Germain).

THE ESSENES WERE THE 'CHOSEN' TRIBE MENTIONED IN THE BIBLE

MASTERS DISCUSSED IN THIS CHAPTER
Noah - St Germain
Tutmoses III - Kuthumi d.1447 BC
Pharaoh Akhnaton (Amenhotep IV) - El Morya 1387-1350 BC
Aaron - St Germain, died circa 1370 BC
King David - Kuthumi c.1010-970 BC
Prophet Samuel - St Germain c.1010-970 BC
King Solomon - El Morya c.970-931 BC

NOTES AND RECOMMENDED READING

Robert Graves, _The White Goddess_, (Faber & Faber, U.K. 1961)
Spencer Lewis, _Rosicrucian Questions And Answers_, (AMORC, U.S.A 1929)
Spencer Lewis, _The Mystical Life Of Jesus_, (AMORC, U.S.A, 1929)
Merrill F. Unger, _Archaeology And The Old Testament_, (Zondervan Publishing House, Michigan, U.S.A 1954)
William Foxwell Albright, _From The Stone Age To Christianity_, (Doubleday Anchor Books, U.S.A, 1957)
Charles W. Hedrick & Robert Hodgson, _Nag Hammadi Gnosticism And Early Christianity_, (Hendrickson Publishers, U.S.A. 1986)
E.A. Budge, _Legends of the Egyptian Gods_, (Dover Publications, U.S.A 1994)
John Allegro, _The Dead Sea Scrolls_, (Penguin Books, U.K. 1964)
Peter Lemesuirer, _The Armageddon Script_, (Element Books, U.K. 1981)
Stephen Quirke, _Ancient Egyptian Religion_, (British Museum Press, 1992)
Daniel J. Boorstin, _The Discoverers, A History of Man's Search To Know His World And Himself_, (Random House, U.K. 1983)
Francis Hitching, _World Atlas of Mysteries,_ (Pan Books, U.K. 1978)
Arthur J. Toynbee, _A Study of History_, (Oxford University Press, U.K. 1934)
John Dominic Crossan, _Jesus, A Revolutionary Biography_, (Harper, U.S.A. 1994)
Peter Dawkins, _The Virgin Ideal_, (Francis Bacon Research Trust, U.K.)
Annie Bessant, _The Ancient Wisdom_, (Theosophical Publishing House, U.S.A 1939)
C.W. Leadbeater, _The Hidden Life In Freemasonry_, (Theosophical Publishing House U.K. 1988)

CHAPTER 5

The Queen of Sheba, & the Ark of the Covenant

'The Kings of Tarshish and of distant shores will bring tribute to him; the kings of Sheba and Seba will present him gifts.' (Psalm 72: 10).

Who was the mysterious Queen of Sheba, argued over by Egyptologists and Biblical scholars for centuries? We know from the Biblical texts that the era in which she lived, was that of King Solomon and we have established in the previous chapter that he lived during the era of the Egyptian Pharaoh Shishak I (Shoshenk/ Sheshonq I).

In the 18th century, St Germain amazed many of his friends by confiding in them that during one of his many past lives, he had known the Queen of Sheba. Considering that St Germain was the prophet Samuel during the era of King David (Kuthumi) and King Solomon (El Morya), this may have been the reincarnation to which he was referring when he had occasion to meet the Queen.

According to information contained in the book titled *The World Atlas of Mysteries* by Francis Hitching:

"The Bible offers a reasonable amount of information about her: 'she came to Jerusalem with a very great train, with camels that bore spices, and very much gold, and precious stones'. The journey was an extremely important one to her, and she went away deeply impressed - 'thy wisdom and prosperity exceedeth the fame which I heard'. But where was the land of Sheba to which she returned?"

The King James Authorized Version of the Bible places it in Arabia (where most archaeologists today think it was) and in Ethiopia, where it was the name of the capital and she is considered to have been both Queen of Egypt and Ethiopia.

We do know that historically speaking, Queen Hatshepsut (Maatkare), who ruled from Thebes, Egypt, c1498 BC until c1483 BC, (at which point of time Tutmoses III became Pharaoh), made a spectacular expedition whose details correspond with the Biblical information of the Queen of Sheba. (Hatshepsut's name translates into 'Foremost of Noble Ladies' and her Throne name was Maat-ka-re meaning

'Truth is the Soul of Re'. As previously stated, she was the stepmother and aunt of Pharaoh Tutmoses III - Kuthumi).

The Lands of Punt and Sheba

The Queen Hatshepsut's voyage to the legendary land of Punt was a location that has also long been argued about by scholars for centuries. The land of Punt, which she recorded as having visited, is thought to have been in the region of northern Somalia, a record of which is carved on the walls of her temple.

Merrill F. Unger, in his book titled *Archaeology And The Old* Testament, informs us as follows:

"*Phut* has been commonly identified with ancient Punt, located south or southeast of African Cush, [Cush was a descendant of Ham, son of Noah], and corresponds with present-day Somaliland. However, Phut occurs in the inscriptions of the Persian Monarch, Darius I the Great (522-486 BC), and its location in Cyrenaica, the region about Cyrene in North Africa west of Egypt, is now certain."

The historian, Josephus, called the capital of Ethiopia, Seba. According to Merrill F. Unger, "Seba is connected with south Arabia through the southwestward migration of the original Cushites [Cush was the father of Nimrod] from lower Mesopotamia, 'the land of Shinar' (Gen. 10:8-12). According to the Assyrian inscriptions this people had migrated to northwest Arabia in the eighth century BC. *Seba, a dialectic variation of Sheba,* is closely associated with the latter as a remote country of the south and also with Egypt and Ethiopia in Africa. Strabo, the noted Greek geographer and traveler (c.63 BC - c.21 AD), located a harbor Saba and a town called Sabai on the west coast of the Red Sea."

"Sheba notably was in southwest Arabia, well known from its own records and classical geographers. The Sabaeans were a great commercial people and spread widely, appearing in northwest Arabia in Assyrian times and in the northern desert."

We know from the Biblical account that the Queen of Sheba was the ruler of an important and powerful kingdom.

"*Sheba* is often mentioned in the Old Testament as a distant people of great wealth, trading in gold, frankincense, precious stones and perfumes (I Kings 10:2, 10; Jer.6:20; Ezek. 27:22; Isaiah. 60:6; Ps. 72:10). Sabaean inscriptions which have been discovered show that these people were a settled and highly civilized people of southwest Arabia with their capital at Mariaba (Saba) about two hundred miles north of modern Aden."

Upon the subject of the Queen of Sheba, Merrill F. Unger writes:

"Although the Queen of Sheba of the Solomonic era has not been attested as yet in south-Arabian inscriptions, there is no valid reason for denying the historicity of either her or her visit to the Israelite monarch."

"It is true that the oldest inscriptions of Saba (Sheba) reach back only to the seventh or eighth century and Assyrian inscriptions do not begin to mention names of Sabaean kings until toward the end of the eighth century."

"However, there is no warrant to doubt that Sheba was an important kingdom or tribal confederacy two or three centuries earlier. Nor is there any reason to dismiss the whole account of the Queen's visit 'as a romantic tale', as generally used to be done. Although queens played little part in the later history of south Arabia, they ruled large tribal confederacies in north Arabia from the ninth to the seventh centuries BC, as the cuneiform inscriptions relate."

That Saba and Sheba were two different places we are able to glean, from the Psalm of Solomon.

'The Kings of Tarshish and of distant shores will bring tribute to him; the kings of Sheba and Seba will present him gifts.' (Psalm 72:10).

F.L. Rawson in his book titled *Life Understood* (1920) writes that "according to Professor Totten, *Tarshish* is one of the names for the Western Isles in the Bible which is Britain."

After many ventures abroad, Queen Hatshepsut returned with an amazing array of exotic plants which included myrrh and frankincense and accordingly botanists and Egyptologists could reach no agreement as to the country of their origin. Her temple was decorated in beautiful motifs of flora and fauna, some African, some Arabian. It has been previously mentioned how Tutmoses III too, decorated his temple that he built, in wonderful designs of flora and fauna and he called it the Botanical Hall.

Queen Hatshepsut versus the Queen of Sheba

The difference in the eras between Queen Hatshepsut, Tutmoses III, and the Queen of Sheba and King Solomon, is approximately some five hundred years. The question arises, is it possible that although the dates do not fit historically, the Queen of Sheba may have been Queen Hatshepsut? And if so, where did King Solomon fit into the picture?

1. We know that Solomon spent time in Egypt. He studied in the great Temples of Egypt and used similar designs to build the Temple in Jerusalem in which to house the Ark of the Covenant.
2. Solomon married an Egyptian princess named Aye, the daughter of the Pharaoh of Egypt, Sheshonq I (Shishak in the Biblical texts).
3. Interestingly, Solomon's mother, wife of King David (Kuthumi) of

Jerusalem, was a 'Sheba', i.e. Bathsheba.

4.   Some theorists believe Sheshonq/Shishak to have been Pharaoh Tutmoses III (Kuthumi).

5.   The Queen of Sheba visited Solomon (son of King David) in Jerusalem.

6.   This visit was possibly during the same era as King David who according to the Bible, 'lived to a ripe old age'.

7.   After the demise of Tutmoses II, who was married to Queen Hatshepsut, she relied upon her Royal Steward, known as Senenmut, who was also the Chief Architect.

8.   Solomon also had great architectural abilities.

9.   According to Egyptian history, Senenmut was also Queen Hatshepsut's chief 'adviser'.

10. According to the Rosicrucian authority, Spencer Lewis, Solomon is referred to 'an adviser in political matters' in Egypt.

11. According to Egyptian history, Senenmut was *tutor* to Hatshepsut's daughter, Neferure.

12. According to Spencer Lewis, Solomon was in Egypt in 952 BC and he was referred to as an *instructor/tutor* to the pharaoh's son.

13. The pharaoh can only have been Shishak/Sheshonq I. If Shishak/Sheshonq I was actually Pharaoh Tutmoses III, it does place him in the same time frame as Queen Hatshepsut. There is no mention of Princess Aye, wife of Solomon and a daughter of Shishak/Sheshonq amongst the Egyptian royal tombs - she would have been buried in Jerusalem where Solomon took her to live after they were married.

14. Senenmut designed his own elaborate tomb in which he was buried in Egypt, accordingly having pre-deceased Queen Hatshepsut by one year.

15. Despite much excavation by numerous archaeologists, the burial place of King Solomon in Jerusalem has never been found, nor that of his father King David. According to Merrill F. Unger in his book: "Excavations at Jerusalem and Palestine in general show how thorough was the damage and destruction wrought by the Chaldean invasions. *Not a trace of the Solomonic temple nor of the palaces of the Davidic kings has remained.*"

16. Hatshepsut's tomb was discovered in the Valley of the Kings in 1916, and investigated by Howard Carter, after which time many strange events occurred that caused a great deal of superstition.

If the chronological dates are incorrect, then it is possible that Queen Hatshepsut was the Queen of Sheba, sometimes referred to elsewhere in the Bible as the 'Queen of the South' which is said to refer to 'Egypt'. We may, therefore, accept that she was Queen of both Egypt and Ethiopia.

And, if Hatshepsut was the Queen of Sheba, then it is also probable that Senenmut was Solomon. Like King Solomon, Senenmut was unrivalled in the administration of the country. The comparisons between Solomon and Senenmut appear to be too many to be 'coincidental'.

The Ark of the Covenant

According to the Ethiopians, after the Queen of Sheba visited King Solomon in Jerusalem, she returned to Ethiopia with the Ark of the Covenant. However, this simply is not true. Why? Because the Prophet Jeremiah rescued it from the Temple of Jerusalem just prior to King Nebuchadnezzar of Babylon invading Jerusalem in 587 BC, and he took it and Jacob's Pillow, to the 'Isles Afar Off'.

In a recent program on the History Channel (2003), an English archaeologist visited Ethiopia in search of King Solomon's mine. He attempted to interview certain priests who purportedly had knowledge of the whereabouts of the Ark of the Covenant in Ethiopia. They were particularly evasive and totally unconvincing.

No doubt the legend will persist until the discovery of the Ark of the Covenant which will be found in a land far away from Ethiopia, when the 'time is ripe'. And, the clue to its whereabouts is that it will be found in the 'Land of the Covenant'.

MASTERS DISCUSSED IN THIS CHAPTER

Tutmoses III - Kuthumi d.1447 BC
Pharaoh Akhnaton (Amenhotep IV) - El Morya 1387-1350 BC

NOTES AND RECOMMENDED READING

Merrill F. Unger, *Archaeology And The Old Testament*, (Zondervan Publishing House, Michigan, U.S.A 1954)

William Foxwell Albright, *From The Stone Age To Christianity*, (Doubleday Anchor Books, U.S.A, 1957)

Francis Hitching, *World Atlas of Mysteries,* (Pan Books, U.K. 1978)

Spencer Lewis, *Rosicrucian Questions And Answers*, (AMORC, U.S.A 1929)

King James Authorized Version of the Bible & Good News Bible.

Comparisons between Egyptian Chronology and Biblical Chronology:

Tutmoses I	c.1524-1518 BC	First pharaoh to be buried in the Valley of the Kings.	Egypt	Pharaoh
Tutmoses III (Kuthumi) (Military leader)	c1504-1447 BC	Buried in tomb in Valley of the Kings.	Egypt	Pharaoh
Hatshepsut	c1498-1483 BC	Buried in tomb in Valley of the Kings.	Egypt	Queen
Senenmut (Architect) (Adviser) (Tutor)		Died year before Hatshepsut & buried in Egyptian tomb he designed, located on the north east corner of Hatshepsut's tomb.		Chief Architect & Royal Steward/advisor to Hatshepsut.
David (Kuthumi) (Military leader)	c1010-c970 BC Same era as the prophet, Samuel - St Germain.	Burial place still unknown. Heir was his son Solomon.	Jerusalem	King
Solomon (El Morya) (Architect) (Adviser) (Tutor)	c970-c931 BC	Married Princess Aye, daughter of Shishak/ Sheshonq. Burial place still unknown.	Egypt & Jerusalem	King
Shishak (Invader of Jerusalem)	c.945-924 BC	Burial place Tanis, Egypt.	Egypt	Pharaoh known as Sheshonq I.
Sheba	Same era as King Solomon.	Visited Solomon in Jerusalem & sought his advice.	Egypt	Queen of Egypt & Ethiopia

CHAPTER 6

The Temple of Solomon, Yahweh & the Astral Gods

"Lilies represented always the flower of humanity. Arranged in line round the edge of the disc they indicated the Great White Brotherhood - the jewels in the crown of mankind, hovering above the human race and directing its evolution."
(C.W. Leadbeater)

According to the Bible, the building of the Temple of Jerusalem commenced in the fourth year of Solomon's reign which was four hundred and eighty years after the 'Exodus' when Aaron (St Germain) and Moses had led the 'Chosen' tribe out of Egypt, to Jerusalem. Biblical chronicles state that Solomon died in c931 BC and that Solomon reigned for forty years. Therefore, his reign would have commenced about 891 BC. It was discussed in a previous chapter that it was Pharaoh Akhnaton (Amenhotep IV) who assisted Moses and Aaron to lead the 'Chosen' tribe out of Egypt. Akhnaton, according to Rosicrucian records, was born in 1378 BC and died in 1350 BC. By deducting the year of Akhnaton's birth, i.e. 1378 BC and the 480 years that Solomon's reign commenced, we have the year 898 BC which is close enough in figures, and also proves that the Pharaoh of that period of the 'Exodus' was Akhnaton.

King Solomon (El Morya), when he built the Temple at Jerusalem, copied the Temple of El Armana which he had built in his incarnation as Pharaoh, Akhnaton.

Kings I: 7 in the Bible informs us that the building of his palace in Jerusalem took thirteen years. However, in Chronicles 2:8 in the Bible we are informed that it took Solomon twenty years to build the Temple. If we add 13 + 20, we arrive at the figure of 33, which once again is symbolic of *Freemasonry*.

Freemasonry traces its antiquity to Solomon's Temple and the rites of Hiram Abif, the Temple Architect. C.W. Leadbeater in his book titled *The Hidden Life In Freemasonry*, states that King Solomon himself appears to be responsible for introducing into Masonry "the original form of the story of Hiram Abif, but not for the insertion of the name which we now use for its hero."

"Solomon for patriotic reasons transferred the theatre of drama to Jerusalem, and centred its interest round the temple which he had built, winning popularity at the same time by bringing his ritual into accordance with that of surrounding peoples, who were mostly worshippers of the Phoenician deity Tammuz, afterwards called by the Greeks, Adonis." (It is from the word Adonis, that we have the word 'Adonai' meaning 'Lord').

According to C. W. Leadbeater:

"Rehoboam, Solomon's son, seems to have taken an intense dislike to Hiram Abif, who had more than once reproved him for arrogance and unworthy conduct; so when after Solomon's death he came to the throne, he took a curious, perverted revenge upon Hiram by decreeing that the victim of the 3rd degree should bear his name for ever. Exactly why this should have afforded satisfaction to Rehoboam it is difficult to see; but perhaps we should hardly hold him responsible for his actions, as he was obviously a decadent, a degenerate of the worst type. His enmity may possibly have shown itself in other ways also, for Hiram Abif presently found it desirable to return to his own country, where he died full of age and honour."

According to Merrill F. Unger in his book titled *Archaeology And The Old Testament*:

"At the time of David and Solomon, both of whom maintained ties of amity with Hiram I of Tyre (c.969-963 BC), southern Phoenicia was consolidated under one king who ruled Tyre, but who bore the official title of 'King of the Sidonians'. From the twelfth to the seventh centuries BC Tyre and Sidon existed as one political entity. Only before and after this period were there two separate states, so that Hiram was a rich and powerful ruler..."

"Moreover, the name Hiram (originally, Ahiram) was a common Phoenician royal name, as is attested by the inscriptions, notably found on the sarcophagus of Ahiram at Byblus discovered in 1923-1924 by a French expedition under M. Montet and dating probably from the eleventh century."

The Plan of the Temple of Jerusalem

From the book titled *The Hidden Life In Freemasonry* by C.W. Leadbeater, we gain knowledge regarding Solomon's Temple. The English Craft ritual says:

"There was nothing in connection with this magnificent structure more remarkable, or which more particularly struck the attention, than the two great pillars which were placed at the porch or entrance. Their original significance dates back much further than this. It is claimed that these two columns originally represented the north and south pole stars."

"They were at first the pillars of Horus and Set, but their names were afterwards changed to Tat or Ta-at, and Tattu, the former meaning 'in strength' (and 'Truth') and the latter 'to establish', the two together being considered an emblem of stability. Tattu is the entrance to the region where the mortal soul is blended with the immortal spirit, and thereby established forever."

"We learn from the Bible that all the decorative work carried out on the Temple was the work of Hiram Abif, a widow's son of Naphtali - a man described in the Biblical account as a cunning worker in brass, who was sent down to Jerusalem by Hiram, King of Tyre, especially in order to do this and other metal work for King Solomon." (In the 16th century when St Columba founded the first major ecclesiastic Celtic centre on the island of Iona, another name for Iona was *Innis nam Druineach* meaning Island of the Cunning Workmen or Sculptors; and still another name by which it was known - *Innis-nam-Druidneach, the Isle of the Druids*. Metals are symbols of Alchemy and brass represents Venus).

Leadbeater further states: "Undoubtedly this man (Hiram) was a true artist, for he took an almost inconceivable amount of trouble to carry out this design exactly as he wanted it. So far as the investigators were able to see, his work was based entirely upon a traditional account of the stone Egyptian pillars which had been handed down from the time of Moses. It did not appear that he had any clear idea of the meaning of these strange decorations, though Moses knew perfectly well the whole system of symbology which lay behind it."

As we have seen, Moses was initiated into the sacred Mysteries by Akhnaton who later incarnated as King Solomon (El Morya) and the motifs used in the decoration of the Temple, were Freemasonic and were traceable back to the Egyptian times.

Returning to comments made by C.W. Leadbeater: "On Tat, the left hand pillar, (of the Temple of Solomon), each link of each chain symbolized what in our Oriental studies we call a branch-race, and the links as they descended became larger and thicker to indicate a deeper descent into matter, until the fourth was reached, when the life-force begins to draw inward and upward, and so its embodiment becomes less material. Each loop of Seven (7) links therefore typified a sub-race, and the seven loops which extended round the pillar, making a festoon, correspond to one of the great root-races, such as Lemurian, the Atlantean or the Arian (Aryan). The whole set of seven festoons hanging one below the other denoted our world-period, one occupation of this planet of ours."

Included in the decorative motifs of Solomon's Temple were pomegranates and lilies.

According to C.W. Leadbeater:

"In Tat the lilies represented always the flower of humanity. Arranged in line round the edge of the disc they indicated the Great White Brotherhood - the jewels in the crown of mankind, hovering above the human race and directing its evolution."

(According to information contained in Peter Dawkins' book titled *Francis Bacon - Herald of the New Age*, Freemasonry is represented by the Pillar or Tau cross [also known as the Hammer]'. Rosicrucianism is signified by the Rose and 'Roses' is sometimes translated as 'lilies or simply as 'flowers').

"The four pendant flower-chains symbolized the Holy Four who reside in Shamballa - the Spiritual King and his three pupil-assistants, the sole representatives on earth of the Lords of Flame who came down long ago from Venus to hasten the evolution of mankind." (It will be remembered that in an earlier paragraph, mention was made of the fact that Hiram Abif was a 'cunning worker in Brass' and that Brass was the symbol of Venus).

Leadbeater then goes onto describe how the various decorations signify different levels of initiation and how they are still current today.

"There are first those on the probationary path, who are aspiring to enter the Path proper, and are doing everything in their power to purify themselves, to develop their character, and to serve humanity with unselfish love *under the guidance of the Masters.*"

"Then come those who have been initiated into the Great White Brotherhood and have thus entered on the Path proper; their lives are dedicated entirely to the service of humanity; in them the bud of human life has opened into flower, and their consciousness has risen in the buddhic principle, which has been described as the truly human expression of man."

"Thirdly come the Arhats, those who have taken the Fourth great Initiation; they are not compelled to reincarnate; if they do so it is quite voluntary; they dip down into human life on this plane simply in order to help."

"According to the historian Josephus's version, the two famous pillars (of Hermes) were entirely covered with hieroglyphics, which after their discovery, were copied and reproduced in the most secret corners of the inner Temples of Egypt, and have thus become the source of its Wisdom and exceptional learning. These two 'pillars' however, are the prototypes of the two 'tablets of stone' hewn by Moses at the command of the Lord."

The authors of *The Hiram Key*, (based on the story of the Freemasons, Knights Templar and Hiram Abif), Christopher Knight and Robert Lomas, discuss how the Rosslyn Chapel of the St Clair family near Edinburgh, Scotland, is decorated with motifs and both the motifs and the design of the chapel plus its pillars are based on the Temple of Solomon. When the Knights Templar were being suppressed in 1313 AD, many of the ones who survived took refuge in Scotland. (In the sequel to this story, *The Dove, The Rose And The Sceptre - In Search of the Ark of the Covenant*, my personal journey to Rosslyn Chapel is discussed and further elaboration is given).

Leadbeater continues: "To the ordinary worshipper in the Temple all this rather complicated ornamentation was merely decorative, but to the initiate it was full of esoteric significance. First, these two pillars were an exemplification of the occult axiom, 'As above, so below', for though they were absolutely alike in every particular it was always understood that they represented respectively the terrestrial and celestial worlds."

According to Merrill F. Unger:

"Despite the fact that no architectural or constructional remains found in Jerusalem can be attributed to Solomon, numerous archaeological finds in the ancient Near East have cast a great deal of indirect light upon the construction of the temple."

"It is now known that the plan of the edifice was characteristically Phoenician, as would be expected, since it was built by a Tyrian architect (I Kings 7.13-15)."

"Similarly ground plans of sanctuaries of the general period 1200-900 BC have been excavated in northern Syria...and the findings have demonstrated that the specifications of the Solomonic structure outlined in I Kings 6-7 are pre-Greek and authentic for the tenth century BC and not to be denied historical genuineness and assigned to the period of Hellenic influence after the sixth century BC, as some critics were accustomed to do."

"The Temple was built by a Canaanite architect from Tyre (Hiram) and it undoubtedly followed the Phoenician models since there was none in Israel to follow. The pillars of Jachin and Boaz, the Sea, the portable lavers, the great altar, the decoration on the walls and objects with figures of cherubim (winged sphinxes), lions, bulls, lilies etc., are all contemporary Canaanite inspiration. The inner part of the Temple was called the 'Holy of Holies' where Yahweh was worshipped."

The Astral Gods had Intercourse with Mortal Women

Continuing with Merrill F. Unger:

"Yahweh was believed to have created astral as well as terrestrial beings and the former were popularly called 'the host of heaven' or 'the sons of God' (*bene El* or *bene ha-Elohim*). This meant simply 'gods' in Canaanite, as is clear from numerous passages illustrated by many parallel Semitic expressions."

"In Genesis 6:1 for example, we have an original myth in which the (astral) gods had intercourse with mortal women, who gave birth to heroes, an idea that often may be illustrated by Babylonian and Greek mythology."

"It is generally recognised by scholars that only part of the early prose passages which mention 'messengers (angels) of God' or 'the messenger of Yahweh' reflect their original sense. In some later passages, the term 'angel of Yahweh' has clearly been substituted for 'Yahweh'."

From information contained in the books written by Madame Helena Blavatsky (such as *The Secret Doctrine* and *Isis Unveiled*) and also in Peter Dawkins' book titled *The Great Vision*, according to the Ancient Wisdom traditions, "mighty souls came to our planet from Venus approximately 18 millions years ago inhabiting the land known subsequently as Hyperborea- 'the Land beyond the North Wind'."

Peter writes: "Establishing this area as their principal home and temple, they then moved across the world to other key areas in order to act as guides and teachers to the young races of humanity. Young humanity was, at the time of this great incarnation of 'God-men' and 'Sun-men', existing and evolving in areas of the world known as Mu, the Motherland."

"As a whole they are known historically as the Third Root Race of mankind, a Race of men that, 18 million years ago, had just began to exist in physical bodies (rather than etheric and astral), to divide sexually into male and female bodies, and to think rationally. They needed, at that dawn of rationality, sexuality and free choice, to be carefully guided, with teachers to answer their questions and to provide allegorical ideas of the life to be aimed for and the experiences to be undertaken."

"During this period the historic (rather than allegorical) story of Adam and Eve took place, followed by the division of Cain from Abel; the latter representing those souls who followed the teachings of the Christ souls, and the former representing those souls who chose otherwise."

"After Mu [also known as Lemuria], the next great epoch of human evolution was in Atlantis, in which humanity is known as the Fourth Root Race. This epoch began about 5 millions years ago. The Atlanteans are the *Nephilim* ('giant's) of the Bible, their ancestor being Seth, the third 'son' of Adam."

"During this period the Christ souls and their disciples - the 'sons of God' - incarnated totally into the dense substance of the planet, and into its human life cycle, taking on dense physical bodies and involving themselves far more completely with the experiences of younger humanity."

"Thus 'the sons of God saw the daughters of men that were fair: and they took them wives of all which they chose.' Their progeny became 'the mighty men, the men of renown', the great initiate-teachers who lived amongst mankind and who established centres of the Ancient Wisdom in Atlantis, to teach the Mysteries of God and lead those who were ready and capable through initiation."

(After the destruction of Atlantis which has been discussed in a previous chapter, Noah - St Germain and his family and priests who escaped before the 'Flood' constituted the 'Fifth Root Race' which was and still is, the Arian/Arian Race).

"From the great Atlantean initiates, particularly Enoch came the ideas and examples of the Sun-King, the Priest-King, and of the royal dynasties and the bloodline. For the Atlanteans and also for the early races of the present Fifth Root Race, the most suitable living example of Truth that these great initiates could give was in the form of a 'Father-Mother' figure - a High Priest and Sovereign Lord ruling his land and guiding his nation of people."

The Book of Enoch (discussed more fully in the following chapter) was discovered in Ethiopia in 1773 by the Scottish explorer, James Bruce. We are informed as follows:

"Enoch was one of the greatest prophets. Thus, in his treatise on the angels, we read: 'We are not to suppose that a special office has been assigned by mere accident to a particular angel: as to Raphael, the work of curing and healing; to Gabriel, the direction of wars; to Michael, the duty of hearing the prayers and supplications of men.'"

Certain chapters in the Book of Enoch "record the descent of two hundred angels on earth, their selection of wives, the birth of their gigantic offspring, and the instruction of mankind in the manufacture of offensive and defensive weapons, the fabrication of mirrors, the workmanship of jewellery, and the use of cosmetics and dyes, combined with lessons in sorcery, astrology, divination and astronomy - all which Tertullian accepts as Divine revelation..."

Yahweh

According to William Foxwell Albright in his book titled *From The Stone Age To Christianity* (1957): "The earliest post-Mosaic version represented Yahweh Himself as leading Israel; the replacement of God Himself by His messenger is orthodox Israelite doctrine, but the use of the term 'Presence' reminds one strongly of the late Canaanite idea that Tanis was the 'presence' (power) of 'Baal' and may have been felt by orthodox Israelite theologians to verge perilously on hypostalizations of deity."

"The enigmatic formula in Exodus 3.14, which in Biblical Hebrew means *'I AM WHAT I AM'*, if transposed into the form in the third person required by the causative *Yahweh*, can only become *Yahweh asher Yahweh/yihweh*, meaning 'He Causes to be what Comes into Existence'. It was also used in the Egyptian texts of the second millennium BC (a god) who causes to be (or who creates) what comes into existence. Both angels and humans were created by God and consequently might be poetically called His 'children'. *Yahweh* is the lord of all cosmic forces, controlling sun, moon, and storm, but not identified with any of them."

MASTERS DISCUSSED IN THIS CHAPTER

Pharaoh Akhnaton (Amenhotep IV) 1378-1350 BC - El Morya
King Solomon reigned c.970-931 BC - El Morya

NOTES AND RECOMMENDED READING

Annie Bessant, _The Ancient Wisdom_, (Theosophical Publishing House, U.S.A 1939)

C.W. Leadbeater, _The Hidden Life In Freemasonry_, (Theosophical Publishing House U.K. 1988)

Merrill F. Unger, _Archaeology And The Old Testament_, (Zondervan Publishing House, Michigan, U.S.A 1954)

William Foxwell Albright, _From The Stone Age To Christianity_, (Doubleday Anchor Books, U.S.A, 1957)

Peter Dawkins, _The Great Vision_, (Francis Bacon Research Trust, Warwick, U.K.)

Peter Dawkins, _Francis Bacon, Herald of the New Age_, (Francis Bacon Research Trust, U.K)

Spencer Lewis, _Rosicrucian Questions And Answers_, (AMORC, U.S.A 1929)

Christopher Knight & Robert Lomas, _The Hiram Key_, (Century, U.K. 1996)

King James Authorized Version of the Bible & Good News Bible.

CHAPTER 7

Thoth, Enoch & the Philosopher's Stone

"I was instructor to Eli and Enoch"
(Taliesin/Merlin/St Germain)

"As above, so below"
(Hermes Trismegistus)

It is noteworthy that in the year 1773, after a period of almost total obscurity lasting fifteen hundred years, the Scottish explorer, James Bruce, discovered in what is now called Ethiopia, *The Book of Enoch* which has been translated by the late Richard Laurence, Archbishop of Cashel, in Ireland. Richard Laurence was formerly Professor of Hebrew at Oxford. He described *The Book of Enoch* as "being a very profound and encyclopedic work on comparative religion and Hermetic philosophy. *The Secret Doctrine* by Madame Helena Blavatsky refers to this edition on thirty-seven occasions."

Enoch also known as Khanoch or Hanoch means 'Initiator' and 'Teacher', as well as 'Son of Man'.

We further learn from the commentary in the back of *The Book of Enoch:*-

"It is declared apocryphal which simply means a *secret* book, i.e. one that belonged to the catalogue of the Temple libraries under the guardianship of the Hierophants and initiated priests and was never meant for the profane. *Apocrypha* comes from the word *crypto* 'to hide'."

"Catholics may disregard its contents, as it is not found in the sacred Canon of their Church; but Protestants, who adhere to the principles of Reformation, and whose tenure of Christianity is therefore contingent on the appeal of reason, must inevitably enroll Enoch among the prophets, or reconsider the supernatural in Christianity."

"The long neglected Book of Enoch now stands in analogous relationship with modern seekers after religious truth; and it remains for its readers to exercise that right of private judgement, to which Protestantism owes its existence, by impartially considering the inevitable modifications of faith involved in the discovery, that the language and ideas of alleged revelation are found in a pre-existent work, accepted by Evangelists and Apostles as inspired, but classed by modern theologians among apocryphal productions."

"Tertullian, who flourished at the close of the first and at the beginning of the second century, whilst admitting that the 'Scripture of Enoch' is not received by some because it is not included in the Hebrew Canon, speaks of the author as 'the most ancient prophet, Enoch,' and of the book as the divinely inspired autograph of that immortal patriarch, preserved by Noah [St Germain] in the ark, or miraculously reproduced by him through the inspiration of the Holy Spirit."

"The Book of Enoch was therefore as sacred as the Psalms or Isaiah in the eyes of the famous theologian, [Tertullian] on whom modern orthodoxy relies as the chief canonist of the New Testament scripture."

We are informed in the introduction in the translation of the Book of Enoch that the book "was written long subsequent to the commencement, and even to the conclusion, of the Babylonian Captivity." [This was the era of King Nebuchadnezzar and the prophet Jeremiah when Nebuchadnezzar, in 587 BC, captured the King of Judah, Zedekiah and his sons, took them to Babylon as prisoners and killed them]. And, "certain sections of the Book of Enoch contain an allegorical narrative of the royal dynasties of Israel and Judah from which Archbishop Laurence constructs a history extending from Saul to the beginning of Herod the Great."

"Chapter xcii records a series of prophecies extending from Enoch's own time to about one thousand years beyond the present generation. In the system of chronology adopted, a day stands for hundred, and a week for seven hundred years. Reference is made to the Deluge, the call of Abraham, the Mosaic dispensation, the building and the destruction of the Temple of Solomon - events which preceded the date at which the Book of Enoch was probably written."

"The 'Learned' (the Initiated), (*Edris*), bore in Egypt the name of 'Thoth', the inventor of arts, sciences, writing or letters, of music and astronomy. Among the Jews, the *Edris* became 'Enoch', who according to Bar-Hebraeus, 'was the first inventor of writing', books, arts and sciences - the first who reduced to a system, the progress of the planets. In Greece he was called Orpheus, and thus changed his name with every nation."

"Enoch is the seventh Patriarch; Orpheus is the possessor of the *phorminx* - the seven-stringed lyre, which is the seven-fold mystery of initiation. Thoth, with the seven-rayed Solar Discus on his head, travels in the Solar boat, the three hundred and sixty-five degrees, jumping out every fourth (leap) year for one day. Finally, Thoth-Lunus is the septenary god of the seven days, or the week. Esoterically and spiritually, *Enoichion* means 'Seer of the Open Eye'."

"Some of the writers interested in the subject - especially Freemasons - have tried to identify Enoch with Thoth of Memphis, the Greek Hermes and even the Latin Mercury. They belong one and all to the same category of sacred writers, of Initiators and Records of Occult and Ancient Wisdom."

(The quotation under the heading of this chapter, by Taliesin, informs us that St Germain was the Instructor to Enoch, which proves that St Germain was far more highly initiated than Enoch).

"*The Secret Doctrine* by Madame Blavatsky teaches us that the arts, sciences, theology, and especially philosophy of every nation which preceded that last *universally known*, but not a universal Deluge (of Noah's time), had been recorded ideographically from the primitive oral records of the Fourth Race, and that these were the inheritance of the latter from the early Third Root-Race before the allegorical Fall. Hence, also, the Egyptian pillars, the tablets, and even the 'white Oriental porphyry stone' of the Masonic legend - which Enoch, fearing that the real and precious secrets would be concealed before the Deluge - were simply more or less symbolic and allegorical copies from the primitive Records. The 'Book of Enoch' is one of such copies and is Chaldean."

"A Highly Initiated adept reached the power and degree, as also the purification, which enabled him to die only in the physical body and *still lead a conscious life* in his astral (etheric) body [which is what the Masters of the Great White Brotherhood were able to 'master']." "When Josephus, speaking of Elijah and Enoch (Antiquities ix.2) remarks that 'it is written in the sacred books that they (Elijah and Enoch) disappeared, but so that nobody knew that they died,' it means simply that *they had died in their personalities*, as Yogis die to this day in India, or even some Christian monks to the world."

According to information contained in Peter Dawkins' book titled *Arcadia*:

"The original knowledge was given to the first sages of Egypt by the 'Gods', and those sages are themselves said to have come as colonists from Atlantis during the last few thousand years of that 'Titanic' period of man's development. In other words, there was a sacred tradition of wisdom knowledge handed down on from the past *via* a line of sages or high initiates, that was said to have come from the great Atlantean sage, Enoch (as he was known to the Hebrews), or Thoth (as he was known to the Egyptians), who 'walked with God' and was raised up into the highest heaven to become the Messiah or Teacher of all mankind. He, in his turn, had received a sacred tradition of wisdom knowledge *via* a line of sages stemming from Adam, the first incarnate man, who had been instructed by God after his fall from Paradise. Enoch was known mystically as 'the seventh from Adam'."

"According to Egyptian sacred lore, there was initially *Ten Divine Dynasties* - 'the reign of the Gods'. These 'Gods' (*Neters*) should be understood as being divine creative principles and archetypes, equivalent to the *Sephiroth* of the Hebraic Cabbala, or the supreme Spirits (*Elohim*) and Archangels of the Judaic-Christian tradition. It should also be understood that Moses, the great law-giver of the Hebrews, was learned in all the knowledge of the Egyptians having been a high priest of On (Heliopolis) and second to the pharaoh [Akhnaton - El Morya] in initiateship and rulership of Egypt, and that it is essentially the same wisdom knowledge that the Egyptians had which was passed on to the Hebrews, *via* Moses."

We learn from Stephen Quirke in his book titled *Ancient Egyptian Religion* as follows:

"The principal difference between Egyptian and foreign cults of Egyptian deities lay in their application to society. In Egypt the priests had, according to Ptolemaic texts on temple walls, to be pure and refrain from the same transgressions as those listed in the 'negative confession' at the judgement of the dead; the purified could then perform the rites necessary to the cult, that is touching the sacred image as it is clothed and fed in the daily ritual and as it is transferred from the temple on festival processions. The cult serviced the universe in a mechanical manner, enabling the king, locally through priests, to keep alive the community of humanity with the world it inhabits."

According to Peter Dawkins:

"The Ancient Egyptian civilisation was carefully planned from start to finish, as a statement and expression of the Ageless Wisdom. There was always, from generation to generation, an inner council of Egyptian sages - the 'prophets' or highest initiates of the land - who knew the plan and were the guardians of it, and responsible for seeing that the plan was carried out as well as possible. Collectively, they were known as *Tat* (Thoth), the 'Word', for they were the living representatives of the Divine Word of Truth which the Egyptians called *TAT*. This high council was composed of the pharaoh plus the dignitaries and prophets of the four principal teaching and initiatory centres of Egypt. These great centres of light and learning were also the principal seats of government. They were located at *Un* (Hermopolis), *Mem-Nefer* (Memphis), *An* (On, or Heliopolis) and *Waset* (Thebes)."

(C.W. Leadbeater wrote that "the Egyptian race was originally dominantly Aryan/Arian and within a few generations the Aryan blood had tinged the entire Egyptian nobility, one of whom was Menes who united the whole of Egypt under one rule and founded at the same time the first dynasty and his great city of Memphis/*Mem-Nefer*.")

Peter Dawkins further adds: "Of this high council, the pharaoh was the chief and 'essence'. He was elected by the council from out of the ranks of the 'blood royal', but only after he himself achieved the degree of prophet. In addition, the heir apparent had to have had a good working knowledge of the eight further grades of dignity that a prophet can attain to, and have 'seen' and understood the archetypal plan in respect of the whole Egyptian civilisation, including especially his own part in it if he became pharaoh."

"He on his own, was also referred to as Thoth, as the whole council was seen to be summed up in him, and he was the ruler of that council; for he, above all others, was intended to be the living and visible representative on earth of the spiritual Truth. He was the 'Son of the Sun God' - the 'Great House' or 'Royal House' (i.e. Temple) in which the Light of God resides and through which that Light is made manifest - which is what *Per-aa* (Pharaoh) means, and also what *Is-Ra-El* means. The Egyptians saw all living things being formed out of matter by the Spirit or Thought of God, which thought provided the Archetype for all living form and its evolutionary life. Perfect form they understood and referred to as the 'temple' of God or, more accurately, as *Is-Ra-El*, 'the temple of the Light of God' *Ra* ('Light') being a term for the Spirit or Thought of *El* ('God')."

From *Legends Of the Egyptian Gods* by Wallis E. Budge we are informed as follows:

"Now, the kings of Egypt were always chosen either out of the soldiery or priesthood, the former order being honoured and respected for its valour, and the latter for its wisdom. If the choice fell upon a soldier, he was immediately initiated into the order of priests, and by them instructed in their abstruse and hidden philosophy, a philosophy for the most part involved in fable and allegory, and exhibiting only dark hints and obscure resemblances to the truth. This the priesthood hints to us in many instances, particularly by the sphinxes, which they seem to have placed designedly before their temples as types of the enigmatical nature of their theology. In like manner, the word 'Amoun', or as it is expressed in the Greek language, 'Ammon' which is generally looked upon as the proper name of the Egyptian Zeus, is interpreted by Manetho to signify 'concealment' or 'something which is hidden'." ('Amen' was derived from 'Ammon' and also means 'hidden' and also the 'hidden god').

According to C.W. Leadbeater, "during the era of Ramesses the Great, when Ramesses was the Master of one of the principal Lodges of the Great White Brotherhood at Memphis, there were in those days, three Grand Lodges of Amen. Each member was the representative of a particular quality."

"One was called the Knight of Love, another the Knight of Truth, and another the Knight of Perseverance, and so on; and each was supposed to become a specialist in thinking and expressing the quality assigned to him."

"These three Grand Lodges worked three distinct types of Freemasonry, of which only one has come down to us in the 20th century. The Master of the first Grand Lodge represented Wisdom, and his two Wardens strength and beauty, as in our Lodges today. The predominant power outpoured was that of wisdom which is perfect love, the quality that is indeed most needed in the world at the present time."

"In ancient Egypt there was an intensity of brotherly feeling between the members of a Lodge which is probably rarely attained now; they felt themselves bound together by the holiest of ties, not only as parts of the same machine, but actually as fellow-workers with God Himself."

"The ritual worked by the Grand Lodges was known as *The Building of the Temple of Amen*. It was indeed one of the most splendid and powerful sacraments known to man. It was celebrated for thousands of years, during which Egypt was a mighty land, but a time came when the egos most advanced in evolution began to seek incarnation in new nations, in which, as in different classes in the world-school, they might learn new lessons. Then this portion of the Egyptian Mysteries fell into abeyance, while the Egyptian civilization grew degenerate and formalized as it became a theatre for the activities of less evolved men."

Peter Dawkins writes in his book *Arcadia*: "The Greeks later translated the name of Thoth as Hermes, and the Great Lord or 'Word of Truth' was referred to them as Hermes Trismegistus ('the Thrice-greatest Word'). The Romans used the name Mercury. Horus (Egyptian *Heru*), meaning Visible Appearance of God', was another name or title of the pharaoh."

The Philosopher's Stone and the 'Emerald Tablet' of Hermes

According to the Rosicrucian authority, Spencer Lewis, upon the death of Akhnaton, Hermes Trismegistus ('Thrice Greatest') continued to protect the sacred Mysteries. "...at the time of the transition of Amenhotep IV, there was a sage named Hermes."

"So great was his learning and yet so mystical his many writings, purposely veiled so that they might be of value only to the future initiates, that the uninitiated minds of future years arose and claimed Hermes a myth, and there are those today who try to establish his identity with the Egyptian god 'Thoth'."

"However, it is the author's pleasure to state now that which has never appeared in print before, and which has perplexed investigators for centuries - the birth date of Hermes Trismegistus - the Thrice Great Man. He was born in Thebes October 9th 1399 BC. He lived to the age of one hundred and forty-two years, dying in the Rosicrucian Monastery at El Amarna, on 22nd March, 1257 BC., and his mummy lies among others in a cachette in the vicinity of El Amarna."

Spencer Lewis relates that during the era of Akhnaton, "Hermes completed his writings, especially the seven books and tablets which were found and brought to light in 400 AD., and which were upon diverse chemical and physical subjects."

'As above, so below' were reputedly the words inscribed upon what is referred to as the 'Philosopher's Stone', inscribed by Hermes Trismegistus. (It is from the word 'Hermes' that we derive the word 'Hermetic').

Hermes was 'the Father of Wisdom' who concealed his books of Wisdom and Science under two stone pillars. An interesting parallel is that the tablets of Moses which were placed in the Ark of the Covenant are also known as two stone pillars.

In the first century AD, the historian Josephus, who spent some time with the Essenes, wrote that the two pillars of Hermes still existed in his own time and that they were built by Seth. Josephus described how the pillars were completely covered with hieroglyphics. They became the source of great Wisdom and knowledge equated with the two tablets of stone, the Covenant, given to Moses and later to Aaron (St Germain) for safekeeping.

The 'Philosopher's Stone' was greatly sought after by the Knights Templar during the Crusades. During the era of the French Revolution, Count Cagliostro who was initiated into the Order of the Rose Cross and the Freemasons by St Germain allegedly discovered the Philosopher's Stone in Arabia.

Apollonius of Tyana, a first century incarnation of St Germain, is reputed to have been in possession of the same Stone, which is sometimes called the 'Emerald Tablet of Hermes'. It was said to have magical qualities and that those who possessed it would have longevity - never having the appearance of aging!

HERMES WAS REFERRED TO BY THE ANCIENT EGYPTIANS AS THE 'LORD OF MAAT', THE 'LORD OF TRUTH'.

MASTERS DISCUSSED IN THIS CHAPTER

Noah - St Germain
Aaron - St Germain
Taliesin/Merlin - St Germain
Apollonius of Tyana - St Germain
King Solomon - El Morya
Pharaoh Akhnaton (Amenhotep IV) - El Morya
Moses - earlier incarnation of Jesus

RECOMMENDED NOTES AND READING

Trans. by Richard Laurence, *The Book Of Enoch*, (Wizards Bookshelf, U.S.A.1976)
Peter Dawkins, *Arcadia*, (Francis Bacon Research Trust, Warwick, U.K)
C.W. Leadbeater, *The Hidden Life In Freemasonry*, (Theosophical Publishing House U.K. 1975)
Madame Helena Blavatsky, *The Secret Doctrine*, (Quest Books, Theosophical Publishing House, U.S.A. 1966)
Annie Bessant, *The Ancient Wisdom*, (Theosophical Publishing House, U.S.A 1939)
Peter Dawkins, *The Great Vision*, (Francis Bacon Research Trust, Warwick, U.K.)

Peter Dawkins, *Francis Bacon, Herald of the New Age*, (Francis Bacon Research Trust, U.K)

Spencer Lewis, *Rosicrucian Questions And Answers*, (AMORC, U.S.A 1929)

E.A. Budge, *Legends of the Egyptian Gods*, (Dover Publications, U.S.A 1994)

Stephen Quirke, *Ancient Egyptian Religion*, (British Museum Press, 1992)

Robert Graves, *The White Goddess*, (Faber & Faber, U.K. 1961)

CHAPTER 8

Egypt & The Ancient Mysteries

"I have been fostered in the land of the Deity"
(Taliesin/Merlin/St Germain)

*"I am everything that has been, that is, and that shall be
And my veil no man hath raised."*
(Athene)

The Egyptian legends and symbols of Osiris and Isis, which are discussed in this chapter, are incorporated into Freemasonry.

Osiris

Between 5000 - 3000 BC, dynastic ruler-ship began in Egypt during which time Queen Isis (one of her symbols was the *Rose*) and King Osiris were worshipped as gods. Isis is equated with the goddess Athena - the goddess of 'Wisdom' otherwise known as 'Sophia' and the legends of Osiris are similar in content, and in particular are equated with the rituals of Adonis (otherwise known as Tammuz) in the Near East, of Orpheus in the Greek Islands, of Dionysus in Hellas - all of which depict death and resurrection, symbolic of eternal life.

Osiris was worshipped as a Sun god - a Solar god (*'sol'* is Latin for 'sun'). Osiris was also worshipped as the god of the Soul - as a Universal embodiment of Soul.

They believed in life after death and resurrection, the story of Osiris being based upon this theory. The Egyptians believed that when the physical body dies, the soul still leads a conscious life in the astral body or 'etheric'. Madame Helena Blavatsky refers to aether as 'primordial Chaos' which Madame identifies as being the spiritual Mother of every existing form and being. From the word 'aether' we obtain the word 'etheric' which is the shining substance of the celestial soul, the body of light.

Osiris was crowned at Suten-henen, a city in which according to Egyptian legend, the great bird, the Phoenix also inhabited; the legendary bird was a symbol of resurrection and immortality, - it rises from its own ashes. When the bird felt death was imminent, it built itself a pyre and died in the flames.

From the ashes there then arose a new phoenix which would fly to the Egyptian city of Heliopolis where it laid the ashes upon the Altar of the Temple of the Sun. This symbol of the phoenix was adopted by the sun-worshipping priests of Heliopolis being symbolic of the sun's daily setting and rebirth. In Egyptian and Freemasonic symbolism, the 'West' where the setting of the sun occurs, represented man's resurrection to a new day. The Druidic Celts of Britain preferred the 'West' coasts where they could observe the 'setting of the sun'.

Stephen Quirke in his book titled *Ancient Egyptian Religion*, relates that "more tangible links connecting the Egyptian influence may be found in the Book of Leinster where 'the seven Egyptian monks in Disert Ullaigh' are invoked, and in the geography written by the Irish monk Dicuil who claimed to have learned of Egypt from a fellow monk. Whatever the substance in these elusive ties, Ireland became the second home of monasticism on the model established in the Egyptian deserts."

From information taken from the book titled *From The Stone Age To Christianity* by William Foxwell Albright, we learn the following:

"Osiris represented the vegetation of the Nile Valley, which dies in the early summer, when dead is submerged under the life-giving Nile inundation, and comes to life again as the inundation subsides. The home of Osiris was in the fresh-water ocean of the underworld, whence the Nile rose at the First Cataract, according to primitive Egyptian conceptions. There the king, the Pharaoh, not only sets and rises again with Re and Horus, but he also dies and comes to life again with Osiris."

"At the same time his living spirit emerges from the mouth of the tomb and flies straight to the never-dying (never-setting) circumpolar stars. The Pharaoh was considered to be the incarnation of the god Re, of the falcon-god Horus (also a solar divinity), and in proto-historic times he became the incarnation of Osiris. Not least he was head of the most absolute monarchies that the world has perhaps ever known, down to the end of the fourth dynasty."

The late Spencer Lewis wrote: "It is not that the Egyptians actually believed that Osiris was a deified individual, or that he actually lived on earth a certain number of years, but to round out the legend he was given an age, and the age was related to observable phenomena, revealing further the fact that Osiris was an allegorical character representing the truths of mysteries. Plutarch stated that 'the number of years that some say Osiris lived, others that he reigned, was eight and twenty; for just so many are the lights of the moon, and for so many days doth she revolve about the circle'."

According to Wallis E. Budge, a well known authority on ancient Egyptian history:

"The characteristics and attributes of both Isis and Osiris changed several times during the long history of Egypt, and a thousand years before Plutarch lived, the Egyptians themselves had forgotten what the original form of the legend was. They preserved a number of ceremonies and performed very carefully all the details of an ancient ritual at the annual commemoration festival of Osiris which was held in November and December, but the evidence of the texts makes it quite clear that the meaning and symbolism of nearly all the details were unknown alike to priests and people."

From information taken from Stephen Quirke's book titled *Ancient Egyptian Religion*, we learn the following:

"The main deities worshipped in the ancient Greek and Latin world, particularly in the heyday of these cults from the third century BC to the third century AD, were those in human form - Isis and a new interpretation of Osiris call Serapis. Serapis was the Greek rendering of Egyptian 'Osir-Apis', that is, the Osiris (i.e. deceased) Apis, a term used in the reign of Nakhthoreb to refer to the Apis bull at Memphis through which Ptah and the creative forces of the Earth could be served in this world."

"Under Ptolemies Serapis became a principal god of Alexandria [founded by St Germain in his incarnation as Alexander the Great], as a deity of the fertile earth, and received a new form in Greek depiction as a bearded man wearing on his head a grain-measure to symbolise his fruitfulness. The theme drew on the perception of Osiris as a grain-god, seen in the sarcophagus texts of Ankhnesneferibra, as much as from the Pharaonic cult of the Apis bull. In Alexandria and through the Greek and then the Latin-speaking world, Isis and Serapis came to embody a pair of natural forces of fertility, male and female."

According to Wallis E. Budge:

"Homer and Thales both learned from Egypt that 'water was the first principle of all things and the cause of generation'. The Nile and all kinds of moisture are called the 'efflux of Osiris'. Therefore a water-pitcher is always carried first in his processions, and the leaf of a fig-tree represents both Osiris and Egypt. The Sun is consecrated to Osiris, and the lion is worshipped, and temples are ornamented with figures of this animal, because the Nile rises when the sun is in the constellation of Leo, the Lion. Horus, the offspring of Osiris, the Nile, and Isis, the Earth, was born in the marshes of Buto, because the vapour of damp land destroys drought."

"An important modification of the cult of Isis and Osiris took place in the third century before Christ, when the Ptolemies began to consolidate their rule in

Egypt. A form of religion which would be acceptable both to Egyptians and Greeks had to be provided, and this was produced by modifying the characteristics of Osiris and calling him Sarapis, and identifying him with the Greek Pluto. Had a high priest of Osiris who lived at Abydos under the XVIII Dynasty witnessed the celebration of the great festival of Isis and Osiris in any large town in the first century before Christ, it is tolerably certain that he would have regarded it as a lengthy act of worship of strange gods, in which there appeared, here and there, ceremonies and phrases which reminded him of the ancient Abydos ritual."

Abydos was a holy city, the ancient cult centre of the god Osiris, situated between Asyut and Thebes where the first Egyptian kings, starting in 3,200 BC were buried. The Pharaoh Seti (1291-1278) who was the son of Ramesses I, built the most remarkable decorative temple there which he devoted to Osiris, Egypt's most popular god. According to C.W. Leadbeater, it was first inhabited by Arian-Egyptians who had come from Arabia.

Rituals

According to Egyptian legends, when Osiris was murdered, his body was cut into thirteen pieces and floated down the Nile in a basket. From the place where his body lodged, there sprouted a huge acacia tree. The legends of the acacia tree, also called *Tamarisk* and *Mimosa*, can be traced back to the ancient Egyptians who considered the tree to be sacred.

Wallis E. Budge states: "There are many places wherein his (Osiris') body is said to have been deposited, and among these are Abydos and Memphis. In what city the cult of Osiris originated is not known, but it is quite certain that before the end of the VI Dynasty, Abydos became the centre of his worship."

"Tradition affirmed that the head of Osiris was preserved at Abydos in a box, and a picture of it, became the symbol of the city. At Abydos a sort of miracle play, in which all the sufferings and resurrections of Osiris were commemorated, was performed annually, and the raising up of a model of his body, and the placing of his head upon it, were the culminating ceremonies."

"At Abydos was the famous shaft into which offerings were cast for the transmission to the dead in the Other World, and through the Gap in the hills close by souls were believed to set out on their journey hither. One tradition places the Elysian Fields in the neighbourhood of Abydos. A fine stone bier, a restoration probably of the XXVIth Dynasty which represented the original bier of Osiris, is now in the Egyptian Museum at Cairo."

Rituals were introduced to change the quality of the novice's soul - to raise his consciousness to a superhuman level in order to make an eternal being out of him. As a result of the ritual undertaken, the human being forsook all fear of death.

He understood the immortality of the soul. The initiate, by raising his state of consciousness (which can be achieved in meditation) to a higher state, could connect with his/hers Eternal Being.

Edgar Cayce wrote: "As this life-force is expanded, it moves first from the Leydig centre through the adrenals, in what may be termed an upward trend, to the pineal and to the centres in control of emotions - or reflexes through the nerve forces of the body. Thus an entity put itself, through such an activity, into association or in conjunction with all that has EVER been or may be. For, it loosens the physical consciousness to the universal consciousness."

Isis

Goddess worship was revered, acknowledged and celebrated throughout the world for at least 20,000 years - long before the rise of the patriarchal religions such as Judaism, and Christianity. The story of the Goddess is the story of the creative source of all life and she is often referred to as the Mother-Goddess; veneration of male deities came much later than that of Goddess-worship.

St Germain explains the meaning of *Genesis* and *Israel* in the book titled *St Germain - Earth's Birth Changes* channelled by Azena Ramanda.

St Germain: *"As we issue forth this understanding, you will recall your grand chronicle, your Bible, the beginning of the beginnings of humanity: Genesis. What be Genesis? It is an anagram - gene of Isis. In this tale, this gene of Isis, there was a ray of light issued from the civilizations that are coming yet again upon your plane to re-institute a new Genesis, a new birthing, a new tale of humanity that is God and knows it is God. The gene of Isis was the institution of the feminine, a receptive energy within Mother Earth. That is why she is a mother. Because she herself is of the essence of female energy, as the Pineal gland becomes stimulated, becoming receptive of the energies of All-That-Is it is being penetrated by the masculine, the solar energy, the Sun God. Do you know what Isis is? It is duplicity of is-is IS."*

"Israel is an anagram, Isis, Ra, Elohim. Isis is the female energy, Ra, the male energy. Elohim the God I AM awareness that interconnects and transmutes the polarities into wholeness, into holiness, if you will."

According to Betty Radice in her book titled *Who's Who In The Ancient World*, the Egyptian goddess, Isis, wife of Osiris, mother of Horus, became one of the most important deities in the Mediterranean world, and her cult spread throughout the Roman Empire. Its special features were its Egyptian professional priests, initiation ceremonies, and processions, all of which are described in the *Golden Ass* by Apuleius. The best preserved temple of Isis is at Pompeii, in which bodies of priests clutching cult objects were found.

Wallis E. Budge wrote in his book titled *Legends Of The Egyptian Gods*:

"To Isis were added many of the attributes of the great Greek goddesses, and into her worship were introduced 'mysteries' derived from the non-Egyptian cults, which made it acceptable everywhere. 'Isis' is a Greek word, and means 'knowledge', and 'Typhon' - the name of her professed adversary, is also a Greek word, and means 'pride and insolence'."

"This latter name is well adapted to one who, full of ignorance and error, tears in pieces and conceals that holy doctrine which the goddess collects, compiles, and delivers to those who aspire after the most perfect participation in the divine nature...this knowledge the goddess invites us to seek after."

"The goddess Isis is said by some authors to be the daughter of Hermes, and by others of Prometheus, both of them famous for their philosophic turn of mind. The latter is supposed to have first taught mankind wisdom and foresight, as the former is reputed to have invented letters and music." (According to Egyptian Heliopolitan doctrine, Isis was the daughter of Keb, the Earth-god, and Nut, the Sky-goddess; she was the wife of Osiris, mother of Horus). Isis being none other, it is said, than Wisdom pointing out the knowledge of divine truths to her votaries. An inscription which the ancient priests engraved upon the base of the statue of Athene at Sais, whom they identify with Isis, reads as follows: *"I am everything that has been, that is, and that shall be and my veil no man hath raised."*

"As the importance of Osiris declined, that of Isis grew, and men came to regard her as the great Mother-goddess of the world. The priests described from tradition the great facts of her life according to Egyptian legends, how she had been a loving and devoted wife, how she had gone forth after her husband's murder by Set to seek for his body, how she had found it and brought it home, how she revivified it by her spells and had union with Osiris and conceived by him, and in due course she brought forth her son...how she reared him and watched over him until he was old enough to fight and vanquish his father's murderer, and how at length she seated him in triumph on his father's throne."

"These things endeared Isis to the people everywhere and as she herself had not suffered death like Osiris, she came to be regarded as the eternal mother of life and of all living things. She made the light to shine, she was the spirit of the Dog-star (Sirius) which heralded the Nile-flood, she was the source of the power in the beneficent light of the moon."

"The message of the cult of Isis was preached by her priests as one of hope and happiness, and coming to the Greeks and Romans, as it did, at a time when men were weary of their national cults...the people everywhere welcomed her with the greatest enthusiasm. From Egypt it was carried to the Islands of Greece and to the mainland, to Italy, Germany, France, Spain and Portugal, and then crossing the western end of the Mediterranean it entered North Africa, and with Carthage as a centre spread east and west along the coast."

According to Stephen Quirke in his book titled *Ancient Egyptian Religion*:

"In Greek and Roman tradition Egyptian deities, and above all Isis, played a role more universal and at the same time more personal; the goddess was available to all who would be her followers and those who served her gained personal redemption. In the second century AD Apuleius wrote an autobiographical account of the Isis cult from the vantage-point of an initiate, in which the Egyptian detail may be contrasted with the Graeco-Roman emphasis on the human rather than the cosmic."

"The initiate had to acknowledge the sinfulness of certain actions, in particular 'enslaving desires' to be replaced by the desire for Isis and 'adverse curiosity' to be countered by the 'quest for truth'; only those deemed capable of the proper behaviour could enter the community of initiates, and the successful applicant was then shown sacred Egyptian texts kept in the sanctuary and underwent a night-time ritual, passing through the underworld and the elements to see the radiant sun in the middle of the night."

"From the night of initiation the person emerged like the sun at dawn... the passage of the sun through the night brings in the union of light and darkness, Ra and Osiris, a new life."

"A temple of Isis was built at Pompeii in the mid-second century BC. Rome's port at Ostia became home to numerous shrines to Egyptian deities in the first century BC, including one of the largest temples to Isis which was closed during the reign of Tiberius (14-37 AD) and reopened under Caligula."

"The complex of temples occupied a site at the modern festival square of Rome, the Piazza Navona, with an avenue of sculpture connecting the temples of Isis and Serapis marked by sphinxes, lions and obelisks brought from Egypt, and in some cases, actually commissioned for the building rather than merely being reused earlier monuments."

"Domitian also constructed a new temple to Isis in Benevento, at the crossroads of inland trade-routes across southern Italy, similarly fitted with an avenue of sphinxes, obelisks and sculpture of the Apis bull, and falcons."

"By opening the mysteries of the underworld from a circle of temple technicians to all who wished to become initiates, the Greek and Roman arena converted Egyptian practice into a different means of approaching gods, one close enough to merge entirely with the rival mystery religions in the Roman Empire during the fourth century AD."

"The Roman Empire embraced Egyptian cults at all levels, from the imperial temples in the capital to shrines at military garrisons as distant as York and London to household shrines such as the fabulous painted room in the Pompeii villa now known as the 'House of Mysteries'."

"This devotion was strongly demonstrated for the last time in the third century AD under Septimus Severus and his successors, who were also among the last emperors to support hieroglyphic workshops and so the productive kernel of Pharaonic religion within Egypt itself. During the fourth century, outside as well as inside their land of origin, the Egyptian cults were eclipsed by a new devotion to Mithras, the invincible sun and, increasingly, by ... Christianity."

According to Wallis E. Budge, "Osiris and Isis were worshipped at Philae until the reign of Justinian, when his general Narses, closed the temple and carried off the statues of the gods to Constantinople [Istanbul], where they were probably melted down."

The Pineal - the 'Third Eye'

Energy moves about the universe at the speed of light, so to energy and light, time is meaningless. "This then is the message which we have heard of Him and declare unto you, that God is light" (John 1:5). Edgar Cayce explained that consciousness operates through energy. All of this was understood by the Ancient Mystics and Initiates in the Temples of Egypt.

The two major hieroglyphs which are most commonly used to identify Osiris are the Throne and an Eye - also called the 'Eye of Horus' and known as the 'Eternal Eye'. We are able to connect through the Pineal, with past, present and the future - the place where time does not move and all time is one. This is known as the *universal consciousness* or 'God'. The Pineal, or 'Third Eye' was a symbol of 'inner vision' - "The Light of the body is in the eye" (Matthew 6:22). It is located in the centre of the forehead and can be seen, visually, by those with the gift of clairvoyance.

Placed within a pyramid/triangle it is an ancient Egyptian symbol utilized by the Freemasons. St Germain was instrumental in the design of the Great Seal of the United States, which portrays among other symbols, the pyramid with the 'Eye' in the missing capstone of the pyramid. On the back of every USA dollar bill is a pyramid with an eye in the middle of it.

According to Wallis E. Budge, "thus their great king and lord Osiris is represented by the hieroglyphics for an eye and sceptre (or throne), the name itself signifying 'many-eyed', as we are told by some who would derive it from the words *os*, 'many', and *iri*, an 'eye', which have this meaning in the Egyptian language." (Apart from the Rose being a symbol of Isis, another was the 'Iris').

Symbols of the Freemasons

C.W. Leadbeater (who in one of his past-lives belonged to one of the principal Lodges during the reign of Ramesses the Great), in his book titled *The Hidden Life In Freemasonry*, informs us that one of the symbols of the Freemasons is "a pair of compasses extended to sixty degrees on the forth part of a circle, with a sun in the centre. The proposition is of course well known, and a practical application of it is widely used by builders, in laying out walls at right angles to each other and in the other work, in the form of a triangle. Plutarch says that a triangle of this kind was frequently employed by the Egyptian priests, who regarded it as a symbol of the universal Trinity. Osiris and Isis being the two sides at right angles to each other, and Horus their product, the hypotenuse."

Another symbol of the Freemasons is the 'ladder'. Leadbeater wrote: "this has many steps, which indicate the virtue by means of which we may ascend to the perfection of the symbolised star. In Egypt those steps were taken to express the initiations leading upwards; but of course these are only two interchangeable methods of expressing the same thing. If we take them to mean initiations, they represent definite steps taken, but if we take them as indicating the virtues, they are the qualifications for initiation."

(In one of Edgar Cayce's readings, he told how the Great Pyramid was of symbolical importance. The empty sarcophagus in the King's Chamber was representative of the fact that the death of the physical body does not mean the death of the soul. Accordingly, above the empty sarcophagus in the King's Chamber are seven stones, probably representative of seven stages of initiation).

Leadbeater continues: "It is a symbol of the Universe, and of its successions of step-like planes teaching from the heights to the depths. It is written elsewhere that the 'Father's house has many mansions'; many levels and resting places for His creatures in their different conditions and degrees of progress. It is these levels, these planes and sub-planes that are denoted by the rungs and staves of the ladder. And of these there are, for us in our present state of evolutionary unfoldment, three principal ones:

1.   the physical plane,
2.   the plane of desire and emotions,
3.   and the mental plane, or that of abstract intelligence

which links up to the still higher plane, or that of abstract intelligence which links up to the still higher planes of the spirit. These three levels of the world are reproduced in man. The first corresponds with his material physique, his sense-body; the second with his desire and emotional nature, which is a mixed element resulting from the interaction of his physical senses and his ultra-physical mind; the third with his mentality, which is still further removed from his physical nature and forms the link between the latter and his spiritual being."

"Thus the Universe and man himself are constructed ladder-wise, in an orderly organized sequence of steps; the one universal substance composing of the differentiated parts of the Universe 'descends' from a state of the utmost ethereality by successive steps of increasing densification, until gross materialization is reached; and then 'ascends' through a similarly ordered graduation of planes to its original place, but enriched by the experience gained by its activities during the process."

"It was this cosmic process which was the subject of the dream or vision of Jacob... *What was 'dreamed' or beheld by him with super-sensual vision is equally perceptible today by anyone whose inner eye (the 'Third Eye' otherwise known as the 'pineal'), has been opened.* Every real Initiate is one who has attained an expression of consciousness and faculty enabling him to behold the ethereal worlds revealed to the Hebrew Patriarch as easily as the uninitiated man beholds the phenomenal world with his outer eyes. The Initiate is able to see the angels of God ascending and descending; that is, he can directly behold the great stairway of the Universe, and watch the intricate but orderly mechanism of involution, differentiation, evolution and re-synthesis constituting the Life-process."

Another symbol of the Freemasons and the Rosicrucians is the circle. Leadbeater writes: "In ancient Egypt long before the time of the Jews, the circle was an emblem with many meanings. First of all, it was the token of the sun-god, Ra; secondly, it bore to the Egyptians the signification of the earth circling round the sun... a portion of the secret knowledge reserved for the ancient Mysteries."

"There was still an older tradition, which held the circle to be the equator and the dot in the centre to be the pole-star, in which the position changes because of the precession of the equinoxes, in which the Egyptians took great interest. The inclination of the chief passage of the Great Pyramid was determined by the position of the pole-star of the period. *This sign was used once more to indicate the all-seeing eye* - an idea easily suggested by the dot in the middle of the circle."

It is important to remember that the Celtic Druidic religion, had its origins in ancient Egypt and many Druids travelled to Egypt to study in the great Temples, bringing the knowledge back with them to Ireland. The Druids worshiped in circles and an example of this is the megalithic Stonehenge. The Egyptians assembled obelisks as phallic symbols of fertility which are also to be found at Stonehenge. Ireland's beloved St Patrick was to introduce the Circle with the Cross and although the significance of this is discussed in greater detail later, suffice to say at this stage, the Cross was symbolic of the Four Directions.

Leadbeater writes: "Another interpretation of this emblem (of the circle) by the Egyptians was particularly beautiful. The three columns, representing wisdom, strength, and beauty, were stated to stand round God's throne, which was the altar itself, which they took to signify love. Thus the circle describes the love of God, and the two lines which bound it are the lines of duty and destiny, or, to put the idea in Oriental terms, of 'karma'. It was said that whilst one kept within the circle of the divine love, and bounded ones actions by duty and destiny, one could not err."

'I Am' - Maat

A simple explanation of 'I AM' is that the ancient Egyptians used the word *Maat* to describe the 'Truth' or the 'perfect understanding of cosmic consciousness'. *Maat* signified wisdom through knowledge which was known as 'illumination'. (As indicated in an earlier chapter, the priests of Egypt who passed their degrees were given the title of the 'Illumined Ones' or the 'Illuminati' who clothed themselves in white robes as a symbol of purity - hence the name the Great White Brotherhood).

According to information contained in Peter Dawkins' book titled *Arcadia*, *Maat-Monad* symbolized the spirit of 'I AM' wherein is stored the memory of every experience undergone from the moment of human reasoning, i.e. 'I AM' meaning that we are all connected to each other via the Universal Cosmic Consciousness of the Creator God whom the ancient Egyptians called *Ptah*.

Think of how many times a day we utilize the phrase 'I am' without consciously realizing that we are stating our connection to the Universal Cosmic Consciousness of the Creator God. The Egyptians used the letter *T* (or the Tau cross) to symbolize the wisdom of *Maat*. The *'T'* was representative of *TAT*, the 'Truth' - the 'Word of God'. When the Master Jesus was crucified, he was placed upon a cross which was shaped the same as the *Tau cross*, this cross being regarded as a symbol of completion.

"THE LIGHT OF THE BODY IS IN THE EYE" (Matthew 6:22)

MASTERS DISCUSSED IN THIS CHAPTER

St Germain

NOTES AND RECOMMENDED READING

William Foxwell Albright, *From The Stone Age To Christianity*, (Doubleday Anchor Books, U.S.A 1957)
C.W. Leadbeater, *The Hidden Life In Freemasonry*, (Theosophical Publishing House U.K. 1975)
Madame Helena Blavatsky, *The Secret Doctrine*, (Quest Books, Theosophical Publishing House, U.S.A.

1966)

Peter Dawkins, _Arcadia,_ (Francis Bacon Research Trust, Warwick, U.K.)

Spencer Lewis, _Rosicrucian Questions And Answers_, (AMORC, U.S.A 1929)

E.A. Budge, _Legends of the Egyptian Gods_, (Dover Publications, U.S.A 1994)

Stephen Quirke, _Ancient Egyptian Religion_, (British Museum Press, 1992)

Robert Graves, _The White Goddess_, (Faber & Faber, U.K. 1961)

Azena Ramanda, _St Germain - Earth's Birth Changes_, (Triad Publishers, Queensland, Australia, 1993).

Betty Radice, _Who's Who In The Ancient World_ (Penguin Books, U.K., 1973)

Francis Hitching, _The World Atlas Of Mysteries_, (Pan Books, U.K. 1978)

CHAPTER 9

The Philosophers & 'Sophia'

"I carried the banner before Alexander"
(Taliesin/Merlin/St Germain)

Having covered some background knowledge of the Masters of the Great White Brotherhood, and their origins, it is time to discuss the Masters' reincarnations as some of the great philosophers, who contributed so much towards our civilization.

According to Robert Graves in his book titled *The White Goddess*:

"The Gnostics, whose language was Greek, identified the Holy Spirit with Sophia, Wisdom; and Wisdom was female."

Peter Dawkins of the Francis Bacon Research Trust describes the philosophy of Sir Francis Bacon.

"The word Philosophy is from the Greek, *Philo-Sophia*, which means 'the love of Wisdom'. A philosopher is described, therefore, as a lover of *Sophia*. But the true Wisdom is Love - the radiance of Love. This is Truth. When the philosopher has discovered the truth and brought it to the light, he or she becomes illumined by the Wisdom, thereby fulfilling the purpose of love by being love. Such a person is a true Gnostic - a Seer or Knower - one who sees and knows truth because he/she has discovered it, is in love with it, and knows it by living and being it."

"*Sophia* = the feminine aspect of Wisdom; that divine Intelligence and Consciousness which allows understanding to develop in man's own mind. *Sophia* is sometimes known as Truth. All true philosophers or Rosicrucians are wed to *Sophia* - the Truth."

"*Christos* and *Sophia*, the radiant and reflective aspects of divine Wisdom respectively, are 'wed' or united with the complimentary aspects of man's nature when made ready or pure enough for the 'marriage' to take place."

According to information contained in Peter Dawkins' book titled *The Great*

Vision: "The words 'Christ' and 'Christhood' refer to the two aspects of Light - Divine Wisdom and Human knowledge respectively - whilst the 'Golden Age' means an era of enlightenment or knowledge of God, which is also synonymous with peace, mercy and justice (or righteousness).."

"Francis Bacon referred to wisdom as divinity. He is probably best known as one of the world's greatest philosophers, although he was also a profound mystic and a supreme poet who attributed most of his knowledge (which was vast) to a divine inspiration and revelation. He consistently emphasized that philosophy should go hand in hand with Divinity, and should serve divinity as a handmaiden serves her mistress - philosophy being the capacity of the loving mind to reflect and understand the light of the heart, and divinity being the light of Love inspired into the human heart."

"Just as science and art are the Twin Pillars of the temple of philosophy, so divinity and philosophy are the Twin Pillars of Life. The balance and union of the two completes the purpose of Existence, just as the Phoenix and Turtle Dove become one flame in their mutual love and then vanish together into the bosom of God. Such union, deliberately and willingly undertaken, is *Yoga*, the conscious union of the human soul with God. It is also known as the Mystical Marriage."

Buddha (circa 566 - 486 BC)

The Master Jesus

Buddha (Siddhartha Gautama) was born to a noble Sakya clan who lived in the basin of the Ganges River in India. His father was King Shuddhodana and his mother was Queen *Maya*. Buddha is reputed to have been an earlier incarnation of Jesus, and his mother Maya, an earlier incarnation of Mary. Like all great Avatars, Buddha taught about reincarnation and that the soul is immortal.

At the time of the birth of Buddha, a great moving star appeared in the heavens, proclaiming his divinity. The same sign appeared in the sky at the advent of the birth of other great avatars, including Socrates (earlier incarnation of Jesus), Mithras, Romulus and Bacchus (Dionysus) who was an incarnation of St Germain, and of course, with the advent of the birth of Jesus - hence the story of the three 'wise' Magi who followed the star in order to find his birthplace and present him with gifts.

In the 16th century the prophet Paracelsus predicted that a supernova would appear in the era of another great avatar's birth. The great avatar was Francis Bacon - St Germain. In 1572, a supernova appeared in the constellation of Cassiopeia which shone more brightly than Venus and was clearly visible in the daylight, remaining there for eighteen months.

What was foretold by the 'Heavens' reflected upon what would occur upon the earth below, and even the initiates into the religion of Mithras (Mithraism), performed rites wearing masks representing the animals of the zodiac.

The Greek Philosophers

During the 6th century BC, the citizens of Greece became very advanced in philosophy and engaged in magnificent intellectual advancement. Many of the Masters incarnated as famous Greek philosophers, who helped to shape our civilization with their profound wisdom and knowledge. Through their studies, they began to master 'fear' and 'control'. The Greeks obtained their knowledge of philosophy, music, astronomy, poetry, art, etc. from the Egyptians, for many of the philosophers studied and were 'initiated' into the 'Greater Mysteries' in the Temples of Egypt. They became known as the wise 'Master Builders' (Masons).

The philosophers believed that to increase in wisdom was to increase in enlightenment, taken from their sacred writings which would lead to eventual 'initiation'. It was their belief that rebirth was passing out of an old condition into a new state; from an old limitation to a new extension of self. The perfection of Self was what the Masters aimed towards and this was only achieved through many incarnations in which they endured all of life's experiences, as does all humanity.

According to the book titled *Who's Who In The Ancient* World, by Betty Radice, Ionias, (the son of Apollo) served in the temple of Apollo in Delphi. Iona was the central coastal area of Asia Minor in historic times, and tradition said that it was colonized by refugees from the mainland at the time of the Dorian invasions. From before 700 BC the Ionians were far advanced in the arts and the early philosophers and scientists were all Ionian, including Pythagoras (Kuthumi) who was the one who laid the foundations of Greek rationalism.

Under the following headings, in chronological order, those philosophers who are known to have belonged to the Great White Brotherhood are discussed.

Pythagoras 6th century BC (c.570 BC - 530 BC)
The Master Kuthumi

Pythagoras was a Greek philosopher who became known as the father of Mathematics and language. In common with all great Avatars, an angel appeared to his mother in a dream and announced that she was to have a special child, one who would be a great benefactor to mankind. He was born in Samos circa 570 BC and there are various legends about him; most equated him with being no mortal man but a god. According to one legend, the mother of Pythagoras was impregnated with the 'spirit' of the god Apollo and he was thus considered to be the son of Apollo. In appearance Pythagoras was said to have been over six feet tall with a body as perfectly formed as that of Apollo.

He studied at Thebes (Greece) and after completing his studies in 531 BC and having passed all the initiations, he entered the *Illuminati* (the Great White Brotherhood of Egypt). From that time onwards, he undertook numerous journeys which included visiting such places as Babylon, Persia, and Hindustan where he stayed for many years.

After finishing his studies with the Brahmins, Pythagoras returned to Crotona where he established a 'Mystery School' and his pupils always addressed him as 'The Master'.

Pythagoras encouraged women to become members and his own wife, Theano, was one of the principal officers of the Grand Lodge which he established at Crotona. Together, they established many local Lodges in Italy and on his visits to Italy, Greece and Gaul (France), Pythagoras encouraged suitable candidates (those who could be trusted and who were in search of the sacred 'Truth' of the 'Greater Mysteries of Life'), to travel to Egypt, in order to be initiated into the great Temples, particularly at Heliopolis, the Temple of the Sun.

Like all great Masters, Pythagoras was a gifted prophet with 'second sight' and was capable of being able to communicate with animals and birds, a gift that he was to retain when he reincarnated as a saint in the 12th century AD, during which time a pet swan formed a very close relationship with him and this will be discussed in a future chapter.

During his numerous travels, Pythagoras is reputed to have visited Marseilles where he was welcomed into the Order of the Druids; however, it is more likely that before his visit, he was already a highly initiated Druid, having been initiated in the Great Learning Halls of Egypt where the Druidic priests were also taught.

Having obtained the highest degrees of initiation in Egypt, it is highly probable that Pythagoras took the teachings to Marseilles and initiated the Celts living there at the time. Marseilles was to be the place that Joseph of Arimathea, Mary Magdalene and their followers visited and taught after they had fled Jerusalem in order to avoid being persecuted by the Romans in 37 AD. (The identity of which Master of the Great White Brotherhood, Joseph of Arimathea was, is revealed in a future chapter).

Pythagoras learned the 'Divine' theory of music and is generally credited with the discovery of the diatonic scale, for he learned that music has great healing power. He understood the philosophy of colour, the principle of which could be incorporated into healing - especially when combined with music and these techniques are being widely utilized today, e.g. in colour healing/therapy combined with meditation music.

He also taught astronomy and the students of Pythagoras worshipped the star Venus which they referred to as the 'Star of the Morning' or 'Lucifer' (meaning 'Light-bearer'), a star which the Knights Templar (Freemasons) continued to revere.

The Essenian community, to which Jesus belonged, followed the teachings of Pythagoras, particularly the usage and interpretation of Pythagorean symbols. Pythagoras considered geometry to be the basis of the whole understanding of the way the universe was formed and the Knights Templar/Freemasons followed the Pythagoras/Hermetic teachings as did the Druids who eventually settled in England and Ireland.

A tradition which the Essenes kept, that had been initiated by Pythagoras, was that women were accorded equal status with men and they could become priestesses; this same tradition was to be found amongst the Celtic Druids.

Pythagoras was a very advanced thinker for his era and he believed that women should be on an equal footing with men. Thus, he encouraged them to become members of his Order of the Great White Brotherhood where they were taught, initiated and also encouraged to hold places of office.

The early Masons who were 'workers in stone' constructed temples, churches and cathedrals based on the mathematical geometrical principles of Pythagoras - notably two of the most famous ones being Notre Dame in Paris and the Cathedral at Chartres in France, both of which are built upon energy Ley lines. Masons built wherever there were major Ley lines of 'serpent/Dragon' energy. By the method of dowsing with a divining rod, the architects would locate the earth's spirit, the earth's subtle energies and find the position where the energies were the greatest. The principle of the Earth's energy was also a teaching of Pythagoras who understood the sacredness of Mother Earth and her energies.

In Kuthumi's incarnation as Sir John Dee, the Magus of the Elizabethan Renaissance and tutor to Elizabeth 1, he, Elizabeth, Sir Francis Drake and Sir Francis Bacon, and many others, belonged to the Dragon Society which revered the Earth's sacred energies. Pythagoras is credited with being the first to introduce the word 'philosopher', for up until that time, they had all been known as wise men called 'Sages' or 'Magis' (Magus/Magicians).

Pythagoras taught that there was one God and that God was the 'Supreme Mind' distributed to all parts of the universe - the 'Intelligence' and the 'Power' within all things. He taught that the four elements of earth, fire, air and water, were permeated by the substance called *ether* - representing the basis of vitality and life. (From the word *ether*, we obtain the word *etheric*).

The Pythagoreans chose the five-pointed star as the symbol of vitality, health and knowledge. Some call this the *Star of David* (whom Kuthumi had once been). It was considered to be an ancient magical sign, sometimes called a pentagram. It is also the symbol of Christ as *Alpha and Omega*.

Socrates (469 - 399 BC)
The Master Jesus

Socrates was a philosopher in Athens, Greece, who believed that he had a duty to teach through the questioning of people's beliefs - teaching that 'Virtue is knowledge'. He taught that we cannot be good until we know what we mean by being 'good' and that full understanding of 'good' ensures that our conduct will be good - the knowledge of which would bring goodness and health of the soul; that it is better to suffer injustice than to be guilty of it; that it is wrong to return evil for evil. Socrates is reputed to have been an earlier incarnation of the Master Jesus, and so we can see that Jesus virtually followed the same teachings in his life as the 'Christ'. The cardinal virtues taught by Socrates were wisdom, temperance, courage and justice.

Plato (c. 429 - 347 BC)
The Master St Germain

Born in Athens in circa 429 BC, Plato became a philosopher, whose numerous works survive to this day, including his knowledge of the existence of Atlantis. He was born into an aristocratic family and his father was believed to have been a descendant of one of the earlier kings of Athens.

Plato became a follower of Socrates (469-399 BC) and accordingly he visited Heliopolis (the Temple of the Sun) in Egypt, where he furthered his studies. He was initiated into the Great Mysteries at the age of forty-nine. This occurred in the Great Halls of Esoteric teaching in Egypt where he was verbally given the highest of teachings and was sent out into the world to teach the work that was requested of him, as Pythagoras (Kuthumi) had done before him. Plato's spiritual views were deeply influenced by Pythagoras.

In one of his works titled *Republic*, Plato describes the joys of after-life in mystical terms. He witnessed the death of Socrates (circa 399 BC) who was accused of atheism and tried in court by the Athenian democracy. There was a similar parallel in Socrates' life as Jesus of Nazareth, the 'Messiah',

Plato dedicated his life to the discovery of 'Truth'. He founded the Academy in Athens in 387 BC which became Europe's first University. As Alexander the Great, St Germain had founded the city of Alexandria with its enormous library which drew students from many countries to study there.

It is the considered opinion of historians, that Alexander the Great cherished a scheme for uniting the East and West in a world empire, one that would be a new and enlightened 'world brotherhood of all men' and these were exactly the same aims of St Germain in his incarnation as Sir Francis Bacon, when in the 16th century AD, he established hundreds of Freemasonic Lodges and the Order of the Rose-Cross throughout Britain, Europe and America. It was also a time when he encouraged both France and America to become 'democratic' societies.

After Plato's death in 347 BC, the continuity of the Greek Mystery Schools was carried on by Aristotle (Kuthumi) who had been one of Plato's most prominent students.

Aristotle (384 - 322 BC)
The Master Kuthumi

Born in Macedonia in 384 BC, Aristotle was the son of a doctor who was a physician to the Royal Court of Macedonia. He studied in Athens under Plato (St Germain) until Plato's death in 347 BC.

Aristotle shares with Plato and Socrates the distinction of being the most famous amongst the Philosophers. In the era of the Master Jesus (who reputedly had once been Socrates), the man who had once been both Pythagoras and Aristotle (namely the Master Kuthumi), reincarnated as John the Beloved, the brother of Jesus. Their father, Joseph, as has previously been established, was an incarnation of St Germain. And so, thus far in the progression of our story, we can see how the pattern of synchronicity emerges.

The writings of Aristotle were on politics, ethics, physics and biology - his fundamental teachings were of 'inspired common sense'. It is noteworthy that Aristotle alleged that since the eagle looked directly into the sun when it ascended, it was regarded as a symbol of spiritual knowledge with respect to its high flight. The 'Eagle' was to become the symbol of St John the Beloved (Kuthumi).

In Athens, in 335 BC, Aristotle established the Lyceum where he taught until his retirement. He died in 322 BC, one year after Alexander the Great (St Germain) who died at the age of thirty-three years in 323 BC.

It is noteworthy that Aristotle wrote of the existence of Terra Australis incognita, an unknown southern land. In his incarnation as Sir John Dee during the 16th century AD, the Master Kuthumi was not only a teacher of navigation who instructed Sir Francis Drake - he was also instrumental in the exploration and founding of colonies. Certain maps which were collected from previous navigators during that period of time, would in a future century (18th century when Kuthumi again reincarnated), assist him in directing others to discover *Terra Australis incognita*...the beautiful land we know as Australia. It was no coincidence that the Master Kuthumi who had once been Aristotle, would sail on a voyage of discovery to find Australia and help to colonize *Terra Australis incognita*!

Alexander the Great (356 - 323 BC)

The Master St Germain

The heroic Alexander the Great (Alexander III) founded the city of Alexandria in Egypt, one that became a great city of learning in which the philosophers lived and studied in the centuries BC. Born in 356 BC, Alexander was the son of Philip II and Olympias and eventually became the King of Macedonia.

According to the author Peter Green in his book titled *Alexander of Macedon*, Alexander was designated as the heir-apparent when his father Philip married Cleopatra Eurydice (not to be confused with the famous Queen Cleopatra circa 70-30 BC).

Cleopatra was only twelve years old when she married Philip and the reason for this marriage was to secure the rich wheat fields along the Nile Delta which she owned. When harvested, these fertile wheat fields, (because of the minerals which washed down in the waters when the Nile flooded), produced the best protein rich wheat in the world, a fact which King Philip recognised, and his son Alexander utilized the wheat products to nourish the troops of his army to sustain them in their numerous battles with their enemies.

The Egyptian soil was so fertile that it contributed to Egypt being a very advanced civilization for its time, developing an advanced network of canals which they diverted from the Nile and utilized as a form of irrigation for their crops, just like the ancient Sumerians had done.

The marriage between King Philip and Cleopatra caused a falling out between he and Olympias at which time Alexander sided with his mother. In due course, a female child was born to Cleopatra and Philip; destiny, however, was on the side of Alexander - succession to the Macedonian throne went exclusively through the male line and had to be pure Macedonian.

When their next child was born, it was a male child; however, Philip had officially recognised Alexander as his heir, and before he could change his mind, Philip was murdered by a king's bodyguard who had a grudge against him. The ambitious Olympias, jealous ex-wife of Philip, having been greatly scorned was suspected of having been in some way involved.

Adding to the suspicion of Olympias having been in some way responsible, was the fact that she obtained a Celtic sword which had been used to stab Philip, and she dedicated it to the god *Apollo*. Alexander, clearly innocent, was upset when he learnt of the death of his father and three of his companions pursued and caught the assassin.

Alexander (St Germain) and Aristotle (Kuthumi)

Olympias had raised Alexander to believe that his destiny was to become king in his own right - destined from birth to win glory and renown, and this he was to achieve. The Greek philosopher, Aristotle of Thrace, who became the **tutor** of Alexander, also encouraged Alexander by implanting in his mind the conviction that his kingship would be justified. Aristotle was an incarnation of the Master Kuthumi and instead of 'educating' Alexander, given the fact that both Kuthumi and St Germain would frequently incarnate into the same time periods, it is more likely that Kuthumi was assisting Alexander to attain his full potential.

Alexander and the goddess Athena

Around 1,000 BC, Egypt was almost bankrupt owing to the fact that the country was being besieged by Assyrian and Persians. However, when Alexander became King of Macedonia in c.336 BC, he was instrumental in removing the despised Persian domination in the Mediterranean and controlling all the Greek cities in Asia Minor.

It was Alexander's dream to create an empire, bound not so much by the power of the sword as by the coherence of a common culture. He had at his command, a large fleet and when in battle, Alexander steered the admiral's flagship himself.

In one of his battles to defeat Xerxes who had invaded Greece, after landing safely in Troy, Alexander *set up an altar to the goddess Athena and dedicated his own armour to her.* In his incarnation as Francis Bacon, St Germain dedicated many of his works to Athena and his mother, Elizabeth I was often depicted as Pallas Athena.

Alexander's Battles and Travels
"I carried the banner before Alexander"
(Taliesin/Merlin/St Germain)

During his time in Egypt, Alexander restored the ancient temples. As a result of the Greek influence introduced into Egypt by Alexander who was possibly assisted by Aristotle, the Greek gods and Egyptian gods merged, at which time the Egyptian god Thoth (Tat) became known as Hermes (who has been discussed in a previous chapter).

Alexander created an incredible international empire with knowledge as well as goods being exchanged throughout his empire from the new city of Alexandria, named in his honour. He was influential in the language of Greek being spoken and written in countries that he occupied, particularly Egypt. In later centuries, the Essenes, some of whom came from Egypt, spoke a mixture of Aramaic and Greek.

In the cryptic verse quoted above, St Germain writing under the pseudonym of Taliesin in the 6th century AD is informing us that he was once Alexander the Great who bore the banner into numerous battles which he fought.

Alexander fought a battle near the River Tigris where he defeated the Persian Emperor Darius in 332 BC and took the Persian title of Great King. He then spent the next few years crossing Afghanistan and penetrating India, particularly the Punjab. Throughout his time in India, Alexander took a great interest in Indian medical lore and was particularly interested in the Indian sages and philosophers.

Alexander and Apollo

The Egyptians traditionally acknowledged Alexander as the son of 'Ammon' and hailed him as a god who had rid them of the Persian invaders. On Grecian coins, Alexander appeared as the god *Apollo* and according to legend, Alexander was said to have had several adventures with beautiful sea maidens (mermaids) and thus mermaids appeared on Phoenician and Corinthian coins.

In the 6th century AD, (according to legend), a beautiful mermaid who was in love with a saint (possibly St Columba) would visit the island of Iona (the Island of the Druids) on the west coast of Scotland.

The Demise of Alexander the Great, 323 BC

According to Peter Green in his book titled *Alexander of Macedon*:

"During a battle in India, Alexander was pierced near his heart by an Indian arrow and was borne away on his shield to the royal pavilion where the arrow was cut out with a sword. A major hemorrhage followed and the attendants were unable to stop the flow of blood. His condition was extremely weak but it was imperative that he appeared to the Indians as alive and still ready to win the battle."

"With iron will Alexander bravely returned to the base camp and waved to his troops as he entered the camp seated on a horse and noise of applause broke across the camp. When he reached the tent, he completely lost consciousness but fully recovered and continued to fight other battles."

In the year 323 BC Alexander was to die of a fever, having never full recovered his health after the arrow wound, although it is thought by some scholars that because of the peculiar symptoms of his death, someone may have poisoned Alexander, possibly one of his rivals.

According to Betty Radice in her book titled *Who's Who in the Ancient World*, Alexander's body was brought to Alexandria and buried, wrapped in gold in a glass coffin in a vast tomb at the cross-roads in the centre of the city, so that Alexander could be its protective deity. This site has never been located and rumours persist to this current time that his body has been seen in tact in a coffin in some underground chamber.

Recently on the History Channel, archaeologists were still searching for his tomb, and no one can agree on the exact location, thus for the time being, it will remain one of the world's mysteries.

After Alexander's demise - the reign of the Maccabees

Following his mother, Olympia's predictions, and possibly with the encouragement and assistance of Aristotle (Kuthumi), Alexander proved himself to be one of the greatest leaders ever known and his feats and contributions to humanity were remarkable. His conquests had spread the Greek culture widely in the Middle East and central Asia, thus his influence lingered for centuries.

Aristotle died in 322 BC, one year after the death of Alexander.

Following the death of Alexander, his empire broke up among the rival claimants. *His generals took control, one of whom was Seleucus who ruled Babylonia.*

If Alexander was poisoned, then the most likely suspect would have been Seleucus. It is of interest to note that Seleucus likened himself to Alexander and even told the story of how his mother was visited in a dream by *Apollo* before his birth.

A descendant of Seleucus was Antiochus III who eventually became the ruler of Palestine. In a future chapter it will be discussed how the son of Antiochus (Antiochus IV) took control of Jerusalem which was the beginning of the Jewish revolt under the Hasmonaean leader, Judas Maccabaeus, whose family were known as the Maccabees and who were feared by the Essenes.

The Essenes considered the Maccabees to be usurpers and surely the truth regarding the person or persons responsibility for Alexander's death, would have been known to them.

Omar Khayyam (d.1123 AD) (Kuthumi) and the Rose

"Look to the Rose that blows about us - 'Lo
Laughing,' she says, 'into the World I blow'
With the seed of Wisdom did I sow,
And with mine own hand wrought to make it grow"
(The Rubaiyat of Omar Khayyam)

Omar Khayyam, an incarnation of Kuthumi, was a great Master of his time, a Persian poet-philosopher who through his poetry, revealed some insight into the Mysteries. His work has been identified with that of Pythagoras whom he had been in one of his previous incarnations and it will also be seen that Omar's talents and abilities were very similar. We also need to bear in mind that Kuthumi had once been the Philosopher, Aristotle.

The multiple talents of Sir John Dee (Kuthumi) in the 16th century AD were discussed in detail in the first chapter, but omitted was the fact that apart from being a brilliant mathematician, he was also a poet and a writer of numerous important works. Sir John Dee was appointed to the Royal Court as Elizabeth's I's astrologer/astronomer. Omar Khayyam was appointed to the Royal Court of Persia as the Royal astronomer.

From information contained in the book titled *Rubaiyat of Omar Khayyam*, we learn that "the Persian Omar Khayyam was born at Naishapur in the latter half of the 11th century AD and died within the first quarter of the 12th century (1123)."

"He was a Master philosopher who wrote about astronomy and invented an astronomical calendar."

"Omar wrote about mathematics, including algebra and was considered to be a genius. His most famous poem of which many will be familiar was the *Rubaiyat*, all very symbolical about roses, wine, bread, cup-bearer, veils etc."

The best translation is considered to have been done by Edward Purcell Fitzgerald (1809 -1883), who declared that "the Persian Mystic, Omar, wrote within his works, many allegories which symbolized an esoteric doctrine such as that of Plato [St Germain] and Pythagoras [Kuthumi] which he dared not and probably could not more intelligently reveal, other than by way of his poetry."

The Gothic cathedrals of Europe and England, apart from being built upon major energy Ley lines, were built upon the principles of the harmonics of mathematics. In other words, they were built upon the principles of Pythagoras.

In the 12th century AD, exceptionally beautiful stained glass was used in cathedral widows, the likes of which have never since been repeated and they are thought to have been a product of Hermetic alchemy. Omar Khayyam was one of those mathematicians and philosophers employed to perfect the Gothic glass which were installed in Cistercian and Carthusian Gothic cathedrals.

Noteworthy is the fact that Edward Purcell Fitzgerald was a friend of Alfred Lord Tennyson's (1817-1904). Also of interest is that according to Paul Broadhurst in his book titled *Tintagel and the Arthurian Mythos*, Alfred Lord Tennyson spent some time staying at Tintagel (the legendary birthplace of Arthur), before he wrote his work *Idylls of the King* which introduced the legendary heroic nature of Tintagel. Tennyson is also famous for his other Arthurian epic, *Morte d'Arthur - The Death of Arthur*. (Alfred Lord Tennyson is reputed to have been a member of the Freemasons and his tomb with a beautifully carved statue of him and his dog above it is in the gardens of the famous Lincoln Cathedral, Lincolnshire, U.K.).

It was in 1136 that Geoffrey of Monmouth wrote *The History of the Kings of Britain* at which time the saga of Arthur and the Holy Grail was introduced and during the era of Omar Khayyam, the First Crusade was launched in 1095 and in 1098 the Cistercian Order to which St Bernard of Clairvaux belonged, was founded in France.

Like the bards and troubadours of that period who disguised their messages and teachings in poetry and song, Omar too disguised his teachings in his poetry.

According to his biographer, Edward Purcell Fitzgerald:

"Omar Khayyam lived and died in Naishapur, 'in winning knowledge of every kind, and especially in Astronomy, wherein he attained a very high pre-eminence. Under the Sultan of Malik Shah, he obtained great praise for his proficiency in science and the Sultan showered favours upon him'."

"When Malik Shah determined to reform the calendar, Omar was one of the eight learned men employed to do it; the result was the *Jalali* era (so called from *Jalal-ud-din*, one of the king's names) - a 'compilation of time' which surpasses the Julian and approaches the accuracy of the Gregorian style."

"Omar was also the author of some astronomical tables, and the French published and translated an Arabic Treatise of his Algebra. His Takhallus or poetical name (Khayyam) signifies a Tent-maker and he is said to have at one time exercised that trade. Many Persian poets similarly derived their names from their occupations. Omar himself alludes to his name in the following whimsical lines:

"Khayyam, who stitched the tents of science,

Has fallen in grief's furnace and been suddenly burned;

The Shears of Fate have cut the tent ropes of his life,

And the broker of Hope has sold him for nothing!"

The only anecdote about Omar's life was printed in the *Veterum Persarum Religion*, p.499:

"It is written in the chronicles of the ancients that this King of the Wise, Omar Khayyam, died at Naishapur in 1123 AD; in science he was unrivalled, the very paragon of his age. Khwajah Nizami of Samarcand, who was one of his pupils, relates the following story: 'I often used to hold conversations with my teacher,

Omar Khayyam, in a garden and one day he said to me:
'My tomb shall be in a spot where the north wind may scatter roses over it'."

The mention of the 'north wind' is interesting. The 'Archangel' Michael controls the North which is Hyperborea and during Kuthumi's incarnation as St John the Beloved, his Essenian angelic title was 'Michael'.

It is also noteworthy that upon the tomb of Edward Purcell Fitzgerald, (the 19th century biographer of Omar), beautiful roses grew from hips taken from the famous rose bushes that once grew on the grave of Omar Khayyam in Naishapur in 1884. (Edward died on June 14th, 1883).

The rose hips were raised at Kew Gardens before being planted on Edward's grave. It was the greatest botanist that the world has ever known, Sir Joseph Banks, (born 1743), an incarnation of Kuthumi, who was President of the Royal Society (an off-shoot of the Order of the Rose-Cross) for fifty years, who nurtured the Royal Botanical Gardens at Kew.

It is also of interest to note that when St George (Kuthumi) whose emblem was the Rose (Red) Cross, died, his friend Constantine the Great, gave instructions for a particular Persian rose to be planted on his grave; it was called *The Rose of Sharon* which had long been an emblem of St George's family. Could Constantine have known of St George's past-life connection with Persia? It would seem so.

Tributes to Omar Khayyam

We further learn of Omar from Edward Fitzgerald's comments:

"It could be said of Omar that he was subtle, strong and cultivated intellect, had a fine imagination and a heart passionate for Truth and Justice."

"He was a free thinker and a great opponent of Sufism and was considered by learned men of the time, to have been a saint."

"His scientific insight and ability was far beyond that of the age and country in which he lived."

"The words in the Rubaiyat have a spiritual interpretation, in other words, they have an allegorical significance."

"Sharastani (1074-1153 AD) who was a distinguished doctor of law and lived in Naishapur, paid tribute to Omar as the greatest scholar of his time, one versed in the philosophy and political theory of the Greeks and who exhorted men to seek the One Author of all by the purification of the senses and the sanctification of the soul."

"Because Omar's teachings were seen as a threat, he concealed his doctrines in a veiled manner because he was in fear of his life. Thus, not for the first time in the world's history, a great scholar and thinker, versed in philosophy, science, mathematics, astronomy and medicine, found it expedient to conform to the orthodox philosophical dialectic of the age, to put away his pen and make a pilgrimage to Mecca."

"If we probe behind the symbol or metaphor, we shall discover a noble philosophy which will guide us through the Mysteries of Life and Destiny."

"The 'Tavern' mentioned in the *Rubaiyat* or *'Caravanserai'* is symbolic of the pilgrimage of the way of Life. Wine is symbolic of the Spirit; the Cup (like the Grail Chalice) is the receptacle of the Spiritual powers poured out in Service: Bread is the Divine Mind (Wisdom) or Food from Heaven; the Persian Nightingale is the Symbol of the Soul, singing in the darkness or hidden depths of man's own being."

"Did Omar know that the earth revolves in space and travels around the sun and that the solar system describes a still greater orbit? The ancient Egyptians possessed this knowledge. May not the Wise Men of the East have been similarly enlightened?"

Omar died in 1123 and the Master Kuthumi reincarnated again in 1140 as Hugh of Avalon, born into a noble family at Castle Avalon in France during which time his father and two brothers were members of the Knights Templar who fought in the Crusades.

His mother, Anne, was likened to a saint because she attended the lepers and washed their sores. Although in his life as Omar, he was likened to being a saint, in Kuthumi's next life as Hugh of Avalon, he was canonized as a saint and more on that particular life will be discussed in a future chapter, for in that era of the Crusades, Kuthumi had a profound influence upon history and upon three Plantagenet kings, namely Henry II, Richard the Lion Heart, John and the Celtic King, William the Lion (St Germain), Defender of the Celtic Faith.

Roger Bacon (c. 1214 - 1294 AD)
The Master St Germain

St Germain reincarnated as Roger Bacon in circa 1214 AD. (His previous incarnation had been as King William the Lion of Scots 1143-1214 during which time he had been a Defender and Guardian of the Celtic faith. In St Germain's incarnation as 'Merlin' he prophesied that he would return as the Lion of Scots).

As Roger Bacon, St Germain was born into a wealthy family in Somerset, England. He studied at Oxford University and the University of Paris where he became a teacher. He was a Master of Alchemy (Chemistry), astrology, astronomy and mathematics. During this period he was also a *Master of the Rose Cross*, at which time he foretold that he would one day reincarnate and discover America.

During his life as Roger Bacon, St Germain laid the foundation for the revolution in science. This took place in the 1500's and 1600's. In his work titled

Epistola de Secretis, there were descriptions of inventions for the future including modern aircraft, automobiles, ships driven by engines and not sail, suspension bridges, submarines and helicopters. The Church of Rome criticized his writings and suspected him of being a wizard/magician. As a result, he was imprisoned in a Paris convent for fourteen years; he died not long after his release in 1292.

St Germain fulfilled the prophecy he had made when he was Roger Bacon, when he reincarnated as Christopher Columbus in the 15th century and discovered America.

As Francis Bacon in the 16th century, St Germain was able to continue the foundations of revolutionary science which he had begun in his life as Roger Bacon, and the foundations of Freemasonry which he had established in his life as St Alban in the 3rd century AD.

MASTER DISCUSSED IN THIS CHAPTER

Plato - St Germain
Alexander the Great - St Germain
Roger Bacon - St Germain
King William the Lion of Scots - St Germain
Christopher Columbus - St Germain
Francis Bacon - St Germain
Buddha - the Master Jesus
Socrates - the Master Jesus
Pythagoras, Master of Mathematics - Kuthumi
St George - Kuthumi
King Arthur - Kuthumi
Omar Khayyam - Kuthumi
Sir John Dee - Kuthumi
Sir Joseph Banks - Kuthumi

NOTES AND RECOMMENDED READING

Betty Radice, *Who's Who In The Ancient World*, (Penguin Books, U.K. 1973)

Arnold J. Toynbee, *A Study of History*, (Oxford University Press, U.K. 1934)

Francis Hitching, *The World Atlas of Mysteries*, (Pan Books, U.K. 1978)

Peter Green, *Alexander of Macedon*, (University of California, Berkeley Press, U.S.A. 1991)

Madame Helena Blavatsky, *The Secret Doctrine*, (Quest Books, Theosophical Publishing House, U.K. 1966)

C.W. Leadbeater, *The Hidden Life in Freemasonry*, (Theosophical Publishing House, U.K. 1975)

Annie Bessant, *The Ancient Wisdom*, (Theosophical Publishing House, U.S.A, 1992)

Robert Graves, *The White Goddess*, (Faber & Faber, U.K. 1961)

Peter Dawkins, *Arcadia*, (Francis Bacon Research Trust, Warwick, U.K.)

Daniel Boorstin,_ *The Discoverers, A History of Man's Search To Know His World And Himself*,

(Random House, U.K. 1983)

Paul Broadhurst, *Tintagel and the Arthurian Mythos*, (Pendragon Press, Cornwall, U.K. 1997)

Edward Purcell Fitzgerald, *The Rubaiyat of Omar Khayyam*, (Collins, U.K., 1974)

CHAPTER 10

The Platonic Academy, 'Arcadia' & Freemasonry

"My name *is a mask*.
I am one yet more than one.
My name is a cipher: it is '1.9' and '9.3'
C.R.C. is an epigram
ST GERMAIN *is a pseudonym*
"*MY ESSENCE IS SILENCE, like the voiceless fragrance of a Rose.
Who can name the Silence?*"

Plato (St Germain) founded his Academy in an olive grove outside of Athens where he reinforced the teachings of Platonism. Olive groves were favourite places, where in later centuries the Essenes would meet at gatherings for their tuition. It has been explained in an earlier chapter that the olive was a symbol of illumination, which bestows peace and knowledge; similarly, the symbology of the 'Dove' and the 'Olive' branch of Noah - St Germain. The moral philosophy of Plato had a great effect upon Roman thinkers plus having an immense influence upon the western world. (From the word Plato, we derive the word 'platonic' and the school of 'Platonism').

It was no coincidence that when Kuthumi reincarnated as Leonardo da Vinci and St Germain reincarnated as Christopher Columbus during the Italian Renaissance period in Florence, they were very dedicated to the Platonic Academy founded by Cosimo de Medici with the encouragement and support of Rene of Anjou, the titled King of Jerusalem.

According to the authors of the book titled *The Holy Blood and the Holy Grail* Michael Baigent, Richard Leigh and Henry Lincoln: "In 1439, while Rene was resident in Italy, Cosimo de Medici began sending his agents all over the world in quest of ancient manuscripts. Then, in 1444, Cosimo founded Europe's first public library, the Library of San Marco, and thus began to challenge the Church's long monopoly of learning. At Cosimo's express commission, the corpus of

Platonic, Neo-Platonic, Pythagorean, Gnostic and Hermetic thought found its way into translation for the first time and became readily accessible. Cosimo also instructed the University of Florence to begin teaching in Greek, for the first time in Europe for some seven hundred years. And he undertook to create an academy of Pythagorean and Platonic studies. Cosimo's academy quickly generated a multitude of similar institutions throughout the Italian peninsula, which became bastions of Western esoteric tradition. And from them the high culture of the Renaissance began to blossom."

"Rene d' Anjou not only contributed in some measure to the formation of the academies, but also seems to have conferred upon them one of their favourite symbolic themes - that of Arcadia. Certainly it is in Rene's own career that the motif of Arcadia appears to have made its debut in post-Christian Western culture."

As we have learned in previous chapters, 'Arcadia' was a favourite theme of St Germain in his incarnation as Sir Francis Bacon. In Peter Dawkins' work titled *Arcadia*, we learn of the poet Percy Shelley's comments: "Shelley acknowledges Francis Bacon as being a great poet, but also he rates Francis together with Plato as being supreme poets. **Did Shelley know or discover more than he let on?** Read the frontispiece to the *Advancement of Learning* (1640) where it compares Bacon to Plato. Here are Shelley's words (from his *'Defence of Poetry'*):

'Poetry is at once the centre of circumference of knowledge...and that to which all science must be referred...A poet is the author to others of the highest Wisdom, pleasure, virtue and glory...Plato was essentially the Poet, the truth and splendour of his imagery, and the melody of his language, are the most intense that it is possible to conceive...Lord Bacon was a Poet. His language was a sweet majestic rhythm which satisfies the senses, no less than the superhuman wisdom of his philosophy satisfies the intellect. It is as rain which distends and then bursts the circumference of the reader's mind and pours itself forth together with it into the universal elements with which is had perpetual sympathy...The language of Plato is that of an immortal spirit, rather than a man; Lord Bacon is, perhaps, the only writer who, in these particulars, can be compared to him.'"

From the work titled *The Great Secret - Count Saint Germain* by Dr Raymond Bernard, A.B., M.A., Ph. D., we learn the following pertinent information:

"The author of the Shakespearian plays must have possessed a large library and had constant access to such reference material for his literary labours. But there is no proof that William Shakespeare ever owned a single book. [The actor, Shakespeare from Stratford on Avon was illiterate and even his Last Will and Testament was signed with a cross. His name was spelt without the 'a'. i.e. 'Shakespere'. Francis signed his works as 'Shakespeare', alluding to the fact that he was the 'Spear-Shaker of the 'Truth']. The author of the Shakespearian plays had revolutionary political opinions and views of governmental reform; a humble actor or playwright could not have expected to have such views in those days. It is clear that some unknown scholar whose learning was encyclopedic and whose station and personal tastes fitted him for such a work was the creator of the plays - *the only scholar of this type who lived in England at this time was Francis Bacon."*

"There is every reason to believe that the author of the plays was a man of large learning; that he had read and studied Homer, *Plato*, Sophocles, Euripides, Horace, Virgil, Lucretia, Statius, Catullus, Seneca, Ovid, Platus, Plutarch, Boccaccio and an innumerable amount of French, Spanish and Danish writers; and since there were no public libraries in those days to which he could resort, he must have possessed a large library, and have gathered around him a literary store commensurate with his own intellectual activity."

"Yet there is no evidence that Shakespeare (the actor) had such a library, for if he did, he would surely have mentioned it in his Will. Another unusual circumstance is that the great literary genius (the actor, Shakespeare who is credited with having written the plays), should have permitted his daughter, Judith, to have grown up and reached the age of twenty-seven years without knowing how to read or write. On this point Donnelly [Ignatius], in his book *The Great Cryptogram* writes:

'It is not surprising that William Shakespere (the actor), poacher, fugitive, vagabond, actor, brewer, moneylender, land grabber, should permit one of his two children to grow up in gross ignorance, but it is beyond the compass of the human mind to believe that the author of Hamlet and Lear could have done so'."

The Freemasons

It has been previously mentioned that Freemasonry was first introduced into Britain in the 3rd century AD by St Germain in his incarnation as St Alban of Verulam.

From my early childhood days I was always curious about the Order of the Freemasons. My Irish grandfather and father were both members but would never divulge any information of its activities.

I was always fascinated with the small suitcase that my father would carry to meetings, which contained a Bible, a strange apron made of chamois and a pair of white gloves, which were enough to make any child curious! I wondered if it was some strange kind of religion.

My grandfather had been a Protestant Sunday school teacher in County Down, Northern Ireland, before he came out to Australia during the Gold Rush days. Upon questioning my father's religious beliefs, my father would reply that he was a 'Gnostic'. For many years I wondered what exactly he meant by that.

The Bible which he left to me was the King James Authorized Version which also had a curious label in the front of it stating that the Bible had been presented to him by the Grand Master of the Lodge. Who? I asked myself many times throughout the years, were the Freemasons and what was a Grand Master?

From that time onwards, with my curiosity fully aroused, some twenty years later, I have managed to discover some of the answers! Finally, I understand what a 'Gnostic' is and I only wish that I had known back then, because I am quite sure my father and I would have had some most interesting discussions based upon this subject.

Over the centuries, the Freemasons often came under suspicion and were attacked because they failed to disclose their members or their activities. (Freemasons recognise each other by a 'secret' handshake).

In recent years, some of the mystery has been removed regarding the Freemasons and the Order of the Rose Cross (Rosicrucians), mainly through the amount of books currently available on the market.

The aims of both the Order of the Freemasons and the Rose Cross are not based upon religion. Anyone may join. Their aim has always been to promote brotherly/sisterly love and work in a more spiritual way towards helping humanity. As modern books will tell you, yes, there have been unworthy members over the centuries, some who joined to further their own gains in a materialistic way which is not the true teachings of these Orders. However, the unworthy ones have been counterbalanced by the numerous worthy ones who have contributed so much and the aims of the Lodges were originally based on the teachings of its founder, Francis Bacon, *The Master of the Mystical Rose* - St Germain.

Famous members of the Freemasons have included:

Charlemagne, King of the Franks, (incarnation of St Germain), (742-814),
Raymond VI, Count of Toulouse (1156-1222),
Roger Bacon (1214?-1294) (incarnation of St Germain),
Dante Alighieri (1665-1321),
Sir John Dee (1527-1608) (Kuthumi),
Giordano Bruno, Italian Philosopher, 1548? - 1600),
Sir Francis Bacon (1561-1626?) (St Germain),
Robert Fludd (1574-1637),
Johan Valentin Andrea (1586-1670),
Sir Christopher Wren (1632-1723),
Benjamin Franklin (1706-1790), (was a friend of St Germain),
Sir Isaac Newton (1642-1727),
Count Alessandro Cagliostro (1743-1795),
Thomas Jefferson, (1743-1826) (third President of the United States),
Mozart (1756-1791),

William Blake (1757-1827) Druid & Poet,
Claude Debussy (1826-1918),
Anton Rubinstein (1829-1894),
And Kings of England and Europe,
And Presidents of the United States.

From the 1600's onwards, many Orders were established under various titles when there was the need to go underground in order to protect the Arcana Teachings of the Great White Brotherhood, which had been handed down through the ages to those worthy of trust.

Charles W. Leadbeater (d.1934) related in his book titled *The Hidden Life in Freemasonry* how he met with the Master Ragoczy (St Germain) in Rome in 1901. Leadbeater revealed that *St Germain (the Master Ragoczy) was and is the Sovereign Grand Master of the Freemasons, but that today's Masons have lost the true meanings and probably have never heard of their original Grand Master who was instrumental in establishing all the original Freemasonic and Rosicrucian (Rose Cross) lodges.*

Francis Bacon's Art of Discovery

It has been said of the Comte de St Germain/Francis Bacon, in well summarized comments made by Manly P. hall in his work titled *Most holy Trinosophia* (available through the Theosophical Society) that: "St Germain was the Grand Master of the old Wisdom, wise in forgotten truths, proficient in all the curious arts of antiquity, learned beyond any other man of the modern world. The mysterious Comte personified in his own incredible achievements the metaphysical traditions of fifty centuries."

"A thousand times the questions have been asked: Where did St Germain secure his astonishing knowledge of natural law? How did he perpetuate himself from century to century, defying the natural corruption which brings priest, prince and pauper alike to a common end? St Germain was the mouthpiece and representative of the Brotherhood of philosophers which had descended in an unbroken line from the Hierophants of Greece and Egypt. He had received the Logos (the Word of God). By his wisdom, he confounded the elders. The life of this man puts to naught the scholastic smugness of two thousand years."

According to Peter Dawkins: "The Baconian Science and Art, which is Rosicrucian (Rose-Cross), has not yet been properly recognised let alone practiced by society at large, and has very little to do with any purely mechanistic, utilitarian and explorative aspects of modern science and society, or with any materialistic philosophy. The aim of Bacon's Art is to discover truth itself, and in particular the ultimate truth, which he recognised as being divine Love - the single summary Law or Desire of the universe. With Bacon's method the discovery of truth goes hand in hand with the practice of truth."

"Science is knowledge, and knowledge is not true knowledge without the practical experience of it. As we can never discover the ultimate truth of Love without practicing love, Bacon's Science is an ethical science, its philanthropic purpose being to relieve the poverty, misery and ignorance of all who suffer in such a state and thereby to glorify God, or Love, through the practice of charity or good works. By this means Love or God, the Truth, is made manifest and known."

"To do this well and efficiently is not necessarily easy, as the history of the human race proves. It is an Art which, when practiced well, produces a Science of Love, which is an Illumination."

Causes and Effects

"It is an Art and Science which requires discovery and practice on many levels of existence, physical and metaphysical, from the outer world of effects to the innermost world of causes. The former is a key to the discovery of the latter, whilst the latter is the creative cause of the former. Since causes produce effects, if we do not like the effects and if we know the causes, by altering or modulating the causes we can change the effects. Likewise, if we discover the supreme Cause, the Law of Love, and learn how to work with it, and if we can put that Law into operation in our lives and surroundings, we can bring about the works of love and produce miracles."

"This is the supreme Art, which is alchemical in nature. It has the capacity to transmute all base matter into spiritual gold, to change all gross and ugly conditions into fine and beautiful ones, and to transform all ignorance into true Science and Illumination. It is an ancient Art, practiced by Sufis and Rosicrucians of all ages - the Adepts or 'Scientists' of the Hermetic Wisdom. The Hermetic Master, Francis Bacon, improved the Art still further, for the benefit of humanity and the whole world. But it has to be practiced. The Art is known by means of itself. This is the great teaching."

St Germain, Shakespeare and the Rose

During the 16th century, a publication of Sir Francis Bacon's *History of Henry the Seventh* was issued in which there is a drawing of Francis Bacon with Rosicrucian roses for shoe buckles, a subtle hint of his association with the Sacred

Teachings of the Arcana.

In a message to Peter Dawkins in 1993, from St Germain, St Germain says that his name is a pseudonym.

"My name *is a mask.*

I am one yet more than one.

My name is a cipher: it is '1.9' and '9.3'

C.R.C. is an epigram

ST GERMAIN *is a pseudonym*

My life is my own,

Yet my life is that of all souls,

A parable of what is, what was and what may be.

My life is my work and my love.

I CANNOT NAME MYSELF,

as the intention of my work is that you should seek,

and by seeking discover me,

and by discovering me, know me.

MY ESSENCE IS SILENCE

Like the voiceless fragrance of a Rose.

Who can name the Silence?"

There are several cryptics contained in the name, one of which is that 'Germain' can be deciphered as 'Je-main' as in French 'Je = **I am**, thus, I AM the main Teacher of the Universe for the Golden Age of Aquarius'.

During the 6th century AD, when St Germain wrote under the pseudonym of *Taliesin*, he informed us in some of the verses left to posterity that: "*I am able to instruct the whole universe. I have been fostered in the land of the Deity [God]. I shall be until the day of judgement on the face of the earth*".

The cryptic of his name of '*Germain*' is his way of telling us that he is a Master Teacher to all intelligences via the 'Universal Cosmic Consciousness' by which we are all connected to the Creator God, and that St Germain is the main Teacher of the New Age of Aquarius.

One of the verses which has previously been mentioned, taken from *The Romance of Taliesin*, reads: "*Is it not the wonder of this world, that I cannot be discovered?*" which is a similar message to that of the one which St Germain gave to Peter Dawkins: "*I cannot name myself, as the intention of my work is that you should seek me, and by seeking discover me, and by discovering me, know me.*"

"*MY ESSENCE IS SILENCE, like the voiceless fragrance of a Rose. Who can name the Silence?*"

As the Master of the New Age of Aquarius, St Germain teaches us the 'Art of Discovery of the Truth' through symbolism given to us in meditation and dreams, the same form of symbolism established so long ago in ancient Egypt. St Germain encourages us to be Masters of our own Path, to seek him and discover the 'Truth' for ourselves.

He is a 'SILENT TEACHER'. To increase our knowledge brings wisdom, which in turn brings 'enlightenment' encouraged by the philosophic discipline of the Masters for the true growth of the soul. When the Master Jesus said "In my Father's House there are Many Mansions", he was referring to the many levels of initiation, which the soul-incarnation undertakes and hopefully reaches new levels each lifetime - the ultimate goal being the perfection of the Self and the release of 'Karma'.

As the *Master of the Mystical Rose*, St Germain was always working behind the 'scenes'. He was the Master of the Muses and their symbol was the red *Rose*, reputed to have grown from the blood of Adonis after he was killed by a boar. 'Scenes' is quite the appropriate word, for as has already been stated, in his incarnation as Sir Francis Bacon, St Germain wrote numerous works including those written under the pseudonym of William Shakespeare - meaning *Will I Am*, *Shaker of the Spear* (of 'Truth'). According to information sent to me by Peter Dawkins:

"The name William is derived from Hwyll, the name of the Welsh Sun-god, who is the Welsh equivalent of Apollo, the Spear Shaker, who shakes his spear of light at the dragon of ignorance. Helm means helmet. All in all the name William Shakespeare means 'the helmet of the Sun God' or 'helmet of Light' - the golden helmet or halo of light belonging to a sainted person - a St George figure or Rose Cross knight."

Athena was not only known as the Goddess of Wisdom equated with *Sophia* but also as the Triple Goddess and one of her symbols, as mentioned in an earlier chapter, was an Owl, equated with the Egyptian word *Hwl* signifying 'wisdom'.

In a future chapter, the origins of the name Bel/Beli/Heli will be discussed for Beli the Great (Mawr/Mor) was an ancestor of King Arthur. Beli was also called Billi, which was a shortened name for William and his name in Old Germanic language meant 'will helmet' i.e. *'helmet of resolution'*.

Francis Bacon's Secret Cipher

It is amazing how many times we tend to quote lines from Shakespeare, for he undoubtedly had a profound effect upon our English language. In January, 1999, it was announced that the BBC listeners had chosen William Shakespeare as Britain's greatest personality of the past 1,000 years. (Sir Winston Churchill was the second).

In the 'Bard' Shakespeare's Sonnet number 33, there is an illusion to him being a Master of Alchemy and it cannot be coincidence that it is numbered 33, which is Francis Bacon's cipher code.

> "Full many a glorious morning have I seen
> Flatter the mountain-tops with sovereign eye,
> Kissing with golden face the meadows green
> Gliding pale streams with heavenly alchemy."

When Francis Bacon (alias Shakespeare) wrote the famous line: *"What's in a name? A rose by any other name would smell just as sweet"*, it is rather cryptic because it can have several meanings. This line could be alluding to the Rosicrucian (the Rose-Cross) lodges and subsequent Freemasonic lodges that he founded. However, it could also allude to the fact that he changed his name and identity many times, but the person remained the same, as did his noble ambitions.

It has previously been stated that Francis Bacon used various codes and ciphers within his plays and poems, however, his prime code was 33 or a series of three's as in the supposed death of St Alban in 303 AD. According to Peter Dawkins, the number 33 is the Elizabethan simple cipher for BACON:

$$B = 2, A = 1, C = 3, 0 = 14, N = 13$$

At Westminster Abbey in London, there is a monument to Shakespeare which was erected in 1841. According to information contained in the book titled *Master R Lord of Our Civilisation* by New Zealand author, Michael Taylor, there is an inscription upon the monument which has encoded within it a message which reads:

'FRANCIS BACON - AUTHOR'

MASTERS DISCUSSED IN THIS CHAPTER

Noah - St Germain

Plato - St Germain

The 6th century Bard, Taliesin/Merlin - St Germain

St Alban - St Germain

Francis Bacon - St Germain

The 12th century Bard, 'Shakespeare' - St Germain

NOTES AND RECOMMENDED READING

C.W. Leadbeater, *The Hidden Life in Freemasonry*, (Theosophical Publishing House, U.K. 1975)

Robert Graves, *The White Goddess*, (Faber & Faber, U.K. 1961)

Peter Dawkins, *Arcadia*, (Francis Bacon Research Trust, Warwick, U.K.)

Peter Dawkins, *The Great Vision*, (Francis Bacon Research Trust, Warwick, U.K.)

Peter Dawkins, *Dedication to the Light*, (Francis Bacon Research Trust, Warwick, U.K)

Michael Taylor, *Master R Lord Of Our Civilisation*, (The Rawley Trust, Christchurch, New Zealand, 1997)

Spencer Lewis, *Rosicrucian Questions And Answers*, (AMORC, U.S.A, 1929)

Isabel Cooper-Oakley, *Comte De St Germain*, (Theosophical Publishing House, U.K. 1985)

Boris Ford, *The Age of Shakespeare*, (Penguin Books, U.K. 1955)

Michael Baigent, Richard Leigh & Henry Lincoln, *The Holy Blood And The Holy Grail*, (Arrow Books, U.K., 1996)

Dr Raymond Bernard, *The Great Secret - Count Saint Germain*, (U.S.A.).

CHAPTER 11

Ancient Mysteries, Parallels in the Bible & The 'Fisher Kings'

"Then he brought me to the door of the gate of the Lord's house
which *was* toward the north; and,
behold, there sat women weeping for Tammuz." (Ezekiel 8:4)
"It is long since I was a herdsman"
"I have been winged by the genius of the splendid crozier"
"And it is not known whether my body is flesh or fish"
(Taliesin/Merlin/St Germain)

According to Irish legend, the descendants of Ham, son of Noah, settled in Ireland which was then known as Hibernia. Many of the Celts had once been the earliest inhabitants of mainland Greece whose culture made them unique as a race and the descendants of Noah, traced their origin of their Greek lineage back to the Trojan hero Aeneas, whose mother (according to mythology) was *Aphrodite*, the goddess of love and beauty.

The most important temple and shrine to the goddess *Aphrodite* in the Mediterranean was in Cyprus, an island which was settled by the Greeks after the Trojan wars. The Greeks identified the planets with gods and goddesses very similar in character to those of the Babylonians. For example, Ishtar became *Aphrodite*, the Morning and Evening Star, whom the Romans called 'Venus'.

Ignatius Donnelly recorded that: "The history of Atlantis is the key of the Greek mythology. There can be no question that these gods of Greece were human beings. The tendency to attach divine attributes to great earthly rulers is one deeply implanted in human nature."

The Worship of Adonis and the Origin of 'Lord'

Part of the Ancient Egyptian Mysteries was that of the worshipping of *Adonis*, who was also worshipped by the Phoenicians, the 'People of the 'Ark' (Arkadians/ Arcadians). In the time of the pharaoh priesthoods, there were twelve levels of initiations and upon attaining the twelfth level the initiate was given the title of *Adon* or the *Rose* Red King. The *initiate was then given the Ankh and the 'Royal Key' to the Books of the Sacred Mysteries.* In latter times the initiations were reduced to seven levels, undertaken by the Knights Templar, members of the Order of the Rose-Cross and the Freemasons.

From *Adonis* came the word 'Adonai' which means 'Lord, and the ancient Egyptians applied this term to their sun-worship. Later, the term was to become 'Christianized'.

According to mythology, *Adonis* was born at midnight on the 24th December and traditionally he was born to a 'Virgin'. He was a beautiful youth who was loved by Aphrodite (Venus), the goddess of 'Love', and was worshipped as a god of vegetation.

Tammuz/Pan and Ishtar

Adonis was also worshipped as the god *Tammuz* who was the husband of the goddess Ishtar. *Tammuz* was equated with the god *Pan* who was regarded as the King of the Deva kingdom, whom Madame Blavatsky referred to as the 'Elementals'. 'Pan' was an Arcadian god, the patron of shepherds and herdsman. He was the son of Hermes (not to be confused with Hermes Trismegistus), and was regarded as the 'Good Shepherd of All'. In Greek, the word pan means 'all'. The Arcadians considered Pan as a special god who presided over Arcadia.

According to Robert Graves, the cult of *Tammuz* originated in Sumer as did the worshipping of Adonis. The other name for *Tammuz* was 'Damu-zi' which meant 'faithful son' and it became a universal religion based on the sufferings of a 'divine son'.

Archaeological evidence has shown that successive cultures down through the ages, such as those of the Minoans of Greece, believed the female form of divinity held the supreme place.

This universal Goddess was given many titles, one of which was, as mentioned above, *Ishtar*. The Goddess is also represented in Minoan art as the Divine Mother, holding up her infant child for adoration and her symbols of immortality, the chrysalis and the butterfly, have been found in Minoan graves in the form of gold amulets.

Zeus's emblem was the double-headed axe - a religious symbol which was utilized in the Minoan world much the same as the cross in the later Christian religion.

Near Tintagel, in the United Kingdom, are ancient inscribed maze patterns believed to be over 4,000 years old and they are of the same design as Minoan mazes found in Crete.

We are told in Ezekiel viii.14: "Then he brought me to the door of the gate of the Lord's house which was toward the north; and, behold, there sat women weeping for Tammuz."

In the book titled *The Hidden Life In Freemasonry*, C.W. Leadbeater informs us that "Moses brought from Egypt the myth of the death and resurrection of Osiris, and that persisted in a modified form until the time of David. Solomon for patriotic reasons transferred the theatre of drama to Jerusalem, and centred its interest round the temple which he had built, winning popularity at the same time by bringing his ritual into accordance with that of surrounding peoples, who were mostly worshippers of the Phoenician deity *Tammuz*, afterwards called by the Greeks *Adonis*."

Leadbeater relates that the Freemasonic legend of Hiram Abif, the Temple Architect employed by Solomon, is considered to be nothing but an adaptation of the myth of *Tammuz* - that Hiram Abif was one of a group of Priest-Kings, and was slain by the others as a voluntary sacrifice at the dedication of the temple, in order to bring good fortune upon the building.

The worshipping of *Adonis* was celebrated in Bethlehem (meaning 'House of Bread' equated with 'House of Wisdom'). 'Bethel' was the original name given to the habitat of a deity and its origins could be traced as far back as the Minoan Greek religion.

Elysium, The Mysteries, The 'Divine Child'

Homer described the after-life (immortality) in 'Elysium', as a world that was perfect.

According to Robert Graves in his book titled *The White Goddess*: "At Arles, in Provence, the cult of the Goddess as a Triad or Pentad of Mothers has survived under Christian disguise until today, when her festival is celebrated from 24th May to 28th May, but now her devotees are largely gypsies." (The name of 'gypsy' originated from 'Egypt').

"As a Triad she has become known as 'The Three Maries of Provence' or 'The Three Maries of the Sea'; as a Pentad she has had Martha added to her company, and an apocryphal serving girl, Sara."

"It seems that these were Christianizations of pre-Christian reliefs on the tombstones of the cemetery of Alyscamps as Arles, in which the Triad, or Pentad, was shown on one pane; and below, on another the soul in resurrection. The scene was explained in the Raising of Lazarus."

"As late as the time of Dante, the cemetery was used in the ancient style. The corpse was laid in a boat, with money in it, called *drue de mourtilage* and floated down the Rhone to Alyscamps. The name Alyscamps has been explained as *Camp Elysiani*, 'the Elysian Fields', but it is as likely that Alys was the ancient name of the Goddess."

In Greek mythology, the tale of the Hesperides (from 'Hesperis' meaning 'West') was also bound up with that of Elysium, the Isles of the Blessed. The Isles were said to be ruled by 'Father Time', otherwise known as *Kronus/Cronus* and in Elysium, time stood still. The inhabitants were immortal and the Golden Age which had vanished from the rest of the world, remained intact.

We are informed by Robert Graves that "the town of Eleusis (from which the Eleusinian Mysteries are said to have originated), where the most famous mysteries of all took place, was said to be named after Attic (Attis) King Eleusis."

"Eleusis means 'Advent' and the word was adopted into the Christian mysteries to signify the arrival of the Divine Child; in English usage it comprises Christmas and the four preceding weeks. The mother of Eleusis was 'Daeira', the daughter of 'Oceanus', 'the Wise One of the Sea', and was identified with Aphrodite, the Minoan Dove-goddess who rose from the sea at Paphos in Cyprus each year with her virginity renewed."

The Enactment of the Shepherds in the Elysian Mysteries

Robert Graves also informs us as follows: "King Eleusis was another name for the Corn god - *Dionysus*, whose life-story was celebrated as the Great Mysteries, the Harvest Thanksgiving in late September."

"At an early stage of the yearly Eleusinian Mysteries, the Divine Child, son of the Wise One who came from the Sea, was re-enacted by people dressed as shepherds and the 'Divine Child' was seated on a harvest basket having originally been rescued from a river bank having sailed there on the harvest basket."

"The myths correspond to those of Moses who was placed in a basket and floated downstream until he was found on a river bank and Osiris who also floated downstream in a basket which lodged on a river bank. Like Moses, Eleusis had no father, only a *virgin* mother, and the symbology of the manger in which Jesus was placed after his birth, is thought to have been derived from these Mysteries."

Reincarnation

The Eleusinian Mysteries venerated the Greek Goddesses Demeter and Persephone, and the mysteries of the cycle of life, death and rebirth. They are thought to have been founded in 1400 BC and managed to survive until about 400 AD at which time they were undermined by Theodosius who set out to destroy all who did not accept the Christian faith. The exclusion of teaching of the pre-existence of the soul and reincarnation began back in circa 563 AD when the early Christian fathers held a council in Constantinople, under the orders of the Roman Emperor, Justinian, and decreed that all clear references to reincarnation be removed.

Aeneas and the Tudors

According to *Who's Who In The Ancient World* by Betty Radice: "the idea of the Elysium Isle was that it was a promise of an after-life provided by the various mystery-cults and the name survives in the Alyscamps at Arles, the celebrated Roman, and later Christian burial ground. In his after-life, the Trojan hero Aeneas re-met his father Anchises in the Blessed Isles. (The Champs Elysees in Paris was named after the Elysian Fields)."

In the following paragraphs we will learn of the connection between the House of Judah to which the Family of the Holy Grail belonged, and the Tudors - the royal House into which St Germain was born in the 16th century AD, as Prince Francis Bacon.

Although this information was given in the first chapter, it is also relevant here. From Peter Dawkins' book titled *The Virgin Ideal* we are informed as follows:

"The Tudors were Welsh sovereigns of an ancient royal lineage, recorded as being descended from the Trojan (Greek) Aeneas (and thus related closely to the Trojans and the Romans), who was himself descended from Judah who was the eldest son of Jacob (who was called Israel) via Judah's second twin son Zarah."

"Thus the British nobility had a common ancestry with the Tribe of Judah and House of David which was reinforced by inter-marriages, of which one marriage in particular was notable - that of a Welsh prince with Joseph of Arimathea's daughter, Anna, from which marriage the Tudors were descended."

We further learn from information contained in Peter Dawkins' book titled *Arcadia*:

"The Tudors formed the ancient royal line of British kings, with a genealogy carefully preserved and recorded by their bards. They traced their line of descent back to the famous King Arthur [Kuthumi], with direct links (via the daughter of Joseph of Arimathea) with the Judaic royal line of David [Kuthumi], and beyond even the later Celts to Hugh the Mighty (also known as Brut, or Brit), who led the original Trojan settlers to 'the White Land' (i.e. Albion) in the second millennium BC, and gave these islands their name 'Britain' (meaning 'The Chosen Land'). This family line provided the 'Crowned Princes' (Cunos) and 'High Kings' (Arviragus) of Ancient Britain, and carried with them the ancient initiatic knowledge."

"The High Kings, all of whom were elected from the 'blood royal' (i.e. the 'Tudor' blood line) and chosen for their strength, wisdom and initiatic powers, bore the hereditary title of 'Merlin'(Myrrdin), as they combined in their office the roles of both High Priest and King."

In an earlier chapter, the origin of the name Anna from the tribe of Mari-anna was explained. Britain is another form of Anna, i.e. Britannia. The High Priests in the Temple of Jerusalem were called by the plural of 'Annas'.

Apollo and Athena

Included amongst Taliesin's cryptic poems was the *Cad Goddeu* in which he mentions having once been a 'herdsman'.

> "It is long since I was a herdsman,
> I have travelled over the earth
> Before I became a learned person.
> I have travelled, I have made a circuit,
> I have slept in a hundred islands,
> I have dwelt in a hundred cities,
> Learned Druids,
> Prophesy of Arthur?
> Or is it me they celebrate?"

All of *Taliesin's* quotations have been taken from Robert Graves' book titled *The White Goddess* and the author is correct when he states that the 'herdsman' referred to in the poem can only be Apollo who was the herdsman to Admetus, the Minyan king of Pherae in Thessaly, several centuries before he set up at Delphi as the 'Leader of the Muses'.

According to Peter Dawkins in his book titled *The Virgin Ideal*:

"In the now little known older traditions or mythologies, Athena is shown as being a Mother Goddess, and as the Virgin Mother she was married to Apollo. Apollo was known as the Chancellor of Parnassus (the Mount of Poetry and Illumination) and the Day Star of the Muses. Athena and Apollo produced as their child, Aesculapius, the Great Healer-Teacher. Athena was also the Goddess of the Arts and Sciences, the Patroness of all Learning."

In his incarnation in the 16th century as Francis Bacon, the writer of the

Shakespearian plays, St Germain was known as the 'Leader of the Muses' of that era. In Greek and Roman mythology the Muses were the Nine Sister goddesses who presided over the arts and sciences and were the poet's inspiration or genius. Originally there were only 'three' and the number 'three' and 'thirty-three' are favoured by Francis Bacon. (Derivatives of the word *muse* are 'music' and 'museum').

Apollo and Arcadia
"And it is not known whether my body is flesh or fish"
(Taliesin/Merlin/St Germain)

According to Robert Graves:
"The origin of where the word 'apple' came from is unknown but the word runs North-west across Europe all the way from the Balkans to Ireland in a form approximating in most languages to Apol. The word Apol is equated to the god Apollo who is the immortal part of Dionysus for Hercules combined Dionysus and Apollo into a single person and apples were offered to him by his worshippers."

"If an apple is halved cross-wise, each half shows a five pointed star in the centre as an emblem of immortality and it also represents the planet of Venus to whom the apple was sacred."

Also, according to Robert Graves, *Apollo* was worshipped as the Dolphin god in Arcadia; therefore, in the quotation mentioned above, by the 6th century Bard Taliesin/Merlin/St Germain, the poet is telling us that he was once worshipped as the god *Apollo*. (In the 16th century, Francis Bacon - St Germain, favoured using the symbol of Apollo, The Muses, Pallas Athena and themes of Arcadia).

Apollo was also equated with the dolphin, as a sea-god, and Mer - as in Merlin, means 'of the Sea'. The Merovingians (derived from the word 'Mer'), claimed their descent from Noah (St Germain) whom they regarded as the source of all 'wisdom' and this belief resurfaced a thousand years later with the Freemasons.

St Germain in his incarnations used similar names to those of his past lives. As we have already established, he was once worshipped as the god *Apollo* and from *Apollo*, we have a derivative thereof - *Apollonius of Tyana*, who in the first century AD was an incarnation of St Germain. (That particular incarnation followed his one as Joseph, the Father of the Grail Family).

According to mythology, *Apollo* was the twin of Artemis and the most popular of the Greek gods. He was known as the god of prophecy and was able to manifest himself in distant places, something St Germain was able to do when he returned in the first century AD as Apollonius of Tyana. The Roman's called *Apollo's* twin sister, Artemis, Diana, later to be worshipped as the goddess of the moon.

Apollo was one of the twelve Olympian Greek gods, a symbol of Light, who is often given the name of the 'sun god' Phoebus, the 'shining one'. *Apollo* was the patron god of archery, medicine, the care of flocks and herds etc. According to mythology, *Apollo* invented the lute (cithara). The lute became *Apollo's* favourite instrument and also became the favourite instrument of the Irish people. It was a difficult instrument to play, because of its numerous strings. The Druids were required to be able to play the lute and it was an instrument upon which the Archdruid, St Columba of Iona, was able to proficiently produce the most wonderful sounds.

(In St Germain's incarnation as the Macedonian King, Alexander the Great, his mother was a worshipper of *Apollo*).

Apollo's son, Iona/Ionias

Apollo had a son whose name was ION or Ionias. Peter Dawkins explains the meaning of *Ion* as follows:

"The letters ION are sacred and are to be found in IONA (the island where St Columba founded his famous monastery in the 6th century AD). The sacred name of St John is derived from the same sacred vowels - I.O.A. as in *JIHOVAH*. I.O.A. as in Iona also means 'Dove' - the Holy Ghost that brings Divine Light into the world of material manifestation."

Many Masters, including Mary and Jesus, had the 'dove' descend upon them.

Symbols in the Irish Book of Kells

The *Book of Kells*, attributed to St Columba in the 6th century AD, was originally written on the island of Iona but when Iona was under threat of invasion by the Vikings, the precious manuscript was transferred to the monastery at Kells in Ireland.

It is truly amazing that the *Book of Kells* has survived for over 1,400 years. The unusual symbols contained within it have mystified scholars for years. There is a portrait of John the Beloved showing him seated upon a throne holding a lighted taper in his right hand which suggest the 'Light' of 'enlightenment'. In his left there is a book which he is holding up, possibly the 'Book of Knowledge'.

Thus with the combination of the lighted taper, the Book and the throne upon which John is seated, there is a subtle suggestion that they are symbols of the hidden 'Truth' of the scriptures to be revealed during the Age of Aquarius by a person of sovereign authority (hence the 'throne').

Numerous other symbols carefully depicted are the Maltese Cross; the Saltire X (St Andrew's cross), St George's cross, the Tau cross, the Phoenix, the Eagle (symbol of John the Beloved - Kuthumi); a human figure held in the clasp of a dragon/serpent; (in Revelations, the 'dragon' represents the Church of Rome. The Lion was the emblem of the House of Judah and in the 1st century AD, the Romans persecuted members of the Royal House of Judah, particularly its Prince - the Messiah - Jesus); a Lion devouring a 'red dragon/serpent'.

Aeneas, Apollo, Arcadia and Pallas Athena

The Family of the Holy Grail was known as the 'Fisher Kings' because of the Piscean (Fish) era in which they lived. However, even though it was the Piscean era, the origins of the symbolism of the fish appear to go back much further in time.

In mythology, *Aeneas* (mentioned in a previous paragraph as being descended from Judah), was the mortal Trojan hero who was the son of Aphrodite whom the Romans worshipped as Venus, the goddess of beauty and love. The Trojan *Aeneas* is credited with having been the original founder of Rome.

According to Robert Graves in his book titled *The White Goddess*: "The name of Pallas became a royal title given to the Peloponnesian kings whose sacred beast was the dolphin." Robert Graves tells of how Pelops (for Peloponnesians) and Pallas are different titles of kings of the same early Greek dynasty.

"The warm-blooded sea creatures such as dolphins are called *cestos*. They are sea creatures with lungs and not cold-blooded fish with gills. To the sea-beast family, according to Aristotle [Kuthumi], belonged all the whales, seals, porpoises and dolphins. The land of the Peloponnesians was once called the Land of Poseidon who was the Achaean god of all sea beasts and fishes. *Arcadia was the centre of the Peloponnesians and Pallas was the god who reigned over them.*"

From whence did dolphins originate?

From the book titled *St Germain - Earth's Birth Changes*, St Germain explains as follows: "The dolphins were upon the land of Atlantis. They did not have the embodiment that they have now. But they understood how to live within the water. They mingled with humanity and merged and blended with land and water. Now the dolphins are here again, assisting humanity in the birth process of life. Through their love and joy they remind you who you are. Have you ever watched one of the dolphins? They behave as though they have not a care in the world and surely they do not. Their squeals are really resonance of children. The Daal universe is the origin of the Dolphins. It is Daal; you would spell it as in Daal-fin. There is much wisdom within your language, you know, if you will only see it."

"Do you know why so many whales and dolphins have beached themselves? It is their utter desire to reach out to you, their brothers and sisters, to be known for what and who they are - equal brothers of humanity. They desire communion. That is why they have been so assisting."

St Germain also explains that the people of Atlantis knew how to breathe underwater like the dolphins and it was from this idea that the aqua-lung was first invented. When St Germain in his incarnation as Apollo became equated with being a dolphin god, it would probably be because he, as a mortal, was able to breathe underwater for long periods of time, having had within his consciousness, the memories of his lifetime in Atlantis.

It is not being suggested that Apollo was ever a dolphin. The people who were worshipped as gods and goddesses had originated from Lemuria and Atlantis and were incredibly advanced in knowledge and technology. They are the ones who established themselves in the ancient land of Sumer, so advanced that their origins have left scholars and archaeologists baffled to explain just how they knew so much. The mythos surrounding them can be explained if we accept that the ancient gods of mythology once existed; it is just that the stories about them handed down by word of mouth over hundreds of centuries became highly exaggerated.

The story of the existence of the Mayan god Quetzalcoatl is undisputed but even he was thought to have come from the sea and returned to the sea. He brought with him amazing knowledge, particularly that of astronomy and established what is now known as the Mayan Calendar.

Quetzalcoatl also worshipped the morning and the evening star which is the planet Venus, (whom the Romans worshipped as Aphrodite). In mythology her mortal lover was the Trojan Anchises and she was the mother of the Trojan, Aeneas. Aeneas married the Latin princess, Lavinia, as recorded by Virgil whose writings influenced such people as Dante and Spenser (a pseudonym of Francis/St Germain).

According to Robert Graves, *"the grandson of Pallas was driven out of Arcadia during an invasion and went to Rome where he formed an alliance with the people of Aeneas, claiming kinship with them in virtue of common descent from Pelops, for the Pelopians had intermarried with the original Arcadians."*

The Sea King, Pallas, reputedly built the Palladium which was a statue of Pallas Athene said to have been sent down from heaven by Zeus to Aeneas, the founder of Troy. In another legend, Aeneas rescued it from the flames of Troy and brought it to Rome where it saved the city on several occasions in early history.

According to Robert Graves, "Hermes was the son of Crios (the Ram) and the Arcadians worshipped Hermes the Ram and acknowledged him as the father of their sea king Pallas. The Orphic (literally meaning 'fisherman') hymn celebrates Zeus ('the father of all gods and men' whose earliest cults are associated with mountain tops and the bringing of thunder and rain whose attribute is a thunderbolt as in Z for lightening), as both Father and Eternal Virgin, a combination of Minerva and Zeus. Minerva is universally identified with Pallas Athena who is the goddess of Wisdom and is the oldest of all the gods." (Zeus was also called Jupiter).

'Wisdom' was considered to be the female (Mother) God, who, as mentioned elsewhere, was known as Sophia. Simon the Magus, one of the disciples of Jesus, was one of the most influential teachers of Sophia who became labelled by the Romans as a 'heretic'. He was also known as a Gnostic - a lover of Sophia.

The Fish

"Listen, and appear to us,
In the name of great Oceanus,
By the earth-shaking Neptune's mace..."
(John Milton)

In a future chapter, the disciples will be discussed. However it is relevant to this chapter to mention that during the era of Jesus, there was a Mystery School operating and certain disciples were initiated into the Orphic Mysteries and Jonah Mysteries (as in the symbolical story in the Bible of Jonah and the Whale). The 'Age of Pisces' which was the 'era' of Jesus was ruled by Jupiter-Neptune.

As Robert Graves points out, "the symbolical 'fish' (such as in the allegorical story of Jonah being swallowed by a whale), had from ancient times, played an important role in the sacred Mysteries. Accordingly, the Jewish Torah or Law which suggests Egyptian influence once held sea-beasts such as the dolphin and porpoise, in reverence. The Jews were tributary once to the Philistines whose god was a sea-beast of many changes named Dagon. One of his other names was Oannes."

"The Philistines conquered the Jews and placed the Ark in Dagon's temple before his own statue and the statue broke into pieces." Robert Graves comments that "the legendary hero who led the Jews into Judea was called Jeshua, son of the Fish."

The 'fish' was also one of the symbols of the Cathars (the 'Johannites' who followed the teachings of John the Beloved - Kuthumi) who were so ruthlessly persecuted by the Church of Rome between the 12th and 14th centuries AD.

In the era of Jesus, the symbology of the 'fish' once again played an important role, and was equated with the ancient Mysteries of Arcadia. According to Robert Graves, the disciples used a secret sign by which to identify themselves. "They would trace the outline of a fish and this became their password signifying that they belonged to the followers of Jeshua (Jesus in Greek) ben (son of) Joseph [St Germain] which was the title of the Anointed One. The passwords used were the first letters of *ichtus* (fish) which stood for *Jesus Christos Theos* and the disciples followed Pythagorean [Kuthumi] asceticism."

In the era of the Messiah, Jesus ben Joseph once again symbolically became the 'son of the fish', because St Germain had once been worshipped as the dolphin god, Apollo, and it seems highly probable that St Germain was once King Pallas whose female counterpart was Athene, the goddess of 'Wisdom' whom the Gnostics called 'Sophia'. For the words of wisdom at the beginning of the Gospel of John (Kuthumi) tell us:

"In the beginning was the Word, and the word was with God, and the Word was God."

According to information contained in Peter Dawkins' book titled *The Great Vision*:

"The Mind of God must first conceive the Divine Thought of Creation. It must become conscious, creating an Idea and Vision of what God desires, which Idea and Vision can then act as the architectural Plan for building the perfect Temple or life-form out of Matter. The first stage of Thought is called 'Creation' - the creation of God's Idea is God's Mind."

"And the spirit of God moved upon the face of the Waters."

"God's Mind became active. Its 'Spirit' became active as Divine Thought. In early Christian texts the Holy Spirit is explained as being the Holy Breath (i.e. Divine Love or Life) and the Holy Wisdom. The Holy Breath utters the Wisdom as the WORD OF TRUTH, radiating it as LIGHT into the heavenly Mind, wherein it is reflected as the perfect vision of TRUTH."

Parallels of the Ancient Mysteries and the Bible

A statue of a wild boar is said to have been placed over one of the gates of Jerusalem in honour of *Adonis*. A key to the cryptic symbolism utilized by Sir Francis Bacon was the use of the 'wild boar'. The boar was equated with *Adonis/ Tammuz* and was sacred to the goddess Diana (a variant of Anna, Athena, Anu, etc.).

According to ancient mythology, *Adonis* was killed by a boar whilst out hunting. The Red *Rose* is said to have grown from the blood of Adonis and became a Kabalistic (Cabalistic) symbol. (One of the poems of Francis Bacon, alias, Shakespeare, was *Venus and Adonis*, which tells of the death of *Adonis*).

The Druids also worshipped the boar as a sacred animal. A boar's head served on a plate was symbolic of 'knowledge' and 'wisdom'. According to the Biblical tradition, Salome requested the head of John the Baptist to be served on a plate. The story of the Head of John the Baptist, like most of the stories in the Bible, is allegorical and contains some of the Ancient Mysteries.

It has previously been mentioned that traditionally, *Adonis* was born at midnight on the 24th December; Bethlehem was celebrated as the traditional birthplace of the Master Jesus, also born on the same day as *Adonis*/Lord in earlier times.

The Divine Child: According to Robert Graves: "The worship of the Divine Child was established in Minoan Crete, its most famous early home in Europe," and that "the Sun-gods Dionysus, Apollo and Mithras were all reputedly born at the Winter Solstice is well known, and the Christian Church first fixed the Nativity feast of Jesus Christ at the same season, in the year 273 AD."

The 'Basket': Robert also writes that: "the Delphians worshipped *Dionysus* once a year as the new-born child, 'the Child in the Harvest Basket', which was a shovel-shaped basket of rush and osier used as a harvest basket, a cradle, a manger."

In the Egyptian legends of *Osiris*, his body was floated down the Nile in a basket.

According to the Biblical tradition, *Moses* was floated down the Nile in a basket.

Although Jesus was not 'floated down the Nile', he was the 'Divine Child', who like *Adonis* and *Eleusis* was born to a 'Virgin' and placed in a 'manger'. In reality however, according to the Rosicrucian authority, Spencer Lewis, their ancient records state that Jesus, as a child of the Essenes, was born in one of their hospices - he was the expected Messiah of whom their prophets had foretold, and all the necessary preparations had been carried out beforehand.

The 'Virgin': The position of the constellation of Virgo was understood by the ancients as giving birth to the Sun on the 25th December, hence the Virgin (Virgo) with the Child of Light. This is the date that Christians celebrate as being the birth of the Son of the Virgin Mary.

Thus, it can be seen that its origins are based upon the ancient 'Mysteries' which have become embodied into Christianity, but whose origins are far older.

Hiram Abif

One of the legendary figures involved in the rites of Freemasonry, of who mention has been given in a previous chapter, was Hiram of Tyre, also called Hiram Abif who was the architect and the Master-Builder of the Temple of Solomon.

According to C.W. Leadbeater, the legend of Hiram Abif forms part of the Third Degree in Freemasonry.

The 'tools' supposedly used by Hiram in the building of the Temple of Jerusalem, namely the compass and the square, were representative of the Macrocosm and the Microcosm and became the symbols of the Freemasons.

According to legend, Hiram divided the men, who were to work upon the temple, into three groups. They were called Entered Apprentices, Fellow-Craftsmen, and Master Masons and were given secret passwords and signs in order to identify their respective excellence in their work or accomplishments; the origins of which have been passed down through the ages to Freemasons.

In an attempt to gain the knowledge of the Master's secret word from Hiram, three Fellow-Craftsmen whose names were Jubela, Jubelo, and Jubelum, assassinated Hiram when he refused to divulge his knowledge. They murdered him at the west gate of the Temple which was symbolic of the setting sun. (It was from Osiris, who was also known as Set, that we acquired the word 'setting'). Each of the names of Jubela, Jubelo and Jubelum are symbolical for they contain the word 'Bel', a god worshipped by the Sumerians as their 'Sun God' and the Celtic Druids continued to worship 'Bel' from which their festival of Beltane was derived.

The three assassins buried Hiram's body and placed a sprig of acacia upon the grave. Later, when King Solomon discovered what had happened, the three men were caught and executed.

Hiram, in common with Lazarus, was 'raised' from the dead. This murder was considered to be a ritualistic one and equated with the Egyptian legends of Osiris, Isis and Horus, containing the key elements of death and rebirth. The legend of Hiram is comprised of a series of Pythagorean numbers. One of the sacred numbers was three, as in the Pythagorean triangle.

In Egyptian, Hermes' name was also Tachut, which in Hebrew is 'Tachat' and which in Greek translates as 'Thoth' meaning 'under' or 'beneath'. The legendary Hiram Abif was buried underneath a sprig of Acacia. The Acacia, which in Australia is called 'wattle', was symbolic of 'immortality. It is also known as the 'thorny bush' from which the 'Crown of Thorns' was made and placed upon the head of Jesus on his way to the crucifixion and obviously, the placing of such a crown, had its own symbolic significance.

According to C.W. Leadbeater, Hiram Abif has been identified with Abibaal, the father of Hiram, King of Tyre and that it is possible that Hiram was not a personal name at all, but a title of the Kings of Tyre, just as Pharaoh was of those of Egypt.

"The name of Hiram Abif is somewhat altered in higher degrees, and even in the Bible it sometimes appears as Huram. A further modification is Khairum or Khurum. Khur by itself means white or noble. There is a variant Khri, which under certain circumstances becomes Khris. This would suggest some possible connection with Krishna and Christ. There are certain passages in the Book of Job where he speaks of the orb of the sun, and the word he uses is Khris."

"It is on record that Hiram, King of Tyre, was the first man who offered sacrifice of fire to Khur, who afterwards became Heracles. Plutarch tells us that the Persians of his day called the sun Kuros, and he connects it with the Greek word Kurios, which means Lord, which we find in the Church service as 'Kyrie eleison'. Khur is also connected with the Egyptian name Horus, who was also Her-Ra and Haroeris, names of the sun-god."

"That Hiram was a widow's son is also a significant fact. Horus as the child of Isis was the reincarnation of his own Father Osiris, and so as a posthumous child might well be described as a widow's son. Though of the tribe of Naphtali, he was born and resided in Tyre, and may well therefore have learned from the Dionysian fraternity which had a centre there."

The name Hermes is derived from 'Herm', which was a form of 'Hiram'.

Maya, Vulcan and Thor

There are various spellings of *Maya*, such as *Mai* which is one of the brightest stars in our constellation. The Roman goddess, *Maia*, was the wife of *Vulcan*, the god of fire equated with *Thor*, the 'god of Thunder' and the Romans worshipped her as one of their nature goddesses. It was from her name that we obtained the month named 'May'. Maya was also equated with the celebration of the Druids of 'May Day', which they called 'Beltane' in honour of the 'Sun god' *Bel.*

Although the brothers, John the Beloved and James are discussed in greater detail in future chapters, it is pertinent at this point of time to mention that in the Bible, they were called by an Aramaic term, *Boanerges* and Jesus referred to them as the 'sons of Thunder'. This terminology applied to a form of 'initiation' which they underwent.

In mythology, the god of Thunder, *Thor*, (also known as *Woden*), was the son of *Odin* who was the Germanic chief god. With the coming of Christianity to Britain, the Anglo-Saxons were forced to adopt the Roman calendar and they named the fifth day, *Thur-Day* for *Thor* - it thus became known as *Thursday. Thor's* frequent companion was *Loki*, the 'fire god' who could disguise himself in the shape of a hawk/eagle.

Nicolai Tolstoy in his book titled *The Quest for Merlin* compares the death of the Norse god, Odin (known as a great god of 'wisdom') to that of the fate of Jesus. Jesus was crucified/hung upon a cross (made from a tree); Odin hung himself from the Cosmic tree - a voluntary death from which he gained resurrection. Odin thirsted in his agony - as did Jesus. Odin screamed at the moment of truth, just as Christ 'cried with a loud voice.'

According to mythology, Maya was the mother of *Faunas*, equated with *Pan*, the Roman god associated with herdsmen and shepherds, woods and pastures, all equated with *Arcadia*. Arcadia was reputed to have been in the mainland of Greece and it was traditionally the home of the god *Pan* (Faunas). During the Renaissance, the pastoral theme of Arcadia was adopted by such artists as Leonardo da Vinci

(Kuthumi), Botticelli, and Nicholas Poussin's - famous for his painting titled *Les Berges d'Arcadie* ('The Shepherds of Arcadia').

Maia, whose name means 'mother', lived in a cave on Mount Cyllene in Arcadia. Homer in Greek mythology refers to *Maia* as one of the daughters of the Pleiades, daughter of Atlas and mother of Hermes by Zeus, and like *Thor*, Zeus was also equated with being a god of Thunder and Lightening. In the Bible, we also find that two of the disciples are likened to gods, such as Zeus.

Dionysus - Bacchus, Orpheus
"I have been in Asia before the building of Rome",
"I have been winged by the genius of the splendid crozier"
(Taliesin/Merlin/St Germain)

In the quotation, 'I have been in Asia before the building of Rome', the Bard, Taliesin/Merlin/St Germain is alluding to the fact that he was once worshipped as the god *Dionysus*, the god whom the Greeks of Thrace worshipped, one that was equated with the *Elysian Mysteries* which, in later centuries became the religion of a submerged society.

The Greek god *Dionysus* was also known as the Roman god *Bacchus* who is said to have been the son of Zeus. According to mythology, *Dionysus* married the king of Crete's daughter, *Ariadne*, and gave her a crown of stars that became known as a constellation after her death. During the Renaissance period, *Ariadne* became another goddess associated with *Arcadia*.

The Cauldron and the Cup:
According to legend, *Dionysus* was taken to Mount Nysa in India where he was taught Mysteries of great secrecy and had a magical cup from whence inspiration came. In the story of the *Romance of Taliesin* (written by St Germain in the 6th century AD), we learn of little Gwion who stirs the magical cauldron, spills three drops on his fingers, licks them and subsequently goes through various transformations and is eventually reborn as Taliesin, owing all his inspiration and possession of all knowledge, from the cauldron.

We find in the legends of the Grail, the famous Grail Cup which Joseph of Arimathea supposedly captured drops of the blood of Jesus.

Correspondingly, in Celtic mythology, Bran the Blessed owned a magical cauldron.

The Cup and the Cauldron are receptacles equated with the attaining of 'Wisdom' or 'Sophia'.

Dionysus carried a magic staff (crozier) entwined with ivy. (Ivy is associated with the Druids as a healing plant). He eventually made his way from Mount Nysa, in India, across Asia and arrived in Greece on a chariot driven by panthers

- the ivy and the panther both being sacred to *Dionysus.* Panthers were associated with the Ancient Egyptian Mysteries and Isis is said to have driven in chariots drawn by panthers.

Robert Graves in his book titled *The White Goddess* informs us that *Dionysus* visited Egypt and was entertained by Proteus, King of Pharos. The Mysteries of the cult of *Dionysus* were eventually to reach Rome and were kept a closely guarded secret. *A symbol of Dionysus was the red Rose equated with the one that grew from the blood of Adonis after he was killed by a boar.*

Orpheus and Dionysus

According to Robert Graves, the revival of the ancient and traditional Mysteries of Eleusis and the invention of Orphism were thought to have become emerged into the Minoan Mysteries of the birth and death and resurrection of Zagreus (the son of Zeus) the 'Divine Child'.

In mythology, Zagreus was a Cretan god who was *usually identified with Dionysus and played an important part in the beliefs of the sect practicing the Mysteries of Orpheus.* From Peter Dawkins' book titled *Francis Bacon - Herald of the New Age* we learn that Francis Bacon, writing under the name of Shakespeare personified *Dionysus.*

"Dionysus is the god of civilization and drama. As such he was considered to be the great playwright, and the founder and patron of the theatre. His festivals consisted chiefly in the representation of the Mysteries as stage-plays. The name Dionysus is composed of two Greek words, Dio meaning 'God' or 'Source of Light' and nyos meaning either 'son' or 'the lame one'."

"The lameness is a cryptic reference to Orpheus as the Rich Fisher King (i.e. the Grail King). *The Hierophants of Dionysus, were considered to be incarnations of Dionysus, and were each known as Orpheus, 'the Fisherman'. That is to say, Orpheus and Dionysus were seen as being identical.'*

"Orpheus, who is the Grail King - the great Fisherman who fishes for the souls of humanity in the waters of the world in order to draw them out into the airy light of heaven - is said to be lame. The lameness is a result of a wound bestowed by humanity upon the world, and the Grail Kingdom (the world) will remain barren until this wound is healed."

"The lameness also occurs in the initiatory story of Oedipus, another character representing the Grail King, who was said to have been born lame, with a hole in his foot.

For this reason Shakespeare (Francis Bacon), in his sonnets, refers to himself as being lame."

"What is more, according to the 17th century historian Camden, 'Bacco', which is the German and Italian rendering of the name 'Bacon', means 'the lame'. It was said by the wits of the period, when Francis Bacon was created Baron Verulam in 1618 and the Viscount St Alban in 1620-1, and it was generally known that he was in debt, that Bacon was 'very lame' as Baron and 'all bones' when Viscount!"

From Peter Dawkins' book *Arcadia*, we learn the following:

"According to *The Schoolmaster*, written by Francis' and the Queen's old tutor, Sir Roger Ascham, **'Euphues'** means 'he that is apt by goodness of wit and appliable by readiness of will to learning.' The name has an affinity with Orpheus, the founder of the Orphic Mysteries, and the Society of the Rose (instituted in order to create a high understanding between people in which all would flourish naturally and war would become impossible). It also has an affinity with Euphorbus, a Trojan hero of whom Pythagoras [Kuthumi] claimed to be a reincarnation."

The 'Land beyond the North Wind'

Traditionally, Apollo was honoured among the Hyperboreans above all other gods. Hyperborea - the 'Land beyond the North Wind' is considered to be Britain and Britain means 'The Land of the Covenant'. According to Robert Graves:

"The Hercules-god of the Orphic mystics was Apollo the Hyperborean. Diodorus Siculus in his quotation from Hecataeus makes it clear that in the sixth century BC the 'land of the Hyperboreans', where Apollo's mother Latona was born, and where Apollo was honoured above all other gods, was Britain...*Ireland, which lay outside the Roman Empire, may have been 'the Land of the Hyperboreans'.*" (The Archangel 'Michael' controls the North - Hyperborea).

According to author Edmund Harold in his book titled *Second Sight*, Kuthumi is the Co-Protector of The Grail, together with the Archangel Michael. However, the Essenes gave their High Priests angelic titles. The title of 'Michael' was allotted to John the Beloved Disciple (Kuthumi).

Although this information will be referred to in a future chapter, it is relevant here to mention that in the 19th century, a Rose-Cross poster was issued in Paris by the Salon of the Rose-Cross, most probably upon the instructions of a certain Joseph 'Peladan' who was the Grand Master at the time. The poster depicts Leonardo da Vinci (Kuthumi) on the right, as 'The Keeper of the Grail' and during that time he was the Grand Master of the Priory of Sion (Zion - Jerusalem). Joseph of Arimathea is to the left, depicted as a Rose-Cross Knight with both hands firmly clasped upon his sword (the 'Truth') and between them is the Archangel Michael upon whose clothing is the Rose-Cross hovering above the 'Grail Cup'. All of this may appear to be very symbolic, but it has great significance. It is noteworthy that Kuthumi in his incarnation as St Patrick was buried in Ireland, along with St

Columba and St Brigid. St Columba had prophesied that they would all be buried together, and the prophecy did indeed come to fruition.

Isis and Cassiopeia

Ancient paintings of the Egyptian Queen, Isis, depict her with a crown of stars upon her head and she is equated with the woman in Revelation in the Bible, written by the Master Kuthumi in his incarnation as John the Beloved Disciple.

"And there appeared a great wonder in heaven: a woman clothed with the sun, and the moon under her feet, and upon her head a crown of twelve stars."

Isis is at the very heart of the ancient Mysteries. We learn from ancient Egyptian inscriptions that Isis is the Virgin immortalized in the constellation of Virgo. She is the World Mother with a serpent under her feet and a crown of stars upon her head; in her arms she carries the young Sun God. To the Egyptians, the serpent represented 'Wisdom' and in the allegorical Biblical story of Eve, the apple and the serpent in the Garden of Eden also represented 'Wisdom'.

Like Isis, Mary, in medieval symbolism was represented as the Queen of Heaven and the 'seat of Wisdom' whose symbol was the *Mystic Rose.* The Rose is also sacred to Isis, symbolic of the 'Tree of Life'.

Isis has always been depicted as the Virgin of the World and is equated with the constellation of Cassiopeia, representing 'Wisdom' as in 'Sophia', known to the ancients as the 'Virgin/Woman with Child' - represented as the celestial virgin with the Sun god in her arms, the significance of which was associated with the annual passage of the sun and the zodiac.

From the book titled *From The Stone Age To Christianity* (1955) by William Foxwell Albright we are informed as follows:

"In the recently discovered Aramaic Proverbs of Akhiquar, from about the 6th century BC, we read: '(Wi)sdom is (from) the gods, and to the gods she is precious; for (ever) her kingdom is fixed in heav(en), for the lord of the Holy Ones (i.e. the gods of heaven) hath raised her'."

"A Jewish counterpart to this is found in Enoch 42:1-2 (second century BC): 'Since Wisdom found no place to dwell, she received an abode in heaven; when Wisdom came to dwell among men and found no abode, she returned to her place and dwelt with the angels'."

"Ben Sir (early second century BC) makes Wisdom similarly say: 'I came forth from the mouth of the Highest, and like vapour I have covered the earth; I have made my abode in the heights, and my throne on a pillar of cloud'."

"Here Wisdom is poetically likened to a breath issuing from the mouth of God and spreading until it penetrates into all recesses. In the Wisdom of Solomon,

Wisdom is called 'a breath of the power of God and an emanation (out-flowing) of the pure effulgence of the Almighty'. Finally in Philo Judaeus we find that Wisdom (Sophia) was the first emanation of God, who created the world and became the mother of the Logos, remaining herself a virgin, since Goddess does not generate in human fashion."

From information contained in Peter Dawkins' book titled *The Virgin Ideal* we learn the following: "The name of the constellation of Cassiopeia means 'the enthroned Lady' - the Queen who inhabits her throne in the heavens - the Virgin Queen, the Celestial Queen, the Queen who is in fact the actual throne itself. Her Arabic name, El Seder, means 'the freed'. In her hand she holds a branch of victory. She is none other than Isis (or Mary), symbolically speaking, who is represented in hieroglyph as a throne - the throne upon which sits her son - husband, the King of Light."

"Every time a star is born in Cassiopeia (i.e. with every nova and super-nova), it is seen as the birth of a child of Light to the heavenly Virgin Queen. Thus, when the 1572-4 super-nova appeared, it was seen as a sign that somewhere on Earth a super-manifestation of the Christ Light was being or was about to be born."

"The super-nova appeared the year that Francis and Anthony Bacon completed their studies and initiatory training in the Platonic Academy at Gorhambury, St Albans, becoming full-fledged 'knights' of the Academy. They then went to Trinity College, Cambridge, in April, 1573, and the star continued to shine brightly for the whole of that first year at Cambridge, the year in which Francis had his great moment, helped by Anthony, he began to plan and prepare the work, secretly."

The Virgin and the Sun God

Mary, in Biblical terminology is depicted as a 'Virgin' and Jesus as the 'Son of God'.

The Celestial Virgin with the Sun god in her arms had its origins back in the time when the ancients divided the life of the sun into four seasons which we know as summer, autumn, winter and spring.

During the various phases, the Sun god, when he was born in the dark of winter, was represented as a dependant infant being nourished until the summer when he had grown into a mature 'Light'.

The Celtic Druids called their summer Llughnsad; Autumn was Samhain; Winter was Imbolc and Spring was Beltane (named after the Sun-god). The birth of the Sun god was celebrated when the darkness of winter could be replaced by the glorious return of the son/sun of light.

In ancient times, the Sun was considered to be a universal deity (god) and it has been previously discussed that the Egyptians believed that the Sun was God and not God that created the Sun.

The annual passage of the sun is through twelve houses of the heavens and it was mentioned in a previous paragraph in this chapter that the initiates of the religion of Mithras, donned masks of animals equated with the twelve zodiacal signs. It was not coincidence that the apostles of Jesus always maintained that there had to be twelve in number and that after Judas betrayed Jesus, they again elected a twelfth member. It is also noteworthy that it was not until the 12th century that the Grail stories began to circulate.

SUMMARY

1. The god who was once worshipped as *Apollo* was an incarnation of St Germain. *Apol* meant 'apple' and it is thought to have been derived from *Apollo* whose worshippers would serve him apples.

2. The word *Aval* also means 'apple' as in *Avalon* and the apple is symbolic of 'Wisdom' (as in the allegorical story of Eve who picked the apple from the Tree of Knowledge in the Garden of Eden).

3. Avalon was the 'veiled' name given to a place/or places where the Sacred Wisdom was taught.

4. The god, once worshipped as *Adonis* (from whence we derive the word 'Adonai' meaning 'Lord') was once an incarnation of St Germain and it was from the blood of Adonis who was killed by a wild 'boar' (the symbol of Francis Bacon), that a beautiful red rose grew; thus the *Red Rose* and the *Boar* became his symbols.

5. The Greek goddess Athena, with her connections to Arcadia, was once widely worshipped all over the Greek world, particularly in Troy and Athens which was named after her. Her prominence dominates the story of the *Masters of the Mystical Rose* as does 'Avalon'.

6. Dionysus was killed by a wild boar and a red rose grew from where his blood had spilt on the ground, thus the *Red Rose* became one of his symbols, as did the *Boar*.

7. After winning a battle victoriously, Alexander the Great (St Germain) set up an altar to Athena.

8. The Hierophants of Dionysus, who were considered to be incarnations of Dionysus, were each known as Orpheus, 'the Fisherman'. That is to say, Orpheus and Dionysus were seen as being identical. Orpheus, who is the Grail King - the great Fisherman who fishes for the souls of humanity in the waters of the world in order to draw them out into the airy light of heaven.

9. Certain of the disciples of Jesus underwent what were known as the Orpheus initiations - they were known as the 'Fishers' of men who recruited followers for the Sacred Teachings.

MASTERS DISCUSSED IN THIS CHAPTER
Noah - St Germain
Apollo - St Germain
Dionysus - St Germain
King Pallas - St Germain?
Alexander the Great - St Germain
Joseph Father of the Grail Family - St Germain
Apollonius of Tyana - St Germain
Merlin/Taliesin St Germain
Sir Francis Bacon - St Germain
King David of the House of Judah - Kuthumi
Pythagoras - Kuthumi
John the Beloved Disciple - Kuthumi
St Patrick - Kuthumi
King Arthur - Kuthumi
Leonardo da Vinci - Kuthumi

NOTES AND RECOMMENDED READING

Robert Graves, _The White Goddess_, (Faber & Faber, U.K. 1961)

Nicolai Tolstoy, _The Quest for Merlin_, (Hamish Hamilton, 1985)

Betty Radice, _Who's Who In The Ancient World_, (Penguin, U.K. 1973)

Azena Ramanda, _St Germain, Earth's Birth Changes_, (Triad Publishers, Queensland, 1993)

Peter Dawkins, _Arcadia_, (Francis Bacon Research Trust, Warwick, U.K.)

Peter Dawkins, _The Virgin Ideal_, (Francis Bacon Research Trust, Warwick, U.K.)

Book of Kells, (Trinity College, Dublin, Ireland)

William Foxwell Albright, _From The Stone Age To Christianity_, (Doubleday Anchor Books, U.S.A. 1957)

Edmund Harold, _Second Sight_, (Grail Publications, Sydney, Australia, 1994)

Michael Howard, _The Occult Conspiracy_, (Rider & Rider, U.K. 1989)

C.W. Leadbeater, _The Hidden Life In Freemasonry_, (Theosophical Publishing House, U.K. 1975)

CHAPTER 12

Origin of the Serpent-Dragon, Glastonbury & St Michael's Mount

"There is a secrecy and silence observed in all Mysteries"
(Tertullian)

The Origin of the Serpent-Dragon

Back in the days of Atlantis, the Masters were known as 'Sons of the Serpent-god' or 'Sons of the Dragon' and these titles were also bestowed upon the Egyptian Hierophants. The 'Serpent' was symbolical of sacred knowledge and the symbol of the two serpents entwined around a staff as an attribute of Hermes Trismegistus (Thrice Greatest) is the emblem of the medical profession, known as the Caduceus.

During the twelfth and thirteenth centuries AD, the Celtic legends written about Arthur and Merlin contained the name of 'Pendragon' which simply meant 'Head Dragon/Serpent' - someone who had become a highly initiated Druidic Priest, having passed all the 'Initiation Ceremonies' which had been handed down from the days of Atlantis through Egyptian 'rites' that were eventually introduced to the Celtic tribes in Ireland and various parts of Britain, such as Glastonbury where the first Celtic Church in Britain was founded by Joseph of Arimathea to teach the ancient sacred Mysteries of the *Mystical Rose*.

The dragon/serpent is an ancient symbol of the highest spiritual essence, embodying not only wisdom, but strength and the divine power of transformation.

When certain of the ancient documents came into the hands of the early Latin theologians, they misinterpreted the meaning of the 'Serpent' and equated the Serpent/Dragon with 'Hell Fire and Damnation', thereby totally misunderstanding that the *'Serpent' was an 'energy force' without which all forms of life would cease to exist.*

Those who are Reiki healers or who perform any sort of natural healing, will understand the natural healing energy field that is freely available to be utilized for healing and those participating in meditation will experience the Kundalini energy which is symbolized by the serpent/dragon energy that lies dormant at the base of the spine until it ascends through the chakras. Those who have read the *Celestine Prophecy* will have some understanding about energy and the auras that emanate from the energy around people, animals, plants, trees and rocks etc.

Satan

The early Church continued throughout the centuries to use such terms as the 'Devil/Satan' and 'Hell' as a means of 'fear' and 'control'.

In her book titled *The Secret Doctrine*, Helena Blavatsky wrote:

"The Devil is now called Darkness by the Church, whereas, in the Bible he is called the 'Son of God (see Job), the bright star of the early morning, Lucifer' (see Isaiah). (The name Lucifer means the 'bearer of light' from 'Lucius' and 'Pher')."

"There is a whole philosophy of dogmatic craft in the reason why the first Archangel, who sprang from the depths of Chaos, was called Lux (Lucifer), the 'Luminous Son of the Morning'. He was transformed by the Church (of Rome) into Lucifer or Satan."

"Hermes was worshipped as the god of Wisdom, known in Egypt, Syria and Phoenicia, as Thoth, Tat, Seth, and Sat-an (the latter *not to be taken* in the sense applied to it by Moslems and Christians). In Greece he was known as Kadmos. The Cabbalists identify him with Adam-*Kadmon* and with Enoch."

The word 'Satan' is also derived from 'Saturn'. Incidentally, the day of the week, Saturday is derived from these names. (Sunday was named after the Sun god).

According to information contained in Peter Dawkins' book titled *The Great Vision*:

"The 'Mother' aspect in Hebrew tradition was called 'Sabbaoth', which is derived from the word for the day of rest or peace - the 'Sabbath' - which is Saturn's (or Satan's day). The whole truth concerning Satan, 'the Adversary', (who was also created as the Crown of God's Creation), and the redemption of Satan from Darkness to Light, is the secret of Divine Intelligence, pierced by the rays of Wisdom shining from the divine Heart and being transformed by the process of life from the darkness of ignorance to the light of knowledge..."

"The mystery-name *Lucifer,* has been grossly misunderstood and its significance horribly distorted and perverted by ignorant and malicious souls. When Jesus said that he 'beheld Satan as lightning fallen from heaven', he was referring to the Divine Immanence incarnating into Matter in order to produce the living soul. Jesus was stating that he had beheld the beginning and origin of all things. There is only one Light, and that is the Son or Thought of God; and there is only one Heaven from which all that Light comes, and that is the Father or Mind of God."

"Lucifer, or Satan, is symbolised by the Serpent. A compound symbol was invented, that of the Dragon, based upon the Serpent symbol, which was used to teach the details of evolutionary life and composition of the soul."

Saturn and Jupiter

From Peter Dawkins' book titled *The Virgin Ideal*, we are informed as follows:
"In Symbology, Saturn represents the invisible Father-God who gives his power and authority to Jupiter, his Son, who dispenses that power as light. Jupiter thus becomes, or is, the symbol of the outpouring of light and his name, Iu-pater, means 'father of Light'. His symbols are thus the thunderbolt or lightening flash (of inspiration, illumination), and the eagle of the higher mind which can dispense such light to other levels and beings."

"Saturn, though, is the invisible, dark source of that light, holding the secret of life - of birth and death, and of time and eternity -hence his symbols of the scythe and hour-glass." (Saturn was also known to the Greeks as *Chronus/Kronus* - Father or Lord of Time).

Jupiter was the principal Roman god, originally a divinity of the sky. He is also identified with Zeus. *Ju* is relation to *Dyeu* meaning 'sky' and *piter - pater* meaning 'father'. (Zeus was the son of Chronus/Kronus).

According to Peter Dawkins:

"When the planet Jupiter conjuncts with Saturn, it is like an outer statement of something happening somewhere upon Earth to do with the transfer of bestowal of light. The sages of old took it as the completion and fulfillment of an initiatory cycle; and in the Jewish tradition (stemming from the Magi of Egypt and Chaldea) a conjunction of Saturn and Jupiter in Pisces signified vitally important occurrences in regard to Israel; namely, the Coming of the Messiah..."

"Saturn and Jupiter conjunct approximately every 19-20 years. The number 19 indicates an initiatory cycle, with 20 completing it, so that 21 really does imply a 'Coming of Age'. 19-20 years is also the Metonic Cycle (c.7,000 days) in which the Sun and Moon return to their original positions relative to each other and the Earth. The Druids and others used this Metonic Cycle as the prescribed period for training and initiation."

The Serpent Energy/Spirit and Feng Shui

In the Book of Revelation, written by St John the Beloved Disciple (Kuthumi), in circa 70 AD, the Archangel Michael is the slayer of the dragon with his mighty sword (symbolical of the 'Truth' to be revealed) and as such, he is equated with St George (Kuthumi) who was also a slayer of the dragon. The Archangel Michael presides over all the sacred areas through which the Mary/Michael energy Ley lines (Serpent/Dragon lines) weave their 'serpentine' energy in Britain. *Dragon* and *Serpent* are synonymous and represent the *Earth Spirit* which our own Australian Aborigines call the *Rainbow Serpent.*

The Chinese call the serpent energy, or Earth Spirit, *Feng Shui,* the study of which has gained a great deal of popularity by Westerners in the latter years. People utilize *Feng Shui* in the décor of their homes and alignment of their gardens. One example is that a mirror placed in the front hall of one's house, facing the front door, is said to ward off angry spirits and create a better energy within the house itself.

Our home is partly on a Dragon line. To the right hand side as one enters the gate and wanders the winding path through the garden, there is a sense of very pleasant 'energy' and it continues all the way up the back to where a very ancient mulberry tree happily grows. We felt the 'energy' from the moment we first embarked upon purchasing the house. All and sundry who have since visited our home over the years, have always remarked about how the place has a 'great feel' to it.

For several years, I just accepted the general overall feeling without giving much thought to its origins. Then, in 1998, upon the occasion of my daughter's 21st birthday, I had ordered from a local party shop, dozens of helium balloons to add to the festivities of her party that evening. When the man delivered the balloons, he said "did you realize that your pathway lies on a Dragon line and that it goes all the way up the back to your mulberry tree?" I just smiled in acknowledgement, having at last received the answer I had sought.

In 1970, when my husband and I lived on the island of Hong Kong, we were fascinated to learn how superstitious the local inhabitants were as to where they built their houses and apartments. Even the gravestones had to face in a certain direction. Our apartment was at the top of Stubbs Road, overlooking Happy Valley, a place where many years before, the government had cut a road through the mountain causing a great deal of alarm amongst the local Chinese, for it was a special place where the sacred serpent/dragon energy dwelled.

During our time there, a major typhoon hit Hong Kong (ironically it was called Typhoon *Rose*). It caused great havoc and devastation as it swept through the colony destroying many shanties and hillside apartments which slid down the escarpments in mudslides caused by the torrential rain, particularly in the area above Happy Valley. It was the belief of the locals that these places had been built where they should not have been and the consequence was the revenge of the 'Feng Shui'. (The word 'Typhoon' was derived from 'Typhon', a mythological monster that was defeated by Zeus' thunderbolts).

According to John Michell in his book titled *The Earth Spirit*:

"A Chinese' geomancer's compass is the instrument by which he determines the correct site for every tomb, temple and house and the correct use for every piece of land, thus preserving the flow of the earth's subtle currents and directing the work of men in accordance with the interest of nature. The rings on the disk relate to the points of the compass, astrological influences and local landscape features. The beautiful, productive and densely populated landscape of old China was a creation of the geomancer's art."

Yin and Yang

The translated meaning of Feng Shui means 'wind and water', the principle of which is a balance of the forces of *Yang* and *Yin* which are the positive and negative energies.

According to Francis Hitching in his book titled *The World Atlas of Mysteries*:

"In Chinese thought, all things are supposed to have an essence that makes them live, drawn from the breath of Heaven (Yang) and the breath of Earth (Yin). Theoretically, productivity is caused by the breath of Heaven descending and mingling with the breath of the Earth. The most auspicious spots are those obtaining a maximum of heavenly breath, and so the configuration on the landscape is important."

"Allied to this is the concept of dragon paths, or *lung-mei*, along which currents of vital power flow. Yin (female) current flows along mountainous ridges and ranges of hills. Yang (male) current runs along valleys and through subterranean channels."

"John Michell, the British antiquarian who has written about the subject at length, says that 'the former ought always to be to the left and the latter to the right, of any town or habitation, which should preferably be protected by them, as in the crook of an elbow'."

"But this was only the beginning of the complexity, since high and abrupt escarpments were considered Yang, and rounded elevations, Yin." (The Yin force of nature, represented by the earth spirit - the serpent energy is a mercurial current which glides in serpentine channels through the earth's crust).

Ley Lines

From further interesting information contained in Francis Hitching's book titled *The World Atlas of Mysteries* we learn that: "in the 1920's, a worthy antiquarian named Alfred Watkins of Herefordshire, U.K. began to offer his theories about a 'ley system' which had once been marked out on the face of Britain, a vein-like pattern of lines that criss-cross each other like a geometric spider's web."

"The megalithic site known as Stonehenge was an accurate observatory. It was noted by Sir Norman Lockyer in his book *Stonehenge and other British Stone Monuments Astronomically Considered*, that a curious geometrical pattern had its apex at Stonehenge. Sir Norman discovered that the line of the midsummer sunrise could be traced backwards exactly six miles to the Neolithic settlement/ religious centre called Grovely Castle. There was an identical distance between Stonehenge and Old Sarum, a similar prehistoric hill-top site on which the original Salisbury Cathedral had been built. When the three places were joined up on a map, a near-perfect equilateral triangle emerged. Surely this was evidence of long-distance planning? And was this knowledge still extant in historic times? For mysteriously, when the new Salisbury Cathedral was built in 1220 AD, it was placed mathematically on the line, exactly two miles beyond Old Sarum."

"Alfred Watkins discovered that Sir Norman Lockyer's triangle could be considered elongated if the midsummer sunrise line was taken beyond the horizons in both directions to join up with other ancient ceremonial sites. Watkins explained that ley lines consisted of some short, some long, but they were in great profusion all over Britain. Checking by foot throughout the countryside, he discovered that the ley lines wound their way through remnants of an ancient civilization that still showed: burial mounds, standing stones, man-made lakes and moats, traditional holy wells, sacred springs, high points of mountains and hills where beacon fires were traditionally lit, old wayside crosses (such as Celtic crosses) at the junction of former trackways, churches built upon the sites of previously pagan religious centres, notches carved on distant hills to mark the direction of the ley, or alongside castles and hill-forts whose ruined walls and ditches could still be seen silhouetted against the sky."

How Ley Lines derived their Name

Ley lines are to be found all over the world but the ones that have been most commonly investigated are those of Britain and Europe, particularly France. According to Francis Hitching, the name Ley line was derived from the word *Eleusis* (as in the *Elysium Isle of the Blessed*). The legendary Greek hero, Aeneas reputedly went to *Elysium* after his time spent on Earth. It was discovered by a Frenchman

(Xavier Guichard) in 1911 when he was researching the origins of ancient European place-names that the one unique one was Alesia.

"In its Greek form of *Eleusis* it dated from legendary pre-Homeric times; in its Indo-European roots Ales, Alis or Alles meant a meeting point to which people travelled. His pursuit of the true meaning of the word, and the origins of the people who first used it, consumed the next 25 years of his life. As Xavier looked more closely into the kind of place which it described, he found there were invariably two identifying features: landscaped hills overlooking rivers, a man-made well of mineral water and from this he deduced that they had all been ancient centres where travellers could stop and drink the life-giving waters."

"Xavier found more than 400 such sites in France alone. He proposed that the whole of Europe, centred on a remote ancient site called Alaise, near Bescancon in southern France, had been divided up into two *roses-des-vents* (which translates into 'roses of the wind' just as Feng Shui translates into 'water and wind') which were compass cards used by Greek geographers: one of 24 lines that attempted to divide the horizon into equal segments; and one of 4 lines that marked the meridian and the equinox, and the winter and summer solstices."

"This implied, he said, a knowledge of latitude and longitude, and the position of the North Pole and the Equator. Moreover, he could trace a common distance between the sites that meant a common unit of measurement." Thus it was from the French name Alaise (containing the word 'lais') that the name 'ley' was derived.

Francis Hitching writes that "Pythagorean [Kuthumi] mathematics suggest that in some way the harmony of numbers, the movement of the celestial bodies, and the key moments in the annual cycle of the Earth's rotation could be made to combine, and to generate an energy whose force can only be dimly felt today - a science of instinct that was essential to the development of mankind."

According to Francis Hitching:

"John Michell, (a writer and researcher who has been at the forefront of the recent movement to gain recognition for the theories of Alfred Watkins), believes that the placing of the churches (on the ancient pagan sites) shows that the planning of leys once took place on an almost unimaginably large scale. If you take a map of southern Britain and impose on it the line of May Day (Beltane), it coincidentally marks the longest possible stretch of unbroken land; astonishingly, the megalithic surveyors may have found this out, for they put many sacred sites along it."

"Avebury, once more imposing and extensive than even Stonehenge, lies almost at the centre of the line; Glastonbury, its steep hill artificially shaped into a three-dimensional labyrinth, lies further to the west; and dotted along the line lie a significant number of churches that are on formerly pagan sites, for they are dedicated to the dragon-killing saints, St Michael and St George."

Glastonbury - 'Avalon'

Anyone who has visited the countryside of Glastonbury, Somerset, (named after the ancient land of Sumer from which we derive our word of 'summer'), will have noticed some of the ancient carvings on the hillsides which feature astrological symbols.

Often they can be viewed whilst driving down the freeways, which have been cut through the hills, but the carvings are much more visible from the air. Glastonbury, itself, has become a Mecca for tourists.

Wearyall Hill which leads up to the famous Tor at the top, lies inside the Glastonbury Zodiac which consists of a circle ten miles (sixteen kilometers) across taking in many of the landscape features which outline the zodiac figures. Of notable interest however, is the fact that the Tor itself, lies in the head of the Phoenix which represents the Age of Aquarius. The Zodiacal carvings include a lion (Leo), a virgin (Virgo), a bull (Taurus), a ram (Aries), fishes (Pisces) to mention just a few.

At the top of the Tor, there are the remains of a chapel, known as the Chapel of St Michael which is another place that is named after the Archangel Michael, (the main building of the chapel was destroyed by an earthquake in the 13th century AD). It is where the Mary/Michael Serpent energy Ley lines meet before again moving onto other strategic places. The chapel was built in 167 AD by the High King Leurug (Lucius, the Great Light) Mawr (Mor) who dedicated it to the Archangel Michael.

The land at Glastonbury which was granted to St Joseph of Arimathea, was given to him by the British Arviragus of the time (a Pendragon - High Priest) Caradoc, (who was married to Venus Julia, daughter of the Roman Emperor, Claudius). Caradoc, whom the Romans called Caractacus, was one of the sons of *Cymbeline* and Cymbeline was otherwise known Bran the Blessed King who was married to Joseph of Arimathea's daughter, Anna. Thus Caradoc was Joseph's grandson.

In 1996, just prior to visiting Britain and climbing the Tor at Glastonbury, in my dream-state one night, I was shown a vision of a book and it was titled *The Sun And The Serpent*. I knew that the book must exist because it seemed to be of significant importance. I spent the next morning telephoning several well known bookshops around Australia, but no-one had heard of it. However, my intuition told me that one day, according to the 'law of the Universe', I would eventually locate it.

After a very enjoyable drive from the ancient Roman town of Bath where we were staying, my family and I arrived at the bottom of the Tor and parked nearby. As I glanced around wondering if we had parked in a secure enough position, I noticed an ice-cream vendor parked on the other side of the road; it was a lovely hot English Summer's day and we decided that an ice-cream would be an ideal treat in which to indulge before we started to ascend the Tor.

As we approached the vendor, he was busily pre-occupied reading a book. Out of sheer curiosity, I leaned over the counter in order to get a close look at the title, whilst we waited for him to serve us. Wonder of wonders - the book in which he was so engrossed was called *The Sun And The Serpent!* Hardly able to contain my excitement, I enquired where he had purchased the book and when he told me of the place in Cornwall, it was only a twenty-minute drive from where we were planning to stay at Newquay one week later.

Before climbing the Tor, we enquired of the ice-cream vendor, the whereabouts of the famous Thorn Tree - there are now varieties of such trees around the base of the Tor and we duly inspected a couple of them. The staff of Joseph of Arimathea that he reputedly planted on Wearyall hill and from which sprouted the Thorn Tree, is known as the Holy Thorn. It is a place where the flow of serpentine energy passes through the Holy Thorn before moving on.

According to information contained in the book titled *The Sun And The Serpent* by Hamish Miller and Paul Broadhurst, "traces of a Roman wharf were discovered on Wearyall Hill which showed that it was once used as a dock in the days of lake villages and it makes plausible the legend that Joseph of Arimathea and his disciples, having come by sea, landed there 'weary-all' on the hill where the thorn bush still grows. Although there cannot be any proof that he did in fact land there, or that he planted his staff in the ground which immediately came to life and blossomed, the legend has been remarkably persistent."

The Tor itself was an ancient Druidic place of worshipping the earth's sacred energies and it is possible that the name may have originated from the god 'Thor' whom the Druids also worshipped.

Mystical Occurrences upon the Tor

Climbing the Tor at Glastonbury is a magical experience and attracts thousands of tourists each year. It rises mystically to a peak. Although steep, it is reasonable easy to climb as it is terraced all around and the only way one could miss one's footing would be to step into the numerous rabbit burrows. Once at the top, the view is spectacular, the stillness is profound, and it is easy to capture the magical mystical quality of the Tor's sacred energies. Far below, all that can been observed is flat land for as far as the eye can see because the Tor was once surrounded by marshes and water, making it an island - also known as *Avalon* (one of the Avalon's).

We sat there for quite some time, absorbing as much as we could and then decided to visit the chapel which was dedicated to the Archangel Michael. As we entered into the remaining tower of the chapel, we observed an ancient carving **of the Archangel Michael with his foot on a dragon,** and one of St Brigit who was the Irish Celtic goddess connected with agriculture and whom the early Church of Rome changed from a 'pagan' goddess to St Brigit. (Brigit is sometimes called Brigid and 'Bride'). Although there was an Irish St Brigid born to a noble family in Leinster in Ireland in the 5th century AD, there was no connection between herself and the 'pagan' goddess.

Prior to meeting Paul Broadhurst, and learning of the strange 'happenings' which occur upon the Tor, my family and I encountered a mystical experience.

As we descended the Tor and reached its base, a curious thing happened. The only vegetation at the Tor is around its base and as we pulled back a bush to cross onto the path, there appeared a most unusual elderly man, who held the branches back so that my two adult children and I, were able to cross over.

He had long white hair, was dressed in a long satin violet/purple robe, and was leaning upon an ancient looking walking stick. He gazed at each of us individually and his eyes mesmerized us, for they had a magical quality about them, almost hypnotic. Even as I write about him, I can still remember his eyes and face so clearly, for he left an everlasting impression.

We are not the fanciful type, but each of us immediately said that the word *Merlin* popped into our thoughts! As we instantly turned around to look in the direction he had taken, which had been that of mounting the Tor, he had simply vanished into thin air!

The Tor, (apart from the Holy Thorn trees around its base), is barren and steeply terraced with no trees to obscure the view, so there was no place that he could go and not be observed. It takes a good twenty to thirty minutes to climb the Tor. As adults, we thought it quite fantastic that it occurred to each of us that he looked like Merlin, and I was so pleased that my two adult children were a witness to such an event, otherwise I would have thought that the Tor and its magical qualities were playing tricks upon my imagination.

Within one week of climbing the Tor, we visited Tintagel, the legendary birthplace of Arthur, and where there is a cave known as Merlin's cave (which can only be viewed when the tide is out). That day, the tide was in and so we visited a local book shop in order to purchase *The Sun And The Serpent* and just as we were exiting the store, I just 'happened' to bump into the co-author, Paul Broadhurst who had just returned that day, from an adventure in Europe, tracing the 'Ley lines'.

Paul invited us to sit down at a nearby table and as we engaged in conversation and told him of our strange experience at the Tor (and of my vision of his book), we were relieved to have Paul inform us that apart from the fact that there are no such things as coincidence, many mystical and strange meetings have been reported from those who have visited the Tor. It was also truly amazing that I had seen his book in a vision and been able to track it down and meet him. The synchronicity of the events that unfolded was incredible.

According to Paul, it is a common experience, even amongst skeptics, to have unusual occurrences of some mystical nature upon the Tor. Sometimes spiritual and unusual shifts in consciousness or 'strange meetings' occur which cannot be explained. It was also curious that the man was dressed in purple, for that is the favourite royal colour of St Germain/Francis Bacon/Merlin.

The Sun And The Serpent by Paul Broadhurst and Hamish Miller is an excellent book written on the subject of the Mary/Michael energy lines. Paul has written several books which include *The Arthurian Mythos* and both he and Hamish are authorities on the Ley lines. The book titled *The Sun And The Serpent*, has illustrations of the *Serpent* energy around all the sacred places and shows how the energy actually 'snakes' its way around the countryside of Britain. According to Paul, there are thirty-three churches in Cornwall dedicated to the Archangel Michael. (There are thirty-three Arch Degrees in Freemasonry; Jesus is said to have died at the age of thirty-three).

The Chalice Well at Glastonbury

When we hear of Glastonbury, we immediately think of its connections with the Grail/Chalice. According to legend, Glastonbury is where St Joseph of Arimathea first took the legendary *Grail* to 'Avalon'. The Grail Cup (Chalice), the famous Cup of the Biblical Last Supper scenario, is reputed to be buried in a well, known simply as the *Chalice Well*, which is situated at the base of Wearyall Hill which leads to the Tor. This Cup was the one handed to John the Beloved Disciple by his brother Jesus in the last supper before the crucifixion. So, having been handed to John the Beloved (Kuthumi), how, we might enquire did the 'Cup/Chalice' come to be connected with Joseph of Arimathea? The relationship between these two men, who played such a prominent role in the Family of the Holy Grail, will be discussed in future chapters.

In their book, Paul and Hamish tell of their experiences of following the Serpent energy from the Tor, to the Chalice Well and onto the great church of St Peter and St Paul in the town of Glastonbury itself. (The church was destroyed by a great fire in 1184 during the reign of the Plantagenet King, Henry II).

Accordingly, "the St Michael serpent curves sharply across to focus on the high altar, within a few yards of what is known as 'King Arthur's Tomb. The energy then projects itself from the Glastonbury Abbey across the countryside to Stonehenge. Where the Chalice Well is situated (at the base of Wearyall Hill where the Tor is) and where the Serpent energy also flows through, a vast amount of water once flowed down from beneath the Tor and pilgrims journeyed there to drink of the healing waters at what was known as 'The White Spring'. Beneath the Tor, where the spring runs from, reasonably large caverns have been found which lends some credibility to the persistent legend associated with the Tor that recalls it as being hollow. Unfortunately, the subterranean passages have collapsed further in, so whatever other secrets are hidden beneath the Tor, will for the time being, remain in the province of speculation."

St George and the Dragon

The analogy of St George depicted with a sword in his hand, (whose emblem is a Red- Rose Cross) slaying a dragon and the Archangel Michael who carries a sword and a shield with a Red (Rose) Cross, who also slays the dragon is obviously about portraying the 'Truth' about the Sacred Teachings and Mysteries.

It is of interest to note that when Joan of Arc (reputedly an earlier incarnation of the Lady Master, Madame Helena Blavatsky), the Maid of Orleans, went into battle, the Archangel Michael also made an appearance to her and her battle flag carried the emblem of the Red (Rose) Cross of St George. In Arthurian legends, King Arthur's (Kuthumi's) sword 'Excalibur' was also symbolic of the 'Truth'. The 'Sword' represents the 'Truth' and the 'Dragon' is the Church of Rome, versus the ancient teachings of the Celts (Druidism) which both the Masters St Germain and Kuthumi were protecting throughout their incarnations.

According to George F. Jowett in his book titled *The Lost Disciples*:

"The Gauls (Celts) were Druids, and their faith held sway all over Gaul, which explains more than anything else, why the land was a safe haven for Joseph [of Arimathea] and the Bethany family."

"Those who have been indoctrinated by the false stories describing the Druidic religion may pause in consternation. The malevolent infamy heaped upon the Druidic priesthood, their religion, with the practice of human sacrifice, is just as untruthful, vicious and vile as the other distortions stigmatizing the ancient Britons."

"On closer examination it will be found that those who uttered vindictive maledictions stand out in Roman history as the dictators of the Roman Triumvirate. Their bestial hatred for everything that was British and Christian deliberately promoted the insidious propaganda to defame the people they could neither coerce nor subdue."

"The influence Druidism had upon the rest of the ancient world, and its peaceful and ready reception of the Christian faith, proves its noble structure.

Hume, the high-ranking British historian acknowledged for his impartiality and the lack of bias in his reporting wrote:

'No religion has every swayed the minds of men like the Druidic'."

"Despising Druidic opposition, the Roman persecutors intensified their malignancy with the British conversion to Christianity. The Emperor Augustus, Tiberius and the Claudian and Diocletian decrees made acceptance of Druidic and Christian faith a capital punishment, punishable by death."

St George is reputed to have made a pilgrimage to Glastonbury during the third century AD, where St Joseph of Arimathea had brought the 'Grail' in the 1st century AD, and founded the first Celtic Church in Britain. More information related to St George is given in a future chapter.

Ireland's beloved St Patrick (Kuthumi) is also reputed to have been an abbot for a while at Glastonbury in the 5th century AD (after he had completed his training with St Germanus - St Germain in Gaul).

St Michael's Mount (named after the Archangel Michael)

"And did those feet in ancient times
walk upon England's pastures green?"
(William Blake)

St Michael's Mount, Marazion in Cornwall, is a beautiful fairy-tale mystical island and when the tide goes out in the summer months, it can be reached on foot across a pathway which would normally be covered by the sea. (On our visit there in the summer, we were half way back at about 4pm when the tide came in with incredible speed and we waded back to Marazion with the water around our knees).

The Mount was once a famous port where sailing ships called in to load their vessels with tin mined in Cornwall. It is an important place associated with legends of the Archangel Michael and the Mary/Michael Serpent energy Ley lines. St Michael's Mount is named after the Archangel Michael. (Marazion is not far from the old smuggler's town of Penzance).

Mara-zion means the 'Sea of Zion/Sion' (Jerusalem) and according to Cornish legend, Joseph of Arimathea, from Jerusalem is reputed to have visited Cornwall in company with Jesus.

In the 5th century AD, there was a Celtic monastery on St Michael's Mount. According to Paul Broadhurst and Hamish Miller in their book titled *The Sun And The Serpent*, "the very name **Penzance** is apparently the modern equivalent of an old Cornish title that means **HOLY HEADLAND.**"

According to Paul, when he and Hamish explored St Michael's Mount following the Mary/Michael Ley lines, "below the terrace, an ancient cross was positioned exactly on the centre of the flow, which overlapped the present building by a few feet on the northern side, but otherwise was perfectly aligned. Here was an impressive testimony to the ancient sanctity of the Mount, with its chapels to St Michael and St Mary built right next to each other."

"The crucial point, though, as had been observed before at Brentnor, Glastonbury and other sites, was 'secret'. Before it was associated with St Michael it (the Mount) had been venerated as a sanctuary of other Solar gods, and had possessed a singular importance. This, we were later to discover, was fully justified. Not only does it mark the flow of the English St Michael currents on their way across southern Britain, but it is unique in that it is also the place where even greater currents of energy flow in from the continent, the energies of a 'European' St Michael Line."

"This other St Michael Line was originally discovered by the French researcher Jean Richer, who noticed an alignment of sanctuaries dedicated to the Greek Sun God Apollo which included Delos, Athens and Delphi...it continued through various other sites in Italy and France dedicated to St Michael, through Mont St Michel (in France), St Michael's Mount, Cornwall and also the remote island of Great Skellig or Skellig Michael, situated just off the west coast of Ireland, where there is a ruined monastery named after the saint."

"Later work on the island of Rhodes (Greece) was to show that the European Michael Line had its solar and lunar components in exactly the same way as its English counterpart (dubbed 'Apollo' and 'Athena' to differentiate between them and 'Michael and Mary'). These energies passed through the sites of ancient temples and fortifications once controlled by the Knights of St John, who went to Rhodes after their expulsion from the Holy Land at the turn of the fourteenth century." [The Knights of St John, named in honour of St John the Beloved who was the Master Kuthumi, used as their emblem, the Maltese Cross].

Once the island was connected to the mainland and when the tide is out, ancient tree stumps can be seen where once a forest had been. According to local legend, back in the 5th century, the Archangel Michael made an appearance to Cornish fishermen just near St Michael's Mount. St Joseph of Arimathea, accompanied by Mary, is reputed to have visited St Michael's Mount in circa 37 AD. Oddly enough, there is no mention of John the Beloved Disciple (Kuthumi) visiting Britain - and yet he was the one who was designated the care of 'Mary' by his brother Jesus at the scene of the crucifixion.

The 'Dragon' Society

During the Elizabethan Renaissance, the son of William Cecil, namely Robert Cecil (who was the sworn enemy of Francis Bacon), purchased St Michael's Mount. One may wonder whether the Cecil's were aware of the Ley lines connected with St Michael's Mount. Did they also belong to the Dragon Society, the Society to which Elizabeth I, Sir Francis Bacon (St Germain), Sir John Dee (Kuthumi), Sir Francis Drake, among others, belonged, the Society which worshipped the Earth's sacred energies? It would seem highly probable because nothing missed the attention of the two Cecil's - they had spies everywhere!

In the book titled *The Occult Conspiracy* by Michael Howard, we are informed that during the 1600's, there was a man named Henry Adams who immigrated to the American colonies from the Devon/Cornwall area of England after being persecuted for having worshipped the Dragon Ley lines. Many of the members of the Dragon society kept their 'pagan' activities concealed by acting as the Puritans and when they fled to the American colonies, they continued to found similar societies.

A Henry Adams in the 19th century made a passionate study of the Middle Ages in France and after an extensive tour of the Ley line areas, wrote his famous work titled *Mont-St-Michel and Chartres* in which he details the Ley lines and discusses their prominence at the Chartres Cathedral and St Michael's Mount in France (not to be confused with the one in Cornwall, England).

The Cathedral of Chartres which Henry visited was dedicated to the Black Virgin, who was a version of the pagan Triple Goddess. The great cathedrals such as Chartres were built upon places where the energy Ley lines were very powerful and the ancient architects and patrons of such buildings, full-well understood the earth's Serpentine/Dragon energies. The cathedrals were constructed by masons and designed upon Pythagorean (Kuthumi's) principles. Those of Notre Dame in Paris (1163-1220) and Chartres (1194-1220) were completed in the reign of Philip Augustus.

According to a letter which Paul Broadhurst sent me, Elizabeth I's own treasurer, Sir Roger North, built a mansion directly on one of the Dragon lines and is buried in the adjacent church, with his feet on a dragon! Paul also related that Sir Francis Drake, who learnt navigation from Sir John Dee, chose to be a member of parliament for Tintagel, the old Pendragon stronghold and that it seems that Sir Francis Drake may also have been privy to certain knowledge of the sacred Mysteries.

The ownership of St Michael's Mount by the Cecils, continued until Robert Cecil's death at which time the Mount again changed hands until it came into the family of St Aubyn, and Sir John Aubyn was a Provincial Grand Master of the

Freemasons.

On the far side of the Island, facing westwards out to sea, is all that remains of the original Celtic monastery...a Celtic cross carved out of stone, somewhat weathered by time but still giving a clue to its ancient history.

The Triple Goddess and the Rose Flame

Although St Brigid actually existed and was taught by St Patrick (Kuthumi) and St Germanus (St Germain), in Celtic mythology Brigit/Brigid appears in many guises and under different names. She is often depicted as the Triple Goddess (detailed in Robert Graves' book *The White Goddess*). The Triple Goddess represents the (1) virgin, (2) mother and (3) wise old woman (crone). The Triple Goddess forms part of the 'Sacred Mysteries'.

From Peter Dawkins' book *The Virgin Ideal* we learn the following important information. "The general concept of virginity used to be summed up or symbolised by those great Goddesses of the past, who were all known as having three aspects. The first aspect was that of the maiden, the second aspect was that of the mother and the third aspect was that of the wise old woman. The triple-Goddess was thus maiden, nymph and crone."

"All the principal Goddesses had these three aspects and in all three aspects they were virgins. That is to say, they would be a virgin maiden, a virgin mother and a virgin old lady. It is very important to understand this in order to know the real meaning of virginity, because during the last Age, the meaning of virginity has been greatly misunderstood and distorted. The names in the West given to these great triple Goddesses have been Isis (of Egyptian tradition), Miriam, Maria or Mary (Hebraic-Christian), Demeter (Orphic), Pallas Athena (Greek), Ceridwen (Druidic), amongst others."

"You may wonder about Pallas Athena. In her original form Pallas Athena was a triple Goddess. She was in one aspect the maiden with her spear, who looked after all heroes on a quest for noble fame or truth. In another aspect she was the wise old lady who looked after the arts and sciences. She was also the mother, until the mother aspect was taken from her and given the name of Aphrodite instead. (Venus was the Greek 'Aphrodite', the goddess of love). But Aphrodite was once part of Pallas Athena, and in her mother aspect, Athena was known as Coronis."

"As the wise old lady or the wise counsellor she was known as Agraulos, and as the maiden she was called Pallas. Then, also in Greece, we have Demeter, who has her triple aspect of maiden, nymph and crone under the names of Core, Persephone and Hecate respectively."

"In Britain, to the Celts the triple Goddess was known as Ceridwen and her three aspects were Arianrhod, Bride or Ave, and Dana or Anna. All these triple Goddesses were virgin mothers of golden children, sons of Light. Isis gave birth to Horus, Mary gave birth to Jesus, Athena gave birth to Aesculapius and Demeter gave birth to Dionysus."

"Many of these names are actually derived from the same root word, originating from the distant past. Horus, Jesus and Dionysus derive from the same root word, Heru or Yesu, which means 'the embodied or ensouled Light'.

"The golden children are the subject of the Greater Mysteries, the Greater Degrees of initiation. They are the fruit of the Lesser Mysteries of Virginity. The virgin mother is the purified psyche and body, the calm, gentle, loving, understanding personality or lower self, healthy in mind and body. When the psyche becomes pure, with a lasting devotion to God, she becomes inspired, impregnated with the Light of God the Spirit - that is, the 'Father'. She then gives birth (from her heart) to a beautiful 'flame' of Light which is her 'child'."

"It is the flame of the heart that is called the golden child, the Christ child, which manifests the Light of the Spirit. It is also known as the Holy Grail (the heart being the Grail Cup), or the Rose of Beauty."

"In tradition the Rose flame is given the name of Yesu (or Jesus) and the Jesus in each of us is the flame that is born from and rises up from our heart centre when we, as persons, reach a perfect stage of harmony and purity of our heart, and that heart is set on fire with perfect love, divine and human. The symbol of the flaming heart, which has been used so much during the Age of Pisces, is a symbol of the virgin mother or psyche giving birth to the Christ child or spiritual soul, the perfect soul consciousness and manifestation of Light. The pure heart is set on fire with love and conscious intuitive awareness, and the Rose flame of love rises up from the heart towards the head."

"Clairvoyantly, using the faculty of celestial or spiritual vision (the vision of the heart), the Rose flame can be seen like a bud to begin with; and then, as it rises higher and higher, the iridescent flame begins to spread out in a way that one can only describe as being like a rose blooming, with petals of etheric light and colour opening and flowing out all the time, in all directions, and yet always preserving the heart of the Rose, the flame shape. Unlike an ordinary rose which blossoms out so many petals and then is finished, the Rose flame of the heart always preserves its central part in the same vesica-like shape however many petals of Light it throws off."

The Vesica Piscis is an oval or almond shape, consisting of two intersecting circles and is found in sacred geometry. Throughout the area of Cornwall where the Mary/Michael Serpent energy Ley lines weave, carvings of this ancient sacred symbol have been found, particularly in ancient churches. The mystical symbol of the Vesica Piscis appears above the archway in the gardens of the Chalice Well at

Glastonbury.

Peter Dawkins further explains: "Eventually the Rose flame soars up right around the head, embracing the head, and when that happens a magical thing takes place in the head. An interaction occurs between the crown and brow chakras resulting in a flash of light which creates a blazing golden-white radiance that shines from the head."

"This is called the corona or crown of glory - the halo which many have seen around the heads of saints. It is so bright, so golden, so powerful, that it effects all levels of vibration, and thus it can even be seen with some of the lower psychic and even the physical senses. It is the light of real joy that shines through the face, the eyes, the radiant smile. The beauty of the corona is beyond description, yet many painters in the past have tried to depict it, and poets and writers have attempted to describe it. It is the crowning of man with the Christ Light - the 'diadem of beauty':

'In that day shall the Lord of Hosts be for a crown of glory, and for a diadem of beauty...' (Isaiah 28:5). Man's own spiritual 'crown of glory' becomes manifest, just as the radiant 'sun of light' becomes manifest in the candle flame. This phenomena is also called 'the countenance of the Lord'."

"The Triple Virgin Goddess in Celtic terms was known as
(1) Arianrhod, (the 'Rainbow'),
(2) Bride or Brigit (dressed in green and white), and
(3) Dana or Anna, the wise old lady."

"Anna, the 'Black Virgin', is traditionally the mother of **Mary, the 'White Virgin' - Mary being the Bride or virgin mother of the golden child."**

The origin of the tribe of 'Anna' and 'Maryanna' was discussed in a previous chapter. In the tradition of Christianity, Anna was the mother of 'Mary'.

Throughout the ancient Knights Templar areas in France, cathedrals and other holy places have been dedicated to the Black Virgin. One of these is the famous Chartres Cathedral, built on an ancient Druidic site. There are also many areas throughout France dedicated to Mary Magdalene including the chapel at Rennes-le-Chateau. In Marseille, where Mary Magdalene journeyed to and accordingly made her place of abode in 37 AD, (accompanied initially by Joseph of Arimathea and Lazarus), there are several places dedicated to Black Madonnas. One is in the crypt of the basilica of St Victor and the underground chapel outside, is dedicated to Mary Magdalene. The cult worship of the Black Madonna is linked to Mary Magdalene and in turn to the worshipping of Isis who is sometimes represented as being black.

Isis was revered by the Knights Templar. She was, as stated elsewhere, equated with the Gnostic 'Wisdom' of *Sophia*. According to the Freemasonic authors, Christopher Knight and Robert Lomas in their book titled *The Hiram Key*, "the Templars were widely reputed to worship something with the curious name of

Baphomet, which was never understood until it was written in Hebrew and the Atbash cipher applied to reveal the word 'Sophia' - the Greek for 'wisdom'."

In the enigmatic parchment discovered at Rennes-le-Chateau and which forms part of its great 'mystery', is the word *Demon* applicable to Asmodeus, a name applied to 'Baphomet' who as stated above, the Freemasons worshipped. Thus, it is very apparent that the Knights Templar and Freemasons **did not worship a 'demon' or a 'devil' - instead, they worshipped 'wisdom'.**

Continuing on with information supplied by Peter Dawkins: "Bride's particular emblem is the white swan, and this is also the emblem of Orpheus, the great Initiate and Founder (or Rekindler) of the Mysteries; for the swan is the symbol of song and music, and of the true initiate (the swan can walk on land, swim in water, and fly gracefully through the air). This of course links with Apollo, whose great attribute is song and music - the music of the heart. Ben Jonson referred to Shakespeare as 'the sweet swan of Avon'. In the word 'Avon' we have the AV of AVE, and the ON which was the ancient name known in Egypt and Sumeria that means 'LIGHT'. Thus in 'AVON' we have AVE, and the Bride, and ON, the 'Light' or Spirit, AVE-ON, the Bride and Spirit." (Note in the above paragraphs, the references to Orpheus, Apollo and Shakespeare, for they were all incarnations of the one person, namely St Germain).

Throughout Cornwall, there are numerous holy wells and springs dedicated to Bride (Brigit) whom the Church of Roman Christianized into a saint, but like Anna (also called Dana) who is equated with the Sumerian and Egyptian goddess Anu, Bride's origins were far older than that. She was worshipped by the Druids as the virgin-goddess who was the patroness of their crafts from whom they received their inspiration and she was also associated with fire-worshipping. Her male counterpart was Bel who was worshipped as the Sun-god, (from whom the Druidic festival of Beltane received its name). The zodiacal constellation of Beltane is Taurus, the bull. (More information regarding the Druids is given in a future chapter).

It was traditional for the Druids to sacrifice young bulls, as a symbol of virility. Beltane was Christianized into May Day, with the May pole being kept as a traditional feature of the yearly ceremony, but the May poles, like the Egyptian obelisks, were phallic symbols signifying 'fertility'.

MASTERS DISCUSSED IN THIS CHAPTER

Merlin/Taliesin - St Germain (6th century AD)
Pythagoras - Kuthumi - (c. 530 BC)
St John the Beloved Disciple - Kuthumi (died 1st century AD)
St George - Kuthumi (3rd century AD)
King Arthur - Kuthumi (6th century AD)
Sir John Dee, the Elizabethan Magus - Kuthumi (16th century AD)
St Joan of Arc - Madame Helena Blavatsky

NOTES AND RECOMMENDED READING

Robert Graves, _The White Goddess_, (Faber & Faber, U.K. 1961)

Paul Broadhurst & Hamish Miller, _The Sun And The Serpent_, (Pendragon Press, Cornwall, U.K. 1994)

Paul Broadhurst, _Tintagel And The Arthurian Mythos_, (Pendragon Press, Cornwall, U.K. 1995)

Peter Dawkins, _The Great Vision_, (Francis Bacon Research Trust, Warwick, U.K.)

Peter Dawkins, _Dedication To The Light_, (Francis Bacon Research Trust, Warwick, U.K.)

Peter Dawkins, _The Virgin Ideal_, (Francis Bacon Research Trust, Warwick, U.K.)

Edmund Harold, _Second Sight_, (Grail Publications, Sydney, Australia, 1994)

George F. Jowett, _The Drama Of The Lost Disciples_, (Covenant Publishing Ltd., U.K., 1980)

Francis Hitching, _The World Atlas Of Mysteries_, (Pan Books, U.K., 1978).

Janet & Colin Bord, _Dictionary of Earth Mysteries_, (Thorsons, U.K. 1996)

Janet & Colin Bord, _Mysterious Britain_, (Paladin, U.K. 1975)

John Michell, _The Earth's Spirit_, (Thames & Hudson, U.K., 1992)

Michael Howard, _The Occult Conspiracy_, (Rider & Rider, U.K. 1989)

Christopher Knight & Robert Lomas, _The Hiram Key_, (Century, U.K. 1996)

Ernest Samuels, _The Education of Henry Adams_, (Houghton Mifflin Co. Boston, U.S.A, 1973)

CHAPTER 13

The 'Archangels' & the Lords of the Seven Rays

The concealed books from Emmanuel's hands
Were brought by Raphael as Adam's gift.
Twelve young men, four of them angels, sent forth from the flower
Of Eve, to give assistance in every trouble, in all oppression.
While they wandered, very great care possessed mankind,
Until they obtained the tokens of Grace."
('Diversified Song 'by Taliesin/Merlin/St Germain)
"I have been winged by the genius of the splendid crozier"
(Taliesin/Merlin/St Germain)
"And Michael, one of the archangels, took me by
my right hand, raised me up, and brought me out to where was
every secrecy of mercy and secret of righteousness."
(The Book of Enoch)

During the 5th century AD, the Archangel Michael, Mary and St Brigid of Ireland, are all reputed to have made appearances at the chapel on top of the Tor at Glastonbury, dedicated to the Archangel Michael. According to author Haroutiun Saraydarian in the book titled *Christ, The Avatar of Sacrificial Love* (1974), the Archangel Raphael was the twin-flame of Mary (mother of Jesus). It is known from certain documents of the Dead Sea Scrolls that the Essenes gave angelic titles to their High priests and therefore, Raphael, was none other than St Germain in his incarnation as Joseph, married to his twin-flame Mary, and they subsequently became the parents of the Family of the Holy Grail.

St Germain's twin-flame is known as the Lady Portia - who may also have been the real St Brigid who was known as 'Mary of the Gaels', whose real name is believed to have been Alice Curtayne. St Germain had contact with her in the 'Land of the Trinity' - Ireland, when in his incarnation as St Germanus of Gaul, he taught St Patrick (Kuthumi). Given also the fact that it was the Archangel Raphael who appeared to me and gave me the message quoted at the beginning of this book, I am quite satisfied that St Germain is Raphael and that 'Michael', was an angelic title given to John the Beloved - Kuthumi.

As discussed in a previous chapter, it was in the 19th century, that a poster was issued by the Rosicrucians depicting Leonardo da Vinci (Kuthumi) as 'Keeper/ Protector of the Holy Grail' holding a 'Scroll'; he is between the Archangel Michael, and another character whose identity will be revealed in a future chapter. Suffice to say at this stage, that the other person was an earlier incarnation of Kuthumi. Therefore, the poster is depicting three incarnations of Kuthumi. According to Edmund Harold in his book titled *Second Sight*, Kuthumi is the Co-Protector of the Grail, together with the Archangel Michael. However, they are one and the same person.

From excerpts taken from the book titled *From The Stone Age To Christianity* by William Foxwell Albright, one of the world's foremost Orientalists and Professor of Semitic Languages at John Hopkins University, form 1959 to 1957, we learn the following information regarding the origins of archangels.

"It is highly probable that the idea of seven archangels was taken from Iranian sources (of Zoroastrian influence)." [The Prophet Zoroaster was an earlier incarnation of the Master we know as Jesus]. "In the earlier books of the Old Testament and the earliest apocryphal and pseudepicgraphical literature there is no where any suggestion that certain angels formed a specially privileged group in the celestial hierarchy, nor do any angels receive personal names identical with those of human beings."

"In Daniel (circa 165 BC) Michael and Gabriel appear, and in Enoch, Uriel, 'God is my Light' and Raphael, as well as many other names, are added. The principal angels (archangels) varies from four to seven, the latter being distinctly later than the former, as is clear from the fact that only these four have genuinely early Israelite (or Canaanite) names, after which all others have obviously been modelled."

"It is curious to note that all four names belong to a type which was in most active use before the tenth century BC and which became archaistic after the Exile. There can therefore, be little doubt that these angelic figures have a pre-history (Israelite or pagan?) which escapes us entirely. We may compare Michael, Gabriel, and Raphael with Enoch, Moses and Elijah respectively. In any case the *idea* of seven chief angels and of their relative station was taken from Iranian sources, since the names are absolutely different in character." (According to the Rosicrucian authority, the late Spencer Lewis, Elijah was an earlier incarnation of John the Baptist who was the Master El Morya who had once been the pharaoh Akhnaton).

The concealed books from Emmanuel's hands
Were brought by Raphael as Adam's gift.
Twelve young men, four of them angels, sent forth from the flower

Of Eve, to give assistance in every trouble, in all oppression.
While they wandered, very great care possessed mankind,
Until they obtained the tokens of Grace."
('Diversified Song 'by Taliesin/Merlin/St Germain)

The word 'Arch' as in 'Archangel' originated with the Arcadians (the People of the Ark/Arc). The Oxford dictionary defines 'archangel' as being of the 'highest rank'. Therefore, these 'Four' young men mentioned above in Taliesin's *Diversified Song* were 'Messengers of the Highest Rank', who could be deemed as Masters of the Great White Brotherhood who belonged to the Essenes.

Robert Graves in his book titled *The White Goddess* explains that "'Emmanuel' refers to Isaiah's prophecy of the birth of the Divine Child from a virgin."

"In *The Book of Enoch*, Raphael is described as the angel of healing and must therefore have been the **chief patron** of the therapeutic Essenes." St Germain, as Joseph, the Father of the Holy Grail Family who belonged to the Essenes, was the Essenes' expected Teacher of Righteousness.

The verses from *Diversified Song* by Taliesin continue:

So did I obtain my Bardic books, Asia's sciences, Europe's too.

I know their arts, their courses and destiny..."

Taliesin knows the destiny of the world. *"I have been winged by the genius of the splendid crozier".* Here we have another verse of Taliesin's. Although the 'splendid crozier (staff)' was a symbol of Dionysus (St Germain), it was also a symbol of the Archangel Raphael who is also the 'overseer' of Mary (wife of Joseph - St Germain).

Considering that Raphael was known as the angel of healing and given that he was St Germain in his incarnation as Joseph, it is easy to see how his son, Jesus, came to demonstrate the 'laying on of hands' to heal (which today we call Reiki).

There is an interesting passage in the Book of Daniel Chapter 12:

"And at that time shall Michael stand up, the great prince which standeth for the children of thy people; and there shall be a time of trouble, such as never was since there was a nation even to that same time: and at that time thy people shall be delivered, every one that shall be found written in the book." (Michael is a great prince! To be a great prince, he must come in human form).

"But thou, O Daniel, shut up the words, and seal the book, even to the time of the end: many shall run to and fro, and knowledge shall be increased."

"Many shall run to and fro, and knowledge shall be increased" is clearly a prophecy that is now coming to fruition. The Age of Aquarius over which St Germain rules as the Lord of the Seventh Ray (the colour of which is 'violet') is the Age of Enlightenment for those who are disillusioned with the inaccuracies of the so-called religion will be led to search for the 'Truth' on a quest for their own 'Holy Grail'.

The Lords of the Seven Rays

Whilst on the topic of Archangels, it is relevant to this chapter to discuss the Lords of the Seven Rays. There are many books currently available explaining the Seven Rays, however, an excellent 'simplistic' explanation is given in Michael Taylor's book titled *Master R Lord of Our Civilisation*:

"Rosicrucian (Order of the Rose Cross), Theosophical and New Age writings talk of a hidden Spiritual hierarchy on this planet. This hierarchy has seven so-called Ray Lords, who each rule over an aspect of life."

St Germain is the Lord of the Violet Ray which symbolises transformation - the Archangel Michael is the Lord of the Blue Ray. It is known as the Ray of Protection and also symbolises the sword of 'Truth'. From Peter Dawkins' book titled *The Mystery Of The Master*, we learn the following:

"There really are souls associated with this one tiny world in the universe whom we can call Masters from our limited angle of perception and relativity. First there is a supreme Master or Lord of the World who has mastered everything which our planetary way of life can offer, but who chooses to stay connected with our planetary life-stream in order to help the rest of us who are still learning to master it."

"Then there are three Great Lords (*Mahachohans*) or Masters who manifest and express the three principal aspects which the Lord of the World has mastered and synthesised in his own being. These are known in some circles as the Manu, the Christ or World Teacher, and the Buddha or Lord of Civilisation; but these names or titles are themselves taken from the names given to cosmic principles which the three Great Lords are manifesting to some degree."

"Each of the three Great Lords deals with the development of one of the three major departments of human life - racial and political development, education or consciousness development, and the development of civilisation or culture. These three are capable of acting and manifesting in seven different ways, and oversee the operation of those seven ways in the world."

"The seven different ways of life expression are usually referred to as the Seven Rays, as distinct from the Pure White Light of which they constitute the spectrum. The Supremely Great Lord is equated with the mastery of the Pure White Light, and the three Great Lords with mastery of the three aspects of the White Light (e.g. brilliance, golden-white, and silvery-white). Then there are the seven Lords (*Chohans*) who are equated with the mastery of the Seven Rays, each one being Master of one particular Ray. Eventually each Ray Master will become a Great Lord; but always the soul will retain the vital memory of its principal line of development; via one or other of the Rays, which memory plays the primary part in moulding the character, approach to life and choice of work of the Master."

"The Masters, Lords, Great Lords and Lord of the World are each best considered as group souls, with one member of each group being chosen at any time to actively manifest to the world what that group represents. The name 'group soul' is a better description than a 'group of souls', for at such a high level of soul development the consciousness of the souls constituting the master group merges as one, whilst at the same time their individuality is preserved. They therefore think as One and act as One, yet at the same time, any individual master soul may perform the role of spokesman and representative of the others."

In the book titled *Morning Light* by White Eagle, we are informed as follows:

"Every secret of your souls is known to the Masters. They work as with one mind, in complete unison; but when they descend to the level of humanity each has his own particular branch of work. Yet at the highest all Masters are *one*. This is because the master-mind is in complete attunement with the universal mind, where truth abides. Radiations of truth go forth from this centre to envelop the whole universe and every individual life."

Continuing with Peter Dawkins:

"The Seven Rays work together in a sequence, in the sense that one of the Rays is dominantly active in turn in any cycle of time, colouring that particular period of time with its quality and influence. For instance, each Age of 2,160 years is ruled by a particular Ray, the dominant one for the Piscean Age being the 6th Ray of Devotion and Idealism. The Master of the 6th Ray therefore played a primary part in assisting human development through the Age of Pisces, which is now in its concluding years. His well-known Avataric incarnation was as Jesus of Nazareth, in which can be found the key to his work and purpose. Like all Masters, he was overshadowed and inspired by, and a channel for, other Masters at a higher level of soul evolution. As a result of his avataric work the Master Jesus is now ascended into even higher levels of consciousness and work, being absorbed into the planetary Christ Group Soul and acting as a World Teacher."

"We are now moving rapidly into the beginning of the Aquarian Age which Age is ruled by the 7th Ray of Purification, Synthesis and Transmutation. It is sometimes known as the Alchemist's Ray, or the Ray of Ceremonial Order and Magic, for it has the ability to sum everything up and bring it to a conclusion in a magical way. It comes into full force at the end of every cycle. In its Violet Flame all life forms and their consciousness have the opportunity of being purified, purged of all dross, and then raised, transmuted and reorganised into a higher and more beautiful form of life expression. For this reason the 7th Ray is sometimes known as the Gateway to Paradise, and the Master of the 7th Ray as the Gatekeeper."

This Master of the 7th Ray, as stated elsewhere, is St Germain - the Lord of Our Civilisation for the Age of Aquarius. The other Chohans of the Seven Rays are Kuthumi, El Morya, Lord Lanto, Serapis Bey, Hilarion, and the Lady Nada.

According to Charles W. Leadbeater in his book titled *The Hidden Life in Freemasonry*:

"The Head of the Seventh Ray is the Master the Comte de St Germain..." "He was Francis Bacon, Lord Verulam in the seventeenth century...and Roger Bacon in the thirteenth... and St Alban. He works to a large extent through ceremonial magic, *and employs the services of great Angels, who obey him implicitly and rejoice to do his will...*" "He is referred to as 'the Head of All True Freemasons throughout the world'. The preservation of the rituals and symbols of Freemasonry was always in the hands of the Chohan of the Seventh Ray, for that is the ray most especially connected with ceremonial of all kinds, and its Head was always the supreme Hierophant of the Mysteries of ancient Egypt."

It has previously been mentioned that Michael controls the North - Hyperborea. We further learn from Peter Dawkins. "The 'North' is known as the Place or Seat of Government, and the 'Mount of Congregation' of the Lord is in the north where the Assembly of the Holy Ones is to be found. The 'North Wind' is also known as *Hyperborea* - 'The Land of the North Wind', and is the source from which the north wind comes. That source is the Heart of God; and this is the secret that is manifesting in the heavens...the lambs of God are they who come from this perfect place of Peace, of Love, bearing the Divine love and its radiant wisdom to the world."

Today humanity may question as to why knowledge of the 'truth' has been kept hidden. A most plausible explanation is given by the English author, Robert J. Scrutton in his book titled *The Message Of The Masters*.

"Surely, we may think, men would welcome such knowledge? Perhaps. Yet it is possible that the information could be either misunderstood or deliberately misrepresented and misapplied in religious practices of ancient times. Men of antiquity were taught that the soul of man lived on when his body died. What use was made of this information by some priesthoods? For thousands of years, information about the spiritual destiny of mankind was withheld because mankind was neither morally nor mentally ready to receive it. In this age, the seal of spiritual revelation was broken and forces applied which enabled man to gain mastery over nature. He used it to make our earth a living hell of struggling, frightened, neurotic people. The answer and its implications could change the entire course of human society. This answer is to be found in recorded history, from its beginning to the present history as seen through the eyes of the Prophets."

MASTERS DISCUSSED IN THIS CHAPTER

Raphael - St Germain

St Joseph - Father of the Family of the Holy Grail - St Germain (died 1st century AD)

St Germanus - St Germain (5th century AD)

Merlin/Taliesin - St Germain (6th century AD)

Sir Francis Bacon - St Germain (16th century AD)

St Mary - the Lady Portia - twin soul of St Germain (died 1st century AD)

St Brigid - 'Mary of the Gaels' possibly the Lady Portia (5th century AD)

Michael - Kuthumi

St Patrick - Kuthumi (5th century AD)

Leonardo da Vinci - Kuthumi (15th century AD)

Pharaoh Akhnaton (Amenhotep IV) - El Morya

Prophet Elijah - El Morya

NOTES AND RECOMMENDED READING

Robert Graves, *The White Goddess*, (Faber & Faber, U.K., 1961).

Peter Dawkins, *Arcadia*, (Francis Bacon Research Trust, Warwick, U.K)

Peter Dawkins, *Dedication To The Light*, (Francis Bacon Research Trust, Warwick, U.K.)

Peter Dawkins, *The Mystery of the Master*, (Francis Bacon Research Trust, Warwick, U.K.

Peter Dawkins, *The Great Vision*, (Francis Bacon Research Trust, Warwick, U.K.)

Peter Dawkins, *The Virgin Ideal*, (Francis Bacon Research Trust, Warwick, U.K.).

Peter Dawkins, *Francis Bacon, Herald of the New Age*, (Francis Bacon Research Trust, Warwick, U.K. 1997)

Haroutiun Saraydarian, *Christ, The Avatar of Sacrificial Love*, (1974)

Edmund Harold, *Second Sight*, (Grail Publications, Sydney, Australia, 1994).

William Foxwell Albright, *From The Stone Age To Christianity*, (Doubleday Anchor Books, U.S.A 1957)

Michael Taylor, *Master R Lord Of Our Civilisation*, (Rawley Trust, New Zealand, 1997)

Robert J. Scrutton, *The Message Of The Masters,* (Neville Spearman, Jersey, U.K. 1982)

C.W. Leadbeater, *The Hidden Life in Freemasonry*, (Theosophical Publishing House, U.S.A 1975)

Richard Laurence, *The Book of Enoch*, (Wizards Bookshelf, San Diego, U.S.A 1976)

White Eagle, *Morning Light,* (The White Eagle Publishing Trust, U.K. 1957)

PART TWO

CHAPTER 14

The Essenes & the Rise & Fall of the Maccabees

"And your Earthly Mother and Heavenly Father
will send their angels to teach, to love and to serve you"
(Gospel of the Essenes)
"The Elect shall possess Light, joy and peace,
and they shall inherit the earth."
(Enoch -Book of Enoch)
"Dissension broke out amongst the ranks of the Hasidim (the Pious Ones, the Holy
Ones, the Saints) who wished to preserve the flame of Divine Truth and eventually broke
up into three basic groups, the Pharisees, the Sadducees and the Essenes (the Holy
Ones)."
(William Foxwell Albright)

The previous chapters have given the reader some indication of the important roles that St Germain he has played throughout our planet's history. Earlier mention has been made of St Germain's incarnation as Joseph, the father of the Holy Grail Family who belonged to the Community of the Essenes and that *the Essenes were the 'Chosen' tribe, mentioned in the Bible for the word 'Essene' comes from the Greek word 'essaios' meaning 'mystic' or 'secret' and the Egyptian symbols of 'light' and 'truth' were represented in the word 'chosen' which translated into Greek, becomes 'Essen'.*

They were the 'Elect' of the Name, the 144,000 (a symbolical number) who shall rise again at the 'End of Days' (the onset of the Aquarian Age). In other words, they will reincarnate again, and know their true purpose and thus play their part to spread their 'Light' to the world for the purpose of restoring the divinity of mankind to earth. All of this is now occurring, and currently termed the 'New Age of Aquarius'.

When the Dead Sea Scrolls were discovered in 1947, at Qumran in the desert of Judah, approximately twenty miles from Jerusalem, tangible proof was provided of the existence of the Essenes. Most of what we know about the Essenes comes from the historian of that time, Josephus (born 37 AD) and from Edgar Cayce (1877-1945). Apart from the information Cayce provided about Lemuria, Atlantis and Egyptian times, Edgar also told a great deal about the life of the Essenes having once lived amongst them as Lucius of Cyrene.

Another modern day scholar, to whom we owe gratitude for his dedication to deciphering the Dead Sea Scrolls of Qumran, is the late John Allegro who published his findings in his book titled *The Dead Sea Scrolls* (1956).

Before the arrival of the long awaited Messiah, Palestine was a land of varied cultures and languages. Those of the Jewish faith were not all Hebrews, due to the fact that the races had interbred after Moses and Aaron (St Germain) had led the 'Chosen' tribes out of Egypt and into Palestine. The Hebrews had intermarried with some of the Arian race which resulted in various castes amongst them and it was because of this that the Hebrews and those of the Jewish faith failed to recognise each other's religions.

Because the Essenes settled in the area of the shores of Galilee, they became classed as Jews by the government. However, according to the Rosicrucian authority, the late Spencer Lewis, they were not Jews by birth, nor were they Jewish by religion. Their 'spiritual' religion had been handed down to them from the ancient temples of Atlantis and the grand patriarch, Noah - St Germain.

Spencer Lewis, who stated that the Essenes were the Rosicrucians of Palestine, informs us in his book titled *The Mystical Life of Jesus*, that there were two major areas where the Essenes established themselves. One in Egypt on the banks of Lake Maoris and the other was in Palestine at Engaddi near the Dead Sea. It was near this area that the Scrolls were found by a young shepherd boy who discovered them hidden in a cave.

According to Spencer Lewis, Lake Maoris was once known as the 'Land of the Roses'. In ancient days, roses and flax grew abundantly in this region. The flax was used to weave the fine white linen for the robes worn by the Great White Brotherhood. (These white robes worn by the Great White Brotherhood were considered to be a symbol of purity, the white being equated with the 'Light').

Not all of the Essenes (the 'People of Light') dwelt at Qumran; some of them had established themselves in Europe (Gaul), England and Ireland, where they set up their priesthoods to continue the teachings of Pythagoras (Kuthumi) and Hermes Trismegistus which became known as *Hermeticism*. These people became known as the Celtic Druids. The Essenes who became the Celtic Druids were the Guardians of the Celtic Church and of the ancient Mysteries.

The Essenes were a very gentle people and because they kept very much to themselves, little was known about them or their activities. The descriptive word of 'gentle people' eventually became 'Gentile' which is the name by which the Jews called them. However, during the era of the Messiah, in order to halt the ever increasing Roman domination over them, the Essenes were forced to have their own band of freedom fighters who were labelled as 'zealots' and the reasons why will be elaborated upon in a future chapter.

According to information contained in the book titled *From The Stone Age To Christianity* by William Foxwell Albright: "I still maintain that the original Essenes came from Mesopotamia in the second century BC and were less affected by Hellenism [referring to its Greek origins and cultures after the time of Alexander the Great - St Germain] than were the larger sects, and insist on the early date of the Gospels, including John [the Beloved]. The priceless documents of the Dead Sea Scrolls have brought a wealth of information and confirmation."

"The dualism of the Dead Sea Scrolls is definitely Iranian (Zoroastrian) in origin and that of the Arkana (Arcana). Earlier Iranian religion was substantially identical in general character and even in detail with that of the Arian faith and essentially like Homeric in Greek religion. At the head of the pantheon stood Ahura Mazda, 'the Lord of Wisdom' who was equated with Mithra, the god of 'Light' and the goddess of fertility, Anahita, 'the Unblemished One'. This period of Iranian religion is reflected by some of the teachings of the Avesta which have been only lightly worked over by later Zoroastrian editors. Somewhere in the ninth or even earlier BC, arose Zarathustra (Zoroaster) who preached a new gospel. According to Zoroaster, the good Ahura Mazda will ultimately prevail over the forces of evil; Ahura Mazda was the great god who created heaven, earth, and mankind."

Education of the Essenes

From early childhood, the children of the Essenes studied to become adepts and were students of the 'Wisdom' of the Avesta teachings which originated from the Persian Avatar, Zoroaster (Zarathustra), born around 650 BC. Incorporated into the teachings of Zoroaster was that of Ahura Mazda, meaning 'the Light of knowledge'.

The Essenian priests were Cabbalists who instructed the community in numerous skills which included the study of astrology, geometry, alchemy (chemistry) and mysticism. They taught the secrets of the universe, the harmonious progression of the heavens. Astronomy was particularly important in the Essenes' education, for according to the famous Philosopher's Stone of Hermes, 'As above, so below', the stars/zodiac are intricately related to events upon the earth - hence the story incorporated into the Bible of the 'Three Wise Magi' who followed the bright shining star in the heavens until they found the birth place of the Messiah. The star was *Cassiopeia* (mentioned in a previous chapter), and was known to the ancients as 'The Woman with Child'. This constellation of *Cassiopeia* produced an unusually bright star every three hundred years and it was the presiding constellation of Syria/Palestine at the time of the birth of Jesus.

According to Spencer Lewis: "Because of the divisions that had arisen among the peoples into sects such as the Pharisees, the Sadducees and their kind, there had arisen the Essenes, who cherished not merely the traditions which had come down by word of mouth, but had kept records of all supernatural experiences - whether in dreams, visions, or voices - that had been felt throughout the experiences of these people."

"These pertained to what you would today call astrological forecasts, as well as all those records pertaining to the coming of the Messiah. *These had been part of the records in Carmel given by Elijah* [El Morya], *who was the forerunner, who was the cousin, John the Baptist* [El Morya]. Hence the group we refer to as the Essenes was the outgrowth of the teachings of Melchizedek, as propagated by Elijah, Elisha and Samuel [St Germain]. The movement was not an Egyptian one, though it was adopted by them in an earlier period and made a part of the whole movement. The Essenes were to aid in the early teaching of the life of the child Jesus, as well as John. For John was more the Essene than Jesus. For Jesus held rather to the spirit of the law, and John to the letter of the same."

John the Baptist (El Morya) had once been the pharaoh Akhnaton, who introduced the idea of immersion into water as a form of purification during initiations. In his incarnation as John the Baptist, El Morya once again introduced the same idea; hence during the era of the Essenes', it became known as 'baptism'.

The Essenes and Spirituality

The Essenes' Teachings were steeped in 'spirituality. They did not worship in buildings, but in the midst of groves of trees where the beauty of nature was in abundance and where they could feel nature's natural energy fields - the earth's spirit (or serpent energy), all around them.

Anything to do with nature was sacred to the Essenes for they appreciated the fact that the 'Creator' was responsible for all the beautiful things upon the earth and the galaxy of stars above in the heavens at night. The Essenes took nothing for granted. None of these wondrous things could be experienced in a room or church specifically built for worshipping - the result would have been completely lack-lustre.

The Druids too, continued the same traditions, for the earth's spirit was around the sacred wells, streams, the landscape and the megalithic stone monuments.

An eloquently beautiful example of the Teachings of the Essenes is quoted further on, from the book titled *The Essene Gospel of Peace* translated by Edmond Bordeaux Szekely. The language in which they were written was Aramaic and Slavonic and at one stage, they had been kept in the Royal Archives of the Habsburgs. (St Germain frequented places where in previous lives, he had hidden documents, and one of these was the palace of the Habsburgs).

The Gospel of Peace provides us with a great deal of information about the Essenes and it is the original manuscript of St Jerome's translation. St Jerome's *Vulgate* consisted of translations of several of the Gospels from the original texts. His real name was St Eusebius (342-420 AD) who became known in England as St Jerome, which in Greek meant 'Sacred name'. His translations of the Hebrew and Greek writings of the Old and New Testaments into Latin formed the main part of the Latin Vulgate Bible. In the 4th century AD, St Jerome was personal secretary to the Pope and as such, he had access to numerous documents hidden by the Vatican. It was not until the 20th century, that Edmond Bordeaux Szekely rediscovered them in the Vatican which had kept the Essenian documents hidden for reasons of their own.

It is noteworthy that according to information in Peter Dawkins' book titled *The Great Vision*, the Gospel of Peace translated by Edmond Szekely from the original Aramaic texts constitutes accurate notes made by John the Beloved [Kuthumi's] personal teachings.

"Follow the example of all the angels of the Heavenly Father and of the Earthly Mother, who work day and night, without ceasing, upon the kingdoms of the heavens and of the earth. Therefore, receive also into yourselves the strongest of God's angels, the angel of deeds, and work all together upon the kingdom of God. Follow the example of the running water, the wind as it blows, the rising and setting of the sun, the growing plants and trees, the beasts as they run and gambol, the wane and waxing of the moon, the stars as they come and go again; all these do more, and do perform their labours."

"And your Earthly Mother and Heavenly Father will send you their angels to teach, to love and to serve you.

The Dead Sea Scrolls Deception - Jesus was a Freemason

In the book titled *The Dead Sea Scrolls Deception* (1991), the authors Michael Baigent and Richard Leigh maintain that the Vatican is suppressing valuable information contained in the Dead Sea Scrolls because their disclosure will undermine vital Christian doctrine.

The authors of the book titled *The Hiram Key*, Christopher Knight and Robert

Lomas after their investigations, believed that "if we were right that there is a direct connection between Freemasonry and the Qumranians, and that the Qumranians were the first Christians, it follows that Christ must have been, in some sense of the word, a Freemason himself. We were aware that this is a notion that will horrify many modern Christians, particularly Roman Catholics, but we did indeed find the evidence that that is exactly what he was."

The authors further relate that when the Jordan Department of Antiquities began their research of the Dead Sea Scrolls between 1951 and 1956, "what they found was the theologian's equivalent to sweating nitroglycerine; the world of Christianity could blow up if the whole thing was not handled with the utmost care. But the lid could not be kept on this explosive issue, no matter how hard the Christian Church tried to do so."

"Those in charge of the research were not independent scholars; they had a faith to protect and an establishment to maintain. Other scholars involved with the scrolls saw evidence that appeared to change the view of Christ and the New Testament, but they were effectively silenced or discredited."

"Accusations of scandal, cover-up and deliberate smothering of the truth have been met by denials and counter accusations of 'over-active imaginations' and 'deliberate sensationalism'. It is a fact that for more than forty years after their discovery, over half of the 800 scrolls discovered have not been published. The academic community was outraged by this unprecedented secrecy of what ought to be public knowledge and after widespread protests, led by the Huntington Library of San Marino, California, the Israeli authorities removed restrictions on public access to the contents of the scrolls in October, 1991. The whole area of investigation concerning Qumran is a minefield for ordinary Christians, so many have preferred to keep away from the subject."

According to the authors Christopher Knight and Robert Lomas: "The positive virtues taught in the Qumran Community were clearly laid out in the scrolls: truth, righteousness, kindness, justice, honesty and humility along with brotherly love. So similar are the three degrees of the Qumran Community to those of Freemasonry that it transcends mere coincidence."

The Masonic writer and member of the Theosophical Society, C.W. Leadbeater, who stated unequivocally that St Germain is recognised as the Head of Freemasonry, adequately described the history of Freemasonry in his book titled *The Hidden Life In Freemasonry*:

"By the exercise of Brotherly Love we are taught to regard the whole human species as one family, the high and low, rich and poor, created by One Almighty Being, and sent into the world for the aid, support and protection of each other. On this principle Masonry unites men of every country, sect, and opinion, and by its dictates true friendship among those who might otherwise have remained at a perpetual distance."

"To relieve the distressed is a duty incumbent on all men, particularly among Masons, who are linked together by one indissoluble bond of sincere affection; hence, to soothe the unhappy, sympathize in their misfortunes, be compassionate in their miseries, and restore peace to their troubled minds, is the grand aim we have in view; on this basis we establish our friendship and form our connections."

"Truth is a Divine attribute, and the foundation of every Masonic virtue; to be good men and true is the lesson we are taught at our Initiation; on this grand theme we contemplate, and by its unerring dictates endeavour to regulate our lives and actions. Hence hypocrisy and deceit are or ought to be unknown to us, sincerity and plain dealing our distinguishing characteristics, while the heart and tongue join in promoting each other's welfare, and in rejoicing in the prosperity of the Craft."

In the Bible, Joseph (St Germain), the father of the Holy Grail Family was described as a 'carpenter' as was Jesus, but a carpenter is also a craftsman - a terminology applied to Freemasonry.

John Allegro made the following remarks regarding the Dead Sea Scrolls.

"Clearing away the deadwood is the first condition of intellectual progress; but whether this generation has the courage or vision to grasp the opportunities of reassessment offered by these miraculous discoveries (of the Dead Sea Scrolls) in the Judean wilderness, remains to be seen." (John Allegro died in 1988).

The Rise and Fall of the Maccabees

In Chapter 9, we learned that St Germain in his incarnation as Alexander the Great was reputedly poisoned and that possibly the heinous crime was executed by one of his rivals, namely his general, Seleucus, who ruled over Babylonia and whose dynasty became known as the Seleucid dynasty (c.323-63 BC).

Included in the Dead Sea Scrolls is the Nahum Commentary which mentions two successors of Alexander the Great - Seleucid kings (identified as Demetrius III who invaded Israel in 88 BC) and Antiochus against whom the Maccabean uprising took place.

The notorious Antiochus IV (175-163 BC) was known as a tyrant king who was a descendant of Seleucus. He took control of Jerusalem which in turn caused a revolt amongst the occupants. In 167 BC, he desecrated the Temple of Jerusalem, and set up an altar to Zeus in place of Yahweh. He endeavoured to abolish the Jewish religion and forbade the observing of the Sabbath. Massacres were committed and captives were taken. Jerusalem was set ablaze in a similar fashion to the way that Nero set fire to Rome over one hundred years later.

The stage was then set for the rise of the Maccabees to lead the Jewish community in a war of independence and we are informed in Maccabees how Judas Maccabeus told his brother Simon to choose reliable men to go to Galilee and rescue the Jews who were in conflict with the Gentiles (Essenes) of Galilee. The Hasmonaeans (Maccabees) led the Jewish revolt in 164 BC against the Seleucid rule and established an independent kingdom in Palestine (Judah).

Having led the Jews to independence and gained a great deal of popularity amongst the Jews as a result, *the Maccabees usurped the priestly office. The ancient priesthood of Zadok was supplanted by the illegitimate Hasmonaean dynasty.* The Maccabean war-leader, Jonathan, (who was the brother and successor of Judas Maccabaeus) was not of the lineage of Zadok.

According to information contained in the book titled *The Hiram Key* written by Christopher Knight and Robert Lomas, the Dead Sea Scrolls recovered from Qumran related how Jonathan Maccabaeus was considered by the Hasidim to be an outrageous choice when he was elected as the High Priest. (In his book titled *From The Stone Age To Christianity*, William Foxwell Albright informs us that the Hasidim were the 'Pious' Holy Ones of the Essenes who rejected the leadership of the Hasmonaeans).

A split occurred amongst the rival priests and continued for the following 160 years, up to, and including the era of the Messiah. In 142 BC, Jonathan Maccabeus whom the Essenes considered to be their arch-enemy was executed by the Seleucid, Trypho, during the time that the Essenes were occupying Mount Carmel and in fear of Jonathan raiding their sacred place. No doubt they were grateful to Trypho for his timely intervention.

According to William Foxwell Albright:

"From the time of Simon Maccabeus (143-135 BC) strife broke out between the Sadducees and the Pharisees, as the two chief parties were thenceforth entitled. For two full centuries, from circa 130 BC to 70 AD, Jewish religious life was characterized by this party conflict in which the Pharisees gained ground steadily at the expense of their more aristocratic brethren, the Sadducees. *Dissension broke out amongst the ranks of the Hasidim (the Pious Ones, the Holy Ones, the Saints) who wished to preserve the flame of Divine Truth and eventually broke up into three basic groups, the Pharisees, the Sadducees and the Essenes (the Holy Ones)."* (The Essenes were of the Zadok/Levi Priesthood - descendants of Aaron - St Germain).

After the Hasmonaean dynasty of Jonathan and Simon Maccabeus, the Essenes were led by their own priests because they believed that the Temple had become corrupted and many of their sacred documents were transferred to Mount Carmel. As a result, they had set up their own Community *which was ruled by their Zadok Priesthood of the Order of Michael.*

Simon Maccabaeus 140 BC

In 140 BC, Jonathan's brother Simon Maccabaeus was elected by his followers as a High Priest and the priesthood was to remain in Simon's house 'until a faithful prophet should arise' (Maccabees 1,14:30-39). Within this statement is the admission of the illegitimacy of Simon's house. Simon and his sons were eventually murdered and the succession was taken over by his grandsons.

Aristobulus I, 103 BC

Then, in the year 103 BC, Aristobulus became the first king of the Jews as well as High Priest and forced all those living in Galilee to adopt circumcision and the Mosaic Law. (He was a grandson of Simon Maccabaeus).

History records the Maccabees as having been a family who held office for several generations (a period of sixty years), until they were finally usurped by the Herodians.

THE ANCIENT PRIESTHOOD OF ZADOK WAS SUPPLANTED BY THE

ILLEGITIMATE HASMONAEAN DYNASTY.

MASTERS DISCUSSED IN THIS CHAPTER
Aaron - St Germain
Prophet Samuel - St Germain
Alexander the Great - St Germain
Joseph the Father of the Holy Grail Family - St Germain
Moses - earlier incarnation of the Master Jesus
Melchizadek - earlier incarnation of the Master Jesus
Prophet Elijah - El Morya
John the Baptist - El Morya

NOTES AND RECOMMENDED READING

William Foxwell Albright, *From The Stone Age To Christianity*, (Doubleday Anchor, U.S.A 1953)
Christopher Knight & Robert Lomas, *The Hiram Key*, (Century, U.K. 1996)
C.W. Leadbeater, *The Hidden Life in Freemasonry*, (Theosophical Publishing House, U.S.A. 1975)
H. Spencer Lewis, *The Mystical Life of Jesus*, (AMORC, U.S.A. 1953)
H. Spencer Lewis, *The Secret Doctrines of Jesus*, (AMORC, U.S.A.1937)
H. Spencer Lewis, *Rosicrucian Questions and Answers*, (Available through Theosophical Bookshops)
Peter Lemesurier, *The Armageddon Script*, (Element Books, U.K. 1981)

John Allegro, *The Dead Sea Scrolls*, (Pelican Books, U.K. 1964)

Michael Baigent & Henry Lincoln, *The Dead Sea Scrolls Deception*, (Touchstone Books, 1993)

Edmond Bordeaux Szekely, *The Essene Gospel of Peace*, (International Biogenic Society, U.K. 1981)

Richard Laurence, *The Book of Enoch*, (Wizards Bookshelf, San Diego, U.S.A 1976)

CHAPTER 15

𝕿𝖍𝖊 𝕸𝖊𝖘𝖘𝖎𝖆𝖍, 𝖙𝖍𝖊 𝕾𝖆𝖉𝖉𝖚𝖈𝖊𝖊𝖘 & 𝖙𝖍𝖊 𝕻𝖍𝖆𝖗𝖎𝖘𝖊𝖊𝖘

*"The teachings of Jesus owe much to Pharisaic thought
and there is little doubt that Jesus was steeped in Essene doctrine and practice."*
(Excerpt from *The Messianic Legacy*)

With the eventual downfall of the Maccabean dynasty, the Essenes were once again faced with a tyrant ruler, namely Herod.

Herod the Great (c.73 - 4 BC)

Most readers would be familiar with the Biblical character, Herod the Great. He is the king discussed by Matthew, who ordered the massacre of all male infants in order to destroy the newly born Messiah, Jesus, although no actual evidence has ever been found to substantiate this event. The story of the order to kill all newly-born male children parallels with that of Moses, and it was probably placed in the Bible to give us a clue as to why the Romans wanted to persecute Jesus and his family. Obviously Herod felt very threatened by the arrival of the prophesied Messiah. Herod did not want to compete with a rival royal family. The Romans were then in domination of Jerusalem.

Herod lived during the same era as Mark Anthony and Cleopatra. He was the son of a man from Idumea named Antipater and a woman from Cyprus, who was the daughter of an Arabian sheik. Herod was not Jewish and commenced his career as a Roman general. Eventually, the Roman Senate made him king in about 40 BC. Such an appointment caused a great deal of resentment, particularly amongst the Jewish community who had always looked down upon the Idumeans as an impure race.

The Herodian family considered themselves to be the royal Roman family. They were usurpers stemming from the time of the Maccabees.

Herod defeated Antigonus, the last of the Hasmonaean kings with the assistance of the Romans in 37 BC. About the same year, Herod married Mariamne, a Maccabean princess, daughter of Antigonus (Herod's rival for the throne), in an attempt to legitimize the lineage, but then murdered her, her mother Alexandra (daughter of Hyrcanus who was a Jewish high priest and Hasmonaean king of the Jews before Antigonus), Alexandra's son Aristobulus (brother of Mariamne) and Mariamne's two young sons, Alexander and Aristobulus. He also murdered his eldest son, Antipater (whose mother was Doris whom Herod had married in circa 47 BC).

The Essenes' Messiah

Under the reign of Herod, the Essenes found their situation intolerable. They began to look forward to their prophesied Messiah. According to the Qumran *Community Rule*, the Essenes expected two separate figures, one a Messiah likened to Moses, and the other a reincarnation of Aaron (of the tribe of Levi), who would be a Zadok High Priest and he would be their 'Interpreter of the Law'. St Germain had once been Samuel, the Zadok High Priest. They also expected a prophet.

Peter Lemesurier in his book titled *The Armageddon Script* informs us that "the priestly Elijah, too, must be reborn amid the community [of the Essenes]. Admittedly, his role would be less exacting than the Messiah's. His task would be merely to preach repentance, to announce the Messiah and to proclaim the imminence of the Kingdom. For this he would need to be somewhat older than the Messiah himself, and consequently might well have to be born to parents who were already adult members of the community." The Messiah would be of the royal bloodline of the House of Judah- the House of David.

Thus the Essenes' prophecy was duly fulfilled.

(1)   The prophet was John the Baptist (El Morya), who in an earlier incarnation had been the prophet 'Elijah'. John was a cousin of Jesus whose parents were Elizabeth and Zachariah. Zachariah, according to Peter Lemesurier, was an Essene priest in the Temple at Jerusalem and Elizabeth too, was a practicing Essene.

(2)   Aaron (St Germain) reincarnated as Joseph, the Father of the Holy Grail Family.

(3)   The Messiah, Jesus, a prince descended from the royal House of David (Kuthumi), who had once incarnated as Moses, brother of Aaron.

Mary (Miriam), the daughter of Anna, becomes the Mother of Jesus

According to Peter Lemesurier: "It was to a girl named Miriam, daughter of one Anna, that the revelation eventually came...he would be a child of what the Essenes termed the 'spirit of Truth'." (The husband of Anna, and father of Mary, was Joachim).

Throughout the Biblical texts, Jesus always maintained that he was the 'Son of Man'. There was no celibacy amongst the Essenes or the priests of the Sanhedrin. They married and fathered children. Even the early Popes of the Catholic Church married and fathered children and it was only in later centuries that the idea of celibate priests was introduced by the Roman religion. In a recent documentary on the History Channel it was revealed that if the priests did not marry and have families, they would leave their money to the Church of Rome - thereby increasing its wealth over the centuries.

Peter Lemesurier makes the following interesting comments: "Word has it that they [Joseph and Mary] had difficulty in finding accommodation... In view of the almost universal Essene presence throughout Palestine, this seems an unlikely tale, even allowing for the secrecy which must have surrounded the plan."

According to Spencer Lewis in his book titled *The Mystical Life of Jesus*: "In the apocryphal gospel called *Protevangelion* written by James, a brother of Jesus, we find reference to the *cave* again in the following words: 'But on a sudden the cloud became a great light in the cave, so their eyes could not bear it'."

"Of the prominent Fathers of the Holy Christian church in the early days, we find that Tertullian (AD 200), Jerome (AD 375), and others, said that Jesus was born in a *cave*."

"Now the facts of the matter are that Matthew [in the Bible] was nearly correct when he said that Jesus was born in a *house*, for the cave in which the child was born was more than an empty excavation under a rock, or a hollow place in the mountainside. The Rosicrucian records and the Essene records have always contained the statement that the child of Mary and Joseph was born in an *Essene Grotto* on the highway near Bethlehem."

There are numerous books available questioning as to whether Jesus really existed. Many people also feel an affinity with the Essenes and their Teachings. In one of my past lives, I was a child of the Essenes and this was shown to me very clearly in a series of visions in 1993 which commenced shortly after my visitation by the Archangel Raphael and the Rose-Cross Knight. Two visions particularly stand out in my memory. The first one of me being present not long after the birth of Jesus and there were many gathered around the young babe in celebration, in fact, it was quite crowded. I was only about eight years old.

The second vision was to do with what happened after the crucifixion. I was sitting on a limestone wall, looking up a narrow street to my right hand side, watching two men who were supporting Jesus between them. I watched them as they carefully came down the steep white limestone cobbled street and saw them enter an opening in a wall almost opposite to where I was sitting, which must have been the place where the tomb was prepared for Jesus.

At the time I didn't understand the visions. Therefore, I sought the help of a well known clairvoyant who informed me in a trance channelling which came from 'Mary', the mother of Jesus that I was indeed a child of the Essenes. The information provided was taped and reads as follows:

"Do you remember being present not long after the birth of Christ? Yes, you do and in the recall of this memory, you also knew me. You must understand my beloved, whose child you were. You were a female child."

"Now it has been suggested by the rather unusual books written of the birth experience of Jesus that we were supposedly alone at that time. This was not true, for there were others around for it was predicted, it had been prophesied. Do you understand?"

"And you were a child, a child of the people, the Community of people that had gathered together and these are the Essenes."

"My Beloved one, you are the daughter of Ruth, do you remember her." (My answer was "no" - for I have no recall of her). "She was the Ruth of the Essenes and she was a trance-channeller and you were her daughter and she is present and stands beside you still. She brings to you love. You also knew Mary Magdalene well."

"And so this child of the Essenes was taught well and trained as an Essene, and it will serve you well, for you also remember your loyalty to them. And so intimately you have had relations with me and Jesus, and you played with Jesus when he was a small child."

"The Essenes were often persecuted. They were an organization that was constantly under fear and threat; they were an organization that brought to this earth, incredible information, information that was given to them by the spirits, information that was gathered and was documented. Much of this information has been destroyed beloved, but you remember it and will return it unto this Earth."

"In past lives you have told spiritual truths and had to hide them - lots of secret information away."

"Your Guide, who has specially chosen to protect and assist you, belongs to the Order of the Knights of St John - he was St John the Beloved Disciple."

Initially, I found the disclosure of who my Guide was, difficult to accept. Although I knew that the visions and visitations which I received were real enough, it was not until I was guided by the Masters to go overseas to visit Ireland and

Britain in 1996, that exact confirmation became very clear. It was during this sojourn overseas that the Master Kuthumi appeared to me in the two countries giving me clarification.

Mt Carmel

At the time of the birth of Jesus, all the documents and records preserved and contained in the Temple of Helios (the Temple of the Sun) were transferred to Mount Carmel. In later centuries, their Sacred Teachings and manuscripts were transferred to Tibet where in the 19th century, as mentioned in an earlier chapter, Madame Helena Blavatsky was taught by El Morya, Djwhal Khul, St Germain and Kuthumi. It was during this time that Helena gathered sufficient information to write her enormous volume of work titled *Isis Unveiled*.

Many great Masters of the Brotherhood studied at Mount Carmel and it was known not only as the 'School of the Essenes' but also as the 'School of the Prophets'.

According to Spencer Lewis in his book titled *The Mystical Life of Jesus*, it is known from Essene records that Jesus completed his official schooling at Mt Carmel when he was thirteen years old (having commenced his tutoring at Mt Carmel when he was six years old). "The record of His entrance into the school at Carmel shows He was entered as Joseph, the son of Mary and Joseph, and the reincarnation of *Zoroaster*, the 'Son of God'."

It is noteworthy that according to Spencer Lewis, discussing Mt Carmel, Pythagoras [Kuthumi] "spent part of his life there, and in the history of his life this retreat of Mount Carmel is referred to as 'sacred above all mountains and forbidden of access to the vulgar'."

Spencer Lewis also informs us about the connection of the Egyptian King Thothmes III, with Mt Carmel, and is referring to Pharaoh Tutmoses III (Kuthumi) (died 1447 BC).

"Those who are students of Rosicrucian history know that Thothmes the Third was one of the great founders of the early mystery schools of Egypt, and a leader in the movement that became the Great White Brotherhood. The Rosicrucian records also point out that Thothmes the Third in the year 1449 BC, conquered Carmel and released it to those who sought to maintain in this out-of-the-way place, a school and monastery for the mystery teachings."

And so, as the story goes, the prophesied Messiah of the Essenes grew to adulthood. According to Spencer Lewis, Jesus travelled a great deal and studied in the Temples of Egypt.

Peter Lemesurier commented upon Jesus journey to Egypt as follows: "An obvious reason for the journey would be to acquire as much as possible of the wisdom of the Egyptian mystery-schools - much as Moses had apparently done before him - which the Carmel Essenes seem to have held in great respect. Numerous traditions and sources, indeed, insist that he was subsequently to visit Persia and India for the same reasons, and even China and Tibet. To this day his alleged 'tomb' is locally revered in Srinagar, Kashmir, and persistent legends also tell of a youthful visit to Glastonbury, in southwest England."

Prior to these journeys mentioned above, when Jesus was twelve years old, he visited the Temple in Jerusalem where he was interviewed by the Priests of the Sanhedrin.

The Priesthood of the Sadducees and the Pharisees

Approximately twenty miles from the Essenian Community at Qumran, is Jerusalem, and it was in Jerusalem that the Temple was established, the Temple where the High Priests of the Sanhedrin assembled.

The Sanhedrin mentioned in the Bible, consisted of a council of High Priests who governed from the Temple and they seemed to have consisted mostly of Sadducees and perhaps a few Pharisees. We gain very little knowledge of the Sadducees and the Pharisees from the Biblical texts and in this chapter we will explore the reasons for the differences between them and the hostility between the two factions.

In order to have some understanding of the Sadducees and their rival party who were the Pharisees, the following paragraphs are quoted from William Foxwell Albright's book titled *From The Stone Age To Christianity.*

"The theology of the Sadducees and Pharisees reflects in large measure different applications of the Greek ways of thinking in the Hebrew Bible. The Pharisees mention existence after death."

"The Sadducees adopted an alternative interpretation and denied life after death. Even among the Essenes we find evidence of indirect Greek influence in the statement in the Scroll of Discipline and in a new emphasis on the distinction between 'spirit' and 'flesh' which goes far beyond anything in the Old Testament."

"By 100 BC (possibly a little earlier), the Communal centre at Qumran had been founded (as we know from the evidence of coins)... and the Essene literature now available to us seems to have been composed during the last century BC."

"It is certain that most, perhaps all, of the books of the New Testament arose in an environment which had been strongly under the influence of the Essenes and related Jewish sectarians. It is now clear that St Paul himself was also strongly influenced from this direction, in spite of his immediate Pharisee background."

"*Even the book of the Apocalypse which shows comparatively little such influence, will probably be found to have been profoundly affected by the Essenes since we have remains of books describing 'heavenly Jerusalem' among the Qumran finds, and it is considered that the book of the Apocalypse is dated around 68 AD; shortly before the Fall of the Second Temple."*

(In the sequel to this story, *The Dove, The Rose And The Sceptre, In Search of the Ark of the Covenant*, the story is told of how and why, John the Beloved who wrote the book of the Apocalypse was forced to go into exile, and that he went to the island of Patmos in 70 AD. In Revelation 1, verse 9, Kuthumi writing as John the Beloved, informs us that he was put on the island of Patmos because he had proclaimed God's word and the truth - in other words, he had preached 'Wisdom').

In order to keep the continuity of the story of the Pharisees, the Sadducees and the Essenes, it is relevant to this chapter to repeat part of passages quoted from William Foxwell Albright which were quoted in the previous chapter.

"From the time of Simon Maccabeus (143-135 BC) strife broke out between the Sadducees and the Pharisees, as the two chief parties were thenceforth entitled. For two full centuries, from circa 130 BC to 70 AD, Jewish religious life was characterized by this party conflict in which the Pharisees gained ground steadily at the expense of their more aristocratic brethren, the Sadducees."

"Dissension broke out amongst the ranks of the Hasidim (the Pious Ones, the Holy Ones, the Saints), who wished to preserve the flame of Divine Truth and eventually broke up into three basic groups, the Pharisees, the Sadducees and the Essenes (the Holy Ones).

Additional information: "Thanks to repeated statements of Josephus (Flavius ben Matthias), supplemented and confirmed by other Jewish and Christian data, we know the essential differences between the Sadducees and the Pharisees. It is very interesting to note that these differences were basically due to the different ways in which groups reacted to the challenge of Hellenic ways of thinking. Their conservative insistence on restricting the scope of canical Hebrew literature had confirmed the Sadducees in their conviction that belief in a future life, in divine judgement, in bodily resurrection, and in an angelic hierarchy were unscriptural and therefore contrary to the religion of the fathers."

"The Sadducees, probably reacting against the stoic attitude of their precursors, insisted on freedom of the human will."

"The Pharisees continued to believe in predestination or providence of God and the free action of man's will. In this respect, it was the Pharisees who carried on the Old Testament tradition and who marked out the delicate but fundamental line which orthodox Christianity was to take. The Pharisees became thoroughly Hellenized and they believed that the poorest man might aspire to become a great scholar if he had enough ability and industry."

In Peter Lemesurier's book titled *The Armageddon Script*, we find that "the Sadducees first emerged into the light of history as a distinct party during the reign of John Hyrcanus I (134-104 BC). Their name appears to derive from the word 'Zadokite', which by then had become a term indicative of priestly legitimacy - an idea having in this case more to do with wishful thinking and the needs of propaganda than with historical accuracy."

"They rejected the 'occult' doctrines espoused by the Pharisees. Even the popular idea of a sudden Divine intervention leading to an imminent Golden Age they continually played down, admitting only that the Kingdom of God, when it finally dawned, would be ushered in (in accordance with scripture), by 'a prophet like Moses'."

Thus it can be seen that somewhere in between lay the doctrines of the Essenes. In the Bible, Jesus is called the 'Nazarene'. From historical records, we know that there was no such place as Nazareth in those days. It was not until centuries later that a town was established and given the name of Nazareth to fit in with the hometown of Jesus, but as St Jerome noted, it was a place occupied wholly by those of the Jewish faith. Jesus was not of that sect at all. There was a sect that did not accept the Jewish faith who became known as the Nazarites or Nazarenes and they mixed with the Essenes, the result of which was that sometimes the Essenes were called by that name.

According to the authors Michael Baigent, Richard Leigh and Henry Lincoln in their book titled *The Messianic Legacy:* "the teachings of Jesus owe much to Pharisaic thought and there is little doubt that Jesus was steeped in Essene doctrine and practice."

It is the valid opinion of the authors quoting Dr Robert Eisenman, Chairman of the Department of Religious Studies at the University of California that "the loyalties of the Sadducees were divided by the time of the era of the Messiah and they consisted of those who clung to their Temple privileges and prerogatives under Herod's reign and continued to do so after his death. It is these latter Sadducees who become known as the Essenes, Zadokites or Zaddikim and the various other appellations that have hitherto confused researchers."

"For Eisenman, there is no distinction at all between the Zealots, Nazareans, Essenes and Zadokites. They all would have been unified by their joint involvement to rid their land of Roman occupation."

Having read the comments of William Foxwell Albright in previous paragraphs, we learnt that the *Sadducees* did not believe in reincarnation and bodily resurrection - so they would have been in total opposition to the religion of Jesus. Therefore, it is very apparent that Jesus and his family were **not** Sadducees.

From the book titled *The Armageddon Script* by Peter Lemesurier, we learn that "the Pharisees were a Jewish group of religious reformers who professed allegiance to the Law of Moses and they became acknowledged as experts on the ancient oral traditions. *At times they became heads of the Sanhedrin or Jewish*

Council, in Jerusalem. Like the Essenes, the Pharisees believed in bodily resurrection. They believed in angels, astrology, alchemy (magic) and everlasting life. Tithing - the giving of one-tenth of one's income to charity - was a firm rule among them."

"Certain professions, notably tax-collecting on behalf of the later Roman occupying power - were barred to them. The Sadducees, for their part, represented the aristocratic faction. They enjoyed the practical advantages of priestly power and a share in the running of the government."

According to the authors of *The Messianic Legacy*:

"JESUS WAS UNQUESTIONABLY A NAZAREAN AND HE SEEMS ALSO

TO HAVE BEEN A ZADOKITE."

MASTERS DISCUSSED IN THIS CHAPTER

Moses - the Master Jesus
Aaron - St Germain
Joseph, (Father of the Family of the Holy Grail) - St Germain
Prophet Elijah - El Morya
John the Baptist - El Morya
John the Beloved Disciple - Kuthumi

NOTES AND RECOMMENDED READING

H. Spencer Lewis, *The Mystical Life of Jesus*, (AMORC, U.S.A. 1953)
John Dominic Crossan, *Jesus, A Revolutionary Biography*, (Harper, U.S.A, 1994)
Brian Grenier, *St John's Gospel*, (St Paul Publications, Australia, 1991)
Martin Meyer, *The Gospel of Thomas, The Hidden Sayings of Jesus*, (Harper, San Francisco, U.S.A, 1992)
Mary Carter, *Edgar Cayce Modern Day Prophet*, (Bonanza, U.S.A 1970)
William Foxwell Albright, *From The Stone Age to Christianity*, (Doubleday Anchor, U.S.A 1953)
Merrill F. Unger, *Archaeology And The Old Testament*, (Zondervan Publishing House, Michigan, U.S.A.1954)
Michael Baigent, Richard Leigh & Henry Lincoln, *The Messianic Legacy*, (Arrow Books, U.K., 1996)
John Allegro, *The Dead Sea Scrolls*, (Penguin Books, U.K 1964)
Peter Lemesurier, *The Armageddon Script*, (Element Books U.K. 1981)
Hershel Shanks, *Understanding The Dead Sea Scrolls*, (University Press, Cambridge, U.K. 1993)
Charles W. Hedrick & Robert Hodgson, *Nag Hammadi, Gnosticism, And Early Christianity*, (Hendrickson Publishers, U.S.A, 1986)
King James Authorized Version of the Bible & Good News Bible

CHAPTER 16

𝕿𝖍𝖊 𝕾𝖔𝖓𝖘 𝖔𝖋 𝖅𝖊𝖇𝖊𝖉𝖊𝖊, 𝖙𝖍𝖊 '𝕱𝖎𝖘𝖍𝖊𝖗𝖘 𝖔𝖋 𝕸𝖊𝖓'

"And when it was day, he called unto him his disciples:
and of them he chose twelve, whom he also named apostles."
"I have suffered hunger
with the Son of the Virgin"
"I was instructor [teacher] to Eli and Enoch"
(Taliesin/Merlin/St Germain)

The Grail family to which the Avatar Jesus, the Messiah, the Christ, belonged were born in the age of Pisces, the Fish, and they were the 'fishers of men', seeking 'initiates' to whom they could teach the sacred Mysteries handed down to them from so long ago.

According to Spencer Lewis:

"We know that the word 'Christ' comes from the Greek word 'Christos' which means 'Messiah'. We find that the word 'Christos' was introduced to other nations when the Septuagint was prepared about 100 BC, and that it was used to translate the word Mashiach which means 'the anointed one', or in its more complete form, Meschiach, meaning 'Jahveh's Anointed.' The word or title 'Christos' had been used in the mystery schools and in the Orient for the name and title of many of the former Avatars. Going back to the Septuagint, we find that the Greek word 'Christos' originally came from the name of one of the Egyptian deities."

The Choosing of the Disciples

According to Spencer Lewis, "the Apostles of Jesus who were carefully selected by Him because of their previous experience in life and their worthiness, were carefully initiated by Him and spiritually developed during the secret conclaves which He held, and which never became a part of the public records of His life."

Matthew 10: These are the names of the twelve apostles: first, Simon (called Peter) and his brother Andrew; James and his brother John, the sons of Zebedee; Philip and Bartholomew; Thomas and Matthew, the tax collector, James son of Alphaeus and Thaddaeus; Simon the Patriot [Zelotes] and Judas Iscariot, who betrayed Jesus. **Mark 4:16:** Simon [Jesus gave him the name of Peter]; James and his brother John [Jesus gave them the name of *Boanerges*, an Aramaic word meaning 'Sons of Thunder']; Andrew, Philip, Bartholomew, Matthew, Thomas, James the son of Alphaeus, Thaddaeus, Simon the Patriot, and Judas Iscariot, who betrayed Jesus. **Luke: 6:13, 14, and 15:** And when it was day, he called *unto him* his disciples: and of them he chose twelve, whom also he named apostles. Simon (whom he also named Peter) and Andrew, his brother, James and John, Philip and Bartholomew, Matthew and Thomas, James the *son* of Alphaeus, and Simon called Zelotes, and Judas *the brother* of James, and Judas Iscariot, which also was the traitor. (Judas *the brother* of James is otherwise known as Thaddaeus).

Additional Information about the Disciples

The original twelve apostles were all Gentiles (Essenes) and were selected from amongst those who were at that time, living in Galilee. The monastery as Mount Carmel (originally founded by El Morya in his incarnation as the prophet Elijah), was presided over by its own High Priests who were known as the Magi (Wise Men), and it was there that the apostles would initially gather to study and be schooled in the Sacred Mysteries.

After the disciples had been trained and certain amongst them had qualified to be 'initiated', they then taught in Jerusalem and other areas within the vicinity.

1.   **Simon Peter, Cephas** (the rock), who resided at Bethsaida. John l: 42: tells us that Simon is the son of John. Simon Peter betrayed Jesus when the cock crowed three times. He was later to become the first Bishop of Rome and was eventually crucified by the Romans. His remains are 'reputed' to be buried beneath St Peter's in Rome; however, in the sequel to this story, *The Dove, The Rose And The Sceptre, In Search of the Ark of the Covenant*, I disclose where they are really buried.

2.   **Andrew, brother of Simon Peter**, both of whom resided at Bethsaida.

3.   **John, the brother of James Boanerges,** is the son of Zebedee and Mary of Galilee. John's more familiar name is John Joseph, the Beloved Disciple, author of the Gospel of John and Revelation. He was also the Master of the Mystical Rose known as Kuthumi.

4.   **Philip from the town of Bethsaida** (the same town where the brothers Andrew and Peter resided). In John l: 45 we are told that Philip meets Nathaniel (who is also elsewhere called Bartholomew) and tells him: "we have found

the one whom Moses wrote about in the book of the Law and whom the prophets also wrote about. He is Jesus, son of Joseph, from Nazareth." The 'we' can only be Simon Peter and his brother Andrew, plus Philip.

Furthermore, because Philip says that they have discovered Jesus who is the expected one according to the prophets, Simon Peter, Andrew and Philip are clearly *not* the brothers of Jesus.

5.   **Bartholomew was also called Nathaniel** whose name means 'Gift of God'.

6.   **Matthew (one of the Four Evangelists)** the 'Tax Collector'. Matthew's name was actually Matthias **Levi.**

7.   **Thomas (also called Didymus meaning 'twin', and Judas)** wrote the Gospel of Thomas which was found included in the Nag Hammadi documents. In John's Gospel 20:24, he is named as 'Thomas' and 'Didymus'. This scenario takes place when Mary Magdalene discovers the missing body of Jesus which is no longer in the sepulchre and John informs us that Thomas called Didymus, who was one of the twelve disciples, was not present. Eight days later, Jesus appeared to the disciples including Thomas.

Because 'Didymus' and 'Thomas' both mean twin, scholars have long debated whether he was a twin of Jesus. However, this seems most unlikely.

He is not the same Judas who **is** the brother of Jesus as told by Mark 6:3, "Is this not the carpenter, the son of Mary, the brother of James, Joses [Joseph] and of Judas, and Simon?" (The brothers are James the Just, John Joseph the Beloved, Judas Iscariot - the 'traitor' and Simon Zelotes - the 'Zealot', the 'Patriot', the 'Magus'). Thomas is reputed to have taught in India in the year 46 AD where he founded churches and he was martyred there in 72 AD.

8.   **James, (a variant of the name is 'Jacob'), brother of John Boanerges** who are the sons of Zebedee and Mary. Their more familiar names are James the Just and John Joseph the Beloved, whose other brothers are Judas Iscariot (not to be confused with Thomas Judas - the twin) and Simon Zelotes (the 'Patriot'). There have been many theories expounded regarding James the Just and the role that he played amongst the disciples.

One theory is that James was Joseph of Arimathea; however it will be seen further on, as recorded by several sources that James was executed in 62 AD and buried in the Kidron Valley; whereas, Joseph of Arimathea was in Britain in 67 AD, and was buried in Britain.

9.   **James the son of Alphaeus:** James' brother is *Judas* (not to be confused with the traitor Judas Iscariot). 'Alphaeus' may not have been an actual person; the name may originally have been 'Orpheus' meaning that James had undertaken an initiation in relation to the Orphic Mysteries discussed in previous chapters. ('Orpheus' literally means 'fisherman').

It is unlikely that this particular James is the brother of Thomas Judas

Didymus because elsewhere we find that James' brother Judas, is also known as the disciple Thaddeus. Thaddeus Judas, like Simon Zelotes and Judas Iscariot, was a freedom fighter for the Essenes. He was eventually beheaded by the Romans in the vicinity of Jerusalem, whereas, as previously mentioned, there is ancient evidence that Thomas Judas Didymus taught in India and was martyred there.

10. **Simon called Zelotes:** (Matthew 13 mentions Simon as being the brother of Judas Iscariot). Elsewhere in the Bible, Simon is also at times referred to as the Canaanite, the 'Magus', the 'magician', and the 'Patriot'.

11. **Judas, the brother of James:** (both of whom are the sons of Alphaeus. Judas is also known as the disciple Thaddeus - sons of 'Alphaeus').

12. **Judas Iscariot:** (Matthew 13 mentions Judas as being the brother of Simon Zelotes).

The Meaning of the Names of 'Zelotes' and 'Iscariot'

The utilization of the name of Judas gives us clues to those so-named as being of the lineage of the House of Judah. The surname of Iscariot was a nickname. Both Judas and Simon Zelotes were labelled as 'zealots' from which the name of 'Zelotes' was derived. 'Iscariot' was a corruption of the word 'sicarii' meaning a small dagger which was the type that the zealots wore around their waist for protection.

It was Judas Iscariot who was the traitor who betrayed Jesus. His role seems to have been not only that of a conspirator, but also that of an extremely ambitious one for he had a great deal of influence upon the lives of Jesus and James the Just and this will elaborated upon in a future chapter.

The Historian Josephus Flavius (37 - 100 AD)

Josephus is often quoted by other authors as being a 'Jewish' historian. His full name was Josephus ben Matthias, (meaning the son of Matthias) whose name in English translates into 'Matthew'. Matthew was a member of the Essenes, as 'initially' was his son, Josephus. If we accept that Jesus was crucified at the age of thirty-three (33) years, then, Josephus was not born until four years later.

Because of his background, Josephus' historical version is sometimes biased and unreliable for he often contradicts himself and the dates that he gives do not always match the appropriate time. However, because the history of which he wrote was so far back in time, apart from his work and the Bible, scholars have little else to draw upon.

Josephus was once a member of the Essenes. He married a Roman woman, lived the high life in a Roman palace, and he was later appointed by the Romans as a governor. Initially, he became a governor of Galilee where many of the Essenes and disciples resided. Thus it will be seen that Josephus had a foot in several camps. He accompanied the Roman soldiers on their attack against the fortress of Masada. What becomes blatantly obvious when reading through Josephus' anecdotes, is his egotistical attitude regarding his own personal achievements and his underlying lack of sympathy for the Essenes and their freedom fighters who fought against the Romans and whom he labelled as 'zealots'.

He was a traitor to his own people and he was virtually another 'Judas'. Josephus also fails to give Jesus recognition as being the Messiah and he was not the only member of this family to do so. There was quite a little family conspiracy taking place as sometimes happens in families where there is a major power play at stake. Greed always ends in corruption and within this Royal House of Judah, there were plots taking place controlled by certain High Priests in position of power.

> **And Jesus, walking by the sea of Galilee, saw two brethren, Simon, called Peter, and Andrew his brother, casting a net into the sea: for they were fishers.**
>
> **And he [Jesus] saith unto them, Follow me, and I will make you fishers of men. (Matthew 4: 18-19).** By this statement, Jesus meant he would have needed their assistance to find recruits to 'initiate'.
>
> **And when he had gone a little further thence, he saw James the *son* of Zebedee, and John his brother, who also were in the ship mending their nets. And straightway he called them: and they left their father Zebedee in the ship with the hired servants, and went after him. (Mark 1: Verse 19).**
> (Zebedee's wife was 'Mary').

It is important to note that they were mending their nets on a 'ship', not a boat, which indicates that it was larger than the ordinary fishing boats, especially considering they had 'hired servants'. Therefore, it must have been a wealthy fishing concern.

Joseph of Arimathea was described as being a rich man who was also closely connected with this family of Zebedee for at the time of the crucifixion, he had prepared a place (tomb) for the body of Jesus to be taken and cared for.

Simon (Lazarus/Zelotes), the Magus, is also elsewhere described as being a son of Zebedee. The mother of Zebedee's children is Mary and elsewhere in the Biblical texts, the Joseph referred to in the following verse, is at times called John. He is John Joseph, the Beloved, named after his father Joseph (St Germain), who is otherwise known as Zebedee.

> **And many women were there beholding afar off, which followed Jesus from**

Galilee, ministering unto him: Among which was Mary Magdalene, and Mary the mother of James and Joseph, and the mother of Zebedee's children. (Matthew 27 verse 55, 56)

'Zebedee' is obviously a symbolic name. When Francis Bacon and Sir John Dee translated the Bible from Greek into English in the 16th century, they may have planted the word 'Zebedee' as a cryptic clue. For example 'Ze' for sons of Zion/Jerusalem; 'Be' for Bacon and 'Dee' for Sir John Dee, the Master Kuthumi who in his incarnation as Leonardo da Vinci, was a Grand Master (Helmsman) of the Order of Sion. *Ze* was part of the word *Zion* and it meant the 'Sons of Light' according to J.J. Hurtak in the book titled *The Keys of Enoch.*

According to English author, Michele Brown, in her historical name book, variants of Sion are Nathanial and Theodore whose names mean 'Tudor' thus equated with 'Judah'. 'Sion' in Hebrew means 'Jehovah has favoured' and its Anglicized version is 'John' and 'Owen.' The name 'Owen' was favoured by the Tudors and in the Grail sagas, the name of the Knight Gawain, is actually 'Owein/Owen'.

It is also possible that 'Z' may have been a code name for the initiates, probably equated with 'Lightning' and Zeus, typifying the 'Ar-Thor' initiations.

'Sons of Thunder' and the Meaning of 'Sons of Jonah'

In order to keep the continuity, it is relevant to this chapter to repeat part of what was explained in an earlier chapter. From information contained in Peter Dawkins' book *The Great Vision* we learn the following:

"It should be noted that when Jesus called James and John *'Boanerges'*, an Aramaic term meanings 'sons of Thunder', he was referring to the Word of God and to the fact that these two disciple-initiates were indeed initiates, baptized with the Holy Spirit. Similarly when he called Peter and Andrew 'sons of Jonah', he was referring to the same Baptism (by IOA, as in Iona, the Dove and initiateship). There was in fact a Mystery school operating amongst the Essenes at the time of Jesus, which led suitable candidates through the paths of initiation - Lesser and then Greater. When an initiate completed the Lesser Degrees and entered the Greater Degrees, he was referred to as a 'son of Jonah', the Dove."

"Another term was also in current usage, but had become misapplied through its popularization; that is 'son of the Torah', where *Torah* is the name for the Law or Word of God, equivalent to the Egyptian *Tot or Thoth* and the Hyperborean *Thor* (as in ArThor)."

"The story that Andrew, and almost certainly the other three principal apostles, were originally disciples of John the Baptist, but were then directed to become disciples of Jesus the Christ, is indicative of the crucial transference from the Lesser to the Greater Mysteries of initiation - the point where those four achieved illumination and became 'sons of Jonah', 'sons of Thunder'."

As indicated in earlier chapters, John the Baptist (El Morya), a cousin of Jesus, introduced 'baptism' which was a form of purification dating back to the era when El Morya had been the Egyptian pharaoh, Akhnaton. His assistant was Hermes Trismegistus (Thrice Greatest).

In the first century, AD, the historian Josephus (Flavius) who in his early life, spent time with the Essenes, wrote that the two pillars of Hermes still existed in his own time and that they were built by Seth. (In the Bible, the original Seth, was the third 'son' of Adam).

Madame Blavatsky wrote that "Hermes was worshipped as the god of Wisdom, known in Egypt, Syria, and Phoenicia, as Thoth, Sat, Seth and Sat-an (the latter *not to be taken* in the sense applied to it by Moslems and Christians). In Greece he was known as Kadmos. The Cabbalists identify him with Adam-*Kadmon* and with Enoch."

According to a thesis by John D. Turner, in the book titled *Nag Hammadi Gnosticism And Early Christianity...* "it is clear that some form of baptismal ritual is peculiar to the Sethians. In particular, the Sethian baptismal water was understood to be of a celestial nature, a Living Water identical with light or enlightenment, and the rite itself must have been understood as a ritual of cultic ascent involving enlightenment and therefore salvation."

"They [the Sethian movement] must have sustained their initial encounter with Christianity as fellow practitioners of baptism, indeed a baptism interpreted in a very symbolic spiritual direction. For example, the Sethian name for their Living Water, itself a conception found in the Johannine [John the Beloved] Christianity (John 4:7-15) is Yesseus Mazareus Yessedekeus, which seems very much like a version of the name of Jesus into which Christians were baptized, perhaps in a three-fold way."

The author also explains that the Johannine texts "portray the exalted Sophia as the fountain or spring from which comes the Word [Logos] like a river, the Mother of the Word through whom the universe came to be. To be baptized in her water is to receive the true gnosis. Thus her Voice is the revelation of the truth."

Turner relates the parallels of verses of John the Beloved and those found in the Gospel of Thomas.

John: 4:14
"He who drinks from the water that I give him,
will never thirst into eternity.
But the water that I will give him
will become in him a spring of bubbling water

for eternal life."

Gospel of Thomas logion 13:

"You have drunk, you have become intoxicated from the
bubbling spring that I have measured out."

Nearly five hundred years after these events, the Master Kuthumi was to
reincarnate as the famous King Arthur. It was a title used when Merlin the Magus
of the 6th century AD, initiated the person whom he anointed as King of the Celts
as King Arthur (meaning Ar-Thor); however, Arthur was not his real name.

In John 1, verse 42, Jesus renamed Simon (Peter) saying:

"Thou art Simon, the son of Jona: thou shalt be called Cephas, which is by
interpretation, A stone."

The Gospel was written in Greek and the Greek word for stone/rock is
'petros'. The meaning of 'Jonas' as having been a form of initiation is equated with
the type of initiation undertaken by the 'sons of Thunder', the Boanerges, John the
Beloved and James the Just (also called the Less) who were the sons of Zebedee
and Simon the Magus is elsewhere mentioned as being a son of Zebedee.

From information contained in Peter Dawkins' book titled *The Great Vision*
we are informed as follows:

"Peter (Simon), John and James (Zebedee, Boanerges) and Andrew were said
to be partners in a fishing concern based at Bethsaida on the north shore of the
Sea of Galilee. The term 'fishermen' refers, in the Orphic Mysteries, to the fully-
fledged initiate who has entered the Greater Degrees of Illumination. The word
Orpheus literally means 'fisherman'."

"It was a term used also in the Druidic Mysteries, which have a kinship with
the Orphic Mysteries. Christianity as we know it was born from a Hebraic womb
into a Greek cultural environment. The Biblical New Testament is filled with
symbols and teachings from both Hebraic and Orphic sources, both of which stem
from Ancient Egypt."

"The 'fisherman' is the Grail initiate, who is able to fish in the ocean of life at
will and catch the mysteries of God - each fish representing the greatest of mysteries
that can be caught, which is man himself: hence the statement by Jesus that these
disciples would be 'fishers of men'. Furthermore, *Bethsaida* (which means 'fisher-
home') was the home of these four fishermen, and Peter's (Simon's) house in
Bethsaida was made a headquarters of Jesus and his disciples."

"Not only was Bethsaida on the northern shore of Lake Galilee, but Galilee
itself is in the northern portion of the land of Israel and represents the 'head' of
the sacred landscape-temple of Palestine; the most northerly point and crown being
the triple-peaked Mount Hermon, called 'the Ancient of Days' by the Jews, referring
to the Heavenly Father...so it was not by chance that the home of Jesus and his
'fishermen' disciples should be at Bethsaida in Galilee."

According to author Betty Radice in *Who's Who in the Ancient World*, Orpheus was the greatest singer and musician conceived by the Greeks and Apollo [St Germain] was said to be the founder of the mystic cult of Orphism.

We are told in Mark 13:3 that Peter (Simon), James, John and Andrew are the recipients of the 'secret revelation' which is obviously alluding to the fact that they had been initiated into the Greater Mysteries. They, along with Peter (Simon) were the pillars of the church in Jerusalem (Gal. 2:9 and 1:18) which shows that they held important positions amongst the Disciples.

'Zebedee' and 'Thunder' is one and the same person for Jesus called his brothers John Joseph and James, the 'sons of Thunder'.

As Zebedee the fisher-man, St Germain in his capacity as a High Priest, would have been known as 'Thunder' and he initiated qualified members into the Orphic Mysteries. Certain of his sons, namely John the Beloved (Boanerges 'son of Thunder') and James the Just (Boanerges 'son of Thunder'), having passed their initiations, would have been eligible to become designated priests who continued to initiate those who were worthy into the Orphic Mysteries which were also Druidic initiations.

The one, who does not seem to have been initiated, was Judas the younger brother; for no-where in the Bible does it state that he was. He was obviously not worthy and probably held some built-in resentment which along with his devious ambitions may have been a contributing factor that led him to assist with the arrest Jesus.

According to information contained in the book titled *Nag Hammadi Gnosticism And Early Christianity*, in a thesis written by Bentley Layton, we are informed that the literary meaning of Thunder is 'Perfect Intellect'.

"...*Thunder* owes its peculiar character to the blending of three ordinary unrelated literary modes: the Isis/Wisdom proclamation, asserting the power, sovereignty, and special knowledge [gnosticism], and special knowledge of the speaker, the philosophical sermon, with its vision of life falling into two neat moral, intellectual, and anthropological options (Two Ways) and exhorting the listener to choose only the higher way; and the riddle, which demands, first, a solution, and, second a re-exegesis [exposition of Scripture] of the entire text as riddle to see how the solution applies. Riddles often speak with a mythic directness that demands the active application of the listener's intellect, in a way that sermons and aretalogies rarely do."

The author, Bentley Layton, mentions the discovery of "a little-known *Gospel of Eve*" which contains a poem that he discourses upon.

"*Thunder, Perfect Intellect* (or simply, Thunder) is a powerful poem of some two hundred verses, originally composed in Greek. This poem has been called unique in the surviving Mediterranean literature, primarily because of its combination of the rhetorical mode of omnipredication (best known from Isis aretalogy) with a logic of antithetical paradox that negates the possibility of taking predication seriously. A few lines from the opening of the poem can serve to remind us of the extraordinary impression made by this most bizarre of all works from the Nag Hammadi corpus:

It is from the power that I, even I, have been sent
And unto those who think on me that I have come;
And I was found in those who seek me.
Look upon me, o you (plural.) who think on me.
And you listeners, listen to me!
You who wait for me, take me unto yourselves,
And do not chase me from before your eyes.
For, it is I who am the first: and the last.
It is I whom am the revered and the despised.
It is I who am the harlot: and the holy,
It is I who am the wife: and the virgin."

"*I have suffered hunger
with the Son of the Virgin*"
"*I was instructor [teacher] to Eli and Enoch*"
(Taliesin/Merlin/St Germain)

In the 6th century AD when St Germain wrote under the pseudonym of Taliesin, the verse above is referring to 'spiritual hunger', not physical hunger and he was implying that he taught Jesus the wisdom of Isis/Sophia (the 'virgin' of knowledge). He had once been the teacher/ instructor to both Eli and Enoch (which proves just how highly evolved a Master he is).

According to John D. Turner's treatise in the book titled *Nag Hammadi Gnosticism And Early Christianity*: "To judge from Irenaeus Haer 1.29 and the four versions of the *Aprocryphon of John* [the Beloved] which represent already Christianized versions of the Sethian myth...the *Aprocryphon of John* first exhibited the following profile. The Father, the invisible virginal Spirit, emitted his female aspect conceived as his Thought (Ennoia) which took shape as his First Thought (or Forethought)..."

The author, Bentley Layton compares the mystery of the verses of the *Gospel of Eve*, to Isis/Sophia.

"Thus Isis grandly claims, 'Isis am I, mistress of every land...It is I who overcome fate'."

On another comparative level, we have John (Kuthumi) in the Bible informing us thus:

'*In the beginning was the Word,[Logos] and the Word was with God, and the Word was God.*

The same was in the beginning with God.
All things were made by Him; and without Him was not anything made that was made.
In him was life; and the life was the light of men.
And the light shineth in the darkness; and the darkness comprehended it not.
There was a man sent forth from God; whose name was John.
The same came for a witness, to bear witness of the Light, that all men through him might believe.'

According to John Turner, in Mark 1, Revelation 12 and the Apocalypse, there is a "basic mythical structure concerning a divine child and his divine mother who are threatened by an evil power, but who are rescued and find safety in the wilderness until the evil power is destroyed. This general pattern could be made to apply not only to Adam and his divine mother or to Seth and his mother Eve, but also to the birth of Jesus, to Mary and their flight to Egypt, and perhaps more remotely to certain aspects of the Isis-Osiris-Horus cycle."

Important points to remember:

1. Zebedee the 'fisherman' is identified in the Bible as being married to Mary, therefore, he is Joseph, (St Germain) and two of his sons are James and John whom Jesus called 'Boanerges', the 'sons of Thunder'. They are otherwise known as James the Just and John the Beloved, (Kuthumi).
2. Simon who is listed elsewhere in the Bible as a 'son of Zebedee' is a brother of Jesus, James, John (Joseph), Judas and the sisters.
3. The younger brother Judas is never mentioned as having undergone any initiations.

ST GERMAIN WAS ONCE WORSHIPPED AS APOLLO AND AS APOLLO HE WAS

THE FOUNDER OF THE ORPHIC MYSTERIES - THOSE OF THE AR-THOR

INITIATIONS EQUATED WITH ZEUS.

MASTERS DISCUSSED IN THIS CHAPTER
Orpheus - St Germain
Apollo - St Germain
Joseph (Zebedee), the Father of the Grail Family - St Germain
Merlin/Taliesin - St Germain
John the Beloved - Kuthumi

King Arthur - Kuthumi
Pharaoh Akhnaton (Amenhotep IV) - El Morya
John the Baptist - El Morya

NOTES AND RECOMMENDED READING

Peter Dawkins, _The Great Vision_, (Francis Bacon Research Trust, Warwick, U.K.)
Robert Graves, _The White Goddess_, (Faber & Faber, U.K., 1961).
Michele Brown, _Baby Name Book_ (History of names), (Greenwich Editions, U.K., 1985)
Betty Radice, _Who's Who In The Ancient World_, (Penguin Books, U.K., 1971).
Charles W. Hedrick & Robert Hodgson, _Nag Hammadi, Gnosticism, And Early Christianity_, (Hendrickson Publishers, U.S.A, 1986)
J.J. Hurtak, _The Keys of Enoch_, (The Academy for Future Science, U.S.A 1977)
King James Authorized Version of the Bible & Good News Bible

CHAPTER 17

𝕿𝖍𝖊 '𝕿𝖊𝖆𝖈𝖍𝖊𝖗 𝖔𝖋 𝕽𝖎𝖌𝖍𝖙𝖊𝖔𝖚𝖘𝖓𝖊𝖘𝖘' & 𝖙𝖍𝖊 '𝕬𝖓𝖓𝖆𝖘' 𝕻𝖗𝖎𝖊𝖘𝖙

"I am able to instruct the whole universe"
"I have been teacher to all intelligences"
(Taliesin/Merlin/St Germain)
"Peace shall be to the righteous; and the path of integrity
shall the righteous pursue,
in the name of the Lord of spirits for ever and ever."
"The Elect shall possess Light, joy and peace,
and they shall inherit the Earth."
(Book of Enoch)
"For everything [of the Essenes] shall be held in common,
Truth and fair humility, and faithful love, and just consideration for one's fellow
in the Holy Council...an eternal planting, a Holy House of Israel,
an assembly of supreme Holiness for Aaron [St Germain]..."
(Excerpt - *The Dead Sea Scrolls* by John Allegro)

The Essenes called themselves the 'New Covenant' and they were a community who were democratically governed. The verses quoted above are rather self-explanatory as to the way in which they conducted themselves and also demonstrate the high level of integrity which they held for Aaron (St Germain).

Back in the days of King Nebuchadnezzar, lived the prophet Jeremiah who prophesied 'The time is coming when I will make a new covenant with Israel and Judah...I will set my law within them and write it on their hearts...No longer need they teach one another to know the LORD; all of them, high and low alike, shall know me...'

In his book titled *The Armageddon Script*, Peter Lemesurier, informs us as follows:

"The Covenant, in other words, would be written indelibly in the consciousness of the faithful in such a way that they could henceforth act out of direct knowledge and of the truth, rather than out of mere second-hand instruction.

241

Intuition and Divine inspiration would once more come into their own, as the prophet Joel had long ago foretold: 'I will pour out my spirit on all mankind; your sons and your daughters shall prophesy, your old men shall dream dreams and your young men see visions...' And the faithful would consequently be inspired by a positive, innate yearning for righteousness, rather than by negative fear of the consequences of neglect. Imbued with this new spirit, they would then find within themselves sufficient strength and conviction to carry out the undertaking which went far beyond all previous attempts to fulfil the Mosaic Law."

The Essenes of Qumran had various names and apart from the Sons of Zadok which are discussed further on in this chapter, they also called themselves 'Sons of Truth, the 'Men of Melchizadek' and 'Sons of Light', or 'People of the Light'. (The Celts of Ireland trace their ancestry back to the tribe of Dan, known in Ireland as the *Tuatha de Danaan* - the 'People of the Light', the children of Anna/Dana/Danu).

The Priest and the Teacher of Righteousness

"I have been on the Galaxy at the throne of the Distributor [God]"
"I have been fostered in the land of the Deity [God]"
"I am able to instruct the whole universe"
"I have been teacher to all intelligences"
"I know the names of the stars from north to south."
"In myriads of secrets, I am as learned as Math...
I know the star-knowledge
Of Stars before the earth (was made)
How many worlds there are...
I shall be until the day of judgement on the face of the earth.
Prophesy of Arthur
Or is it me they celebrate?"
(Taliesin/Merlin/St Germain)

Continuing with Peter Lemesurier:

"For the Teacher of Righteousness was held to have been instructed by the mouth of Yahweh Himself. In his heart 'God sets (understanding) that he might interpret all the words of His servants to the Prophets, through whom He foretold all that would happen to His people and His land.' **To him Yahweh [God] had revealed 'all the mysteries of the words of His Servants the prophets'** and it was therefore the task of the Teacher and his successors to 'measure out all knowledge discovered throughout the ages, together with the Precept of the age', and to 'do the will of God according to all that has been revealed from age to age.'"

"For the Teacher, in consequence, set himself the daunting task of studying and meditating upon all the prophecies relating to the current times, which historical events had convinced his compatriots were the **long-predicted Last Times, the culmination of world-history, immediately leading up to the promised Golden Age.**" (Bold-type has been utilized for the sake of emphasis).

The Essenes of Qumran believed that the *Teacher of Righteousness and his group would form the family of the new 'Israel' - the 'Elect', the 'Chosen' ones.* The Dead Sea Scrolls related how the 'Sons of Zadok', were the 'Chosen of Israel', the 'Elect of the Name', who shall arise again in the end days.

According to John Allegro "The Essenes' own leader was called the *Teacher of Righteousness* and they called themselves the *Sons of Zadok,* or the *Children of the Light* in contradistinction to their religious opponents, the *Children of Darkness.*"

An ancient scroll which pre-dated the finding of the Dead Sea Scrolls belonging to the Essenes was discovered in Cairo in 1897 and it became known as the *Damascus Document.* This document contained the laws of the Essene Community which mention the fact that their sect was ruled by priests called the Sons of Zadok. (In Hebrew, the word Zadok meant 'Righteous').

As mentioned elsewhere, St Germain had once been the prophet Samuel, the Zadok High Priest who anointed David (Kuthumi) as King of the House of Judah.

John Allegro informs us that the *Teacher of Righteousness* of the Qumran Community had access to the Sacred Mysteries and this is mentioned in the commentary of the prophet Habakkuk: "to whom God made known all the secrets of the words of His servants, the prophets." (The Book of Habakkuk was found in Cave 1 at Qumran).

Thus, the *Teacher of Righteousness* was a 'revealer of mysteries and knowledge'. In other words, he was an instructor into the Arcane (secret) Mysteries, one whom the Essenes knew had incarnated many times before.

According to John Allegro "the Teacher of Righteousness had the responsibility of passing on these secrets to his followers and in another Qumran commentary is referred to as the 'Mediator of Knowledge' and he is probably the author of the hymn who styles himself as 'Mediator of Knowledge in the wonderful Mysteries'."

We are further informed in the *Manual of Discipline*: "He will purge by His Truth all the deeds of Men, to give to the upright insight into the knowledge of the Most High and into the Wisdom of the sons of Heaven, to give the perfect way of understanding. Thus, the Spirit of Truth enlightens man to an understanding and insight and mighty wisdom which believe in all the works of God."

The Dead Sea Scrolls tell of two men who will appear in the 'Last Days' (the onset of the Age of Aquarius). One is spoken of as the 'Star' and the other is the 'Sceptre', a king from the lineage of the House of David (Judah). Clearly these prophecies indicate that the Star is St Germain and the Sceptre is Kuthumi who had once been King David.

From the Book of Daniel we learn that the Book of Knowledge is to be sealed until the 'Last Days' and in the Book of Revelation of John the Beloved (Kuthumi), the book has its seven seals opened by the Angel/Teacher or Revealer of the Mysteries. In Luke 8:17 we are informed "For nothing is secret, that shall not be made manifest; neither any thing hid, that shall not be known and come abroad."

Throughout this story, reference is given to 'Wisdom' being otherwise called 'Sophia' and also 'Pallas Athena'. The Teacher of Pallas Athena is St Germain and his works of the 16th century when he incarnated as Sir Francis Bacon began the teaching of 'Wisdom', of 'enlightenment'; works which often incorporated the name of Pallas Athena. It was during the Elizabethan Renaissance that Francis Bacon laid the ground work for the Advancement of Learning and for the new Golden Age of Aquarius.

It is known from the *Damascus Rule* that the community of the Essenes was governed by a hierarchy, the head of which was designated the title *mebaqqer,* or 'Guardian'. Peter Lemesurier in his book titled *The Armageddon Script* informs us that the Dead Sea Scrolls confirm that, even at the Essenes' annual meeting on the Feast of the Renewal of the Covenant, the 'Guardian' in charge of the whole assembly was to "be one who had **'mastered all the secrets of men and the languages of all their clans'."**

John Allegro and other scholars of the Dead Sea Scrolls admit that one of the difficulties of identifying characters mentioned in them is that actual names of individuals are rarely given - only titles alluding to the character of the person.

The Essenes' Zadok High Priest, whose name was anonymous, is described in the Scrolls as both **'The Priest' and 'The Teacher of Righteousness'.** But which High Priest could he have been?

And, furthermore, where was the place where he would become the *Interpreter of the Law? A place where he would once again be a magistrate/judge as he had been in his incarnation as the Zadok High Priest, Samuel?*

The 'Annas' Priest of the Sanhedrin, the 'Interpreter of the Law'

"I am able to instruct the whole universe"
"I shall be until the day of judgement on the face of the earth."
(Taliesin/Merlin/St Germain)
"For everything [of the Essenes] shall be held in common,

Truth and fair humility, and faithful love, and just consideration for one's fellow in the Holy Council...an eternal planting, a Holy House of Israel, an assembly of supreme Holiness for Aaron [St Germain]..."
(Excerpt - *The Dead Sea Scrolls* by John Allegro]
The Sovereign Lord [supreme ruler] said, "**Those priests belonging to the tribe of Levi who are descended from Zadok, however, continued to serve me faithfully in the Temple ...**"

(Ezekiel 44:15, Good News Bible]

Annas the Elder

We have ascertained that the Essenes' expected Teacher of Righteousness would be a reincarnation of Aaron (St Germain) and that the prophecy was fulfilled when St Germain reincarnated as Joseph, the father of the Messiah and the Grail Family.

From the hints given about Zebedee being a wealthy fisherman who had a 'ship' (not a 'boat') and servants, we know that whatever his occupation was, he was both a prominent and respected member of the community. Not only that, he was also the father of Jesus (Levi), John the Beloved (Levi), James the Just (Levi), Simon Zelotes (Levi), Matthew (Levi) and Judas (Iscariot). It will be seen further on that with the exclusion of Jesus, five of the sons of 'Zebedee', the 'Fisherman', became High Priests of the Sanhedrin. We have learned that the connotation of 'Fishermen' meant that the disciples were gathering 'initiates' for the Orphic/Jona Mysteries.

The only High Priest of that era, who adequately fits the requirements and description, was the High Priest whom the historian Josephus (Flavius) described as being a very powerful, wealthy and highly respected member of the community who had servants.

Josephus in his *Antiquities* recorded that at the time of the birth of Jesus, **the head of the Levi/Zadok priests was Annas, the Elder High Priest of the Sanhedrin in the Temple of Jerusalem.**

Joseph, the Father, was the Elder Priest Annas, the title of which is the plural of '**ANNA**' whose ancient origins have been discussed in previous chapters. Thus, it was no mere coincidence that the Priests used the ancient title of '**ANNA**' whose origins could be traced back to the Arian race and the tribe once known as the Mari-Annas.

('Mari' is another name for 'Mary' and consider how many Maries are included in the Grail family and also the fact that Anna was the maternal grandmother of Jesus. Joseph of Arimathea married an Anna and they named their daughter Anna. This was the same Anna who married Bran the Blessed King of Britain and founded the continuity of the Grail dynasty - the future Celtic kings and Saints of Britain).

According to the Bible, the profession of Joseph (the Father) was that of a 'carpenter' (as well as a fisherman - a 'fisher of men'). Commenting on the word carpenter, Peter Lemesurier wrote that "the word was also used in contemporary esoteric literature as a cipher code for 'scholar'; and thus for an **interpreter of the scriptures**."

Peter also relates that carpentry was a 'craft'. Craft, as mentioned elsewhere in our story, is a terminology of Freemasonry.

As the anonymous *Teacher of Righteousness*, the 'Interpreter of the Scriptures' of the Essenes, he was also expected to become the 'Interpreter of the Law' and the main place where the 'Law' was 'interpreted' was the Temple of the Sanhedrin where he would naturally have held a position of power.

Commenting upon the Essenes' Teacher of Righteousness, the author Peter Lemesurier in his book titled *The Armageddon Script* wrote: "Historically, however, few interpreters have had their intuitive gifts for biblical exegesis trusted so implicitly as the sect's Teacher of Righteousness. This undoubted fact suggests that not only was he a man of enormous presence and of overwhelming and contagious conviction, but that his prophetic interpretation had proved astonishingly accurate even during his own lifetime. It would not be too surprising if the latter were the case, since, his whole approach seems to have centred on the *deliberate fulfillment* of prophecy. This fact, plus the operation of the Law of Self-Fulfillment, would probably have been more than enough to give rapid factual credence to his prophetic gifts."

(According to William Foxwell Albright in his book titled *From The Stone Age To Christianity*, Samuel the prophet, who was the Zadok High Priest, was also a judge/magistrate, an 'interpreter of the Law' and "was even considered to be a diviner/seer").

"Yet it needs to be borne in mind that the Teacher was still attempting to do two things at once - to interpret *and* prophesy. This is by no means an easy task, even at the best of times. But the Essenes clearly had good and cogent reasons for holding their Teacher's gifts in high regard. Undaunted by the difficulties, therefore, the Teacher continued to pursue his awesome mission."

Additional Information about the Levi Priesthood

From the book titled *From The Stone Age to Christianity* we are informed as follows:

"The Tabernacle and the Ark were under the charge of the Levi priesthood, who perpetuated their Egyptian traditions as late as the early 11th century, when the two sons of Eli are called Hophini and Phinehas, both Egyptian names."

"At the head of the priesthood stood the chief priest, called in our earliest sources simply as 'the priest', since early Israel seems to have consistently eschewed honorific titles. We know from the inscriptions of Ugarit that the head of the local priesthood was called *rabbu kahinima* meaning 'chief of the priests', as early as the 14th century BC."

"Only the exceptional head of a priestly system could also become a leader of his people in war and peace. In times of crisis or danger, there had to be magistrates whose decision in civil cases would provide a court of appeal for tribesmen who felt themselves oppressed. Leaders arose, heads of clans and priests such as Eli and the prophet Samuel [St Germain]."

"FOR NOTHING IS SECRET, THAT SHALL NOT BE MADE MANIFEST; NEITHER

ANY THING HID, THAT SHALL NOT BE KNOWN AND COME ABROAD."

(LUKE 8:17)

MASTERS DISCUSSED IN THIS CHAPTER

Aaron of the House of Levi - St Germain
Prophet and Zadok High Priest Samuel - St Germain
Teacher of Righteousness, (Annas the Elder High Priest of the Sanhedrin), - St Germain
Joseph, (Zebedee) the Father of the Family of the Holy Grail - St Germain
Francis Bacon of the House of Tudor - St Germain
King David - Kuthumi
John the Beloved Disciple - Kuthumi

NOTES AND RECOMMENDED READING

John Allegro, *The Dead Sea Scrolls*, (Penguin Books, U.K 1964)
Peter Lemesurier, *The Armageddon Script*, (Element Books U.K. 1981)
Hershel Shanks, *Understanding The Dead Sea Scrolls*, (University Press, Cambridge, U.K. 1993)
William Foxwell Albright, *From The Stone Age To Christianity*, (Doubleday Anchor Books, U.S.A, 1957)

Charles W. Hedrick & Robert Hodgson, *Nag Hammadi, Gnosticism, And Early Christianity*, (Hendrickson Publishers, U.S.A, 1986)

Merrill F. Unger, *Archaeology And The Old Testament,* (Zondervan Publishing House, Michigan, U.S.A 1954)

Robert Graves, *The White Goddess*, (Faber & Faber, 1961)

King James Authorized Version of the Bible & Good News Bible

CHAPTER 18

The Sons of the Elder High Priest 'Annas'

"Is not this the carpenter, the son of Mary,
the brother of James and Joseph,
and of Judas, and Simon?
And are not his sisters here with us?..."
(Mark 6:3)

According to Josephus (37-100 AD) in his *Antiquities*, the immediate family of Annas the Elder had dominated the high priesthood for most of the preceding decades. **To have five sons all become high priests of the Sanhedrin, had never happened before.**

It has been mentioned in earlier chapters that according to Josephus, Aaron [St Germain] the brother of Moses, served as the first High Priest, and after his death was succeeded by his sons, from whence time came the law that only those related to Aaron by blood, could serve as a High Priest.

Jesus visits the Temple of the Sanhedrin in Jerusalem

In Luke 2:41-51: we are told that when Jesus was twelve years old, he was taken to the learned High Priests of the Sanhedrin in Jerusalem who examined him for his abilities. They considered him to be an exceptionally bright child and were most impressed with his intelligence. He remained there for three days. When questioned by Mary, his mother, as to why he remained there for so long, Jesus replied:

"Why is that you have come looking for me? Didn't you know that I must be about my Father's business?"

The 'Father' is obviously Annas the Elder High Priest whose title was 'the Father'. It would be natural enough that Jesus would have been examined by him considering the fact that he was the 'Head' of the Sanhedrin; however he was also his real father.

Jesus learns of his Father's demise

We are informed by Spencer Lewis that it was during his stay in India that Jesus learned of his father, Joseph's death and at the time he was fifteen (15) years old.

"Messengers informed Him..." "According to the several translations of the message which He sent by the Essene messengers to His mother, it read as follows:

'Beloved mother: Be not grieved, for all is well for father as with you. He has completed his present work here on earth, and has done so nobly. None in any walk of life can charge him with deceit, dishonesty, nor wrong intention. In his period of life here *he has completed many great tasks and is gone from our midst truly prepared to solve the problems that await him in the future.*"

'Let your soul be busy in meditation and contact with him...I am sure that my brothers will care for you and supply your needs and I am always with you in mind and spirit.'"

As mentioned elsewhere, Joseph (St Germain) the Father of the Holy Grail Family had his next incarnation as Apollonius of Tyana in the 1st century AD, a long life in which he continued to teach the Ancient Mysteries. Therefore, it is most interesting to learn from Spencer Lewis that in later years, Jesus (the 'missing years' of Jesus being mentioned in the Bible) studied in Greece under the personal direction and care of Apollonius, who opened up the ancient records of Grecian lore for Jesus.

Out of the six sons of Annas the Elder (Joseph), Jesus did not become a member of the Annas High Priests.

The Remaining 5 Sons of Annas the Elder (St Germain)

The names of the five sons of Annas the Elder High Priest who were High Priests in the Sanhedrin were (1) Eleazar, (2) Mathias, (3) Theophilus, (4) Jonathan Annas, and (5) Annas the Younger. The following is a list of additional information regarding them. It becomes obvious that Eleazar replaced Annas the Elder in 15 AD, which is the year that Jesus learned of his father, Joseph's (St Germain's) demise.

1. ELEAZAR - Simon (Lazarus) High Priest 15 AD = SIMON ELEAZAR, THE MAGUS, THE 'GNOSTIC'

The Essenes were very much a close community who wished to remain uninvolved in anything of a political nature. However, upon further investigation it becomes evident that there were several included amongst the disciples of Jesus who appear to have participated in both politics and fighting, in order to defend the Community of the Essenes against the domination of the Romans.

One of these disciples was Simon Eleazar Levi who belonged to the Zadok/ Levi priesthood of the Essenes. Simon is allotted various names in the Bible including the 'Magus', the 'Magician'. The fact that Simon was called a 'Magus' tells us that he belonged to the Great White Brotherhood, who during the era of Jesus were given the title of the Magi, meaning wise magicians.

Sometimes Simon is referred to as Simon Levi. Moses and Aaron, as stated elsewhere, were of the tribe of Levi and according to the ancient Law by which the Essenes abided, only those who were descendants (or reincarnations) of the Levi tribe and the Zadok tribe could serve as High Priests in the Temple of Jerusalem. Noteworthy is the fact that the original Eleazar was one of the sons of Aaron (St Germain) during the era of Moses (an earlier incarnation of Jesus).

From the book titled *From The Stone Age To Christianity* by William Foxwell Albright, we learn that "few problems in the history of religion are so elusive as the question of Proto-Gnosticism and Judaeo-Gnosticism. Since the earliest literary remains of Gnosticism proper do not antedate the second century AD. **The earliest Gnostic was Simon Magus.** However, there is now direct evidence that some of the central ideas of the Gnostic system go back into the ancient Orient. The central figure of Gnostic mythology is that of Sophia 'Wisdom'. At all events, the elements were at hand and by the middle of the first century AD they had already been fitted into the first known Gnostic system by **Simon Magus.**"

The title of *Magus* was only granted to one who had attained the very highest degree of initiation in the Mystery School that was operating during the era of Jesus. A *Magi* had to have proved himself to be a Master of astrology, the arts and sciences and was a person who was very highly evolved. The scholars who wrote the book titled *Nag Hammadi, Gnosticism, And Early Christianity*, one of whom was Charles W. Hedrick, stated that the Dead Sea Scrolls are Gnostic in their content and that "the early church fathers traced the origins of Gnosticism to **Simon Magus** (Acts 8 verse 10), whom the early priests of Rome considered **'the father of all heresies'.**"

It was Simon Eleazar, the Magus, the 'Gnostic' mentioned in the previous paragraphs concerned with 'Sophia' - 'Wisdom', who with Joseph of Arimathea, accompanied the three Maries, to Marseilles in 37 AD before Joseph continued on with Mary, the Mother, to Glastonbury where the first Celtic Church in Britain was established and which was dedicated to Mary. One of the reasons that Simon accompanied the Grail family was because he was a member - he was Simon the brother of Jesus as mentioned in the Bible, Mark 6:3.

According to the book titled *St John's Gospel* by Brian Grenier:

"A family that was dear to the heart of Jesus was Martha, Mary and Lazarus (El-eazar = 'God helps')."

Lazarus was a corrupted version of Eleazar. The authors of *The Messianic Legacy* Michael Baigent, Richard Leigh and Henry Lincoln discuss the fact that in John's Gospel, "there is mention of another Simon, Simon Bar Jonas which would normally mean 'Simon son of Jonas', even though the man's father is elsewhere identified as Zebedee." (The sons of Zebedee have been discussed in a previous chapter - they were the sons of Joseph [St Germain] and Mary).

Simon Eleazar (the Magus) Levi, not only held an important position amongst the disciples, but he was also known to have been an outstanding freedom fighter for the Essenes, at which time he was given the title of Simon the Zealot (Zelotes), the Patriot who was one of the 'sons of Zadok'. Simon was loathed and feared by Josephus (Flavius).

Simon Eleazar, **Levi**, the Magus became a High Priest for a time; however, because of his activities as a freedom fighter (a zealot), (for according to the historian Josephus, he led a revolt against the governor of Judah who was Pontius Pilate) pressure was put upon the priesthood who were in the unenviable position of also having to please the Romans and the result was that Simon was deposed.

2. MATTHIAS - Matthew Levi (High Priest in 42 AD)

Matthew's name is a variant of the name Matthias which means 'gift of Jehovah'. (He is not to be confused with the Matthias in the Bible who replaced Judas the traitor). Matthew became a High Priest in 42 AD.

Matthew in the Biblical texts is described as a 'son of Alphaeus'. However, the probability is, like all the other applied titles of 'sons of', that Alphaeus was another title of the Orphic (meaning 'Fisherman') Mystery initiations, the origins of which could be traced back to the founder of the Orphic Mysteries, Apollo (St Germain).

There were four Evangelists; Matthew (Matthias Levi) was one of them. And so, he was not only a son of Annas the Elder High Priest (Zebedee/Joseph) but he was a disciple of Jesus and also his brother.

3. THEOPHILUS

The names given in the Bible were originally in Hebrew, Aramaic and Greek before they were translated into English. It seems highly probable that Theophilus may have been derived from Theodore which means 'Gift of God' and the name is a variant of Tudor (as in *Judah*). The name 'Theodore' may have been combined with the Greek word *Philos/Philus* as in 'philosopher' and thus the translated meaning of his name may have been that Theophilus belonged by lineage to the House of Judah/Tudor and that he was in fact, a philosopher.

Also of important significance is the fact that another name for Theodore is Jonathan, from which the name 'John' is derived.

According to an historical book of names by Michele Brown from whence the explanation of these names has been taken, Michele writes that the name of 'John' is also a variant of Sion/Zion (as in the House of Sion).

It is noteworthy that St Luke (the Evangelist) who was also the author of the Acts addresses the Gospels to Theophilus, and addresses him with the title of 'Your Excellency' which shows that Theophilus was a person whom the disciple Luke, held in high esteem. Furthermore, Theophilus must also have been in a high position to be addressed as such. According to information contained in Robert Graves' book titled *The White Goddess*, there was during the era of Jesus, one known as Theophilus, a well known historian/philosopher who wrote in Greek which was also, as previously mentioned, the language in which the Gospels were written.

Theophilus also became one of the Annas High Priests for a brief term, and therefore it is safe to presume that Luke was addressing this same Theophilus as 'Your Excellency'. Theophilus was otherwise known as John Joseph, the Beloved Disciple, and the 'lover of Sophia' - 'Wisdom'.

Robert Graves discusses how one known as Barnabas was preaching the Gospel of Jesus during that era who he equates with Theophilus. Barnabas is recorded in Acts 4:36 as also being known as *Joseph from the tribe of Levi.*

The name of Barnabas means 'One who encourages'.

Another explanation for the name of Barnabas which is quoted in the Bible is 'the son of consolation' (The Acts 4:36). And still another name ascribed to him is Joseph Barsabbas meaning 'son of the father' who would have been 'Joseph'.

We learn a great deal about Barnabas in the Acts of the Apostles (written by Luke) and his full name was Joseph Justus Levi. He founded what became known as the original Christian Church, in Antioch. According to Spencer Lewis in his book titled *The Mystical Life of Jesus*, the original Church where the apostles gathered in groups and where they taught, was called the 'Christine Church'. Joseph of 'Arimathea' founded the first Christian Church in Britain at Glastonbury in

37-38 AD.

(In 52 AD, the Emperor Claudius offered the hand of his daughter, Julia Venus, to Caradoc, whom the Romans called Caractacus. Caradoc was the grandson of Joseph of Arimathea. Caradoc's mother was Joseph's daughter, Anna, who married Bran the Blessed King, otherwise known as Cymbeline and also known as Cunobelinus. During this time in Rome, according to information taken from Peter Dawkins' book titled *The Great Vision*: "Caradoc established the first above-ground Christian Church in Rome and it became known as the 'Home of the Apostles' - the most fashionable and cultural centre in Rome, a place where St Paul [Saul] made his home for eight years and where St Peter frequently visited." Because Joseph of Arimathea's grandson had established this first Christian Church in Rome for the Apostles, and because Joseph of 'Arimathea' is known to have lived until at least 70 AD, we can presume that he too, made frequent visits to his family in Rome).

Joseph Justus Barnabas was classed as being a Levi. In Acts 15:25, Barnabas is referred to as "our beloved Barnabas". It becomes very evident in the Acts that he was a very important personage amongst the apostles and it would appear that his true identity was that of John Joseph (Kuthumi) the Beloved Disciple and brother of Jesus whose Greek name was Theophilus, the philosopher, 'His Excellency'. In earlier incarnations, Kuthumi had been Pythagoras - the Greek philosopher and the Father of 'Maths' (as in mathematics), Aristotle - the Greek philosopher, and Lao Tze - philosopher and founder of the Taoist religion. Thus it was not the first time that he had been a philosopher.

Someone who worked closely with Theophilus (alias John Joseph, the Beloved disciple) was Joseph of Arimathea, the name of which also contains 'thea/theo'. The reason that they would have worked closely together was because Theophilus was a member of the Sanhedrin, as was Joseph of Arimathea whom Luke (23:50) describes as follows:

"And, behold, there was a man named Joseph, a counsellor; and he was a good man and a *just*: (The same had not consented to the counsel and deed of them)"; [meaning the members of the Sanhedrin]. The probability is that there is a clue in the name of 'Justus'. Phonetically, 'Justus' is 'Justice' and Joseph of Arimathea is described as being a 'just' man, and an honourable counsellor. The terminology of 'just' therefore pertains to 'justice' and 'Justice' pertains to the 'Law'. It was in the Temple of Jerusalem that the Sanhedrin who were the counsellors, assembled to mete out 'justice'.

The organization that Joseph Justus Levi (otherwise known as Barnabas) established was as we have already seen, known as the Christine Church, and it consisted of an inner circle of disciples including John Mark (St Mark the Evangelist - cousin to John the Beloved and the rest of the Holy Grail Family) and Lucius of

Cyrene (possibly Luke the Evangelist who may have been Edgar Cayce who wrote the Acts of the Apostles for Edgar stated that he had been Lucius of Cyrene, an Essene and one of the followers of Jesus). 'Lucius' means *Bearer of Light*.

It was at this time that the Cross was adopted as the symbol of their special Church, but it did not have the crucified body of Jesus upon it, instead it had a 'ROSE' in the centre - as a symbol of the ancient teachings by the Masters of the Mystical Rose.

The Essene Brotherhood, as part of the Great White Brotherhood, had always used the cross as a symbol. According to Spencer Lewis, this device originated as a mystical or esoteric symbol in the days of Akhnaton (El Morya), when he was pharaoh of Egypt and "he used the cross in his Mystery Schools as an emblem of the body of a man with arms outstretched, representing the physical man with his *sufferings* and trials of earthly life."

"At the time between the adoption of the cross as a symbol of man's physical body and the formation of the Christine Church, a rose was added to the cross as a second element in the mystical symbol. The *rose* was likened unto the soul of man, because of its gradual unfoldment, beautiful perfume, and richness of colour and manifestation of maturity. By adding the rose to the cross, the esoteric meaning of the combined symbol was that the soul-personality evolves through sufferings, trials, tribulations, and incidents of the physical body and physical existence."

So far, three sons of Annas the Elder High Priest have been discussed, namely Eleazar Levi, (Simon the Magus, the 'Gnostic'), Matthias Levi (Mathew, the Evangelist) and Theophilus, the Philosopher (John Joseph the Beloved Disciple). They were all sons of Zebedee, the 'fisherman', who cast their nets for initiates. It is now time to discuss the remaining two.

4. JONATHAN ANNAS (High Priest 37 AD)

(Variants of the name Jonathan are Nathaniel, Theodore, Tudor, Matthew and Sion)

Jonathan Levi became the High Priest of the Sanhedrin for one year in 37 AD; a year after Josephus Caiaphas had been replaced.

Considering that three of the sons Annas the Elder have so far been identified as also being disciples of Jesus (i.e. Simon Eleazar/Lazarus, Matthias - Matthew the Evangelist and Theophilus - John Joseph the Beloved Disciple), the second last missing link is Jonathon whose full name may have been Jonathan James. (The last missing link is Judas Iscariot). It seems highly probable that Jonathan Annas was James the Just. The name of Jonathan also contains the word Jona and it will be remembered that 'sons of Jona' was a terminology applied to those who had undergone initiations into the Greater Mysteries of the Secret School in operation during the era of the disciples.

After the death of Annas the Elder, James (Jonathon Levi Annas?) may then have been in charge of initiating others into the Orphic Mysteries. During this time, his older brother, the Annas High Priest, Theophilus (John Joseph the Beloved Disciple), also known as Joseph Justus Levi Barnabas, was busy founding secret churches which taught the Sacred Mysteries of the Arcana, those of the *Mystical Rose*.

James the Just was executed in 62 AD, and the events regarding this tragedy will be discussed in the following chapter. Suffice to say at this stage, why he was executed remains a great mystery and the reasons can only be guessed at. He obviously played a very important role but at some point in time, after the crucifixion, there was a falling out between James and Judas Iscariot, the 'traitor', the younger brother of both James and Jesus.

5. ANNAS THE YOUNGER

The following chapter is devoted to the exploits of Annas the Younger.

SUMMARY

So far it has been established that those of the Priesthood of Levi (Levites) who belonged to the High Priesthood of the Sanhedrin (excluding Annas the Elder who died in the year 15 AD and then reincarnated as Apollonius of Tyana), were:

1. Eleazar = Simon *Levi* Lazarus (whose name would originally have been Simeon, named after his famous ancestor), became a High Priest in 15 AD for one year when Tiberius became the third Roman Emperor.

2. Theophilus = John the Beloved Disciple (Kuthumi), the 'Philosopher', also known in the Bible as Joseph Justus Barnabas Levi. In Acts 15:25, Barnabas is referred to as "our beloved Barnabas". Joseph Justus Barnabas founded the original Christian Church, in Antioch, known as the Christine Church and they adopted the Cross with the Rose in the centre.

   Joseph of Arimathea established the first 'Christian Church' in Britain, at Glastonbury in 37 AD. It is noteworthy that Joseph of Arimathea's grandson, Caradoc/Caractacus, (whose mother Anna was Joseph of Arimathea's daughter), established the first above-ground Christian Church in Rome in circa 45 AD, and it became known as the 'Home of the Apostles' - "the most fashionable and cultural centre in Rome, a place where St Paul [Saul] made his home for eight years and where St Peter (who had first visited Rome in 44 AD) frequently visited."

3. Jonathan *Levi* = James the Just who was a High Priest in 37 AD. Jonathan's name is important because it tells us of his family connection to the House of Judah/Tudor.

The other names of his brothers also give us clues to their ancestral lineage, particularly Judas whose name pertains to the House of Judah. The name 'Jonathon' also contains 'Jona' which tells us that he underwent the 'Jona' initiations.

4.   Matthias (Matthew) *Levi* succeeded as High Priest in 42 AD.

5.   Annas the Younger was a High Priest for three months in 62 AD.

As the story unfolds about this family, it becomes obvious that a split amongst them occurred.

Gauging Who was Who

It has previously been discussed that according to William Foxwell Albright in his book titled *From The Stone Age To Christianity*, from the time of Simon Maccabeus (143-135 BC) dissension broke out amongst the ranks of the Essenes, the 'Holy Ones' and eventually broke up into three basic groups and below is a simplified list of exactly 'who was who'.

1.   **The Pharisees**: "Believed in bodily resurrection. They believed in angels, astrology, alchemy (magic) and everlasting life. Tithing, the giving of one-tenth of one's income to charity was a firm rule amongst them. Certain professions, notably tax-collecting on behalf of the later Roman occupying power were barred to them". (Excerpt repeated from *The Armageddon Script* by Peter Lemesurier).

Matthew (Levi): Proof that the disciple Matthew Levi, (the Evangelist) who was a brother of Jesus could **not** have been a Pharisee relies upon the fact that he is listed in the Bible (as if to give us a clue) that he was a 'tax collector'.

John (Levi) the Beloved, (who was a brother of Matthew, Simon, James the Just, Judas and Jesus), appears **not** to have belonged to the Pharisees either. From reading the verses quoted below, it is also apparent that John had his own disciples, and that Jesus to whom the conversation is directed, had his own separate disciples:

"Now John's disciples and the Pharisees were fasting; and the people came and said to him, [Jesus] 'Why do John's disciples and the disciples of the Pharisees fast, but your disciples do not fast?" (Mark 2:18). This verse is virtually segregating them into three different groups, i.e. the Pharisees, John's disciples and those of Jesus.

Jesus (Levi) was an Essene and it seems doubtful that he belonged to the Pharisees for it is interesting to note that there are several passages in the Bible where Jesus condemns the Pharisees.

St Paul (Saul), a Roman, was converted to Christianity, although not known to be a member of the Sanhedrin, he **was** a Pharisee. It is the opinion of scholars that his teachings were totally different to those of Jesus. In fact, in Acts 15, it becomes apparent that the apostles gathered together in a meeting to discuss the rightness correctness of Paul's teachings and doctrine, for they did not approve.

Josephus Flavius, (the historian) once a member of the Essenes, rejected them and became a member of the Pharisees. Josephus was the son of Matthias (Matthew).

2. **The Essenes**: Like the Pharisees, the Essenes believed in bodily resurrection and they also believed in angels, astrology, alchemy (magic) and everlasting life. **Jesus (Levi)** believed in 'The Resurrection and the Life' (John 11).

3. **The Sadducees**: Rejected the 'occult' (secret) doctrines of the Pharisees and the Essenes, and denied life after death (reincarnation) and bodily resurrection. The Sadducees would have been in total opposition to the religion of Jesus. Therefore, it becomes very obvious that Jesus and his family were **not** Sadducees.

Annas the Younger is listed as a strict Sadducee. He was the one who was responsible for the death of James the Just, (who was the brother of Jesus, Matthew, Simon and John the Beloved). Could this Annas Priest called 'the Younger' have been the *"Son of Destruction"* mentioned in the Bible?

"THE EARLIEST GNOSTIC WAS SIMON MAGUS"

MASTERS DISCUSSED IN THIS CHAPTER

Aaron - St Germain
Prophet Samuel (Zadok High Priest) - St Germain
Joseph (Zebedee) - The Father of the Holy Grail Family - Annas the Elder High Priest - St Germain
Apollonius of Tyana - St Germain
John the Beloved Disciple (Theophilus) - Kuthumi
Mark the Evangelist and Disciple - Djwhal Khul

NOTES AND RECOMMENDED READING

William Foxwell Albright, *From The Stone Age To Christianity*, (Doubleday Anchor Books, U.S.A, 1957)

Charles W. Hedrick & Robert Hodgson, *Nag Hammadi, Gnosticism, And Early Christianity*, (Hendrickson Publishers, U.S.A, 1986)

Merrill F. Unger, *Archaeology And The Old Testament,* (Zondervan Publishing House, Michigan, U.S.A 1954)

Peter Lemesurier, *The Armageddon Script*, (Element Books U.K. 1981)

John Dominic Crossan, *Jesus A Revolutionary Biography*, (Harper, San Francisco, U.S.A, 1994)

George F. Jowett, *The Drama Of The Lost Disciples,* (Covenant Publishing Co. Ltd., London, U.K. 1980)

Michele Brown, *Baby Name Book*, (Greenwich Editions, U.K., 1985)

Josephus, *Thrones of Blood*, (Barbour & Co., U.S.A. 1988)

Brian Grenier, *St John's Gospel*, (St Paul Publications, Australia, 1991)

King James Authorized Version of the Bible & Good News Bible

CHAPTER 19

𝕿𝖍𝖊 'Wicked Priest' & the 'Son of Destruction'

"When I was with them
I protected them in your name that you gave me,
And I guarded them, and none was lost
Except the son of destruction..."
(John 13:10)
"Men and Brethren, this scripture must needs have been fulfilled,
which the Holy Ghost by the mouth of David spake before
concerning Judas, which was the guide to them that took Jesus"
(Acts 1:16)

The Omission of the Maccabees in the Protestant Bible

It is interesting that the story of the Maccabees which consists of two books, has been omitted from the King James Version of the Bible, and that their story is told in the Roman Catholic Bible.

The authors of *The Hiram Key* questioned: "Why should this be so? The fact that these two books are missing from the King James Bible actually told us a lot. There must be a very important reason why the Catholic Bible represents the story of the Maccabean Revolt and the Hasmonaean high priesthood as legitimate, and the King James Bible does not recognise any of it as scripture at all."

"What was wrong with these works, and what could the far-later compilers of the Protestant Bible possibly have known that could cause them to drop these long accepted works, supposedly inspired by God?"

"The only people who knew that the rise of the Hasmonaean high priests and kings was illegitimate were the Members of the Qumran Community who despised these false high priests and their political panderings to the Romans."

The answer lies in the fact that the appointment of Jonathan Maccabaeus as High Priest was totally unacceptable to the Essenian Community because

Jonathon, who was the brother of Judas Maccabeus, was not of the line of Zadok. The original Zadok had been the High Priest, Samuel, an incarnation of St Germain, during the era in which he anointed David as King of the House of Judah. The sons of Zadok were the 'Chosen of Israel' and the 'Chosen of Israel' were St Germain's people, the Essenes.

In his incarnation as Sir Francis Bacon of the House of Tudor, when he translated what became known as the King James Version of the Bible, he and his assistant Sir John Dee, who had once been John the Beloved (Kuthumi), knew the truth regarding the illegitimate lineage of the Maccabees. And furthermore, St Germain had once been the Essenes' anonymous Teacher of Righteousness.

The Dead Sea Scrolls of the Essenes mention the 'Wicked Priest, and the 'Spouter of Lies' and some authors consider him to have been Jonathan Maccabeus; however, it is more likely that this person was a priest during the era of the Messiah.

Division within the Family of the House of Judah/David

We are informed by the late Spencer Lewis in his book titled *The Mystical Life Of Jesus* which was written in 1929, long before the discovery of the Dead Sea Scrolls of the Essenes in 1947, that at the time of the Messiah, Jesus, born to Mary who was the daughter of Anna and Joachim, the Essenes represented **"the group of most highly evolved and spiritually trained beings on earth."**

Within this royal family of the House of Judah, there was a great deal of rivalry occurring, based upon ambition. It is apparent that the historian Josephus, who was a member of the Pharisees, had a particularly negative attitude towards the Annas priests, but then, he did disregard his own people and become a Roman citizen so therefore, he could hardly have written favourably about the Annas priests whom the Romans only just tolerated.

The Pharisees did not believe in life after death, therefore some of their teachings were not in accord with those of the Essenes. Noteworthy is that according to the historian, Josephus (Flavius), Josephus Caiaphas (the High Priest in power at the time of the crucifixion of Jesus), was the son-in-law of Annas the Elder.

Certain texts within the Bible tell us that Jesus rejected both the Pharisees and the Sadducees which would help to explain why he did not become a member of the Annas High Priests in the Temple of Jerusalem, which is where they resided.

We are also informed by Matthew (Matthias) 14, (verses 53-58) in the Bible, that Jesus was rejected at Nazareth, his home town. After they rejected him, Jesus said to them: "A prophet is respected everywhere except in his home town and by his own family. Because they did not have faith, he did not perform many miracles there."

It is evident that there was conflict with the Teachings of Jesus and those of the High Priests in the Temple of Jerusalem. Certain of the priests did not like Jesus because he preached a philosophy that was different from theirs. Possibly they resented the fact that he knew more about the Ancient Teachings than they did, for as we have learned previously, Jesus had travelled widely and been initiated in the Great Pyramid in Egypt into the Great White Brotherhood.

As his popularity grew and the crowds continued to follow him, the priests perceived that Jesus was undermining their authority. These priests however, did not include his brothers, who were not only High Priests of the Sanhedrin, but also his disciples, Simon Lazarus (Eleazar), James the Just, John the Beloved and Matthew. The remaining brother, the youngest one mentioned in the Bible namely, Judas Iscariot was his enemy.

Mary Magdalene and the Year of the Crucifixion

Matthew 13:55-56: **"Is not this the carpenter's son? Is not his mother called Mary? And are not his brothers James [the Just, the Less] and Joseph [John Joseph, the Beloved] and Simon [Lazarus/Eleazar/Zelotes] and Judas [Iscariot]. And are not all his sisters with us?"**

It was in 15 AD that Simon Eleazar (Lazarus) otherwise known as Simon the Magus, the Gnostic Teacher of Wisdom, succeeded his father Annas the Elder High Priest and became an Annas High Priest, the same year that Tiberius became the Roman Emperor. (The other names of Tiberius were Julius Caesar Germanicus and he remained as the Roman Emperor until 37 AD).

Then in 18 AD until 36 AD, Joseph Caiaphas was an Annas High Priest of the Sanhedrin.

At the time leading up to the scenario of the crucifixion of Jesus, Martha and Mary Magdalene were residing at Bethany on the outskirts of Jerusalem with their brother Lazarus who was Simon Eleazar - an Annas High Priest of the Sanhedrin. It has previously been explained that he was also known as the Magician (Magus), Zelotes - Zealot.

John Dominic Crossan made the following pertinent comments in his book titled *Jesus, A Revolutionary Biography*: "Please do not think I am imagining Jesus going there [to Bethany] to raise Lazarus from the dead..." "But that family is very special. *It is a family of siblings; we never hear of a father or mother.*" (The story of Jesus raising 'Lazarus' from the dead was a form of initiation which Simon underwent).

'This family' was by then, old enough to have fled the proverbial 'nest'. Joseph, the father had died in 15 AD and Mary, the Mother, may have been living with

Jesus, for later we will see that at the scene of the crucifixion of Jesus, that he entrusted the care of his mother to John the Beloved (Theophilus), his brother.

Mary Magdalene may have been the eldest daughter and she was a priestess amongst the Essenes. Mary considered Jesus to be her 'Teacher'. George F. Jowett in his book titled *The Drama of the Lost Disciples* informs as that "the identity of Mary Magdalene with Mary of Bethany is a subject of controversy, but the French Church regards them as one."

According to Peter Dawkins, in his book titled *The Great Vision*:

"Mary of Bethany/Mary Magdalene, Martha and Lazarus [Simon Eleazar] were the beloved younger sisters and brother of Jesus and when Mary in her role as priestess anointed her elder brother Jesus on his head and feet, she anointed her Rabboni ('beloved teacher') for having knowledge of the events that would lead to his crucifixion, Mary intuitively grasped the situation and anointed him with the precious spikenard ointment. By this deed, Mary was following the ancient tradition that went back as far as the Egyptian days of anointing the Egyptian Kings/Pharaohs. The symbolism of anointing signified the recognition of the fact that her brother Jesus was a royal brother, a prince of the House of Judah, in the manner of a Priest-King who was the rightful heir to the Throne of Salem ('Peace')."

Mary Magdalene was a 'Gnostic' - a Lover of 'Sophia' Wisdom

In common with her brother Simon Lazarus (Eleazar), Mary Magdalene was also a Gnostic. According to a thesis by Douglas M. Parrott which appears in the book titled *Nag Hammadi, Gnosticism, And Early Christianity*: "The presence of Mary (presumably Mary Magdalene) in other gnostic dialogues (*Dialogue of the Savior, Gospel of Mary, Pistis Sophia*) and her absence from tractates that are orthodox suggests that she functioned in gnostic circles simultaneously as the representative of the female followers of Jesus as a symbol of the importance of women among the Gnostics. Occasionally, to be sure, other women are mentioned (*Pistis Sophia; Gospel of Thomas*, logion 61), but Mary predominates. In the *Sophia of Jesus Christ* the representative character is quite clear, since she is the only one of the seven named."

The author then refers to *Pistis Sophia I-III*. "Three female disciples are named: Mary (Magdalene), Martha, and Salome. Mary, the mother of Jesus, is also named. Mary Magdalene predominates throughout as the most frequent and insistent questioner of Jesus. At one point she takes the lead and represents all the disciples to Jesus. At another point the opposition between her and Peter is emphasized. There she states her fear of Peter, because he threatens her and hates 'our race' (the gnostics? Women?)."

John the Beloved Disciple and James the Just - 'Gnostics'

"John (the Beloved) also figures prominently and, in fact, is named along with Mary as surpassing the other disciples...here then he should be included amongst the **gnostic** disciples."

It is noteworthy that the author also mentions that John, (a **'gnostic'**) is the son of Zebedee. The author also links James the Just as being James the 'son of Zebedee', a **gnostic**, and points out that "it is worth recalling that our knowledge of James the son of Zebedee is very limited - he may well have played an important role among the disciples before his martyrdom (as James the Just)."

Matthew (Matthias) - a 'Gnostic'

Douglas M. Parrott also questions why Matthias (Matthew) would have been chosen by the **Gnostics?** The answer is clearly because he also was one of the sons of Zebedee, who was also an Annas High Priest, and a disciple of Jesus, otherwise known as Matthew, one of the Four Evangelists.

Continuing with Douglas M. Parrott: "When Peter appears (in the Gospel of Mary and *Pistis Sophia IV* and *I-III*), he is portrayed as opposing the female (and **gnostic**) disciples, particularly Mary Magdalene."

The Betrayal of Jesus

According to Merrill F. Unger in his book titled *Archaeology And The Old Testament*:

"About 63 BC Rome came into world ascendancy and dominated the scene through and beyond the New Testament. Thus the Romans became the overlords of Judea (Judah)."

The Jews were *not* responsible for the crucifixion of Jesus. The event was brought about by the Romans. The Roman method of death was by crucifixion, whereas the Jewish method was by stoning. The Romans were anti the Essenes, particularly their Druidic religion, and especially those who belonged to the royal family of the House of Judah. And, Jesus was a prince of that family.

In the events leading up to the arrest of Jesus, Jesus knew that he was going to be betrayed and by whom. From the Biblical accounts, we know that Judas Iscariot betrayed Jesus for thirty pieces of silver and that he was bribed to do so by certain of the *Sadducee* Priests of the Sanhedrin who no doubt pandered to the

Romans. It has been pointed out elsewhere in our story that Annas the Younger High Priest of the Sanhedrin was a strict *Sadducee.*

Judas aided and abetted the corrupt priests, encouraged by Josephus Caiaphas to betray Jesus. Judas was the brother-in-law of Caiaphas and Caiaphas was a strict *Sadducee.* (As mentioned elsewhere, Joseph Caiaphas was the son-in-law to Annas the Elder High Priest. Caiaphas was the Head priest from 18 to 36 AD).

The common denominator here, is the connection to the Sadducees which both Judas and Annas the Younger had, and the fact that they were both in their own way, responsible for the death of two brothers, namely Jesus and James the Just. Why? What were the reasons?

Not until the Dead Sea Scrolls were discovered did we learn of the existence of the *Wicked Priest - the 'Spouter of Lies'*, whom the late John Allegro identified as being Jonathan Maccabee which is a very plausible theory.

However, another one who could also be identified as the *Wicked Priest* and the *Spouter of Lies* is Judas, the traitor who denied that he would ever betray Jesus. Therefore, a more plausible theory would be that Judas was in fact the younger brother of the Grail family of Priests who was otherwise known as Annas the Younger High Priest of the Sanhedrin.

Judas probably resented being the youngest in the family with a long way to climb up the ladder of succession, and Caiaphas was a personal enemy of Jesus who had held a position of power for nearly two decades. It can easily be seen that he resented Jesus' rise to power and the attention he was gaining.

Was Judas the Traitor really put to Death?

Judas Iscariot, the zealot, (who carried a dagger, namely a 'sicarii' from which the name 'Iscariot' was derived), was, as the Bible points out, a 'traitor'.

When reading the Gospels there are conflicting stories regarding the death of Judas. Only two of the Gospels, namely the Acts (written by Luke whom it appears was Lucius of Cyrene, the Beloved Physician who was an incarnation of Edgar Cayce), and Matthew (Matthias who was a High Priest of the Sanhedrin as well as becoming one of the Evangelists), discuss this particular event. It is of significant importance that the Gospel of John (Kuthumi) makes no mention of the actual death of Judas.

Version 1: In Matthew 27 we are told that Judas regretted betraying Jesus, and returned the thirty pieces of silver to the chief priests of the Sanhedrin. By this, we know that in the first place he was bribed by them to betray Jesus. Judas threw the coins down in the Temple and went off and hanged himself. The priests decided it was blood money, collected the coins and bought a potter's field to bury strangers in!!!

Version 2: We are told in Luke (who was the author of the Acts whom he addresses to 'Dear Theophilus') in Acts1:18; that: "when Judas received the money for his evil act, it was he who bought a field, and in the field he fell down and all his bowels spilt out."

Firstly, if the priests decided that the money was blood money, they still had no qualms about using the money to buy a field - all in all, it is a very strange story. Secondly, it was a peculiar thing for Judas to do - buy a field. He was a zealot, and a rebel who according to Josephus (Flavius) made frequent raids as a 'robber'. Judas would have been considerably wealthy having stored some of his hoard and not needed thirty pieces of silver. The thirty, like thirty-three, must be a symbolical number.

Which story are we to believe? Did Judas really die? Or, was he the one known as the 'Prodigal Son', the one forgiven for his misdeeds? Once forgiven, he may have improved for a time but then reverted back to his old ways. It would seem that Judas was the youngest son because that is how he is listed in the Bible. Annas the Younger is specifically called the 'Younger'.

According to the Gospel of John the Beloved (Kuthumi), Judas showed no remorse for his act of treachery. (Josephus Flavius described Annas the Younger as bold and insolent). Brian Grenier in his book titled *St John's Gospel* makes an interesting observation when he says:

"John reminds us frequently of Judas' perfidy (see 6.64, 70-61, 12-4; 13-21; 18:15) and going a step further than the other evangelists, he presents a harsh portrayal of Judas. He presents him as a representative figure of those 'disciples' [of Jesus] who returned to their former way of life and no longer accompanied him (6.66)." (Note: the verse and chapter number mentioned is 666, which represent the so-called 'Beast of Revelation' of which there are numerous meanings).

"Equally notable by its absence is any reference to Judas' remorse. It is in the context of another meal, the Last Supper, that Jesus takes with 'his own' that we find the most damning indictment of Judas in John's Gospel. Addressing his Father, Jesus prays:

'When I was with them I protected them in your name that you gave me, and I guarded them, and none was lost except the son of destruction, in order that the scripture might be fulfilled.' (17:12)."

John 6. 24: 'But there are some of you that believe not. For Jesus knew from the beginning who they were that believed not, and who should betray him.'

Brian Grenier continues: "There is no place for the traitor's kiss in the Johannine [John the Beloved] scheme of things; for Jesus is always in control of the situation. This is the place where Jesus' glory is revealed. He takes the initiative, and, as he utters the divine name I AM, the minions of earthly power fall at his feet (John 18:6)."

"Wherein lies the tragedy of Judas? The theme of rejection of Jesus is introduced into the Gospel as early as the prologue. 'He came to what was his own, but his own people did not accept him'. (1:11). Even his own chosen disciples (with one notable exception), desert him in his time of need, and Peter denies him three times; but of Judas alone is it stated that he betrays him."

The 'notable exception' was the one who wrote this particular Gospel, namely, John Joseph, the Beloved Disciple - the Master Kuthumi who makes such a point about the betrayal of Jesus. The Gospel of John was written in circa 70 AD and it would be quite understandable that he wrote in the way he did, for Judas had betrayed his own brother Jesus, and, if Judas was also known as Annas the Younger, he had also ordered the execution of James the Just in 62 AD, John's other brother.

If Judas the traitor was also the son known as Annas the Younger (who is never named), then it would make sense that, not content with having helped lead to the arrest of one brother, namely Jesus, he managed to scheme his way into a more powerful position - that of elected High Priest of the Sanhedrin, (in 62 AD) so that he could persecute another of his brothers. As Judas the traitor, he was under the influence of the Sadducees and as Annas the Younger High Priest, he was a strict Sadducee.

Therefore, not only could he be called by the Essenes, the *Wicked Priest*, the *'Spouter of Lies'*, but he is also adequately described as the 'SON OF DESTRUCTION'.

Joseph Caiaphas and Pontius Pilate

Both Caiaphas and Pontius Pilate were replaced within the same year, 36 AD. (Pontius Pilate governed for ten years from 26 to 36 AD).

In his book titled *Jesus A Revolutionary Biography*, John Dominic Crossan makes the following pertinent points. "Pilate, in other words, was dismissed from office for excessive cruelty or unnecessary brutality..." "And we may well suspect the same reason for Caiaphas' simultaneous dismissal. My point is not that Pilate was a monster. He was an ordinary second-rank Roman governor with no regard for Jewish religious sensitivities and with brute force as his normal solution to even unarmed protesting or resisting crowds."

"Like any Roman governor he was also careful to distinguish between the rich and the poor, the powerful and the powerless, the important and the unimportant, the aristocrat and the peasant. In the New Testament gospel accounts Pilate is completely just and fair. He wished to acquit Jesus but was forced, reluctantly and against his will, to crucify him..." "And he held lengthy discussions with Jesus during which he repeatedly proclaimed his innocence of any crime worthy of death."

The late Spencer Lewis made important observations in his book titled *The Mystical Life of Jesus.* "Caiaphas would appear to have been a spy for the Roman government if we are to judge by the secret reports that he made to Rome regarding the activities of Jesus. On the other hand, he may have been merely a personal enemy, for he certainly did everything possible to keep Rome informed about Jesus and to make it difficult for Jesus to continue His work. Even though Caiaphas was an eminent leader of the Sanhedrin, he did not represent this body in the reports he made, nor in the attitude he assumed. It is even indicated that Caiaphas went so far as to present large sums of money for the purpose of procuring evidence and making sure that a warrant would be issued by Rome for the arrest and trial of Jesus."

"The one outstanding point in connection with the crucifixion of Jesus is the use of the cross. **That one thing tells the story that Rome had ordered His death, and that it was a Roman punishment and not a Jewish one, for the Jews would have stoned Him, in their usual manner,** had they desired to get rid of this man for any reason. The fact that His death was ordered in the Roman manner and at the hands of those officially delegated to carry out the death sentence in a legal manner, indicates that the whole affair was not one of mob violence or religious persecution on the part of the Jews, but a sentence officially proclaimed at Rome." (Bold type has been utilized for the sake of emphasis of an important statement).

"The only offense that can be attributed to Jesus throughout His whole career was a political offense from the Roman point of view. The Roman army in Israel and the spies maintained by the Romans made it possible for that government to take stringent measures whenever there seemed to be a traitor in their midst or a possible uprising."

The wife of Caiaphas is not mentioned by Josephus, but she was a sister of James the Just and the other members of the Family of the Holy Grail. It is a probability that she was either Martha or Mary Magdalene. Perhaps which ever female it was, became the 'estranged' wife of Caiaphas which may to some degree have influenced his anger directed towards the family of the Holy Grail. As we have already ascertained, just prior to the crucifixion, Mary and Martha were living with their brother Simon Lazarus (Eleazar) in Bethany - no mention of any spouses.

Three years after the crucifixion, in 36 AD, Jonathan Levi (presumably otherwise known as James the Just), was the Annas High Priest who replaced Joseph Caiaphas. It would be natural enough that Caiaphas greatly resented his replacement, because Caiaphas had ruled over the Sanhedrin longer than any other High Priest.

The following year, Mary Magdalene, Martha and their brother Lazarus

(Simon Eleazar), departed with their mother, Mary, in the company of Joseph of Arimathea for Marseilles leaving behind Judas the 'traitor'. It becomes apparent that it was deemed to be no longer safe for the immediate family of the Holy Grail to remain domicile in the country of their birth.

Although a split had occurred within this royal family of the House of Judah, Caiaphas the 'in-law' and Judas Iscariot obviously maintained close contact with one another over the successive years, awaiting an opportunity to get rid of James the Just, an opportunity which presented itself in 62 AD.

CONCLUSION

ANNAS THE YOUNGER, THE 'WICKED PRIEST', THE 'SPOUTER OF LIES' WAS JUDAS ISCARIOT, THE 'TRAITOR'

MASTERS DISCUSSED IN THIS CHAPTER

Aaron, brother of Moses - St Germain
Annas the Elder High Priest of the Sanhedrin (Zebedee/Joseph), St Germain
Apollonius of Tyana - St Germain
The Master Jesus
Pythagoras - Kuthumi
John the Beloved (Theophilus) - Kuthumi
John Mark - Djwhal Khul

NOTES AND RECOMMENDED READING

George F. Jowett, _Drama Of The Lost Disciples_ (Covenant Publishing Co. Ltd., London, U.K. 1980)
Peter Dawkins, _The Great Vision_, (Francis Bacon Research Trust, U.K.)
Charles W. Hedrick & Robert Hodgson Jr. _Nag Hammadi, Gnosticism, And Early Christianity_, (Hendrickson Publishers, U.S.A. 1986)
John Allegro, _The Dead Sea Scrolls_, (Penguin Books, 1964)
Peter Lemesurier, _The Armageddon Script_, (Element Books, U.K. 1981)
Mary Carter, _Edgar Cayce, Modern Day Prophet_, (Bonanza, U.S.A. 1970)
William Foxwell Albright, _From The Stone Age To Christianity_, (Doubleday, U.S.A, 1953)
Merrill F. Unger, _Archaeology And The Old Testament_, (Zondervan Publishing House, Michigan, U.S.A. 1954)
Spencer Lewis, _The Mystical Life of Jesus_, (AMORC, U.S.A. 1929)
Spencer Lewis, _The Secret Doctrines of Jesus_, (AMORC, U.S.A. 1937)
Spencer Lewis, _Rosicrucian Questions And Answers_, (AMORC, U.S.A. 1929)
John Dominic Crossan, _Jesus, A Revolutionary Biography_, (Harper, U.S.A 1994)
Josephus, _Thrones of Blood_, (Barbour & Co., U.S.A. 1988)
Brian Grenier, _St John's Gospel_, (St Paul Publications, Australia, 1991)
King James Authorized Version of the Bible and Good News Bible

CHAPTER 20

The Death of James the Just 62 AD

"...the priests found him standing beside the columns of the temple, beside the mighty corner stone. And they decided to throw him down from the height, and they cast him down."
(The Second Apocalypse of James)

In order to keep the continuity of the parallel between Judas and Annas the Younger, we need to move forward some twenty-nine years after the scenario of the crucifixion.

Curiously, there is no mention of James the Just being present at the scene of the crucifixion of his brother Jesus. In 38 AD, a year after the departure of the 'Bethany' group consisting of Mary the Mother, Mary Magdalene, Martha, Lazarus (Simon Eleazar) and Joseph of Arimathea, James the Just (presumably Jonathan Annas) of whom it could be said was one of the 'shadowy disciples' (the other one being John Joseph the Beloved who was the Annas High Priest known as Theophilus), was in Jerusalem and it was there that Paul first met him.

Frequently, the historian Josephus (Flavius) refers to Jonathan Annas (Levi) as being a zealot who was an incredible annoyance to certain Roman officials. He played a vital role as a freedom fighter on behalf of the Essenes.

The latter name of *'Just'* as allotted to James in the Bible appears to be a clue that he belonged to the Annas Priests, where 'justice' pertained to the 'Law'. It will be recalled that the brother of James the Just, John Joseph the *Beloved* is in the Acts referred to as Joseph *Justus* Levi whom the disciples called 'their *Beloved* Barnabas'.

To re-cap what has been mentioned elsewhere, Joseph (Annas the Elder), the Father of the Holy Grail Family had six sons:
1. Jesus (Levi).
2. John the Beloved (Levi), one of the Four Evangelists.
3. James the Just (Levi).

4. Simon Levi (Lazarus/Eleazar, the 'Zealot', the 'Patriot', the Magus - 'magician' etc.)
5. Matthew (Levi), one of the Four Evangelists.
6. Judas Iscariot (Levi) (the 'traitor').

Of these six sons, with the exclusion of Jesus, five of them became Annas Priests of the Sanhedrin in the Temple of Jerusalem and according to Josephus, "to have five sons all become high priests of the Sanhedrin, had never happened before." This serves to prove that the family of 'Annas' was a very powerful one and they were Levi/Zadok High Priests as was the requirement for those who served in the Temple.

It will be recalled that it was Jonathan Levi Annas who replaced Joseph Caiaphas in 36 AD for a short time as the chief High Priest of the Sanhedrin.

The 'Shadowy Disciples'

According to Peter Lemesurier in his book titled *The Armageddon Script*:
"One of his [Jesus'] chief secret supporters, it seems was an influential member of the Jerusalem Priesthood by the name of Johanan (John), the shadowy 'Beloved Disciple' who seems to have been a major source for the author of the fourth gospel. Together with Jesus' younger brother Jacob (James the Just), he appears to have played an important behind-the-scenes role in the affairs of Jesus and his cell of followers, possibly during the whole of their time together. Indeed, since the normal Essene practice was to appoint a central executive body consisting of twelve laymen led by three priests, it seems quite likely that Jesus, James and John were the group's controlling triumvirate, or, in the Essene parlance, the 'Foundations of the Community' - respectively the Master (*maskil* or *mebaqqer*), the Supervising Priest and the more secularly orientated Steward (*mebaqqer 'al melekheth ha-rabbim*) described in the sect's original *Damascus Rule*."

The Zealots - the 'Freedom Fighters
James the Just stoned to Death in 62 AD

There was a great deal of animosity which existed between Josephus Flavius, Eleazar (Simon Lazarus/Zelotes) and his brother Jonathan. Josephus Flavius accused them of being zealots who carried daggers (sicarii - short curved swords) under their clothing. They carried these weapons out of necessity in order to defend their rights and their people, the Essenes, who were being persecuted by the Romans.

According to Edgar Cayce in the book titled *Edgar Cayce Modern Day Prophet* by Mary Ellen Carter: "Even the two or three Essenes among His disciples, forgot themselves often enough to provoke incidents. At this time, Jerusalem was occupied by the Romans very much as France in our century was occupied by the Nazis..."

During the first year of Nero's reign, in 54 AD (after the death of Claudius), the procurator of Jerusalem was Felix and according to Josephus Flavius, Felix (the Roman procurator of Jerusalem), loathed and feared both Jonathan Annas and his brother Eleazar (Simon Lazarus).

Jonathan "persisted in telling him how to run the country and devised a plot to have him killed." (Felix Marcus Antoninus was procurator of Jerusalem from 52 to 60 AD. He was the judge of St Paul Acts 14 and kept him in prison for two years, hoping for money for his release).

From *The Armageddon Script* by Peter Lemesurier we learn the following pertinent information: "With the death of Claudius in 54 AD, the tension was redoubled as the infamous Nero succeeded to the Imperial throne. Now the guerilla-actions started to broaden into a general class-warfare. Private armies representing rich and poor, the established and the dispossessed, confronted each other in the streets. The ordinary priests, who had sided with the common people, were deprived by the Sadducean authorities of the rations to which they were entitled. And it was ostensibly for speaking up on their behalf that James, the brother of Jesus, was now seized by agents of the ruling High Priest, pushed over the parapet of one of the eastern pinnacles of the Temple and finished off by stoning in the Kidron valley below."

Thus it is evident that James the Just rubbed many officials the wrong way, just as Jonathan Annas managed to do. Owing to the antagonism to Roman officials shown by both James the Just and Jonathan Annas, it seems too much for co-incidence that they were not the same person.

John Dominic Crossan quotes from the *Antiquities* of Josephus (Flavius).

"Upon learning of the death of Festus, Caesar sent Albinus to Judaea as procurator. The king removed Joseph [the son of Simon Eleazar/Lazarus/Magician/Zelotes the Essenes' zealot freedom fighter], from the high priesthood, and bestowed the succession to this office upon the son of Annas, who was likewise called Annas...The younger Annas...was rash in his temper and unusually daring. He followed the school of the Sadducees, who are indeed more heartless than any of the other Jews...when they sit in judgement. Possessed of such a character, Annas thought that he had a favourable opportunity because Festus was dead and Albinus was still on the way. And so he convened the judges of the Sanhedrin and brought before them a man named James, the brother of Jesus who was called the Christ, and certain others. He accused them of having traversed the law and delivered them up to be stoned."

"Those of the inhabitants of the city who were considered the most fair-minded and who were strict in observance of the law were offended at this. They therefore secretly sent to King Agrippa urging him, for Annas had not even been correct in his first step, to order him to desist from any further such actions. Certain of them even went to meet Albinus, who was on his way from Alexandria, and informed him that Annas had no authority to convene the Sanhedrin without his consent...King Agrippa, because of Annas' action, deposed him from the high priesthood which he had held for three months, and replaced him with Jesus the son of Damascus."

According to the authors of *The Hiram Key*, Christopher Knight and Robert Lomas:

"The New Testament has been assembled to exclude details of the assassination, but a gospel rejected by the Emperor Constantine, *The Second Apocalypse of James*, does record the event as follows:

'...the priests found him standing beside the columns of the temple, beside the mighty corner stone. And they decided to throw him down from the height, and they cast him down. And...they seized him and [struck] him as they dragged him to the ground. They stretched him out, and placed a stone on his abdomen. They all placed their feet on him, saying, 'you have erred!' Again they raised him up, since he was still alive, and made him dig a hole. They made him stand in it. After having covered him up to his abdomen, they stoned him'."

The authors further state that Hegesippus, a second- century Christian authority, wrote:

"So they cast down James the Just, and they began to stone him since he was not killed by the fall; but he kneeled down, saying: 'Oh Lord God, my Father, I beseech thee forgive them, for they know not what they do.' While they were thus stoning him, one of the priests of the sons of Rechab, of whom Jeremiah the prophet testifies, cried out, 'Stop! What do ye? The Just is praying for you.' But one of them...smote the head of the Just One with his Club.'"

According to Daniel Boorstin in his book titled *The Discoverers, A History Of Man's Search To Know His World And Himself*, James was executed in Jerusalem and in the 9th century AD, his remains were transferred to Spain (Compostella) where the cult of St James began.

The conclusion regarding James the Just is that he was Jonathan Levi, the High Priest of the Sanhedrin who replaced Caiaphas in 36 AD, for one year. James angered certain Roman authorities and members of the Sadducees who worked closely with the Romans. This probably initially came about with his activities as a zealot freedom fighter, defending the Essenes.

James would have been seen as a rival by his younger brother Judas Iscariot

(Annas the Younger). What is apparent is the fact that the conflict that the disciples/ apostles had with the Sadducees was mainly over their opposite beliefs. Whatever James' activities were, he had an important role to play and he would have carried it out to the fullest, unfortunately to his own detriment.

ALL THE SONS OF ANNAS THE ELDER HIGH PRIEST WERE OF THE TRIBE OF LEVI/ZADOK.

MASTERS DISCUSSED IN THIS CHAPTER
Annas the Elder High Priest/Zebedee/Joseph - St Germain
John the Beloved - Kuthumi

NOTES AND RECOMMENDED READING

Peter Lemesuirer, *The Armageddon Script*, (Element Books, U.K. 1981)

John Dominic Crossan, *Jesus A Revolutionary Biography*, (Harper, San Francisco, U.S.A, 1994)

George F. Jowett, *The Drama Of The Lost Disciples*, (Covenant Publishing Co. Ltd., London, U.K. 1980)

John Allegro, *The Dead Sea Scrolls*, (Penguin Books, U.K., 1964)

Josephus, *Thrones Of Blood*, (Barbour & Co., U.S.A. 1988))

Daniel Boorstin, *The Discoverers, A History of Man's Search to Know His World And Himself*, (Random House, U.K. 1983)

H. Spencer Lewis, *The Mystical Life of Jesus*, (AMORC, U.S.A., 1929)

H. Spencer Lewis, *The Secret Doctrines of Jesus* (AMORC, U.S.A., 1937)

H. Spencer Lewis, *Rosicrucian Questions and Answers*, (AMORC, U.S.A 1929)

Good News Bible & King James Authorized Version of the Bible

CHAPTER 21

The 'Beloved Disciple' & the 'Son of Consolation'

"And, behold, there was a man named Joseph,
a counsellor; and he was a good man,
and a just: (The same had not consented to the counsel and deed of them);
he was Joseph of Arimathea..."
(Luke 23:50-51)

The 'Gnostic' Druids

Not long after the crucifixion of Jesus, the apostles gathered in a room in Jerusalem to discuss the replacement of Judas Iscariot, the 'traitor'. Included in the group was Simon the Patriot (Acts 1 verse 13) who is otherwise Simon Zelotes (the Zealot - Lazarus/Eleazar, the 'Magus' - the 'Magician' Gnostic teacher of 'Sophia' - wisdom); and Jesus' other brothers, James the Just and John the Beloved; these latter two are most aptly described as the 'Shadowy Disciples'.

According to George F. Jowett in his book titled *The Drama Of The Lost Disciples*, both Lazarus (Eleazar) and Joseph of Arimathea were Druids, as was Mary Magdalene, her sister Martha; so obviously their brothers, James the Just and John the Beloved were too. And we have learned in a previous chapter, that Mary, Simon (Lazarus/Eleazar), James the Just, and John the Beloved were all 'Gnostics'.

Throughout the centuries the knowledge, teachings and true meaning of the Celtic Druids has been greatly misconstrued. With the advent of the Roman form of Christianity arriving in Britain, the Druids, like the Essenes, were also in need of protecting their sacred religion. The Romans called the Essenes 'heathens' and 'barbarians'. The latter word that they used to describe them was fairly close to the truth, for 'bar' in Hebrew means 'son of', and they were the sons of the Arians because they belonged to the Arian race.

In an earlier chapter, George F. Jowett was quoted as follows:

"The influence Druidism had upon the rest of the ancient world, and its peaceful and ready reception of the Christian faith, proves its noble structure. Hume, the high-ranking British historian acknowledged for his impartiality and the lack of bias in his reporting, wrote: **'No religion has ever swayed the minds of men like the Druidic'.**"

"Despising Druidic opposition, the Roman persecutors intensified their malignancy with the British conversion to Christianity. **The Emperor Augustus, Tiberius and the Claudian and Diocletian decrees made acceptance of Druidic and Christian faith a capital punishment, punishable by death.**"

The Druids were labelled as 'pagan'. It was only when the early Church of Rome gained a strong foothold in Gaul (France) and Britain, that they changed the meaning of 'pagan' to mean something 'heathen' and many who were considered to be 'heretics' were given these labels, particularly the Druids. In actual fact the word 'pagan' is from the Latin word *paganus* which means a *rural district* and *countryman*.

Anyone who was actually gifted with special powers of natural healing, prophecy or studied astrology was destined to be persecuted with the resultant abhorrent death by slow burning on a pyre whilst they were still alive. The word *occult* became something to be feared when it is actually defined in the Oxford Dictionary as something *esoteric* or *hidden*, from the Latin *Occulto - cult -* 'to hide'.

However, despite the superstition and persecutions, the original *Arcana* Teachings of the *Mystical Rose* continued to grow and blossom, protected by the Druids.

The 'Beloved Disciple'

Kuthumi in his life as John the Beloved was a disciple whose activities were veiled and under various names. In the previous chapter, part of this information below was quoted; however, it is also relevant to this chapter.

According to Peter Lemesuirer in his book titled *The Armageddon Script*:

"The tradition underlying the provision of the Qumran *Community Rule* [of the Essenes], was that the sect's governing council should contain twelve lay members. Yet, following the same source, the group should have been headed by three priests. Of these, Jesus, as Priest-Messiah, would clearly have been one. And indeed, there are hints in the surviving literature of two other shadowy priest-figures hovering in the background - Jacob (James), the widely-revered Nazarite and younger brother of Jesus, surnamed The Just; and John the Priest, the influential host of the Last Supper whom the fourth gospel calls the Beloved Disciple."

Who was the mysterious Joseph of Arimathea, the 'secret disciple'?

"And after this Joseph of Arimathea, being a disciple of Jesus, but secretly for fear of the Jews, besought Pilate that he might take away the body of Jesus: and Pilate gave *him* leave. He came therefore, and took the body of Jesus." (John 19:38).

"When the even was come, there came a rich man of Arimathea, named Joseph, who also himself was Jesus' disciple. He went to Pilate, and begged the body of Jesus. Then Pilate commanded the body to be delivered. And when Joseph had taken the body, he wrapped it in a clean linen cloth, And laid it down in his own new tomb, which had been hewn out in the rock: and he rolled a great stone to the door of the sepulcher, and departed." (Matthew 25: 57-60).

"And, behold, *there was* a man named Joseph, a counsellor; *and he was* a good man, and a just: (The same had not consented to the counsel and deed of them;) *he was* Joseph of Arimathea..." (Luke 23: 50-51, Italics quoted as in the King James Authorized Version of the Bible).

From the verses above we learn that Joseph of Arimathea was a disciple of Jesus, and John (Kuthumi) informs us that he was a 'secret' disciple.

Joseph's most outstanding achievement was that he became known as the First Master of the Grail which he brought to Glastonbury where he founded the first Celtic Church in Britain in c.37 AD. The *Rose* and the *Grail* were synonymous and Joseph was a *Master of the Mystical Rose.*

Another important aspect regarding the role of Joseph of Arimathea was that he was able to take care of Jesus after the crucifixion. He was obviously on good terms with Pontius Pilate, because when Joseph requested the body, it was given to him without any qualms.

One of the reasons that he had so much influence was that he was a member of the Annas Priests of the Sanhedrin - an honourable counsellor, a 'just' man.

He was of the priesthood of Levi/Zadok. Hence he was a member of the Essenes and he was both a disciple of Jesus and a member of the High Priests of the Sanhedrin.

Barnabas, otherwise known as Joseph Justus Levi in the Bible whom the disciples address as 'their Beloved Barnabas', established the first Christian Church at Antioch which became known as the 'Christine Church', and as we have learned in a previous chapter, they adopted the Rose and the Cross as their symbol.

An interesting point is that the Bible *specifically* defines Barnabas as being *'the son of consolation'.* Of consolation to whom?

Jesus Entrusts the Care of His Mother, Mary, to John His 'Beloved Disciple'

When Jesus therefore saw his mother, and the disciple standing by, whom he loved, he saith unto his mother, "Woman, behold thy son!"

Then saith he to the disciple, "Behold thy mother!" And from that hour that disciple took her unto his own *home*. (Italics utilized in John 21: 26-27).

There is no other logical explanation as to why Jesus addressed his mother Mary at the crucifixion referring to his Beloved disciple as 'He is your son' and then to the disciple 'She is your Mother'. And from that time, the disciple took her to live in his own *home*. This would only make sense if Mary was the mother of John Joseph the Beloved who presumably was the second eldest son, otherwise the other brothers and sisters would have taken care of Mary.

James the Just, was also known as James the Less, probably giving us clues that he was younger than John, otherwise the care of their mother would have been given to James, for it was not until 62 AD that James was executed.

Confirmation regarding the Beloved Disciple is reaffirmed by Hans-Martin Schenke, Professor of New Testament Literature and Theology at Humboldt University, Berlin, whose thesis appears in the book titled *Nag Hammadi, Gnosticism And Early Christianity*:

"The observation about John 19:26-27, where Jesus entrusts his mother to the Beloved Disciple, reveals its full relevance. While all the other Beloved Disciple scenes of the Fourth Gospel (of John) are designed to reveal the superiority of the Beloved Disciple to Peter (Simon), *this scene serves 'only' to make the Beloved Disciple the brother of Jesus.*"

Joseph of Arimathea

We need to question why an acquaintance of the family was given the important task of taking the body of Jesus off the cross and transporting him to a newly built tomb, specially prepared; one that Joseph of Arimathea, owned. Why did the family not have their own tomb? Was Joseph of Arimathea merely an acquaintance? According to custom, the body should have been taken care of by the closest male relative of the family, such as the next male in line.

We know that John Joseph, the Beloved Disciple, was given the care of Mary, therefore, how did it come to be that it was Joseph of Arimathea, almost a *complete stranger*, who accompanied Mary to Glastonbury in 37 AD, just four years after the crucifixion? The answer is clearly because the Beloved Disciple and Joseph of

Arimathea was the same person. John Joseph is the 'Secret Disciple' who took Mary to live in his own *home*. He was clearly the 'Son of Consolation' to his mother Mary, after the crucifixion.

Joseph of Arimathea was a member of the Sanhedrin, an honourable counsellor, a 'just' man. The one known as Joseph Levi was also given the name of 'Justus'. Phonetically, 'Justus' is 'Justice' and this word pertained to the High Priests of the Sanhedrin.

It is important to note that Joseph was a 'secret disciple'. Another word for 'secret' is 'Arcana'. The Oxford Dictionary definition is as follows: 'hidden', 'secrecy', 'obscurity', 'revealed religious truth', 'one beyond human intelligence'. All of these words describe the 'secret disciple', namely John the Beloved who was Kuthumi, a Master of the Great White Brotherhood, the Brotherhood of 'higher intelligence'. He was a *Master of the Mystical Rose* who taught the knowledge of the sacred Arcana, of 'Sophia', and therefore his activities were kept 'secret' whilst he endeavoured to reveal 'religious truths'.

When Jesus was arrested we are informed by John 18:15 as follows:

"And Simon Peter followed Jesus, and so did another disciple; that disciple was known unto the high priest, and went in with Jesus into the palace of the high priest."

The palace of the high priest belonged to Caiaphas. The 'disciple' who followed Jesus into the palace, would have been John Joseph the Beloved Disciple, in his capacity as a High Priest of the Sanhedrin, known by his Greek name as Theophilus, the philosopher, the 'lover of Wisdom'.

He accompanied his brother, Jesus, to Pilate, and it would have been at this point of time that he made arrangements with Pilate for Jesus to be taken off the cross and taken to Joseph's own specially prepared new, previously unused, tomb. As a High Priest of the Sanhedrin, John the Beloved (Theophilus, the son of Annas the Elder High Priest), he would have had a certain amount of influence over Pilate.

According to the Book of John, chapter 19, Mary Magdalene was the first to discover that the body of Jesus was missing. She ran to inform Simon and 'the other disciple whom Jesus loved' (i.e. the 'Beloved Disciple'). John was second after Mary to inspect the sepulchre.

In a previous life, the 'Beloved' brother of Jesus, namely John Joseph *Levi*, had been King David whose name as stated elsewhere, means 'Beloved'.

Another clue which we are given is that Joseph of Arimathea brought myrrh to attend the body of Jesus. This gift he had brought to the infant Jesus, when he was one of the elderly wise men (the 'Magi') known as Baltazar, before his next incarnation as the brother of Jesus.

Zebedee's Princely Sons

In the events preceding the crucifixion, Jesus informed his disciples three times that one of them would betray him. After the third time, Mary approached Jesus with a request prior to the Last Supper.

Matthew 20:20-11: Then the wife of Zebedee came to Jesus with her two sons, bowed before him, and asked him a favour. "What do you want?" Jesus asked her. She answered, "Promise me that these two sons of mine will sit at your right and your left when you are King."

As we have seen in previous chapters, these two sons of Mary were John the Beloved and James the Just, who were the ones referred to as the *Boanerges*, the 'Sons of Thunder' because they had become 'initiates' into the Greater Degrees of the ancient Egyptian rites.

It is noteworthy that after the mother of Zebedee's children, Mary, had requested of Jesus that they may sit next to him in their appropriate positions that Jesus replied:

"You will indeed drink from my cup" Jesus told them, "but I do not have the right to choose who will sit at my right and my left. These places belong to those for whom my Father has prepared them." (Matthew 20:25).

These verses would make sense only if the two younger brothers were princes within their own right. These two priest brothers were John Joseph the Beloved (Theophilus Levi) and his brother James the Just (Jonathan Annas Levi), the sons of Zebedee (Joseph otherwise known as Annas the Elder High Priest of the Sanhedrin) and Mary.

"But Jesus called *unto him*, and said, Ye [You] know that the princes of the Gentiles exercise dominion [sovereignty/supreme rule] over them, and they that are great exercise authority upon them." (Matthew 21:25)

Firstly, Jesus is mentioned by Mary in the verses of Matthew, as being a King.

Secondly, Jesus mentioned the words 'princes of the Gentiles' by which he meant 'princes of the Essenes' who were commonly known as the 'Gentle' people from whence the name 'Gentile' was derived (According to Edgar Cayce, who was Lucius of Cyrene in the era of Jesus, John the Beloved and his brother James Zebedee were Essenes).

Thirdly, it was John the Beloved who, at the famous scenario of the Last Supper, was designated the position of sitting on the right hand side of Jesus. He was therefore the next prince. James the Less, sat on the left hand side and would have been designated the third prince in line after Jesus, which is another reason why his younger brother Judas Iscariot (Annas the Younger) may have plotted to have James killed in order to secure a closer step up the rung of the ladder to succession.

The Solution of the 19th Century Rose-Cross Poster
And
Leonardo da Vinci's (Kuthumi's) Painting of the Last Supper

Reference has been made earlier to a 19th century Rose Cross poster, a copy of which features in the book titled *The Occult Conspiracy* by Michael Howard. The poster depicts three people. On the left hand side, is Joseph of Arimathea, donned in a Knights Templar uniform with the Rose Cross.

We need to bear in mind the significance of this symbolism because during the era of Joseph of Arimathea, the Knights Templar were not in existence. However, it was John the Beloved/Joseph Levi Justus alias Joseph of Arimathea (Kuthumi) who founded the First Christian Church at Antioch with the Cross and the Rose as its symbol.

In the poster, Joseph of Arimathea is clasping the sword firmly in both hands - representing the 'Truth'. His right hand is on the top of the sword. In the scenario of the Last Supper, John the Beloved was designated to sit on the right hand side of Jesus.

The Archangel Michael, who is placed in the centre, is also adorned with a Rose Cross, and he is supporting the Chalice/Grail Cup, the responsibility of which was handed to John the Beloved during the Last Supper. This same 'Chalice' is reputed to have been hidden at the Chalice Well in Glastonbury, England.

On the right hand side, is Leonardo da Vinci, holding a scroll tightly in his right hand thus depicting the 'Truth to be revealed' as in the opening of the 7th Seal in Revelations, written by John the Beloved.

All of this symbolism reveals the Master Kuthumi as being the First Master of the Grail, for he was Joseph of Arimathea; 'Michael' was the Essenian angelic title allotted to him as John Joseph the Beloved Disciple; and Leonardo da Vinci, also an incarnation of the Master Kuthumi, became the Grand Master (Helmsman) of the Order of Sion/Jerusalem during the Italian Renaissance.

When the Rose Cross poster was issued in the 19th century, the man who was head of the Order of the Rose Cross at that time was Joseph Peladan, a name which may have been utilized by St Germain.

Leonardo da Vinci's (Kuthumi's) painting of *The Last Supper* (1497) took four years to complete and he obviously put a great deal of thought into the symbolism conveyed.

Next to Jesus, on his right hand side, there is a figure which is obviously a female for not only does she look female, but she has a pink satin or silk fabric shawl draped partly over her. Some believe this to have been Mary Magdalene, but it could also have been Mary, the Mother of Jesus and John. Traditionally, there should be twelve disciples at the Last Supper; however, the inclusion of the female makes up the total of twelve. For some obscure reason, Leonardo has portrayed the painting in this way.

Interestingly, Jesus, the female (Mary?), and two other apostles (possibly John the Beloved and James the Just) are robed in similar blue clothing. For some (symbolic?) reason, Jesus is only half-robed in this blue coloured apparel. There is a third disciple also partly robed in blue that will be mentioned further on. Perhaps the blue colouring is designating the brothers of Jesus. In symbolism, Mary's colour is blue, representing her as the as the 'Queen of Heaven'.

It stands to reason that Mary would have been the prominent female at the Last Supper, given the fact that she was the Mother of the Family of the Holy Grail. Leaning next to her is one of the disciples, also dressed in blue. He appears to be comforting her and he may have been John the Beloved. He is in third position along the table to the right of Jesus.

The lady's countenance is indeed poignantly very sad, as a mother's would be. Her hands are folded on the table as if in recognition of the inevitable. There is also what could be termed a whimsical expression upon her face as if she will be contented for John to take care of her.

It was at the Last Supper that Jesus announced that he would be betrayed by one amongst them.

On close inspection of the painting, it appears that the person seated next Jesus on his *left* hand side (who is not robed in blue), has temporarily seated himself there in order to talk to Jesus, (perhaps in an effort to convince Jesus that he would not be the one to betray him), and this may have been the disciple, Peter who was to deny knowing Jesus.

On the left hand side behind Jesus, is a disciple with his finger upraised in a gesture. Leonardo has utilized this gesture in several of his paintings and it is considered to represent an underground stream of knowledge and wisdom. This may have been Simon (Lazarus/Eleazar), the Gnostic teacher of Sophia - Wisdom, whom the Church of Rome, as we have learned in an earlier chapter, considered to be the 'Father of all Heresies'. Therefore, Leonardo has depicted him as best he could by way of such symbolism representing Simon despising the Church of Rome.

Possibly it is the disciple James the Just (robed completely in blue) who is just a little further along the table from Simon. James is not seated, but standing as if ready to move back into his proper position i.e., to the immediate left of Jesus, where the disciple who is probably Peter, is seated next to Jesus. Both James' hands appear to be pointing towards the person seated next to Jesus on his *right* hand side, and he does not seem to be happy with the situation to hand. This person sitting on the right hand side of Jesus, is next to the female (Mary?), and is also partly robed in blue. He is clutching a small leather pouch in his hand - obviously symbolic of the thirty-pieces of silver which he obtained for betraying Jesus. Therefore, he is Judas Iscariot, the 'Traitor' (Annas the Younger).

John the Beloved's hand is resting reassuringly on the shoulder of Mary? as the 'Son of Consolation' would do, and in his other hand, is a knife facing towards the back of Judas. Why? Because as we have read earlier, Brian Grenier in his book titled *St John's Gospel* stated:

"John reminds us frequently of Judas' perfidy (see 6.64, 70-61, 12-4; 13-21; 18:15) and going a step further than the other evangelists, he presents a harsh portrayal of Judas. He presents him as a representative figure of those 'disciples' [of Jesus] who returned to their former way of life and no longer accompanied him (6.66). "Equally notable by its absence is any reference to Judas' remorse. It is in the context of another meal, the *Last Supper*, that Jesus takes with 'his own' that we find the most damning indictment of Judas in John's Gospel. Addressing his Father, Jesus prays:

'When I was with them I protected them in your name that you gave me, and I guarded them, and none was lost except the son of destruction, in order that the scripture might be fulfilled.' (17:12)."

John 6. 24: 'But there are some of you that believe not. For Jesus knew from the beginning who they were that believed not, and who should betray him.'

Brian Grenier continues: "There is no place for the traitor's kiss in the Johannine [John the Beloved - Kuthumi] scheme of things.."

In a vision, regarding this famous painting of his, Kuthumi showed me the words OUT OF PLACE.

It then became obvious that Leonardo da Vinci (Kuthumi) has deliberately seated some of the disciples out of place. John should have been designated the right hand side next to Jesus, but instead Judas, the 'Son of Destruction' is there clutching his ill-gotten gains (the money pouch of thirty pieces of silver). And, the disciple seated on the left hand side of Jesus, is Peter who when questioned by the Roman soldiers, denied knowing Jesus. Therefore, Kuthumi has depicted in his painting of the *Last Supper*, the two figures in closest proximity to Jesus, who were the ones that ultimately betrayed him.

Conclusion

From the word 'Arimathea' we are able to ascertain certain of its meanings.

1. It contains the beginning of the word 'Arian' and the Grail family was of Arian descent.
2. 'Ari' means 'noble' as in 'aristocrat' and it will be remembered that the Master Kuthumi had once been the Greek philosopher, Aristotle.
3. Thea/Theos' means 'a lover of Sophia' - a 'lover of wisdom', (also called 'Athena'). Hence, John Joseph the Beloved (alias Joseph of Arimathea) was given the Greek name of Theophilus in his capacity as the Annas High Priest of the Sanhedrin - an 'honourable counsellor'. 'Theo' is also a shortened version of Theodore which according to an historical book of names by Michele Brown is another name for Tudor. It has elsewhere been explained that 'Tudor' and 'Judah' were synonymous.
4. According to Robert Graves in his book titled *The White Goddess*, 'Math' means 'treasure'. One of the definitions of 'treasure' contained within the Oxford Dictionary is "A 'beloved' or highly valued person."
5. 'Math' is also a shortened version of 'mathematics' and the 'Father of Mathematics' was Kuthumi in his incarnation of Pythagoras, whose teachings the Essenes followed. John Joseph of Arimathea was the 'Secret Disciple' to whom the 'treasure' of the Grail family was entrusted, namely their Mother, Mary, for symbolically, Mary was the Grail Cup - the 'container' who had given birth to the Grail family.
   Within the Arthurian literature is the story of Sir Gawain and the Green Knight, written by an anonymous author during the 14th century AD (circa 1390). In the tale, Gawain encounters a Knight and enquires his name. In reply he is told that the Knight's name was
   (a) Joseus (another name for Joseph).
   (b) Joseus' lineage is that of Joseph of Arimathea.
   (c) Joseus' uncle was King Fisherman, and
   (d) Joseus' father is King Pelles.
   (e) 'Pelles' another name for *Pallas* synonymous with 'Athena- 'Wisdom' - *Sophia*. From these clues we are able to ascertain the relationship of the knight to the mysterious Joseph of Arimathea.
1. Apart from having a daughter named 'Anna', John Joseph (of Arimathea) in continuing the family tradition of 'Naming Patterns' also had a son whom he named 'Joseph'.
2. The one referred to as 'King Fisherman' was Jesus.
3. The knight was Jesus' nephew, Joseus (Joseph) named after the knight's father, Joseph of Arimathea.
4. John Joseph the Beloved (alias Joseph of Arimathea) also known as Theophilus, the

284

'lover of Sophia' was the First Master of the Grail and thus he was also King Pelles (Pallas), the bearer of 'Wisdom' - the bearer of 'Sophia', and a 'Defender of the Faith', which was Druidic/Celtic.

When St Germain reincarnated as Merlin in the 6th century AD, at which time he anointed Kuthumi as 'King of the Celts' and a 'Defender of the 'Faith', Merlin's mother was Princess Eithne (another version of 'Athena' the Goddess of 'Wisdom'), and his father's name was a Celtic version of 'Pelles/Pallas'.

JOHN THE BELOVED DISCIPLE WAS JOSEPH OF ARIMATHEA

MASTERS DISCUSSED IN THIS CHAPTER

Joseph the Father of the Grail Family (Annas the Elder/Zebedee) - St Germain
Merlin - St Germain
King David - Kuthumi
Pythagoras - Kuthumi
Aristotle - Kuthumi
Balthazar - Kuthumi
John the Beloved Disciple alias Joseph of Arimathea - Kuthumi
King Arthur - Kuthumi

NOTES AND RECOMMENDED READING

Brian Grenier, *St John's Gospel* (St Paul Publications, Australia, 1991)

George F. Jowett, *The Drama Of The Lost Disciples*, (Covenant Publishing Co. Ltd., London, U.K. 1980)

Michael Howard, *The Occult Conspiracy*, (Rider & Rider, U.K 1989)

Charles W. Hedrick & Robert Hodgson Jr., *Nag Hammadi, Gnosticism, And Early Christianity*, (Hendrickson Publishers, U.S.A 1986)

John Dominic Crossan, *Jesus A Revolutionary Biography*, (Harper, San Francisco, U.S.A, 1994)

King James Authorized Version of the Bible, and Good News Bible

CHAPTER 22

After the Crucifixion & the Final Resting Place of the Messiah

"Father, if thou art willing, remove this cup from me;
Nevertheless not my will but Thine will be done."

There is a strange clue in the Gospel of John 19:38-39:

"...And there came also Nicodemus, which at the first came to Jesus by night, and brought a mixture of myrrh and aloes, about an hundred pound in weight."

This was an incredible amount of spices and it will be seen further on that these would have been utilized to heal the wounds of Jesus.

In the first edition of *The Masters of the Mystical Rose, A History of the Grail Family*, I did not reveal the following because at the time when I began writing the book in 1993, I felt that it would have been far too controversial. However, in eleven years since, many theories regarding the life of Jesus have come to light. Whether Jesus actually survived, married and fathered children, will no doubt be an on-going mystery; however, it is interesting to note the following information given by the late Spencer Lewis who in his book titled *The Mystical Life of Jesus* informs us of events which occurred after the crucifixion.

"Just before sunrise, Yousef [Joseph] of Arimathea and other Essenes who had been hiding nearby approached the tomb when the guards were trying to protect themselves from the rain under the shelter of some cattle houses at some distance. Using the means they had previously provided, and taking advantage of the laxity of the officials in sealing the doorway properly, they caused this great stone to be thrown over, and the doorway to be opened. When they entered the tomb, they found Jesus resting easily, and rapidly regaining strength and vitality."

"In the Book of John [Kuthumi] in the Bible, we have one of the interesting facts concerning the crucifixion which appears in the ancient records from which I am quoting, and which incident is often overlooked by the most critical of the

Bible students. It is that although it was common practice to break the bones in the body of every crucified person, and to cause their bodies to hang upon the cross for several days so there would be no possibility of the body remaining alive, nevertheless the body of Jesus was taken down without the bones being broken, even though the soldiers broke the bones of the two criminals that were upon the crosses nearby."

"This was not an oversight on the part of the soldiers by any means, for not only did they fulfil the law by breaking the bones of the two criminals, but they had been so accustomed to this procedure for many years that we cannot believe that after having performed their duty with the other two, they would forget the practice, momentarily, in the case of the third body upon the cross. The ancient records, to which I have been referring, state that when the soldiers were notified that the body must be taken down immediately because a release had come, and that everything must be done to permit Jesus to regain His consciousness and strength if He had not passed through transition, they realized that they were not to injure, torture, or in any way affect the case and comfort of Jesus, but to relieve Him as quickly as possible from the agony in which they found Him."

In the above-mentioned paragraphs, Spencer Lewis has made some very valid points. He then relates how Jesus was administered to by the Essenes and nursed back to health and also points out that the original 'Apostles' Creed' stated that Jesus was "on the third day brought to life from the dead", and that in the version of later centuries, it was changed by certain church officials to "suffered under Pontius Pilate, was crucified, dead and buried."

"The appearance of Jesus in the midst of His Disciples on various occasions during His period of recuperation constitutes, in several cases, a mystical demonstration of the ability of the Master to project His personality and consciousness to places distant from His physical body. Such demonstrations of the higher spiritual laws as this were common not only to Jesus, but many of the eminent Avatars of the past, and, in fact, some of His Apostles and Disciples and many of the brethren of the Great White Brotherhood made themselves visible to others at distant points very often."

The Master St Germain in various incarnations such as his one as Apollonius of Tyana and that of St Germain, was able to achieve the same and his ability to be able to be in different places simultaneously, was well documented during the 18th century. It has also been discussed in a previous chapter that according to Spencer Lewis, Jesus visited Apollonius and was tutored by him.

According to Spencer Lewis, Jesus continued for a while to teach his Disciples in private and then one night Jesus "appeared among the High Priests in the monastery at Mt Carmel, and retired to the rooms that had been set aside for Him as his sanctum; and the door of His public life was closed to mankind."

"The disappearance of Jesus from public sight closing His public work and public mission as *The Christ*, was not the end of His existence on the earth plane in the *physical body*. This is definitely stated in so many ancient and reliable records that it is surprising that the Holy Fathers of the Christian church attempted to make His ascension a *physical* fact, and proclaim it the end of His earthly career. In many of the discussions of the Council of the church in the first centuries after Christ, there were *frank admissions* on the part of the greatest authorities that Jesus lived to be fifty, sixty, or even seventy years of age."

"It was not until the doctrine of the Resurrection of the *body* and the Ascension of the *body* in a physical sense appeared to be an important theological necessity that these early church fathers decided, in their high Councils, to eliminate all references to the activities of Jesus after the Ascension, and make the Ascension appear to be the culmination of His *physical* existence, as well as of His *Christly* mission."

"The ancient records of the Great White Brotherhood and other records in the Rosicrucian archives clearly show that after Jesus retired to the monastery at Carmel, He lived for many years, and carried on secret sessions with His Apostles and devoted Himself, through meditation and prayer, to the formulation of doctrines and teachings which His Apostles should give to the world."

Initiations of Jesus

In his book titled *The Great Vision*, Peter Dawkins of the Francis Bacon Research Trust, explains about the initiations which Jesus underwent leading up to the crucifixion.

"The Gospel story of the life of Jesus, as with all scriptures, is allegorical and complex. It can be interpreted truly in many different levels and from many viewpoints. Truth is truth, but it transcends human dogma and limited human understanding. It needs to be approached with **compassion** and **humility** - the two great qualities which it is said that the Christ souls are emphasizing for us at this period in humanity's evolution:

I am the Spirit of Humility:
To every voice I bend the knee,
And listen well that I might know
What to do and where to go.

"Jesus of Nazareth, a personal incarnation of the Christ soul known as Jesus Christ, fulfilled all natural laws and achieved Christhood *as a new personality* before he began his so-called Christ-mission for that life-time - a Christ-mission that lasted but three years, if the dates are taken as being strictly historical as well as allegorical.

During those three years he demonstrated to his disciples, and through them to the whole world, the seven great initiations of life that man can, will and does undertake."

"Hence, although being already in a state of Christhood when he called his disciples together and began his three-year mission, he yet portrayed the first three initiations of the Lesser Mysteries that precede and give rise to the final four initiations of the Greater Mysteries of Christhood. Although Christed, his work was nevertheless to act out dramatically, for the benefit of others, the pre-Christhood stages of initiation. And, although he was already a *Mahachohan* ('Great Lord') of the 7th degree of Initiation - a fully Christed One - yet his work as Jesus as Nazareth was to show the other degrees of Christhood (4th, 5th and 6th) leading up to the 7th, after he had portrayed the 1st, 2nd and 3rd initiations."

First Jesus portrayed the **1st Initiation**, related to the *Water* Element and involved with purifying and controlling the emotions, and learning to desire and love truly from the heart. This is referred to as **Baptism**: hence, even though he did not need to in one sense, Jesus submitted to his cousin John's symbolic baptism in the river Jordan, for the benefit of others, as an example of the true path to follow. The baptism in the Jordan was an act of dedication - the beginning of initiation, in which the soul hears the Word of God and sets out to follow its guidance. Afterwards came the Temptations in the Wilderness, testing the true motives of the would-be initiate."

"When the portrayal of the 1st Initiation was completed, and Jesus had assembled his circle (or school) of 120 disciples, establishing his home in a spacious house in Capernaum, he then began the portrayal of the **2nd Initiation** by calling the Twelve Apostles, consecrating them and giving them the Word. Then followed the period of careful teaching and development of understanding. The 2nd Initiation is represented by the *Air* element and, and is involved with purifying and controlling the thoughts, becoming aware of and understanding truth."

"The **3rd Initiation**, which is signified by the element *Fire*, is concerned with putting into practice all that one has learnt to love and understand, surrendering one's will totally to the Will of God, and thereby learning to serve God and all God's creatures according to the Will of God, which is perfect Love. It requires self-sacrifice, and so Jesus portrayed this 3rd Initiation of **Crucifixion** by enacting it out in real life in terms of the ancient symbols used to describe this initiatory event."

"After entering Jerusalem in glory as king, he was literally and willingly crucified on a tree that had been made in the form of the cross used in the Mysteries - the Romans having adopted traditional symbols used to teach the Mysteries and perverted them into horrific means of execution. This 3rd Initiation is prefigured in Israel's history by the Kings, David [Kuthumi] and Solomon [El Morya], whose glory was followed by the conquest, break-up and scattering of the Twelve Tribes that made up the nation of Israel - just as the Twelve Apostles scattered when Jesus was taken for trial and execution." (What happened to the so-called 'Lost Tribes of Israel' is explained in the sequel to this story, *The Dove, The Rose And The Sceptre - In Search of the Ark of the Covenant*).

Peter Dawkins explains that the "lower self or personality of Jesus of Nazareth suffered and died on the cross in the culmination of this 3rd Initiation, and was buried in a tomb." "On the third day he arose, reborn in his new spiritual form, as *Jesus*, the Christed soul. This was his demonstration of the **4th Initiation** called **Resurrection**, which is the start of the Greater Christ Mysteries of Initiation. The 4th degree is the degree of the Adept."

"Progressing systematically through the 4th Initiation, teaching his disciples every step of the way, he then portrayed the **5th Initiation**, called **Ascension**. This is the degree of the Master soul, the 4th degree of the Adept simply being preparatory to the Higher Mysteries - a state of childhood. In the 5th Initiation the Christ-child becomes a Christ-man."

"The Ascension from the Mount of Olives - the Mount of Christhood - that stands to the east of Jerusalem, took the Master Jesus into the sphere of Unification with the Christ Light, his individual form of light dissolving into a more universal form of light, disappearing as such from the sight of his disciples. The 'cloud' that 'received him out of their sight' was a cloud of radiance which is nevertheless a veil or 'cloud' that conceals the Absolute. The **6th Initiation** is **Unification** with the Christ Glory. It is the degree of the *Chohan* or Lord of Light, who oversees the direction and operations of that particular 'Ray' of Light that he has become at-one with."

"The Christ is essentially Spirit - the spiritual Light of God. It is the Divine Idea or Holy Wisdom that fills the Mind of God - the radiant Son of the Father. The Father is the Divine Mind, the Son is the Bliss Consciousness of that Mind, and the two are essentially One. When Jesus is referring to his Father in Heaven, he is referring to the Christ-Spirit and the Mind of God in which the Spirit dwells. 'I and my Father are One'. This is a statement referring (a) to the Christ Spirit and the Divine Mind of God, which are the One Holy Spirit; and (b) to the Christed soul, Jesus, and the Holy Spirit, the Spirit being the 'Father' to the soul, and the Christ soul being the 'Son' of the Spirit."

The shape of the cross upon which Jesus was crucified, is known as the Tau equated with the ancient Egyptian days. From Peter Dawkins' book titled *Francis Bacon - Herald of the New Age*, we learn that "Freemasonry is represented by the Pillar or Tau Cross."

In a thesis written by Harold W. Attridge contained in the book titled *Nag Hammadi, Gnosticism, And Early Christianity*, the author discusses the *Gospel of*

Truth. "Jesus, the Christ, came to enlighten those in darkness and show them a way, which is the truth. In the process, he was persecuted...and 'nailed to a tree'. While both the language and the conceptuality would be familiar to most Christians, the text continues and throws a new and surprising light upon the historical event of Christ's passion. By being 'nailed to a tree', Christ becomes 'a fruit of knowledge of the Father'. This trope suggests a further allusion to the tree of knowledge in the garden of Eden, for Christ, as the fruit of knowledge, 'did not become destructive'. Through the symbolical reinterpretation of the death of Christ effected here, the general soteriological principle of the text once again emerges. While the *Gospel of Truth* does not, in a strictly docetic fashion, deny the reality of the physical death of Jesus, it does 'correct' the familiar interpretation of that death as an atoning sacrifice."

Ascension

The 'Age of Aquarius' is considered to be the 'New Age of Enlightenment' and Ascension is a frequently discussed topic, although it is unlikely that many truly understand the concept.

In simplistic terms, when Jesus resurrected he changed his frequency and the reason he told Mary Magdalene not to touch him when he 'appeared' to her, was because he had not completely anchored his 'Light' body. The disciples who saw him immediately afterwards did not recognise him at first because the Light Body is precisely as it says 'a lighter body that does not consist of the density of the third dimension in which we all exist.

The process of Ascension was how Jesus raised his body beyond the frequency vibration of the physical senses but could still materialize when he wished to do so, just by changing his frequency vibration. The crucifixion was symbolic of Resurrection/Ascension and this was exactly what Jesus was endeavouring to demonstrate - the existence of immortality to humanity.

Over the last two thousand years, religion has become totally distorted and today many are seeking the 'Truth' as many books currently on the market, prove. It is human nature to find a plausible explanation for something we do not fully understand. Such is the case in the number of theories currently being expounded. These theories consist of what really happened after the crucifixion. Some state that Jesus was substituted by Simon the Cyrene (who carried the Cross) but in John's (Kuthumi's) Gospel we are told that Jesus carried the Cross all the way and because we are informed by Kuthumi that this was the case, we are thus being informed by a Master of what actually did happen.

Somewhere along the way, as a result of the false teachings of the early

Roman Church which have led to so many misunderstandings, we have been misled. Jesus was a Master, a true Master of the Great White Brotherhood, who are sometimes called 'Ascended Masters' and this is why the disciples referred to him as 'Master'. He mastered the Ascension process during his lifetime.

The numerous appearances of the Lady Master, Mary, that have taken place, such as the visitation received by the 'Children of Fatima' and St Bernadette of Lourdes, are just further examples of how Masters have the ability to manifest/materialize themselves at will. However, their appearances are not of a solid state, as in third dimensional existence, they are of a lighter form which could be described as 'holographic'. The form is such that one is able to see through them because it is 'etheric'. They appear with beautiful radiant colours around them which emanate from their auric field.

Because the Master Jesus was such a highly evolved soul, his energy field (auric field) extended some enormous distance from his body and anyone coming within this field was flooded with that Divine Love energy. However, those who suffered from such things as guilt with no love of self became judgemental, and as a result, they felt totally uncomfortable in his presence.

This explanation is a perfect example of 'Light' versus 'Dark', the two polarities - positive energy versus negative energy and the two, like water and oil, do not mix; they are exact opposites. This is also an example of what was meant by the 'Anti-Christ'. It could be said that this was demonstrated in the Biblical story of Jesus versus Judas.

The term 'Anti-Christ' does not apply to any one particular person, such as some figure in the Middle East, rising to power who would become known as the 'Anti-Christ'. The terminology means those who accept the teachings of Jesus within their own soul versus those who do not. They then become their own 'Anti-Christ's' experiencing the 'Dark' versus the 'Light' of their own consciousness and thus they begin their own Armageddon within their own consciousness.

The greatest saying which covers all, is:

"Do unto others as you would have done to you", - if we all followed this simple rule of integrity, the world would be a far better place.

The Final Resting Place of The Messiah

According to Spencer Lewis: "The ultimate passing or transition of the great Master Jesus is recorded in the ancient records as having occurred peacefully and in the presence of the brethren of the Brotherhood in the monastery at Carmel. His body remained in a tomb on the mount for several centuries; but it was finally removed to a secret sepulcher guarded and protected by His brothers."

Qualifying the reasons why many records of the Rosicrucians have not been made public, Spencer Lewis wrote:

"It is not strange that the Rosicrucian records have contained these facts for many centuries, and it is not true that the Rosicrucians have willfully and deliberately concealed these facts, nor held secret the fact that they possessed ancient records of this kind; but up to recent years the best translators and workers on new variations of the Christian Bible and Christian history have refused to examine the Rosicrucian records of the records contained in the archives of India, Egypt, and other lands, on the basis of either prejudice or ecclesiastical condemnation."

"That it will continue to be condemned and criticized is taken for granted, but the criticism of truth *cannot* destroy it, and there are thousands of Christians in the world today who say that their faith has been strengthened by and through a better and more intimate, as well as a more sympathetic, understanding of the mystical life of Jesus."

New Gospel Discovery

It was reported in the newspapers in 1997, that a lost gospel was found in the Berlin museum by a researcher named Paul Mirecki. He discovered it in 1991 in the Berlin's Egyptian Museum. The manuscript adds to the New Testament Gospels of Matthew, Mark, Luke and John in which there are details of conversations between Jesus and his disciples held after the Resurrection and descriptions of the stages of Jesus' ascension, plus it offers more information about what happened afterwards. There are some subtle changes and quotes. In Luke 22, Jesus says "Father, if thou art willing, remove this cup from me; nevertheless not my will but Thine will be done."

The reference to the removal of the cup could mean the removal of the 'Grail Cup' of responsibility, in order that John Joseph, the Beloved Disciple (alias Joseph of Arimathea) would continue the work of the Grail Family, during which time he became -

'THE FIRST MASTER OF THE GRAIL'

MASTERS DISCUSSED IN THIS CHAPTER
Apollonius of Tyana - St Germain
John the Baptist - El Morya
John Joseph the Beloved Disciple alias Joseph of Arimathea - Kuthumi

NOTES AND RECOMMENDED READING

Peter Dawkins, *The Great Vision*, (Francis Bacon Research Trust, U.K)
Peter Lemesuirer, *The Armageddon Script*, (Element Books, U.K. 1981)
Mark Age, *1001 Keys To The Truth*, (U.S.A 1976)
Spencer Lewis, *The Mystical Life Of Jesus*, (AMORC, U.S.A, 1929)
John Dominic Crossan, *Jesus A Revolutionary Biography*, (Harper, U.S.A. 1994)
King James Authorized Version of the Bible, and Good News Bible

CHAPTER 23

The Marriage in Cana & Cryptics in the Bible

John 2:

Verse 1:   And the third day there was a marriage in Cana of Galilee; and the mother of Jesus was there.

Verse 2:   And both Jesus was called, and his disciples, to the marriage.

Verse 3:   And when they wanted wine, the mother of Jesus saith unto him, They have no wine.

Verse 6:   And there were set there six waterpots of stone, after the manner of the purifying of the Jews, containing two or three firkins apiece.

Verse 7:   Jesus saith unto them, Fill the waterpots with water. And they filled them to the brim.

Verse 9:   And when the ruler of the feast had tasted the water that was made wine, and knew not whence it was: (but the servants which drew the water knew); the governor of the feast called the bridegroom.

Verse 11:   This beginning of miracles did Jesus in Cana of Galilee, and manifested forth his glory; and his disciples believed in him.

The Biblical reference to the 'marriage in Cana' is reputed by recent authors to have been the 'wedding' of Jesus and Mary Magdalene. The story of the 'marriage in Cana' was an allegorical one and was an alchemical marriage, the whole event being written in the symbolical language of Pythagorean mathematics.

Another symbolic clue is that the word 'Cana' forms part of the word 'Arcana' and as has been discussed throughout this story - the Arcana were the Sacred Teachings of the Essenes who were the Rosicrucians of Palestine. The Gospel story of Jesus, as with all scriptures, is allegorical and complex. The Masters, particularly St Germain and Kuthumi, encourage us to find the truth within the statements in the Bible thus revealing some of the 'veiled truths'.

If Mary Magdalene was the real sister of Jesus, and it seems highly probable that she was, considering that she *was* the sister of 'Lazarus' (Simon Eleazar - the Magus, the 'magician', the zealot, the patriot etc.) and resided with him and their sister Martha at Bethany, then she could not have married Jesus at what recent authors refer to as the 'Wedding in Cana'.

The 'Marriage in Cana' was symbolizing the 'Alchemical marriage of water and wine. The word 'Alchemy', originates from the Egyptian 'Land of Khem' which the ancient Greeks called 'Khemia' from which we derive the word 'chemistry'.

It is noteworthy that the 'Marriage in Cana' is only mentioned by John the Beloved (Kuthumi) in the Book of John, and although current authors writing about the Grail Family, refer to this occasion as a 'wedding', it does not state this in the Book of John (John 2). It distinctly says 'there was a marriage in Cana of Galilee', **not** a *'wedding'*. Within this statement lies a clue that it was an 'alchemical marriage', not a real one for the Masters were able to use their powers of manifestation and transmutation.

We are actually given several clues.

1. The symbology of the numbers, (which incidentally, are frequently used throughout the Gospel of St John and the Book of Revelation).
2. The Alchemical element of water.
3. Wine.
4. The bridegroom without the bride - symbolic of an alchemical marriage.

1. THE PYTHAGOREAN SYMBOLOGY OF THE NUMBERS 3, 6 & 9

Number three was the sacred number of Pythagoras (Kuthumi). It is the first number which is greater when multiplied by itself than when added to itself. For example, $3 + 3 = 6$, however, when cubed it becomes $3 \times 3 = 9$. In considering the symbology of the marriage in Cana, we are told firstly, that the event occurred on the third day when Jesus requested the servants to fill six jars with water (which he turned into wine). The number six consists of two lots of three e.g. $3 + 3 = 6$.

*The number six was particularly sacred to the Ancient Orphic Mysteries. It was known as a 'hexad', **the symbol of marriage** because it formed a union of two triangles, one masculine and one feminine.*

There were six days of initiation in the 'Chemical Marriage' and on the 7th day the participants had completed their trials of initiation. (The Chemical Marriage is discussed further on in this chapter).

By adding the 6 wine jars and the 3 (for the third day) we have the number 9. The number nine is the Pythagorean symbol of Man and it symbolises 'completion' having conquered all three levels: spiritual, mental and physical in mastership of one's self. In the Bible, the ointment that Mary Magdalene of Bethany used to anoint Jesus was said to have cost 300 days' wages. There were the 3 Wise

Magi who visited the infant Jesus bringing him 3 gifts. Alchemy has 3 basic principles, Sulphur, Salt and Mercury (quicksilver).

THE PYTHAGOREAN NUMBER EIGHT AND NUMBER THIRTY-THREE

The number 'three' is twice contained in 'thirty-three' and was a number often used by Francis Bacon, as we have seen in previous chapters, for the cipher code of the name of Bacon spelt out the number 33.

There are 33 degrees of Freemasonry.

Jesus was said to have been crucified at the age of 33.

The wise King Solomon (El Morya) is said to have ruled for 33 years.

Alexander the Great (St Germain) accordingly died at the age of 33 years.

St Alban (St Germain) reputedly died in 303 AD, although that date is now recognised to be purely symbolical pointing to the fact that he was a Master of the Mystical Rose of that period, at which time he introduced Freemasonry into Great Britain.

According to both Aristotle (Kuthumi) and Pythagoras (Kuthumi), the number eight was also sacred. The symbolic Lotus has eight petals - eight paths which lead to spiritual perfection. The number eight is formed of two circles. It is comprised of the number thirty-three, because by reversing one of the three's and placing it opposite the other, thirty-three becomes an eight.

2. WATER

Water is one of the four primeval elements. It was as we have learned, used symbolically for baptismal initiations as far back as the days of Pharaoh Akhnaton (El Morya) who returned in the era of Jesus as his cousin, John the Baptist. Continuing the tradition from the ancient Egyptian days, purification by water is used as the first initiation, hence babies are usually traditionally baptised not long after their birth.

In Alchemy, water is represented by an inverted Pyramid, and astrologically it is associated with Pisces, the Fish. These events took place during the Piscean era which was the era prior to the Aquarian Age to follow. Water is also a symbol of the power of bodily emotional and spiritual cleansing, hence when we weep, we weep tears consisting of water and salt. Salt is also alchemical as in SAL and salt is also a crystallization of water from something that was previously liquid.

3. WINE

After the 'marriage in Cana', the next important occasion was the Last Supper at which the 'Grail Cup' was filled with wine which was symbolical of the 'Wine of Life'; firstly Jesus and the disciples shared the bread amongst them as a symbol of the 'Bread of Life' or 'Divine Wisdom' being symbolic of spiritual nourishment.

The ancient Greeks regarded wine as the blood of Dionysus and made sacrifices of wine to the gods, such as Bacchus. It was considered a symbol of 'spiritual knowledge' and of the abundance of God's gifts which also became equated with immortality.

The Persian poet, Omar who was discussed in an earlier chapter (and who was an incarnation of Kuthumi), sang the praises of both wine and bread in his poem the *Rubaiyat of Omar Khayyam*.

"Come, fill the Cup, and in the Fire of Spring
The Winter Garment of Repentance fling:
The Bird of Time has but a little way
To fly - and Lo! The Bird is on the Wing."

"Here is a loaf of Bread beneath the Bough,
A flask of Wine, a Book of Verse - and Thou
Beside me singing in the Wilderness -
And Wilderness is Paradise enow."

In Alchemy, as previously stated, marriage is symbolical of a union; as in chemistry, it is a combination or fusion of elements. The symbolical bridegroom was Jesus, the Christed One, who performed an alchemical miracle. In John 2:11, we are told:

"This beginning of miracles did Jesus in Cana of Galilee, and manifested forth his glory; and his disciples believed in him."

This was His first demonstration of what we today label as 'miracles'. Anyone who has studied the ancient wisdom of the Theosophical Masters such as Madame Helena Blavatsky, will understand the conceptual theory involved in the power of manifestation. All Masters of the Great White Brotherhood, through the teachings of the Ancient Wisdom, were able to use the power of manifestation as they had done in the ancient days of Atlantis and Lemuria. It is recorded that Madame Blavatsky manifested diamonds into a plain gold ring for one of her friends. The grand Alchemist was St Germain who is recorded as having utilized the powers of manifestation to transmute base metals into gold and small inferior diamonds and jewels into large flawless ones.

In the word 'Cana' we have the sacred sound Ca (Ka) as in Cabbala (Kabbala). According to information contained in Peter Dawkins' book titled *Arcadia*:

"The word Kabbala or Cabbala means 'the Received Light or Wisdom' which is derived from Ka [also CA]."

'Cana' also contains the word 'An' (as in ANA) within it. From Peter Dawkins' book titled *The Great Vision*, we are informed as follows:

"In Hebraic-Christian tradition, the God-name for the Divine Mind (or Heavenly Father) is AN, whilst that for the Divine Mother (or Earthly Mother) is ANNA. AN is sometimes spelt ON from which we derive our word ONE from this mystery name."

4. THE (AL)CHEMICAL MARRIAGE

In the 16th century, an author published a work known as *The Chemical Marriage*. The name under which he published this work was Johann (John) Valentine Andrea whose work made reference to and was identical with that of Christian Rosenkreutz (Rose-Cross) who was born in 1378.

According to Dr Raymond Bernard's work titled *The Great Mystery Comte St Germain*:

"Christian Rosenkreutz was a mask of Francis Bacon, its true founder, who was the author of the Rosicrucian Manifestos, the 'Confessio' and 'Fama Fraternitatis' which he sent to Germany and which were published in 1615 by Valentine Andrea, a German theologian whose name he used in connection with his Rosicrucian writings. From the time that he wrote the Rosicrucian Manifestos and issued them through Valentine Andrea in Germany, eight years before his feigned death in England and passage to the Continent, Francis Bacon was the moving spirit of Rosicrucianism during the 18th century, as he was its founder during the 17th, as well as the leader of Freemasonry."

"In evidence that St Germain, or, as he was previously called, Francis Bacon, was the true founder of Rosicrucianism, who was symbolically represented under the form of the mythical figure of Christian Rosenkreutz, is the statement in the Rosicrucian Manifestos that he was born in 1378 and lived one hundred and six years, which meant that he had died in 1484. It is claimed that when his tomb was opened one hundred and twenty years later, it was found to contain the works of Paracelsus, which is impossible since the latter was born in 1493, and hence his writings could not have gotten into the tomb of a man who died nine years previously. This would indicate that the story of Christian Rosenkreutz was allegorical, not historical as pointed out by Manly Hall in his *The Enigma of the Rosicrucians*."

"The mysterious book that appeared at about the same time as the Rosicrucian Manifestos - *The Chemical Marriage of Christian Rosenkreutz* which was published by Valentine Andrea in Germany whilst Francis Bacon was still in

England, was undoubtedly a product of Francis Bacon's secret Society."

According to the biographer of Sir Francis Bacon, the late Alfred Dodd in his book titled *Francis Bacon's Personal Life Story:*

"There is another significant fact which should not be overlooked in dealing with the concealing labours of Francis Bacon and St Albans (he had once been St Alban) as the cradle of Speculative Art. The Town Coat of Arms for St Albans is the Cross of St Andrew."

"A St Andrew's Cross formed the Arms of Johann Valentine Andrea, i.e. St Andreas (or St Andrew), who is supposed to be the writer of the Fama Fraternitatis (1614) ['Frater' means 'brother'] and the Founder of Rosicrucianism. Andrea was not, however, the real author or the Founder. He was a Mask for someone else who used the Cross of St Andrew in one of the Higher Masonic Degrees as a 'Knight of St Andrew'. We thus get a most suggestive hint of the connection between Freemasonry and Rosicrucianism and also between English and Scottish Masonry with its ancient centre of St Andrews. The Cross shows the real origin of the Continental Rosicrucian Manifestos - St Albans' and the writer, Francis Bacon."

In the Appendix of Alfred Dodd's book, we learn that "the real John Valentine Andrea never claimed the writings as his and expressly disavowed them. The truth is that they were written as propaganda booklets by Francis Bacon, and, since it would have been too dangerous to publish them in a small place like England, they first ran in manuscript there, secretly passing from hand to hand, were then translated by Andrea and published in German, and eventually in English and printed by 'Eugenius [You genius] Philalethes, the pen-name of Thomas Vaughan, a Mystic, a Freemason and a Rosicrucian, who knew the Secret Authorship and printed it on the Title Page for those who had eyes to read... 'Lo! A Prince, Frater Francis Bacon.'"

The name of Christian Rosenkreutz is reputed to have been a pseudonym for Christian Rose-Cross, (C.R.C.). This was also possibly what St Germain was referring to when he gave a cryptic message to Peter Dawkins which is worth repeating:

"MY NAME is a mask. I am one yet more than one. My name is a cipher: it is '1.9' and '9.3'. C.R.C. is an epigram.

MASTERS DISCUSSED IN THIS CHAPTER

St Alban - St Germain
Christian Rosenkreutz - St Germain
Francis Bacon - St Germain
Pythagoras - Kuthumi
Aristotle - Kuthumi
St John the Beloved Disciple - Kuthumi
Omar Khayyam - Kuthumi

Pharaoh Akhnaton (Amenhotep IV) - El Morya
King Solomon - El Morya
John the Baptist - El Morya

NOTES AND RECOMMENDED READING

Alfred Dodd, *Francis Bacon's Personal Life Story*, (Rider & Co., U.K., 1949, 1986)
Dr Raymond Bernard, *The Great Secret - Count Saint Germain*, (U.S.A.).
Robert Graves, *The White Goddess,* (Faber & Faber, U.K. 1961)
Annie Bessant, *The Ancient Wisdom*, (Theosophical Publishing House, U.S.A 1992)
Madame Helena Blavatsky, *The Secret Doctrine*, (Quest Books, Theosophical Publishing House, U.S.A, 1966)
Edward Fitzgerald, *Rubaiyat of Omar Khayyam*, (Collins, U.K. 1974)
Peter Dawkins, *The Great Vision*, (Francis Bacon Research Trust, Warwick, U.K.)

CHAPTER 24

The Persecution of the Christians & the Battle of Masada

"I know about the Emperor when he was half-burnt"
(Taliesin/St Germain)

"And did those feet in ancient time,
Walk upon England's mountains green:
And was the Holy Lamb of God,
On England's pleasant pastures seen!
And did the Countenance Divine,
Shine forth upon our clouded hills?
And was Jerusalem builded here,
Among these dark Satanic Mills?"
(William Blake)

"I have been on the White Hill
in the court of Cynvelyn (Cymbeline)
(Taliesin/Merlin/St Germain)

After the scenario of the crucifixion, the Essenes were still under threat of persecution by the Romans who wished to eradicate the royal family of the House of Judah. Thus, it was deemed necessary to protect the immediate Grail family, hence the reason for the journey to Marseilles (Gaul) of Mary Magdalene, Martha, Lazarus (Simon Eleazar), Mary their mother, and her son John the Beloved (alias Joseph of Arimathea).

According to George F. Jowett in his book titled *The Drama Of The Lost Disciples*, the apostle Philip had preceded their visit to Gaul to make preparations for their arrival. The others remained in Gaul whilst Joseph and 'Mary' sailed for Britain from the port of Marseilles, and are considered to have arrived in 37 AD.

George F. Jowett wrote: "This was not an accident. It was the beginning of the new destiny long prophesied."

"There are still people who insist that the British story is a superstitious myth without foundation, just as they continue to debate that the Bible is untrue. They are as mentally fogbound as the Victorian historians who could not understand how, why or where there could be any connection between the ancient British and the continental races, and less with the prophecies and people of the Bible."

"The Gauls were Druidic, and their faith held sway over all Gaul, which explains more than anything else why the land was a safe haven for Joseph and the Bethany family, as well as the many other converts who had previously found refuge there, after a safe escape from Judea..."

The Founding of the First Christian Church in Britain

"Long before Joseph arrived in Britain, the scandal of the cross was known to them and had become a cause of grave concern to the Druidic Church. The swiftness with which the Druidic delegates journeyed to Gaul to meet Joseph shows how concerned they were to obtain first-hand information. Contrary to the fallacious story of later historians, there was no argument, civil or religious, no bloodshed. It was an open acceptance that elected Joseph of Arimathea to the head of the Christ-converted British Church."

"From then on the Druidic name and the old religion in Britain and Gaul began to be superseded by the Christian name, which the British created to identify the accepted Christ faith, formerly known as 'The Way'. Joseph was the unseen power behind the throne, as he had been on that black night in the Sanhedrin and the following four years in Judea. All rallied around him eager to begin proclaiming the Word to the world."

"The first Christian Church above ground (in Britain) was erected 38-39 AD."

This was not the first time that Joseph of Arimathea (John the Beloved) had visited Britain, because according to ancient legends, he was at one time accompanied by Jesus, which would make sense, because after all, they were brothers. The poet William Blake, who was a Grand Master of the Order of the Rose Cross and also a member of the Order of the Druids, wrote his famous poem which is quoted at the beginning of this chapter. According to the *Oxford Anthology of English Literature Vol. II*, the verse 'dark satanic mills' does not apply to industrial mills but 'mills of the mind'. It is noteworthy that in Paul Broadhurst and Hamish Miller's book titled *The Sun And The Serpent*, in the introduction given by John Michell, William Blake had addressed a meeting of Jews, 'where he informed them that all their priestly traditions had come down to them from the Druids'. Blake's authority for these statements was the 18th century antiquarian and Druid revivalist, William Stukeley." (Stukeley also claimed that 'Abraham was the father of all Druids'.)

The Founding of the Roman Catholic Hierarchy

"The Roman Catholic hierarchy was founded *circa* 350, after Constantine, and not until centuries later was the Papal title created. Until then, the head of the Roman Catholic Church was still a Bishop. The title of Pope, or universal Bishop was given to the Bishop of Rome by the wicked Emperor Phocas, in the year 610 AD. This he did to spite Bishop Ciriacus of Constantinople, who had justly excommunicated him for his having caused the assassination of his predecessor, Emperor Mauritus."

"Gregory I, then Bishop of Rome, refused the title but his successor, Boniface III, first assumed the title of Pope. Jesus did not appoint Peter to the headship of the Apostles and expressly forbade any such notion as stated in Luke 22:24-26."

Caradoc and Cymbeline

According to one of the Arthurian legends, Joseph of Arimathea passed the guardianship of the Grail Cup to Bron (another name for Bran) **who was his son-in-law**, Bran the Blessed King, the Archdruid High Priest who is better known as *Cymbeline.*

In earlier years Bran/Cymbeline had married Joseph's (John the Beloved's) daughter Anna, and one of the sons of this marriage was Caradoc whom the Romans called 'Caractacus'. In order to cement relations between the Romans and the Brits, Claudius offered the hand of his daughter Venus Julia, to Caradoc. Caradoc married her and they settled in Rome where the first above-ground teaching centre, known as the 'Home of the Apostles' was established.

Cymbeline, was an Archdruid High Priest who had fought many battles against the Romans who were invading Britain. He gained the title of 'Blessed King' because of the high esteem which the people held for him. Cymbeline ruled over the southern area of Britain known as Siluria in the first century AD. Another name by which he was known was *Cunobelinus, 'Cuno'* meaning 'Crowned Prince'.

From Peter Dawkins' book titled *Arcadia*, we review the following pertinent information which is very relevant to this chapter. Please note the prominence which the Master Kuthumi, First Master of the Holy Grail, has played in his various incarnations, mentioned in the following paragraph.

"The Tudors formed the ancient royal line of British kings, with a genealogy carefully preserved back to the famous King Arthur [Kuthumi], with direct links (via the daughter of Joseph [Kuthumi] of Arimathea) with the Judaic royal line of David [Kuthumi] and beyond even the later Celts to Hugh the Mighty (also known as Brut or Brit), who led the original Trojan settlers to 'the White Land' (i.e. Albion) in the second millennium BC. They gave these islands their name of 'Britain' (meaning 'The Chosen Land'). This family provided the 'Crowned Princes' (Cunos) and 'High Kings' (Arviragus) of ancient Britain and carried with them the ancient initiatic knowledge. The High Kings were elected from the 'blood royal' (i.e. the 'Tudor' blood line)."

The story of Bran the Blessed King is told in the collection of 6th century AD stories written by Taliesin/Merlin (St Germain) which in later centuries became known as the *Mabinogion*. The majority of stories feature the Four Branches of royal families.

The Four Royal Houses were:
1. Siluria (the royal house into which Anna, Joseph of Arimathea - John the Beloved's daughter married),
2. Camulod,
3. Dalriada (Ireland)
4. Gwynedd, (Wales)

Apart from some of the characters who may be mythological, historical ones are from time to time mentioned in the *Mabinogion* and these include Owein, son of Urien of Rheged, and Caswallon who was the king of the Catuvellauni tribe whose capital became the city of Verulam, today known as St Albans (as discussed in previous chapters).

The Royal Family Branch

1. The story of the First Branch of the royal family in the *Mabinogion* was concerned with the birth, death and exploits of Pwyll (meaning Pallas/Pelles) and his son Pryderi who historically was possibly 'Brideri', the High King of Gwynedd (Wales) who ruled from c.538-565 AD. Pelles/Pallas is introduced into the Arthurian legends as King Pelles. Sir Lancelot's wife, Elaine, was the daughter of King Pelles of Ireland.

2 In the Second Branch is the story of Branwen, the sister of Bran who marries King Matholwch of Ireland. In Celtic mythology, 'Bran' means 'raven' and his sister 'Branwen' meant 'white raven'; the raven, like the eagle and the owl, were the birds that were 'seers' and the Druids considered them to be sacred. Both the raven and the eagle can spot the tiniest movement upon the earth below as they fly high in the sky, whereas the owl at night can do the same.

In the story of Bran and Branwen, Bran fought many battles in Ireland, one of which he was forced into battle against his sister's husband who had been mistreating Bran's sister. Included amongst the seven people who accompanied Bran the King of Ireland on the journey to rescue his sister, was Taliesin/Merlin and we are told this in one of his verses contained in the *Romance of Taliesin* - "*I was with Bran in Ireland*".

One of the numerous legends about 'Bran' was that he had a magic cauldron from which 'wisdom' could be supped. The symbology of the 'cauldron' was used in Francis Bacon's play (when he wrote under the pseudonym of 'Shakespeare') *Macbeth* in which the three (3) witches stirred the cauldron muttering: "*Bubble, bubble, toil and trouble*". The cauldron has also become equated with the Grail being a 'dish', 'plate' or a chalice. Like many of the other names ascribed to the so-called gods of the race of the Tuatha de Danaan, such as Mor (as in Dagda Mor), 'Bran' too became a name incorporated into the family tribal groupings, such as the name Gabran (Ga-bran). The historical name of their ancestor was King Beli (Heli) Mawr which is also 'Mor'.

2.   The Third Branch of the royal family tells of the children of Llyr, also 'Lear' (which is another character about whom Francis Bacon was to write about under the name of *Shakespeare* - namely, his famous play *King Lear*). Caswallon (62-48 BC) was the son of Beli Mawr (Mor) and he was an historical king at the time of the Roman invasion led by Julius Caesar. Caswallon's son was King Lear, who married Pernadim and they became the parents of Bran the Blessed, the Archdruid High Priest, of Siluria (Wales). His more familiar name is Cymbeline/Cunobelinus and he married Anna, the daughter of John Joseph the Beloved (alias Joseph of Arimathea). Their sons were Caradoc (Caractacus) and Prince Linus.

Francis Bacon, writing under the name of Shakespeare, was also to write his work *Cymbeline*. Francis Bacon/St Germain knew all of these characters because he had once been the Merlin of the 6th century who had written about them under the pseudonym of *Taliesin*.

4.   The Fourth Branch of the royal family tells of the story of the children of Don/Dana/Danu/Anna whose origins could be traced back to the ancient Sumerians and to the tribe who called themselves *Marianna (Mary/Anna)*. The family is that of *Math* and *Arianhod* who are the children of *Don* meaning 'a lord' and the name of 'Don' or 'Donn' also applied to a brave man.

In order to save confusion with the variants in names, below is a brief summary:

Beli Mawr (Mor) the Great was Lord of the Britons c.132-72 BC.

One of Beli's grandsons was King Lear who married Pernadim.

King Lear and Pernadim's son was Bran the Blessed High King, (Cunobelinus) known as Cymbeline.

Bran the Blessed (Cymbeline) married Anna, daughter of Joseph of Arimathea (alias John Joseph the Beloved).

Anna and Cymbeline had a son Caradoc.

Caradoc was the Pendragon (Head Military Leader) whom the Romans called Caractacus. He married the Roman Emperor, Claudius' daughter, Venus Julia. Caradoc was the grandson of Joseph of Arimathea (alias John Joseph the Beloved Disciple).

Throughout the history of the Arthurian legends, there have been times when Arviragus, Caradoc and Arthur are said to have all been different names for the one person. The confusion obviously came about because 'Arviragus' was a title meaning 'High King'. 'Pendragon' and 'Merlin' were titles given to those who were highly initiated into Druidism.

It was Caradoc who granted the land at Glastonbury upon which Joseph of Arimathea (John the Beloved) built his first church in Britain.

Not far from where the church was built (the remains of St Joseph's church can still be seen today), is the famous Chalice Well.

The Rose Cross given by Joseph of Arimathea (Kuthumi) to Caradoc

We learn from Peter Dawkins in his book titled *The Great Vision* the following pertinent information:

"Caradoc, the son of Cymbeline [Bran the Blessed High King] was the first to bear the title 'Defender of the Faith' which was given to him by Joseph of Arimathea, together with the 'Long Cross' to display on his coat of arms. The 'Long Cross' was the 'Red' or 'Rose Cross', displayed on a white (or silver) background and it was used as the badge of the elected Christian King."

"All Christian Kings of Britain adopted the Rose/Red Cross as their symbol, together with the title 'Defender of the Faith' - a title which echoed the old Druidic motto and war-cry, 'The Truth against the World'. Since the time of Caradoc, the Rose/Red flag has always been the Christian flag of the British Church. It was to become known as the St George's Cross."

(It will be recalled that mention has been made in an earlier chapter that St George was an incarnation of the Master Kuthumi. He became the first Christian martyr for having defended the Christians against the Roman persecutions).

According to George F. Jowett in his book titled *The Drama of the Lost*

Disciples:

"The banner of the Cross under which Caractacus led the British troops for nine years was to be unfurled at Rome and accepted by the Romans as their national insignia. It was the family of Caractacus who first unfurled that standard at Rome...in the end the Silurians conquered Rome for Christ."

"The royal boundaries of the Silures were divided into two sections. The Arviragus ruled over the southern part of England, and Caradoc (Caractacus), over Cambria, the region that is now Wales. Each was king in his special domain but in time of war they united under a Pendragon or Commander-in-Chief, agreed upon by the people."

"There was to be a second separate planting of the Christ Seed in Britain about twenty years after Joseph of Arimathea's arrival. Independent of the Josephian Mission it was also to be sponsored by the Royal Silurian House, in Wales, by the father and family of Caractacus, under the commission of St Paul. It originated in Rome, where this same family was to be the divinely ordained instruments."

Caradoc was a High King of royal blood who was appointed Head Dragon (Pendragon) by the Druidic council when his father Bran (Cymbeline/Cunobelinus) abdicated in favour of his son. The father of Caradoc, the Archdruid High Priest, Bran, spent the rest of his years dedicated to being a 'Defender of the Faith'. Caradoc became a military leader of the Britons who led the British armies against the Romans during their mammoth invasion of Britain (42-52 AD) in which the Romans hoped to stamp out the seat of Druidism and thus the Celtic Church.

When the Roman invasion of Britain began in 42 AD, Britain became a province of the Roman Empire.

Caradoc became the King of the Catuvellauni who were a tribe that lived near what is now called St Albans. (St Germain's next known incarnation after his one as Apollonius, was that of St Albanus - St Alban, born of Roman parents in Britain in the 3rd century AD. St Albans was the original town of Verulam and in the 16th century AD, Francis Bacon - St Germain, was given the title of Baron Verulam, Viscount St Albans by King James I of England. Bacon's family home was Gorhambury, near St Albans).

After years of resistance against the invading Romans, at which time he was given the support of two Welsh tribes, the Silures and the Ordovices, Caradoc was forced to take refuge with the Brigantes of Yorkshire. His father, Cymbeline (Bran the Blessed) had also led battles against the Romans. When Caradoc sought refuge with the Brigantes, he was betrayed by their Queen who had him placed in chains and delivered to the Romans, accompanied by his father, Bran, who was also captured. (It was during their time spent in Rome at the royal palace of Claudius, that Caradoc was offered and accepted the hand of Claudius' daughter, Venus Julia).

The origin of Bel/Baal and Heli/Beli

Anna and Bran the Blessed had another son whose name was Beli (Heli). The names of Cymbeline and Cunobelinus also contain the word 'bel'. It is of interest to note that the lineage of Joseph (the Father of the Grail family, namely St Germain), is mentioned in the Bible, Luke 3, 23: "And Jesus himself began to be about thirty years of age, being (as was supposed) the son of Joseph which was the son of Heli."

Heli in Celtic is a variant of 'Beli' equated with the legendary early British King, Beli Mawr (Mor). It has already been established that the House of Tudor originated from the House of Judah and could trace its lineage back to the ancient British king, Beli Mawr the Great. He ruled Britain approximately 72 BC.

In the *Mabinogion*, (Beli Mawr/Mor) appears as a king of Britain who was the founder of the Welsh royal line - the Silures, the lineage into which Anna, the daughter of Joseph of Arimathea married.

Considering the fact that Anna named one of her sons 'Beli' which also meant 'Heli', it would appear that the tradition of carrying on the family names was continued. (This was held to be a common tradition amongst the Celtic families and in Ireland it was known as the 'Naming Patterns').

Through this genealogy, it is probable that Joseph, the Father of the Grail Family (St Germain), whom the Bible tells us so little about (which of course arouses our curiosity as to his origins), was a prince who was a son or grandson of Beli (Heli) Mawr (Mor), the Great. This was not after all, the first time that St Germain was born a prince. There was still a later time in the 6th century AD when he was born a Celtic Prince, and still later on in the 16th century when he was born a royal prince of the Tudor lineage. These royal families could trace their lineage back to Princess Tea Mor Tephi of the Royal House of Judah, (whose story is told in the sequel to this story, *The Dove, The Rose And The Sceptre - In Search of the Ark of the Covenant*).

One of St Germain's famous works which he wrote under the masked name of Shakespeare, was as previously mentioned, *Cymbeline, King of Britaine*. It is noteworthy that Alfred Lord Tennyson, who was the Poet Laureate of Britain for over forty years, was so impressed with this work that upon his death, and after his body had been laid out, a copy of *Cymbeline* was placed with him.

A variant of the name Beli (Heli) is the Phoenician word 'Baal' which meant 'Master' and reference to 'Baal' is found in the Old Testament. It is also called 'Bel' and the Druidic festival of Beltane derived its name from the Phoenician word

'Baal'. When the Roman form of Christianity came to Britain, the festival of Beltane was changed to May Day and was originally considered to be a 'pagan' festival for the May Pole was a symbol of fertility.

From the book titled *From The Stone Age To Christianity* by William Foxwell Albright, we learn that: "originally, both Baal and Yahweh were lords of heaven and senders of rain and they were both storm-gods (like 'Thor') and givers of fertility. The name of Yahweh eventually replaced 'Baal'."

According to information contained in Peter Dawkins' book titled *The Great Vision*; 'BAL' (sometimes written as BEL) is found in many sacred traditions and languages, such as Druidic, Arabic, Phoenician, Greek, as well as Hebrew. In Arabic, Phoenician, Hebrew and Greek, the numerological cipher of BAL (sometimes written as BEL) = 33, (B = 2, a = 1, l = 30)."

Cymbeline

"I have been on the White Hill
in the court of Cynvelyn (Cymbeline)
(Taliesin/Merlin/St Germain)

We learn from the above quotation that St Germain visited the court of Cymbeline in Britain and this would have been during the time that St Germain had reincarnated (after his life as Joseph, the Father of the Grail family), as Apollonius, the wonderful Holy Man who spent time in Rome preaching the wisdom/teachings of the Essenes. (According to Betty Radice in her book titled *Who's Who In The Ancient World*, the character 'Polonius' in Shakespeare's play *Hamlet* is thought to have been derived from 'Apollonius'.

(White Hill mentioned in the above verse, was where the palace was situated and it was painted with white-wash, hence its name. 'White Hill' was the original name for the Tower of London).

St Peter first visited Rome in 44 AD and St Paul consecrated the second priestly son of Caradoc (Caradoc was the son of Cymbeline/Bran the Blessed), Prince Linus, as the first Bishop of Rome in 58 AD. St Paul lived for eight years at the 'Home of the Apostles' in Rome and it became a most fashionable and cultural centre. John Joseph the Beloved (alias Joseph of Arimathea) would have made visits there also, not only to be with his family, but also to have meetings with the Apostles. In Rome, he would also have had meetings with St Germain in his incarnation as Apollonius.

When Claudius died in 54 AD, Nero became the emperor and chaos reigned. Nero hated the Christians and Jews with a passion and he was notoriously unstable. He ordered his procurator, Albinus, to tax the Essenes and the Jews heavily and the freedom fighters (the zealots) were rebelling, desperately wanting their freedom from the Romans and all the injustice that they had incurred.

After the Great Fire in 64 AD, when Nero accordingly accidentally set Rome ablaze, the sadistic, unhinged emperor tried to blame the event upon the Christians and subsequently increased his endless persecutions. The zealot rebels led by Simon Magus (Lazarus/Eleazar) the son of the Elder High Priest Annas (Joseph - St Germain), stepped up their protests. Apollonius (St Germain's next incarnation following that of Joseph) was in Rome at the time.

In 66 AD, Nero expelled the philosophers from Rome. Just prior to this event, Apollonius (St Germain) was charged with high treason. However, when the charges were brought before Nero, they mysteriously and 'miraculously' disappeared from the parchment when it was unrolled. Apollonius travelled to Spain and Damis, one of his disciples, implied that whilst in Spain, Apollonius conferred with certain activists who later led the revolt against Nero.

It was rumoured that Apollonius and Eleazar (Lazarus) helped to bring about the downfall of the evil Nero. This would explain the verses that St Germain wrote in the 6th century under the pseudonym of Taliesin/Merlin: *"I know about the Emperor when he was half-burnt"*.

During the persecutions by Nero, all except for Claudia (daughter of Caradoc and Venus Julia), all her royal family living in Rome plus thousands of other Christians were martyred, and the early Christian Church in Rome, the 'Home of the Apostles' was virtually wiped out.

Roman Harassment in Britain

When Nero came into power in 54 AD, many serious events occurred. By this time, the Celtic Church at Glastonbury which John Joseph established had been operating for almost thirty years.

In 60 AD, Queen Boudicea of the Iceni tribe (Norfolk, England) had her own problems with the Roman invaders. Her royal household was plundered and her daughters were raped by Roman soldiers. Enraged, she organised her own battle against the Romans fighting a battle against them at Colchester and then at Verulam (later to be called St Albans), where she was defeated.

Then, in 61 AD, the deranged Nero issued orders for the destruction of the Druidic settlement on the island of Mona (Anglesey). According to Robert Graves in his book titled *The White Goddess*, in the year 61 AD, the Roman general, Paulinus, conquered Anglesey and cut down the sacred oak trees in order to prevent the Druids worshiping their god Baal/Bel/Beli and accordingly the name of *Cymbeline* means 'the Hound of Bel'.

The island of Mona was a sacred home of the Druids. 'Mona' was the last stronghold for the Druids who maintained considerable political power.

It is rather curious that one of the paintings of Leonardo da Vinci (Kuthumi) is the Mona Lisa (now displayed at the Louvre in Paris). In fact, according to a recent programme on the History Channel, it was Leonardo's favourite painting which he took with him when he went to live at Le Clos-Luce, Amboise in France,

Mona Lisa is known as the lady with the 'enigmatic' smile upon her countenance, obviously placed there for a reason by the artist. Perhaps Kuthumi purposely gave her the name of Mona and added the mysterious smile, alluding to his past-life as John the Beloved (alias Joseph of Arimathea) for he was alive during the era of the destruction of the Druidic settlement of Mona. According to an historical book of names by Michele Brown, 'Mona' means 'noble one'. The name of 'Arimathea' contains 'Ari' which means 'noble'.

When the Celtic monastery at Anglesey was destroyed, the one at Glastonbury would have become a major centre of learning and it is probable that many of the documents that had been stored at Mona were rescued and brought to Glastonbury. The next important Celtic monasteries in Britain were not founded until the 5th and 6th centuries, and these were established by the Masters of the Great White Brotherhood, namely Kuthumi in the 5th century, and St Germain in the 6th century.

After the Druidic settlement of Anglesey was destroyed in 61 AD, one year later, in 62 AD, James the Just was put to death in Jerusalem by Annas the Younger High Priest of the Sanhedrin - Judas Iscariot - the traitor, the Essenes' 'Wicked Priest', the 'Spouter of Lies'.

The following year, in 63 AD, Mary Magdalene is reputed to have died in Gaul (France) and she was buried at St Maximins.

The Battle of Masada near Jerusalem in 67 AD
And the Attack on Qumran in 68 AD

In 67 AD the Essenian zealots launched a successful attack on Herod's former city, Masada, and the following year, in 68 AD, the Roman Emperor Titus Flavius Vespasian (who succeeded Nero), in retaliation, issued instructions for his son Titus to attack Qumran, by which time the Essenes had carefully placed their precious scrolls in sealed jars and hid them in the surrounding caves so that they could be found in later centuries when it was deemed that the 'time was ripe' for such a discovery.

Then, in 70 AD the Romans led by Titus began a massive invasion upon Jerusalem at which time the Temple was destroyed and any inhabitants still within the city, were slaughtered. And so, like the Cathars in later centuries who were cruelly persecuted by the Church of Rome, thousands of Essenes suffered and also died as a result of Roman persecution.

The Sadducee Priests no longer had a Temple or any power; their time of finding favour with the Romans, was over.

MASTERS DISCUSSED IN THIS CHAPTER

Joseph - The Father of the Grail Family (Annas the Elder) - St Germain
Apollonius of Tyana - St Germain
St Alban - St Germain
Taliesin/Merlin - St Germain
Sir Francis Bacon (Shakespeare) - St Germain
John the Beloved Disciple (alias Joseph of Arimathea) - Kuthumi
St George - Kuthumi
King Arthur - Kuthumi

NOTES AND RECOMMENDED READING

Robert Graves, _The White Goddess_, (Faber & Faber, U.K., 1961)

George F. Jowett, _The Drama Of The Lost Disciples_, (Covenant Publishing Co. Ltd., London, U.K. 1980)

Peter Dawkins, _The Great Vision_, (Francis Bacon Research Trust, U.K.)

Peter Dawkins, _Arcadia_, (Francis Bacon Research Trust, U.K.)

Arnold J. Toynbee, _A Study Of History_, (Oxford University Press, U.K. 1934)

Betty Radice, _Who's Who In The Ancient World_, (Penguin Books, U.K. 1973)

Gwyn & Thomas Jones, _The Mabinogion_, (J.M. Dent & Son, U.K.)

Josephus, _Thrones Of Blood_, (Barbour & Co. U.S.A 1988)

William Blake, _Jerusalem_, (Oxford Anthology of English Literature, Oxford University, U.K. 1973)

Paul Broadhurst & Hamish Miller, _The Sun And The Serpent_, (Pendragon Press, Cornwall, U.K., 1994)

CHAPTER 25

The 'Beast' 666

"And I saw as it were a sea of glass mingled with fire and them that had gotten
the victory over the Beast..."
(John 15:2)

It is of interest to note that the English author, Robert Graves wrote in his
work titled *The White Goddess* that the riddle in the thirteenth chapter of the
Apocalypse is:

"Here is wisdom. Let him that hath understanding count the number of the
Beast: for it is the number of a man and his number is 666. I vaguely remembered
from my school days, the two traditional solutions of St John's cryptogram. They
are both based on the assumption that since letters of the alphabet were used to
express numerals in Greek and Hebrew alike, 666 was a sum arrived at by adding
together the letters that spelt out the Beast's name."

"The earliest solution, that of the second century bishop Irenaeus, is
LATEINOS, meaning 'The Latin One' and so denoting the race of the Beast; the
most widely accepted solution is NERON KESAR, namely the Emperor Nero
regarded as Antichrist."

Although the *Apocalypse* of John the Beloved (Kuthumi) was written in
Greek, Robert Graves had a vision of Roman numerals that appeared to him, flashed
upon a wall:

D.C.L.X.V.I. which the author knew was DOMITIANUS CAESAR LEGATOS XTI
VILITER INTERFECIT. 'Domitian Caesar basely killed the Envoys of Christ'.

Robert explains: "In the first place I had been aware that the *Apocalypse*
was referred to by most Biblical scholars to the reign of Nero (54-67 AD), not to
that of Domitian (81-96 AD) and yet my eye read '*Domitianus*'. Now I remembered
that Nero's original name, Domitius was Nero's original name before the Emperor
Claudius adopted him into the Imperial family and changed his name to Nero
Claudius Caesar Drusus Germanicus, and that he hated to be reminded of his

plebian origin."

"St John the Divine [Beloved] would naturally not have respected Nero's feelings and the use of D.C. for N.C. would have served to protect the secret. The word Viliter was recognizable as a word of condemnation."

Robert Graves further states: "When I came to scrutinize the *Apocalypse* text, I found in the margin a cross-reference to *Chapter XV, verse 2*, which runs:

'And I saw as it were a sea of glass mingled with fire and them that had gotten the victory over the Beast, and over his image, and over his mark, and over the number of his name, standing on the sea of glass, having the harps of God.'

"The 'image' is the one mentioned in the previous context: apparently the meaning is that Christians were martyred who loyally refused to worship Nero's statue. So, 'them that had gotten the victory of the Beast and over his image and over his mark and over the number of his name' were the Envoys of Christ who refused to be terrorized into Emperor worship, and who when sacrilegiously slain were carried straight up to Paradise. The *Apocalypse* was originally written in the time of Nero's persecutions."

According to Betty Radice in her book titled *Who's Who In The Ancient World*:

"Nero was not only extremely vain but he reputedly started the great fire that destroyed half of Rome in 64 AD. After the Fire of Rome, Nero built his famous Golden House on an extravagant scale in a royal park, overlooking an ornamental lake, later filled in and covered by the Colosseum. In its forecourt stood a huge statue of himself as the sun-god."

Robert Graves' solution to the riddle of 666 was that the statue of the Beast (Nero) reflected on the ornamental lake which had the appearance of a sea of glass. "In Hebrew the letters TRJVN which add up to 666 (*Tav* = 400; *Resh* = 200; *Yod* = 10; *Nun* = 50), form the common cipher-disguise in Talmudic literature for Nero (*trijon* means 'little beast'). It is possible that the first version of the *Apocalypse* was written in Aramaic before 70 AD in which 666 was a cipher meaning 'Little Beast', which pointed to Nero. When it was re-written in Greek, the cipher 666 was given a new solution and one that any intelligent person could understand without recourse to Hebrew: namely DCLXVI."

John the Beloved wrote of many of the events of which he was a witness to, and obviously he was in Rome at the time of the fire in 64 AD, and the martyrdom of the Christians. No doubt he would have been resident at the Home of the Apostles in Rome and there he would have met up with Apollonius (St Germain).

The next ruler after Nero was Vespasian upon whom Apollonius had a great deal of influence. It was during the era of Vespasian that John the Beloved was exiled to Patmos in 70 AD, by Vespasian because of his activities involved with fighting the Romans and defending his people the Essenes, and it was there that he wrote the Book of John and Revelation. He then returned to Glastonbury and as Joseph of Arimathea, he was buried there with his mother, Mary.

From the book titled *The Message Of The Masters* by Robert J. Scrutton, we learn another opinion regarding *Revelation*.

"We cannot understand the case behind the rise and fall of ancient civilization if we continue to remain blind to the meanings and warnings. The first many-headed beast refers to the worship of wealth in the ancient world. The second beast, said St John, 'exercised all the power of the first beast before him, and causes the earth and those who dwell therein to worship the first beast, whose deadly wound was healed'. 'And he caused all, both small and great, rich and poor, free and bond, to receive a mark in their right hand, or in their foreheads' - the grasping hand and the profit-motivated mind. 'That no man might buy or sell, save that he had the mark, or the name of the beast, or the number of his name' - credit, cheque book or banknote number?"

"St John the Divine/Beloved most definitely invites the reader to reflect upon the meaning of this chapter. After saying that no man may buy or sell with the mark, or *number* of the beast, he ends with his pertinent saying:

'Here is wisdom. Let him that hath understanding count the number of the beast: for it is the number of a man; and his number is Six hundred score and six.' Economic thralldom, the despotism of systems and man's inhumanity to man by no means exhausts the hidden meanings of the number 666. It has many mystical, psychological and geometrical meanings. In antiquity it was used to indicate or provide natural proportions, strength and beauty of Nature and the works of man, and also to indicate the spiritual powers that could raise man to godhead or make him lower than a beast. The Christians and the Hebrews used a language of numbers and symbols - gematria, numerology and Qabbalah (Cabbala) - evolved by earlier philosophers, to give expression to information obtained in dreams, visions and intuitions, in ratios of geometry. 'Here is wisdom', in the number 666, says the Apostle John."

"For example: Solomon's Seal, which has been accredited with magical powers, was once known as the symbol of wisdom and power that shaped a spiritual diamond from human dross. Its number was 666, the number of divine alchemy that changes crude metals into gold. The 666 of the two interlaced, equilateral triangles also gave the lines, angles, curves and flying arches of some of man's most glorious architecture. It was foundational to an extensive mathematical geometry in the realms of the spherics: in the unification of the platonic solids and the triangulation of them, and gave the fundamental rectangles of dynamic symmetry to curves and spirals in great works of art and architecture."

"The number is fundamental to the proportions of Gothic architecture. Cesariano mentioned three rules for designing churches. The first fixed overall length and breadth by means of the Vesica Piscis, the second provides the subdivision of the plan in actual bays, and the third determined the heights of the various parts of equilateral triangles. The shape of the Vesica Piscis is obtained from the overlapping of two circles of equal radius, when the circumference of one touches the centre of the other. This gives the extent of the ground plan, with the height, shape and proportions of the various parts of the church determined by a hexagon or the triangles of Solomon's Seal in each circle, and overlapping with the six points of either figure touching the circumference of its circle."

"The overlapping of the two circles was said to express the overlapping of spiritual and human consciousness, the overlapping of spirit and matter typified in Gothic architecture, and spiritual consciousness, or route from empirical consciousness to universal consciousness."

"The second dragon from the earth of human greed when Christian and Islamic kings, merchants and even Popes went secretly to Lombard insurers and pawnbrokers to mortgage jewels for loans of gold, or credit notes to finance trade and war, willingly paid the high interest demanded."

"What the Apostle John meant to convey when he wrote that 666 was the number of a *man*, may be that given by the Christian Gnostics and other apostles, whose writings were rejected or destroyed by the Roman Church. The persecuted Christian Gnostics identified 666 with the imperial rule of Rome and later with the Roman Church as the antithesis of the Christ-Spirit, the Beast. This was because the Roman Church oppressed the Gnostics and rejected the writings of the apostles on the teachings of Jesus the Christ which might undermine its rule and power."

St Peter became a martyr when he was taken prisoner during the persecution of the early Christians and was crucified upon the orders of the Emperor Nero. According to Peter Dawkins in his book titled *The Great Vision*:

"Despite later Roman Catholic claims, neither St Peter nor St Paul were ever Bishops of Rome; their work and responsibility were far greater than that. Neither were they responsible for the way the Church of Rome went when it was corrupted by power politics in the 6th century onwards. Thousands of other Christians were martyred during the persecutions instigated by the Emperor Nero, and the early Christian Church in Rome was virtually wiped out."

The Sole 'Keepers of Divinity'

According to Madame Helena Blavatsky in her book titled *The Secret Doctrine*:

"The Sacred Teachings (of the Arcana) were, at least, partially known to several of the Fathers of the Church. Some of the doctrines of the Secret schools, though by no means all, were preserved in the Vatican, and have since become part and parcel of the Mysteries, in the shape of disfigured additions made to the original Christian programme by the Latin Church. Such is now the materialized dogma of the Immaculate Conception. This accounts for the great persecutions set in motion by the Roman Catholic Church against Occultism, Masonry and *heterodox* mysticism generally."

Despite the great secrecy and care that was taken by those who received the Arcana knowledge of the *Mystical Rose*, sometimes through the centuries, the knowledge did fall into the wrong hands. It resulted in much confusion of the Sacred Teachings, of which many became distorted by priests of the early Church of Rome, for by maintaining religious control over the population, the church reigned supreme.

The early Churchman of the medieval world ingratiated themselves into positions of power and control. They corrupted the true meanings of the *Arcana* Teachings, and by means of using 'fear' as a form of control over the population of their diocese, they became very wealthy whilst the people starved from poverty as a result of floods and famines. In order to 'save their souls' from going to 'hell' (which does not exist), they donated whatever they could to the Church. Because of the great control they achieved through corrupt means, particularly in keeping the population ignorant of the true Teachings, the early Church Fathers established themselves as the sole gatekeepers of 'divinity'.

Through ignorance and superstition, people who performed miracles were labelled as 'heretics' by the priests, but, ironically, were later to be recognised as saints and usually within a short space of time of their transition. Amongst these saints were St Alban (St Germain) and St Thomas Becket (reputed to have been El Morya). Pilgrimages were made to their tombs and the miracles which occurred were recorded. Other personages who assumed important roles in their lifetimes and who were later to be recognised as saints were St Ninian, St Mungo and St Hugh of Lincoln.

Those who sought the 'Truth' in the Middle Ages were tortured and persecuted in the most horrible fashion by the Church of Rome and it is rather ironic that these were 'religious' persecutions carried out in HIS name. However, the Mystics of the ancient Wisdom did prevail, albeit in the greatest of secrecy using symbolism, and under different names and methodology.

The people whose history is discussed in this story, like all historical figures, have at times been treated unkindly by biased authors. The English authors see history from their point of view, the Scottish from theirs, the Irish from theirs, the Welsh from theirs, the French from theirs and so on and so forth. It will also be found that if history books have been written by someone of a religious denomination, there is usually some form of biased opinion given.

An example is an old book printed in the early 1900's by a priest for his students in which he stated categorically that the religion of the Church of Rome, was the 'one and only religion'; the others were not to be taken seriously. He wrote about the various popes and the wealth which the Church of Rome had accumulated over the years, as something of which to be proud. The Inquisition set up by Pope Innocent III, which murdered hundreds of thousands of people who were considered to be 'heretics' because they did not belong to the 'one and only' religion, was in the author's opinion, a "necessary evil."

It is noteworthy that in September, 1998, the newspapers reported the following:

"The Vatican has prepared a document in advance of the millennium asking for a pardon for its 'sins' over 2,000 years, including outrages perpetuated in God's name during the Crusades. The thirty-five page paper is said to analyse 'acts of violence and repression' prohibited by the Catholic Church's teachings but committed by its institutions. The writing is intended as the basis of a request for pardon which the Pope will pronounce at a solemn Mass in Rome on 8th March in 1999."

"For the first time, the Crusades have been mentioned among the Church's wrongs in a list which has been dubbed '2000 years of horrors'. But the document and its list of wrongs, which includes the burning at the stake of the Dominican preacher, Savonarola in 1498, the Czech religion reformer Jan Hus in 1415 and the philosopher Giordano Bruno in 1600, is not final."

From Peter Dawkins' book titled *Arcadia*, we learn the following pertinent information:

"In May 1583, Giordano Bruno came to England from France for a two-year visit. Famous for being an exponent of the Hermetic (derived from Hermes Trismegistus) art of memory, amongst other things, he had come direct from the Court of Henry III with letters of introduction from the French king to his ambassador in London and lodged for the duration of his stay in England with the French ambassador. Bruno probably enjoyed a kind of diplomatic immunity, for he was able to publish some of writings in England which any native country would not have been allowed to publish openly. Sir Philip Sidney brought Bruno from Oxford to meet Sir John Dee [Kuthumi]."

"Bruno's ideas were entirely in accord with those of Francis Bacon, both of whom sought right back beyond Christianity, Hebraism, and the philosophers of Ancient Greece, to Ancient Egypt as the earliest available source and outstanding practical example of a truly great scientific-religious Wisdom tradition, in which God was seen as being present in all Nature."

Prophets and Seers

In ancient times, sages were consulted regarding the future and in today's society clairvoyants and psychics have gained popularity. The word 'Seer' literally means a 'see-er'.

The ancient Egyptians and the Greeks would consult their Seers/Prophets. Kings and Queens did likewise. (Queen Elizabeth 1st astrologer was Sir John Dee - Kuthumi). Prophecies by saints were recorded for the future and many of them came true within their life time, such as the prophecies of St Columba.

In the 16th century, Ursula Southiel (1488-1561), otherwise known as Mother Shipton of Knaresborough in Yorkshire, made a series of predictions which included the 'downfall of Rome'. Ursula married Tobias Shipton - hence her name 'Mother Shipton'. She became a well known seeress in the area. The locals considered her to be a witch and she did eventually end up living in a cave which still exists and is a tourist feature of the quaint town of Knaresborough. The water that drips down the side of the rocks in the cave is considered to have special properties and over the aeons, people have tied notes of paper containing their wishes to branches of trees nearby, hoping their prayers will be answered. Mother Shipton successfully prophesied Henry VIII's invasion of Northern France in 1513, and the destruction of the Spanish Armada: *"The Western monarch's Wooden Horses Shall be destroyed by the Drake's forces."*

St Malachy also predicted the final downfall of the Church of Rome.

From the book titled *Prophecies of St Malachy and St Columbkille* (Columba), we learn that Malachy's family name was O'Morgair. He was born into a noble family in Armagh, Northern Ireland, in 1094 - the same country where St Patrick [Kuthumi] lived and taught in the 5th century AD. Unlike many of the saints, the life of St Malachy is well documented because his contemporary and close friend was St Bernard of Clairvaux (patron of the Knights Templar who studied the *Arcana*) who was his biographer. St Bernard belonged to the Order of the 'White Monks' - the Cistercians who robed themselves in white robes like the Essenes and Druids. He described Malachy as distinguished for his meekness, humility, and modesty. He also told of how Malachy foretold the day and hour of his death. It is of interest to note that St Malachy's prophecies consisted of one hundred and twelve popes from Malachy's time onwards.

The book from which this information has been obtained was written in 1969 and stated: "The prophecies of Malachy have almost come to an end; just three more popes and -

De Mediate Lunae (meaning 'Of the half moon'),

De Labore Solis (meaning 'From the toil of the sun' or 'Of the eclipse of the

sun'), and, Gloria Olivae (meaning 'The Glory of the Olive'),
will have joined the other 108 pontiffs thus anticipated or prophesied by
Malachy."

In 1958, John XXIII was elected as Pope. He died in 1963. The next Pope
was Paul VI (1963-1978). In 1978, John Paul II was elected and was the first non-
Italian Pope since Adrian VI (1522-1523) of the Netherlands. The Pope has suffered
a great deal of ill health in recent times and, as previously mentioned, in 1999 he
was to offer an apology for the 'wrongs' committed by the Church of Rome. He
may well be the one whom St Malachy prophesied as 'Gloria Olivae'. The Olive
branch has always been associated with peace.

According to Malachy's prophecies, after the one known as 'Gloria Olivae',
there will only be one more Pope - *Petrus Romanus* (Peter of Rome) or it could
refer to someone who is equated with being like a 'Rock' or 'Stone' for that is the
true meaning of 'Petrus'. Below is the prophecy of Malachy concerning the last
Pope.

"*In the final persecution of the Holy Roman Church there will reign Peter
the Roman, who will feed his flock among many tribulations; after which the seven-
hilled city will be destroyed and the dreadful Judge will judge the people.*"

It is interesting that St Malachy had such a close association with St Bernard
of Clairvaux - he even died in the arms of St Bernard when he fell ill from a fever on
one of his visits to Clairvaux. St Bernard features in future chapters of this story,
but suffice to say at this stage, his teachings were those of the Celtic faith and he
would have been one of the Masters of the Great White Brotherhood.

In his book titled *The Occult Conspiracy*, Michael Howard wrote: "The
relationship between the Pope and the Grand Masters was an explosive one. It
could be nothing else. The Church regarded the members of the secret societies
as spiritual anarchists who were agents of a Satanic conspiracy against organised
religion. The Freemasons and the Rosicrucians (Order of the Rose Cross) on the
other hand, accused the Church of suppressing the true teachings of Jesus of
Nazareth. One of the first victims of the intolerance of the early Christian Church
was Celtic Christianity."

MASTERS DISCUSSED IN THIS CHAPTER

Apollonius of Tyana - St Germain
St Alban - St Germain
Sir Francis Bacon - St Germain
John the Beloved Disciple (alias Joseph of Arimathea) - Kuthumi
St George - Kuthumi
King Arthur - Kuthumi
Sir John Dee - Kuthumi
St Thomas Becket - El Morya

NOTES AND RECOMMENDED READING

Robert Graves, *The White Goddess*, (Faber & Faber, U.K., 1961)

George F. Jowett, *The Drama Of The Lost Disciples*, (Covenant Publishing Co. Ltd., London, U.K. 1980)

Peter Dawkins, *The Great Vision*, (Francis Bacon Research Trust, U.K.)

Peter Dawkins, *Arcadia*, (Francis Bacon Research Trust, U.K.)

Peter Bander, *Prophecies of St Malachy and St Columbkille*, (Colin Smythe Ltd., U.K. 1979)

Betty Radice, *Who's Who In The Ancient World*, (Penguin Books, U.K. 1973)

Madame Helena Blavatsky, *The Secret Doctrine*, (Quest Books, Theosophical Publishing House, U.S.A, 1966)

William Foxwell Albright, *From The Stone Age To Christianity*, (Doubleday Anchor Books, U.S.A 1957)

Michele Brown, *Baby Name Book*, (Greenwich Editions, U.K., 1985)

The West Australian Newspaper, 28th September, 1998

Michael Howard, *The Occult Conspiracy*, (Rider & Rider, U.K. 1989)

Robert J. Scrutton, *The Message Of The Masters*, (Neville Spearman, Jersey, U.K. 1982)

CHRONOLOGY OF EVENTS

c. 530 BC:	Pythagoras - Philosopher and Father of Mathematics (Kuthumi).
469-399 BC:	Socrates, Greek Philosopher (earlier incarnation of the Master Jesus). He lived during the era of Plato (St Germain). Some of his teachings were not acceptable to the local hierarchy and he was executed. Plato is said to have witnessed the execution.
c.429-347 BC:	Plato, Greek Philosopher (St Germain).
384-322 BC:	Aristotle, Greek Philosopher (Kuthumi) - became the tutor of Alexander the Great (St Germain).
356-323 BC:	Alexander the Great (St Germain).
c.323-63 BC:	Seleucus, rival and general of Alexander the Great ruled over Babylonia and his dynasty became known as the Seleucid dynasty.
167 BC:	Antiochus IV, a descendant of Seleucus, took control of Jerusalem, causing a revolt amongst its occupants. Jerusalem was set ablaze and the stage was set for the rise of the Maccabees.
164 BC:	The Hasmonaeans (Maccabees) led the Jewish revolt against the Seleucid rule and established an independent kingdom in Palestine (Judah). The Maccabees usurped the priestly office. The ancient priesthood of Zadok was supplanted by the illegitimate Hasmonaean dynasty.
142 BC:	The enemy of the Essenes, Jonathan Maccabeus was executed by the Seleucid, Trypho.
140 BC:	Jonathan's brother, Simon Maccabeus was elected as a High Priest by his followers and was to remain in Simon's house, 'until a faithful prophet should arise' (Maccabees 1, 14:30-39) - an admittance of the illegitimacy of Simon's house.
103 BC:	Aristobulus I became the first king of the Jews. He was the grandson of Simon Maccabeus. They remained in power for a period of sixty years until they were usurped by the Herodians.
c.100 BC	The Essenes Communal centre at Qumran was founded around this time, or possibly a little earlier, according to the archaeologist, William Foxwell Albright.
c. 132 -c72 BC:	Beli (Heli) Mawr (Mor), Lord of the Britons. Exact dates are not known. He was possibly father or grandfather of Joseph (St Germain), the Father of the Grail Family. The Bible informs us that Joseph was the son of Heli (which is also Beli in Celtic).
c. 36 BC:	Birth of Joseph (St Germain), son of Heli. It is possible that he was actually born in Britain.

c. 73 - 4 BC: Herod the Great - King of Judea. In 37 BC, Herod defeated Antigonus, the last of the Hasmonaean kings with assistance from the Romans. Herod was the son of a man from Idumea named Antipater and a woman from Cyprus who was the daughter of an Arabian sheik. He was not of royal birth, and became a puppet king of the Romans.

43 BC: Herod married Mariamne, a Maccabean princess, daughter of Antigonus (the rival of Herod), in an attempt to legitimize the lineage. However, he eventually murdered her and her family.

c. 7 BC: Birth of the Messiah, Jesus. According to the Bible, Jesus' birth occurred during the reign of Herod who upon learning of the birth, issued a decree that all infant male children be killed, for he saw the Royal House of Judah, of which Jesus was a prince, as a threat to his own 'created' royal house. The fact that Jesus is said to have died at the age of 33 may have been a symbolical number relating to his association with Freemasonry. He was said to be a 'carpenter', but carpentry is a 'craft' and one of the terminologies found in Freemasonry, is 'Craft'. According to the Rosicrucian authority, Spencer Lewis, Jesus survived the crucifixion, lived for many years, and died at Mt Carmel.

(Unknown date AD) John Joseph of Arimathea's daughter, Anna, married Bran the Blessed who was also known as Cymbeline and was the Archdruid High Priest known as the High King or Arviragus who was also given the title of Pendragon (meaning 'Head'). He was descended from Beli Mawr (Mor).

15 AD: Eleazar (Simon/Lazarus/Zelotes), the Magus (Magician), succeeded his Father, Annas the Elder (Joseph - St Germain), as High Priest of the Sanhedrin. According to Spencer Lewis, Jesus was 15 years old when he heard of his father, Joseph's demise. He had been travelling for 3 years, since he had first been interviewed by the High Priests of the Sanhedrin when he was 12 years old.

18 AD: Joseph Caiaphas became High Priest of the Sanhedrin.

33 AD: At the scene of the crucifixion, Jesus handed over the care of Mary to John the Beloved.

36 AD: The reign of the High Priest of the Sanhedrin, Caiaphas, who was responsible for the persecution Jesus, ended.

37 AD: Joseph of Arimathea (John the Beloved) and his brother Simon Eleazar (Lazarus) escorted their Mother, Mary, plus their sisters Mary Magdalene and Martha, to Marseilles. Notably missing were their brothers, James the Just and Matthew (Mathias) who became

High Priests of the Sanhedrin. Their youngest brother, Judas Iscariot (the Traitor), would become the Annas High Priest of the Sanhedrin, for 3 months in 62 AD, at which time he was responsible for the murder of his brother, James the Just.

37 AD: Joseph of Arimathea (John the Beloved) the brother of James the Just, continued on to Britain from Gaul, taking his mother Mary, with him.

Caradoc, who was the Arviragus at the time, granted the land at Glastonbury to Joseph of Arimathea (John the Beloved) who was his grandfather. There he was to build the first Celtic Church in Britain. Joseph of Arimathea was known as the 'First Master of the Grail'. As John the Beloved, he was handed the Grail Cup of responsibility by his brother Jesus at the scenario of the Last Supper, just prior to the crucifixion - thus he became the 'First Master of the Grail.

41 AD: The Roman Emperor, Caligula was murdered.

Claudius (Tiberius Claudius Nero Germanicus) succeeded as Emperor of Rome.

42- 52 AD: Caradoc became the military leader (Pendragon) of the British and led the British armies against the Romans in their mammoth invasion in which the Romans hoped to stamp out the seat of Druidism and Christianity.

42 AD: Agrippa appointed Matthias (Matthew) Levi son of Annas the Elder High Priest, as High Priest of the Sanhedrin.

43 AD: Roman conquest of Britain by the Emperor Claudius.

44 AD: St Peter made his first visit to Rome.

45 AD: Caradoc married the Emperor of Rome's daughter, Venus Julia. In Rome he became known as 'Caractacus'.

52 AD: Caradoc/Caractacus was taken prisoner by the Roman Emperor Claudius because of his continuous fighting against the Romans whilst they and he were in Britain. He was released and he and his family were given a palace in Rome in which to reside. During his time in Rome, he established the great cultural centre which was known as the 'Home of the Apostles'.

54 AD: The Emperor of Rome, Claudius, died and was succeeded by Nero. The Essenes' zealots banded together to protect their people from persecutions.

58 AD: Caradoc's son was Prince Linus who was consecrated as the first Bishop of Rome by St Paul.

60 AD: Queen Boudicea of the Iceni tribe (Norfolk, England) had her royal household plundered and her daughters raped, by the invading Romans. She fought a battle against them at Colchester and then at Verulam (St Albans) in 61 AD, at which time she was defeated.

61 AD: Nero issued instructions for the main Druidic centre of Mona, Anglesey, to be destroyed.

62 AD: James the Just was executed in Jerusalem upon the instructions of Annas the Younger (Judas Iscariot - the 'traitor').

63 AD: Mary Magdalene died and was buried at St Maximins, in France (Gaul).

63 AD: Joseph of Arimathea, (John Joseph the Beloved Disciple, who was First Master of the Grail) returned to Britain, having visited Gaul and Jerusalem.

64 AD: The great fire of Rome occurred at which time Nero stepped up his persecutions of the Christians. St Germain in his incarnation as Apollonius was brought before Nero on charges which were subsequently dropped and Nero banned all philosophers from Rome.

68 AD: Death of Nero.

70 AD: St John the Beloved (Joseph of Arimathea) was exiled from Rome by the Roman Emperor, Vespasian, to Patmos where he wrote the Book of John and the Book of Revelation

c. 80 AD: St John the Beloved (Joseph of Arimathea) died in Great Britain.

79 AD: Death of the Roman Emperor Vespasian (Titus Flavius) who had ruled from 69 AD. He brought peace to a harassed city and stability to the empire. He commenced the building of the Temple of Peace and of the great Flavian amphitheatre in the grounds of Nero's Golden House, later to become known as the Colosseum after the huge statue of Nero.

PART THREE

CHAPTER 26

The Celtic Druids & Avalon

"Still think Briton's
That Arthur liveth
And dwelleth in Avalon."
(Layamon circa 1170 AD)

Dr Martin Evidson, a research consultant to the department of forensic pathology at Sheffield University U.K., who has written an article in an edition of *British Archaeology*, shows that the English people are mostly Celtic in their ancestry. Previously, they had always been thought to have been Anglo-Saxon in their origins. Through a genetic study, it seems that there may not have been a mass invasion of Anglo-Saxons after all.

It was reported in *The Times* (20th April 1997) that "instead of a massive invasion by the Anglo-Saxons, the Germanic settlers came in only small numbers, leaving most of the native Celtic-speaking population undisturbed. The result of which proves that the English are not predominantly the descendants of Germanic peoples, but come from the same indigenous stock as the Welsh and Cornish."

The article further stated: "the latter were never driven to the west of the country by Anglo-Saxon hordes, as legend has it. The English were Celts."

According to Dr Evidson, "the genetic evidence does not support the hypothesis of the widespread destruction or displacement of the native population by invaders from what is now Germany; the myth of kinship grew with the subsequent construction of English history."

The Christianization of Gods and Goddesses

When the Church of Rome made its presence felt in Britain, it Christianized many of the gods and goddesses whom the Celtic Druids worshipped. In 601 AD, owing to the fact that the people of Britain had followed the old ways for thousands of years and were not willing to be 'converted', Pope Gregory who upon finding that he was unsuccessful in his ambition to convert the whole of Britain, instructed his ambassadors who visited Britain not to destroy pagan temples and customs but to incorporate them into the Christian theology. As a result, many of the pagan gods and goddesses that the Druids worshipped were then called saints.

One of these was St Brigid who has been discussed in a previous chapter and another was 'Anna', revered as the Celtic Earth Mother, derived from the goddess Anu, who became St Anna. In Greece, where the goddess Venus was worshipped, Venus became St Venere and the gods Mercury and Dionysus became St Mercourios and St Dionysus. The Sun-god Helios became St Elias.

Before the coming of Christianity, giants and gods/goddesses were the heroes of the old Irish folk tales, many of which became exaggerated as they were passed down by word of mouth over the years (rather like 'Chinese Whispers') and it was not until Christianity started to make itself known in the Celtic regions that any of these myths were actually written down.

The monks in the monasteries, taught people to write and the stories had by then, been told and retold around the firesides in the long winter months, starting at *Samhain* (1st November). This was later to be called 'Halloween', the festival of All Souls.

Listed below are a few examples of how 'pagan' (meaning 'country man') celebrations, became 'Christianized'.

The eve of Samhain on the 1st November became known as All-Hallows Eve (Halloween).

The Winter Solstice which was the shortest day of the year on December 21st or 22nd was celebrated as the Goddess giving birth to a new sun. This became a Christianized version of the birth of Jesus, the Son of the Virgin, on the 25th of December, which we now call 'Christmas'.

The Celtic festival of Imbolc on the 1st February was later Christianized into Candlemas Day. It originally represented the end of winter and the beginning of days of increasing light and it became associated with the goddess Brigit, a goddess of fertility.

The Celtic festival of Beltane on May 1st, named after the 'pagan' god BEL BAL/BAAL became May Day, a time when it was the beginning of summer and joyful celebrations were held in honour of Mother Earth and the fertility of the land.

Easter became a Christianization of the Spring Equinox festival which was calculated by the first full moon occurring around the 21st of March, the date of the Equinox.

The Summer Solstice June 21st - 22nd became St John's Day (June 24th).

The Order of the Celtic Druids & the Seasons

Many of the stories handed down by word of mouth were of the various waves of Celtic and other tribes that had invaded Ireland from around 1,000 BC and these stories were a way of preserving the knowledge of their ancestors. The Druidic priests or instructors were called *Gwydd* but it was necessary to distinguish between the priests and the instructors so the priests were called the *Der-Wydd (Druid)* and the superior instructor was called *Go-Wydd* or *V-Vydd (Ovate)* and went by the name of *Beirdd* which is the origin of **Bard**. These were the Teachers of the Ancient Wisdom, or 'Greater Mysteries' and the most highly initiated ones were given the title of **MERLIN**.

It is generally believed that the word *Druid* is derived from the Irish word *Drui* which means *Men of the Oak Trees*. We obtain the word 'Gaelic' from the 'Gauls' and the Gaelic word *druidh* means 'wise man' or 'magician' as in 'Magus', which is exactly what Merlin was! For the Merlin that we are discussing in this story was St Germain, a Master of the Great White Brotherhood.

The Druid priests were able to predict the future and they also acted as medicine men, using herbal medicines from nature and the natural energy field. They believed in nature spirits, *'Elementals/Devas'* and considered the rivers, springs and holy wells to be sacred for they believed that they were protected by earth-spirit goddesses. All trees, particularly oak trees were sacred also.

Druids of the Emerald Isle, who were mainly concerned with healing, were robed in green and called the Order of the Ovate.

The second division was the *Bards/Beirdds* who robed themselves in violet-blue to represent 'truth' and 'harmony'. The third division was the *Druid (Derwyddon)* and they always dressed in white robes, reminiscent of the robes worn by the Great White Brotherhood who studied in the Temples of ancient Egypt.

It sometimes took as long as twenty-five years to become fully qualified at which time they became known as *Archdruids* and they were vowed to secrecy. In Britain there were usually only three or four Archdruids situated in scattered areas which were also strategic from the point of view that the Archdruids were the overseers and could be depended upon for sorting out any problems within their communities.

At dawn on the 25th December, each year, the Druids would rise early to watch the birth of the Sun, which they regarded as their 'Sun god' and great celebrations were held. Winter, (Imbolc) in the northern hemisphere officially begins on February 1st but the cold frosts and the snow begin in December. At Beltane (May 1st) which is the astrological month of Taurus when spring burst forth in all its glory, bonfires were lit on hilltops to celebrate the fruitful germination of their crops.

The Druids celebrated *two* solstices, the new and the full moon and the 6th day of the moon were sacred periods and it is believed that the 'initiation' ceremonies took place only at the two solstices and the two equinoxes. This would have been when their Arthor's or Pendragons (head leaders - chiefs) were chosen, probably by a Merlin.

It was traditional to celebrate *eight* festivals in all, whereby the first four were called Sun Feasts. These were Midwinter, Spring Equinox, Midsummer and Autumn and by using their calendar system, the Druids were able to judge when to plant their crops, when to harvest them and when to leave the fields fallow, in order to rest them. Observations of the rising and setting of the sun and the stars was always completely predictable.

An example of the way the ancient megalithic monuments correspond to the passage of the Sun, the Moon, the stars and planets can be seen at Stonehenge on the Salisbury Plain and at Druid's Ring at Dromberg not far from Cork in Ireland where the stones are aligned to the winter solstice sunset. The example of implementing a calendar by observation of the stars, was utilised by the ancient Egyptians who marked the first day as the one when the star Sirius (the Dog Star) could be seen rising.

The teachings of the Druids incorporated the philosophy of Pythagoras and they worshipped a Madonna or Virgin Mother with a Child in her arms, who was sacred to their Mysteries as has been explained in a previous chapter. Many sanctuaries throughout Britain and Ireland were considered to be sacred places where the Druids would meet to celebrate the return of the 'Sun' after the long darkness of winter. It was common for the sanctuaries to contain stone obelisks which were actually phallic symbols of fertility and evidence of this can be seen at Stonehenge. The Druids understood that the Sun god was fertilizing the Mother Goddess, Earth, and that the fruits of their labours in regard to crop planting, would flourish. All that they knew of the sacredness of the land, the Sun, the Moon, the Stars, had been passed down to them from the ancient people of Sumer.

Spring was followed by Summer (from the name 'Sumer'), known as *Llughnsad* which began on the 1st day of August, which astrologically is the sign of Leo, the Lion. Autumn was known as *Samhain* and commenced on the 1st day of November; the astrological sign of Scorpio. Winter (*Imbolc*) which commenced on the 1st day of February, was the astrological sign of Aquarius. On sacred hills throughout the land, beacons were lit as a form of celebration for each season and many of the sacred hills are in alignment with the Dragon/Serpent energies of Mother Earth.

The *Druids* was the name given to the 'priesthood' of the Celtic people. Their work was far more important than just belonging to a priesthood for like the Essenes, they were teachers, bards (poets), seers (prophets), diviners of the earth's sacred energies, judges, doctors and Magis.

The Influence of the Zodiac, and the Four Evangelists

"I know the names of the stars from the
North to the South
(Taliesin/Merlin/St Germain)

The Druids would follow the paths of the sun and the moon through the twelve signs of the Zodiac. The seasons were thus divided accordingly. As mentioned previously, there were eight festivals of the year. Four of these fell in fixed signs of the zodiac: the astrological signs of Aquarius - the 'The Man who is the Water bearer', Taurus - the 'Bull', Leo - the 'Lion', and Scorpio - the 'Eagle'. These are the signs of the four Evangelists represented in the Irish *Book Of Kells* written by St Columba. (The *Book Of Kells* includes such symbols as the 'Saltire' - St Andrew's Cross, the 'Maltese Cross', the 'Tau Cross' and the 'Cross of St George').

From information contained in Peter Dawkins' book titled the *Virgin Ideal* (written in 1980), we learn the following pertinent information:

"The upright cross of the Rose-Cross otherwise known as the St George Cross and the Saltire Cross otherwise known as St Andrew's Cross mark the eight principal festival points in the cycle of the Age. The St George Cross or Rose Cross marks with its vertical shaft, the midpoints of Winter (i.e. the Winter Solstice or Christmas) and of Summer (i.e., the Summer Solstice or Midsummer). With its horizontal bar it marks the mid-points of Spring, (i.e. the Spring Equinox) and of Autumn (i.e. the Autumnal Equinox). The Saltire or St Andrew's Cross marks the beginning of Winter (i.e. Samhain, the Festival of Peace), the beginning of Spring (i.e. the Festival of Imbolc or Candlemas), the beginning of Summer (i.e. Beltaine/ Beltane or May Day), and the beginning of Autumn (i.e. Lammas or Lugnasadh)." (Lugnasadh was named after the Celtic god of Light, Lugh).

"These eight festivals divide the Age into eight sections as they do the ordinary year. An Age is an estimated period of approximately 2,160 years, each Age being dominated by one of the twelve signs of the Zodiac, as the Point of Aries recesses through the twelve Signs of their constellations. The Age, like the year, is divided into four principal 'seasons', each of about 540 years, and these are further sub-divided into eight distinct periods of 270 years each, when terrestrial and cosmic energies ebb and flow between the beginning/ends and the mid-points of each season (i.e. the Solar festivals). In addition to this main pattern of energy flow and its influence on the evolution of both the body and the psyche of the world, there are also the twelve zodiacal periods or 'months' each of 180 years, three to a season."

"Right now, in AD 1980, we are just emerging from the Scorpio phase and beginning to enter the Sagittarian month which will 'shoot' or raise up the golden seed of consciousness and life to new evolutionary heights of the new born 'Golden Age'. For us, the Aquarian Age properly began about AD 1890, and we have been passing through 'the years of Fire' ever since."

The elements of 'Fire', 'Water', 'Air' and 'Earth' were believed by the ancients to be the essential energy forces that sustain the world. The astrological signs for 'Fire' are Aries - the 'Ram' ruled by Mars, and Leo - the 'Lion' ruled by the Sun. The 'Water' signs are Sagittarius - the 'Archer' ruled by Jupiter, Pisces the 'Fish' ruled by Neptune/Jupiter, Cancer the 'Crab' ruled by the Moon, and Scorpio whose symbol is a scorpion or an eagle and is ruled by Mars/Pluto. The 'Air' signs are Aquarius - the 'water bearer' ruled by Saturn/Uranus, and Gemini - the 'Twins' ruled by Mercury. The 'Earth' signs are Libra - the 'scales' ruled by Venus, Capricorn - the 'Goat' ruled by Saturn, Taurus - the 'Bull' ruled by Venus, Virgo - the 'Virgin' ruled by Mercury. According to Druidic tradition, the cycle of the Moon was represented by the four fire festivals which fall approximately in the central portion of each season.

Continuing on with further information contained in Peter Dawkins' book titled *The Virgin Ideal*:

"From 1890 onwards, various groups and movements involved with the search for spiritual truth and wholesome values have been blossoming forth, whilst at the same time very great difficulties and hardships have been appearing in the world, such as the two world wars, population explosions leading to famine and seemingly insoluble economic disparagement, social and political revolutions and reforms and so on: all in all, it could be said, 'Nation shall rise against nation, and kingdom against kingdom and great earthquakes shall be in divers places, and famines and pestilences; and fearful sights and great signs shall there be from heaven." (Matt.24; Mark 13; Luke; 21)."

"If you were to think of a time when great tribulations with a spiritual re-emergence began to take place in earnest, you would probably settle for the date 1890 or turn of the century, the middle of the Scorpio period, the Samhain festival of the Age marking the threshing point when the grain is separated from the chaff. This was the time when so many 'Spiritual' movements searching for truth began in the world, including, I might mention, the Francis Bacon Society. Theosophical and Anthropsophical movements, and many others, started to emerge into the light of day at that time, and countless others have been coming together, blending their seeming differences in a synthesis of enlightened consciousness and activity, and gradually a world-wide brotherhood of man has been steadily emerging, transcending all national, cultural and linguistic difficulties."

A Visit to Druidic Sites of Worship in Ireland

One of the fascinating places which my family and I visited in Ireland in 1996 was Blarney Castle, a fifteen minute drive from Cork. The grounds of Blarney are exceptionally beautiful and are much larger than I had imagined. Our first stop was at the castle itself where we did the usual 'touristy' thing and kissed the 'Blarney Stone', which one legend states, was originally part of the *Stone of Destiny.*

The legend of 'Blarney' is said to have been derived from the time of Queen Elizabeth I, who when impatient with the length of Lord Blarney's explanations, exclaimed "This is all Blarney - what he says, he never means." Thus, according to legend 'kissing the Blarney Stone' at Blarney Castle will result in sudden eloquence of speech!

There is a lovely Manor House not far from the castle which is well worth a visit. After a most enjoyable tour of the house, we ventured into the grounds. Here, deep in the forest, we discovered a Druidic grove, in a wooded dell surrounded by ancient oak trees. Under the trees was a large circle of very ancient stones and a dolmen which the Druids had in times long ago, used as their sacred place of worship.

The Dolmen were enormous stones which were sometimes used to mark graves or considering the size of some of the megalithic (from the Greek word *Megalith* meaning 'great') stones, it is thought that certain sites were deliberately chosen in preference to carting the stones. As the sun filtered light downwards through the towering yew and oak trees, it seemed to illuminate the ancient stones, creating an eerie atmosphere in which the ancient presence of the Druids could be felt.

Most of the curious rocks and stones in the forest at Blarney have stood there for over 2,000 years. With the tall overhead trees, the sun filtering through creating different tones of green in the growth surrounding the circle, the scenery held the enchantment of a fairy glade where the Irish 'little people' - the leprechauns inhabit - according to Irish legend!

Another place of interest where the ruins of an ancient Druidic monument exist is at Glandore, not far from Cork. Called 'Druid's Ring', it consists of a circle made of stones and an altar stone, aligned to the winter Solstice sunset (Imbolc). It was excavated in the 1950's and although on a far smaller scale when compared to Stonehenge which we were later to visit when we returned to England, it was well preserved and impressive.

Strange stones, dolmens, megalithic sites (like those of Stonehenge), are not confined to England alone. Ireland is reputed to have an estimated 1,200 sites, all of which have left people extremely curious as to the reasons why and how they were constructed.

Another of the numerous fascinating places in Ireland is New Grange. The entrances to the burial chambers are aligned so that the sun enters only on a specific day of the year; e.g. the winter solstice when the sun is reborn from the earth. Situated in the Boyne valley (famous for the Battle of the Boyne), in County Meath, New Grange is thought to have been built about 3000 BC. In the burial chamber itself, the rays of the sun filter through from the entrance on midwinter solstice morning at which time a spiral carving at the end of the tomb, is illuminated. Unfortunately, we were there in summer and were therefore unable to witness this amazing event which occurs annually.

New Grange is a place where many curious symbols are carved on large stones and where a white quartz wall was discovered. The reasons for its existence remain a mystery. At many prehistoric sites in Cornwall, there is also evidence of quartz having been used. One particular place is in West Penwith where a stone in Boscawen-un circle consists of white quartz.

Quartz is known to generate energy and the Druids considered it a sacred crystalline mineral. Uluru, where our main Australian energy grid is centred, is reputed to contain red quartz crystal somewhere within it. Considering that it is the focal point for the *Rainbow Serpent* energy, in common with the numerous megalithic sites throughout Britain and Ireland, especially Stonehenge, there may indeed be some kind of alignment with energy ley lines which the quartz attracts.

In common with our own Australian Aborigines (who are descendants of Lemuria), the Druids considered the dwelling places of the spirits of their ancestors, as 'sacred'. Our own Aborigines are known to have existed at least as far back as 30,000 BC and Uluru at Ayres Rock in central Australia is the birthplace of their legendary *Rainbow Serpent* and is therefore, the most sacred place to the Aborigines in the whole of Australia. In the many legends regarding the *Rainbow Serpent*, the common theme is one of an ancestral spirit of sacred significance which was a symbol of fertility, the father and mother of all forms of life - the Mother Earth. This sacred worship of the land was revered by all of the ancient cultures throughout the world, including the American Indians.

Two famous people who were members of the Druids were the poet William Blake and Winston Spencer Churchill who joined the Order of the Druids in 1908.

Symbols across the Landscape

Throughout the landscape of Cornwall, there are key alignments of sites marked by special stones, either naturally or deliberately placed, which date from 3,000 BC. Like Stonehenge, many of them are aligned to significant astronomical events.

Those inhabitants, the Celtic Druids of ancient times, left behind for us, puzzles to solve, often carved into the landscape. Even today, we are confounded by the mystery of these and other phenomena such as the mysterious 'crop circles' which have appeared all over Britain, with symbols incorporated into them.

In his book titled *Rising Out Of Chaos*, Simon Peter Fuller relates how he received detailed information (from etheric guides) informing him that in 1987, the phenomenon that was soon to focus world attention would be 'crop circles'. Simon writes "we were told then that from 1988 onwards, numerous huge shapes would start appearing in the cornfields of south-west England. They are known elsewhere in the world, but nothing in the quantity or complexity as seen in England."

"By their very presence and number in this particular area, and at this crucial moment, they signify in symbolic language that the transformation of human and planetary consciousness has begun. Mother Earth, it appears, is speaking to us, and much of the symbology she is using is recognizable to awakening people and, significantly to indigenous peoples. I have shown pictures of crop circles to the Oromo and Samburu in African, Maoris in New Zealand, Aborigines in Australia and American Indians. These same symbols appear in *their* cultures, and even in their cave paintings!"

"Despite all subsequent attempts to discredit or sabotage them, the 'corn circles' defy all intellectual and mechanical theories: they simply *are*. Scientific tests do in fact show that the bent but still growing crops have undergone a change in molecule structure - and no faker has yet been able to reproduce that!"

It is of interest to note that Simon Peter Fuller describes in his book his close association with Sir Winston Church since his early childhood and that Sir Winston is one of his 'Guides'. According to Simon, "through the rapidly-expanding younger generations of Winston's family, I was privy to the special intimacy with the old man that was reserved for his grandchildren. (Simon lived on the adjoining estate). My greatest accomplishment at school again involved Winston Churchill."

Later in his story, Simon tells of sometime after the death of Sir Winston, Simon became aware that it was Winston who was one of his Spirit Guides, and how it was not mere coincidence that from his early youth, Winston had profoundly influenced him. (Simon Peter Fuller, like Hamish Miller and Paul Broadhurst, work with the earth's sacred energies).

Avalon

It was discussed in an earlier chapter that 'Avalon' means the 'Isle of Apples' and that according to Robert Graves in his book titled *The White Goddess*, 'aval' originated from 'apol' and the legends of Apollo whose worshippers donated apples to him. (St Germain was once worshipped as the god 'Apollo' and when he incarnated as Apollonius the name was a derivative of Apollo).

'ON' was a Temple in Egypt where the ancient Teachings of the Sacred Arcana, the teachings of the *Mystical Rose* were taught to the Masters of the Great White Brotherhood.

There were many 'Avalons', for they were the Celtic monasteries founded throughout Britain and even Europe. In the era of King Arthur and Merlin, the following places mentioned were directly connected with the Arthurian legends.

1.   The island of Tintagel (pronounced Tin-taa-gel) in Cornwall, the supposed birthplace of Arthur.
2.   St Michael's Mount, Marazion, Cornwall.
3.   Glastonbury.

Avalon - The Burial Place of Joseph of Arimathea

The Celtic monasteries discussed above were, as stated, all Avalons, where the sacred teachings of the Arcana were taught. So, where was the First Master of the Grail buried? Well, according to authors Hamish Miller and Paul Broadhurst in their book *The Sun And The Serpent*, in a book by the Reverend C. Dobson entitled *Did Our Lord Visit Britain as They Say In Cornwall, Somerset*, the quotation which was made by a fellow ecclesiastic, the Reverend L.S. Lewis, revealed the actual discovery of Joseph of Arimathea's remains:

"The Vicar of Glastonbury tells us that Joseph's body remained buried here (St Joseph's Chapel - the old 'Mother Church') until AD 1354, when Edward III gave his licence to John Bloom of London to dig for it, and the Abbot and monks consented. There is the statement of a Lincolnshire monk in 1367 that his body was found. They placed it in a casket let into a stone sarcophagus, which was placed in the east end of St Joseph's Chapel, and it became a place of pilgrimage. There is a written record of the sarcophagus being still in position in 1662 when the chapel had become partially ruined. Owing to fear of puritan fanaticism prevalent at the time, it was secretly removed into the Parish Church churchyard, and its identity was concealed by the pretence of the initials on it, J.A., which stood for John Allen. In 1928, the present Vicar of Glastonbury found it half buried in the soil, and had it removed into the church, and its construction bears out the accounts of a silver casket which could be raised and lowered, and shows other marks of identity."

Thus, we now know where John Joseph, the Beloved Disciple (alias Joseph of Arimathea) who was the First Master of the Grail, is buried - not far from the famous Chalice Well where he reputedly hid the Grail Cup/Chalice. There is no

Chalice buried there; the story is symbolical about the Grail Teachings of the Arcana and the *Mystical Rose*. Kuthumi, during the era of Jesus, was a *Master of the Mystical Rose* who established the first 'Christine' Church at Antioch whose emblem was the Rose and the Cross. Then he later established the Celtic Church at Glastonbury - Avalon. King Arthur was buried at one of the other Avalons which will be disclosed in a future chapter. Suffice to say at this stage, it was on an island surrounded by water, and not far from the mainland.

JOHN THE BELOVED ALIAS JOSEPH OF ARIMATHEA WAS BURIED AT GLASTONBURY

THE MASTERS DISCUSSED IN THIS CHAPTER
Merlin - St Germain
John the Beloved alias Joseph of Arimathea - Kuthumi
King Arthur - Kuthumi

NOTES AND RECOMMENDED READING

Robert Graves, *The White Goddess*, (Faber & Faber, U.K., 1961)
Peter Dawkins, *The Great Vision*, (Francis Bacon Research Trust, Warwick, U.K.)
Peter Dawkins, *The Virgin Ideal*, (Francis Bacon Research Trust, U.K., 1980)
Barry Cunliffe, *The Celtic World*, (Bodley Head, U.K., 1979)
Barry Cunliffe, *The Ancient Celts*, (Oxford University Press, U.K. 1997)
Henri Hubert, *The Rise Of The Celts*, (Keggan, U.K. 1934)
Henri Hubert, *The History Of The Celtic People,* (Bracken Books, U.K. 1992)
John Michell, *The Earth Spirit*, (Thames & Hudson, U.K., 1975)
Paul Broadhurst & Hamish Miller, *The Sun And The Serpent*, (Pendragon Press, Cornwall, U.K., 1994)
Paul Broadhurst, *Tintagel And The Arthurian Mythos*, (Pendragon Press, Cornwall, U.K., 1995)
Arnold J. Toynbee, *A Study Of History*, (Oxford University Press, U.K., 1934)
Emile Legouis & Louis Cazamian, *A History of English Literature*, (J.M. Dent & Sons, U.K., 1945)
Simon Peter Fuller, *Rising Out of Chaos*, (Kima Global, South Africa)

CHAPTER 27

The Continuity of the Celtic Church &
The Masters of the Mystical Rose

"For a day and a year in stocks and fetters"
(Taliesin/Merlin/St Germain)

When the world of what was considered by the early Church of Rome to be 'pagan' religion collapsed, the Celtic Church of Ireland, although monastic in form, remained far more closely connected with the teachings of the ancient Greeks and Egyptians, some of whom had come to Ireland as the early Druids.

Celts moulded 'Christianity' to fit their own social heritage, instead of allowing it to break up their native tradition. The pre-Christian Bardic Schools of the Druids, instead of being abolished when the monastic schools were established, were simply reorganized under the inspiration of St Columba. The mystical traditions endured, 'veiled' in the terms of Egyptian myths still available for those who were able to perceive the 'Truth'.

The Druids were the forerunners of the Celtic Christian Church whose minstrels and travelling bards/poets preserved the Sacred Teachings and secretly spread them from court to court, not only in Ireland but in Gaul (France).

Many of the Sacred Teachings were spread by those who were later to be recognised as saints. Upon the demise of one saint, another would reincarnate to further the plans for the stability and protection of the Celtic Church. These saints were great teachers and founders of churches whose work and spirit survived and inspired those who came after them. One of these great teachers, although not canonized as a 'saint' was Apollonius (St Germain) who has been mentioned in previous chapters.

Apollonius was born in Cappadocia and his career was that of a very wise Holy Man who performed numerous miracles. According to legend, *the mother of Apollonius was visited by an angel in a dream who informed her that she was to have a special child, a great messenger who would be known as Apollonius.* In a later incarnation in 521 AD, when St Germain reincarnated as Merlin, his mother had a similar angelic visitation, informing her that she was to have a special child.

As Apollonius, St Germain spent his years teaching the Sacred Mysteries of the Arcana, possibly at the Home of the Apostles, in Rome, before it was destroyed during the persecutions. He had a great following because of his wisdom and the miracles which he performed. He travelled far and wide to such places that included India, where he spent some time with the Indian fakirs. Throughout his travels, he collected many followers who, in turn, taught the Sacred Mysteries which had been passed on down throughout the centuries.

There is no recorded date for the death of Apollonius, but it is known that he lived in Rome during the era of Nero and it was earlier discussed that he would have spent time at the 'Home of the Apostles' which had been founded by Caradoc, the son of Anna (Joseph of Arimathea - John the Beloved's daughter), and Bran the Blessed King who was otherwise known as Cymbeline.

Because Taliesin/Merlin/St Germain specifically informs us that he was 'at the White Hill' (Tower of London which was a palace), at the court of Cymbeline (Bran the Blessed), we know that he would have visited London from time to time.

To place things in perspective, Nero had persecuted the Christians and was responsible for the great fire that destroyed half of Rome in 64 AD. Mary Magdalene died in France one year prior to this event. (It was during the reign of Nero that Apollonius was arrested and brought to trial, however, the writing upon the scroll containing the complaints against him, mysteriously vanished. Apollonius was released, and, shortly afterwards, Nero banned all the philosophers from Rome. Apollonius went to Spain and according to his companion Damis, gathered recruits to assist his people, the Christians against Nero).

The last years of the public life of Apollonius were spent travelling and teaching, with Damis assisting him. When he finally departed from his friend, he did so obscurely, sending him to Rome with a message for the Emperor. Damis never forgot his parting words:

"Damis, whenever you think on high matters in solitary meditation, you will see me."

(This would have been referring to the 'inner vision' which is achieved through meditation and apart from etheric manifestations, is the other form in which the Masters can be perceived, just as our 'guides/guardians' are. In a future chapter it will be seen that St Germain and his soul mate would communicate with each other through their 'inner vision').

Apollonius (St Germain) and the 'Emerald Stone'

Reference has been given in earlier chapters to Hermes Trismegistus and the famous 'Emerald Stone', written about in some of the Arthurian legends and a little more information is now relevant.

The Stone is reputed to have been brought from Atlantis to the ancient Temple of the Sun (Heliopolis) in Egypt, by members of the highly initiated Priests who fled to Egypt from Atlantis prior to the Deluge of the 'Noah' era.

According to legend, in the 18th century, during the era of the French Revolution, this famous Emerald Tablet was re-discovered by an Arabian initiate with whom Count Cagliostro studied before he was initiated into Freemasonry by the Comte de St Germain.

An earlier discovery of the Emerald Tablet in a cave was said to have been made in the 1st century AD by Apollonius.

According to Egyptian legends, the body of Hermes was interred in the Valley of Hebron and the Divine Emerald Tablet was buried with him. It was mentioned in an earlier chapter that the historian of the 1st century AD, Josephus, recorded that the famous Stone of Hermes Trismegistus was known to be in existence amongst the Essenes during the era of Joseph (St Germain), the Father of the Holy Grail family. Josephus described how the pillars were completely covered with hieroglyphics.

According to the Rosicrucian authority, the late Spencer Lewis, during the era of Akhnaton [El Morya], "Hermes completed his writings, especially the seven books and tablets which were found and brought to light in 400 AD., and which were upon diverse chemical and physical subjects."

The 'Emerald Stone' became incorporated into the folklore of King Arthur in the 13th century AD, when Wolfram von Eschenbach wrote his *Parzival* in which he claimed that the Emerald Stone had fallen from Lucifer's crown and it was saved by angels who carried it to earth from which time onwards, it was to be protected by the 'Grail' family.

'Lucifer' (Lucipher) as mentioned elsewhere in our story, means the 'Light Bearer' and is another name for Venus. (The early Church of Rome totally corrupted the meaning of Lucipher, turning him into 'Satan' and it will be remembered that it was discussed in an earlier chapter that other names allotted to Hermes were Tat, Thoth, and Sat-An).

The legends associated with Apollonius as having found the Emerald Stone in a cave and its later connections with Count Cagliostro in the 18th century AD prove that it was indeed protected by the Grail family. St Germain often retrieved objects/documents containing valuable information which had been secreted in case they came into the wrong hands.

According to St Germain in the book titled *Twin Souls & Soulmates* channelled by Claire Heartsong, when being questioned:

Question: "As I understand it, you are saying that even during your youth as Francis Bacon you became aware of soul memory, including your life as Joseph?" [The Father of Jesus].

St Germain: "Indeed, not only soul memory, beloved, but that which I had buried in a variety of places, actual tangible records that I had laid up for myself at a later time."

Whether the Emerald Stone actually existed or whether it was symbolically the fabled 'Philosopher's Stone of Hermes Trismegistus with which it has been equated, the early Knights Templar definitely believed in its existence and went in search of it, for, according to legend, those who found it and looked upon it would have eternal youth!

St Albanus (St Alban) d. 209 AD (St Germain)
(During the era of Emperor Septimus Severus)
'For a day and a year in stocks and fetters'
(Taliesin/Merlin/St Germain)

The next known reincarnation of St Germain after his life as Apollonius was as St Albanus (Alban) who had been briefly mentioned in previous chapters. According to the *Penguin Dictionary of Saints* by Donald Attwater and Catherine Rachel John, St Alban was venerated as the first martyr in Britain. The first known reference to him was in the 5th century AD *Life of St Germanus of Auxerre* by Constantius, translated by F.R. Hoare in the *Western Fathers* (1954). (St Germanus was an incarnation of St Germain in the 4th century AD).

We are informed by C.W. Leadbeater in his book titled *The Hidden Life In Freemasonry* that Albanus was born into a noble Roman family at the town of Verulam in England, during the third century AD. He served in Rome for several years and undertook initiations into Freemasonry and also became proficient in the Mitharaic (Mithras) Mysteries which were so closely associated with Freemasonry. So once again, we find St Germain serving time in Rome.

It was Verulam in England that St Germain introduced the 'Craft' of Freemasonry.

The grandfather of Cymbeline (Bran the Blessed), was, as mentioned elsewhere, Caswallon, whom Caesar called Cassivellanus, the King of the Catuvellanui tribe who ruled just north of the Thames and their city was just near St Albans (which was then called Verulam). Caswallon became a High King (Pendragon) of Britain who successfully fought Caesar's advancing army at which time Caesar withdrew from Britain in September 54 BC.

Caswallon moved his capital to the British-Roman town of Verulam which was later to become associated with the legends of St Albanus (Alban). In the 16th century, Francis Bacon's home was at Gorhambury, near St Albans and it was no coincidence that King James I, bestowed upon him the title of Baron Verulam, Viscount of St Alban, in 1621.

According to Donald Attwater and Catherine Rachel John, St Alban's death is sometimes given as 303 AD; however, a recent study uses the Turin manuscript to show that he was martyred in 209 AD. He is thought to have been beheaded by the eldest son of Septimus Severus (reigned 193-211 AD) during the time of the Roman occupation of Britain.

The verse of Taliesin *"for a day and a year in stocks and fetters"* is referring to one of St Germain's lives as having experienced being a prisoner and may have been during his life as St Alban. The reason for his imprisonment was for protecting a monk against so-called 'heresy'. It is considered that the date of St Alban's death being given as 303, was symbolic of his connection with Freemasonry, i.e., **'33'** and it will be remembered that Francis Bacon's name deciphered by code = **33.**

(It is of interest to note the connection of St George becoming equated with the Archangel Michael, the mighty slayer of the Dragon. In his book *The Sun And The Serpent*, the author Paul Broadhurst of Pendragon Press, Cornwall, relates that many of the Ley lines pass through ancient churches of which 10 are dedicated to St Michael and/or St George and 23 to St Mary. This gives a grand total of '33').

In his next known reincarnation after that of St Alban, St Germain as St Germanus of Auxerre, led a battle on two occasions, against the invasion of the Saxons in Britain during which time he returned to the tomb of St Alban where he extracted documents which had been hidden there from his previous life as St Alban (died 209 AD).

St George (280 - 304 AD) (Kuthumi)

The next *Master of the Rose* protecting the Celtic Church and the ancient teachings of the Rose-Cross was St George whose family originally came from Cappadocia where 'coincidently' Apollonius (St Germain) was born in the previous century and had taught the Sacred Mysteries in the 1st century AD during the reign of Nero.

According to the *Penguin Dictionary of Saints* by Donald Attwater and Catherine Rachel John, St George was one of the most famous of the early martyrs. "The beginning of his veneration began in Palestine at Diospolis (Lydda) where George was apparently martyred there in 304 AD. The popular legend that surrounds George is that during that era he was a knight from Cappadocia who rescued a princess from a dragon after which time, the kingdom became Christianized."

"The legends of St George as the slayer of the dragon were known in Ireland and Britain, long before the Norman Conquest. Saint George's Flag with the white background and the Red Cross has often been regarded as a general Christian banner. Some equate the 'dragon' with being that of the early Church of Rome and it was not long after the death of St George that his close friend Constantine the Great came into power and saved the Christians."

According to Peter Dawkins: "Some authorities claim that the families of Joseph of Arimathea and George were kinsmen and that they were linked in some way."

This would make sense from the point of view that Joseph of Arimathea was John Joseph, the Beloved, the Master Kuthumi and he reincarnated as St George, again a 'Defender of the Faith' who once again did his best to protect the Christians from persecution. It will be remembered that as John the Beloved he recorded the 'Beast' in Revelation whom the English scholar/poet Robert Graves concluded was none other than 'Nero', who slaughtered thousands of Christians.

St George is reputed to have made a pilgrimage to Glastonbury. It is noteworthy that St Patrick (Kuthumi) is reputed to have spent time as an abbot at Glastonbury in the 5th century AD after he had completed his training with St Germanus (St Germain) (c.378 - 430 AD) in Gaul, (France).

During the reign of Diocletian, the Emperor who reigned prior to Constantine the Great, Galerius Maximus, was the co-Emperor of the eastern empire who persecuted the Christians and imprisoned and tortured St George. The Emperor Diocletian was strongly under the influence of the co-Emperor of the eastern empire, Galerius Maximus who was completely over-zealous in his persecution of the Christians. George was a defender of the Christians and because of this, he was arrested, imprisoned and eventually beheaded in 304 AD.

From information contained in Peter Dawkins' book titled *The Great Vision*:

"Druidism accepted Christianity (not the Roman kind) with ease, seeing in it a natural fulfillment of their own teachings. The Druidic colleges, vibrant centres of religion and learning, soon became Christian colleges that sent out missionaries all over the known world, founding Bishoprics in numerous cities of importance. It was these missionaries and their teachings that alarmed Rome and precipitated the massive Roman invasions of Britain in an attempt to destroy what the Romans saw as the main centre of Christian teachings and evangelism."

"The Romans were unable to defeat the Britons entirely or stop the Christian missions, despite the decades of war and persecution (43-86 AD) and eventually a treaty was concluded that incorporated the British as allies of the Roman Empire, recognizing most of the British native freedoms, and kingly prerogatives. The peace that ensued lasted until the Diocletian persecutions, circa 300 AD."

Constantine the Great (Flavius Valerius Constantinus)
(Roman Emperor 306-307 AD)

By the 4th century AD, there were many rival emperors fighting to occupy the Roman throne and persecutions of the Christians were continued. During the era of St George, there emerged a man who was to play a decisive role in the history of the Roman Empire and Christianity - his name was Constantine the Great.

According to the Penguin book of *Who's Who In the Ancient World* by Betty Radice, Constantine was the son of Constantius Chlorus and his wife Helena, who was believed to be a British princess.

Madame Blavatsky in her book *The Secret Doctrine* informs us as follows:

"The days of Constantine were the last turning-point in history, the period of the supreme struggle that ended in the Western world throttling the old religions in favour of a new one; every issue was blocked up, every record that hands could be laid upon were destroyed. However, fragments of the Secret Wisdom survived geological and political cataclysms to tell the story and every survival shows evidence that the Secret Wisdom was once the one fountain head, the ever-flowing perennial source, at which were fed all its streamlets - the later religions of all nations, from the first down to the last."

"This period, beginning with Buddha [earlier incarnation of the Master Jesus] and Pythagoras [Kuthumi] at the one end and the Neo-Platonists and Gnostics at the other, is the only focus left in history wherein converge for the last time the bright rays of light streaming from the aeons of time gone by, unobscured by the hand of bigotry and fanaticism."

Constantine was originally a 'pagan' member of the worshipping of the Sun god and he followed the teachings of ancient Egypt. In common with the Essenes and the Druids of Ireland, he followed the teachings of the Greek philosopher, Pythagoras, (Kuthumi).

Not surprisingly, Constantine's conversion to Christianity would appear to have been influenced by St George (Kuthumi) and it could not have come at a more appropriate time in history. As we have learned thus far, St Germain in his incarnation as Apollonius had done his best to protect the Christians from persecutions by Nero. St Germain also had a great deal of influence over the Roman Emperor, Vespasian (69-79 AD) who succeeded Nero. Probably under the influence of Apollonius, Vespasian built the 'Temple of Peace' in Rome and it is rather ironic that in his incarnation as St Alban, St Germain was beheaded by the Romans.

According to Peter Dawkins:

"Constantine the Great was a friend of St George (280-304 AD) whose father was the governor of Cappadocia (where Apollonius was born in the 1st century AD). George's father was an officer in the army of the Emperor Diocletian and his mother's family at Lydda which is en route to Jerusalem, had received a visit in the 1st century AD by the Apostle Peter (Simon) which resulted in the family being converted to Christianity (not the Roman style Christianity but the Christianity established by Jesus before it became corrupted by the early Church fathers). When Constantine became the Emperor in 311 AD he banned the execution of the Christians and gave them back their land which had previously been confiscated."

"Constantine declared St George to be the patron saint of all Christendom and founded the Order of Constantinian's Angelic Knights of St George, the first chivalric Order in which St George was honoured."

According to Betty Radice in her book titled *Who's Who In The Ancient World*, Constantine defeated his rival Maximus (Galerius) in 312 AD which is commemorated by the Arch of Constantine near the Colosseum in Rome. He transferred the capital of the Empire to Byzantium and renamed it after himself, as Constantinople (now known as Istanbul).

Isaiah and the Rose

Upon the instructions of Constantine, a rose bush was planted at the sepulchre of St George (Kuthumi) - the 'Rose of Sharon', which was the emblem of St George's family.

When Kuthumi founded the first Christian Church at Antioch, the symbol of the Rose in the centre of the Cross, was adopted.

Also upon the tomb of Persian Poet/Philosopher/Mathematician, Omar Khayyam (Kuthumi) who makes frequent mention of the 'Rose' in his famous poem the *Rubaiyat* was planted the 'Persian Rose'.

According to Peter Dawkins:

"The Persian rose of the single variety became the original emblem of England and later the Tudor Rose. As the original emblem of England, it preceded the white and red roses of Lancaster and York, and later the Tudor rose, which developed their symbolism from the Rose of Sharon."

The reference in Isaiah in the Bible, to Carmel may be referring to where the original sacred documents of the ancient Mysteries were kept. The words 'blossom as the rose' are possibly a reference to the Rose of Sharon, the Red-Rose of St George which later became the Tudor Rose emblem and was associated with the Sacred Teachings of the Rose Cross which the Masters taught.

Isaiah '33'

Isaiah '33' reads like a prophecy for the future. It is also of significant importance that it just so happens to be one of the sacred numerical ciphers used by Francis Bacon. The 'Rose' and' 'Sharon' are mentioned in verses 5 - 9:

"The Lord is exalted; for he dwelleth on high: he hath filled Zion with judgement and righteousness. And wisdom and knowledge shall be the stability of thy times, *and* strength of salvation: the fear of the Lord *is* his treasure. Behold, their valiant ones shall cry without: the ambassadors of peace shall weep bitterly. The highways lie waste, the wayfaring man ceaseth: he hath broken the covenant, he hath despised the cities, he regardeth no man. The earth mourneth *and* languish: Lebanon is ashamed *and* hewn down: Sharon is like a wilderness; and Bashan and Carmel shake off *their fruits.*"

'Sharon is like a wilderness' and 'Carmel shakes off fruits' may mean that these are the teachings of the Teacher of Righteousness, so revered by the Essene Community that will once again 'blossom', particularly through the writings of Francis Bacon which include many messages of the Rose-Cross Teachings.

These Sacred Arcana Teachings, the *'fruits'* which were once stored at Mount Carmel, are equated with those of the Rose-Cross. As Annas the Elder High Priest, the *Teacher of Righteousness*, St Germain may have written the Book of Isaiah for the Essenes religion was that of the Rosicrucians and he would have known that in his future lives, he would continue these Sacred Teachings of the *Mystical Rose.* As he informed us in his verses of Taliesin *"I have been Teacher to all Intelligences, I am able to instruct the whole Universe, I shall be until the day of Judgement upon the face of the Earth."*

It will be recalled that Mount Carmel was where the sacred documents were once kept by the Essene Community and that it was originally established by El Morya in his incarnation as Elijah who in an earlier incarnation had once been the Pharaoh Akhnaton who introduced the symbol of the Rose and the Cross in ancient Egypt during the era of Hermes Trismegistus. In keeping with the prophecies of the Essenes, El Morya returned as the forerunner to Jesus, as his cousin John the Baptist.

St Germanus (c.378-448 AD) (St Germain)

The next known incarnation of St Germain after his one as St Alban was as Germanus (Germain), the Bishop of Auxerre in Gaul (France). Germanus was born of Gallo-Roman parents. He was the son of Rusticus and Germanilla, and his family was one of the noblest in Gaul.

During his time in Rome (where he had once been in his incarnation as Apollonius in the 1st century AD) St Germanus studied to become a lawyer. The theme of continuity runs through St Germain's life, having once been the Prophet Samuel who was a magistrate/judge, and also in his life as Joseph, the Father of the Holy Grail Family, he was the Essenes' Teacher of Righteousness, who practiced the 'Law' under the title of Annas the Elder High Priest of the Sanhedrin at the Temple of Jerusalem. And then in later life as Sir Francis Bacon, he became a lawyer.

Germanus married Eustachia, a lady of noble birth. Eventually, he returned to Gaul where, in 418 AD he was appointed the position of Bishop of Auxerre, much against his will. He at once made radical changes to his mode of life and proved to be a bishop of exceptional ability.

Germanus also became a provincial military commander. The Pope of the time was *St Celestine I* who in 429 sent St Germanus to Britain after he had received a plea from the Britons.

On two occasions Germanus defended the Britons by leading a battle against the Picts and the Saxons who were invading them and whilst in Britain, he visited the tomb of St Alban at Verulam. It was also recorded that as late as 448 AD, fourteen years after his first visit to the tomb of St Alban in Britain, Germanus paid a second visit, obviously to retrieve documents that had been hidden. Interestingly, Germanus built a church at Auxerre, in honour of St Alban (whom he had once been).

St Germanus educated St Patrick (Kuthumi) at Auxerre, and when Patrick had passed his final exams, Germanus sent him back to Ireland to teach and found numerous Celtic monasteries. St Patrick, the patron saint of Ireland, was the precursor (harbinger) to St Columba, a royal prince of Ireland whose ancestors had all been crowned upon the Stone of Destiny at Tara, Ireland's Camelot.

Germanus died at Ravenna on the 31st July, 448 AD, where he had journeyed to plead with the emperor on behalf of the people of Amorica (now Brittany), who were in conflict with the imperial viceroy of Gaul. He was buried at Auxerre, and when his tomb was opened up many years later by Charles the Bald, his embalmed body was still well preserved. Charles the Bald was a grandson of Charles the Great (Charlemagne) and Charlemagne (768-814) is said to have been an incarnation of St Germain. We will learn more about St Germanus' activities in a future chapter.

MASTERS DISCUSSED IN THIS CHAPTER

Samuel the Prophet - St Germain (BC)
Joseph the Father of the Grail family (Annas the Elder) - St Germain (d.15 AD)
Apollonius of Tyana - St Germain (lst century AD)
St Albanus (Alban) - St Germain (3rd century AD)

St Germanus - St Germain (5th century AD)
Merlin/Taliesin - St Germain (6th century AD)
Charlemagne the Great - St Germain (8th century AD)
Sir Francis Bacon - St Germain (16th century AD)
Pythagoras - Kuthumi (c.530 BC)
Joseph of Arimathea (John Joseph the Beloved) - Kuthumi (1st century AD)
St George - Kuthumi (4th century AD)
St Patrick - Kuthumi (5th century AD)
Omar Khayyam - Kuthumi (11th century AD)

NOTES AND RECOMMENDED READING

Donald Attwater and Catherine Rachel John, *Penguin Dictionary of Saints*, (Penguin Books, U.K. 1995)

Peter Dawkins, *Arcadia*, (Francis Bacon Research Trust, U.K. 1988)

Edward Purcell Fitzgerald, *Rubaiyat of Omar Khayyam*, (Collins, U.K., 1974)

Isabel Cooper-Oakley, *Comte De St Germain*, (Theosophical Society, 1985)

Alfred Dodd, *Francis Bacon's Personal Life Story*, (Rider & Co., U.K., 1949, 1986)

Azena Ramanda & Claire Heartsong, *Twin Souls & Soulmates,* (Triad Publications, Queensland, Australia, 1994)

Madame Helena Blavatsky, *The Secret Doctrine*, (Quest Books, Theosophical Publishing House, U.S.A, 1966)

Paul Broadhurst and Hamish Miller, *The Sun And The Serpent*, (Pendragon Press, Cornwall, U.K., 1994)

C.W. Leadbeater, *The Hidden Life In Freemasonry*, (Theosophical Publishing House, U.K., 1975)

Betty Radice, *Who's Who In The Ancient World*, (Penguin Books, U.K. 1971)

R. H.C. Davis, *A History of Medieval Europe*, (Longman, U.K. 1970)

F.J. Dennett, *Europe A History*, (Linehan & Shrimpton, Melbourne, Australia, 1960)

Robert Graves, *The White Goddess*, (Faber & Faber, 1961)

CHAPTER 28

Brief Early History of Ireland

"The time shall come O Brendan
When you would feel it painful to reside in Erin (Ireland)
The sons of kings shall be few in number
And the Literai [Literary] *shall be deprived of dignity"*
(St Columba)

It is believed that before the sinking of Atlantis, Ireland was once part of a great continent that was joined to what we today call America. Various specie of plant life, particularly the iris, is unique to parts of America and is also found in Ireland. Once, Ireland was joined to Britain. Parts of Northern Ireland and Scotland are very similar and the island of Iona between Scotland and Northern Ireland is believed to be one of the oldest islands in the world.

The Irish Celts claimed that they had inherited their great love of music, poetry and learning from the 'People of Light', the Tuatha de Danaan. Their chief god was Dagda Mor (Mawr). The Celts are thought to have arrived before 600 BC and they brought with them complex, clearly defined laws and religion. The *Book of Invasions* written in the 9th century AD is the earliest first account of the arrival of the Celts.

They had arrived in separate waves at least six centuries before Christ and many of these tribes were from the ancient land of Sumer and were originally the Arcadians/Phoenicians, considered to be the 'People of the Covenant'. The first of these people were known as the 'Pretani' and the other name that they called themselves was the 'Cruithin' which is the Irish Celtic form of Pritani/Pretani or Prydyn from which Britain was named.

The word 'Cruithin' is the Q-Celtic (Gaelic) form of the word Pretani which implied an ancient population group. When the Irish colonized parts of Scotland and the Isle of Man, the Gaelic of these areas was known as Q-Celtic. The descendants belonging to this race of people were known as the Dalriata tribes who dominated the north-eastern Ulster area, particularly Tyrone, until the 9th and 10th centuries AD.

When the second wave of Celts arrived in Ireland, they called themselves the *Euerni* who became known as the *Ulaid*. To the Greek and Roman cartographers, the island was called *Ierin* and in Latin it was called *Hibernia*. Eventually it became known as *Eire Land*, and subsequently, Ireland.

The Celtic inhabitants were known as the Gauls or Gaels and the last major Celtic settlements in Ireland took place about 50 BC. The inhabitants of Ireland at that time, called these people the *Gaodhail* or *Gaeil* which in English, translated into 'Gaelic'. The influence of the Gaels was quite powerful over the next three hundred years and by the 5th century AD, they were the dominant tribe throughout most of Ireland. During these centuries, they founded numerous dynasties and tribal groupings which continued until the Norman invasion. As the Gaels progressed to the west of Ireland, they also expanded their territory towards the north. They made their presence felt on the western coasts of Britain in the 4th and 5th centuries and in the south-west of Wales which was known as the Silures.

They progressed as far as the islands of Man, Orkney, Shetland, and down to Cornwall and Devon. Evidence of their expansion is the distribution of Ogham stones which were memorial stones and virtually all such stones found in the British Isles are of Irish origin.

The early Celts were largely nomadic and Ireland was once densely covered by forests, which were inhabited by wild animals such as wolves, boars and deer. Owls dwelled in the trees and the crystal streams were full of salmon. All of these creatures became incorporated into the Druidic folklore. Merlin was said to be able to turn himself into an owl or a salmon whenever he wished - they were both symbols of 'wisdom'.

There were no towns or cities and the houses resembled beehive-like dwellings made out of wood and thatched with turf, whereas, Ireland's royal palace of Tara in County Meath was made out of mud and wattle. All that remains of Tara today are a series of shallow banks and mounds covered by grass.

Tara was once Ireland's Camelot where the High Kings ruled and were often challenged by rival tribal clans for their position. The High Kings surrounded themselves with bards, courtiers and minstrels who would recite and sing the legends of the Irish people. These legends survived in this manner until finally when the monks arrived in Ireland, the legends were written down by the scribes. By then, the stories had been handed down by word of mouth for numerous centuries and as such, became exaggerated to some extent. However, behind the myths there was always some element of truth.

It is historically known that in Ireland, there were two distinct tribes; the southern tribes were called *Eoghanacht* which translated into the 'People of Egan' in honour of their ancestor Eogan which in English translated into 'Owen'. (The name of *Yawain*, the knight mentioned in the Arthurian legends, was a variation of 'Owen' and in future centuries, an 'Owen' of this tribe, was to become Owen Tudor, of Wales who married Catherine of Valois whose son Henry 6th was the great great grandfather of Francis Bacon/Tudor).

The Tribe of Ui Neill (Niall) (O'Neill)

Oh Derry, my beloved Derry!
My place of abode, the solace of my existence!
Woe betide the man, O God, thou whose ways are unsearchable,
Who is destined to despoil my Derry!
I am Columba, a descendant of the Illustrious Niall"
(St Columba)

In the midlands, west and north, the tribe called themselves *Connachta* or 'People of Conn' who was another of their ancestors. The area in Ireland where they settled became known as Connaught. The continuity of the names of the families was handed down from generation to generation and the most important of the *Connachta* tribes were the Ui Neill (originally 'Niall' and later to be called O'Neill). They were the ruling family claiming descent from Niall Noigiallach who was descended from 'Conn'. Niall is usually credited with the conquest of most of Ulster.

The sons of Niall set up their own dynasties in the north-west of Ireland and they were known as the *Cenel Conaill* and the *Cenel Eoghain (Owen)*. 'Cenel' was used to describe a wide family group embracing all great noble families of royal blood.

St Columba was born into this family and their lineage of descent is written in the mythology of the *Tuatha de Danaan*, the 'People of Light' from the 'Blessed Isle', thought to have been 'Elysium'- a place singled out by the gods for eternal happiness where their ancestor the Trojan hero Aeneas re-met with his father Anchises. (It will be remembered that the 'Ley' lines were named after *Alesia* from which the words *Ales, Alis or Alles* were derived and which in its Greek form was 'Eleusis').

According to Robert Graves in his book titled *The White Goddess*, the Tuatha de Danaan were a confederacy of tribes in which the kingship went by matrilineal succession, some of whom invaded Ireland from Britain in the middle Bronze Age. According to the *Book of Invasions* the Tuatha de Danaan had been driven northwards from Greece as a result of an invasion upon Syria and eventually made their way to Ireland via Denmark, hence the name the 'Kingdom of the Danes'.

Descendants of the tribe of the Tuatha de Danaan who lived in the Glens of Antrim, Ireland, were the people of Dal Riata which eventually became one word - Dalriata. Over the centuries in which their dynasties had been founded, they were attributed various tribal names, one of which was the 'kinsmen of Gabran' (Bran).

There was rivalry between the Ulaid tribal groups, the Dal Fiatch in east Down and the Cruithin in Antrim who considered themselves to be the 'true Ulstermen' although they all belonged to the same original dynasty. The Dal Fiatch claimed the title of the Ulaid; however, this was strongly disputed by the Cruithin who occupied the territory of Derry (meaning 'oak trees').

In the 5th and 6th centuries, the rise of the Ui Neill took place with the conquest of several kingdoms stretching from Sligo Bay on the west coast, north to Inishowen in Donegal and then eastwards to the Irish Sea.

As the separate dynasties emerged, they became known as the northern and southern Ui Neill, but they were still the people of Dalriata and kinsmen of the tribe of Gabran. Many smaller divisions existed and were known as *'Tuath'* of which there were one hundred and fifty throughout the country. They each had a ruler who owed allegiance to the king of the province who generally belonged to the *Eoghanacht* (Egan/Owen) or the Ui Neill family.

With the arrival of Christianity brought by the Church of Rome to Britain and Ireland, it posed problems for the Gaelic society, for apart from the numerous other conflicts that evolved; they were not willing to be separated from their kin by monastic communities.

The end solution, was to give the most powerful churchmen, such as bishops and abbots, a status that was equivalent to that of the king of a *Tuath* which resulted in the church gaining a great deal of power and wealth.

Thus it was fortunate that several Masters of the Great White Brotherhood reincarnated into this time period (later to be recognised as saints) to protect the Celtic Church and the Sacred Teachings of the Druids, from becoming corrupted and labelled as 'pagan' by the early Church of Rome.

The Irish monastic communities built in a similar fashion to their Sumerian ancestors and their monasteries consisted of groups of detached huts and beehive cells. The island of Iona was a good example of the way in which the monks lived and it was built upon the instructions of St Columba. The majority of monks were bi-lingual in Latin, Gaelic, proficient in Hebrew and Greek as well and the services were conducted in both Latin and Gaelic. Many of the monks were distinguished in poetry, philosophy, science, healing and astronomy. They also had an appreciation of the fine arts and valued the music and poetry by their Bards.

Although the transportation of the Stone of Destiny, the sacred Stone upon which all the Kings of Tara stood upon to be crowned, is discussed in greater detail in a future chapter, it was because of the constant competition amongst the tribes to claim for themselves the High Kingship of Tara, that by the early 500's AD, it was deemed necessary to establish a small tribe of the People of Dalriata in Argyll, Albany, which was on the west coast of what later became known as Scotland. Hence the reason that Fergus Mor mac Erc transported the Stone to Scotland. (Albany was derived from 'Alba' meaning 'white', not in a racial sense, but equated with 'Light' because these people were the descendants of the 'People of Light', the Tuatha de Danaan).

In the 6th century AD, a royal prince of this tribe was born in Northern Ireland. His name, as mentioned elsewhere, was Columba and he was a prophet who foresaw the eventual downfall of Tara and its kings. The prophecy at the beginning of this chapter was made by him, to his friend Brendan. Both of them were later to be recognised as saints.

Another important person who made great contributions during this era and was later recognised as a saint, was St Columbanus. He was born in c.543, some twenty years after the birth of St Columba and over the years, had contact with him.

Columbanus was born in Bangor, County Down and studied with St Comgall. St Columba had also been a student with St Comgall who founded the monastery at Bangor. Columbanus (probably under the instructions of St Columba), established a cluster of monasteries in Burgundy, France, and introduced his own Irish monastic rule. He celebrated Easter according to a method of reckoning which was still employed in Ireland but which had been discarded by Rome. Columbanus was chastised by Pope Gregory and in turn, he chastised the Pope.

This area in Burgundy was where in later centuries, the Knights Templar became well established and it was the area where St Hugh of Avalon was born in the 12th century. The French city of Avallon/Avalon (Avallonnais) dates back to Merovingian times (their emblem was the 'bear'). It was the capital of the region and was part of the kingdom of Aquitaine. Thus it can be seen that St Columbanus would have been most influential in this part of Burgundy, for he established the Teachings of the Celtic Church of Ireland there, establishing his own Irish monastic rule and he was not in any way influenced by the Pope who regarded Columbanus as a 'heretic'.

NOTES AND RECOMMENDED READING

William Francis Collier, *Central Figures In Irish History*, (Trinity College, Dublin, 1891)
Robert Graves, *The White Goddess*, (Faber & Faber U.K., 1961)
Florence Marian McNeil, *Iona*, (Blackie & Sons, Glasgow, Scotland, 1920)
John Grenham, *Clans And Families of Ireland*, (Bramley Books U.K., 1993)
Arnold J. Toynbee, *A Study of History*, (Oxford University Press, 1934)

Donald Attwater and Catherine Rachel John, *Penguin Dictionary of Saints*, (Penguin Books, U.K. 1995)

The Book of Invasions, (Dublin Library, Kildare Street, Ireland)

Barry Cunliffe, *The Celtic World*, (Bodley Head, U.K., 1979)

Hubert, *The Rise Of The Celts*, (Keegan, U.K., 1934)

Peter Bander, *The Prophecies of St Malachy and St Columbkille*, (Colin Smythe, U.K., 1969)

CHAPTER 29

Ireland's Beloved St Patrick (Kuthumi)

"I was in the buttery in the land of the Trinity"
(Taliesin/Merlin/St Germain)

From the book titled *Central Figures In Irish History* by William Francis Collier, L.L. D., Trinity College, Dublin, written in 1891, we are informed that Patrick's name was originally "*Succat* meaning 'strong in war'. The Saint later in life assumed the Latin name of *Patricius* (Irish *Patraic*), by which alone he is celebrated as the Patron-Saint and 'Apostle' of Ireland.

"Born at Nemthur, where Alculaid or Dumbarton afterwards stood, Patrick was the son of Conchessa (said by some to have been a sister of St Martin of Tours) and of Calpornius, who, though in orders as a deacon, filled also the civil office of *decurio* or magistrate under the Roman government."

Patrick's (Kuthumi's) formative years were spent in Northern Ireland after having been captured and brought to Connaught, the area belonging to the tribe known as the *Cruithin* whose origins were discussed in the previous chapter.

According to Irish legends, when Patrick was approximately sixteen years old, he was captured by the powerful tribe of Ui Neill (O'Neill) whose High King at Tara was King Conall, a great grandfather of St Columba. Patrick is recorded as having 'baptised' Conall, however, it was more than likely than he 'initiated' King Conall.

After his years spent in Ireland, Patrick escaped to Gaul (France) where he was trained at the monasteries of Lerins and Auxerre. His principal teacher was St Germanus (an incarnation of St Germain) who was the Bishop of Auxerre and who visited Britain and commanded an army in combat with the Saxons and the warring Picts.

Patrick was considered to be unsuitable for his vocation in the priesthood because he had no time for the contrived authority of the Roman bishops and nor did his teacher, St Germain (Germanus). It is highly probable that Patrick was initiated into the Order of the Druids when he spent time with St Germain in Gaul which was an area where the Druids had long been established. As far back as the days of Pythagoras (Kuthumi), he reputedly visited Gaul and was welcomed by the Druids and it was Marseilles in Gaul where the Druids had settled, that he first ventured to as Joseph of Arimathea, (John the Beloved), with the remnants of the Family of the Holy Grail, before journeying on to Britain with his mother, Mary.

Patrick was much more concerned with the Orders of the Celtic Church and in common with other saints he had the gift of prophecy. His teachings were different in many more respects from those of Rome and his writings indicate a distinct tendency towards the Arian tradition of the Essenes.

According to Madame Blavatsky in her book *The Secret Doctrine*, the Arians inherited all their valuable knowledge of science, the hidden virtues of precious stones, alchemy (chemistry), science, physics, astrology, and astronomy, from the Atlanteans.

Patrick travelled the land of Ireland for almost thirty years, supervising the building of Celtic monasteries and churches. He refused to persuade his converts to relinquish their beliefs in their mythological heroes and heroines which had been incorporated into their legends and although the Church of Rome have done their best to ascribe to the fact that Patrick leaned towards their teachings, the Irish know differently. He was a true Celt, who protected their sacred heritage. In the sequel to this story, *The Dove, The Rose And The Sceptre - In Search Of The Ark Of The Covenant*, further information is given about St Patrick, including documented facts that although they later became worshipped as Roman Catholic Saints, neither he nor St Columba were of that religion. Historical evidence shows that Patrick was quite a rebel, especially where the Church of Rome was concerned.

The areas that Patrick is known to have lived and worked in were Saul in County Down, Derry, Armagh, Templepatrick and Croagh Patrick. Some of these areas became significant centres of learning where churches and monasteries were built amongst the sacred oak groves of the Druids.

In Ireland, St Patrick taught 'Mary of the Gaels' who eventually became known as St Brigid. Mary was of noble birth, a princess who was born in Leinster. She worked with her mother attending to lepers and the poor and it was said of her that she could perform miracles.

One of her jobs was to churn butter. In order to feed the poor, Mary (Brigid) and her mother kept a stock of supplies in the 'buttery'. Taliesin/Merlin/St Germain wrote in one of his verses referring to his past incarnations:

"I was in the buttery in the land of the Trinity" (Ireland) which proves that during his incarnation as St Germanus, he visited Ireland, possibly to see both St Patrick and Mary. Mary would have belonged to the Great White Brotherhood and may have been St Germain's twin soul, the Lady Portia who had been his wife,

Mary, when he was Joseph, the Father of the Holy Grail family. The 'Shamrock' - Ireland's emblem consists of a three-leaf clover and it is said that St Patrick utilized the shamrock to explain the Trinity but this is a false myth. The first time that the shamrock was associated with Patrick was on coins issued by the Roman Catholic Confederation of Kilkenny in 1645.

It was not until the 6th century that Patrick's life was written about and there was much confusion about the Saint's activities. Scholars tracing his history have had to rely upon a mixture of Patrick's own writings, oral tradition and claims by various monasteries.

Patrick's personal writings were modest to the extreme. His established his headquarters at Saul, near Downpatrick which is where he first landed on his return to Ireland. Saul's Latin name was Stabulum, and in Irish *Sabhal*- meaning a 'stable'. It was at Saul that Patrick built his first Celtic church in Ireland.

In those days, there were no towns in Ireland, only communes and so Patrick created bishoprics, almost three hundred and fifty in total. These established centres became 'major centres of learning' which is exactly what the island of Iona was to become almost one hundred years later.

Patrick and his scribes were reluctant to abandon many of the Celtic traditions and it is not clear just how the Roman scribes were able to pin down the most basic elements of the Celtic language and literature and incorporate some of their own Roman mythology into the Celtic religion, especially in the way that they made saints of some of the gods and goddesses who had not only been worshipped by the Celts, but by the Romans as well. A further example of this was the goddess of the sacred wells 'Co-vianna' whom the Romans changed to St Anna.

Being of Irish Celtic ancestry, second generation Australian, and having spent some time living in Northern Ireland in 1967, I have felt always felt a close affinity to St Patrick. On a return journey to Ireland in 1996, I traced the footsteps of Patrick to many famous places that are attributed to him.

A significant historical place of interest connected with St Patrick is Ballintubber Abbey, which like Iona and Stonehenge, is a symbol of Irish heritage, dating back beyond Christian times to the Irish Celtic forebears. The Abbey is about an hour's drive north of Galway, before Sligo and is delightfully scenic.

Local inhabitants have restored the Abbey to its former, if not better, glory and it is situated in a beautiful part of the country. Even though it was summer time when we made our visit, the landscape around was a glorious emerald green, the green that Ireland is so famous for. At the Abbey is a holy well where pilgrims were baptised by Patrick and although it is now situated in the middle of a golf course alongside the Abbey, the well managed to convey a magical feeling of its spiritual antiquity.

In the Abbey grounds there is a beautiful statue of St Patrick and beyond it is the beginning of the track that leads to the famous holy mountain of St Patrick, called Croagh Patrick. Like the Tor at Glastonbury, it can be seen rising majestically pointing heavenwards, beckoning the traveller to climb and explore its mystery. Hundreds of pilgrims annually travel on foot, retracing the journey that Patrick so frequently made.

The guided tour begins at the Abbey itself and crosses over many fields where unnamed tombs and mounds signify the sadness of the loss of many lives during the 'Great Potato Famine'. At the top of the mountain, is a small chapel dedicated to St Patrick and the whole area has a wonderful inspirational feeling about it.

Ballintubber means the town-land or homestead of the well of St Patrick. On the site of the present abbey, St Patrick founded one of his churches in 441 AD after his return from journeying to the holy mountain of Croagh Patrick. Thus for 1,500 years, a church has occupied the site of the present day Abbey.

The Abbey was founded by King Cathal (Cathaoir) Mor O'Connor. He was of the royal lineage of O'Connors, kings of Connacht. Originally, the Abbey was occupied by travelling priests. The sanctuary was dedicated to Mary and the Apostle St John the Beloved (Kuthumi).

In his time, Patrick had endeavoured to meld Christianity with the pagan Celtic religion, in order to please both Celtic Druids and the Church of Rome and in this he was highly successful; however, as already mentioned, his leaning was towards the Celtic people. As a roving Bishop, he worked in many of the so-called 'pagan' areas of the North of Ireland.

St Patrick and the Celtic Cross

When we visited St Patrick's Abbey at Ballintubber, our guide informed us that the Celtic Cross, which is a cross within a circle, was designed by St Patrick to please both the Church of Rome and the Celtic Druids. By using the cross it pleased the Church of Rome, and the incorporation of the circle pleased the Celtic Druids who always worshipped in a circle. Apart from its connections with the Sun and the Moon, the circle was considered a symbol of absolute perfection.

The Cross represented the Four Directions. The 'Circle' enclosing the 'Cross' was symbolic of Paradise and the Tree of Life. It was also called '**THE ROSE OF THE WINDS**'. The Ley lines have been discussed previously, however, it is relevant here to briefly review information contained in Francis Hitching's book *The World Atlas Of Mysteries*: "Xavier found more than 400 such sites in France alone. He proposed that the whole of Europe, on a remote ancient site called Alaise, near Bescancon in southern France, had been divided up into two *roses-des-vents*."

'ROSES-DE-VENTS' translates into *'ROSES OF THE WIND'* and from the word Alaise, the word 'lais' and 'Ley' lines were derived, the name given to the Earth's Serpent Energy.

Patrick is credited with having rid Ireland of snakes/serpents, except there were none. He certainly would not have 'rid Ireland of the Serpent Ley lines' but he did do his best to keep the religion of the Roman Church out of Ireland, for in the Book of Revelation, the Serpent and the Dragon represented the Church of Rome. The legends of St George and the Archangel Michael were also indicative of eradicating the 'Dragon' - the early Church of Rome.

(Merlin was credited with having advised 'Vortigern' who was having trouble making the walls of his fortress stand up without constantly falling down, that the problem was two dragons, one white and one red which were confined underneath the earth where the tower was being erected. This legend maybe directly connected with the Serpent/Dragon Ley lines).

It was no mere coincidence, but Divinely ordained, that having founded the first Celtic Church at Glastonbury, in his incarnation as Joseph of Arimathea (John the Beloved) Kuthumi continued to protect the 'Celtic Faith' by becoming Ireland's 'Beloved' St Patrick who founded the first Celtic Church in Ireland, at Saul.

In his next incarnation, he would become the one known as King Arthur, of the legendary 'Holy Grail' fame, who stood upon the ancient symbolic *Stone of Destiny* at Avalon, in order to be crowned King of the Celts, and 'Defender of the Faith'.

Patrick paved the way admirably for future saints to follow in his footsteps. He was a much beloved man and is fondly remembered by Celtic people all around the world who celebrate his feast day each year as 'St Patrick's Day' on the 17th March.

In the 5th century AD, St Patrick and St Brigid (Mary of the Gaels) prophesied the future coming of the 'Dove from the North', one who would make major contributions towards saving their Celtic heritage and in a prophecy made by the 'Dove of the North' in the 6th century AD which came to fruition, curiously, the two saints mentioned above and the 'Dove from the North' were buried together in Ireland. Why? The answer is revealed in the sequel to this story, *The Dove, The Rose And The Sceptre...*

MASTERS DISCUSSED IN THIS CHAPTER

Merlin/Taliesin - St Germain
St Germanus - St Germain
Pythagoras - Kuthumi
John Joseph (of Arimathea) - Kuthumi
St Patrick - Kuthumi
King Arthur - Kuthumi

NOTES AND RECOMMENDED READING

William Francis Collier, _Central Figures In Irish History_, (Trinity College, Dublin, 1891)

Robert Graves, _The White Goddess_, (Faber & Faber U.K., 1961)

Francis Hitching, _The World Atlas of Mysteries_, (Pan Books U.K., 1978)

Rev. Thomas A Egan, _The Story of Ballintubber Abbey_, (Ballintubber Abbey, County Mayo, Ireland)

Madame Helena Blavatsky, _The Secret Doctrine_, (Quest Books, Theosophical Publishing House, U.S.A, 1966)

Anthony M. Wilson, _St Patrick's Town_, (Isabella Press, Belfast, Northern Ireland, 1995)

Donald Attwater and Catherine Rachel John, _Penguin Dictionary of Saints_, (Penguin Books, U.K. 1995)

Barry Cunliffe, _The Celtic World_, (Bodley Head, U.K., 1979)

Hubert, _The Rise Of The Celts_, (Keegan, U.K., 1934)

CHAPTER 30

The Legends of Merlin & Arthur

"Germanus was able to get the troublesome teachers banished and hence forward, says
Bede, 'the faith was maintained uncorrupted in these parts for a long time'."
(*Penguin Dictionary of Saints* by Donald Attwater & Catherine Rachel John)

Apart from Taliesin in the 6th century AD, the earliest sagas of Merlin and
Arthur were written by Geoffrey of Monmouth who was brought up in a Benedictine
monastery near Monmouth of which he was an archdeacon in Llandaff (Wales)
and was later appointed as bishop of St Asaph in 1152. His most famous works
written in Latin were *Historia Regum Britanniae (The History of the Kings of
Britain)*, written in c.1136, which contained the first full-length story of Arthur, and
Vita Merlini (The Life of Merlin), written in c.1148, some six hundred years after
the events. It is important to remember that Geoffrey confused dates, eras, events
and names and some six hundred years later, fused them into one exciting romantic
tale, and although readily acceptable at the time, is now considered to be mostly
fictitious.

The Life of Merlin tells of Merlin's adventures and his eventual madness.
However, Gerald of Wales (Giraldus Cambrensis) who was born of noble birth and
a descendant of the People of Dalriata wrote that there were two Merlins; one was
a prophet/magician and the other was a wild man who lived in the woods - probably
he preferred the life of a hermit. The Merlin, in whom we are interested, was the
prophet/magi. The Venerable Bede (c.637-735), a monk and historian, who was a
friend of St Columba's biographer, the Abbot of Iona, Adamnan, wrote that during
Arthur's time, there was a great deal of conflict between the Britons, Picts, Angles
and the Scots who were the people of Dalriada - Columba and Arthur's kinsmen.

When delving back so far into history, the sources upon whom most scholars
have relied upon have been Bede, Gildas, Adamnan, and Geoffrey of Monmouth.

According to authors Donald Attwater and Catherine Rachel John in their
book titled the *Penguin Dictionary of Saints*, the historian "Gildas whose name

meant 'Wise monk' is famous as the author of the work called *De Excidio Et Conquestu Britanniae* ('Concerning the Ruin and Conquest of Britain'). In it, warning lessons are drawn from the history of Britain under the Romans."

The work was written somewhere between 516 AD and 547 AD and he died in 570 AD which places him in the exact time frame of the Arthur (c. 530 - 608 AD) and Merlin of this story of the *Masters of the Mystical Rose.*

According to the above mentioned authors, Gildas visited Ireland and had considerable influence upon the development of the Irish Church. "Some scholars now incline to the belief that the *De Exidio* was not wholly written by Gildas, but that part of it was added just after his time."

If the work which Gildas wrote is considered to be not wholly his own, then the Merlin of the 6th century AD, namely St Germain, who resided in Ireland at that time, was probably the author or co-author as may also have been of a book of Geoffrey of Monmouth's which will be discussed further on in this chapter.

Both Gildas and the Welsh *Cambrian Annals* recorded that an 'Arthur' was defeated by the Saxons at Mount Badon in 516 AD. (It will be remembered that St Germain in his incarnation as St Germanus also fought the Saxons). The same source recorded that Arthur and his enemy son Mordred were both killed in a battle in 537 AD.

The name of Mordred, Arthur's son, may be a clue to his lineage. For example, *Mor* is a variation of *Mawr* as in Beli Mawr, the legendary king of Briton to which the family of Arthurs (Ar-thors) belonged who were the 'kindred of Gabran'.

Historically, that particular Arthur (remembering that it was a designated title given to Pendragons - chief military leaders), may have been Comgall of the clan of Gabran of Dalriata who ruled as High King from 506 until his death in 537 AD.

The recorded date of 537 AD would appear to be too much for mere coincidence. King Comgall was a descendant of Fergus Mor (Mawr) mac Erc who first brought the Stone of Destiny from Tara to Scotland.

All these High Kings who belonged to the kindred of Gabran (dating back to Bran the Blessed King - Cymbeline) were kings of Dalriata and Dalriada. Historically it is known that Comgall's next successor was Gabran.

The Origin of Vortigern

Geoffrey of Monmouth wrote of a character that was called 'Vortigern', briefly mentioned in the previous chapter. However, this person did not actually exist; it was only a title meaning an 'overlord'.

The clan of Gabran of the tribe of Dalriata, Ireland and Dalriada, Scotland, considered themselves to be free warriors, freemen, free-masons and they belonged to the Order of the Druids. The smaller divisions of their tribes were known as the *Tuatha* who each had their own over-lord (Vortigern) who in turn, owed his allegiance to a High King who belonged to the tribe of *Eoghanacht* or the *Ui Neill.* These people, through Celtic mythology, traced their ancestors back to the *Tuatha de Danaan,* the *Children of Anna* known as the *People of the Light.* Before their stories were finally written down during the 6th century by the monks at the Celtic monasteries, all the tales were verbally handed down from generation to generation.

During the fifth century the Romans had withdrawn from Britain for the last time and Britain was left to fight the Picts, Scots, Danes and Irish. According to tradition, they were saved by the arrival from Amorica (Brittany) by Constantine II, who with the assistance of his three sons, drove the Jute Hengist (c.450) from England. The sons were Constantine, Ambrosius and Uther, (later to be called 'Pendragon').

Upon the death of Constantine, his elder son Constantine (III) took the throne. Constantine chose 'Vortigern' as his chief adviser.

Vortigern, the 'Overlord' was terrified of the Picts and made an alliance with them and with the warlords, allowing them to settle in Kent and Northumbria. Historically, Hengist was the leader of the invading Anglo Saxons and he and his brother Horsa, settled in Kent.

The problem with historical sources is that it is difficult to discover any that agree on the exact dates that these events took place. However, according to Nennius (516-570 AD) 'Vortigern' began his reign in 425 until his death in 464 AD.

Ambrosius Aurelianus

Those readers who are familiar with the legends of Arthur and Merlin will remember that one of characters in the same time frame as 'Vortigern' about whom Geoffrey of Monmouth wrote, was Ambrosius Aurelianus, supposedly one of the sons of Constantine II of Amorica, (Brittany in Gaul), (France), from a family of Roman consuls. The 'Prince of the Sanctuary' was a designated title allotted to a High Archdruid Priest who was a 'Guardian of the Faith', and Ambrosius Aurelianus was given this title.

Could it be mere coincidence that St Germanus (St Germain) who was born of Gallo-Roman parents, was a military commander (Pendragon) who reputedly died at Ravenna in 448 AD where he had journeyed to plead with the Roman consul in Gaul on behalf of the people of Amorica (now Brittany), who were in conflict with the imperial viceroy of Gaul? It was in 448 AD that the Britons had appealed to the Roman consul in Gaul to give them assistance.

Could it be mere coincidence that as a military commander (Pendragon), Germanus, on two occasions, commanded an army which fought battles defending the Britons against the warring Picts and Anglo Saxons - the same era in which Ambrosius Aurelianus is said to have fought them?

Surely this would have been yet another time that St Germain was 'Defender of the Faith', trying to establish peace?

For if Nennius' date of 'Vortigern' (who began his reign as an 'overlord' in 425 AD until his death in 464 AD), is correct, then this places St Germanus in the same time frame as 'Ambrosius Aurelianus' who fought against the Picts and the Saxons.

It certainly seems to be all too much for just co coincidence!

According to Geoffrey of Monmouth, Ambrosius Aurelianus was a Pendragon; in other words he was a head military commander. The probability is that Ambrosius Aurelianus may have been a fictitious name or it could have been the Roman name for St Germanus.

If it was a fictitious name, it is noteworthy that according to an historical book of names by Michele Brown, 'Ambrosius' means 'immortal', 'divine' and was the 'nectar of the gods'. Another character about whom Geoffrey of Monmouth wrote, was one called 'Emrys Merlin' and according to Michele Brown, 'Emrys' means the same as 'Ambrosius' - 'divine' - 'immortal'.

We are informed by the authors Donald Attwater and Catherine Rachel John in their book titled the *Penguin Dictionary of Saints* that St Germanus was sent from Gaul to the island of Britain where he vanquished the false teachers.

"Germanus was able to get the troublesome teachers banished and hence forward, says Bede, 'the faith was maintained uncorrupted in these parts for a long time'."

This only serves to prove that Germanus was a 'Defender of the Faith'.

It has previously been discussed that on both occasions that Germanus visited Britain, he visited the tomb of St Alban and it will be remembered that St Alban was a previous incarnation of St Germain.

In a vision, St Germain showed me the name of 'Merlin' and how to transpose the 'M' by splitting the 'M' into two AA's and then he told me that Ambrosius Aurelianus was a coded name applicable to an important place in time. To me, this was confirmation that he had been the one known as Ambrosius Aurelianus.

Thus, it could be deemed that the names of Ambrosius and Emrys Merlin which both have the same meaning pertaining to 'divine' and 'immortal' gods, were a major clue that these two characters were Masters of the Great White Brotherhood.

From Peter Dawkins' book titled *The Great Vision*: "Merlin or Myrddin, meaning 'Wise Man' was a title given to Ambrosius (i.e. Merlin Ambrosius) who was known as 'Prince of the Sanctuary' because of his holiness and wisdom."

Geoffrey of Monmouth claimed that he was translating his story about Merlin and Ambrosius Aurelianus from an old and unknown British book. It will be recalled that it was mentioned at the beginning of this chapter that Geoffrey was brought up in a Benedictine monastery near Monmouth and that he became the bishop of St Asaph in Wales in 1152.

It is indeed highly probable that if the old book existed, it had been hidden somewhere in the monastery of St Asaph, because in about 553 AD, St Kentigern (c.518-603) had founded the monastery of St Asaph. (St Kentigern was fondly given the nick-name of 'Mungo the Beloved One'. He was trained at the school of St Serf in Fife, and made his centre at Cathures, now called Glasgow). It is noteworthy that in about 581, Kentigern was visited by St Columba who was working in the area of Strathclyde. In all probability, the book may have been written by St Columba and hidden in the monastery of St Asaph - the reason it may have been St Columba will be made clearer in Chapter 33, for St Columba knew Merlin well.

In Alfred Lord Tennyson's *Percival's Quest*, Percival gave up his knighthood to become a monk. Soon before his death, he told his story of the Holy Grail to a kindly, practical-minded fellow monk whose name was 'Ambrosius'. St Germanus apart from all his other attributes, was also a monk.

The conclusion is therefore that Ambrosius Aurelianus who was designated the title of 'Prince of the Sanctuary' and was a 'Pendragon' (chief military commander), was Germanus. He would also have been a 'Merlin' who initiated Patrick as a 'Merlin'.

Because St Germanus (Ambrosius Aurelianus) had been the principal teacher of St Patrick (Kuthumi), it is reasonable to presume that from time to time, St Germain called upon Kuthumi to assist him, even in battle. This is not as far-fetched as it seems, because when St Germain became the 'Merlin' of the 6th century AD, at which time he anointed Kuthumi as 'Arthur', King of the Celts, they both accompanied each other in battles fought on Irish and Scottish soil.

It is noteworthy that St Germanus sent St Patrick to the area of Caithness in Scotland when the Picts were out of control.

According to Florence Marian McNeil in her book titled *Iona*, St Ninian also worked among the Picts in Galloway and he accomplished much more than he has been credited with. His foundations have been traced all over the south and east of Scotland and as far north as Caithness. He was sent by St Germanus to control the southern Picts in Galloway (Albany/Scotland). By the mid-fifth century AD, the earlier work achieved by St Ninian in these areas was practically undone by the invading hordes of Jutes, Angles and Saxons. St Patrick (c385-461AD) and St Ninian (born c350-432AD) were in the same period of time and it is highly probable that some of the Arthurian and Merlin legends were written about them.

When St Germain reincarnated as Merlin in the 6th century AD, he actually did accomplish restoring peace amongst the Picts of the North.

The 'Merlin' of this era, made certain prophecies. We know that St Germain was a prophet and a Seer in all his incarnations which have previously been discussed throughout this story. According to Geoffrey of Monmouth, Merlin conveyed great stones from Ireland in memory of Ambrosius Aurelianus and they were miraculously erected on the Salisbury Plain - this great monument became known as Stonehenge.

Historically, this is incorrect because Stonehenge existed for thousands of years before Merlin's time. The clue here however, is that Merlin was very familiar with Ireland and as St Germanus he had visited Ireland to see St Patrick and St Brigit, because in his verse of Taliesin (when he became the Merlin of the following century), he told us: *"I was in the buttery in the land of the Trinity"* and the 'buttery' was where St Brigid and her mother kept supplies for the lepers and the poor.

The Merlin of the 5th century AD

Just suppose that St Patrick (Kuthumi) became incorporated into the legends of Ambrosius Aurelianus, written by Geoffrey of Monmouth. Within any legends and myths there are always some elements of truth; therefore we need to sift through what are known facts and see if there are any similarities.

Merlin was reputed to have been kidnapped when he was a young boy, and taken as a slave, which is exactly what happened to St Patrick.

In Mary Stewart's book, *The Crystal Cave*, the author also tells of how Ambrosius was the father of Merlin and of how in his early youth, Merlin had been kidnapped and taken over the sea to his father Ambrosius.

Historically, Patrick was kidnapped twice.
(a)   From Amorica (Gaul) to Ireland.
(b)   From Ireland to Amorica.

St Germanus (Ambrosius Aurelianus) had several common denominators with the family of St Patrick:

1.   He became a *lawyer*, under the Roman government, and was born of *Gallo-Roman* parents of *Amorica*.
    In the *Brittonum Historia*, when Ambrosius is questioned about his race, he replies "My only father comes of the race of the Roman consuls."

2.   Calpornius, the father of Patrick, who was married to Conchessa (said by some to have been a sister of St Martin of Tours - Gaul) was a *magistrate* under the *Roman* government in *Amorica*, Gaul.

According to William Francis Collier in his book titled *Central Figures of Irish History* (1891) (transcribed from Patrick's own writings), Patrick was travelling to Amorica in Gaul when he was seized by British marauders, and carried off to Dalriada in Ireland where he was sold as a slave.

After about six or seven years in bondage, Patrick whilst sleeping one night, heard a voice in his head, informing him that two hundred miles away, a ship awaited which would carry him away from the Irish shore. Patrick made his way to the ship and after three days at sea, they touched land in Gaul.

Patrick tarried with these pirate mariners for sixty days who also wanted to keep him as a slave, and then he managed to escape and made his way to his parents in Amorica where he dwelt with them for some time. Eventually, he journeyed to meet up with St Germanus [Ambrosius Aurelianus] who trained and educated him for his mission.

Then, once again, he had another prophetic enlightenment. This also occurred in a dream whilst he was sleeping. "He saw in his sleep a man named 'Victoricus' coming from Hiberio (as the Saint always calls Ireland) with many letters in his hand. This figure gave a letter to the dreamer, who read therein the words, 'The Voice of the Irish'. 'We pray thee, holy youth, to come and henceforth walk amongst us'."

"Obeying this dream, Patrick crossed the sea, arriving in Ireland."

MASTERS DISCUSSED IN THIS CHAPTER
St Alban - St Germain
St Germanus (Ambrosius Aurelianus) - St Germain
Merlin - St Germain
St Patrick - Kuthumi

NOTES AND RECOMMENDED READING

William Francis Collier, L.L.D. *Central Figures Of Irish History,* (Trinity College, Dublin, 1891

Mary Stewart, *The Crystal Cave*, (Hodder, U.K.)

Geoffrey of Monmouth, *The Vita Merlini*, (trans. J.J. Parry, University of Illinois, 1925)

T.H. White, *The Once And Future King*, (Collins, U.K. 1958)

T.H. White, *The Book of Merlin*, (Collins, U.K. 1978)

Chrétien de Troyes, *Arthurian Romances*, (trans. Owen, Dent, U.K. 1987)

Geoffrey of Monmouth, *The History of the Kings of Britain*, (edited by L. Thorpe, Penguin, 1966)

Arnold J. Toynbee, *A Study of History*, (Oxford University Press, U.K., 1934)

Donald Attwater and Catherine Rachel John, *Penguin Dictionary of Saints,* (Penguin Books, U.K. 1995)

Gwyn & Thomas Jones, *The Mabinogion*, (J.M. Dent & Son, U.K.)

Robert Graves, *The White Goddess*, (Faber & Faber, U.K., 1961)

Barry Cunliffe, *The Celtic World*, (Bodley Head, U.K., 1979)

John Grenham, *Clans and Families of Ireland, The Heritage and Heraldry of Irish Clans & Families*, (Bramley Books, U.K., 1993)

Florence Marian McNeill, *Iona*, (Blackie & Sons, Glasgow, Scotland, 1920)

David Day, *The Quest For King Arthur*, (De Agostini Editions, U.K., 1995)

Michele Brown, *Baby Name Book* Historical Book of Names (Greenwich Editions, U.K. 1985)

Peter Dawkins, *The Great Vision* (Francis Bacon Research Trust, Warwick, U.K.)

Anthony M. Wilson, *St Patrick's Town*, (Isabella Press, Belfast, Northern Ireland, 1995)

CHAPTER 31

The Knight 'Patrise' & the 'Perilous Seat'

"O what can ail thee, knight-at-arms,
Alone and palely loitering?"
(*La Belle Dame sans Merci* by Jonathan Keats)

Within the Arthurian legends written by Sir Thomas Malory in his *Morte d'Arthur*, there is the story of a brave knight from Ireland called *Patrise* who is obviously St Patrick. *Patrise* lived during the era of Sir Lancelot and his kinsman Sir Bors (which may be a play on words for the 'Boar' was an animal sacred to the Druids thus giving a hint that this family was a Druidic one), who agreed to defend Queen Guinevere. Lancelot was married to Elaine, daughter of a king of Ireland (King Pelles) and it was Lancelot and Elaine's son who became Sir Galahad.

Because of the reference to Patrise (Patrick) living during the time of Sir Lancelot and Sir Bors, we can place the era during the period of St Patrick's life who was born in c. 386 AD and died in 461 AD. Sir Lancelot's and the Irish princess, Elaine's son, Sir Galahad was the person destined for the 'Perilous Seat'. The 'Perilous Seat' could only have been the 'Stone of Destiny'.

Lancelot and Galahad

Did Lancelot and Sir Galahad really exist?

Those readers who are familiar with the story of *Camelot* will remember that Sir Lancelot was the valiant knight who fell in love with the beautiful Guinevere who was King Arthur's wife. The Queen saddened by the eternal triangle in which she had become entangled, left both Arthur and Lancelot and became a nun.

This story is also told in Sir Thomas Malory's *Morte d'Arthur* and in Chrétien of Troyes' *The Knight of the Cart*. It was Chrétien who first introduced the idea of

Camelot and it was Eleanor of Aquitaine who introduced the idea of 'Camelot' into the court of her husband, Henry II, Plantagenet, King of England. 'Camelot' signified a time of 'knights in shining armour' rescuing 'damsels in distress' symbolic of chivalry being introduced into Britain. Women, up until that point of time, were treated as mere 'chattels'.

Chrétien lived at the court of Marie of Champagne, who was one of the daughters of Eleanor of Aquitaine from her first marriage to King Louis VII of France. Marie was married to the Count of Champagne and she would have been the authoress known as Marie of France who also wrote Grail romances such as the *Lay of Sir Launfal* in 1189. According to Emile Legouis in the book titled *A History of English Literature* (1945), Marie wrote her work at the court of Henry II (her step-father).

The Court of Champagne in France was a centre for esoteric and Cabbalistic Teachings of the Arcana and thus the Teachings of the *Mystical Rose*. The Count of Champagne was a member of the Knights Templar who journeyed to the Holy Land, and upon his return, gave a portion of his land to St Bernard where the Abbey of Clairvaux was built. The Cistercian Abbot, St Bernard (c.1090-1153 AD) was the patron of the Knights Templar. In the 13th century (1215-1235), Cistercian scribes compiled the *Prose Lancelot* or *The Vulgate Cycle*, a massive work that was written in French.

In circa 1172 AD, Chrétien of Troyes wrote the work titled *Le Chevalier a la Cherrette - The Knight of the Cart*, which introduced Lancelot for the first time and told the story of the 'Ordeal of the Sword Bridge', wherein Lancelot heroically rescues Guinevere - the story of which was commissioned by Marie.

According to Emile Legouis: "Allowing for the part of Chrétien de Troyes, the conclusion is that the British cycle was evolved principally by the Anglo-Normans, and that Walter Map, who was half-Norman and half-Welsh, presumably welded together the Arthurian legend and the legend of the Holy Grail. He is credited with giving the cycle its religious and moral character in that he represents Guinevere, Arthur's wife, as an adulteress, and her lover, Lancelot, as unworthy, by his sin, to accomplish the quest for the Holy Grail, which was reserved for his son, Galahad. The *Queste del Saint Graal, Lancelot du Lac,* and *Mort d' Arthur* are attributed to Walter Map."

"The powerful imaginative leaven of this story, the most beautiful and varied of all those in the minds of the English when they again began to write, must not be forgotten. It was a story all the more stimulating to them because it was set in their own country, and they believed it to be national."

Chrétien claimed to have attained his knowledge for the story from monks who had assisted King David I of Scots to rebuild his abbeys and churches. King David was the son of Malcolm Ceann Mor (Canmor) and St Margaret (who introduced the cult of St Andrew, and the symbol of the famous X, the 'saltire' which became the national emblem of Scotland). King David's grandson was William the Lion of Scots, an incarnation of St Germain.

Lancelot's Quest

In Chrétien's story, Lancelot went in search of Guinevere, and upon the quest for the *Holy Grail* and the *Grail Castle*. The Queen left him various clues along the way, like a scavenger hunt. During his search for Guinevere:

1. Lancelot often refers to the 'Perilous Seat' which could only be the 'Stone of Destiny'.

2. Lancelot visits an abbey at Glastonbury where the tomb of St Joseph of Arimathea lies. (It has been established in a previous chapter that Joseph's tomb was at Glastonbury).

    As he stood in the abbey 'alone and palely loitering', a voice tells Lancelot that he is not the one 'destined' for the 'Perilous Seat' but from the death of Jesus Christ there would be 454 years until the arrival of the 'destined one' to whom the 'Perilous Seat' belonged and it would be occupied by Lancelot's son, Sir Galahad.

    It has been mentioned in an earlier chapter that according to the Rosicrucian authority, the late Spencer Lewis, Jesus survived the crucifixion - however, we do not know the date of his actual death. Therefore, we will rely upon the year 33 AD as being the year alluded to in Chrétien's story.

    By adding 454 + 33 we are given the clue that the year of the arrival will be approximately 487 AD and we may be able to identify Galahad and his father, Lancelot. (The names which the characters were allotted were just pseudonyms, disguising their real identity). 'Lance' is another name for a 'spear' - a 'Shaker of the Truth' as in 'Shakespeare' and we can assume that Lancelot was a 'Defender of the Faith'.

3. The voice at the abbey informed Lancelot of his royal lineage and that his grandfather was the son of St Joseph of Arimathea. We know from the other Grail legends that Joseph had a son named Joseph.

    Lancelot and his son Galahad were direct descendants of Joseph of Arimathea - in other words, of John Joseph the Beloved Disciple whose daughter, Anna, had married Bran the Blessed King (Cymbeline) and founded a family of 'Guardians of the Grail'. It will be remembered that John Joseph's grandson, the son of Cymbeline and Anna, was Caradoc (Caractacus) and John Joseph (of Arimathea) bestowed upon him the honour of being the Second Master of the Grail, John Joseph having been the First.

It is relevant to repeat here, what has been mentioned earlier.

Within the Arthurian literature is the story of *Sir Gawain and the Green Knight*, written by an anonymous author during the 14th century AD (circa 1390). In the tale, Gawain encounters a Knight and enquires his name. In reply he is told that the Knight's name was:

(a)   Joseus (another name for Joseph).

(b)   Joseus' lineage is that of Joseph of Arimathea.

(c)   Joseus' uncle was King Fisherman, (who is Jesus).

(d)   Joseus' father is King Pelles. 'Pelles' is another name for *Pallas* synonymous with 'Athena- 'Wisdom' - *Sophia*. The father of Joseus was John the Beloved alias Joseph of Arimathea, whose brother 'King Fisherman' was Jesus.

4.   Sir Lancelot's wife, Elaine, was an Irish princess, the daughter of King Pelles.

5.   On his quest for Guinevere and the Grail Castle, Lancelot visited a 'sandy strand' somewhere on an island off the coast of the 'Waste Land' through which he had journeyed en route. (The area of Stirling, Scotland was once known as the 'Waste Land'). His journey takes him through many 'perilous' places. The importance of the 'Sandy Strand' is emphasized as if from this, we may be able to identify exactly where the Grail Castle was.

This significant clue is identifiable and will be revealed in a future chapter! Interestingly, Malcolm Canmor and his wife Margaret were to restore many of the important buildings upon this island of 'Avalon', which had been destroyed by raiding Norsemen.

Chrétien of Troyes wrote Lancelot's name as 'the Ancelot', derived from the Latin word Anguselus which in Celtic becomes Aengus/Angus. (According to an historical book of names by Michele Brown, Angus is thought to have been derived from the Trojan hero, Aeneas). Because Lancelot was given the title of the 'Angus', it would mean he was an important chieftain, a Pendragon of royal blood whose lineage could be traced back to the Judah/Tudor family.

Which King was born about 487 AD who may have been 'Galahad' destined for the Perilous Seat?

1.   Fergus Mor mac (son of) Erc who took the Stone of Destiny to Scotland from Tara was High King in the early 500's AD. The Stone of Destiny was moved many times and numerous kings were crowned upon it, thus it certainly fits the description of the *Perilous Seat*.

2.   Fergus Mor mac Erc's ancestors were the Grail family and Sir Lancelot's ancestors were also the Grail Family. Although Fergus reigned in the early

part of 500 AD, he would have been born around 487 AD. Therefore, the probability is that Fergus was Sir Galahad, the son of Lancelot, and they were the descendants of Beli Mawr (Mor).

Malcolm Canmor, his son King David of Scots and David's grandson King William the Lion of Scots, were also descendants of Mor Erc. As mentioned in a previous paragraph, Chrétien of Troyes claimed to have received the knowledge about Lancelot from monks who had assisted King David of Scots to rebuild his abbeys and churches.

High Kings of Dalriada to whom the Stone of Destiny Belonged
(Kindred of Gabran - House of Ui Neill/Niall)
(Excerpts taken from *Monarchs, Rulers, Dynasties and Kingdoms of the World* by R. Tapsell and *Clans and Families of Ireland,* by John Grenham)

NIALL (Neill) NOIGIALLACH died circa 450 AD - was the great great grandfather of St Columba who ruled as High King (Pendragon) of Royal Tara.

CONALL Crimthainne [Crimthin] reigned as King of Tara in c. 450 AD and was the great grandfather of St Columba. Conall was the one who was baptised/initiated by St Patrick (Kuthumi). According to William Francis Collier in his book titled *Central Figures of Irish History* (1891), Conall had a brother, Layary, who had a daughter Princess Eithne the Fair who was also baptised/initiated by St Patrick. It is possible that it was this Eithne who married Phelim mac Fergus and they became the parents of St Columba.

Conall was succeeded by Fiachnu mac Niall who then became the High King of Dalriada, Ireland in late 400's AD. (Ui Niall later became the name O'Neill and MacNeill).

FERGUS MOR MAC ERC (Son of Erc Mor) reigned early 500's AD as King of Dalriata, Scotland. The brothers of Fergus were reputedly Eochaidh who was High King of Tara (and was killed in a battle); and Murtagh mac Erc who subsequently became the High King of Tara. Fergus may have been the youngest. It was his older brother Murtagh who gave permission for Fergus to take the Stone of Destiny to Scotland and thereby establish his own kingship. When Fergus crossed over to Scotland with the Stone of Destiny, he was accompanied by many of the tribe of Dalriata which in Scotland then became 'Dalriada' and the dynasty eventually achieved sovereignty over the Picts.

Fergus belonged to the kindred of Gabran and his clan occupied the areas of Kintyre, the Isle of Gigha and Jura. (The name Fergusson was derived from 'sons of Fergus', who became the chiefs in Ayrshire, Argyll).

Because Columba's father's name was Phelim mac Fergus, he would have been one of the sons of Fergus but may not have been the elder whom it would appear, was Domangart.

c.500's: Domangart mac Fergus (Son of Fergus).

506-537 AD: Comgall (brother or son of Domangart). This Comgall would appear to have been the 'Arthur' who was killed in the Battle of Mount Badon in 537 AD at which time his son 'Mordred' was also killed.

Because the date of Comgall's death is given as 537 AD, it coincides with the date given in the *Cambrian Annals* and by Gildas, as being the death of an Arthur who was killed in battle at Mount Badon.

521: Columba Crimthin was born in Donegal to Princess Eithne and Prince Phelim mac Fergus.

537-559 AD: Gabran (father of Aedan).

559-574: Conall mac Comgall (son of Comgall).

Conall mac Comgall ruled in the same era as Brideri c.538-565 who ruled Gwynedd, Wales, (who was possibly the 'Pryderi' branch referred to in Taliesin's Four Branches of families). According to William Francis Collier in his book titled *Central Figures In Irish History*, Conall was a cousin of St Columba, who granted him the gift of the island of Iona, over which the monarch ruled.

563: Columba sailed to Iona.

574-608 AD: Aedan mac Gabran (son of Gabran) ruled.

608-630 AD: Eochaidh Buide (son of Aedan) ruled.

The Stone of Destiny and Tara

As we have seen throughout this story, the Stone of Destiny is reputed to have been the original Jacob's pillow upon which he received the vision that all his future descendants would be of the House of David. The Stone was eventually brought by the Prophet Jeremiah in c. 587 BC, to the Royal Palace of Tara, where all the High Kings were crowned upon it and with the anointing as such, came the responsibilities to protect the Grail Teachings of the Arcana. The hill of Tara's more ancient name was *Rach Cormac*.

In Tibet, the goddess *Tara* was worshipped as their *White Goddess* and she became known as the mother of the Tibetan people, just like *Anna* was considered to be the mother of the Irish Tuatha de Danaan. According to Stephen Beyer in his book *The Cult of Tara*, Tara is the principal superhuman being in Tibet who might be called *divine* without further qualification. She is prayed to by millions; her help in all adversity is divine.

As a female goddess she was considered to be mightier than the Buddhas and Bodhisattvas. In a Tibetan hymn she is addressed as the 'mother who gives birth to all the Buddhas of the three times'. The Tibetan 'cult of *Tara*' is considered to have been brought from India and it is not known just how far back in time it originated. In Celtic mythology, the god *Taranis* was the god of 'Thunder' equated with Thor as in Ar-thor and it is possible that Tara was named after this particular god and furthermore, that 'initiations' were undertaken there.

The Royal Palace of Tara was considered to be Ireland's Camelot. An ancient manuscript called *The Magical Stone of Tara* tells the story of the High King Conn (Conall) of the Hundred Battles who went to Tara at sunrise. He was accompanied by three Druids and three Bards. Conn enquired of his Druids as to what the Stone was called and from whence it came. The Druids informed him that it was called the 'Fail' or 'Destiny' and that it came from the mystical Isle of Destiny.

From that time onwards, the Stone became known as the 'Stone of Destiny' and in the Arthurian legends, it was the 'Perilous' Stone. The Stone of Destiny was moved several times and eventually it was placed at Scone near Perth in Scotland and the Celtic kings continued to be crowned upon it.

Then, in the 15th century AD, it was stolen by King Edward I of England, during the era of William Wallace of *Brave Heart* fame. Edward gave instructions for a throne to be built in which the Stone of Destiny was to be placed underneath. The throne with the Stone of Destiny was then taken to Westminster Abbey and from the time of its installment, all the future kings and queens of Britain were crowned upon it.

The first Scottish king to be crowned upon it was James VI, Stuart King of Scots, who thus became James the 1st of England. In accordance with the Biblical prophecies, this occasion united Ireland, Scotland, Wales and Britain. The Stone of Destiny was returned to Scotland in 1996, by the Royal family and it is currently exhibited in Edinburgh Castle.

The Legend of the Stone of Destiny

The legend of the Stone of Destiny stated that if ever the Stone should be moved again, it would be the fall of a dynasty, but also, Scotland would regain its rightful independence. In September 1997, one year after the Stone was removed to its rightful place in Scotland the people of Scotland voted to achieve the right to have their own parliament once again. (For an update on the Stone of Destiny and the prophecies regarding it and the 'Overturns' see the sequel to this story, titled

The Dove, The Rose And The Sceptre, In Search Of The Ark Of The Covenant).

Sir Thomas Malory - Morte D'Arthur
The War of the Roses and the Priory of Sion

According to Florence Marian McNeill in her book written in 1920, titled *Iona*, Phelim mac (son of) Fergus was a great-grandson of Niall (Noigiallach) who ruled as High King of Royal Tara from 379 to c.450AD. Phelim mac Fergus was the father of Prince Columba. (According to an historical book of names 'Phelim' is a variant of Pelles/Pallas).

In the account given by Sir Thomas Malory (d.1471), Sir Galahad was described as belonging to the kindred of Joseph of Arimathea and he was a grandson of Pelles for his mother Elaine, Lancelot's wife, was the daughter of King Pelles of Ireland.

Sir Thomas Malory was not an author, so just how did he come by this knowledge?

He was a knight in service to Richard Neville, the 16th Earl of Warwick and was also a Member of Parliament for Warwickshire. He originally began campaigning for the Yorkists. For some unknown reason, Malory swapped sides from the Yorkists to the Lancastrians, whereby he was later imprisoned on 'trumped up' charges and from 1451 AD, he spent most of his life in confinement. He was accused of numerous crimes, but it is thought that because of his political activities, he was framed.

Whilst imprisoned, Malory translated and adapted his work of over twelve hundred pages of script from the immensely long French cycles of the Arthurian romances, which glorified the quest for the *Holy Grail* as the quest of the Knights. He was not known as a writer, but rather as a knight who distinguished himself during the War of the Roses.

According to Emile Legouis in the book titled *A History of English Literature*:

"Among the prose versions of old romances published by Caxton [who invented the printing machine], there was one which was to be not only food for the people but also a feast for the fastidious. Caxton was well inspired on the day he printed Sir Thomas Malory's *Morte d'Arthur*. He tells us that when he had published the noble feats of Hector of Champagne, and Godfrey de Bouillon, he was 'instantly required' by 'many noble and divers gentlemen' also to imprint those of Arthur who belonged to the realm of England."

"In reply, he pleaded that 'diver's men hold opinion that there was no such Arthur,' yet allowed himself to be persuaded. The translation he used was ready to hand, having been made by Thomas Malory, knight, Member of Parliament and Lancastrian, who shared the misfortunes of his party and died in 1471. His translation was completed in 1469, and published in 1484."

"Malory represents himself as translating a French book. In truth he seems to have had recourse to many books, so that his *Morte d'Arthur* is a compilation. He has brought together scattered romances and co-ordinated them, without eliminating the traces of disparity."

"Despite the immense Parentheses which recount the separate adventures of Sir Balin, Sir Pelles, Sir Palomides, Sir Bors...we can distinguish in his work the lines of a dominant story, that of Arthur, which is logically followed by the tale of the Sangreal [Holy Grail]. The charm of this prose is that it is made up of poetic reminiscences inherited from a long line of earlier poems."

There is the likelihood that whilst Malory was imprisoned, he was coerced by Margaret of Anjou into translating the French version of *Morte d'Arthur (The Death of Arthur)*. Margaret was married to Henry VI, Plantagenet King of England and was the daughter of the famous Rene, Count of Anjou, who was also the titled king of Jerusalem whose ancestor, Godfrey de Bouillon, was the conqueror of Jerusalem in 1099, during the Crusades at which time he took the title 'king of Jerusalem'.

According to the authors Michael Baigent, Richard Leigh and Henry Lincoln in their book titled *The Holy Blood And The Holy Grail*, Rene was the grand Helmsman of the Priory of Sion [which was an offshoot of the Order of the Rose Cross and of the Freemasons]. The Priory of Sion (another name for Jerusalem), had been established by Godfrey de Bouillon during the First Crusade. Although he became the titled king of Jerusalem, he preferred to be called 'The Guardian of the Holy Sepulchre'.

"There was a secret order behind the Knights Templar which created the Templars as its military and administrative arm. This order, which has functioned under a variety of names, is most frequently known as the 'Priory of Sion'. It has been directed by a sequence of Grand Masters whose names are among the most illustrious in Western history and culture. Although the Knights Templar were destroyed and dissolved between 1307 and 1314 AD, the Priory of Sion remained unscathed. Acting in the shadows, behind the scenes, it has orchestrated certain of the critical events in Western history."

The Earl of Warwick, Richard Neville (who was the employer of Sir Thomas Malory), was often referred to as the 'king maker' who had ambitions to have a Lancastrian king upon the throne. The House of Lancaster was a branch of the Plantagenet family and the House of York was an English Royal House which was also related to the Plantagenet royal lineage, thus the War of the Roses was really a battle between two rivalling dynastic families.

Margaret, the daughter of Rene of Anjou, was a member of the Angevin dynasty from whom the Plantagenets were descended and her husband, Henry, as previously stated, was a Plantagenet. This family believed themselves to be related dynastically to the family of the Holy Grail and believed in their own destiny as such. The Priory of Sion of which her father Rene, was the Grand Helmsman, was concerned with the lineage of the House of Judah - the House of David.

According to Emile Legouis in the book titled *A History of English Literature*, relating back to the 12th century: "The Norman and Angevin kings remained intellectually continental and French until they lost Normandy and Anjou in 1204. Many of the best French writers of the time lived at their court; many of the principal works of the 12th century were composed there. The reign of Henry II (1154-99) marks the zenith of this literary glory."

During the War of the Roses, Margaret sided with the Lancastrians. Her husband, Henry, was unfortunately given to bouts of insanity and at one stage, in 1456, Margaret sided with Richard, 3rd Duke of York, when she left Henry and dispatched a force which clashed with Richard Neville, the 16th Earl of Warwick.

The first engagement of the War of the Roses between the House of York and the House of Lancaster took place in May 1455 at St Albans (the original area of Verulam), where St Germain had once lived as St Alban.

Henry had been captured in a battle in March 1460 and Richard, 3rd Duke of York, who was one of England's most powerful nobles, forced Henry to acknowledge him as his heir. As fate would have it, Richard was slain in battle in December of the same year, and instead of Henry and Margaret's son, Prince Edward, becoming heir to the throne, Richard the 3rd Duke of York's son, Edward, became King Edward IV of England. Henry's loyalty was strongest towards the Lancastrians who were defeated by the Yorkists at Towton in 1461, at which time Margaret and Henry fled north to take refuge in Scotland.

Then in 1465, Margaret allied herself with Richard Neville, Duke of Warwick, who had fled to France, possibly to Margaret's father, Rene of Anjou, because this was where Margaret took refuge and she and Neville were in league with one another.

Rene I was the second son of Louis II, King of Naples, Duke of Anjou and Sicily. He was a superb manuscript illuminator, an accomplished poet, artist and musician. His sister, Mary, was the wife of King Charles VII of France. Rene's ancestry could be traced back to Geoffrey, the Count of Anjou who in the year 1128 married Matilda, the daughter of the Plantagenet King, Henry I of England.

Henry I, was the founder of the great dynasty of kings through his son Henry II and Eleanor of Aquitaine, the mother of Marie of Champagne at whose court, Chrétien of Troyes resided during the time that he wrote his Grail Romances.

In an earlier chapter it was mentioned that Rene, as King of Naples, was a very close friend of Cosimo de Medici and encouraged him in the founding of the Platonic Academy in Florence, which promoted the sacred Teachings of Arcadia and thus of the *Mystical Rose*.

Rene also played an important role in assisting Joan of Arc (1412-1431), (an earlier incarnation of the Lady Master, Madame Helena Blavatsky) to whom the Archangel Michael made appearances telling her of her destiny. (After Joan of Arc's victory, King Charles VII of France created his own Scots Guard for protection. These Scots Guard became members of the *Order of St Michael* and later a branch of this Order was established in Scotland and gave their allegiance to the French Crown. The members were made up of distinguished families in Scotland, including some Stuarts and it was through them being members of the *Order of St Michael* that the young Scottish nobles received their training and initiations into Freemasonry).

It was during the War of the Roses that St Michael's Mount at Marazion in Cornwall was taken possession of by the Earl of Oxford. He and his men entered St Michael's Mount disguised as pilgrims. They were given supplies of ammunition and plenty of provisions by the Earl's friends and relations who lived in the area of Marazion.

The Earl of Oxford was eventually captured and St Michael's Mount was regained by King Henry VII. Fights for possession of the Mount continued until the time of Queen Elizabeth I (the mother of Francis Bacon), at which time the Mount was sold to the enemy of Francis Bacon, namely Robert Cecil who was his cousin.

As discussed elsewhere, the Mount was, and still is, a main area where the energy Ley lines intersect and it would have been one of the places where members of the Dragon Society would meet. (The Dragon Society worshipped the earth's sacred energies and according to the author Michael Howard in his book titled *The Occult Conspiracy*, its members included Sir John Dee [Kuthumi], Elizabeth I, Sir Francis Drake and Francis Bacon). The fact that Robert Cecil acquired the Mount would indicate that he too belonged to the same society.

In conclusion upon the subject of Sir Thomas Malory, there is no other literary work that he ever achieved except the translation of *Morte d'Arthur*, which contained the legends of the Grail Family which could be traced back to Joseph of Arimathea (John the Beloved - Kuthumi) of Jerusalem.

The links between Margaret, her father Rene - Grand Helmsman of the Priory of Sion (Jerusalem), Richard Neville, the Duke of Warwick, and his knight Sir Thomas Malory, whose source of his French manuscripts has always been such a mystery, are too much for mere coincidence. They obviously came via Rene of Anjou who was obsessed with the Grail legends so bound up with the Stone of Destiny, the 'Perilous Seat', of which Sir Thomas Malory wrote.

CONCLUSION:

Sir Lancelot's son, Sir Galahad was Fergus Mor mac Erc (son of 'Erc') who first brought the 'Perilous Seat' - the 'Stone of Destiny' to Scotland. Fergus reigned as Pendragon in the early 500's AD which means he would have been born about 487 AD which was the approximate time allotted for the birth of Sir Galahad.

Fergus Mor mac Erc (alias Sir Galahad), was the one 'destined' to take the famous throne to Scotland and from that time onwards, all the High Kings of Scots were crowned upon it. Chrétien of Troyes' romantic work *Erc and Enide* would have been based upon this particular 'Erc'. According to an historical book of names by Michele Brown, 'Enid' was an English form of Eithne, (Athena).

The true identity of Merlin and Arthur of the 6th century are still to be revealed!

MASTERS DISCUSSED IN THIS CHAPTER

Merlin/Taliesin, 'Defender of the Faith' - St Germain
St Alban, 'Defender of the Faith' - St Germain
William the Lion of Scots, 'Defender of the Faith' - St Germain
Francis Bacon, 'Defender of the Faith' - St Germain
Joseph of Arimathea (John the Beloved), First Master of the Holy Grail - Kuthumi
St Patrick, 'Defender of the Faith' - Kuthumi
King Arthur 'Defender of the Faith'- Kuthumi

NOTES AND RECOMMENDED READING

Emile Legouis, *A History of English Literature*, (J.M. Dent & Sons Ltd., U.K. 1945)
Chrétien de Troyes, *Arthurian Romances*, (trans. Owen, Dent, U.K. 1987)
William Francis Collier, L.L.D. *Central Figures Of Irish History*, (Trinity College, Dublin, 1891
John Grenham, *Clans and Families of Ireland, The Heritage and Heraldry of Irish Clans & Families*, (Bramley Books, U.K., 1993)
R.Tapsell, *Monarchs, Rulers, Dynasties and Kingdoms of the World*, (Thames & Hudson, U.K.).
Alfred Lord Tennyson, *Morte d'Arthur*, (The Oxford Anthology of English Literature, Oxford University Press, U.K., 1973)
Sir Thomas Malory, *Morte d'Arthur*, (The Oxford Anthology of English Literature, Oxford University Press, U.K., 1973)
Mike Dixon Kennedy, *Celtic Myth & Legend*, (Blandford, U.K. 1996)
Michael Howard, *The Occult Conspiracy*, (Ryder & Ryder, U.K. 1989)
Michael Baigent, Richard Leigh & Henry Lincoln, *The Holy Blood And The Holy Grail*, (Arrow Books, U.K., 1996)
Michele Brown, *Baby Name Book* Historical Book of Names (Greenwich Editions, U.K. 1985)
Donald Attwater and Catherine Rachel John, *Penguin Dictionary of Saints*, (Penguin Books, U.K. 1995)

John St Aubyn, *St Michael's Mount.*

Elizabeth Hallam, *The Plantagenet Encyclopedia*, (Tiger Books International, U.K., 1996)

Stephen Beyer, *The Cult of Tara*, (University of California Press, 1978)

T.H. White, *The Once And Future King*, (Collins, U.K. 1958)

T.H. White, *The Book of Merlin*, (Collins, U.K. 1978)

David Day, *The Quest For King Arthur*, (De Agostini Editions, U.K., 1995)

Geoffrey of Monmouth, *The History of the Kings of Britain*, (edited by Lewis Thorpe, Penguin, 1966)

Geoffrey of Monmouth, *The Vita Merlini*, (trans. J.J. Parry, University of Illinois, 1925)

CHAPTER 32

St Columba & Iona

"The reason I love Derry is for its peace,
for its purity
and for its clouds of angels from one end to the other"
"In Iona of my heart, Iona my love,
Instead of monk's voices shall be lowing of cows"
(St Columba)

Whilst Princess Eithne was sleeping one night, an angel appeared to her in her dream-state. The angel stood before her and offered her a robe of exquisite beauty and then took it from her and spread it out till it covered the mountains, lochs and forests, reaching across the sea as far as Albion (Scotland).

From this sign, the mother knew that her child was to be the child of whom the prophecies of St Patrick and St Brigit had foretold in the previous century....her child was to be the 'Dove' of the North of Ireland.

As has been established in previous chapters, it was common for parents to receive an angelic visitation when the birth of a great avatar was imminent, or a sign would appear in the sky such as a large star as in the case of the birth of Jesus. A new star was symbolic of the birth of a 'Child of Light'.

Thus, on the 4th December, 521 AD at Gartan, a wild mountainous district in Donegal, Columba was born. Upon his birth, the child was given two names. The first name was *Crimthan* in honour of his great grandfather who was Conall Crimthainne (Crimthin) meaning 'fierce as a wolf', and the second name was *Columba* (Latin for *'Dove'*).

It was discussed in the previous chapter that Columba was of noble lineage, descended from the Royal House of Neill (Niall). His father, Phelim mac Fergus, was a great grandson of Niall, High King of Ireland. Niall's son, Conall Crimthin, who was Columba's great grandfather, was the one who was baptised/initiated by St Patrick (Kuthumi) and it was this same family who reputedly captured Patrick and brought him to Ireland. Columba's father Phelim mac Fergus appears to have been a son of Fergus Mor mac Erc (son of 'Erc) who brought the Stone of Destiny from Tara to Argyll. It was established in the previous chapter that the one known as Sir Galahad in the Arthurian legends, may have been Fergus for it was he who crowned himself upon the Stone of Destiny in Argyll, the Stone which could adequately be called 'the Perilous Seat', and possibly his father, Erc, was Sir Lancelot.

As mentioned elsewhere in our story, Sir Lancelot's wife, Elaine, was an Irish princess whose father's name was King Pelles. Therefore, it is not coincidence that Columba's father was called Phelim, for according to an historical book of names, Phelim means Pelles/Pallas. Neither could it be coincidence that Columba's mother's name was Eithne, which is a variant of 'Athena', the goddess of 'Wisdom' who is so closely associated with Arcadia and whose male counterpart is Pallas.

Also discussed in the previous chapter, was the fact that the great grandfather of Columba, Conall Crimthin, had a brother, Layary, who had a daughter, Princess Eithne the Fair, who was also baptised/initiated by St Patrick (Kuthumi). In all probability, it was this Princess Eithne who married Phelim mac Fergus and became the mother of Columba.

By lineage of descent, Columba was a royal prince who could have become the High King of Dalriata in Ulster, Ireland; however, his destiny was already planned and it did not include kingship. Later to be called *Colum Cille, Dove of the Church*, this special child, Columba, was destined to protect the Celtic Church and its sacred traditions, such as the Druidic teachings handed down from the ancient days of Egypt.

Prince Columba was furthering the work that John the Beloved (alias Joseph of Arimathea who was the Master Kuthumi), had commenced when he founded the first Celtic Church at Glastonbury in 37 - 38 AD.

During the 6th century, the Church of Rome was anxious to continue converting the whole of Britain to its own doctrines and dispense with what they considered 'pagan' religions such as the Celtic Druids. It was an important era in history which once again, required the reincarnations of some of the Masters of the Great White Brotherhood.

In the era that Prince Columba was born into, Justinian was the Emperor of Rome; Gregory who was later to become Pope, was still a law student in Rome, and Europe was in a state of upheaval.

Columba's Early Education - The Order of the Bards

"I was Bard of the Harp
to the Don (Lord) of Llychlyn (Dublin)
(Taliesin/Merlin/St Germain)

Columba's scholastic abilities became very apparent when he was still a child. He was therefore placed in the care of St Finnian at an ecclesiastical school at Movilla in County Down and it was there that he was later ordained as a deacon. At the monastic school of St Finnian, Columba became a member of the *Order of the Bards.*

Through his initial training, Columba was to always retain the love that he had acquired for the old poetic tales, the mythology of his race. He became a poet/bard of very high renown. Columba was also an accomplished 'initiate' into the 'Greater Mysteries'.

After his tutorage with St Finnian, Columba moved to Leinster where he studied the native literature from a Bard of that province *and then proceeded to Glasnevin near Dublin before returning to his native Ulster.*

The verse quoted under this heading by Taliesin, tells us that whoever Taliesin was, (although we know he was Merlin), he served for a time as a Bard at the court of the Lord of Dublin. Could he have known St Columba?

One of Columba's numerous talents was the power of organization, a talent that he was to put to excellent use in a future incarnation. He was a prophet and a brilliant student who displayed his incredible talents at a very early age.

By the age of twenty-four, Columba established a monastery at Derry (meaning Oak Grove), on a site that had been given to him by one of his kinsmen of the clan of Ui Neill. Prior to this, Columba had visited Tours in Gaul (now France) from whence it is thought he obtained the ideas which he incorporated into the monastery at Derry.

The chosen site was situated in a grove of oak trees because the 'oak' was very sacred to the Druids and Columba insisted that as few as possible were to be cut down to make way for the monastery. The Druids of Columba's time had a love of the arts and a passion for music. They were a people steeped in mysticism, that dominating sense of the unseen with a conviction of the existence of the spiritual world. This they held in common with the Essenes, and like the Essenes, they wore white robes as a symbol of purity.

Columba's early education was such that it enabled him to carry out all his ambitions to the fullest. He was ahead or a 'Head' of his time. Columba was a highly 'initiated' member of the Order of the Druids and became an Archdruid. Wherever Columba travelled in Ireland, he founded monasteries of which over three hundred are ascribed to him and the most famous of these monasteries in Ireland, were Durrow and Kells.

Scholars who have studied the *Book of Kells* consider that the author/artist was St Columba. Two other splendid manuscripts attributed to him are the *Catharch*, a Psalter in the Library of the Royal Irish Academy, and *The Book of Durrow*, the Gospels in the library of Trinity College Dublin.

According to William Francis Collier in his book titled *Central Figures In Irish History*, the word 'Catharch' meant 'Fighter' and the *Catharch* was carried through a hundred battles as the sacred Talisman of the Ui Neill clan. "It consists of fifty-eight parchment leaves, enclosed in a silver case."

Columba also wrote numerous prophecies, hymns and poems.

His biographer, Adamnan recorded how Columba spent a great deal of his time reading, writing and using his artistic skills upon the documents that are now antiquities, having survived almost in tact some 1,400 years later.

This affirms that Columba was not only a scribe (author) but a renowned poet and it is of interest to note that **not only was he a member of the Order of the Druids, but he was to defend the Order of the Bards at the Convention of Drumceat in 575 AD.**

The Book of Kells

At this stage in our story, it is pertinent to discuss the Book of Kells attributed to St Columba.

In 1996, my family and I visited Trinity College in Dublin where the 6th century AD Book of Kells is housed. We stood patiently in the queue in the room which is kept specifically darkened so as to prevent the light from fading the famous manuscript of the Four Evangelists.

As my eyes became adjusted to the darkness, I suddenly began to see a red glow and gradually my Master Teacher, a Master of the Mystical Rose, began to manifest himself in front of me in etheric form, until his rose-red uniform with its gold crosses down the front of the jacket where normally buttons would be, became very apparent.

I could feel his wonderful energy surrounding me and the experience was just as profound as the summer's evening in 1993, when he had first appeared to me in my garden by the pool at which time I could smell the divine scent of 'roses' where there were none growing.

He was so visible to me when I was only a matter of minutes away from viewing the Book of Kells, that I became agitated when a woman in front of me stepped backwards and through him. I then realized that he was invisible to anyone else in the room, except me.

The significance of this moment startled me incredibly. By acknowledging his presence to me since the first time that I had left Australia, I knew that I had been divinely guided to be there. I knew then, just how important were the symbols contained within the Book of Kells, e.g. *St George's (Kuthumi's) Cross,* the *Maltese Cross* and the *Saltire -* St Andrew's Cross (X).

I was already very familiar with my Guide's blue mantle with the Maltese Cross on the back, however, I knew in that profound moment that the gold crosses down his jacket were not only symbolic of the *Saltire* but also of the sacred Pythagorean X, and I knew that Pythagoras had once been Kuthumi. Thus, with a feeling of great humility and wonderment, I knew for certain at last who the Knight of the Order of the Rose Cross was, for I know his symbols well.

Within the space of three weeks, Kuthumi was again to make another important appearance to me, this time in England, yet again giving me further confirmation and it wasn't long after that, as pieces of the jig-saw puzzle finally began to fall into place - particularly with the synchronicity and visions which occurred, that I realised why I was required to write this story of *The Masters of the Mystical Rose.*

Later, when we visited the Dublin museum to see the famous Ardagh Chalice, and the Tara Brooch, there, in the foyer in a large glass display cabinet, was a uniform of the Knights of the Order of St Patrick which was also very similar to the one my Guide wears - black trousers, rose-red jacket and a blue mantle.

The chivalric Order of St Patrick (Kuthumi) was founded in 1783 until 1908, being an Irish equivalent of such English institutions as the Orders of the Bath, and the Garter - Freemasonic Orders. The valuable insignia of the Grand Masters of the Order of St Patrick were kept in Dublin Castle. A photo in the book titled *Clans and Families of Ireland* depicts the main jewel of the Order as an oval medallion filled with precious stones. In the centre is a red rose-coloured Saltire Cross (or Pythagorean X), suspended from a magnificent gold chain beginning with a red rose, and alternated by intricate gold filigree knots, harps and finishing with a red rose. Unfortunately, the beautifully jewelled collar was stolen in 1908 and has never been recovered. Its whereabouts still remain a mystery!

Columba's Journey to Iona

In Columba's era, what is now Scotland was divided into several small principalities; North and South of the Grampians were the Northern and Southern Picts; in the South-West were the Britons of Strathclyde and the Picts of Galloway; in the South-East were a group of English settlers (Angles) whose king fortified the rock of Edwin's Burg (Edinburgh); and lastly, there was a colony of Scots or Gaelic Celts, who had crossed from Ireland in the 5th century and spread over what is now Argyll (Land of the Gaels) and the adjacent isles.

According to William Francis Collier in his book titled *Central Figures In Irish* History: "**These Scots, of the tribe of Dalriata Ireland (Dalriada Scotland) to which race Columba belonged, were destined to give to the land of their adoption its name, its Royal House and its religion**".

After the death of St Ninian, who had been sent to work amongst the Picts by St Germain in his incarnation as St Germanus, the Picts then lapsed back into their old ways.

They were a much more powerful tribe, who after a major victory in 560 AD, were nearly successful in expelling the Scots of Dalriada in the area of Argyll.

It was in 560 AD, three years prior to the arrival of Columba in Albany (Scotland) that the Scots settlers of Dalriada suffered a crushing defeat at the hands of Brude, King of the Northern Picts. Brude was the son of Maelchon who was the ruler of all the lands north of the Forth and the Clyde.

The Scottish people of Dalriada's king, a kinsman of Columba and of the kindred of Gabran, had been slain and there was danger that the whole colony would be wiped out.

At the time that Columba decided to establish a monastic Centre of Learning on the island of Iona, there had not only been numerous invasions by the Picts from the North, but also by the Saxons in the Argyllshire area of Albany (Scotland) where the people of Dalriada had established themselves. The channel which separates County Antrim where the People of Dalriata belonged and Argyllshire where the People of Dalriada settled is only twelve miles wide and the houses of Kintyre can be seen from the Irish coast opposite. Iona lay on the borderland between the country of the Picts and the realm of the Scottish Dalriada. (It is just off the coast of Mull, and in these modern days, just a mere ten minutes by ferry).

It is generally considered that this threat to his people of Dalriada was the main reason for Columba leaving his beloved Ireland, in order to save his kinsmen.

Although Columba was born a prince, who could have become a High King and probably even ruled from the seat of the royal palace of Tara, it was at this point of time in his life, that Columba had to make choices. We are informed by William Francis Collier in his book titled *Central Figures In Irish History* as follows:

"At this period of Columcille's [Columba's] life, a question seemed to tremble in the balance, whether his path of life should lie amid crowns and swords, or amid the gentler victories of the crosier and the missal; for in those times a man of royal lineage never knew at what hour he might be summoned to wear a crown - too often of blood and thorns."

"In the veins of Columcille the hot warrior-blood ran red; but he was not destined to wield the sword."

Before his departure for Iona, Columba on behalf of his own people in Antrim was involved in a tribal skirmish with the High King of Sligo, King Diarmid, who imprisoned Columba. According to William Francis Collier, he escaped but was pursued by soldiers lurking in the woods.

"He struck into a pathless region, and as he went on his way, the silence of the lonely hills fell like dew upon his fevered brain, and soothed him into song. There is no sweeter or more pious utterance in the ancient Irish tongue than Columcille's *Song of Trust*, composed during this perilous moor-land journey to the North."

And so in 563 AD, at the age of forty-two years, the prince of the northern Ui Neill of Dalriata, along with twelve companions (disciples), crossed the sea from Ireland to Albany, Argyllshire in western Scotland in a coracle made of wicker and hides, which was the mode of sea transport in those days.

Upon his arrival in Albany, Columba's first mission was to control the out of control Picts and bring them into line. The court of King Brude was at Inverness in the north of Scotland and St Columba carefully chose two trusted friends to accompany him, Kenneth and Comgall.

The 'Perilous' Journey undertaken by Columba

The journey undertaken by Columba to visit Brude sounds not unlike the one that Sir Lancelot in the Arthurian legends, undertook. According to the author of the *Book of Iona*, Florence Marian McNeil:

"The route lay due north-east through the Great Glens of Alban and through a continuous line of long, narrow lochs, now linked by the Caledonian Canal. So wild a region with its dark, brooding mountains and primeval forests, could be traversed only on foot and the whole adventure must have involved *perils* of water, *perils* of robbers, *perils* in the wilderness known to the apostles of old."

Within the legends of Lancelot, the word *perilous* occurs numerous times. Lancelot comes to a 'perilous bridge', a 'perilous chapel', a 'perilous castle', a 'perilous ford', a 'perilous forest', a 'perilous river', a 'perilous seat' to be occupied at a future time after the death of Jesus, by Lancelot's son, Sir Galahad. This 'perilous seat', as has been established, was the Stone of Destiny taken by Fergus Mor mac Erc to Albany, Scotland in circa 500 AD. On a visit to Dunstaffnage Castle in 2001, I learned that the coronation of Fergus upon the Stone of Destiny took place at Dunstaffnage where it was first housed. Later it was transported to Iona.

Returning to the story of the 'perilous journey'... Columba and his two companions, Kenneth and Comgall, arrived safely at the court of Brude where they were greeted by King Brude's chief Druid, Briochan. Briochan at first encouraged Brude to refuse them admittance, however, Columba showed Briochan a certain 'cross' whereupon the doors which Briochan had bolted, flew open as if by magic!

Within the Arthurian legends, there is mention of a 'pagan' named *Bademagus*, which is obviously a pun for 'Bad Magus' or 'Bad Magi'. In other words, the person was a member of the Druids, but considered to be an undesirable one. Bademagus was thought to have been the deputy of King Urien of Gorre. King Urien is more likely to have been King Brude of the Picts and Bademagus the influential Chief Druid of his Court, whose name was Briochan.

Although Columba and his two monks initiated the conversion of King Brude of the Picts and his clan, it was to be King Aedan mac Gabran who would sign the alliance at the Convention of Drumceat at Derry in Ireland in 575 AD. It was at this same Convention that Columba as an *Archdruid* was to defend the Order of the Bards.

The result of the meeting was to ensure that King Brude of the Picts and his people would maintain peaceful relations with the People of Dalriada and from that time onwards, Brude was to remain a staunch friend of King Aedan and Columba. It was Columba who had rescued Aedan from the impositions placed upon him and his people by Aedh mac Ainmuirech who was the rival King of Tara who is discussed in the following chapter.

As a result of Columba establishing Iona, it was to become the major Celtic monastic centre for the next two hundred years to which people travelled from far and wide, to study the ancient Mysteries and Sacred Teachings and undertake various initiations.

Another name for Iona was *Innis nam Druidneach* meaning the Island of the Cunning Workmen or Sculptors (Masons) and still another name by which it was known was *Innis-nam-Druidneach* - 'The Isle of the Druids'.

The Hebrew word *Iona* corresponds to the Latin *Columba* and both mean the *'Dove'*. It was not the first time in history that the symbolism of the Dove was equated with Masters of the Great White Brotherhood - it will be remembered that Noah's (St Germain's) symbol was the 'Dove of Peace'.

Thus the angelic visitation to Eithne (Athena), Columba's mother, came to fruition. The 'Dove from the North' of Ireland, did indeed spread the sacred Teachings from Ireland to Scotland.

Something that Merlin and Columba had in common was that they were both prophets and many of their prophecies came true within their own lifetime.

Considering that Merlin and Columba were both Druids and Bards who lived in the same time period of the 6th century, it would seem reasonable to assume that they would have known each other, and/or maybe they were even educated at the same educational institutions. The monastic educational centres available in those days were few and far between. There were those in Gaul, such as Auxerre where St Germain had been a bishop in the 5th century and the others were in Ireland.

Columba, being a royal prince, would have known King Arthur and therefore he would have known the *Merlin* who trained Arthur to be a High King of the Celts and a 'Defender of the Faith'.

MASTERS DISCUSSED IN THIS CHAPTER

Noah - St Germain
Taliesin/Merlin - St Germain
King Arthur - Kuthumi

NOTES AND RECOMMENDED READING

Florence Marian McNeill, *Iona*, (Blackie & Sons, Glasgow, Scotland, 1920)

John Grenham, *Clans and Families of Ireland*, (Bramley Books, U.K. 1993)

Peter Bander, *The Prophecies of St Malachy and St Columbkille*, (Colin Smythe, U.K., 1969)

Ian Grimble, *Scottish Islands*, (British Broadcasting Commission, U.K., 1985)

R. Tapsell, *Monarchs, Rulers, Dynasties and Kingdoms of the World*, (Thames & Hudson, U.K.)

Barry Cunliffe, *The Celtic World*, (Bodley Head, U.K. 1979)

Donald Attwater and Catherine Rachel John, *Penguin Dictionary of Saints*, (Penguin, U.K., 1995)

William Francis Collier, *Central Figures In Irish History*, (Marcus Ward & Co. U.K. 1891)

Lesley Whiteside, *In Search of Columba*, (Columba Press, Dublin, 1997)

CHAPTER 33

King Arthur, Merlin, & Avalon

"Tara which you now see so prosperous,
Shall be covered with grass - all its buildings as well as its elevated site,
It shall not be long ere it becomes a desert..."
(St Columba)
Three times the fullness of Prydwen, we went on sea
Three times the fullness of Prydwen, we went with Arthur
(Taliesin/Merlin/St Germain)

"And lo! they took Arthur,
And swiftly they bare him down,
And softly him laid down,
And forth began their sailing.
Then it was accomplished.
What Merlin said would happen,
That great woe would follow
On Arthur's forthfaring.
Still think Briton's
That Arthur liveth
And dwelleth in Avalon.
(Layamon circa 1170 AD)

"Prophesy of Arthur,
Or is it me they celebrate?
(Taliesin/Merlin/St Germain)

It has been established in the previous chapter that when Columba was born a prince, he could have become a High King and probably even ruled from the royal palace of Tara, whose eventual downfall he prophesied. However, he chose instead to become a monk in order to establish hundreds of Celtic monasteries and protect the traditions of the Celtic Druids, from the encroaching Church of Rome. And, shortly in this chapter, we will see that in order to do this, he utilized a pseudonym for his writings.

From an article which appeared in *New Dawn* magazine, January, 1997, based upon information supplied by the Life Science Fellowship in Melbourne, we learn the following pertinent information:

"Communities of Celtic Christians, who refused to bow to Imperial Rome, continued for several centuries. Reviewing Celtic Christianity we discover that it was quite unlike both Roman Catholicism and evangelical Protestantism. Christianity was mystical and esoteric, insisting on a way of life that unites, rather than vain theologies that divide. The following are some of the special features of the Celtic Church:

1. A profound respect and care for the environment and a desire to live in harmony with the natural world.
2. A love of solitude and silence was always a hallmark of Celtic spirituality.
3. A passion for scholarship and learning. This feature, inherited from the Druids, was responsible for the 'Golden Age' of faith and learning in *Ireland*, and enabled Celtic monasteries to re-ignite the flame of learning in Europe.
4. Simplicity was a strong feature of the Celtic Church.
5. Not being burdened with the excessive structure and law of the Roman Church, the Celtic Church relied on personal relationships for internal cohesion and for mutual support. The importance of family and clan that so permeate the secular life of the Celt carried into the Church. A particular manifestation of this was the 'Anamchara' or 'Soul-Friend', someone with whom one could share all, and from whom one could count on for sound advice. The Anamchara could be either ordained or a lay person, of the same or other gender. St Brigid of Kildare said: 'A person without an Anamchara is a body without a head'."
6. Much more than any of the Churches, the Celtic church upheld the equality and dignity of women. There are letters from Roman Church authorities criticizing the Celtic Church for the fair and just treatment of women that the Celts practiced in ecclesiastical affairs. Brigid, the Patron St of Ireland, was a Bishop."

"The Celtic Church points us back to a lost heritage. By retracing our steps, we may yet discover that inner dimension of the Message of Jesus the Christ, so vital for modern Man, if he is to connect with his inner self."

The people we have to thank for establishing the early Celtic Church and its traditions firmly in Ireland who were later recognised as saints, have previously been discussed, but the one who achieved the most was the 'Dove from the North', namely, Columba.

At the time that Columba founded the monastery on the island of Iona, it acquired great prestige and soon became the ecclesiastical head of the Celtic Church in Ireland and Scotland.

Merlin and Arthur

'By Johannes (John) the Diviner (Divine) I was called Myrddin (Merlin)
"Prophesy of Arthur or is it me they celebrate?"
(Taliesin/Merlin/St Germain)

It is important to remember that Merlin was a very highly initiated Druid, a poet, and a prophet of renown. Merlin wrote his poetry under the pseudonym of Taliesin and upon reviewing information given in the first chapter, according to Robert Graves in his book titled *The White Goddess*:

"The poet who called himself Taliesin, Chief of Bards, was well versed in Latin, French, Welsh, English, the Irish Classics, Greek and Hebrew literature too. Whoever Taliesin was, he was hiding an ancient religious mystery - a blasphemous one from the Church of Rome's point of view - under the cloak of buffoonery, but had not made his secret altogether impossible to guess."

"It was done this way deliberately, with the medleys reading like nonsense only because the texts had been deliberately confused, doubtless as a precaution against them being denounced as 'heretical' by some Church officer. During the 6th century AD, whoever Taliesin was, he spent much of his time as a guest of various Celtic chiefs and princes to whom he wrote complimentary poems. The author of the poems was a paganistic cleric with Irish connections and he was connected to the ancient House of Tewdwr (Tudor)."

The authority on Freemasonry and Rosicrucianism, Manly Hall wrote that:

"Taliesin was an ancient scholar and a Druidic priest who had passed through all the 'Mysteries' which have been preserved from antiquity."

Gwyn and Thomas Jones in their introduction of *The Mabinogion* (which contains the stories of Taliesin) wrote the following pertinent information:

"The 'author' was considered to be the heir of bards and storytellers unnumbered. He was a great artist which no competent judge has ever denied. The natural turn of his mind was towards harmony and proportion and one senses in him at all times, sanity and the spacious mind."

"He wrote the finest Welsh prose of his age, a *grand master* who never for one sentence intrudes the veil of style between the reader and what is read. The author achieved the effect of illumination and extension of time and space which lies beyond the reach of all save the world's greatest writers. *He was an artist who concealed his art.*"

"Frequently we recognise an assumption on the author's part of a knowledge

we do not possess. Its best stories give what only a genius can do and this genius was a Celtic one."

St Germain in his incarnation as Francis Bacon, who wrote under the pseudonym of Shakespeare - the 'Shaker of the Truth' was the greatest Bard the world has known since Taliesin!

By now it should have become obvious to the reader that Taliesin went to great lengths to disguise within his poems, his true identity even though he tells us that he was Merlin.

The Merlin of the 6th century AD was St Columba who was the 'Dove from the North', the one who was prophesied by St Patrick (Kuthumi) and St Brigid (whom in all probability was the Lady Portia, the twin soul of St Germain).

When Taliesin wrote: "By John the Diviner (Divine) I was called Merlin", he was referring to the fact that the person who had once been John the Divine, the Beloved Disciple, had reincarnated into the 6th century AD and knew the poet as 'Merlin'. They had known each other during the 1st century AD when John had been the Beloved/Divine disciple alias Joseph of Arimathea (Kuthumi), who was Joseph's (St Germain's) son, and Joseph was the Father of the Holy Grail Family.

In the first chapter, part of the Lady Portia's story of St Germain was discussed. The channelling of Claire Heartsong in the book titled *St Germain Twin Souls & Soulmates* is very relevant at this point of time in our story.

Portia is telling of St Germain's incarnation as Sir Francis Bacon:

"He was a lad who took a number of grand pilgrimages. He followed the steps of a previous embodiment that he had known as Merlin - one of the Merlins. There was with him in the court one who previously had walked with him as Arthur (King)."

The person was Sir John Dee - Kuthumi who assisted Francis Bacon in the translation of what became known as the King James Authorized Version of the Bible.

In the first chapter of our story, Dr Raymond Bernard in his book titled *The Great Secret Count Saint* Germain was quoted thus:

"The King James translation of the Bible and the Shakespeare Plays - the two greatest masterpieces of the English language, which did so much to make this language what it is - were both the creations of Francis Bacon; and while his editorship of the Bible is easier to understand, his authorship of the Shakespeare Plays is generally not admitted."

"Yet both literary productions reveal themselves, by their unique superior excellence, to have had a common author."

Like the Essenes' Teacher of Righteousness, it was the task of Merlin (writing under the name of Taliesin), to reveal the great secrets of the world, transmitted in such a way, that those who did not understand his poetry and messages, would not be able to misconstrue them.

"I was with Bran in Ireland'

(Taliesin/Merlin)
Three times the fullness of Prydwen, we went on sea
Three times the fullness of Prydwen, we went with Arthur
(Taliesin/Merlin/St Germain)

It has been mentioned in an earlier chapter that it was Geoffrey of Monmouth (Wales) who wrote the story of Merlin and Arthur in the 12th century AD, six hundred years after the historical events had taken place.

Commenting upon Geoffrey of Monmouth, Emile Legouis in the book titled *A History of English Literature* (1945) wrote: "Geoffrey is, in large part, the creator of the Arthurian legend. His book is a work of imagination in disguise, and it is impossible to say to what extent tradition helped him. But it was certainly with an historian's gravity that he wrote out his fables."

"Following Nennius so far, he makes Brutus, the father of the Britons, into the great-grandson of Aeneas, who came to Britain and there founded Troynovant, or New Troy, afterwards called London."

"But the most curious parts of his story are those which concern Arthur, represented by the heroic defender of the Britons, and Merlin, whose prophecies he collects."

"Arthur appears as the conqueror of the Anglo-Saxons, the Picts and the Scots. He brings Ireland, Iceland, Scandinavia, and Gaul under his imperial rule. Ever victorious, he lives during the 6th century."

About 580 AD, Aedan mac Gabran (d.608 AD) is reputed to have led an expedition to the Orkneys, which lie far off the northern coast of Scotland. He embarked on a long series of raids on neighbouring territories and conquered a considerable part of the kingdom of the Picts as far as the North Sea.

In Chapter 30, mention was made that Geoffrey of Monmouth claimed that he obtained the knowledge for his works, from an old and unknown British book and that Geoffrey became the bishop of St Asaph in Wales in 1152. St Kentigern (c.518-603 AD) had founded the monastery of St Asaph. It was St Kentigern who received a visit from St Columba in about 581 AD, who had been working in the Strathclyde area. Therefore, it seems highly probable, that Merlin/St Columba was the original author of the book, and that he gave it to St Kentigern who hid it in the monastery at St Asaph where it was to remain until the 12th century AD until it came into the hands of Geoffrey of Monmouth. It was during the era of St Kentigern, that St Germain in his incarnation as St Columba wrote the first poem about Arthur, writing under the pseudonym of Taliesin.

In the quotation under this heading, *Prydwen* about which Taliesin wrote, was King Arthur's magic ship upon which Arthur and *Merlin*, the Bard, the Prophet who was the confidant of Arthur, made several journeys across the sea between Ireland and Scotland.

When *Taliesin/Merlin* wrote the verse: "*I was with Bran in Ireland*", the 'Bran' he was referring to was Aedan mac Ga-bran, St Columba's cousin. The descendants of Fergus Mor mac Erc, were known as the Cenel Gabran. They were descended from Princess Tea Mor Tephi and her husband Prince Heremon (Eochaidh). Princess Tea Mor Tephi was the daughter of Zedekiah of the House of Judah, and just prior to the Fall of Babylon when Nebuchadnezzar invaded the city, she accompanied her ward and great great grandfather, the prophet, Jeremiah, to Ireland, taking with them the Stone of Destiny.

According to Florence Marion McNeil in her book titled *Iona*:

"Columba has been accredited with martial propensities and was concerned with more than one battle fought on Irish soil."

Columba returned numerous times from Iona, to Ireland in a diplomatic capacity to settle differences between the rival clans of Dalriata in Ireland. There was fierce rivalry between the Northern and Southern Ui Neill and at times, the Cenel Conaill sought to dominate the Southern Ui Neill.

Prophecy of St Columba

The rival High King of Tara was Aedh mac Ainmuirech of the clan Cenel Conaill, Over-King of the Northern Ui Neill. Because of the numerous clans who were competing with each other and the constant changes of High kingship in Ireland, Columba paid a visit to Aedh and warned him with a prophecy of the future. Present at the meeting was Aedan mac Gabran, a cousin of St Columba who was also of the clan of Ui Neill.

Ainmuirech confronted Columba in a haughty and vain manner. Parts of the prophecy of Columba are quoted at the commencement of this chapter and the remainder follows:

> *Though it is today in the enjoyment of prosperous affluence*
> *O Tara, the flourishing seat of monarchy,*
> *Prosperity will forsake its hills*
> *It is the penalty which the acts of princes earned,*
> *That Tara shall be devoid of a house for ever.*
> *I assure you in serious verity*
> *Oh Tara, the flourishing seat of monarchs;*
> *That there is not tonight in the wide expanse of Banba [Ireland]*

A place, alas! Fated to enjoy such brief stability...
It is the penalty which the acts of princes earned,
That Tara shall be devoid of a house forever..."

Columba foretold the downfall of Tara, then the most magnificent seat of royalty in Europe. He clearly expressed to Ainmuirech, the misery and current instability of human affairs. After hearing the prophecy, Ainmuirech agreed to back down on some of the issues at stake, particularly to free Aedan, the son of the King of Albany, namely Gabran, from the tribute which had long been imposed upon his people. (Gabran had succeeded Comgall in 537 AD and ruled until 559 AD, at which point of time, he was succeeded by Conall mac Comgall who ruled until 574 AD. It was this Conall who was also a cousin of Columba, who granted him the island of Iona).

It was to Columba's advantage that he was of royal descent, and his kinship connections with the noblest families of Ireland and Scottish Dalriada, made him a political power. He had also established himself as a statesman and by winning the Picts over to the Celtic Church; he had secured peace between other tribes, thus preparing the way for political union. This was a major step in his endeavour to unite all the clans of the Scots so that they could learn to live in peace and harmony. In his previous incarnation as St Germanus (Ambrosius Aurelianus), about whom Geoffrey of Monmouth wrote, St Germain had been drawn into battle to defend the Britons from the Picts of the North.

Some centuries later, Tara was no longer the seat of a king or chief and all that remains of this once great palace, are mounds covered in grass which is exactly what Columba prophesied.

Other Prophecies of St Columba which came to fruition

According to Geoffrey of Monmouth, during *Merlin's* lifetime, King Urien of Rheged and his son *Owein* ('Yvain' in the romantic tales of the Knights), mounted an army against the Angles and was accompanied by Rydderch (Roderick) Hen, King of Strathclyde. He belonged to the Four main clans ruled by kings.

King Roderick was in the same era as St Kentigern who was on good terms with Roderick and worked in the Clyde district for many years. It was Roderick who procured his consecration as bishop in about 540 AD.

The other spelling of his name was King Rodercus Rydderch Hen whom St Columba prophesied 'Rex' meaning 'king' *would die at the Battle of Arthuret in 573 AD.* The prophecy came true. They were defeated by the Northumbrians in 573 AD, one year before Aedan mac Gabran was crowned as King of Dalriada, Scotland, by St Columba.

Poems and songs alluding to and thus recording this battle are attributed to the famous Taliesin (St Germain).

Columba also prophesied accurately about the sons of Aedan mac Gabran; two would be killed and the youngest would survive and take his place. This was Eochaidh Buide who became king of the Picts after Aedan's death in 608 AD.

The Anointing of Aedan in 574 AD as High King of the Celts of Dalriada

Comgall reigned until 574 AD which was the year that Columba anointed Aedan as King of Dalriada. It is highly probable that the one who was slain in a battle with King Brude of the Northern Picts in 560 AD, prior to Columba taking the 'Perilous' journey northwards to make peace with Brude, was Aedan's father, Gabran. (It was recorded that the King of the Scots who was slain was one of Columba's own kinsmen).

Columba was born in 521 AD and he would have been aged fifty-three when he anointed Aedan as King of Dalriada.

The legends of Merlin tell of how he raised Arthur since he was a child. As the Merlin of the time, and the Chief Archdruid High Priest, Columba would have raised Arthur to become a future King and Pendragon (military commander) which is exactly what Aedan became. It is evident that Aedan was too young to succeed his father, Gabran, which is why after Gabran's demise, Conall mac Comgall reigned in his stead.

It was common practice for bright young children to be tutored by the Druids from an early age. When Aedan grew to maturity and qualified, he was initiated as an 'Ar-thor'.

So where was Aedan mac Gabran crowned? Well, according to Florence Marian McNeill in her book titled *Iona* which was published in 1920:

"On this Stone - the old Druidic STONE OF DESTINY, sacred among the Gaels before Christ was born Columba crowned the King of Argyll, the King of the Gaels, Aedan mac Gabran. This was the earliest recorded royal coronation in Great Britain and it took place at Iona."

Having trained Aedan since he was young, Columba as the Merlin of the time, the wise Magi, the chief Archdruid High Priest, the Seer, the Prophet whom the kings and chiefs consulted, the greatest Bard of his time, the genius who disguised himself by writing under the name of Taliesin, the Merlin who was often seen to be surrounded by angels, having 'initiated' Aedan into the Greater Mysteries, the 'Orphic' Mysteries so often spoken about in previous chapters, created him an 'Arthor'. This accomplishment St Germain had carried out back in the 1st century

AD, when he was Joseph, also known as Annas the Elder, the Essenes' *Interpreter of the Law* during which time Kuthumi had been his son John the Beloved whom Jesus called one of the sons of 'Thunder'.

Once so long ago, St Germain in his incarnation as Samuel the Prophet, the Zadok High Priest, had anointed Kuthumi as King David of the House of Judah.

The pseudonym of Taliesin meant 'Radiant Brow' which would have described the beautiful halo of energy which was around St Germain, for he was a Master of the Great White Brotherhood, the *'Teacher to all Intelligences'* etc.

Avalon

The island of IONA was Avalon. It was also the place where Aedan was taken over the sea to be buried in 608 AD, hence the story of King Arthur being ferried across to an island.

Iona, Glastonbury, St Michael's Mount and Tintagel, all these places were once Celtic monasteries where the sacred Mysteries of the Mystical Rose where taught by the Masters of the Great White Brotherhood.

The Master of the Mystical Rose, Kuthumi, having once been John Joseph the Beloved alias Joseph of Arimathea, founded the first Avalon at Glastonbury and as we have seen in a previous chapter, his remains were buried there. As King Arthur, he was buried at another Avalon, namely Iona, and in the era of the Crusades, he would be born at another Avalon - one in Gaul (France).

The Graves on the Island of Iona

According to Florence Marian McNeil, many of the graves on the island of Iona are marked by flat stones upon which curious motifs are carved which include 'bear' symbols and abbots croziers (staffs). Upon the stones belonging to the women are such emblems as shears, mirrors and combs.

In the story of *Culhwch and Olwen* which is included amongst the works of Taliesin, whilst Culhwch goes in search of his bride Olwen in Ireland, he encounters the same implements that are carved upon the tomb slabs of the women buried at Iona, who were Druids.

The story of *Culhwch and Olwen* written by St Germain under the pseudonym of Taliesin is also full of boars and piglets. From Peter Dawkins' book titled *Arcadia* we learn the following pertinent information:

"The family crest of the Bacon family was the 'Boar'. The boar is the incarnate 'truth' which is hunted after...serving the boar's head on a platter with an apple, was symbolic of knowledge. Druids were known as 'boars', as a title of distinction. The boar is the male and the sow is the female, and the pig is the young swine. The swine when raised for slaughter, used to be known as the hog, the earliest form of which can be found in the Welsh language such as *hwch*, [as in Culhwch] which is derived from the sacred words, *Hava-Oc*, meaning 'Bride - Spirit'. Interestingly (as the key to all truth lies in language), the Welsh for pig is *beak*, which is etymologically the same as *peak* (French, *pique*) which means a 'point', 'pike' or 'spear'."

"The sow is an ancient symbol of wisdom-knowledge, as the feminine counterpart to the spiritual authority depicted by the boar. The sow was known as the Great Mother, and is a symbol of Venus. She represented the Mysteries in the form of Truth. She was imagined as moving (even flying!) over the surface of the earth, and from time to time she dropped a litter of piglets. Whenever and wherever she did, a Mystery School sprang up - the pigs becoming the initiates and then the adepts as they grew up."

According to Florence Marian McNeil:

"On the island of Iona are interred 48 crowned kings of Scotland, 4 of Ireland and 7 of Norway. The records are found in the *Chronicles of the Picts and Scots* and from Adamnan's time when he wrote the biography of *Saint Columba*. Among the numerous kings buried at Iona was Aedan mac Gabran. Also amongst the other famous kings buried there is *Macbeth*, recalled in the Shakespearian lines: Rosse: 'Where is Duncan's body?' Macduff: 'Carried to Columskille, (Columcille - 'the Dove of the Church, otherwise known as Columba), the Sacred storehouse of his predecessors and guardians of their bones.' Macbeth was laid to rest beside his reputed victim. Duncan's son, Malcolm Canmor (Ceanmor) was the first to break the tradition of royal burials at Iona - his body lines in Dunfermline. There were a total of 60 kings believed to be buried at Iona."

The Angels visit Columba

There is a hill on Iona that was called Angel's Hill and I had the most pleasant experience of visiting there in 2001 (see sequel to this story titled *The Dove, The Rose And The Sceptre, In Search Of The Ark Of The Covenant*).

According to Adamnan, the biographer of St Columba, it was witnessed by several monks that from time to time, the saint was visited by angels. At such times, he was seen praying with his hands spread out to heaven; and raising his eyes heavenwards towards the sky, suddenly a marvellous thing happened. Four Holy Angels, citizens of the Celestial world, clad in white garments, would come flying to him with wonderful speed and stood around him. After some conversation with the Blessed man, the heavenly angels sped swiftly back into the high heavens.

Angel's Hill was also where the Feast of St Michael took place, a time when fires were lit as beacons for the celebrations that took place.

On Sunday the 9th June, 597 AD, Columba departed his life to be with his angels and was probably met by the one who first appeared to his mother Eithne, the one who informed her that she was to have a special child, the 'Dove of the North' who would achieve so much for the Celtic people.

The account of St Columba's death was recorded and is a most moving one. Diomit, the Saint's attendant, saw from a distance an 'angelic Light' which filled the Church. The Light quickly faded and groping in the darkness, he found the Saint lying on the floor.

Generally, the concept of the numerous legends about Merlin is that Merlin does not really die, he becomes invisible, and he is simply hidden in a prison of air - in other words, he is in the etheric realms where he becomes an 'observer'.

The Black Stones of Iona

Columba's tomb is said to have originally been his stone pillow. His shrine was frequently transported between Ireland and Scotland in an effort to preserve it from the numerous raids carried out by the Vikings upon the island of Iona.

It is noteworthy, that King William the Lion of Scots (about whom Merlin made a prophecy *"A new conqueror in Scotland shall be named and crowned Lion...the Lion shall hold the Balance and stretch his palm over Scotland..."*) helped to restore Iona, as had his great grand father, Malcolm Ceanmor. (William the Lion was a reincarnation of St Germain. William was born during the era of the Crusades and he was the 'Celtic Defender of the Faith', a Pendragon - a military leader of that time).

According to Florence Marian McNeill, "...near St Columba's tomb stood formerly one of the most ancient and sacred of Iona's relics - the Black Stones of Iona, so called, not from their colour, but from the black doom that fell on any who dared to violate an oath sworn upon them."

"So recently as the reign of James VI (Stuart) who became James I of England, two clans who had spent centuries in bloody feuds, met there and solemnly pledged themselves to friendship. The last of these stones disappeared about 100 years ago. There is the tradition that the Coronation Stone in Westminster Abbey was originally one of the famous Black Stones (the Stone of Destiny). Its legendary history is very ancient for it is believed to have been reverenced as Jacob's pillow by the tribes who brought it from the East in the first wave of Celtic emigration."

Attributes of Columba

According to Florence Marion McNeil:

"The political effects of Columba's mission are not to be ignored. His royal descent and his kinship with the noblest families of Ireland and the Scottish Dalriada would alone have made him a power politically; but, apart from this, the first ten years of his labours in Scotland established him as a statesman no less than as a religious leader of uncommon gifts."

"In winning over the Picts, he had secured peace between the tribes and prepared the way for political union. Columba's reputation for wisdom and saintliness was such that he was frequently called upon to settle disputes between the clans; the King of Strathclyde consulted him regarding his future and when the King of the Scottish Dalriada died, it was Columba who appointed his successor, Aedan, who went to Iona for consecration at the saint's hands..."

"In 575 AD at the famous Convention of Druim Cett in Ireland, Columba accomplished three objects of note: firstly, the 'staying of the Bards', secondly, he gave exemption to women participating in military service, and thirdly, he achieved political independence for the Scottish Dalriada."

Columba's biographer, Adamnan, recorded how much children and animals loved Columba and to the end Columba was lord and servant of all. He taught family values and unconditional love. The distinctive feature of the system that operated on the Island of Iona was that the teachings embraced those of the East and the monastery was not destined for recluses. The monks were allowed to marry and their wives lived with them on the island.

The missionaries of the North and South willingly yielded obedience to Iona and were loyal to Columba's authority; he always allowed them their individual liberty and freedom of judgement.

Columba - 'Author'

As a major centre of Learning, there were many wonderful ancient books and documents which were housed at Iona where the monks enjoyed a tremendous education. People travelled from far and wide to Iona where they, as Druidic monks, were taught poetry, philosophy, alchemy (chemistry), science, music and astronomy. They were all bi-lingual in Latin and Gaelic and like Columba, were proficient in Hebrew and Greek as well. Right up until the time of his death in his 77th year, his love of writing continued.

In addition to the founding of hundreds of monasteries and extensive missionary activity which sometimes took him to Gaul (where he had been St

Germanus [St Germain] in the previous life-time), Columba is credited with having written over three hundred books and translated numerous copies of the Bible by hand as well as composing numerous hymns and poems. Apart from his large poetical output, he was highly skilled in the art of copying manuscripts.

According to Lesley Whiteside in her book titled *In Search of Columba*:

"Columba was a scholar, whose range of reading put him in touch with the religious thought of the Old and New Testaments and of theologians of the intervening centuries, up to his own time. Needless to say, the chief object of his attention was the Bible, which he read in both Jerome's Vulgate and its Old Latin predecessor. He would also have been familiar with Jerome's commentaries, works of the Apocrypha such as the Book of Enoch, and patristic authors such as Athanasius and Cassian." Lesley adds that Columba established a very fine library in which the monks studied.

"It was by Columba's example that Iona and other Columban monasteries developed a wonderful tradition of copying biblical manuscripts. The scribe already occupied a special place in Irish society but the illustrator's art also rose to prominence as he was given ample scope to exercise his imagination in decorating the manuscripts."

Columba/Taliesin was the greatest scribe and poet of his time - a genius!

Columba's gifts

He was also gifted with the most incredibly beautiful voice and his singing could be heard for miles. He was also a master at playing the difficult Irish Lute.

St Germain in the 17th and 18th century was credited with the most wonderful singing voice and he could play any instrument with great dexterity, as well as write equally as well with both hands simultaneously. He also composed operas and he played the violin brilliantly.

'Columba's Second Sight'

According to Florence Marion McNeil:

"Stories of Columba's visionary powers abound in his biographer, Adamnan's pages. In our modern civilization, what is called 'second sight' is generally regarded as mere superstition. Yet even amongst the classes we called educated, especially in our Celtic fringes, there are not a few who believe it to be a 'quickened inner vision', a veritable 6th sense, as real as the physical senses or more so. To one who marvelled at his power, Columba replied: 'Heaven has granted to some to see on occasion in their mind, clearly and surely, the whole of earth, and sea and sky'."

Columba - 'Miracle worker'

Columba's biographer, Adamnan, also recorded that when there was a drought, Columba would successfully summon the rain. Adamnan was the Abbot of Iona from 679 until his death in 704 AD, thus he had every opportunity to search out the facts relating to Columba's life and work. His biography of the founder of Iona has been described as 'the most complete biography that all Europe can boast of, not only at so early a period, but even through the whole of the Middle Ages'.

Columba - Nature Lover and 'Healer'

The Archdruid Priest, Columba revered nature and he loved to wander all over the island of Iona and it is indeed a very beautiful, special and spiritual place.

His favourite flower was the Hypericum which grew in abundance on the island of Iona. This beautiful golden flower which was very hardy and could survive the Atlantic storms that from time to time, lashed the shores of Iona was given the name of St John's Wort and also Aaron's Beard. St Columba is reputed to have utilized the plant for healing people and animals.

The 'Sandy Strand'

In a previous chapter, the 'Perilous' journey which Sir Lancelot undertook when he went in search of Queen Guinevere, was discussed. He visited a 'sandy strand' somewhere off the coast of the 'Waste Land' through which he had journeyed en route and he was upset when he found Guinevere's comb. It was mentioned earlier in this chapter that according to Florence Marian McNeil, many of the graves on the island of Iona are marked by flat stones upon which curious motifs are carved. Upon the stones belonging to the women are such emblems as shears, mirrors and combs.

The area of Stirling, (Argyllshire) in Scotland, was once known as the 'Waste Land'. In the story of Lancelot's search, the emphasis was placed on the 'sandy strand' as if it was an important clue and it was!

Florence Marian McNeill's description of Iona is as follow:

"Iona is situated off the coast off the west coast of Argyllshire, and separated from the south-west coast of Mull by a narrow sound about half a mile across. The coast-line is varied; there are cliffs and caves and a sheltered bay, and *to the north lies a great stretch of dazzling silver sand which is referred to as the 'sandy strand'.* This tract is called in Gaelic, the 'Machiar' and is made up of shelly sand."

After the Demise of St Columba

Immediately upon learning of the news of the death of St Columba of Iona who had established the greatest learning centre of its kind in the 6th century AD, Pope Gregory the First perceived such an occasion as a golden opportunity to halt the spread of the Celtic faith.

According to Peter Dawkins:

"St Augustine was sent over to Britain on a mission to the unconverted Saxons by the Bishop of Rome in 597 AD, at the time when the new title of Supreme Pontiff was being foisted onto the Roman Bishop, and tried to coerce the Bishops of the British Church into accepting the authority of the Bishop of Rome. Their reply to Augustine was:

'We have nothing to do with Rome. We know nothing of the Bishop of Rome in his new character as Pope. We are the British Church, the Archbishop of which is accountable to God alone, having no superior on earth.'"

Francis Bacon (St Germain), writing later on this subject said:

"The Britons told Augustine they would not be subject to him, nor let him pervert the ancient laws of their Church. This was their resolution and they were as good as their word, for they maintained the liberty of their Church for five hundred years after this time and they were the last of all Churches in Europe that gave up their power to the Roman Beast, and in the person of Henry VIII, that came of their blood by Owen Tudor, the first that took that power away again."

Continuing with Peter Dawkins:

"Even with the 'Romanisation' of England through the spread of the Roman Catholicism, the original British Church never died out and it guarded its secrets - the esoteric mysteries of Christianity - against the perversion of the Roman Catholic hierarchy until such time as the Roman dominance could be shaken off and the real Truth revealed publicly."

The Antiquity of Iona

According to Florence Marian McNeill: "The geology of Iona is remarkable. The island is immeasurably older, not only than the surrounding islands, but also than the highest mountains and most of the dry land on earth. During the great earth-changes of the Tertiary period, the fact of the globe attained, with minor differences, its present configuration.

"When our planet from a flaming mass of combustion like the sun, shrivelled into a globe with a solid crust, and the first oceans condensed in the hollows of its surface, then it was that the Achaean rocks of which Iona and the Outer Hebrides consist, were formed on the sea bottom. They contain no fossils for as far as it is known, no living creature as yet existed in the desolate waste of waters, or the primeval land."

"They were hard, rugged and twisted; and in Iona, as elsewhere, marble has been developed by the vast heat and pressure they have undergone...The great Ice Age has also left its mark, for the glaciers from the hills of Mull reached out over the Sound, and, as they melted, boulders of red granite, scraped from the Ross, dropped out of the ice along the eastern shore of Iona."

"The beginning of Iona is almost the beginning of the world itself."

The Tuatha de Danaan, the 'Children of Anna', the 'People of the Light' always claimed that they came from the 'Blessed Isle' and perhaps Iona was once a part of the Elysiums.

MASTERS DISCUSSED IN THIS CHAPTER

The Prophet Samuel & Zadok High Priest - St Germain
Joseph, Father of the Holy Grail Family & Annas the Elder High Priest, the 'Teacher of Righteousness' - St Germain
St Columba (The Bard Taliesin/Merlin) - St Germain
King William the Lion of Scots - St Germain
Sir Francis Bacon (The Bard 'Shakespeare') - St Germain
King David of the House of Judah - Kuthumi
John the Divine/Beloved (alias John Joseph of Arimathea) - First Master of the Grail - Kuthumi
King Arthur - Aedan mac Gabran - Kuthumi

NOTES AND RECOMMENDED READING

Robert Graves, *The White Goddess*, (Faber & Faber, U.K., 1961)
Florence Marian McNeill, *Iona*, (Blackie & Sons, Glasgow, 1920)
John Grenham, *Clans And Families of Ireland*, (Bramley Books, U.K., 1993)
William Francis Collier, *Central Figures In Irish History*, (Marcus Ward & Co. U.K. 1891)
Peter Dawkins, *Arcadia*, (Francis Bacon Research Trust, Roses Farm, Warwick, U.K.)
Donald Attwater and Catherine Rachel John, *Penguin Dictionary of Saints*, (Penguin, U.K. 1995)
Geoffrey of Monmouth, *The History of the Kings of Britain*, (edited by L. Thorpe, Penguin, 1966)
Daniel J. Boorstin, *The Discoverers, A History of Man's Search To Know His World And Himself*, (Random House, U.K. 1983)
E. MacNeill, *Celtic Ireland*, (1921), Dublin Library, Kildare Street, Ireland.
The Prophecies of St Malachy and St Columbkille, (Colin Smythe Ltd., 1969 U.K.)
Ian Grimble, *Scottish Islands*, (British Broadcasting Corporation, U.K., 1985)

Emile Legouis, *A History of English Literature*, (J.M. Dent & Sons Ltd., 1945)
Lesley Whiteside, *In Search of Columba*, (Columba Press, Dublin, 1997)

CHAPTER 34

The Knights Templar & the Cathars

"I am the Fountain of Light,
I am the Universe,
I am all Consciousness,
I am the Spirit of Light,
Deep unconditional and forever,
My Gift to the Light which is around me
is the spark of all life;
I carry it freely, generously.
In purity of the Soul"
(Prayer of the Cathars)

Having discovered the identity of Arthur and Merlin, we now move on in time to discuss the Knights Templar and the Cathars, known as the Albigensians - the 'People of Light' who were so closely linked with the Holy Grail.

At the beginning of the 19th century, a gifted young German author and historian, Otto Rahn, wrote an important historical book about the Cathars of southern France and their connection to the Holy Grail. He maintained that hidden within the Grail Romances were the Sacred Teachings of the Cathars and that the Holy Grail was a symbolic initiation. And more importantly, the Cathars followed the Teachings of St John the Beloved and called themselves 'Johannites'.

The Uniform of the Knights Templar

Because the Knights Templar form part of this story, it is therefore interesting to know what their uniforms were like. From the book titled *Order of the Knights of St John of Jerusalem* by Vaclav Mericka, we are informed that the "Order of the Knights of St John were established in the years 1113 to 1118, shortly after the founding of the Kingdom of Jerusalem. Another important order of the knighthood was the *Order of the Knights Templar* who derived their name from the Temple of Solomon in the vicinity of their headquarters."

"The Knights of the Order of St John (the Beloved) originally wore black mantles embroidered with white eight-pointed crosses, while the sur-coat or vest, the garment worn underneath the mantle, was red and was also the colour of their banner. In the 1700's the sur-coats of medieval habits were changed into uniforms consisting of coats or jackets, the rose-red colour being maintained. Knights of St John and Knights of Malta wore black trousers, red coats/jackets and dark blue mantles embroidered on the back with the eight point Maltese Cross."

"The origin of heraldry and its application is linked with the Crusades and dates roughly from the middle of the 12th century AD. The Crusades themselves constituted the period in which religious orders of knighthood were established. Heraldry came into being because the knights who took place in the Crusades wore pictorial insignia by which to recognize each other. They adorned their standards with these insignia and bore them on their shields. And because at that time the noblemen who were members of the newly-founded religious orders of chivalry wore special habits, heraldic coats of arms were used as distinguishing symbols of the badges of orders too. From the historical point of view, the most important period is that of the first and second Crusades in the years 1096-1098 and particularly in 1146-1148 when insignia were first systematically used in the Kingdom of Jerusalem."

"The oldest of these associations was established in 1113 and 1118, shortly after the founding of the Kingdom of Jerusalem. It was the *Order of the Knights of St John of Jerusalem* and developed from the charitable services provided at the hospital of St John in Jerusalem. The first Superior of the Order is said to have been Gerard - perhaps as far back as 1099, when Godfrey de Bouillon conquered Jerusalem. From the ranks of knights, the Grand Master was elected, and later, Grand Priors who headed eight Grand Priories of Zion, [meaning 'Jerusalem']."

"The Knights of St John did not limit their activities to the Holy Land where they had originated, but with the help of ecclesiastical authorities, and later with considerable assistance from secular powers, they spread to other countries, the so-called 'provinces' of Europe of that time; soon, powerful and important branches were established there. At first the Knights of St John moved to Limassol on Cyprus, later to Rhodes - hence the name, the Knights of Rhodes - and finally under the Emperor Charles V, after fierce battles with the Turks, they settled in Italy and from the year 1530, on Malta. But their history did not end there, for the Reformation had a considerable influence on their fate and the Knights of St John split into a Catholic branch known as the Knights of

Malta, whilst the original *Knights of St John* spread to the Protestant countries."

"The Order collapsed at the beginning of the 14th century following a serious conflict with the King of France and with the *Order of the Knights of St John*. The property of the Templars was taken over by the Knights of St John, while the members and representatives of this powerful Order were physically liquidated. Only in Spain and Portugal was the Templars' order absorbed by the newly established *Order of Christ*. The insignia of the Order retained in essence the original Templars' Cross with only minor alterations."

According to Michael Howard in his book titled *The Occult Conspiracy*:

"Following the suppression of the Templars in the 14th century, the Order in Portugal was exonerated of all guilt...instead of disbanding, as the Order was forced to do in most European countries, the Knights Templars in Portugal were reformed. This new Order took the name of the *Knights of Christ* and survived until at least the late 16th century. Its members included several famous navigators and explorers and it is said that the father-in-law of Christopher Columbus belonged to the Order." It is claimed that Christopher Columbus - St Germain, also belonged to the same order. Columbus married Felipa Perestrello, who was the daughter of the former Grand Master of the *Knights of Christ* which was the same Order of the Knights Templar.

C. W. Leadbeater in his book titled *The Hidden Life In Freemasonry* wrote:

"St Germain, under the name of Baron Hompesch, who was the last of the *Knights of St John of Malta*, was the man who arranged the transfer of the island of Malta to the English."

Information contained in the New Dawn magazine of March, 1998, which quoted a manuscript, written on Greek parchment, said to be a copy of the original dating from 1154 AD, claimed that Hugues de Payen, [who in all probability was the St Germain], the First Grand Master of the Templars, was initiated into the esoteric wisdom of the Templars. [This was the sacred Teachings of the Arcana].

"Up to about the year 1118 AD, (i.e. the year the Order of the Temple was founded), the mysteries and hierarchic Order of the initiation of Egypt, transmitted to the Israelites by Moses, then to the Christians by Jesus, were religiously preserved by the successors of St John." [Who was the Master Kuthumi].

"These mysteries and initiations, regenerated by the evangelical initiation, were a sacred trust which the simplicity of the primitive and unchanging morality of the Brothers of the East had preserved from all adulteration. Concerning the Knights Templar, this document tells us that due to the 'justice', 'virtues', and the 'charity of Hughes de Payen,' the Templar Grand Master was invested with Apostolic Patriarchal power and placed in the legitimate order of the successors of St John the apostle [the Beloved]. Such is the origin of the foundation of the Order of the Temple and of the fusion in this Order of the different kinds of initiation of the

Christians of the East designated under the title of Primitive Christians or Johannites."

An informative article which appeared in New Dawn magazine in August, 1997, written by M. Sabheddin, was presented as a tribute to Otto Rahn and his Quest for the Holy Grail. (Otto Rahn is discussed under the heading of the Cathars further on in this chapter).

"In the 19th century, European writers, heavily influenced by the papal condemnation of the Knights Templar, depicted the discredited warriors of the Knights Templar as a veritable satanic brotherhood involved in a vast conspiracy of evil. A popular conspiracy theory, heavily promoted today with right-wing Christian circles, continues to see the Templars of the 19th century agents of evil."

"Ironically, this theory...relies directly on the writings of the 19th century reactionary Catholics and their early 20th century popularizes. Added to this is a very selective and quite uninformed reading of the works of Freemasonic historians, particularly the American Albert Pike."

The Cathars

The Cathars were originally known as the Albigensians or men of Alba, the 'White Land' (equated with the 'People of Light' and not to be taken in a racial sense). The Essenes, the community to which the Grail family belonged, also called themselves 'the People of Light' as did the Irish Tuatha de Danaan.

It can thus be seen how continuously this description was used to describe people who fought for the 'Truth' against the 'Darkness of ignorance'.

The people during the Middle Ages were disenchanted with the Church of Rome's corrupt administration and the way it displayed its riches. Thus, the alternative they sought was to join the Cathar movement.

One of the teachings of the Cathars was that each individual was responsible for their own soul - their own 'Karma', which would have been an inspiring alternative to the Church's doctrine of 'Original Sin'. 'Spirituality' offered a new kind of independent freedom, similar to what is re-occurring in today's society.

The Cathars, who were also closely associated with the Knights Templar, were members of a Gnostic (from the Greek word *gnostikos* meaning 'knowledge') community whose religious views outraged the early Church of Rome.

How the Cathars Derived their Name

The name of the Cathars is thought by some to have originated from the Greek 'Katharos' which means 'pure'. The Cathars called themselves 'good Christians', or 'friends of God'; the locals called them 'Parfaits' meaning 'good men' and the Slav word for them was 'Bogomil'. The country in which the name had been established the longest was Bulgaria, where one known as 'Bogomil' preached in circa 950 AD. It is thought that he real name was 'Theophilus' and it will be recalled that during the 1st century AD, the Master Kuthumi was the Annas High Priest whose Greek name was Theophilus. His other name was John the Beloved (alias Joseph of Arimathea).

Bogomilism did not disappear from the Balkans until the Turkish conquest which started in 1463 AD and ended in 1481 AD.

It is important to remember that the Cathars followed the teachings of John the Beloved and that they called themselves the 'Johannites'. Therefore, it stands to reason that Bogomil/Theophilus was an incarnation of the Master Kuthumi. It has been mentioned in an earlier chapter that the Masters often retained the same names in their reincarnations as those that they had in their past lives.

In the 9th century, Johannes (John) Eriugena was born of Scottish parents in Ireland as indicated by his pseudonym - 'Eriugena' meaning 'Irish born'. *He was the greatest philosopher of his time, responsible for the Carolingian Renaissance, whose like was not seen again in Western Christendom until the Italian Renaissance of the 15th century, during which time Kuthumi reincarnated as Leonardo da Vinci, the 'Lion of Vinci' at which time he became the Grand Helmsman (Master) of the Priory of Sion (Zion).*

John travelled to Gaul (France) and was appointed by the French King Charles I, (who was Charlemagne the Great - St Germain), as the main teacher and head Philosopher of the Royal Court School in France. (It will be remembered that in the 11th century AD, when the Crusades first began, the Master Kuthumi incarnated as the Philosopher, Mathematician, and Astrologer who was appointed to the Royal Court of the Shah of Persia as the head teacher. It will also be recalled that the Master Kuthumi again attained the name of John in the 16th century AD, when he reincarnated as the Royal Astrologer to the Court of Elizabeth I, mother of Francis Bacon - St Germain, where he was the brilliant mathematician known as Sir John Dee who named his son, Arthur).

John was commissioned by the French King Charles I to translate into Latin the Neoplatonic works of Dionysius. Because he did not submit his work to censorship, although King Charles thoroughly supported him, John came into conflict with Pope Nicholas I. One of his works was called *De Divina Praedestionation* which was about 'Divine Predestination' concerned with an individual's free will determining their destiny and he also asserted that there was no such thing as 'hell' and 'damnation'.

In his opus *De Divisione Naturae* written in circa 867 AD, John of Ireland (Eriugena) dared to present Philosophy as an independent discipline on an equal footing with Theology, and to declare that where philosophic reason and theological authority conflict, reason and not authority, must prevail.

John wrote that all human beings would become pure spirits and his writings as such, were considered to be 'heretic' by the Pope and against all the teachings of the Church of Rome. He died in 877 AD and 'Theophilus' otherwise known as 'Bogomil' was circulating the teachings of John the Beloved to the Cathars in circa 950 AD, and this, in all probability was his next incarnation after his one as John Eriugena. By 1225 AD Pope Honorius III ordered the works of Eriugena to be burnt.

It will be remembered that in an earlier chapter from information taken from William Foxwell Albright's book titled *From The Stone Age To Christianity*, we learned that the Arians established themselves in Cappadocia (the city where St Germain incarnated as Apollonius of Tyana in the 1st century AD) and that one of their older cities was Khattusas (Boghazkioi) which held a position of predominance by the beginning of the 15th century BC.

One of the monastic Orders founded by St Bruno at La Grande Chartreuse in France was the Carthusians, which phonetically is similar to 'Khattusas'.

'Khatti' is the original of the name 'Hittite' which appears in the Old Testament. It seems highly probable that the Khatti people were, in later centuries to become known as the 'Cathars'. The Church of Rome referred to them as the 'Cat' people.

From Peter Dawkins' book titled *The Great Vision* we learning the following:

"From 1080-1260 a great civilizing impulse began to blossom from the stormy difficulties of the Dark Ages. The Mediaeval world had truly emerged. Catharism flowered in the south of France. The troubadour movement, nourished by the bards from the north and the culture of the south, grew with it, purposefully influencing and guiding the formative period of chivalry and moral precepts into knighthood, and their controlling hand, with the founding of many religious Orders of Knighthood (such as that of the Templars, Hospitallers, Teutonic Knights etc.,) so the esoteric brotherhoods were working to inspire and guide the Orders of Chivalry with the deeper teachings and wisdom."

"The Templars in particular, in this period, became an organization able to lead aspirants into the real Christ Mysteries and initiations, to turn military zeal into a passion for harmony and order, tolerance and peace. Roman Catholicism tried to extend its power and unite the many kings and emperors under its single domination, to create a Holy Roman Empire in reality (or 'Christ's Kingdom on earth' as they called it); and this period is particularly marked by the various Crusades, launched in an effort to win back the 'Holy Land' from the 'infidel' and to exercise papal dominion over the temporal rulers of Christendom in the process."

"At the same time the 'Johannite' (John the Beloved) brethren worked more gently to bring about a Kingdom of the Holy Grail, a Kingdom of true Love, throughout Christendom and beyond. Whilst the growth of royal power, of priesthood and chivalry grew apace, so did the merchant classes and artisans, and the Guilds that were introduced, similarly influenced. Eventually greed and jealousy brought about a severe persecution of the esoteric brotherhoods by orthodox Church and State and a Crusade was launched against the Cathars which virtually wiped out the bright, gay culture of Languedoc and Provence."

MASTERS DISCUSSED IN THIS CHAPTER

Christopher Columbus ('Order of the Knights of Christ) - St Germain
Baron Hompesch, ('Last of the Knights of St John of Malta') - St Germain
St John the Beloved alias Joseph of Arimathea, First Master of the Holy Grail - Kuthumi

NOTES AND RECOMMENDED READING

Vaclav Mericka, *Book of Orders & Decorations*, (Hamlyn, U.K. 1975)

Michael Howard, *The Occult Conspiracy*, (Ryder & Ryder, U.K. 1989)

Peter Dawkins, *The Great Vision*, (Francis Bacon Research Trust, U.K. 1985)

Rene Nelli, *The Cathars*, (Editions Quest, 13 Rue du Breil, Rennes, France)

Excerpts from *New Dawn* Magazine, July - August, 1997: *Otto Rahn & The Quest For the Holy Grail*, by M. Sabheddin.

Excerpts from *New Dawn* Magazine, March - April, 1998: *The Secrets of the Knights Templar*, (Life Science Fellowship, P.O. Box 12116, A'Becket Street, Melbourne, Victoria, Australia, 3000)

Michael Baigent, Richard Leigh & Henry Lincoln, *The Holy Blood And The Holy Grail*, (Arrow Books U.K. 1996)

Simon Peter Fuller, *Rising Out Of Chaos*, (Kima Global, South Africa, 1994)

C.W. Leadbeater, *The Hidden Life In Freemasonry*, (Theosophical Publishing House, U.K. 1975)

Michael Baigent, Richard Leigh & Henry Lincoln, *The Holy Blood And The Holy Grail*, (Arrow Books, U.K. 1996)

Arnold J. Toynbee, *A Study of History*, (Oxford University Press, U.K. 1934)

F.J. Dennett, *Europe, A History*, (Linehan & Shrimpton, Melbourne, Victoria, Australia 1960)

CHAPTER 35

The Persecution of the Cathars

It has no fabric but understanding.
It has no rivals because it is non-competitive.
It has no ambitions, it seeks only to serve.
It knows no boundaries for nationalisms are unloving.
It is not of itself because it seeks to enrich all groups and religions.
It acknowledges all great Teachers of all ages who have shown the Truth of Love.
(Prophecy of the Cathars)

In the 13th century AD, Montsegur, where the Cathars resided, was one of the most significant strongholds in Languedoc. The castle was built in 1204 AD, at the highest point of a spur of rocks known as 'Pog'.

Catharism was a dualistic religion emanating from Asia Minor in the 10th century which was particularly well received. As a result, at a time when the Church was ostentatious about its wealth and its priests were leading dissolute lives, the Cathars, poorest of the poor and leading ascetic lives, soon became a threat to the Kingdom.

Thus the Pope, with the support of the King of France, inaugurated a Crusade against the 'heretics' which was to last for nearly a century.

The Cathars of Albi were savagely persecuted when in 1209, Pope Innocent III preached the Albigensian Crusade (1209-29) in the Languedoc area in which the Cathars resided. Although numerous Cathars were slain, the crusade failed to stamp out those whom the Church of Rome labelled the 'heretics' and this led to the setting up of the Inquisition whose cruelty by torture almost completely eradicated what was known as Catharism, by the 14th century. The same fate was dealt out by the Catholic Church to the Knights Templar in the 14th century.

According to information contained in the book titled *A History of Medieval Europe*, by R.H.C. Davis, at the commencement of the persecutions of the Cathars, the root of the problem may have escalated as follows:

"On 15th January, 1208, the papal legate, Pierre de Castelnau, was murdered at a crossing of the Rhone near St Gilles. Rightly or wrongly, it was universally believed that the murder had been committed at the instigation of Raymond VI, Count of Toulouse. Raymond was a typical product of what all good churchmen considered to be the decadent and immoral civilization of the towns of southern France. He was the idol of the troubadours and the paragon of courtly love. He himself was suspected of heresy, and was said to have received the murderer of the papal legate in public and to have congratulated him on his deed. Though excommunicated, he remained unrepentant."

"In these circumstances it seemed to Innocent [Pope], and indeed to the vast majority of Christians, imperative that some definite action should be taken. He therefore approached Raymond's feudal overlord, Philip Augustus, King of France, and enjoined him to confiscate his lands as a heretic. From Innocent's point of view, all would have been well if only Philip had agreed to play the part allotted to him. Unfortunately however, he refused, since, being already at war with King John of England and the Emperor Otto IV, he could not afford to dissipate his military strength in the south. Innocent therefore took the matter into his own hands and preached a Crusade against the Albigensians."

"The call to arms met with a wide response. The barons of northern France coveted the wealth of Languedoc, and were only too eager for a holy war in which the prizes were both tempting and conveniently near to hand, and on 24th June, 1209, a vast army assembled at Lyons. Once the Crusade had been launched, there was a massacre at Beziers and *auto-da-fe* at Minerva (1210), and nothing could stop the progress of the holy war. Even though many of the greater barons, such as the Duke of Burgundy, eventually returned to their fiefs, the lesser barons, under Simon de Montfort, continued the war of conquest and won a decisive victory at Muret (1213)."

Simon de Montfort was proclaimed Count of Toulouse by Rome in 1213 AD. His son, Simon de Montfort became the 6th earl of Leicester. He was born in Normandy and went to England in 1229. He married Eleanor, the sister of Henry III Plantagenet King of England, and according to Elizabeth Hallam in her book titled *The Plantagenet Encyclopedia*, Simon was fully invested with the earldom of Leicester in 1239. It is noteworthy that in the 16th century, Francis Bacon - St Germain was to become the son of Robert Dudley, Earl of Leicester.

Sir Winston Churchill and other great statesmen and historians, recognised Simon, Earl of Leicester, as being the *father of the English Parliament.*

In 1244, Raymond VII, the Count of Toulouse, promised the King that he would destroy the castle at Montsegur. On the 1st March 1244, the besieged occupants made an abortive attempt to escape. Then, on the following day came the surrender. The Cathars were given fifteen days respite, at the end of which they had to choose either to renounce their beliefs, or to be burnt at the stake. On the 16th March, the Cathars were burnt alive and the name of Montsegur became a legend.

Otto Rahn gave a public lecture about the Cathars in 1938. From the article in *New Dawn* magazine, July, August, 1997, we learn that a local newspaper reported on his talk:

"The Albigensians (Cathars) were exterminated. Two hundred and five leading followers of the Light-Bearers were burnt on a huge pyre by Dominicans in the south of France after a large-scale priestly Crusade in the name of Christian clemency. With fire and sword, the Lucifer doctrine of the Light-Bearer was persecuted along with its followers. The Albigensians were dead, but their spirit lives on and has an effect today through new devotion and rejuvenated enthusiasm. The Vicar of Christ could truly burn men; but he was mistaken if he believed that he burned along with them their spirit, devotion and longing."

"This spirit became alive again before many men yesterday, powerfully, visibly, in Otto Rahn, a descendant of the old Troubadours." It will be remembered that Lucifer came from the word Lucipher - meaning 'Light Bearer' and that the word never meant the 'Devil' or 'Satan'; only the Church of Rome corrupted its true meaning.

The article further stated: "In 1244, the heretical Cathars had made their last heroic stand against a Catholic crusade which finally triumphed in their destruction. Tradition affirms that on the night before the final assault, three Cathars carrying the sacred relics of the faith, slipped unnoticed over the wall (of Montsegur). They carried away the magical regalia of the Merovingian King Dagobert II and a cup reputed to be the Holy Grail."

As was mentioned in an earlier chapter, one year before the millennium, the Pope made a formal apology on behalf of the Roman Catholic Church for many of the atrocities that have been carried out in the past. During the Middle Ages, the attitude of the Church of Rome seemed to be that the 'end justified the means'.

In a book written in the early part of the 1900's by a Roman Catholic priest, he described the Albigensians as "having the most peculiar and queer doctrines which were leaking into Christendom from the East. It was destroying the Christian (Catholic) faith in Languedoc and the local clergy had too much wealth and too little learning to be able to fight it successfully."

"St Dominic [Guzman] preached against it with considerable results. St Dominic and his friars worked tirelessly to defeat the errors which were menacing the European mind and established Christian philosophy and theology on firm and rational foundations. It was due to them, more than to anyone else, that the 13th century was the golden age of mediaeval civilization." (St Dominic also came into contact with St Francis of Assisi whose life is discussed further on in this chapter).

"It was not really surprising that such heretics as the Albigensians were persecuted. Mediaeval heresy was never a mere difference of opinion, but always a revolutionary doctrine, tending to the over-throw or alteration of all existing institutions. They became a sort of secret society, eating away at the very vitals of Christendom and the fear and hatred they aroused were multiplied tenfold."

The priest further commented that: "The most dangerous of these heresies and the one that in the end provoked the Church into setting up the Inquisition, was that of the Albigensians (so-called Albi, a town in southern France, which was one of their chief centres). This doctrine had come from the East - it was a revival of a teaching which had been driven out of Europe under the Roman Empire."

"It was impossible to tolerate Albigensianism. Religious authorities considered it a cancer on society. Despite the massacres that took place, if there must be persecution, some such efficient instrument such as the Inquisition is probably the best way of keeping it within some sort of limits." It is rather ironical that the Pope who instigated the crusade against the Albigensians (Cathars) was called Pope Innocent III!

Further information contained in Peter Dawkins' book titled *The Great Vision* informs us as follows:

"But instead of stamping out the 'consolamentum' of the Cathars and 'science' of the troubadours, the persecution, severe though it was, stimulated a dispersion of the Cathars and troubadours to Italy northern France and Germany, where their influence had already reached. It was a catalytic action - a radiance of light carrying seeds of light into all the kingdoms of Christendom (c. 1260-1440) - and it had a direct motivating effect on the dawning of the European Renaissance. Added to this was the persecution and dissolution of the Knights Templar by the pope and the king of France in 1306-1312 AD, with the same effect as with the Cathars. Through the trouveres of northern France, the minnesingers of Germany, the poets of the Sicilian court and the bards of Britain, the Renaissance neared its birth."

Through intense investigations, "**Otto Rahn traced the Cathars who guarded the Holy Grail back to the Druids who were the forerunners of the Celtic Christian Church, beginning with Joseph of Arimathea and Glastonbury, one of the 'Avalon's.**"

Otto discovered that the secret traditions and wisdom of the Cathars was spread throughout the medieval courts of France in the 11th and 12th centuries AD by the bards and wandering minstrels whom he maintained, **were all members of the Order of the Druids** and hence their connection with the Cathars. Otto also discovered that the **sacred Teachings of the Cathars was called 'Johannite Christianity'** for it was based on the Teachings of St John the Beloved, the disciple whom Jesus loved and together shared the knowledge of the sacred Mysteries.

This of course is quite logical considering that it has already been established in earlier chapters of this story that John and Jesus were brothers, the sons of Joseph who was St Germain. It was also believed that the Cathars had in their possession, the original version of St John's gospel so we can assume that it came into their possession at some stage, by direct authority of the *Master of the Mystical Rose*, Kuthumi and St Germain.

Another article written in New Dawn magazine in March, 1998, gave additional information about the 'Johannites'.

"Back in 1842 the historian Ragon admitted that the Templars learnt from the 'initiates of the East' a 'certain doctrine' which was attributed to St John the Apostle. He wrote: 'they renounced the religion of St Peter [Roman Catholic Church] becoming 'Johannites'. **The Cathars who were also called 'Johannites' claimed to inherit their secret Gnostic teachings from the apostle John.** Support for an association between the Cathars and Templars is found in their mutual use of certain grottoes in the Pyrenees. Some researchers even claim that caverns near the Cathar fortress of Montsegur are covered with Cathar and Templar symbols'."

The article further states: "**The Celtic Christian communities, in their showdown with the Roman papacy invoked the mystical and apocalyptic St John as the source of their authority.** In the New Testament the Gospel of John gives the clearest presentation of Jesus' mission and the nature of the Christ. John is also the disciple associated with the End of Time, the millennial kingdom. True Christian mystics, both inside and outside the Catholic ecclesiastical structure, identified with the hidden Church of John rather than the worldly Roman Church of Peter. The Church of Peter is that of the Pope. The hidden Church of John is mystical and esoteric. By trying to suppress and even deny the Church of John, the exoteric Church of Peter forfeited the mysteries of Christ. Christianity and Western civilization lost touch with their mythic soul."

"We know that the Knights Templar dedicated themselves to the recovery of the esoteric community established by Jesus the Christ. Their loyalty being to the hidden community (*ecclesia*) of John the Beloved, rather than to the exoteric Church [the Church of Rome]. The Pope may claim to derive his authority from the apostle Peter, **but in the eyes of the Templars, he presided over a corrupt and despotic regime far removed from the real message of Jesus.**"

(Excerpts have been quoted from article in New Dawn magazine, March, 1998, titled *The Secrets of the Knights Templar* by the Life Science Fellowship, P.O. Box 12116, A'Beckett Street, Melbourne, Vic 3000).

Continuing with the story of Otto Rahn (from the article in New Dawn magazine):

"The deeper that he delved into the mysteries of the Grail the more he realised that the Holy Grail was an emblem set up in opposition to the Teachings of the

Church of Rome who had so cruelly persecuted the Knights Templars and the Cathars. He became convinced that the Roman teachings of Lucifer being Satan were totally incorrect. Lucifer means the 'Bearer of Light' and he saw the Grail as a symbol of 'Light'. Lucifer stood in opposition to the god of Darkness which Rahn realised, were those teachings of the Roman Church and in the interest of peace, he gave a lecture in 1938 defending the hundreds of Cathars, 'Light Bearers' who had been burnt on a pyre in the south of France upon the instructions of the Church of Rome. The Cathars, like the Essenes, studied the Teachings of the Cabbala and their applied 'wisdom' was given the name of *Sophia* from whence the word *Theosophical* was derived, meaning 'God-knowledge' or 'Wisdom of God'."

Peter Dawkins explains about the mystery of *Sophia* in his book *The Great Vision.*

"It is important to realise that there are three aspects to Divine Thought: namely, the Word (or Will), the radiant Wisdom, and the reflected Intelligence. Then we should realise that the Word itself contains the very Idea of this triune Thought, which Trinity is then radiated as the Light of Divine Wisdom, and then reflected as the Vision of Divine Intelligence."

"The Word (*Logos*), the Light *(Christos)* and the Vision (*Sophia*) each themselves contain the Word, the Light and the Vision in their own respective ways. Man is associated with *Sophia*, the reflected Intelligence or Vision of Truth, as the summation and crowning principle of all that *Sophia* means; but as *Sophia* he also incorporates the whole triune Thought of God (*Logos, Christos* and *Sophia*) as a Reflection or Vision of Truth. The mystery of Man lies in the 'fulfilment of God's idea. There cannot be a complete reflection of the Christ Light until the Vision itself embodies all that is in the Holy Wisdom [*Sophia*]." (It is of interest to note that 'Bethlehem', the town where Jesus, John the Beloved and his brothers and sisters were born to Joseph [St Germain] and Mary, meant *The House of Bread* meaning *The Place of Wisdom*)."

Sadly at the age of thirty-five years, having bravely disclosed his findings in his book, Otto Rahn was killed and his death remains a mystery. The author of the article on Otto Rahn quoted from Miguel Serrano's book titled *Book of Resurrection.*

'Amor'

Accordingly, "in the days of the Cathars and the initiated knights of the Grail, 'love' did not mean the same thing as it has come to mean today. *Amor* (Love) was a cipher, it was a code word. *Amors* spelt backwards is Roma [Rome]. That is, the word indicated, in the way in which it was written, the opposite to Roma, to all that Rome represented. Also *Amor* broke down into 'a' and 'mor', meaning *Without-death*. That is, to become immortal, eternal, thanks to the way of initiation of Amor. A way of initiation totally opposed to the way of Rome...This is why *Roma* destroyed *Amor*, the Cathars, the Templars, the Lords of the Grail, everything which may have originated in the 'Hyperborean Blood Memory' and which may have had a polar, solar origin."

The beautiful prayer at the beginning of this chapter was the one used by the Cathars.

The Cathar Prophecy

A friend whose lineage could be traced back to the Cathars, toured through the Cathar region of Montsegur with the author of *Rising Out Of Chaos*, Simon Peter Fuller. Ross kindly sent me the Cathar Prophecy of 1244 AD, a legacy left in the hope that the values for which it stands would once again be instilled in mankind. Fortunately, it survived because most of the Cathars; documents were destroyed by the Church of Rome. It reads as follows:

"The last of the Cathars were burnt by the Inquisitors of the Roman Catholic Church at Montsegur, Languedoc, France in 1244 but they left this prophecy that the Church of Love would be proclaimed in 1986."

It has no fabric but understanding.

It has no rivals because it is non-competitive.

It has no ambitions, it seeks only to serve.

It knows no boundaries for nationalisms are unloving.

It is not of itself because it seeks to enrich all groups and religions.

It acknowledges all great Teachers of all ages who have shown the Truth of Love.

Those who participate practice the truth of Love in all their beings.

There is no walk of life or nationality that is a barrier.

Those who are, know.

It seeks not to teach but to be, and by being, enrich.

It recognises the planet as a Being of which we are a part.

It recognises that the time has come for supreme transmutation, the ultimate alchemical act of conscious change of the ego into a voluntary return to the whole.

It does not proclaim itself with a loud voice but in the subtler realms of loving.

It salutes all those in the past who have blazoned the path but have paid the price.

It admits no hierarchy or structure for no-one is greater than another.

Its members shall know one another by their deeds and being and by their eyes and on no other outward sign save the fraternal embrace.

Each one will dedicate their life to the silent loving of their neighbour and the environment and the planet whilst carrying out their task however exalted or humble.

It recognises the supremacy of the great idea which may only be accomplished if the human race practices the supremacy of love.

It has no reward to offer here or in the hereafter save the ineffable joy of being and loving.

Each shall seek to advance the cause of understanding, doing good by stealth and teaching only by example.

They shall heal their neighbour, their community and our planet.

They shall know no fear and feel no shame and their witness shall prevail over all odds.

It has no secret, no Arcanum, no initiation, save that of true understanding of the power of Love and that, if we want it to be so, the world will only change if we change ourselves first.

All those who belong, belong. They belong to the Church of Love.

In summary of the Cathars, it is rather ironic that a group of people whose main objective was to teach the power of Love, which is what the Master Jesus sought to teach us, were so cruelly annihilated.

St Francis of Assisi (1182 - 1226 AD)

In 1210 AD, Pope Innocent III had been introduced to Francesco Bernadone, who was later to become known as St Francis of Assisi, whom he hoped would become a role model for the Church.

Francis was born into a wealthy middle-class family and in his youth, he served in a war against Perugia after which time he chose to live a life of poverty. When he sold his possessions, his father brought a court action against him. Francis then renounced his patrimony and declared that from that day forward, his Father would be the one in Heaven.

He gathered a small retinue around him whom he called the 'frati'; the English translation was 'friars'. The religion of Francis was not of the conventional kind for he did not join any Order and he and his monks travelled barefoot around the countryside, preaching as they went. In the times that Francis was not travelling, he lived the life of a hermit.

It was the hope of the Church of Rome that Francis would join with St Dominic Guzman (who was earlier mentioned in this chapter) and that the followers of the two saints would form a spiritual army against the heretics, such as the Albigensians (Cathars).

Francis refused and did not want any position of authority, however, as previously mentioned, St Dominic upon Orders from the Church, helped to persecute the Cathars. Gradually, the Church of Rome began to intervene on a more frequent basis, wanting to bring the Order that Francis had established, under the one umbrella. Francis became concerned that his original Order would become corrupted, although even until his death he declared his faith in the priests of the Roman Church.

He retired to live as a hermit in a small hut and insisted on owning only one tunic and a bible. Two years before his death, he was inflicted with the stigmata. Marks appeared on his hands of where the nails had been driven into the Cross at the time of the crucifixion of Jesus. Earlier in his life, Francis had shunned lepers but his attitude changed after his conversion and he attended both the sick and the lepers. St Francis had a close affinity with all animals and birds and was dearly loved both those around him.

St Francis was obviously one of the Masters of the Great White Brotherhood, whom some say was the Master Kuthumi. It does not seem logical however, that the Master Kuthumi would have become so closely affiliated with the Church of Rome and declared his belief in them.

Furthermore, a Master who had once been Pythagoras, John the Beloved (alias Joseph of Arimathea) and King Arthur would have been a more highly evolved soul, one who would not have needed to produce the so-called miracle of the stigmata, upon his body. The one who wrote the Book of Revelation would have had no need to inflict such pain upon himself subconsciously induced as a form of penance. Nor do I believe that Kuthumi would have shunned lepers.

In his incarnation as John the Beloved (Joseph of Arimathea), the *First Master of the Grail,* Kuthumi had founded the first Celtic Church in Britain in *defiance* of the Church of Rome. As St George he had *fought* the Romans in order to save the Christians who were being persecuted and as a result of his bravery, he was *executed* by the Romans. As Arthur, he was the Guardian of the Celtic Church, the Pendragon of that time.

Therefore, another person of that same era who had an incredible impact on history was an incarnation of the Master Kuthumi. The reasons for this assumption will be explored in the following chapter and the readers may form their own conclusions.

The importance of John the Beloved, the Master Kuthumi, has been demonstrated throughout this chapter and his prominent role as the First Master of the Holy Grail, is not to be underestimated.

MASTERS DISCUSSED IN THIS CHAPTER

Pythagoras - 'Father of Mathematics' - Kuthumi
St John the Beloved alias Joseph of Arimathea, 'First Master of the Holy Grail' - Kuthumi
St George, 'Defender of the Faith' - Kuthumi
King Arthur (Aedan mac Gabran), 'Keeper of the Holy Grail' - Kuthumi
Theophilus ('Bogomil') preached the Teachings of John the Beloved to the Cathars- in all probability Kuthumi

NOTES AND RECOMMENDED READING

Peter Dawkins, _The Great Vision_, (Francis Bacon Research Trust, U.K., 1985

Arnold J. Toynbee, _A Study of History_, (Oxford University Press, U.K., 1934)

F.J. Dennett, _Europe, A History_, (Linehan & Shrimpton, Melbourne, Australia, 1961)

R.H.C. Davis, _A History of Medieval Europe_, (Longman U.K. 1970)

Excerpts from New Dawn Magazine, March 1998: _The Secrets of the Knights Templar_, (Life Science Fellowship, P.O. Box 12116, A' Becket Street, Melbourne, Victoria, 3000).

Michael Baigent, Richard Leigh & Henry Lincoln, _The Holy Blood And The Holy Grail_, (Arrow Books, U.K., 1996)

Michael Baigent & Richard Leigh, _The Temple And The Lodge_, (Corgi Books, U.K., 1996)

Michael Baigent, Richard Leigh & Henry Lincoln, _The Messianic Legacy_, (Arrow Books, U.K., 1996

Christopher Knight & Robert Lomas, _The Hiram Key_, (Century Books, U.K., 1996)

Spencer Lewis, _Rosicrucian Questions And Answers_, (AMORC, U.S.A 1929 available through Theosophical Society)

C.W. Leadbeater, _The Hidden Life in Freemasonry_, (Theosophical Publishing House, U.K. 1975)

William Foxwell Albright, _From The Stone Age To Christianity_, (Doubleday Anchor Books, U.S.A, 1957)

Peter Simon Fuller, _Rising Out Of Chaos_, (Kima Global, South African 1994)

Rosemary Ellen Guiley, _Encyclopedia Of Mystical & Paranormal Experience_, (Grange Books, U.S.A, 1991)

Rene Nelli, _The Cathars_, (Editions Quest, 13 Rue du Breil, Rennes, France)

Michel Roquebert, _Cathar Religion_, (Editions Loubatieres, France)

Lily Deveze, _A History of France_, (Carcassonne, 1964)

Elizabeth Hallam, _The Plantagenet Encyclopedia_, (Tiger Books, U.K., 1996)

CHAPTER 36

The First Grand Master of the Knights Templar

"Due to the 'justice', 'virtues', and the 'charity of Hughes de Payen,' the Templar Grand Master was invested with Apostolic Patriarchal power and placed in the legitimate order of the successors of St John the apostle [the Beloved]. Such is the origin of the foundation of the Order of the Temple and of the fusion in this Order of the different kinds of initiation of the Christians of the East designated under the title of Primitive Christians or Johannites."

(Excerpt New Dawn Magazine March 1997)

We have read in the previous chapter of the Cathars who were persecuted in the 13th century AD, and it seems too coincidental that the Carthusian Order has the same name. According to David Hugh Farmer in his book titled *Saint Hugh Of Lincoln*:

"The Carthusian Order formed an integral but independent part of the movement of reformed monasticism which arose in the late 11th century, mainly in Italy and France, and flourished especially in the 12th century."

"Some communities, like the Cistercians, originated as breakaway movements from older established monasteries. Others resulted from a group of disciples attaching themselves to a renowned master."

St Bernard of Clairvaux (1090 - 1153 AD)

St Bernard was born into a noble family and was responsible for having built the Cistercian Abbey of Clairvaux. He was a unique mystical man who was known to perform miracles and also was able to balance his religious and political affairs. It was due to his noble background, that he became involved with the Knights Templar as their patron. They were incorporated as a religious Order at Troyes in 1128, at which time he preached the Second Crusade (1147-1149). St

Bernard drew up the rule of conduct for the Knights Templar. Pilgrims en route to the Holy Land were administered to by the Hospitallers of St John (named after St John the Beloved) whose emblem was the Maltese Cross. St Bernard also integrated the Celtic Church with his Cistercian Order.

From the article titled *The Secrets of the Knights Templar* which appeared in New Dawn magazine in March, 1998, we are informed as follows:

"The monastic traditions of the West, shaped by St Bernard, fostered a rebirth of spirituality. The earliest Biblical writings and mystic texts preserved in the monastic Orders later inspired Europe's greatest visionaries...Joachim of Fiore, Paracelsus, Giordano Bruno and popular movements such as the Brethren of the Free Spirit." (Reference was made in an earlier chapter to the fact that Giordano Bruno visited Sir John Dee - [Kuthumi] and Sir Francis Bacon [St Germain] during the Elizabethan Renaissance, and that he was a Grand Master of the Order of the Rosicrucians who was persecuted by the Church of Rome).

Through his noble lineage, Bernard was also related to Hugues (Hugh) de Payen who was instrumental with the aid of Godfroi (Godfrey) de Bouillon in establishing the Order of the 'Poor Knights of Christ', which originally consisted of only nine men. According to information contained in the *Hiram Key* by Christopher Knight and Robert Lomas, Hugues de Payen was accompanied on his journey by Andre de Montbard who was the uncle of St Bernard.

The Order of the Cistercians as they developed under St Bernard became extremely numerous and was a party to be reckoned within the politics of both State and Church; even one of Bernard's monks, Eugenius III, became a pope. Both the Cistercians and the Carthusians had their origins dating back to the 11th century in Burgundy.

Credit has also been given to St Bernard for giving assistance to Scotland's Celtic Church.

Sir Hugues (Hugh) De Payen (1070 - 1136 AD)

Hugh was born of noble birth in the Champagne area of France and he went into service as a knight with the Count of Champagne who was his cousin.

(It was mentioned in an earlier chapter, that Marie of France, the daughter of Eleanor of Aquitaine by King Louis VII of France, wrote several Grail romances between 1155 and 1190, and she was married to the Count of Champagne during the era of the Crusades. It was at the Court of the Count of Champagne that Chrétien of Troyes also resided and wrote his Arthurian romances. Marie's stepfather was Henry II, Plantagenet King of England and her half brother was Richard the Lion Heart). Hugh paid a visit to Henry I, Plantagenet King of England

and was given a warm welcome.

Hugh was the First Grand Master of the Knights Templar, a Master of the Grail, (following in the footsteps of John the Beloved alias Joseph of Arimathea) and his Order was founded in 1118 AD. (The Knights Templar patron was the Cistercian, St Bernard of Clairvaux 1090-1153, who interestingly was twenty years younger than Hugh de Payen). In 1118 AD, Hugh and his Knights Templar joined the Crusades. (The First Crusades commenced in 1095).

Throughout the time that the Knights spent in Jerusalem, they were given the support of Baldwin II who became the titled king of Jerusalem and the Count of Anjou. The Knights appointed themselves as guardians of the roads leading to Jerusalem and established their lodgings on the site of Herod's Temple at which time they conducted themselves in a most secretive manner. There is much speculation as to the motives of these knights for it is thought that they spent their nine years there tunnelling through solid rock to reach the 'Holy of Holies' in Jerusalem in an effort to gain the stored treasures and documents or even the Ark of the Covenant. Whatever treasures they retrieved are reputed to be hidden somewhere beneath the Chapel.

Hugh de Payen married Katherine St Clair in 1101, and was given Blancradock, Scotland as part of the dowry. In a later century, in 1446, Sir William St Clair donated the land at Rosslyn where the famous Rosslyn Freemasonic Chapel was built. The Chapel took forty years to build and was never fully completed.

In 1128, Hugues de Payen, had a meeting with King David I of Scotland not long after the Council of Troyes. (King David I was to become the grandfather of King William the Lion of Scots who was an incarnation of St Germain who also supported and granted land to the Knights Templar in Scotland).

Local legend in Roslin, Scotland, tells of an enormous treasure whose hiding place will not be revealed until the day when a trumpet blast shall awaken 'a certain Lady of the ancient house of St Clair from her long sleep'. The question arises; will it be discovered in Scotland or elsewhere in the British Isles? Too much attention has been focused upon Rosslyn in recent times and the clues which lead to Rosslyn Chapel could all be a red-herring.

All the evidence points to Hugh de Payen the First Grand Master of the Knights Templar, as having been an incarnation of St Germain. It stands to reason that having once been the Father of the Family of the Holy Grail that St Germain would become the First Master of the Knights Templar whose Order was so bound-up with Freemasonry.

Hugh, the 'First Grand Master of the Knights Templar', who had married into the Scottish family of St Clair, the family which donated land in Scotland to the Knights Templar, died on the 24th May, 1136 AD, and St Germain's next incarnation was as King William the Lion of Scots, a 'Defender of the Faith'

(1143-1214), who as previously mentioned, donated land to the Knights Templar.

William the Lion's (St Germain's) grandfather, David I, was the youngest son of Malcolm Canmor and Margaret, who was the granddaughter of King Edmund. David married Matilda, a wealthy heiress who was the daughter of the 2nd Earl of Northumberland. From this marriage David secured land in six English counties and founded many monasteries.

Much of David's earlier life was spent in England, at the royal court and when he became David King of Scotland, he was given a great deal of Norman support. In gratitude for the support given to him by certain Norman nobles, such as Fitz-Alan, (who later became Stewards/Stewarts of Scotland), they in turn, were granted gifts of land.

The lineage of Malcolm Canmor, father of King David could be traced back to the People of Dalriata and Dalriada - the tribe to which Prince Columba (St Germain) belonged. It was Malcolm Canmor who gave the St Clairs the Barony of Roslin where the now famous Rosslyn chapel of the Knights Templar was built in the year 1446 AD, and as previously mentioned, the St Clairs in turn, donated some of their land to the Knights Templar.

According to information supplied by the present Earl of Rosslyn, in a booklet I obtained whilst visiting the Chapel in 2001, William St Clair came to England with his first cousin, William the Conqueror and fought with him at the Battle of Hastings in 1066.

William the Conqueror reigned as King of England from 1066-1087 AD, after his Norman invasion known as the famous Battle of Hastings. William's youngest son became Henry I (1068-1135 AD), Plantagenet King of England who married Edith of Scotland. Edith was the daughter of King Malcolm of Scots, otherwise known as Malcolm Canmor (also Canmore) and St Margaret. In Scotland, Malcolm was the 'Defender of the Celtic Faith'.

King Henry 1st (Plantagenet) arranged a marriage between his daughter Matilda and Henry V, Holy Roman Emperor, and after his death in 1128 AD to Geoffrey IV, (1113-51 AD), the count of Anjou. Geoffrey was the grandson of King Baldwin II of Jerusalem. Accordingly Geoffrey was fond of wearing a sprig (*planta*) of broom (*genista*) in his hat which is how the name *Plantagenet* was derived. (Geoffrey and Matilda's eldest son became Henry II, Plantagenet King of England).

William St Clair escorted the bride of Malcolm Canmor, the Saxon princess, Margaret, from the court of Hungary, (where she had been raised), to Scotland. He was made cup-bearer to Queen Margaret and obtained a life interest in the barony of Rosslyn. William St Clair had a son Henry St Clair who accompanied Godfroi de Bouillon to the Holy Land in 1096.

Henry St Clair's son, also named Henry was the first of the St Clairs to live at Rosslyn and he was knighted by King David I and was sent by King William the Lion (St Germain) as ambassador to Henry II, Plantagenet King of England.

As Merlin in the 6th century AD, St Germain prophesied that he would one day return as the 'Lion of Scotland'. King William the Lion (St Germain) was the son of Henry 6th Earl of Northumberland and it is a rather curious fact that in St Germain's life as Sir Francis Tudor Bacon, his real father, Robert Dudley, was the son of Lord Northumberland. William succeeded his brother Malcolm IV (1141?-1165) as King in 1165 and reigned as King of Scotland until his demise in 1214 AD.

Omar Khayyam (Kuthumi) and the Old Man of the Mountains

It was into this same era that Kuthumi incarnated as Omar Khayyam (? - 1123 AD), the poet/philosopher/mathematician who was the Royal Astrologer at the court of the Shah of Persia and he also made a pilgrimage to the Crusades where he no doubt met up with Hugh de Payen.

One of Omar's associates was Malik Shah, the grandson of Toghrul Beg the Tartar, who had wrested Persia from the feeble successor of Mahmud the Great, and founded the Seljukian (Turkish) Dynasty, which finally roused Europe into the Crusades. Omar's other close friend was Nizam-ul-Mulk, Vizier to Alp Arslan and Malik Shah. Nizam-ul-Mulk met Omar Khayyam when he became the pupil of one of the wise men of Naishapur, at which time he and Omar undertook the study of the Koran, the sacred book of the Muslims.

From the article titled *The Secrets of the Knights Templar* which appeared in New Dawn magazine in March 1998, we learn the following:

"The truth is that the Knights Templar were established to fulfill a spiritual ideal entrusted to them by St Bernard. This secret mission amounted to a rediscovery of the original Middle Eastern sources of Christian mysticism. Furthermore, these knights were members of a religious order; their name 'guardians of the Holy Land' assumed a higher meaning. We know that each of the different authentic Traditions has its own Holy Land, counterpart of the ideal Holy Land, symbol of the Primordial Tradition itself. In the case of the Templars the city of Jerusalem was not only the centre of the Mosaic tradition but also the image of the spiritual state for which it stood. We can easily understand how in these conditions the temporal and regal power was alarmed by the fraternization between Christians and Muslims which transcended all doctrinal differences. The 19th century French Catholic occult writer Elphias Levi concluded that the Templars' spiritual vision threatened the whole world with an immense revolution."

The same article quoted Julius Evola, the author of *The Legacy of the Grail*:

"Moreover, the Templars were charged with keeping secret liaisons with Muslims and being closer to the Islamic faith than to the Christian one. The 'secret liaisons' allude to a perspective that is less sectarian, more universal, and thus more esoteric than of militant Christianity. The Crusades, in which the Templars played a fundamental role, in many aspects created a supra traditional bridge between West and East. The crusading knighthood ended up confronting ethics, chivalrous customs, ideals of a 'holy war' and initiatory currents. Thus the Templars were the Christian equivalent of the Arab Order of the *Ishmaelites*."

Another associate, with whom Omar had studied in his youth, was Hasan Ben Sabbah. In later years, Hasan demanded a place in the government with the Sultan of Persia who employed Omar as the Court's Royal Astrologer and teacher. However, Hasan ben Sabbah became discontented with his life and dissociating himself with Omar, he plunged into a maze of intrigue, which resulted in him trying to overthrow the Sultan.

Within Edward Fitzgerald's version of the *Rubaiyat of Omar Khayyam*, there is a commentary which was written about the life of Omar.

"It was recorded by Nizam-ul-Mulk that he met Hakim Omar Khayyam who was endowed with sharpness of wit and the highest natural powers. One of the other students that studied with them was Hasan Ben Sabbah. Hasan became the head of the Persian sect of the *Ismailians*, a party of fanatics who had long murmured in obscurity but rose to an evil eminence under the guidance of his strong and evil will."

"In 1090 AD he seized the castle of Alamut, in the province of Rudbar, which lies in the mountainous tract south of the Caspian Sea; and it was from this mountain home that he obtained evil celebrity amongst the Crusaders as 'THE OLD MAN OF THE MOUNTAINS'."

"The terror spread through the Mohammedan world; and it is yet disputed whether the word *Assassin* which they have left in the language of modern Europe as their dark memorial, is derived from the *hashish* or opiate of hemp-leaves (the Indian *bhang*), with which they maddened themselves into the sullen pitch of oriental desperation."

"One of the countless victims of the Assassin's dagger was Nizam-ul-Mulk himself, the old school-boy friend."

New Dawn magazine March-April edition of 1998 quoted Dr Bussell from his book titled *Religious Thought and Heresy in the Middle Ages*:

"It cannot be disputed that the Templars had 'long and important dealings' with the Assassins and were therefore suspected of imbibing their precepts and following their principles.'

"From the middle of the 12th century the Assassins operated in close proximity to the Templars, and for a number of years they paid an annual tribute of gold to the knights. Oriental historians confirm a close relationship existed between the Assassins and the Templars. They remark that the same two Orders had the same colours (white and red), the same organization, the same hierarchy of degrees. While in Palestine, one of the leading Templar knights, Guillaume de Montbard, [an uncle of St Bernard] was even rumoured to have been initiated by a Grand Master of the Assassins."

"The Assassins were the most powerful secret society operating throughout the Middle East. In Syria, where they held a string of fortresses, their chief or Grand Master became known to the Crusaders as the OLD MAN OF THE MOUNTAINS. From his mountain stronghold at Alamut, 'the eagle's nest' in northern Persia, the Assassin Grand Master presided over a network of initiates sworn to a politico-religious vision inspired by a secret wisdom tradition. The authoritative work *The Concise Encyclopedia of Islam*, states that the first Old Man of the Mountains, Hasan Sabbah, built his empire through the propagation of *Ismailism*, a Gnostic-dualistic creed which teaches that out of an unknowable God...a series of emanations called 'intellects' emerged which culminated in the creation of the world. Hasan Sabbah's Assassins were known in the Muslim world at the time as the *Ta'limmiyyah*, (the people of the secret teaching'), the *Batiniyyah*, ('the people of the inner truth') or the *Fidaiyyah* ('the self-sacrifices), in recognition of their esotericism and non-attachment to earthly life. Some authorities say the name 'Assassin' given to them by their enemies, derives from the Arabic *Assasseen*, meaning 'guardians'."

"Their castles in northern Persia and Syria were almost impregnable. When orthodox Muslim armies conquered Syria, the Syrian Assassins offered to ally themselves with the Crusaders and to become Christians. This offer was declined by the Crusaders, who may well have realised that, whatever religion the Assassins outwardly professed it would be no more than an outer garment."

"Their 'conversion' to exoteric religion could not be expected to affect their inner and secret beliefs. The Assassins highly valued knowledge - both spiritual and earthly. They amassed great libraries and acquired scientific instruments. When Mongol hordes eventually defeated the Assassins and overran Alamut, they discovered a grand centre of learning and scientific knowledge."

According to Edward Fitzgerald, the biographer of Omar Khayyam, we learn that Omar and his student companions, who included Hasan Ben Sabbah, were pupils of Imam Mowaffak of Naishapur but that Hasan Ben Sabbah was greatly influenced by his father, Ali, who was considered heretical in his creed and other doctrines. The path which Hasan chose, the part of the fanatic Ismailians whereby he became known as the Old Man of the Mountains', may have arisen from the influence of his father. However, he must have also retained some of his earlier esoteric teachings from the great teacher, Imam Mowaffak. Undoubtedly, Omar (Kuthumi) also, would have had some esoteric influence upon Hasan Ben Sabbah.

There were two major Muslim powers in the Near East during this time and they were at war with each other. They were the Seljuks who were advancing westwards and the Fatimid caliphs of Egypt - Palestine lay between them. The Seljuks had captured Jerusalem in 1070 and in 1099 the Fatimids had succeeded in recovering it. On the 15th July, 1099, there was no serious opposition and the Crusaders, led by Godfrey (Godfroi) de Bouillon, captured Jerusalem, thus he became known as the 'King of Jerusalem'.

Henry II Plantagenet (1133 - 1189 AD)

Henry II of England was the son of Geoffrey Plantagenet, count of Anjou, and the Empress Matilda. (He became King of England in 1154 AD). Henry II of England was the count of Anjou, the duke of Normandy and ruler of Anjou, Poitou and Aquitaine.

Eleanor of Aquitaine, who became Henry 11's wife, was one of the wealthiest land owners of the time. She was an outstanding ruler, the patron of poets and musicians of Aquitaine. When Eleanor became the Queen of England, she established a court like the old Arthurian days and hence the flood of writings by authors who wrote upon the subject of Arthur and Merlin.

It was from his marriage to Eleanor, that Henry acquired vast domains thus adding to his power and prestige in France. He was far wealthier in his holdings than his overlord Louis VII (c.1121-80) of France which often caused friction between them, apart from the fact the Eleanor was Louis' ex-wife. Eleanor and Henry produced five sons, William, Henry, Richard, Geoffrey and John, and three daughters, Matilda, Eleanor and Joan.

In order to defend and rule his lands, Henry had to be constantly on the move, followed by his large retinue of Knights. He had great abilities as a warrior and an administrator which earned him widespread respect. By 1170 AD, he had gradually changed and clarified the common law and dismissed incompetent sheriffs who were the king's representatives of the English counties.

Philip of Alsace, count of Flanders (d.1191) was a friend of Henry II, Plantagenet King of England. Philip was a member of the Knights Templar who took part in the Crusades. It is generally considered that during his time in the Holy Land, Philip came across an important document which was passed into the hands of Wolfram von Eschenbach who wrote *Parzival* in which Wolfram identified the Knights Templar as modern Grail Knights.

The two people mentioned in the discovery of the Grail story, whose names Wolfram disguised under pseudonyms, are believed to be Hugh de Payen (1070-

1136 AD) and the Count of Champagne. Wolfram seems to have gone to great lengths to conceal names, places and events which was exactly what the bards and minstrels of the Middle Ages did, in order to prevent being persecuted for extolling the 'truth'. (The capital city of Champagne was Troyes where Chrétien c.1150-1195 AD, who also wrote many Grail romances, resided). Accordingly, Chrétien was a close friend and relative of Hugh de Payen.

According to the authors of the book *The Holy Blood And the Holy Grail*, Michael Baigent, Richard Leigh and Henry Lincoln, "the Order of the Temple was established in 1118 and it is clearly on record that the count of Anjou - father of Geoffrey Plantagenet - joined the Order in 1120, only two years after its supposed foundation, and in 1124 the count of Champagne, did likewise."

"At least three of the nine founding knights, including Hugues de Payen, seem to have come from adjacent regions, to have had family ties, to have known each other previously and to have been vassals of the same lord. This lord was the count of Champagne. The count of Champagne donated the land on which St Bernard; patron of the Knights Templar, built the famous Abbey of Clairvaux; and one of the nine founding knights, Andre de Montbard, was Saint Bernard's uncle."

"In Troyes, the capital of Champagne, the court of the count of Champagne was an influential school of Cabalistic and esoteric studies which had flourished since 1070. It was at the court of Troyes that the Templars were officially incorporated."

Clearly the court was a centre where the Mysteries of the sacred Arcana of the *Mystical Rose*, were taught; a centre that attracted many of the Order of the Knights Templar and European nobles and a centre that may have been one of the European Avalons.

MASTERS DISCUSSED IN THIS CHAPTER

Joseph, Father of the Holy Grail Family - St Germain
Sir Hugh de Payen, First Grand Master of the Knights Templar - in all probability St Germain (1070-1136 AD)
King William the Lion of Scots - St Germain (1143-1214 AD)
Omar Khayyam - Kuthumi (d. 1123 AD)

NOTES AND RECOMMENDED READING

Elizabeth Hallam, *The Plantagenet Encyclopedia*, (Tiger Books, U.K., 1996)
David Hugh Farmer, *Saint Hugh Of Lincoln*, (Honywood Press, U.K., 1992)
Ian Grimble, *The Scottish Isles*, (British Broadcasting Corporation, U.K., 1985)
F.J. Dennett, *Europe, A History*, (Linehan & Shrimpton, Melbourne, Australia, 1961)

R.H.C. Davis, *A History of Medieval Europe*, (Longman U.K. 1970)

Excerpts from New Dawn Magazine, March 1998: *The Secrets of the Knights Templar*, (Life Science Fellowship, P.O. Box 12116, A' Becket Street, Melbourne, Victoria, 3000).

Michael Baigent, Richard Leigh & Henry Lincoln, *The Holy Blood And The Holy Grail*, (Arrow Books, U.K., 1996)

Michael Baigent & Richard Leigh, *The Temple And The Lodge*, (Corgi Books, U.K., 1996)

Michael Baigent, Richard Leigh & Henry Lincoln, *The Messianic Legacy*, (Arrow Books, U.K., 1996

Christopher Knight and Robert Lomas, *The Hiram Key*, (Century Books, U.K., 1996)

Arnold J. Toynbee, *A Study Of History*, (Oxford University Press, U.K., 1934)

Michael Howard, *The Occult Conspiracy*, (Ryder & Ryder, U.K. 1989)

Edward Fitzgerald, *Rubaiyat of Omar Khayyam*, (Collins, U.K. 1974)

Daniel J. Boorstin, *The Discoverers, A History of Mans' Search To Know His World And Himself*, (Random House, U.K., 1983)

CHAPTER 37

St Hugh of Castle Avalon (1140-1200 AD)

"The most beautiful sacerdotal figure known to me in history"
(Ruskin giving his opinion of St Hugh)
"His particular blend of strength and gentleness, austerity and hospitality, scholarship and closeness to nature, accessibility and intransigence made him a saint of all times and of all seasons."
(Biographer, David Hugh Farmer giving his opinion of St Hugh)

A centre of Learning in the Burgundy area of France during the Crusades in the 11th and 12th centuries was *Avalon*.

In the Bibliography of the book titled *The Holy Blood And The Holy Grail* by Michael Baigent, Richard Leigh and Henry Lincoln, the authors write:

"It is interesting that the French city of Avallon dates back to Merovingian times. It was the capital of a region, then a comte, which was part of the kingdom of Aquitaine. [Eleanor of Aquitaine married Henry II, Plantagenet of England]. It gave its name to the whole region - the Avallonnais."

According to Hugh's biographer, David Hugh Farmer, "Hugh was a Burgundian by birth. He came not from French but from Imperial Burgundy. His father William was the "Sieur [Lord] of Avalon, a knight of the feudal family of Graisivaudan who spent most of his life in the service of the emperors. Hugh's mother, Anna, was the daughter of the Lord of Theys and their home was the Castle Avalon." Further information contained in David Farmer's book informs us that Hugh's father and two brothers, Peter and William were members of the Knights Templar.

Hugh of Castle Avalon was born three years before King William the Lion of Scots. King William the Lion of Scots as mentioned elsewhere, was an incarnation of St Germain (1143-1214 AD) and it appears very probable that he had in a previous life, been the First Grand Master of the Knights Templar, Sir Hugh de Payen, who like Hugh of Avalon, was born of noble birth in Burgundy.

Hugh assisted his mother, Anna, who was much loved by all and renowned for her care of the sick and the poor. From an early age he would help her to wash the sores of the lepers. Following his mother's early death, Hugh's father William of Avalon took his young son to a small monastery at Villarbenoit, near Grenoble, in the company of other sons of nobility and it was there that Hugh was initially educated. Later on, he made the decision to join the Order of the Carthusians as a monk in 1159 AD and he spent the early years of his life in France, beginning as a deacon in charge of the tiny parish of St Maximin which was the village closest to Avalon. It was at St Maximin that Mary Magdalene's remains were preserved in the Abbey. Maximin had been included amongst the party which Joseph of Arimathea (John the Beloved - Kuthumi) escorted to Marseilles Gaul.

The district in which Hugh lived was called the Dauphine. After the fall of the Roman Empire, this territory comprised the southern part of the kingdom of Burgundy. In subsequent centuries it was successively part of the dominions of the Carolingian kings, part of the new Burgundian kingdom of Arles and a possession of the counts of Vienne whose title Dauphine, gave the region its name and it was to later become incorporated with France.

During his time in France, Hugh was called upon to nurse a Cistercian archbishop, Peter of Tarentaise who would often visit the Grande Chartreuse where Hugh had become ordained as a priest. It was St Bernard of Clairvaux who had given the appointment of archdeacon to Peter of Tarentaise. Peter had the reputation himself of being a miracle healer and he established hospices for travellers. The original biographer of Hugh, Adam, wrote of the close friendship that was established between Hugh and Peter and it was thought that Peter discussed much of his own life and probably that of his patron, St Bernard of Clairvaux, with Hugh.

On his many visits to France, Henry II of England, (who was also the duke of Normandy), had established a close friendship with Hugh of Avalon. According to David Farmer, "Henry's affection for Hugh had been so well known that some had thought him to be his illegitimate son. The chronology of such an attribution is impossible. Henry was fifty-six when he died and by then Hugh was forty-nine."

Henry II had a falling out with his best friend Thomas a Becket (reputed to have been an incarnation of the Master El Morya), who was the archbishop of Canterbury. When the trouble between Thomas and Henry had reached a stage where the issues seemed to be unsolvable, unfortunately, due to a misunderstanding about Henry's instructions, some of Henry's knights murdered Thomas in 1170 AD in his own cathedral at Canterbury.

It was not long after his death, that miracles occurred at his tomb and pilgrims came from far and wide. Chaucer's *Canterbury Tales* was written in honour of Thomas a Becket. It is of interest to note that Chaucer translated a work called the *Roman de la Rose* ('The Rose of Rome') into English. Could Chaucer have also been familiar with the ancient teachings of the *Mystical Rose?* On a diplomatic mission to Italy in 1372-3, Chaucer discovered the works of Dante which had a major influence on his poetry. (Dante belonged to the Order of the Rose Cross). Geoffrey Chaucer (c.1340-1400) was married to Katherine of Swynford's sister. (Katherine became the third wife of John of Gaunt and her descendants were the Lancastrians who took part in the War of the Roses. Katherine is fondly remembered in the book by the same name written by Anya Seton and Katherine's tomb is in Lincoln Cathedral).

In 1180, (two years before the birth of Francis of Assisi), after serving forty years in France in the Burgundy area of the Knights Templar, Hugh was brought to England by Henry II to become the abbot of the Carthusian priory of Witham, near Bath, and not far from Glastonbury. It was because of Henry's administrative skills that he recognised in Hugh of Avalon, similar abilities.

During the second half of his life, Hugh became the confident of nobles, kings and the friend of Jews. Having spent the first forty years of his life in France and made this important decision to remain the rest of his time residing in England, Hugh was to spend the duration of his life humouring and settling disputes between the three Angevin kings at which time he was often privy to the most confidential information and plans formulated by these kings, (Henry, Richard and John).

Hugh made several return trips to France on behalf of Henry and formulated many influential friendships. According to information contained in David Hugh Farmer's biography of Hugh, after six years serving as prior at Witham, Hugh was appointed by Henry as Bishop of Lincoln Cathedral in Lincolnshire. He was enthroned as bishop on the Feast of St Michael, 29th September, 1186. A week earlier, he had been consecrated at Westminster Abbey in St Catherine's chapel on the feast of St Matthew on the 21st September. Special days such as these, were chosen because the bishops were believed *to be the successors of the Apostles in the English Christian Church.*

There were two important factors about Hugh's appointment. One was that the king had chosen him and the second was that Hugh's initial reluctance to accept the position offered to him, was overcome by the intervention of the priory of the Grande Chartreuse who for political and religious reasons, saw the installation of Hugh as a bishop of England, as being most advantageous. The politics at this time were mainly to do with the Crusades.

Hugh was the first French bishop ever to be installed in England. His appointment to Lincoln Cathedral proved to be a brilliant success. There were many times that Hugh opposed Henry II on numerous issues, such as his forest laws about which Hugh was concerned for the unfair taxes placed upon the people who lived in or around the vicinity of the forests and he managed to prevent them from being taxed.

This period of time in history was during the days of 'Robin Hood and his merry men'.

Queen Guinevere, King Arthur and Sir Lancelot of the 12th century AD

Henry II (1133-1189) had first met Eleanor of Aquitaine when she was the wife of King Louis VII of France who was Henry's feudal overlord. She divorced Louis and within eight weeks, married Henry. Henry was only nineteen years of age at the time and she was considerably older. He became King of England when he was twenty-one.

When the marriage of Eleanor of Aquitaine and Henry began to fail, Hugh tried to mend it for them but by then the rift was too great and Eleanor returned to France. Both Eleanor and Henry were known for their 'affairs'; neither could stay faithful to the other. Eleanor though, caused Henry much consternation for she turned his sons against him.

David Farmer made the following comments, "The fact that his wife, the brilliant but unreliable Eleanor of Aquitaine, and his sons all opposed him more or less constantly in his last years must have brought him much disappointment."

Accordingly, Henry's mistress was the 'Fair Rosamund', daughter of Walter de Clifford and Hugh on more than one occasion, informed Henry II of his disapproval of the relationship.

Interestingly, Walter Map who was mentioned in an earlier chapter was the satirical chancellor of Lincoln, appointed prior to Hugh's arrival there and he and Hugh became close friends. It was also mentioned earlier that in circa 1172 AD, Chrétien of Troyes wrote the work titled *Le Chevalier a la Cherrette - The Knight of the Cart*, which introduced Lancelot for the first time and told the story of the 'Ordeal of the Sword Bridge', wherein Lancelot heroically rescues Guinevere - the story of which was commissioned by Marie who was the daughter of Eleanor of Aquitaine and step-daughter of King Henry II, being the daughter of King Louis of France.

The comments made by Emile Legouis in his book titled *A History of English Literature* (1945), are also relevant to this chapter in keeping with the continuity.

"Allowing for the part of Chrétien de Troyes, the conclusion is that the British cycle was evolved principally by the Anglo-Normans, and that **Walter Map**, who was half-Norman and half-Welsh, presumably welded together the Arthurian legend and the legend of the Holy Grail. He is credited with giving the cycle its religious and moral character in that he represents Guinevere, Arthur's wife, as an adulteress, and her lover, Lancelot, as unworthy, by his sin, to accomplish the quest for the

Holy Grail..." **The *Queste del Saint Graal, Lancelot du Lac,* and *Mort d' Arthur* are attributed to Walter Map**. It was a story all the more stimulating to them because it was set in their own country, and they believed it to be national."

Although the origins of the knight, Sir Lancelot have previously been explored and explained, and that they consist of a combination of legends and names over different periods of time, it is possible that Walter Map in his version, was having a 'pun' on Henry II, and his wife, Eleanor of Aquitaine. It was she who first introduced the idea of chivalry into the Plantagenet Court, based upon the Arthurian legends. The Plantagenet Court was Eleanor's 'Camelot'. Therefore, she may have been portrayed as Queen Guinevere.

Historically, the real King 'Arthur', as we have already learned, was Aedan mac Gabran, who had lived some six hundred years earlier in the 6th century AD, was according to some sources, married to a Pictish Princess from Scotland. Therefore, if in Walter Map's story, Eleanor was Queen Guinevere, then King Henry II was portrayed as the King Arthur of the 12th century. Walter's Sir Lancelot was a French Knight - and Eleanor of Aquitaine, upon leaving Henry, fled back to France; so perhaps Walter Map's Sir Lancelot was King Louis.

According to David Farmer, "Strict churchmen who had not been satisfied by the dissolution of Eleanor's marriage to Louis regarded the children of Henry's union with Eleanor as 'The Devil's Brood'."

The legendary story of Arthur, Guinevere and Lancelot depicted the eternal triangle. In the story of King Arthur, when he found out about his adulteress wife, Guinevere, he became a very lonely saddened man which is precisely what happened to Henry II.

Elizabeth Hallam in her book titled *Chronicles of the Crusades* (1989) wrote that Eleanor was an 'imprudent woman', whom it is alleged, was unfaithful to her husband Henry. Accordingly, Eleanor, as some stage, was rumoured to have had an affair with Raymond, Prince of Antioch.

Lincoln Cathedral

At the time that Hugh was appointed as bishop of Lincoln, the Cathedral had recently been severely damaged by an earthquake. Hugh searched for a master-mason and acquired an architect to rebuild the cathedral, namely Geoffrey of de Noiers. Stone had to be quarried and transported from a nearby source. Masons were needed to cut, shape and carve it.

Hugh was one of the first to introduce pointed arches into an English building. According to David Hugh Farmer "...when the nature and the scale of Hugh's achievements is studied closely, it can be seen that it was in all probability the most important in the history of the cathedral between 1073 and the late thirteenth century. Unfortunately, the full history of the building of Lincoln has never been written."

"Modern visitors to the splendid pile of Lincoln cathedral cannot fail to be impressed by its immense size, beauty and delicacy. Its harmony of design, the combination of strength and delicacy, of size and grandeur with the exquisite execution of the smallest detail and the striking contrasts of light and shade, recall the mixture of austerity and courage, gentleness and courtesy which made the Burgundian bishop one of the most popular saints. Hugh actually worked on the building himself, carrying a hod with stones and mortar."

It was mentioned in an earlier chapter that Kuthumi, in his previous incarnation as the Poet, Philosopher, Mathematician and royal Astrologer, Omar Khayyam, (? -1123 AD), was employed to design and make the Gothic stained-glass which was installed in many of the 12th century Gothic cathedrals. The glass was of such beautiful luminosity that the likes of it have never been seen since and the secret of how it was made has long ago vanished. According to tradition, only those who knew the secret of Alchemy were able to perfect such glass. Kuthumi, as Pythagoras, was the Master of Mathematics. As Omar, he was a Master Mathematician. All the ancient Cathedrals were built on Pythagorean mathematical principles as well as being built on Ley lines.

Hugh's design and overseeing of its construction made his building one of the most important to be erected in England during the last part of the 12th century and to this day, it remains as a fine memorial to him. Built high on a hill it can be seen from miles around, especially considering that the area of Lincolnshire is so flat.

It is of interest to note that during the Second World War, the brave English pilots who flew over Germany on night missions, returned via Lincoln guided by the top of the spire of the cathedral.

Hugh loved children and they were especially fond of him. Another lovely attribute of Hugh's was that he continually visited the sick amongst who were the lepers and just as he had done in his youth when he accompanied his mother Anna, Hugh washed, dried and kissed their feet. He also provided them with food, drink and was generous in providing them with money. He would visit the hospices where the lepers were and sit amongst them giving comfort with kindly words and motherly tenderness.

He was credited with giving away a third of his yearly income to help the poor and infirm. Accordingly, in those days many people did not bother to bury their dead, they just left them along the way side, especially the lepers. Hugh would take it upon himself to personally bury the bodies and he would inform his priests that *"God would immediately send his angels to guard the soul on its return to its creator, and thus being happily reunited, it would blossom again to enjoy ever eternal renewal."* This recorded statement of Hugh's clearly defines how he believed in reincarnation.

One of Hugh's close friends in his early days at Lincoln, was Baldwin (died 1190 AD) archbishop of Canterbury who had previously been a monk at Ford Abbey in Devon. Baldwin was not only a member of the Order of the Cistercians (the Order to which St Bernard of Clairvaux had belonged) but was also a Knight who took a prominent part in the Third Crusade. He was also possibly a cousin of Baldwin, count of Flanders (1171-1205) who was also the emperor of Constantinople.

One year after the capture of Jerusalem, the majority of the Knights Templar returned to their homes, leaving Baldwin the First with about three hundred knights with which to defend the city. The small coastal town remained in the hands of the Muslims and was still to be captured. He enlisted the help of the Genoese fleet in 1101 and then Venice, the trading rival of Genoa, also lent its fleet in 1110. But even with the country conquered, there was still the problem of governing and defending it.

Baldwin, the archbishop of Canterbury, was a favourite of Henry II and his son Richard the Lion Heart. When the Third Crusade was imminent in which Richard the Lion Heart was to play a major role, Baldwin set up a meeting at which time Hugh of Lincoln was present and approved of the Crusade to protect the Holy Land. Hugh was asked to join the Crusades, however, it was deemed necessary for him to give stability to his diocese.

Baldwin journeyed to Wales to preach the Third Crusade, accompanied by Gerald of Wales (Giraldus Cambrensis), who was the son of a Norman knight and bishop-elect of St David's in Wales. Whilst he was away on the Third Crusade, Baldwin founded a hospice called St Thomas at Acre and died during the siege at Acre in 1190.

Richard the Lion Heart King of England
And William the Lion of Scotland (1143-1214 AD) 'Defender of the Faith'

"A new conqueror shall be named and crowned Lion....the Lion shall hold the Balance and stretch his palm over Scotland..."
(Merlin/St Germain 6th century AD)

Not long after Henry II's death which occurred on the 3rd September, 1189, Hugh of Lincoln attended the coronation of Richard I the Lion Heart, so named because of his valour during the Crusades. In December of the same year, Hugh of Lincoln and Geoffrey Plantagenet, archbishop elect of York (who was the illegitimate son of Henry II), were given the important task of escorting William I, the Lion, King of Scotland (1143-1214) to Canterbury to greet Richard. William the Lion (St Germain) of Scotland and Hugh of Lincoln (previously of Avalon) were very close friends and William often consulted Hugh upon important issues.

Eleanor of Aquitaine sided with William who hoped to re-obtain Northumberland and Cumbria, which was lost to England in 1157. However, he was defeated on the battlefield and captured. William had little choice but to sign the *Treaty of Falaise* which recognised the English King as the Lord of Scotland but when Richard the Lion Heart became King of England, William paid money to him to have the Treaty annulled. During his time of captivity, the High Steward of Scotland, Walter Fitz Alan attended to the affairs of Scotland. (The name of Steward was later to become that of Stewart and Stuart).

After William the Lion was freed, he requested Pope Clement to declare the Church of Scotland (Albany) independent from the Church of Rome. In this he was unsuccessful for after considerable delay, in 1188 Pope Clement III replied that the Scottish Church would be subject to Rome.

King William joined forces with France against England in what was the first Franco-Scots alliance and he was a supporter of the Knights Templar, as had been his grandfather David I, who had granted land in Scotland, to the Templars in the area of Argyll. He was able to subdue the areas of Caithness. Sutherland in the late 12th century and the Scandinavian Western Isles were added to Scotland by the *Treaty of Perth* in 1266.

William the Lion of Scotland died at Stirling Castle, Scotland, in 1214 AD.

Mention was made in an earlier chapter of Captain Sir James Stirling who founded the Swan River Settlement, which he named after Perth in Scotland. He was a descendant of David I of Scotland. The Stirling descendants were prominent members of the Scottish Freemasons and one of their earlier ancestors, became famous as Lord Provost of Glasgow in the troubled times of Charles II. Another of Sir James Stirling's ancestors was Walter who played a prominent part during the reign of Mary Queen of Scots.

Richard the Lion Heart introduces the British National Emblem Of the St George Cross

When Richard became King of England after the death of his father Henry II, he spent many years away from England fighting the Holy Wars of the Crusades in order to win Jerusalem back from the Muslims. Richard is reputed to have only spent six months of his reign in England for which he has received much criticism from historians. He was a member of the Knights Templar and he travelled in their ships and resided at their castles during his sojourns in Europe. He sold Cyprus to the Templar Order and the island for a time, became their official seat.

Richard was captured by Leopold V duke of Austria who surrendered him to the Holy Roman Emperor Henry VI, and he was imprisoned at a castle in Germany. This event took place on Richard's return from the Holy Land. He was held for ransom and it was Hugh of Avalon in Burgundy who became St Hugh of Lincoln, England, who held the important meetings which raised the money for Richard's release.

According to information contained in Peter Dawkins' book titled *The Great Vision*:

"Richard I vowed to refound the old British 'Arthurian' Order, and he promised to make any knight who could successfully scale the walls of Jerusalem during the Crusades, a 'Companion of St George'. His Knight Companions were to be distinguished by wearing the light-blue thongs like a garter around their knees, bound tightly on or just below the knee, to remind the knight never to flee. This insignia was previously used by the Druids, and its deeper meaning was defending the Truth. (The British Pendragon was described as an 'elected man of the garter', leader of your ranks'). Richard instituted the battle-cry 'For St George', esoterically meaning the same as the Druidic battle-cry. His knights carried his personal banner with his device of the Red Cross on a White Field - the flag which has now become the British Ensign."

"Richard I died before he could fittingly found his Order of the Round Table, but successive Kings of England implanted the ideal more firmly into the young English nation. Richard II ordered that every soldier should be distinguished by wearing the Red (Rose) Cross of St George, and from his time until the 16th century, the Red Cross was borne as a badge over the armour of each English soldier. Edward I renewed the ancient tournaments which had fallen into abeyance since Arthur's time and, with one hundred knights at the Round Table gathering at Kenilworth Castle, he revived the Arthurian glories."

"Edward III made the next big step, and he actually managed to carry out Richard I's cherished scheme. He refounded 'The Most Noble Order of St George and the Garter', as a 'society, fellowship and college of knights', having for its purpose 'Good Fellowship'. The Knights of this Order were also known as 'The Knights of St George and the Blue Garter'. The Order originally included ladies, who were known as *Dames de la confraternite de St George*. There were twenty-six Knight Companions, including the King and his Queen (i.e. 13 x 2 in total), epitomizing the Christ presiding over his Zodiac in such a way as to show the male-female aspects of each part. They were to show fidelity and friendliness towards another. The light-blue garter presented Amity and Courage; the gold collar, having twenty-six garter links encircling twenty-six *Roses of Sharon* tied together with gold knots, representing the bond of Faith, Peace and Unity."

It will be recalled that the *Rose of Sharon* was planted upon the grave of St George (Kuthumi) and also upon the grave of Omar Khayyam (Kuthumi). The same is mentioned in Isaiah 35: "The wilderness and the solitary place shall be glad for them; and the desert shall rejoice, and blossom as the rose. It shall blossom abundantly, and rejoice even with joy and singing; the glory of Lebanon shall be given unto it, the excellency of Carmel and Sharon, they shall see the glory of the Lord and the excellency of our God."

According to the author Peter Lemesurier, in his book *The Armageddon Script*, 'Lebanon refers to the Essenes *Community Rule* in which the true Temple was represented by the community itself and was known as 'Lebanon' where 'the men of perfect holiness' dwelt who are elsewhere in the Scrolls, referred to as 'the Poor' and 'the sons of Zadok', while the revered founder of the whole movement is almost always referred to anonymously as 'the Teacher of Righteousness'.

King John (1167-1216 AD)
"An incompetent king will pull down the walls of Ireland"
(Merlin - St Germain)

Whilst Richard was away fighting the Crusades, his younger brother John took over the as ruler of England and history has not painted a particularly kind picture of John. Richard had chosen his nephew Arthur, duke of Brittany, as his successor whilst he was away fighting the Crusades. John in his resentment, plotted against Richard and when he heard of Richard's captivity, he attempted to prolong it and he is thought to have been behind the plans which led to the alleged murder of Richard's appointed successor.

William the Lion (St Germain) again attempted to regain Northumberland and Cumbria to be returned to Scotland when John became King of England and thus became the Lord of Scotland; however, by 1209 he still had no success.

In the 6th century AD, Merlin had predicted that an incompetent king during the 13th century would *'pull down the walls of Ireland'*. The prediction came true. John became lord of Ireland. In 1210, John led a campaign in Ireland at which time he successfully established royal authority. One of his main castles was built on the picturesque Shannon River in Limerick and is known as King John's castle which today has been turned into a museum displaying exactly how the knights of the olden days lived and fought.

The Last Days of St Hugh of Lincoln

At the time that John became King of England in 1199, he requested Hugh of Lincoln to take another journey abroad, the purpose of which was to end the hostility between himself and Philip, King of France. Shortly after this, Hugh obtained permission to make an extended pilgrimage to a series of famous shrines and monasteries in his homeland. One of the places he visited was La Motte which was the centre of the Order of the Hospitallers. The Hospitallers were the Knights of the Order of St John (the Beloved, the Master Kuthumi).

When Hugh arrived at Grenoble, the bishop and people came out to welcome him as one of their own. His long pilgrimage had tired him to such a degree that on his return to England, he knew his time was near.

It had been a long career and the years of being friend and advisor to the three Angevin kings had also taken its toll. Knowing that death was imminent, Hugh gave precise instructions that he was to be buried in front of the altar of St John the Baptist, in the northern most chapel of the eastern part of the Cathedral that he had been instrumental in building.

This was a common request for anyone who had been a Knight Templar or connected with Freemasonry. At the erection of all stately or superb edifices, it is customary to lay the first foundation stone in the north-east corner and this tradition is steeped in the history of the Freemasons.

Amongst the important visitors who came to Hugh's deathbed was King John who was very distressed to see his friend Hugh, so ill. He offered to help Hugh in any way he could. On the 16th November, 1200 AD, Hugh died in the house of the bishops of Lincoln in London and the funeral procession took five days to reach Lincoln Cathedral where he wished to be buried.

In the foothills a mile from the city, they were met by the kings of England and Scotland, the archbishops of Canterbury, York, bishops, abbots, nobles, clergy, and magnates. The Jewish community of Lincoln also gathered to pay their respects to Hugh who had helped them on many occasions, particularly when he had bravely, personally defended them during a bloodthirsty riot in Lincoln in 1189. There was an immense crowd of people that had seldom been seen before. King John and other magnates carried his coffin on their shoulders.

The King of Scotland, William the Lion (St Germain), was overcome as he helped to carry the coffin. Thus was the scene for Hugh who was the most notable bishop of that period of time in the Middle Ages, loved and revered by all who knew him.

Although Hugh was known to have performed numerous miracles during his lifetime, others took place for various people on and after the day of Hugh's burial. From that day onwards up to and including the present era, pilgrims have journeyed to Lincoln Cathedral to his tomb and miracles have continued to occur.

According to David Farmer, "It was certainly appropriate that the burial of Hugh in 1200 should have been one of almost unprecedented solemnity, attended by rich and poor alike."

St Hugh and the Swan

During Hugh's lifetime, he had a close affinity with birds and animals, not unlike St Francis of Assisi who was born in the same era. However, a special story is about a white swan at his manor in Stow.

This story is especially dear to me because once, I had never heard of St Hugh of Lincoln. In 1996 during meditation one afternoon, I had a vision of a flock of swans that looked more like geese, except they were swans. One of them left the flock, came up very close to my vision and smiled at me. He was so unusual because he was larger than the average swan and was most unusual in appearance.

The swan's beak was bright yellow, where normally it would have been black, and his eyes were almost human. His feathers on the lower part of his body were incredibly white and there was no swelling like a swan would have on its beak. From his neck up to his head, he was covered in bright yellow feathers. It was the most incredible vision and at the time, I had no idea what it meant. According to a book of symbols, the swan was a symbol of celestial beings of the 'Other-world' and of St Hugh of Lincoln.

Eventually, I was led to take the journey to England and to St Hugh's tomb, still unaware that there was any connection to him and a 'real' swan.

A mythological Celtic tale concerns the story of King Lear's children who were turned into swans, to remain that way until St Patrick (Kuthumi) was the release them in a future century.

The visit to the Lincoln Cathedral was a most spiritual and memorable one which incurred some amazing experiences, including a manifestation of the second appearance upon my overseas journey, of my spiritual Guide.

Six weeks earlier, when my family and I had arrived at Heathrow airport in England, en route to Dublin, we missed the connecting bus to take us to Gatwick where we were to connect with a flight to take us to Ireland. We finally managed to locate a local tour bus which took us to our destination. Not long after boarding the bus, the tourist guide came up to us and said:

"Whilst in England, you should go to Lincoln Cathedral and when you get there, don't forget to look for the green man and the Lincoln Imp!" Then she continued on down the aisle to chat with the other passengers.

My daughter and I laughed thinking this was all very 'Celestine Prophecy' stuff, as we still had not decided whether we should go all the way to Lincoln just because of the strange vision of the Swan of St Hugh of Lincoln which I had received some six months previously.

Some weeks later, when we were leaving Ireland, a taxi driver mentioned to us that considering the fact that we were en route to Chester, Lincoln Cathedral would be well worth a visit. Thus, we were again reminded that we should visit Lincoln, and taking into consideration the vision I had received, we decided that three messages in all must mean that we were definitely to take the journey there. However, it still seemed a long way to go.

The second day after our arrival in the beautiful ancient town of Chester, where in 607 AD a great battle was fought between King Athelfrith of Northumbria and the Welsh leader Scromail, we finally decided to take a day's journey to Lincoln, not knowing in the least what to expect when we reached there.

Lincoln cathedral stands out for miles as one approaches it through the fens of Lincolnshire. It truly is a beacon and beckons one to explore its beauty. As we entered the enormous Cathedral, we were amazed by the thousands of 'pagan' carving with which it was decorated and as we stood gazing around, not knowing where exactly to begin to look for St Hugh's tomb, a priest appeared from nowhere, stood beside us and said, "have you espied the Green Man and the Lincoln Imp as yet?"

He then directed our gaze to the panels above where we were standing and there they were, carved so long ago by the ancient masons. It was explained to us that the masons took carte blanche about what they carved and that the Green Man was a Druidic symbol of fertility - the Imp had similar features to the Green Man.

Completely in awe of all these 'coincidences', I then enquired of the priest the whereabouts of St Hugh's Tomb, and behold, it was just in front of us and almost below the 'pagan' symbols of which we had first been informed about upon our arrival at Heathrow airport! My daughter and I looked at each other in sheer amazement, whilst at the same time thinking, "was this all there was to it? Had we journeyed all this way just to view these strange carvings of which we had seen similar ones in so many other ancient cathedrals?"

Suddenly, near the tomb, in the darkest corner, the familiar red glow started to emerge and my Guide, my teacher, the *Master of the Rose* began to manifest as he had done at Trinity College. As I gazed at him, I couldn't help but wonder what the significance of him appearing to me in front of St Hugh's tomb, was. Soon, his image faded and I was left feeling very puzzled as to why I had been brought to this Cathedral, a place so far from my home in Australia.

As we were leaving, I was drawn to purchase a book from the Cathedral bookshop titled *Saint Hugh of Lincoln* by David Hugh Farmer. When we at last returned to our hotel in Chester that night, although feeling rather over-awed by the day's events not to mention the long drive, I began to read through the book with the greatest of interest and intrigue for that historical period of the Crusades and the Knights Templar, seemed so familiar to me, like some far back distant memory of a past life.

The reader can imagine my overwhelming surprise and emotions when I reached the final chapter and learned of St Hugh's swan which became his symbol.

Gerald of Wales, who like Hugh was of noble birth and was related through lineage to Fergus Mor Mac Erc, wrote a biography of his close friend Hugh, as did Hugh's monk, Adam, who always attended him. The story of the swan described by Gerald and published in David Hugh Farmer's book, was exactly as I had seen the swan in my vision and I humbly realised why I had been guided to visit Lincoln cathedral and I knew then that St Hugh had been an incarnation of the Master Kuthumi.

"A swan suddenly arrived one day which had never been seen before. In a few days it had fought all the other swans there; being larger and heavier than them. It was about as much larger than a swan as a swan is larger than a goose; but in everything else, especially its white colour, it closely resembled a swan except that it was not only larger but also did not have the usual swelling and black streak on its beak."

"Instead, that part of its beak was flat and bright yellow in colour, as also were its head and the upper part of its neck. This royal bird of unusual appearance and size suddenly became completely tame when the bishop arrived. It let itself be captured without difficulty and was brought to the bishop for him to admire. When he fed it, the bird used to thrust its long neck up his wide and ample sleeve so that its head lay on Hugh's breast; for a little while it would remain there, hissing gently, as if it were talking fondly and happily to its master and asking something from him."

"Whenever the bishop returned after one of his usual absences, for three or four days before the swan displayed more excitement than usual. It flew over the surface of the river, beating the water with its wings and giving vent to loud cries. From time to time it left the pond and hastily strode either to the hall or the gate as if going to meet its master on his arrival."

"Curiously enough, it was friendly and tame to nobody except the bishop; it kept everyone else away from its master when it was with him by hissing at them and threatening them with wings and beak, emitting loud croaks as is the habit of swans. *It seemed determined to make it quite clear that it belonged only to him and was a symbol sent to the bishop alone.*"

"The keepers of the manor would know when the bishop was coming as soon as they heard the swan's unusual cries. On his last visit to the manor house in 1200, the swan would not meet Hugh. It was hanging its head with a general air of wretchedness giving it the appearance of suffering grief. Afterwards, people realised that it was taking its leave of its master for the last time. The swan realised that St Hugh was soon to leave his earthly mission and it survived for some years after Hugh's death, continuing to mourn its master."

Attributes of St Hugh

Included amongst Hugh's many attributes was the fact that he was fearless, independent and was well able to stand up to kings. He fought hard for human rights and was described as being a unique person and a unique saint. According to the tribute paid to him by his modern-day biographer, David Hugh Farmer, "Hugh's unusual combination of qualities has made him so appealing down the centuries *that Ruskin thought him 'the most beautiful sacerdotal figure known to me in history'. His particular blend of strength and gentleness, austerity and hospitality, scholarship and closeness to nature, accessibility and intransigence made him a saint of all times and all seasons."*

The Cathedral at Lincoln is a fine tribute to Hugh who was a friend of children, animals and birds, lepers, of kings, Knights Templars and the Jewish community. According to David Farmer, whilst Hugh was stationed at Grande Chartreuse in France, he had tamed squirrels and at Witham in England, a bird called a burnet was his close companion. "In this Hugh resembled other saints like Cuthbert and Godric, as well as Francis of Assisi (1182-1226) and Antony of Padua."

Hugh greatly encouraged learning and according to Gerald of Wales, the Lincoln schools were second only to those of Paris. In fact, "at Paris itself, near the end of Hugh's life the students flocked to acclaim him as their patron."

"Trained lawyers, Adam tells us, also admired Hugh's skill and integrity as a judge: on particular occasions he showed special knowledge of the laws of the sanctuary, of the rights and privileges of his see concerning knight-service and the traditional tribute of a cloak to the king..."

"Such knowledge and skill were unlikely qualities in one who had lived a contemplative monastic life until the age of forty-six. *What was his intellectual background and how did he acquire these particular attainments?"*

Paul Broadhurst, of Pendragon Press, Cornwall whom I met in Cornwall, wrote to me offering additional information regarding St Hugh. Paul's comments were as follows:

"Your idea that Hugh was Masonic in inspiration is not so strange, as Templarism and Grail hunting was of course, at its peak at around that time. The Chateau de la Grand Chartreuse near Avallon where he was born (which is now a Tibetan Buddhist monastery), was once quite a place. Evidently the locals experienced a vision of Saint Hugh and Saint Bruno with 12 disciples, wandering

through the Alpine countryside."

"Later the place was to become a great centre. And amongst other things, there was a foundry established there where they made the finest steel (Damask) in Europe for the Knights Templar. All very Arthurian! The fact that Hugh then went on to have a certain amount of influence on British royalty would seem to emphasize this. Hamish Miller and myself are planning a trip to Grande Chartreuse for purely by 'coincidence' (apart from your information regarding Saint Hugh), we have received a letter from a lady studying at the monastery, who has asked us to come and give a lecture there, oblivious of course, to the fact that we were being 'led' there by dowsing! (For the Serpent/Energy Ley lines in that area)."

(St Bruno was the original founder of the Order of the Carthusians at La Grande Chartreuse in France in 1084 and Henry II founded two Carthusians houses, the one at Witham in Somerset and another in France).

Conclusion:

In concluding this chapter, important points of interest are as follows:

1. St Hugh of Avalon became St Hugh of Lincoln, the first French bishop ever to achieve such a high position and whose life was centred in him being in the most strategic position. His influential importance during this era, knew no bounds. His kindness, love for humanity, peace-making abilities, charitable works and healing abilities, were unlimited.

2. At the beginning of his career, Hugh joined the Order of the Carthusians in 1159 AD. He became a deacon, in charge of the parish of St Maximin which was the village closest to Avalon. As Joseph of Arimathea (John the Beloved), Kuthumi had escorted the 'Bethany' party to Gaul (France) including Mary Magdalene, whose remains were preserved in the Abbey of St Maximin where Kuthumi, in his life as Hugh of Avalon, was deacon.

3. The area of Burgundy was associated with the Knights Templar. It was the area in which Sir Hugues (Hugh) de Payen, the First Grand Master of the Knights Templar, was born, and, all evidence points to Hugh de Payen having been the Master St Germain. During that era, Kuthumi had been the philosopher, Omar Khayyam.

4. Hugh of Avalon's Order of the Carthusians was affiliated with that of the Order of the Cistercians established by St Bernard at Clairvaux; the land of which had been granted to him by the Count of Champagne, who employed Hugh de Payen as a knight. (Hugh de Payen had married Katherine St Clair whose family granted lands to the Knights Templar and whose ancestor, William St Clair built the Rosslyn Freemasonic Chapel in 1446 in Scotland, near Edinburgh. Some of the Knights Templar are buried there). St Germain,

in his incarnation as William the Lion of Scots, continued to protect St Bernard's Order in Scotland and Hugh of Lincoln and William were close friends. And, William was a 'Defender of the Faith'.

5.   Hugh's father and brothers were members of the Knights Templar.

6.   Castle Avalon in France, where Hugh was born, would have been one of the Avalons, one of the places of the sacred Teachings of the Arcana and the *Mystical Rose.* As we have previously learned, as King Arthur (Aedan mac Gabran), Kuthumi was buried at 'Avalon' which was the island of Iona where he had also been crowned as King, by St Columba - St Germain.

7.   Hugh of Avalon/Lincoln became a close friend and adviser to at least five kings and many nobles. He was also a confident of many prominent bishops and archbishops of that era.

8.   Another good friend of Hugh's, who became one of his biographers, was Gerald of Wales whose ancestry could be traced back to Fergus Mor mac Erc who brought the Stone of Destiny from Ireland to Scotland.

9.   Hugh's friends and associates may have been responsible for writing some of the Grail legends of that era, particularly *Walter Map* who was with Hugh at Lincoln Cathedral. It was during a time when the legends of Arthur and Merlin were prolifically written about and an era when the Knights of the Round Table was re-established by Henry II, Eleanor of Aquitaine and their Knight Templar son Richard the Lion Heart who was a 'Defender of the Faith' and who carried the Rose-Cross as his symbol when he fought in the Holy Lands defending Jerusalem.

10.   Another of Hugh's other close friends was the Cistercian, Baldwin who was the archbishop of Canterbury who was also a member of the Knights Templar who fought in the Crusades. Baldwin was possibly a cousin of Baldwin, the count of Flanders who was the emperor of Constantinople.

11.   The Lincoln Cathedral was designed by Hugh, although he employed an architect and masons. The building was based on the concepts of the European cathedrals and he also helped to build it. It was the first of its kind, introducing the unique arches into English architecture. According to the authors Paul Broadhurst and Hamish Miller in their book titled *The Sun And The Serpent* and also the author Michael Howard in his book titled *The Occult Conspiracy*, all the major cathedrals of Europe were built on energy Ley lines, particularly the one at Chartres and the Notre Dame in Paris. Many in England are also built on the Ley lines.

12.   The Master Kuthumi had once been Pythagoras and all the major cathedrals were based on Pythagorean mathematics which produced musical harmony within the spheres of their design. Masons, who travelled around working on the construction of such cathedrals, eventually became known as

Freemasons. The interior of the Lincoln Cathedral is carved with numerous figures which the early Church of Rome would have labelled as 'pagan', such as the 'Green Man and the 'Imp'. Some of these features are to be found in the Rosslyn chapel, near Edinburgh.

MASTERS DISCUSSED IN THIS CHAPTER

St Columba/Merlin - St Germain
Hugues de Payen, in all probability - St Germain
William the Lion of Scots - St Germain
Pythagoras - Kuthumi
John the Beloved (alias Joseph of Arimathea) - Kuthumi
Omar Khayyam - Kuthumi
St Hugh of Avalon and Lincoln - Kuthumi
St Thomas a Becket - El Morya

NOTES AND RECOMMENDED READING

David Hugh Farmer, _Saint Hugh Of Lincoln_, (Honywood Press, U.K., 1992)

Donald Attwater and Catherine Rachel John, _Penguin Dictionary of Saints_, (Penguin, U.K. 1995)

Ian Grimble, _The Scottish Isles_, (British Broadcasting Corporation, U.K., 1985)

Elizabeth Hallam, _The Plantagenet Encyclopedia_, (Tiger Books, U.K., 1996)

Elizabeth Hallam, _Chronicles of the Crusades_, (Weidenfeld and Nicholson, Ltd., London, U.K.)

Michael Baigent, Richard Leigh & Henry Lincoln, _The Holy Blood And The Holy Grail_, (Arrow Books, U.K., 1996)

Michael Howard, _The Occult Conspiracy_, (Ryder & Ryder, U.K. 1989)

Paul Broadhurst and Hamish Miller, _The Sun And The Serpent_, (Pendragon Press, Cornwall, U.K. 1995)

Arnold J. Toynbee, _A Study Of History_, (Oxford University Press, U.K., 1934)

Malcolm Uren, _Land Looking West_, (Oxford University Press, U.K., 1948)

J.C. Cooper, _An Illustrated Encyclopaedia Of Traditional Symbols_, (Thames & Hudson, U.K., 1979)

Emile Legouis, _A History of English Literature_, (J.M. Dent & Sons Ltd., U.K. 1945)

Frank Kermode, John Hollander, _The Oxford Anthology of English Literature_, (Oxford University, U.K., 1973).

Edward Fitzgerald, _The Rubaiyat of Omar Khayyam_, (Collins, U.K., 1974)

CHAPTER 38

The Last Grand Master of the Knights Templar & Rennes-Le-Chateau

'Neither a borrower nor a lender be.'
'ET IN ARCADIA EGO'

Those readers who are familiar with the book titled *The Holy Blood And The Holy Grail* by Michael Baigent, Richard Leigh and Henry Lincoln, will remember the history of the downfall of the Knights Templar - of the persecution of Jacques de Molay who was the last Grand Master of the Knights Templar, Hugues (Hugh) de Payen having been the First Grand Master.

According to the authors of *The Hiram Key*, Christopher Knight and Robert Lomas: "In our trawl through post Jewish-war literature, we came across a wide-spread belief, known as 'Bereshit Rabbati', that the power of prophecy would return to Israel in 1210 AD...in 1244, just thirty-four years after the power of the prophecy was to return to Israel, an infant was born into a family of minor nobles in eastern France; his name was Jacques de Molay. The young knight had a clear sense of mission and he joined the Knights Templar at the earliest age possible - twenty-one. He did well and developed a reputation for organisation underpinned by rigorous discipline and rose to be the Master of the Temple in England before being made Grand Marshal with responsibility for military leadership of the Order. Few people can have been surprised when Jacques de Molay was elected as Grand Master of the Knights Templar in 1292, the highest office."

St Germain reincarnated in circa 1214 as Roger Bacon and he was a Grand Master of the Order of the Rose Cross in England. As mentioned above, Jacques de Molay rose to be the 'Master of the Temple' in England and no doubt he was assisted and influenced by St Germain. (Roger Bacon died in 1294 AD).

By the 13th century AD, the Templars had become very powerful, particularly as the international bankers of Europe, lending money to not only the royal families of Europe but also to the Vatican (just as the Medici family had done).

One of the 'borrowers' was the French King Philip IV, (ironically called 'The Fair') who owed a great deal of money to the Templars and he not only resented this, but also the fact that the Templars had become more powerful than the monarchy. With the assistance of Pope Clement V, the king plotted to bring about the arrest of Jacques de Molay and this occurred on the 13th October, 1307 which was a Friday and reputed to have been the origin of the foreboding of 'Black Friday'. Knowing that he was soon to be arrested, Jacques is thought to have destroyed many of the important documents belonging to the Knights Templar.

The Pope issued orders for the 'lenders' - the Templars, to be arrested. The arrests were based upon false accusations and the whole scenario was like a re-enactment of one from the past....that of orders carried out upon the instructions of an earlier Pope, who rather ironically was called Pope Innocent III, which led to the arrest and persecution of the Albigensians, otherwise known as the Cathars.

From the *Plantagenet Encyclopedia* by Elizabeth Hallam we learn that the Templars' leader, their Grand Master, Jacques de Molay (1243?-1314 AD) who had distinguished himself in defending Palestine against the Syrians, and when the Templars were driven from the Holy Land to Cyprus in 1291, was arrested, imprisoned and tortured for seven years before he was finally burnt at the stake on the side of the River Seine in Paris in 1314 AD.

From the book titled *The Occult Conspiracy* written by Michael Howard, we are informed as follows:

"In Germany, Portugal, Switzerland and Aragon the Templars were declared innocent and in Cyprus, where the Order had its headquarters, all the knights were acquitted of the charges brought by King Philip (the Fair). Before his execution, de Molay had nominated a trusted Knight called Larmenuis as his successor and told him to secretly organize the Order and gather together its scattered knights."

"It is from this point in history that the Templars disappeared effectively from public view. They emerged in the following centuries as a clandestine organization working underground promoting the occult (secret) tradition and subversive politics."

In the book titled *The Holy Blood And The Holy Grail*, the authors Michael Baigent, Richard Leigh and Henry Lincoln state that "H.P. Blavatsky (Madame Helena) and Rudolf Steiner, spoke of an esoteric 'wisdom tradition' running back through the Rosicrucians (Order of the Rose Cross) to the Cathars and Templars - who were purportedly repositories of more ancient secrets still."

According to Peter Dawkins in his book titled *Arcadia*:

"It is thought that the Bacon family (into which Francis was adopted), derived their name from the Bascoigne family who were the Lords of Molay in France.

Jacques de Molay made this family famous by being the last publicly known Grand Master of the Knights Templar."

If St Germain was in fact Hugues de Payen, (1070 - 1136 AD), the First Grand Master of the Knights Templar, then Jacques de Molay (1243?-1314), the last Grand Master of the Knights Templar, was Kuthumi for it is known that during this era, St Germain was the philosopher/inventor/scientist, Roger Bacon (1214?- 1294). It was not the first time that Kuthumi had been a martyr, the previous known time having been as St George whose emblem was the Rose-Cross.

It stands to reason that the Master Kuthumi who had once been John the Beloved (alias Joseph of Arimathea), the 'First Master of the Holy Grail', would become the 'Last Grand Master of the Knights Templar'.

If Jacques de Molay, the 'Last Grand Master of the Knights Templar' was an incarnation of the Master Kuthumi, then the Shroud of Turin once contained his body. The authors of the *Hiram Key*, Christopher Knight and Robert Lomas maintain that Jacques was tortured upon the orders of the Pope and King Philip of France in the same style of the way that Jesus was, even up to having a 'mock' crown of thorns placed upon his head.

The body (still alive) was wrapped in a long piece of linen - and taken to a family who nursed him back to health. The shroud remained in the care of the family for some ages. It was later to become known as the Shroud of Turin.

Recent evidence supports the theory of the authors of *The Hiram Key*, because forensic tests carried out suggest that the Shroud only dates back to approximately 600 - 700 years AD, not 2,000. Jacques died in 1314 and therefore the calculation fits adequately. It is rather ironic that in Kuthumi's incarnation as John the Beloved, it was his brother Jesus, whose body was also placed in a long piece of white linen. History obviously had a way of repeating itself for members of the Grail family! According to the same authors in their book titled *The Second Messiah*, Jacques of Molay was the 'Second Messiah'.

It was fortunate that after the arrest of Jacques de Molay, and the other thousands of Knights Templar, that some of them managed to escape by way of ships which belonged to them that were kept at the seaport of La Rochelle. From there they sailed to Scotland where the Order was never dissolved. Some of these Templars are said to have fought on the side of Robert Bruce at the Battle of Bannockburn which took place the same year that Jacques de Molay had been captured and put to death, in 1314 AD.

The Templar army was led by the Grand Master of the Scottish Templars, Sir William St Clair who was the 'guardian' of that period of time, of Roslin where the Rosslyn Freemasonic chapel was established.

There is a great deal of evidence available today, which attests to the fact that the Knights Templar did settle in Scotland, particularly near Argyll where there are graves and tomb carvings showing Templar figures in the church at Kilmartin.

According to information sent to me by Peter Dawkins:

"The connection of the Freemasons with the Rosicrucians is allegorized in the thirty-three degrees of the Ancient and Accepted Scottish Rite of Freemasonry, wherein Craft Masonry constitutes the first three degrees and the Rosicrucian level begins with the 17th degree onwards. This itself is patterned on an earlier scheme used in Scotland when the Knights Templar took sanctuary there in alliance with Freemasonry - the Templars being the Red Cross Knights or Rosicrucians. The simple cipher signature of FRANCIS BACON = 33."

Rennes-Le-Chateau
'ET IN ARCADIA EGO'

Before closing upon the subject of the Knights Templar, it is important to discuss Rennes-le-Chateau in France and its connections to them. Within this area are many Roman remains, which can still be seen, such as paths of stone leading from Carcassonne towards Spain via Rennes-le-Chateau.

The Visigoths, driven back by the Huns of central Europe, established the prosperous town of Rhedae. In 410 AD, after having pillaged Rome and taken possession of the enormous treasure of Jerusalem which had been brought back by Titus in the year 10, the Visigoths inhabited the entire south of Gaul and also Spain where they created the most powerful kingdom of the entire western world with Toulouse as their capital.

Clovis I

In this particular era of history, all the people of Western Europe were Arians and this included Clovis I (died 511 AD) who was ruler of the Franks who were renowned for their golden hair and their kings wore it long as a sign of their royal birth.

Clovis led the 'Merovingians' or 'Franks' and defeated the Visigoths at Vouille. They then set fire to Toulouse and forced the Visigoths to retreat to Carcassonne. Not far from Carcassonne is the village of Rennes-le-Chateau. The Merovingians once inhabited the area around Rennes-le-Chateau and quite recently, when a mechanical digger was working on a road many tombstones from a Merovingian cemetery were discovered.

According to the authors of *The Messianic Legacy*, Michael Baigent, Richard

Leigh and Henry Lincoln, someone who belonged to the Priory of Sion with whom they made contact, acknowledged "the Merovingians to have been of Judaic descent, deriving from the royal line of David." And furthermore, that they traced their ancestral lineage back to Noah.

The Visigoth kingdom eventually weakened and the only land which they were left with was a piece stretching from Carcassonne to their new capital of Toledo, which was invaded by the Arabs, but the invasion was prevented by Charles Martel of Poitiers. Northern Gaul was occupied by the Frankish people (now known as the French) and under their great teacher Clovis (486-511), they took possession of southern Gaul as well. By 500 AD, Italy was an Ostrogothic kingdom, Gaul a Frankish kingdom, and Spain a Visigothic kingdom.

Upon the demise of Clovis I, his kingdom was divided amongst his sons; however, they and their sons fought amongst themselves and ended up assassinating each other.

Charles Martel (688 - 741 AD)
St Germain

Charles Martel was born in 688 AD, the illegitimate son of Pepin of Herstal and is reputed to have been an incarnation of St Germain. He is credited with having been the founder of the Carolingian Empire.

Charles' main determination was to weld the Franks together and in a series of campaigns, he defeated his adversaries and distributed lands and positions amongst men upon whom he could rely. The value of his work was seen in the crushing defeat upon the Moslems.

In 732 AD the viceroy Abd-ur Rahman led a Moslem army across the Pyrenees and swept northwards over France. However, the Franks were well equipped and their leader, Charles Martel, had prepared them to deal with this invasion. They met the Moslems near Poitiers (this battle is some called the battle of Tours) in one of the decisive conflicts of history and drove them back to the foothills of the Pyrenees.

During the long hours, the Arab horsemen charged again and again the iron-clad line of the Franks, but they failed to break it and eventually the bare remnant of them fled southwards, leaving their leader dead upon the field. This was a turning-point. The Moslems held Spain, and for the moment, part of southern France. The problem of security in the Mediterranean world had changed dramatically, and the danger area had shifted from the West to the East.

After his victory, Charles earned the nickname of 'Martel' - 'the Hammer'. He confiscated lands held by the Church of Rome and appointed his own bishops. According to Frankish custom, Charles divided his power between his sons,

Carloman and Pepin III (known as 'the Short').

Between 639 AD and 751 AD, the Merovingian dynasty still reigned over the Kingdom of the Franks. In the 7th century the kingdom was divided into three parts called Neustria, Austrasia and Burgundy. Aquitaine was also part of the Frankish kingdom. There were constant wars between the feudal nobles of Neustria, Austrasia and Burgundy and during his reign, Charles Martel was Mayor of the Palace of these kingdoms from circa 717 to 741 AD, and he ruled on behalf of the Merovingian King, Theuderic IV.

In 747 AD, Carloman chose to become a monk and left Pepin as sole ruler. Pepin was not in the true sense, King of the Franks by birth. Pepin approached Pope Stephen II and enquired as to whether he could be elected as a king. Upon the Pope's agreement, Pepin was consecrated by St Boniface and the consecration was repeated by the Pope himself.

Charlemagne the Great 'Defender of the Faith'
St Germain

Pepin III died in 768 AD. His son Charles ruled alone until his death in 814 AD. He is better known as *Charlemagne the Great* and he was one of the most important of all the Frankish (Merovingian) kings. Charlemagne is reputed to have been an incarnation of St Germain. He considered it his duty to not only protect his subjects but to educate them. He surrounded himself with learned men and established a School of Learning at his palace where the arts could be cultivated...rather reminiscent of St Germain's days as St Columba.

In the year 800 AD, Pope Stephen III crowned Charles the Great (Charlemagne) as Emperor of the West - he thus became King Charles I of the Franks (France) and according to Einhard, Charlemagne's biographer, the Pope's action took him by surprise. By being crowned Emperor of the West, Charlemagne was invested with full temporal authority over the Christians and had the corresponding duty of protecting them. Thus once again, it could be deemed that St Germain was a 'Defender of the Faith'. It is noteworthy that in his incarnation as Alexander the Great, St Germain's ambition was to unite the West. Not everything is able to be achieved in one life time - it takes many. For example, in his life as Roger Bacon, St Germain prophesied that he would one day return and discover America - this he achieved when he reincarnated as Christopher Columbus.

When the Franks finally drove back the Arabs and the Visigoths towards Spain, Charlemagne gave the city of Carcassonne to one of his leaders, thus creating the first Count of Carcassonne with Rhedae being part of his lands.

In the 11th century AD, there were many disputes for the possession of

Rhedae and then in 1209 AD, Simon IV de Montfort and his crusaders set fire to it, whilst pursuing their inquisition against the Cathars. The city of Rhedae was eventually destroyed but the city of Carcassonne on the River Aude in Languedoc, still remains.

Charlemagne died in 814 AD.

The Chateau

From information contained in *The Holy Blood And The Holy Grail*, we learn the following:

"In pre-historic times the area around Rennes-le-Chateau was regarded as a sacred site by the Celtic tribes who lived there; and the village itself, once called Rhedae, derived its name from one of these tribes."

The name of Rhedae is believed to have originated from the Gallic word 'Reda' meaning a 'four-wheeled chariot'.

The small village of Rennes-le-Chateau consists of houses tucked around the Chateau and the church of St Magdalene. According to further information contained within the book titled *The Holy Blood And The Holy Grail*:

"The Chateau was once the ancestral home of Bertrand de Blanchefort, fourth Grand Master of the Knights Templar who presided over the famous order in the mid-twelfth century. Rennes-le-Chateau and its environs had been the ancient pilgrim route, which ran from Northern Europe to Santiago de Compostella in Spain, and the entire region was steeped in evocative legends, in echoes of a rich, dramatic and often blood-soaked past."

Possession of the Chateau changed hands several times, and eventually a family called Voisins became the owners and they began the construction of the present Chateau, the old Chateau having been almost completely destroyed. The last of the family of Voisins was Blanche de Marquefave whose mother had married a Spanish Lord. Blanche married Pierre d'Hautpoul and the dowry he received was the barony of Rennes at which time he took the title of Seigneur de Blanchefort. The last Marquise d'Hautpoul de Blanchefort, Marie, was left a widow with no male heirs and died at the Chateau of Rennes in 1781 AD , at the age of sixty-seven.

Accordingly, Lady d'Hautpoul de Blanchefort was the trustee of a great secret which had been passed down in her family from generation to generation. Having no sons, she decided to impart her secret, along with some documents of considerable importance, to her confessor, Antoine Bigou, the local parish priest in Rennes-le-Chateau.

When the priest heard the confession, he was greatly disturbed and he decided to hide the documents in the Visigoth pillar which held up the altar in the church of St Magdalene. In 1791 AD, he had a large gravestone placed on the tomb of the Marquise, engraved with Latin inscriptions one of which, 'ET IN ARCADIA EGO', was in Greek lettering. This translates into 'Even in Arcadia I am found.'

During the French Revolution, Antoine was forced to flee to Spain where he died not long afterwards. However, before his demise he confided his secret to a priest. The secret has given rise to much debate. Some say that it was concerned with an enormous treasure, once owned by the Cathars, or that they possessed something of sacred value. According to the authors of *The Holy Blood And The Holy Grail*:

"There was also the vanished treasure of the Knights Templar, whose Grand Master, Bertrand de Blanchefort, commissioned certain mysterious excavations in the vicinity. According to all accounts, these excavations were of a markedly clandestine nature, performed by a specially imported contingent of German miners. If some kind of Templar treasure were indeed concealed around Rennes-le-Chateau, this might explain the reference to 'Sion' in the parchments discovered by Sauniere."

"Until 1188 the Order de Sion and the Order of the Temple are said to have shared the same Grand Master. Hugues de Payen and Bertrand de Blanchefort, for example would thus have presided over both institutions simultaneously. In 1188 the Order of Sion is said to have modified its name, adopting the one which it has allegedly obtained to the present - the Prieure de Sion ('Priory of Sion')." In an earlier chapter, it was discussed that it is highly probable that Hugh de Payen, as 'First Grand Master of the Knights Templar, was an incarnation of St Germain.

Eventually, the important secret handed down by the last family member who belonged to the Chateau at Rennes, was given to a priest named Berenger Sauniere who began restoration work of the church, during which time a certain person under a disguised name, was sent on an important mission to Rennes by the Comtesse de Chambord who was originally a 'Habsburg'. His name was Monsieur Guillaume and he frequented Rennes-le-Chateau during the restoration work and proffered the enormous sum of 3,000 francs in return for the finding of any precious documents hidden in the church. In actuality, Monsieur Guillaume was Johann of Habsburg, Archduke of Austria.

Seigneur d'Hautpoul who, upon his marriage to Blanche adopted her family name of Blanchefort, had been tutor to the Comtesse de Chambord's husband, and had tried to have him placed upon the throne of France in the place of Louis XVII, the legitimate son of Louis XVI. The Comtesse had been widowed two years previously and it is of interest to note that her husband had been a pretender to the Crown of France, and was the last descendant of the Bourbon family, the Habsburgs. Was there some secret they knew which would have legally entitled him to have become the next King of France?

Mention has been made in an earlier chapter of St Germain's close associations with the Habsburg family of Austria. From *St Germain - Twin Souls & Soulmates*, in a channelling given to Claire Heartsong by the Lady Portia, St Germain's twin soul, we learn that during the era of St Germain: "So it was that this one, with a number of other ones, was privy to many, many books and records of bygone eras and they went on pilgrimages together. They went to what had become known as Alexandria and other temple sites in Egypt, the Holy Land, Asia Minor, Greece, Italy, Germany, Austria and Switzerland, where some of these records were hidden away by the Habsburgers in their courts."

Thus, the question may well be asked, "Where was St Germain during the time that Johann (John) of Habsburg, had been sent as an emissary of the Comtesse de Chambord, to Rennes le Chateau?"

It is recorded that in 1757, St Germain was in France and spent time with Louis XV who gave him rooms at the Royal Chateau of Chambord, where he was allotted a laboratory and taught students the study of Alchemy (chemistry). Thus, in answer to the question posed in the previous paragraph, we are able to connect St Germain with the family of Chambord and also with the Habsburgs.

We can be certain that if the documents concealed at Rennes-le-Chateau were as important as they appear to have been, then the Master would not have been far away. As the *Master of the Mystical Rose*, he would have gone to any lengths to protect the secret documents discovered at Rennes. He may have been the one who via the Comtesse de Chambord (who was a member of the Habsburg family), gave instructions for an emissary to be sent to Rennes-le-Chateau. In a future paragraph, it will be seen that after his important discovery, Berenger Sauniere had a meeting with the Rosicrucians (Order of the Rose Cross) in Paris and from that time onwards, he reputedly became incredibly wealthy.

According to the authors of *The Holy Blood And The Holy Grail*:

"But perhaps the most consequential visitor to the unknown country priest was the Archduke Johann von Habsburg, a cousin of Franz-Josef, Emperor of Austria. Bank statements subsequently revealed that Sauniere and the archduke had opened consecutive accounts on the same day, and that the latter had made a substantial sum over to the former."

The authors further relate that "although deposed in the eighth century, the Merovingian bloodline did not become extinct. On the contrary it perpetuated itself in the direct line from Dagobert II and his son Sigisbert IV. By dint of dynastic alliances and intermarriages, this line came to include Godfroi de Bouillon who captured Jerusalem in 1099, and various other nobles and royal families past and present - Blanchefort, Gisors, St Clair (Sinclair in England), and *Habsburg Lorraine*. At present, the Merovingian bloodline enjoys a legitimate claim to its rightful heritage." (It will be recalled that the First Grand Master of the Knights Templar, Sir Hugh de Payen, married into the St Clair family of Roslin, where the Rosslyn

Freemasonic Chapel was later established).

"The true origins of the Merovingians claimed descent from Noah whom they regarded even more than Moses, as the source of all their Biblical wisdom and this belief resurfaced a thousand years later in European Freemasonry."

Also according to the authors, the Merovingians claimed direct descent from ancient Troy and even further back to ancient Greece in their land known as Arcadia. As we have seen in previous chapters, Noah was an incarnation of St Germain, and St Germain was the founder of 'Freemasonry' which he introduced into Britain in the 4th century AD, when he incarnated as St Albanus (St Alban) of Verulam.

The Hunt for the 'Treasure'

The priest, Sauniere, became active in his hunt for the 'treasure', thoroughly searching the old church whilst another priest who also knew the secret, Henri Boudet, published an unusual book titled *The True Celtic Language and the Stone Circle of Rennes-les-Bains*' which aroused a great deal of criticism and it was reputed that the secret that Henri Boudet was keeping could be the cause of major upheavals.

Accordingly, during his search of the church, Sauniere discovered a container filled with pieces of gold and other treasure. He was also said to have discovered a tube containing two parchments and a manuscript in code. During the restoration that was carried out by Sauniere, an elderly helper whilst climbing the bell tower of the Church of St Mary Magdalene, noticed something shining which had been thrown down on its side. It was a canister in which a rolled-up parchment had fallen out. The old man, who was unable to read, gave it to Sauniere to translate and thus the saga began.

In March, 1891, Sauniere visited Paris where he stayed for five days during which time he was introduced to Emile Hoffet who was a famous Freemason and also to a Joseph Peladan who founded the *Order of the Rose Cross of the Temple and the Grail* in 1891. They both became frequent guests of Sauniere at Rennes-le-Chateau. But what exactly was it that they found? Was it treasure or was it a document of enormous importance? What becomes obvious is that the secret was a 'Grail' one, one that was associated with the Great White Brotherhood of the *Masters of the Mystical Rose*.

Sauniere died in 1917, and Marie Denarnaud died in 1953. Before her death, Marie burnt certain private papers that belonged to Sauniere.

And so, it could be supposed that the secrets died with them. But such is not the case. Many clues are to be found in a painting in which Sauniere was particularly interested; interested enough that he procured a copy of it from the Louvre in Paris. It is called *The Shepherds of Arcadia* by Nicholas Poussin.

In the sequel to this story, *The Dove, The Rose And The Sceptre, In Search of the Ark of the Covenant*, a great deal more is disclosed about the secrets of Rennes-le-Chateau and their relevance to the discovery of the Ark of the Covenant hidden in 'Arcadia'.

ET IN ARCADIA EGO - 'Even in Arcadia I am found'.

Twins

According to local legends, Sauniere discovered a document which either disclosed that Jesus and Mary Magdalene were married, or that Jesus was a twin. However, as has been discussed earlier, it is highly probable that Mary was the sister of Jesus. The 'Truth' is sometimes rather difficult to find, and it is up to the readers to draw their own conclusions.

No doubt the debate of the marriage of Mary and Jesus will continue for many years to come and there is no definite proof. However, it will be remembered that the 'Wedding at Cana' mentioned in the Bible which many authors now claim was their marriage, was a symbolical story demonstrating the power which Jesus had in being able to turn water into wine. It states in the Bible that 'there was a marriage at Cana'. There was no bride and groom mentioned. The marriage was an 'Alchemical' one.

Were there really twins in this Grail family? Has it been a secret known to a select few which has long been covered up?

Scholars have long debated whether Thomas Didymus was a twin because his name means 'twin' 'twin' as if it was some clue deliberately placed in the Bible.

There are several stories about twins in the Bible, thus genetically speaking, twins were in the Grail lineage. For example:

1.   Isaac (son of Abraham) and Rebecca had twin sons, Esau and Jacob (whom the Lord re-named 'Israel').
2.   Jacob's grandsons were Ephraim and Manasseh.
3.   Tamar and Judah had twin sons, Zarah and Pharez.

According to information contained in the book titled *The Messianic Legacy* by Michael Baigent, Richard Leigh and Henry Lincoln:

"The suggestion that Jesus had a twin brother was one of the most persistent and tenacious of the ancient 'heresies'. Nor did it ever completely disappear, despite repeated attempts to extirpate it. During the Renaissance, for example, it surfaced repeatedly, albeit in a somewhat garbled form. It is conspicuous in certain of Leonardo da Vinci's works, especially 'The Last Supper'. As we have seen in earlier chapters, Leonardo was an incarnation of the Master Kuthumi and he had once been John Joseph, the Beloved Disciple (alias Joseph of Arimathea - First Master of the Holy Grail). He would have known the truth about the twins.

It is a probability that Thomas was given the name of Thomas Didymus ('twin twin') in order to detract from the identity of the real twin. However, it is unlikely that Thomas was a brother of Jesus, although he may have been a cousin. He is not included in the Biblical texts as a member of the immediate family.

Mark 6:3: "Is not this the carpenter, the son of Mary, the brother of James, and Joses (Joseph) and of Judas and Simon?" The brothers of Jesus, who have been mentioned in a previous chapter, were James the Just, John Joseph the Beloved, Judas Iscariot - the 'traitor' and Simon Eleazar/Lazarus - Zelotes - the 'Zealot'.

Thomas is reputed to have taught in India in the year 46 AD where he founded churches and he was martyred there in 72 AD.

There is always the possibility that Mary Magdalene was the twin of Jesus. She has unfortunately always been portrayed by the Church of Rome as a harlot, and they did not hold women in high esteem in those days. It is known that Jesus was very close to Mary and that some of the other disciples resented her because of his affection for her. If Mary was the twin of Jesus, it would help to explain her prominence in the churches and shrines that have been dedicated to her, for even in Lincoln, England, across the road from the Lincoln Cathedral there is an ancient church dedicated to her.

Her prominence however, in the Grail legends and in the churches and shrines dedicated to her throughout the Templar areas of France suggest that her role was much more than she has been accredited. Considering the way the Church of Rome felt about Mary Magdalene, painting her as a 'scarlet' woman, makes one think that they were trying to hide something.

According to Michele Brown in her book containing the meaning of historical names, the old pronunciation of 'Magdalene' was 'maudlin' which, because Mary Magdalene was a patron saint of penitents, came to mean 'tearful'.

In the Magdalene church at Rennes-le-Chateau, beneath the altar, Mary Magdalene is depicted in tears, kneeling in a grotto in front of a cross formed of two branches (Mary and Joseph's twins?), of which one is alive. Mary died in 63 AD, nine years before Thomas was martyred in India in 72 AD. So why would she be depicted as weeping for a twin who did not die until 72 AD? However, she could have been weeping for her twin brother Jesus.

Why did the early Church of Rome injure Mary Magdalene's reputation in such a way? What were their motives? What did they fear?

As we have previously seen, this Grail family who were Essenes, and members of the Order of the Rose Cross, were under persecution by the Romans and fled to Marseilles. One of the reasons that instigated their flight may have been because the Romans *knew* that Mary was a twin of Jesus. In all the Gospels relevant to Mary Magdalene, she is always close at hand, particularly during the crucifixion scenario. Thomas is not mentioned at all as being in attendance and one would surmise that if Thomas was the twin of Jesus, that it would have been to him, and not John the Beloved, that Jesus handed over the responsibility of his mother, Mary. It was also Mary Magdalene (and not Thomas) who discovered that the tomb was empty.

Continuing with information contained in *The Messianic Legacy* regarding 'twins' we find that "the theme recurs in subsequent painters, including Poussin...and in the decorations commissioned by Berenger Sauniere for the church at Rennes-le-Chateau, both Mary and Joseph are depicted one on each side of the altar holding a Christ-child."

MASTERS DISCUSSED IN THIS CHAPTER

Noah - St Germain (BC)

Alexander the Great, (whose ambitions were to unite the Western world), (356-323 BC), - St Germain

Joseph, (Father of the Family of the Holy Grail), (died circa 15 AD) - St Germain

Hughes de Payen, (First Grand Master of the Knights Templar) (1070-1136 AD) - possibly St Germain

St Alban, (introduced Freemasonry into Great Britain), (died 209 AD) - St Germain

Roger Bacon, (prophesied discovery of America), (1214?-1294 AD) - St Germain

Charlemagne the Great (united the Western world), (768-814 AD) - St Germain

Christopher Columbus, (discovered America), (1451-1506 AD) - St Germain

Francis Bacon - St Germain, (Head of Freemasonry and the Order of the Rose Cross) - St Germain (1561-1626? AD)

John the Beloved (alias Joseph of Arimathea, First Master of the Holy Grail), (died circa 80 AD) - Kuthumi

St George, (martyr and 'Defender of the Faith') (280-304 AD) - Kuthumi

Jacques de Molay (Last Grand Master of the Knights Templar) (1243?-1314 AD) - possibly Kuthumi

Leonardo da Vinci, (Grand Master of the Priory of Sion - Jerusalem), (1452-1519 AD) - Kuthumi

NOTES AND RECOMMENDED READING

Peter Dawkins, *Arcadia*, (Francis Bacon Research Trust, U.K.)

Michael Howard, *The Occult Conspiracy*, (Ryder & Ryder, U.K. 1989)

Elizabeth Hallam, *Chronicles of the Crusades*, (Weidenfeld and Nicholson, Ltd., London, U.K.)

Elizabeth Hallam, *The Plantagenet Encyclopedia*, (Tiger Books, U.K. 1996)

Michael Baigent, Richard Leigh & Henry Lincoln, *The Holy Blood And The Holy Grail*, (Arrow Books, U.K., 1996)

Michael Baigent, Richard Leigh & Henry Lincoln, *The Messianic Legacy*, (Arrow Books U.K. 1996)

Christopher Knight and Robert Lomas, *The Hiram Key*, (Century Books, U.K., 1996)

Christopher Knight and Robert Lomas, *The Second Messiah*, (Century, London, U.K. 1997)

R.H.C. Davis, *A History of Medieval Europe*, (Longman U.K. 1970)

Michele Brown, *Baby Name Book*, (Greenwich Editions, U.K. 1985)

Daniel J. Boorstin, *The Discoverers, A History of Mans' Search To Know His World And Himself*,

(Random House, U.K., 1983)

F.J. Dennett, *Europe, A History*, (Linehan & Shrimpton, Melbourne, Australia, 1961)

PART FOUR

CHAPTER 39

Elizabeth 1ˢᵗ, Lord Robert Dudley & Their Tudor Princes

"Oh God, thou has set to rule us a woman, whom nature
hath formed to be in subjection unto man, and whom thou
by thine holy apostle commandest to keep silence and not
to speak in congregation. Ah, Lord! To take away the empire
from man and give it to a woman, seemeth to be an evident
token of thine anger towards us Englishmen!"
(Thomas Becon)

*"...he was delivered in great secrecy... My heart ached for the sibling who was born. The
young maiden who was a lady in waiting took the wee babe."*

('Portia', twin soul of St Germain, excerpt from *St Germain, Twin Souls & Soulmates*)

It is relevant at this point of time to show that Francis Bacon, who was an incarnation of St Germain, underwent the trials and tribulations which most of us have at one time or another experienced. History has painted a rather unkind picture of his mother Elizabeth I, and Francis Bacon too, has had his share of criticism in the centuries since, when historians and scholars have failed to see the 'real' man behind the 'mask'.

Now that we are in the 21ˢᵗ century, taking into consideration the accumulated knowledge that has been written about Elizabeth and the Tudor era, we need to take a more sympathetic outlook of the times in which they lived and the acute circumstances of intrigue which surrounded them.

This particularly applies to Sir Francis Bacon/St Germain whose heart thirsted for the good of mankind. Since the time of the great Avatar, the Master Jesus, no man ever lived upon the earth in the last 2,004 years who had nobler aims than Francis Bacon. Therefore, it is very important to show the underlying currents that led to many of the tragic events that occurred within their lives. They were living in a time when England was constantly under the threat of invasion. Both Elizabeth and Francis were individually schemed against by many in their own royal circle and both had many tragedies occur in their lives.

It was 'fateful' circumstances which brought Elizabeth to the throne of England. History regards Elizabeth as a 'great' but difficult woman. Many factors need to be taken into consideration including her childhood which was fraught with unhappiness and danger.

Turning the clock back some years, in 1527, Henry VIII's first wife, Catherine of Aragon was forty-two years old and past child-bearing. So far there had been one child of this marriage, a daughter, 'Mary'. Mary was sickly owing to the fact that she had genetically inherited her father's disease of syphilis. Henry wanted a son and as his eyes roamed over the lovely ladies of his court, they fell upon Anne Boleyn.

In order to obtain a divorce from Catherine, Henry sought the advice of Cardinal Thomas Wolsey who was to approach the Pope on Henry's behalf. Two years dragged on with little success and the frustrated and angry Henry, deprived Wolsey of his office.

Hampton Court Palace, alongside the Thames, was the original home of Cardinal Wolsey and it was built on a site leased from the Knights Hospitallers. Special apartments were provided for Henry and Catherine of Aragon for their visits. Henry became especially fond of this luxurious residence and it could be said that he 'coveted' it because when Wolsey failed to secure Henry's divorce, he was stripped of his lands and possessions including Hampton Court. Wolsey died in 1530, just before he was to be tried for treason.

Henry then appointed a new chancellor, Sir Thomas More (reputed to be an incarnation of the Master El Morya), whose unfortunate story was told in the movie *A Man For All Seasons*. Without going into a great deal of unnecessary detail, Sir Thomas More also greatly displeased the King because he would did not approve of Henry's actions, so Thomas Cromwell was eventually elected Chancellor of the Exchequer and he was the one who hurried the divorce through which was not acceptable to the Pope.

An Act was past that severed the church from Rome which in effect, created the Church 'of' England as against the church 'in' England. By then, in 1533, Henry had already secretly married Anne Boleyn, who accordingly was already pregnant with Elizabeth.

When Elizabeth was born on the 7th September, 1533, Henry still desperately wanted a male heir for the throne of England and Anne had thus far only produced a daughter, instead of a male heir.

According to Elizabeth Jenkins in her book titled *Elizabeth And Leicester*:
"When she was two years and eight months old her mother Anne Boleyn

was beheaded on a five-fold charge of adultery. Just before her arrest, the Queen was seen in the courtyard of Greenwich Palace holding up her little girl in her arms, in a despairing attempt to win a smile from the angry King as he stood frowning in a window above them. Three days later she was committed to the Tower, where her head was cut off."

Her father declared Elizabeth a 'bastard' child, after he had his marriage to Anne Boleyn annulled. Elizabeth Jenkins relates that from the great King, Princess Elizabeth's admired and dreaded father, she had received an upbringing which combined the intensive education due to a very clever child with the rigorous social training of a Princess. Her intellect and her personal magnetism, her learning and acquirements had come to her from King Henry VIII; and from him she also received a nervous injury so deep-seated and severe that it had life long implications.

In the following years, there occurred the death of Jane Seymour when Elizabeth was only four years old, and then when she was only eight years old, King Henry's fifth wife, Katherine Howard, her mother's cousin, her young, enchanting step-mother, was beheaded.

Jane Seymour died after giving birth to their son Edward VI - considered to be the heir to the throne and thus the future King of England. But alas, Edward, like his half-sister Mary, was a sickly child, having also inherited syphilis from their father who had given it to their mothers before the children were born. Poor children, the 'sins of the father' were being reaped upon them. It was a disease that was particularly rife during this era and Henry's children became the unfortunate victims, for alas, penicillin had not then been discovered.

After the Succession Act of 1544, Elizabeth had been third in line to the throne. To Elizabeth, being third in line to the throne at the time, it would have seemed highly inconceivable that she would ever become Queen.

Henry VIII died 28th January, 1547, and his son Edward VI inherited the throne - Elizabeth's progression towards accession was now second in line.

According to Elizabeth Jenkins in her book titled *Elizabeth And Leicester.*

"On the evening of July 6th, 1553, a fearful tempest swept London; lightening and thunder racked the sky, torrential rain drowned the streets, at 6 o'clock the summer evening was dark as night." At that hour King Edward died (aged 16 years), and Lady Jane (aged 17 years), then the wife of Guildford Northumberland, reigned for only nine days.

Unlike his half-sister, Mary, (who was a devout Catholic), Edward had been a devout Protestant. The powerful nobles of the court were concerned that if Mary became Queen of England, then the Catholic Church would gain a strong hold again.

And thus, Mary became Queen of England in 1553. By the autumn of 1558, it became evident that Queen Mary would not live long, and she died childless on the 17th November, 1558 at the age of forty three years.

The Throne of England now belonged to Elizabeth, twenty-two years after the death of her mother Anne Boleyn. Elizabeth reigned from 1558-1603, a long forty-five years of Britain having a female ruler. Having been brought up in a court of political intrigue, in which her own mother had been plotted against and condemned, some say 'framed', Elizabeth was very aware of her tenuous position. She never felt secure, having been declared a 'bastard' child by her own father, Henry Tudor, and having the knowledge that her own father was instrumental in having her mother beheaded, did not make for a particularly happy childhood. Elizabeth had neither the love of a mother nor father to raise her and in the future, this was to have serious repercussions in regard to her maternal feelings towards her own sons.

Unfortunately for Elizabeth, she was raised in a male dominated society, many of who resented having a 'female' upon the throne. Apart from all the nefarious plots and dramas which occurred within Elizabeth's royal court, another unfortunate occurrence for her was that she was 'female'. The people had always expected to have a king to rule over them - as did the church, politicians and courtiers of that era. The general feeling of her acceptance can be summed up in a quotation of a certain Thomas Becon, who declared to God his feelings on the matter.

As the Queen of England, given the fact that men saw her as 'only' a woman, flawed and ineffective, Elizabeth felt the need to prove herself to be an even better ruler than any previous king, especially her father, and throughout her life, her political skills were constantly being tested. Whenever anything went wrong politically, it was blamed upon Elizabeth because she was a 'woman'. It seemed to her best interest to model herself on being a 'Virgin Queen' - the 'virgin' meaning 'pure'.

According to Peter Dawkins in his book titled *Arcadia*, Elizabeth's name in Hebrew is *Eli-Sheba* meaning 'consecrated to God' and this was the attitude that Elizabeth wished to display. She wanted to be the epitome of a female goddess and was often depicted as the goddess 'Athena', sometimes called 'Gloriana' and Elizabeth wished to be seen as the 'Great Mother of Her People.'

For Elizabeth, there was no such thing as 'stability' in her life, and there would come a time when the proverbial 'last straw' would eventuate, bringing her to such a state of remorse, from which she was never to recover.

The Secret Marriage of Elizabeth 1st and Robert Lord Dudley

According to the late Alfred Dodd, biographer of Francis Bacon, in his book entitled *Francis Bacon's Personal Life Story*, the parents of Francis Bacon were Queen Elizabeth Tudor and Lord Robert Dudley (known as the Earl of Leicester), whom she married in a private, undisclosed ceremony at the house of Lord Pembroke. However, there appear to have been two marriage ceremonies, at different time periods as we shortly shall see.

In 1553, when Elizabeth's half sister, Mary (known aptly as 'Bloody Mary', who was the daughter of Henry VIII and Catherine of Aragon), became Queen of England upon the death of her young half brother Edward VI (who was the son of Henry VIII and Lady Jane Seymour), Mary issued orders for Elizabeth and the Dudley family, including Robert, to be imprisoned in the Tower of London, charged with 'treason'. (Robert Dudley was born in 1532, one year before Elizabeth who was born on the 7th September, 1533).

According to information contained in the late Alfred Dodd's book titled *Francis Bacon's Personal Life Story:*

"Members of Elizabeth's household were imprisoned and tortured to obtain evidence that she had conspired to subvert the existing order. A warrant was actually drawn up for her execution, but the Governor of the Tower refused the responsibility because of a flaw in the warrant."

"So real was the peril that Elizabeth told the French ambassador, when adverting to this period, 'that she desired of her sister but one request, that she might have her head cut off with a sword, as in France, and not with an axe, after the present fashion'."

"At the beginning of her imprisonment she was very rigorously confined in the Bell Tower but later she was allowed full liberty of the Tower and its grounds. She thus met Destiny in the person of Lord Robert Dudley, who was lodged at Beauchamp Tower and who was daily expecting the same fate that had overtaken his father, Northumberland, and his brother, Guildford. He (Lord Robert Dudley) had been one of Elizabeth's playfellows in childhood."

At the time, Dudley was married to Amy Robsart. They were married in 1550 when Robert was eighteen years old and he was twenty-one when he was imprisoned with Elizabeth in the Tower.

From Peter Dawkins' book titled *Dedication to the Light*, we are informed as follows:

"According to Francis' cipher history, whilst the Princess Elizabeth was in the Tower, the Gaoler was persuaded to allow messages to be exchanged between Elizabeth and her childhood friend, Robert Dudley (who was imprisoned in a separate cell with his brothers). Finally the Gaoler was induced to allow a secret meeting between Elizabeth and Robert. Elizabeth was taken to Robert's cell, where he had an itinerant priest awaiting, and here Elizabeth was cajoled to undergo a form of marriage with Robert, so that united in such a way they might meet death together - an ignominious death which they both expected to be imminent, but which in fact never came about."

"Rumours of this private and irregular 'marriage' eventually circulated, despite its secrecy, but they remained as rumours."

Lord Robert Dudley and Elizabeth were released in the summer when the Catholic Philip of Spain visited England for his proposed marriage to Queen Mary. The prospect of the visit placed Mary in a more charitable mood. As 'Bloody Mary' she was not often seen to be so charitable. Her mother, Catherine of Aragon, was the daughter of Queen Isabella and King Ferdinand of Spain, who were responsible for personally commencing the Spanish Inquisition; they were anti the Protestants and also banished all Jews from Spain.

After the death of Queen Mary on 17th November, 1558, Elizabeth was crowned as Queen of England in 1559.

From Elizabeth Jenkins' book titled *Elizabeth And Leicester*, we are informed as follows:

"That Robert Dudley was greatly in the Queen's confidence was already clear. It was confirmed by his being entrusted with a peculiar errand. Dr John Dee [Kuthumi], a remarkable man who had many academic distinctions, was also an astrologer and a setter-up of horoscopes. Elizabeth was very much interested in the occult. During Mary's reign, Dee had been up before the Privy Council for casting the Princess's horoscope, which in the hands of a competent practitioner, must inevitably have foretold the Queen's death at no long-distant date. The new Queen wished that he should choose an auspicious date for her coronation. Lord Robert Dudley was sent to him on this mission, and Dee advised January 14th, 1559."

Shortly after Elizabeth's accession, she bestowed upon Robert Dudley, the title of Earl of Leicester, and Master of the Horse. He was thus in constant personal attendance upon her.

The Venetian ambassador made the following comments about Elizabeth and Robert: 'a very handsome young man towards whom in various ways the Queen evinces such affection and inclination that many persons believe that if his wife, who has been ailing for some time, were perchance to die, the Queen might easily take him for her husband.'

Another European ambassador remarked: "Sometimes she speaks like a woman who will only accept a great prince, and then they say she is in love with Lord Robert and will never let him leave her side."

The Venetian ambassador wrote: "My Lord Robert Dudley is in very great favour and very intimate with her Majesty. In this subject I ought to report the opinion of many, but I doubt whether my letter may not miscarry...wherefore it is better to keep silence than to speak ill."

According to Elizabeth Jenkins: "In these weeks of high summer (1559), while Dudley engrossed the Queen entirely and she was scarcely seen, on the 17th July there was had up before the justices Ann Dowe, of Brentwood, sixty-eight years old, known as Mother Dowe who spent most of her time on the road. Five weeks before, at Rochford, in a house on the green beyond the parsonage, where she went to mend a fan, the wife of that house said in her hearing that Dudley had given the Queen a new petticoat that cost twenty nobles. In answer to this Mother Dowe had said the Queen had no need of a coat for she was able to buy one herself. Three days later in the same parish she met one Mr Coke riding on a horse. 'What news, Mother Dowe?' he said. She repeated the story about the petticoat to which Coke replied: 'Thinkst thou it was a petticoat? No, no, he gave her a child, I warrant thee.'"

('Mr Coke' mentioned above, may well have been Edward Coke who was related to Robert Cecil through marriage, and like Cecil, he was a sworn enemy of both Francis Bacon and his younger brother, Robert, Earl of Essex. Like Cecil, Coke knew the secret of the parentage of Francis, and perhaps he had learned of it first hand from 'Mother Dowe' in the village where the Dudley's resided).

The news soon spread around the village and it was the village where Dudley's wife Amy Robsart lived and it is thought that she heard the gossip from her servants. On the 8th September 1560, (two years after Elizabeth's succession to the throne and the day after Elizabeth's birthday), Amy was found at the bottom of a stone staircase, dead - her neck broken by the fall.

It has been said of Amy that she was suffering from cancer. The verdict was death by misadventure. When neighbours were interviewed, they thought that no foul play had taken place. Whatever the truth was, suspicion fell upon Robert Dudley and it was to haunt him for the rest of his life.

History books relate the great love-match that was between Elizabeth and Robert Dudley, and there have been many debates over the years as to whether the Queen and Robert did marry.

According to the late Alfred Dodd's in his book titled *Francis Bacon's Personal Life Story:*"On the 12th September of the same year (1560) [5 days after the death of Robert Dudley's wife, Amy], Dudley and the Queen were privately married at Brooke House, Hackney, the home belonging to the Earl of Pembroke - Sir Nicholas and Lady Bacon being witnesses".

The Secret Birth of Francis Bacon
St Germain

"...he was delivered in great secrecy... My heart ached for the sibling who was born. The young maiden who was a lady in waiting took the wee babe."

('Portia', twin soul of St Germain, excerpt from *St Germain, Twin Souls & Soulmates*)

Alfred Dodd, biographer of Francis Bacon in his book titled *Francis Bacon's Personal Life Story* wrote the following:

"On the 22nd January, 1561, there was born in London the world's greatest genius, born not for an age but for all time."

According to information contained in Dr Raymond Bernard's work titled *The Great Secret Count Saint Germain* regarding the birth of Francis Bacon, it was the intention of the Queen to dispose of the child. Sir Nicholas Bacon (whose wife Lady Anne was the Lady in Waiting to the Queen) persuaded the Queen to let them adopt Francis because Lady Anne had given birth to a still-born child. Francis was substituted for Anne's dead son and she raised him as if he was her true son. There were many witnesses to this secret birth, but they were sworn upon fear of death, to maintain their secrecy.

According to Dr Raymond Bernard:

"There exists in the British Museum an engraving depicting the confinement of Queen Elizabeth. As was customary at a royal birth, the entire court was present but they were bound in secrecy concerning the event on pain of death. This was kept as a state secret. Later, Francis discovered it, but he too feared to openly express this secret; as Alfred Dodd so convincingly shows, he concealed it in Shakespeare Sonnets which he wrote."

According to the late Alfred Dodd:

"The Queen's intimacy with Leicester resulted in another child known to history as the Earl of Essex. The two men, (Francis and Robert), knew each other as brothers; and an examination of their photographs shows a marked resemblance to each other and also to their father, Earl of Leicester. (On the other hand, there is no resemblance between the physiognomy of Francis and that of Lord or Lady Bacon - his foster parents). (But between the pictures of Bacon and his mother, Queen Elizabeth, there is a strong resemblance also)."

Throughout the turbulent years of the reign of Elizabeth I, Robert Dudley, Earl of Leicester, did his utmost to persuade Elizabeth to acknowledge him as her husband

Alfred Dodd comments: "From the outset, she [Elizabeth] regarded herself as the secret wife of Dudley...she knew that Dudley was disliked by the great nobles and an open marriage would have jeopardized the State. Moreover, she was not going to yield up the reins of the Kingdom to anyone."

"In short, she was not prepared to hand over the helm of the Kingdom to a partner. She felt she could accomplish the critical task of saving England far better than anyone else. What her father had done, she could do. She was a Tudor. She was also going to have love in her life. She was going to know what it was like to be a wife and a mother: but it was a secret life, a concealed experience, a thing apart; to the world she would be known as 'THE VIRGIN QUEEN'. She would keep all her opponents guessing until the situation cleared."

It was the continued hope of the Court and Parliament (who were unaware of her secret marriage to Dudley), that Elizabeth would one day marry, and thus they would make her consort, King of England, thereby having the 'male' ruler they so wished for. Throughout her life, these scheming people never ceased plotting to find a husband for her. Elizabeth declared that even if she was to find a suitable husband, she would remain Queen. They then reconciled themselves with the fact that even if she refused to recognise a future husband as a King of England, there would at least be a 'son' by such a union who would inevitably become heir to the throne.

Another problem was a religious one. At the time that Elizabeth became Queen, the country was still recovering from her father Henry VIII's dispute with Rome. Elizabeth was now head of the Church of England and the people did not want her to marry a European prince that was of the faith of the Church of Rome, as her father Henry had previously severed those ties.

According to Peter Dawkins, when Elizabeth became Queen of England, it was an occurrence that enabled the reformation of the English Church to continue so as to return it to the original model of the Celtic Church, which was the Church of the Brits or Albions, before the invasion of Rome and the subsequent conversions to Catholicism.

Her whole life consisted of plots and intrigues, in which many schemes were involved in attempting to bring about her assassination. For this reason, she needed her own intimate circle of friends whom she trusted, that would become spies in order to protect her and the throne of England. Thus, Elizabeth kept certain courtiers infatuated and loyal to her by utilizing her feminine wiles. Many of the courtiers that she had inherited were elderly ones who had served her father Henry VIII. Fortunately, they had sons who came to serve her at court. Because she paid too much attention to Robert, Lord Essex, a man so much younger than herself, rumours were rife about their relationship; but the relationship was not so strange after all, when we take into consideration the fact that he was her youngest son of whom she was particularly fond.

Francis learns of his true Parentage

At the age of fifteen years, Francis accidentally learnt the secret of his birth.

According to Peter Dawkins of the Francis Bacon Research Trust, in his book titled *The Great Vision*, "Francis received a devastating blow which affected his whole life dramatically. Francis discovered who his natural parents were and who he rightly was. The knowledge did not change his philanthropic views and purposes, but the manner of discovery and what it signified made an immense difference to his thoughts, emotions and the manner in which he could afterwards conduct his life and work. The sudden and unintended revelation burst explosively into his (and others) consciousness with an uncontrolled force that caused dread lips to be sealed for evermore, inaugurating a chain of crucifying events that were to have the profoundest effect on mankind."

"The story of this royal revelation is, naturally, only to be found told by Francis himself in his ciphers, but he recounts the story in full and in at least two different ciphers, each checking against and enhancing the other. In his 'Word Cipher' account the dire emotional impact is experienced to the full, as he pours out his heart to his future readers in a faithful and detailed report of the events as they occurred and as they were actually experienced by him at the time, hiding very little."

"In his 'Bilateral Cipher' account he provides summaries and additional details, but in this latter cipher the emotion is on the whole reserved and kept out of the way. Not all that Francis recorded in cipher has been deciphered yet, and there are various details and missing sections of the story here and there..."

"Into every generation is born a soul filled with malice, deformed spiritually and often physically as well, as a kind of countermand and adversary to any generous and light-filled impulse. For every movement we make, there needs to be an opposite movement of resistance to make this step possible. Every Jesus has his Caiaphas, and every knight his dragon, Francis Bacon had Robert Cecil."

"From childhood Francis and Robert had detested each other, Francis loathing the malice in Robert and Robert loathing Francis through envy and jealously. Both boys were born with highly developed intellects, but there the likeness stopped. Francis had also a kind heart, filled with love and good-will, a generous disposition, and was endowed with a noble spirit, a handsome form and bearing, and was well liked by people of all walks of life. Robert Cecil on the other hand, was born deformed, an unsightly hunchback who was feared and disliked by his contemporaries, and whose heart was filled with envy of the fortune of others and malice towards them in revenge for his own mishap."

"As the two boys were frequently in each other's company - Francis being the adopted son of Lady Anne Bacon and Robert being the elder child and only son of Lady Anne's sister, Lady Mildred Cecil, wife of Sir William Cecil (Lord Burghley) - it was Francis with all his gifts who became the principal target of Robert Cecil's poisoned mind. Both Francis and Anthony Bacon were hated by Robert Cecil, and Robert early on made a vow publicly expressed, to see the ruin of those two devoted brothers, his cousins. To this 'short-list' he added that of Robert Devereux, the Queen's second son, when he discovered that Francis and Robert Devereux were in fact royal brothers, rightful sons of the Queen."

It is noteworthy that a poem attributed to Edmund Spenser was titled *Mother Hubbard's Tale*, but all evidence points to it as having been written by Francis Bacon under Spenser's name, for he also wrote the *Shepherd's Calendar* under Spenser's name. (*The Shepherd's Calendar* is discussed further on in our story).

According to the foreword, by Ernest Rhys given in the book titled *The Shepherd's Calendar and Other Poems by Edmund Spenser* (1932), the "fox in the parable is intended for Burghley (Cecil)... indeed, the satire was dangerously outspoken."

In the poem, the poet is telling of his grief, his betrayal by a fox who was "crafty and unhappy witted."

>"The fox, that first this cause of grief did find...with words unkind.
>The evil plight that doth me sore constrain,
>And hope thereof to find due remedy?
>Hear, then, my pain and inward agony..."

The events came about because Queen Elizabeth happened to overhear court gossip between one of her maids and Robert Cecil, disclosing the truth about Francis Bacon's parentage. In anger, the Queen proceeded to beat the maid at which point of time, Francis walked into the room and seeing all the commotion, went to the maid's defence and attempted to diffuse the situation to hand. This in turn, caused the Queen to speak venomously to Francis, as we shall see further onwards.

Continuing with information supplied by Peter Dawkins:

"The whole cause of the royal revelation lay in the maliciousness of the twelve-year old Robert Cecil who had wanted to avenge himself upon the Queen and one of her ladies-in-waiting, due to an incident in the hall of the castle where the Court was assembled one fateful day in August, 1575. Even Robert Cecil had not entirely foreseen what his spite of the moment would lead to. But let us allow Francis [St Germain] to tell the story in his own words - first in the Bilateral Cipher."

'....Queen Elizabeth, who as hath been said previously, publicly termed herself a maiden-queen, whilst wife to the Earl of Leicester. By the union, myself and one brother were the early fruits, princes by no means basely begot, but so far were we from being properly acknowledged, in our youth we did not surmise ourselves other than the son of the Lord Keeper of the Seal, Nicholas Bacon, in the one case, and of the Earl of Essex, Walter Devereux, in the other.'

'Several years had gone by ere our true name or any of the conditions herein mentioned came to our knowledge. In truth, even when the revelation was in a measure accidental - albeit 'twas made by my mother - her wrath over one of my boy-like impulses driving her to admissions quite unthought, wholly unpremeditated, but, when thus spoken in our hearing, not to be retracted or denied...'

'I am indeed, by virtue of my birth, that royal though grossly wronged son to our most glorious yet most faulty - I can find no stronger terms - Queen Elizabeth, of the stock that doughty Edward fully renowned. Of such stock Henries Fifth, Seventh and Eighth, historic battle kings came, like branches sent from the oaks. My true name is not as in some back pages it was given, but Tudor. Bacon was only foster parent to my early youth, yet was as loving and kind to me as his own son, careful of my education, and even aspiring to my high advancement. But to Mistress Anne Bacon, ever quick with her sympathy and wise to advise, I do owe a greater or warmer gratitude, since she did much more truly and constantly guard, guide, protect and counsel me.'

'Moreover, to her I owe my life...it was by her intervention that the hour of nativity did not witness my death. Her majesty would truly have put me away privily, but Mistress Bacon, yearning over helpless baby-hood, saved me, having held over me a hand of protection. My attempts in after years to obtain my true, just and indisputable title of Prince of Wales, heir-apparent to the throne, must not however be thought or supposed to indicate that I held myself disinterested of these obligations, offered affront to these kind benefactors, or in any way conducted myself in such manner as would either cast reflections upon my breeding or do discredit to my birth.'

'It may clearly be seen that it was the most commonplace of ideas - an action barely ambitious because 'twas simply natural. But it failed most sadly, for the would-be Virgin Queen, with promptness (not liking our people's hearts to be set upon a king), before my ABC's even were taught to me, or the elements of all learning, instructed my tutors to instill into my young mind a desire to do as my foster father had done, aspiring to high political advancement, look for enduring renown there; not dreaming, even, of lack wherein I should look for many honours, since I was led to think I was born to nothing higher.'

'Of a truth, in her gracious moods my royal mother showed a certain pride in me when she named me her little Lord Keeper, but not the Prince - never owned that that be truly the rightful title I should bear, till Cecil did sorely anger her and bring on one of those outbreaks of temper against one of the ladies in her train who, foolish to rashness, did babble such gossip to him as she heard at the Court. In her look much malicious hatred burned towards me for ill-advised interference, and in hasty indignation said:

"You are my own born son, but you, though truly royal, of a fresh and masterly spirit, shall rule nor England nor your mother, nor reign over subjects yet to be. I **bar you from succession forevermore my best beloved first-born that blessed my union with** - no, I'll not name him, nor need I yet disclose the sweet story concealed thus far so well men only guess at it, nor know of a truth of the secret marriages, as rightful to guard the name of a Queen as of a maid of this realm. It would well beseem you to make such tales skulk out of sight, but this suiteth not your kingly spirit. A son like mine lifteth hand nere in aid to her who brought him forth; he'd rather uplift craven maids who tattle whenever my face (aigre enow ever, they say) turneth from them. What will this brave boy do? Tell a, b, c's?"

'Ending her tirade, she made me rise. Tremblingly I obeyed her charge, summoned a serving-man to lead me to my home and to Mistress Bacon.'

In Francis own words in the Word Cipher he informs how the Queen reacted to him defending the maid from her blows.

'The wrath of the enraged Queen like an earthquake fell upon my head and, my lord, I'll tell you what, all my glories in that one woman I forever lost. The Queen like thunder spoke: "How now, thou cold-blooded slave, wilt thou forsake thy mother and chase her honour up and down? Curst be the time of thy nativity!"

'I stood aghast and most astonished. Then she said again: "Slave! I am thy mother. Thou mightest be an emperor but that I will not betray whose son thou art; nor though with honourable parts thou are adorned, will I make thee great, for fear thyself should prove my competitor and govern England and me."'

"Fool! Unnatural, ungrateful boy! Does it curd thy blood to hear me say I am thy mother?" And into her eyes fierce, scornful, nimble lightnings dart with blinding flame.'

Whilst this entire tirade of verbal abuse was being poured upon Francis by his mother, standing nearby listening was Robert Cecil Burghley.

Francis seeks solace and validation from his adoptive mother, Lady Bacon

Francis wrote: 'Stupefied, I abruptly rise, turn, and as my tears made me blind, with uncertain steps cross the Court, and by means of one of the several posterns leave the castle and swiftly toward the city walk; and as my feet ascend the hill, mindless of the way, I thought I will go to the worthy lady up to whom all this time, I have believed to be my mother - mistress Anne Bacon, the wife of that renowned and noble gentleman, Sir Nicholas Bacon.'

When Francis finally arrived at the Bacon home, he informed Lady Bacon of all that had occurred and begged her to confirm everything. According to Peter Dawkins, dissolving into tears, Lady Anne confessed that "he was indeed the Queen's son but that the Queen and Leicester had promised to allow her to adopt and raise Francis as her own child, never revealing the story of his natural birth."

"She went on to disclose the whole story of Elizabeth and Robert Dudley's love for each other; their first (bigamous) marriage whilst imprisoned in the Tower of London during Mary's reign; how Francis was conceived...how they had married for the second time - this time legally, but in secret at the house of Lord Pembroke, with Sir Nicholas, as Chief Judge of the Realm, performing the ceremony in front of two other witnesses, Lady Anne herself, and 'Lord Puckering'; and how Francis' birth followed on from this, thus making him 'nobly' born and legally the rightful heir to the throne of England."

The following day, as if to add insult to injury, the Queen sent Robert Cecil with a message that Francis was to make attendance upon the Queen. Francis, still in a state of shock and wondering if this time, he fate was truly sealed, took his time which of course, further antagonized her by the time he finally arrived.

According to Alfred Dodd, "Queen Elizabeth had threatened Francis' death if he ever divulged the fact of his being her son, which she had angrily confessed to him when he had greatly displeased her.... all the witnesses of the Earl of Leicester's secret marriage with her were dead, and all demonstrating papers had been destroyed."

According to Peter Dawkins, Francis wrote the following comments about Robert Cecil, and the reader will see the similarity of the poem of *Mother Hubbard's Tale*, attributed to Edmund Spenser but obviously written by Francis about the grief caused him by the 'fox'.

"A fox, seen oft a Court in the form and outward appearance of a man named Robert Cecil - the hunchback must answer the Divine Arraignment to my charges against him, for he despoiled me ruthlessly. The Queen, my mother, might in the course of events which followed their revelations regarding my birth and parentage, without doubt having some natural pride in her offspring, have shown to us [referring to Francis and his younger brother, Robert, born in 1566 who later became Earl of Essex], no little attention had not the crafty fox aroused in that tiger-like spirit the jealousy that did so torment the Queen, that neither night nor day brought her respite from such suggestions about my hope that I might be England's king..."

As we have seen, Elizabeth was pregnant with Francis when she again married Robert Dudley. The marriage was legitimate because Amy had died leaving him a widower. Therefore, Francis, although conceived out of wedlock, was born in wedlock and thus titled to become the Tudor King of England.

Elizabeth's relationship with Francis was often strained (to say the least). When he was around her at Court in his younger days, before he discovered that he was her real son, she fondly called him her 'little Lord Keeper'. Obviously after the devastating truth was revealed to Francis, nothing could be the same between them. It was indeed a time for a period of great adjustment for them both. Elizabeth was growing older, and she became bitter as the years went by. As for Francis, he excelled - everything was a learning curve and he learned to stay positive in order to achieve his goals, of which there were many. It was to be in the latter years, when his brilliance and intellectual ability really began to show, that the Queen started to fear him, fuelled on by unjust rumours and lies fed to her by Robert Cecil and his father.

Thus the scene was set for a life of turmoil and intrigue within the Baconian and Tudor circle.

Sir Thomas More - El Morya

Still upon the subject of the Tudor era, it is appropriate to discuss Sir Thomas More who is included in the great collection of Masters of the Great White Brotherhood who reincarnated into the 15th century AD.

Sir Thomas More was born in 1478 and was raised in the household of John Moreton, Archbishop of Canterbury. The Archbishop recognised the young child's excellent potential and predicted that he would one day become a great man. He sent young Thomas to be educated at Oxford University where Thomas became one of the most accomplished classical scholars of his generation in Latin and Greek.

According to Peter Dawkins in his book titled *Dedication To The Light*:

"Sir Thomas More was right at the centre of affairs and acknowledged as England's leading exponent, writer and philosopher of the 'New Learning', who received a constant stream of visitors from both home and abroad who visited More's Platonic Academy of Learning."

It was during this period of time that Sir Nicholas Bacon, the adoptive father of Francis, was greatly influenced by Sir Thomas More. As a result, Sir Nicholas Bacon established his own small Platonic Academy at Gorhambury near St Albans, which was their place of residence. It was no mere coincidence that Francis Bacon was to be raised by this special family so involved with the Teachings of Plato, whom St Germain had once been. There is a pattern to everything and everyone.

Another admiral achievement of Sir More was that he was a pioneer of women's education for, up until that time, women were treated as mere chattels and not worthy of being educated.

Sir Thomas More published his famous *Utopia* in 1516, in Latin which purported the idea of the ideal Commonwealth. The story described an imaginary nation witnessed by a traveller who had voyaged to America which had been discovered thirteen years previous by Christopher Columbus (St Germain). There were veiled prophecies contained within this work, premonitions of things to come, such as euthanasia, religious tolerance, and women becoming priests.

This period was time of cultural revival known as the Renaissance, which had begun in Florence during the era of Rene of Anjou, Duke of Naples (and the titled King of Jerusalem/Sion). It has been discussed in earlier chapters that it was Rene who influenced Cosimo de Medici to found an Academy in Florence where the teachings of Plato were studied.

It cannot be mere coincidence that Sir Thomas More was raised in the household of the Archbishop of Canterbury, John Moreton, who was a friend and defendant of Henry VII (Tudor) and his wife Margaret (the great grandparents of Francis Bacon). For, in a past-life, Sir Thomas More (El Morya) is reputed to have been St Thomas a Becket, who in that particular lifetime was the Archbishop of Canterbury!

Henry II is reputed to have reincarnated as Henry VIII. As we have read in previous chapters, Henry II was exceptionally fond of women, which is one of the reasons his wife, Eleanor of Aquitaine, left him and returned to France. We know from history just how fond Henry VIII was of women, because after all, he did have SIX wives not to mention numerous affairs hence the reason his unfortunate children, Mary and Edward developed syphilis.

According to the authors of *The Holy Blood And the Holy Grail*, the original first independent Grand Master of the Order of Sion was Jean de Gisors (John of Gisors) (1133-1220). He was a wealthy landowner and vassal of King Henry II of England. The authors were able to confirm that Jean de Gisors met with Thomas a Becket at Gisors in 1169. Therefore, it is highly probable that Thomas was also a member of the Order of Sion.

In common with Thomas a Becket who had a falling out with Henry II and was murdered in his own cathedral at Canterbury by some knights who were in the service of Henry II, Sir Thomas More had a falling out with Henry VIII, the result being that Henry VIII issued orders for Sir Thomas More to be executed. It has been mentioned elsewhere throughout this story of the history of the *Masters of the Mystical Rose* that it was common for Masters who reincarnated to retain the same or similar names by which they were called in past-lives, and in this case we have:

Henry II, and Henry VIII,

Thomas a Becket and Thomas More...Coincidence?

It is noteworthy that Moreton, the Archbishop of Canterbury who raised Thomas, took the side of the Lancastrians during the War of the Roses, and then spent time in exile living at the court of Margaret of Anjou, whose father Rene,

Count of Anjou has featured so prominently in this story. He had once been the Grand Master (Helmsman) of the Order of Sion.

Because Sir Thomas More refused to attend the coronation of Anne Boleyn, he great displeased Henry.

Before his sentence was passed, Thomas More spoke of his commitment to a 'Universal Church' whose powers neither prince nor Parliament had any right to determine. When he was beheaded, it was an act that shocked the whole of Western Europe. He was one of the earliest victims of the English Reformation, a man much loved, and respected by all who knew him; one who sacrificed himself for his principles, as all Masters of the Great White Brotherhood have done.

MASTERS DISCUSSED IN THIS CHAPTER

Francis Bacon - St Germain
Sir John Dee - Kuthumi
Sir Thomas a Becket - El Morya
Sir Thomas More - El Morya

NOTES AND RECOMMENDED READING

Elizabeth Jenkins, *Elizabeth And Leicester*, (Victor Gollanz Ltd, U.K. 1961)
Peter Dawkins, *The Great Vision*, (Francis Bacon Research Trust, Warwick, U.K.)
Peter Dawkins, *Arcadia*, (Francis Bacon Research Trust, Warwick, U.K.).
Peter Dawkins, *Dedication To The Light*, (Francis Bacon Research Trust, Warwick, U.K)
Alfred Dodd, *Francis Bacon's Personal Life Story*, (Rider & Company, U.K., 1986).
Dr Raymond Bernard, *The Great Secret - Count Saint Germain*, (U.S.A.).
Isabel Cooper-Oakley, *Comte De St Germain*, (Theosophical Publishing House, U.K. 1985)
Azena Ramanda and Claire Heartsong, *St Germain Twin Souls & Soulmates*, (Triad Publications, Qld., Australia, 1994).
Ernest Rhys, *The Shepherd's Calendar And Other Poems by Edmund Spenser*, (J.M. Dent & Sons Ltd., U.K. 1932)
Christopher Haig, *Elizabeth I*, (Longman, U.K.)
Elizabeth Hallam, *The Plantagenet Encyclopedia*, (Tiger Books, U.K. 1996)

CHAPTER 40

The Romance of Francis Bacon (St Germain)

"Shall I compare thee to a Summer's Day?
Thou art more Lovely and more Temperate:
Rough winds do shake the Darling Buds of May,
And Summer's Lease hath all too short a Date."
(Sonnet 43 by Francis Bacon alias Shakespeare)
"Certain events occurred which were to determine the course of European
history and eventually World history."
(Peter Dawkins - *The Great Vision*)

According to the late Alfred Dodd, when Francis aged fifteen years old and had learned the truth about his royal birth, he was then banished from court and sent by his mother, Queen Elizabeth to France. He was accompanied by Sir Amyas Paulet who was to protect him, watch over him.

"While at the French court, he fell in love with Marguerite of Navarre who was then taking steps to be divorced from her husband..."

Catherine de Medici (1519 - 1589 AD)
And the Massacre of the Huguenots

The daughter of Lorenzo de Medici was Catherine de Medici, who became Queen of France (1547-1559). Unfortunately, Catherine did not inherit her father's noble traits or those of her great grandfather, Cosimo. She married the Duke of Orleans who became the King of France in 1547 (known as Henry II) and upon the death of her husband, Catherine ruled as regent for her son Charles IX, until he was old enough to become King in 1563, but even then Catherine continued to be a dominant figure.

History records her as a very powerful, sinister woman who became a major force in French politics. She was a Roman Catholic who was anti the Huguenots (Protestants) and plotted to assassinate the Protestant leader, which led to the death of some fifteen thousand Huguenots in France, a most unfortunate occurrence in history. Two brothers, who were ancestors of my husband's family, were prominent members of these Huguenots in France who managed to escape to Holland where they became liberators for a short time and then were forced to flee to County Down in Northern Ireland, at which time they changed their name.

What is fascinating about Catherine de Medici is that she was the mother of Marguerite of Valois whose marriage she had arranged to the Protestant King Henry of Navarre, who was later to become Henry IV, King of France. Being an arranged marriage, it comes as no surprise that it was a loveless one! Henry's affections were otherwise inclined, and accordingly the marriage was never consummated.

According to information contained in Peter Dawkins' book titled *The Great Vision*:

It was in this year, 1572, that the supernova of Cassiopeia shone brightly in the sky, day and night, and as Peter Dawkins so aptly phrased it, "certain events occurred which were to determine the course of European history and eventually World history." The same star is considered to have been the one that shone brightly in the sky during the birth of the Messiah, Jesus, some 1,500 years previously.

"On Monday, August 18th, 1572, the Princess Marguerite de Valois, sister of the feeble and neurotic Catholic King of France, Charles IX, and daughter of the powerful and ruthless Queen Mother, Catherine de Medici, was married in great pomp to the Huguenot King of Navarre, Henri de Bourbon. The marriage festivities continued in great style until Thursday August 21st. It was followed the next day by the attempted assassination of the Admiral of France, Gaspard de Coligny, a Huguenot and Queen Catherine's imminent rival as the principal influencer of Charles IX's mind and actions. The final result of this botched attempt was the ghastly massacre of all the now-indignant Huguenot followers of Henry de Navarre, who had come to Paris as guests for the great wedding."

"The massacre was begun by the order of Charles IX, persuaded by his mother, Catherine de Medici, at midnight on Sunday 24th August, St Bartholomew's Day. It was mercilessly carried out by the Catholic soldiers and citizens of Paris. At least five thousand people were murdered - two thousand in Paris and three thousand in the provinces, at a very conservative estimate. It was one of the most notorious events in European history, but the atrocity helped to unite the Huguenots and other Protestants, and gave them increased determination to fight for their cause. The outbreak of the fourth war of religion in England inevitably followed, and in England had far-reaching effects on the mind and policies of Queen Elizabeth and her people, as also on Henri of Navarre (who was one day to become Henri IV of France). Sir Nicholas Bacon [the adoptive father of Francis Bacon] even supported a Bill in Parliament for the expulsion of all Frenchmen resident in England."

Marguerite of Valois (1553 - 1615 AD)

"Shall I compare thee to a Summer's Day?"
(Sonnet 43, Francis Bacon alias Shakespeare)

The deep love which Francis felt for Marguerite had blossomed from the time of his early youth when he spent time at the French Court.

It is fascinating that Marguerite should be the granddaughter of Lorenzo de Medici and the great-granddaughter of Cosimo de Medici, who had founded the first Platonic Academy during the Italian Renaissance in the previous century. The Medici family always played an important role in St Germain's life and even when he faked his death as Francis Bacon in 1626 and fled to the Continent, where he assumed the title of the Prince Ragoczy (Francis III) of Hungary, he was under the protection of the Medici family.

I wonder if St Germain knew in his incarnation as Christopher Columbus, during which time he was given financial assistance by Lorenzo de Medici for his voyages of discovery that he would in a future life, fall in love with Lorenzo's granddaughter?

From Peter Dawkins' book titled *Arcadia* we are informed as follows:

"Right at the start of the *Shepherd's Calendar* (written by Francis Bacon under the name of Spenser), in the Argument that commences in the January Aecologue, is the plain statement that Colin Clout (the author, Francis Bacon), is still suffering from his unrequited love, and that Rosalinde in the poem shadows (i.e. veils) the name of the one he loves."

A straight and meaningful anagram of 'Rosalinde' is 'Daisie lorn'. Daisy in French is *Marguerite*; 'Lorn' means 'lost'. Thus 'Daisie lorn means 'Lost Marguerite', which is an extremely good description of the author's love, whom he has lost. That this is Francis Bacon's love, Marguerite de Valois, is confirmed by the statement that she is the 'Widow's daughter of the glen, for Valois is not only a district (hence a 'borough') of Northern France, but *de Valois* infers 'of the Valley' which is the same as 'of the Glen'. Furthermore, Marguerite de Valois was the daughter of Catherine de Medici, widow of Henry II of France - not just any widow, but the Queen Mother. As such, not only was Marguerite the 'Widowe's daughter', but she was also of 'no meane house' and a foreigner. To add even further detail, Marguerite de Valois was the wife of Henry de Navarre, and thus the Queen of Navarre, even whilst being the object of Francis' love.'"

According to the late Alfred Dodd, who was considered to be the greatest modern day authority of his era on the Shakespeare-Bacon controversy: "The royal blood of the House of Valois, the most literary family in France, flowed in Francis' veins from his great-grandmother, Catherine de Valois, widow of Henry V, whose second husband was Owen Tudor. Their son Henry was Elizabeth's (the First's) grandfather. It is worth noting also that the education of Henry VIII was personally superintended by the illustrious Margaret Beaufort, his grandmother, who, as Countess of Richmond, was a patron of Caxton's [inventor of the printer] successor, Wynkyn de Worde, who printed her books and translations."

"S. A. E. Hickson in *The Prince of Poets*, says:

'The hereditary predecessors of Queen Elizabeth show that there breathed in the genius of her Royal Veins, the valour and virile wisdom of the Plantagenets, the distinguished literary taste of the French House of Valois, the indominatable will of the Tudors, the devout learning of Margaret, and the wit of Anne Boleyn.'"

"The galaxy of various women, talented, brave, beautiful, accomplished, witty, learned, affectionate and devout, which surrendered the cradle when Francis was born, is astonishingly remarkable: Eleanor of Castile, Isabella of France, Philippa of Hainault, Katherine Swynford [whose tomb lies in the Lincoln Cathedral and who is fondly remembered in the story *Katherine* by Anya Seton], Margaret Beaufort, Catherine de Valois, Elizabeth Woodville, Elizabeth of York, Anne Boleyn, Queen Elizabeth. 'They formed a real constellation of living women', says Hickson."

The beautiful, dark haired Queen Marguerite was described as being brilliantly clever, a genius who strongly reflected the spirit of the French Renaissance with the support that she gave for church reform and religious liberty...all of which is quite understandable, considering that she had in her, the noble blood of Lorenzo and Cosimo de Medici. She was a prolific writer and her major work was *The Heptameron* which was a collection of seventy stories.

When the young Francis Bacon arrived at her French court, Marguerite was in the process of divorcing Henry. According to Alfred Dodd, "Tradition says that when Francis first saw Queen Marguerite, he swooned away, so affected was he by her loveliness or as the Theosophists would explain it, *by the shock of recollecting that they had met before in a previous life.* In a book published in 1621, six years after her death, written in Latin under the mask name of 'John Barclay' entitled *John Barclay his Argenis*, Francis tells of his feelings about fair Marguerite."

"There is not, however, anything very remarkable in the fact that Francis and Marguerite should fall in love with each other. While she was a beautiful woman he had an equally striking personality, with a mind far beyond his years and was physically a mature adult. In view of her extraordinary mind, her literary aspirations, her wide knowledge and range of reading, and the outstanding fact that her cast of intellect was more akin to Francis Bacon's than that of anyone else at the French Court - save Ronsard - it is inconceivable that such persons with so much in common would not be rapidly drawn together by the sheer force of mental gravitation."

"They were both geniuses of similar tastes, both had their private problems through husband and mother, both needed sympathy, both longed for the ideal things of life and their establishment on earth and both were of the Blood Royal...though one was under a cloud as a concealed Prince. Her beauty of mind and intellectual gifts were apparently only equalled by her physical charms, for Brantome in a perfect panegyric of her life wrote:

'To speak of the beauty of this rare Princess: I believe that all those who are, will be, or ever have been, will be plain beside it and cannot have beauty...No Goddess was ever seen more beautiful...To suitably proclaim her charms, merits, virtues, God must lengthen the earth and heighten the sky, since space...is lacking for the flight of her perfections and renown'."

"His handsome face and alluring ways were sufficient to capture the heart of any woman - maid or wife. There can be little wonder that love flamed between Francis and Queen Marguerite at first sight."

"The *Marguerite Sonnets* were the beginnings of the mysterious body of verse known today as *Shake-speare's Sonnets*. They became literally and truly his Sonnet-Diary. It was written in secret and kept, so the author tells us, 'in sure Wards of Trust that to my use my Jewels of Emotion might unused stay'. (Sonnet Diary 105)."

"We can see through the amber of his thought and note the fossils that lie there imprisoned for all time - some beautiful, and some repellent, for crises were many during his pilgrimage...and some were very bitter. That is the reason why we can definitely say that Francis Bacon was passionately attached to Marguerite of Navarre. He left his sacred Sonnet-Diary to be revealed generations after all his contemporaries had passed away - the immortal love-songs of the world's greatest poet."

"From his contact with Marguerite he acquired the habit of clothing his emotions in imaginative terms. They were truly the beginnings of what was described by Francis Bacon's friends as 'Living Art'. They knew his secret, the art of writing poetry of perfection. He was a highly sensitive soul who suffered the rapture and agony of varying conflicting emotions all his life. He suffered more intensely than the average man. Few have been placed on the rack of fate more than the concealed Prince who wore the Bacon mask...He won tranquility of mind and soul by spilling his agitations on paper, weaving round them in ink a garment of beautiful images - so tenuous and fanciful, so broadly conceived, that they became jewels of passion that could be used by universal man."

"So skillfully has the poet precipitated his thought round the irritating *motif* that had called his emotions into action that his iridescent pearls, precious because they had grown out of his heart's blood, had a cosmopolitan appeal...to all nations, to all time, to all men. They served vastly different feelings. They appealed to different emotions. And therefore men have ever read into the flashing jewels on the finger of Time vastly different interpretations. The original concrete irritation in the heart of the pearl, enfolded in words that sparkled different meanings, lay hidden and unknown, which was what the author intended. His real thoughts, the cries of his soul, were far too sacred, too precious, too dangerous, to be thrown on the highways of the world, either in his own age or to the immediate generations that followed."

"His first two Sonnets to Marguerite tell the entire story of his passion. He writes to her as a person fully acquainted with his birth-secret. He says that for the moment the Stars do not favour him. He cannot boast of 'Public Honour' and Proud Titles' which are justly his." "The First Sonnet (43 - xviii) has long been regarded as the finest Love-Sonnet in the English Language."

Her Love...Immortal

"Shall I compare thee to a Summer's Day?
Thou art more Lovely and more Temperate:
Rough winds do shake the Darling Buds of May,
And Summer's Lease hath all too short a Date:
Sometime too hot the Eye of Heaven shines,
And often is his Gold Complexion dimmed:
And every Fair from Fair sometime declines,
By Chance or Nature's changing Course untrimmed;
But Thy Eternal Summer shall not fade
Nor lose possession of that Fair thou Owest;
Nor shall Death brag Thou wander'st in his Shade,
When in Eternal Lines to Time Thou growest:
So long as men can Breathe or Eyes can See,
So long Lives THIS, and This gives Life to Thee."
(Sonnet 43)

From Peter Dawkins' book titled *The Great Vision*, we learn more of how Francis felt about Marguerite:

"I look into the lady's face, and in her eyes I find a wonder, or a wondrous miracle, and nor heard nor read so strange a thing - a shadow of myself formed in her eye, and in this form of beauty read I - love!"

Marguerite: 'Speak then, my gentle Prince; and canst thou love?"

Francis: 'Nay, ask me if I can refrain from love, for I do love thee most unfeignedly.'

Marguerite: 'But I love you with so much of my heart, that none's left to protest, my gentle lord.'

Francis: 'Oh happy shall he be whom Marguerite loves.'

Marguerite: 'Then never say that thou are miserable, because, it may be, thou shalt be my love. Boldness comes to me now, and brings me heart; Prince Francis, I have loved you night and day, for many weary months.'

Francis: 'Why was my Marguerite so hard to win?'

Marguerite: 'Hard to seem won; but I was won, my lord, with the first glance; that ever pardon me, if I confess much you will play the tyrant: I've come to join thee, and leave the king. I'll be thine, for I cannot be mine own, nor anything to any, if I be not thine.'"

"In the Second Canto to Marguerite, Francis writes 'Some Glory in *their BIRTH*, some in their Skill, Wealth, Bodies' Force, Garments, Hawks, Hounds, or an adjunct Pleasure wherein it finds a joy above the rest. But these particulars are not my measure, all these I better in one general Best. *Thy LOVE is better than HIGH BIRTH TO ME...*"

Prince Francis is summoned home to England
By his Mother Elizabeth 1st

According to Peter Dawkins:

"As happened so many times in Francis' life, just as the prize seemed won and in his grasp, it was snatched away from him at the critical moment. The summons from Queen Elizabeth was for him to return home immediately, with no delay, and he was to set out for England the very next day...it turned the sweetness into bitter gall. Francis did indeed return to England filled with hopes and plans of a future marriage with Marguerite, but Marguerite's tender hopes were dashed, her heart mortified, her offering of love seemingly repudiated. Not even one night would, or could, Francis stay with her, even though she pleaded that he might do so. What a mistake, perhaps he made, yet - there was actually no hope for the marriage."

Alfred Dodd wrote that "the remaining Sonnets in the Canto give a wonderful insight into the poet's (Francis') psychic and psychological knowledge. They not only show that he was familiar with the wonderful powers of the mind but that he, himself, had a developed Sixth Sense which brought him *en rapport with the unseen world beyond our normal senses*. Francis indicates that he had a knowledge of telepathy, clairvoyance, the human etheric body which often transversed the astral place at night-time which 'could jump both sea and land'; as soon as THINK where he would be."

"All this esoteric information is quietly told in his confession of love and his torment at his journeying away from her (Marguerite). When Francis the lover retires to rest he goes in thought on a pilgrimage to her and sometimes he suggests her double or spiritual body visits him, for his 'Soul's Imaginary Sight' (clairvoyant perception) presents thy Shadow to my Sightless View' - he sees her etheric body by the light of her aura. 'Is it thy Spirit that thou send'st from Thee so FAR from Home into my deeds to pry?' he asks."

(A modern day book which tells of the author's ability to astral travel at will to distant places just by 'thinking' oneself to the place is titled *Journeys Out of the Body* by Robert A. Monroe).

According to Alfred Dodd:

"Francis never married his Marguerite but he treasures her in his heart as an ideal, and in the last four Sonnets he mingles her as an idealized Love with other Loves - literature, (Free) masonry, his wife Alice (whom he married late in life), the Earth-mother, all that have taken possession of his life during the marching years. The last Sonnet he writes about her was after she had passed to the Higher Life. He says he knows the lost Ideal is not dead. She still lives."

"Francis Bacon was warm-hearted, emotional, sensitive, and, as is the way with exceptionally fine-fibred natures, he could not bare his heart to the world and betray his innermost feelings. But he did discharge his feelings in a way unique that only a genius could have imagined...the manipulation of a Sonnet carrying in his heart the truth of the particular emotion that called it into being; and he also made a provision for the Secret of the Sonnets not to be known to the general world for long generations until all the principal actors were dust, when no harm could be done to anyone by the Diary's disclosure." (These Sonnets which the author refers to consisted of eight wonderful Sonnets written to Marguerite).

"He later wrote 'Romeo and Juliet' as an autobiography of this experience, just as 'Hamlet' (the philosopher-prince) was equally autobiographical."

According to Peter Dawkins, after the great disappointment of being separated from Marguerite, Francis then recorded in his private writings:

'From that day I lived a doubtful life, swinging like a pendant branch to and fro, or tempest tossed by many a troublous desire. At length I turned my attention from love, and used all my time and wit to make such advancement in learning or achieve such a great proficiency in studies that my name as a lover of Sciences should be best known and most honoured, less for my own aggrandizement than as an advantage of mankind, but with some natural desires to approve my worthiness in the sight of my book-loving and aspiring mother, believing that by thus doing I should advance my claim and obtain my rights, not aware of Cecil (Robert), his misapplied zeal in bringing to her Majesty's notice, to conceive in her mind that I had no other thought save a design to win sovereignty in her life-time.'

'I need not assert how far this was from my heart at any time, especially in my youth, but the Queen's jealously so blinded her reason that she, following the suggestions of malice, showed little pride in my attempts, discovering in truth more envy than natural pride, and more hate than affection.''

Thus, the 'first' great love of Francis Bacon's life was not to be, however, Marguerite is now immortalized for all time in the beautiful Sonnets.

'Their life [Romeo and Juliet] was too brief - its rose of pleasure had but partly drunk the sweet dew of early delight, and every hour had begun to hope unto sweet love, tender leaflets in whose fragrance was assurance of untold joys that the immortals know. Yet 'tis a kind of fate which joined them together in life and in death.'

'It was a sadder fate befell our youthful love, my Marguerite, yet written out in the plays it scarce would be named our tragedy since neither yielded up life. But the joy of life ebbed from our hearts with our parting, and it never came again into this bosom on full-flood-tide. O we were Fortune's fool too long, sweet one, and art is long....'

'Far from angelic though man his nature, if his love be as clear or as fine as our love for a lovely woman (sweet as a rose and as thorny it might chance), it sweeteneth all the enclosure of his breast, oft changing a waste into lovely gardens which the angels would fain seek. That it so uplifts our life who would ere question? Not he, our friend and adviser...Sir Amyas Paulet.'

'It is sometimes said, "No man can at once be wise and love", and yet it would be well to observe many will be wiser after a lesson such as we long ago conned. There was no ease to our suffering heart till our years of life were eight lustres. The fair face liveth ever in dreams, but in inner pleasures only doth the sunny vision come.''

(*Bilateral Cipher of Francis Bacon, pp.79-80 (Romeo and Juliet, undated Quarto).*

(Extracted from Peter Dawkins' book titled *The Great Vision*)

St Germain's Twin Soul

"One day, just beyond my twelfth birthday, I was in my father's vineyard....I chanced to look just across the way and beheld the form of a man...I said unto him, 'My dear brother, I am your mirror'.

Hand-in-hand we walked that night..."

(The Lady Portia, Twin Soul of St Germain)

(Excerpt from St Germain *Twin Souls & Soulmates*)

Many years passed, during which time Francis mourned his lost love, and then at the time of the reign of James I (Stuart) of England who succeeded to the throne after the death of Elizabeth, we learn from Alfred Dodd, that Francis, dressed in Royal Purple, mysteriously married a young lass named Alice Barnham on the 10th May, 1606, nine years before the death of his beautiful Marguerite.

According to Alfred Dodd in his book titled *Francis Bacon's Personal Life Story*, Francis met Alice, a 'commoner' when she was eleven years old. (Alice was born in 1592). It could be said that a 'commoner' was someone of a humble background and in the book titled *St German Twin Souls & Soulmates*, Portia, the twin-soul of St Germain, Portia tells of when the time finally arrived for her to reincarnate in order to assist St Germain: "I chose to be born as all humanity is, to be humble, to be as a child, to embrace humanity to my heart - to be no different than you, my brothers and sisters. I retained enough of the knowing and had about me angels and beings who assisted me to remember who I am and why I had come into the Earth-plane again."

To quote the words of Alfred Dodd: "It is a matter of interest - destined to become more as the years advance - to know something about Alice - the girl-wife of the world's greatest intellectual genius. She is passed over in silence by the majority of biographers as though she were of little account."

According to Alfred Dodd, Francis met Alice whilst he was touring the country when he visited the family estate at Aylesbury at which time she was about eleven years old. He waited until she was fourteen years old before he married her.

Alfred Dodd raised the important question: "It is an amazing puzzle to me that not a single biographer has commented on the fact that a man of forty-six - the ripest scholar and genius ever known - married a girl barely fourteen. Not one has asked, 'How came it about? How did he come to announce his intention to marry Alice Barnham to the king (James) when she was a mere child of eleven? Is there not a manifest mystery here that demands an explanation?"

"Not a single writer has ever tried to probe the reason. They have slurred over the disparity of ages as though it were the most natural thing in the world for a man of forty-six to wed a child of fourteen. It is obvious that when forty-six weds fourteen there is 'something' concealed deep below the facts."

From the book titled *St Germain Twin Souls & Soulmates*, we learn a little of Portia's story relating to the years after the birth of Francis Bacon, which she had witnessed from the etheric dimension.

"Years passed and I continued to look down, longing to romp and play with this one. He saw me with inner vision and he wished to draw me into his experience, but I said it was not time yet. Other ones such as myself in the ethers, participated and from time to time manifested and taught this wee lad and opened him far beyond his years or beyond the capacity of those around him who were indeed great beings. This one had a work to do and it was agreed by the councils that a great focus would come through him to be embodied and exemplified, that would entorch the entire court of England with a new thought, a new capacity to perceive life."

"...at the birth of the Aquarian Age, I knew that I had a part to play in this, so I chose to delay my coming until the appropriate hour and then there was the descent into an embodiment here..."

Portia then tells the story of how she met St Germain in her father's vineyard in the country, when she was still a young child of about twelve years of age, and they recognised each other, at which time she said to St Germain: "My dear brother, I am your mirror" (meaning 'twin soul').

Questions were posed to St Germain by Claire Heartsong about his meeting with Portia.

St Germain:	"We knew one another before."
Q:	"Was she in a physical embodiment or an etherical...?"
St Germain:	"In an embodiment. We knew - she better than I..."
Q:	"You mean while you were living the life of Francis Bacon, you met Portia?"
St Germain:	"Yes, she lifted her frequency into a grand understanding of who she was, so that we might facilitate [promote/assist] one another."

And so, after all these years, the question posed by the late Alfred Dodd has at last been answered. St Germain married his twin soul Alice Barnham who was an incarnation of the Lady Portia. This would help to answer Alfred's question as to why the greatest genius the world has ever known, chose to marry one so young, when he could have had the choice of any noble lady. Portia informs us that she chose to be born of 'humble' origins, and Alice was of 'humble' origins because she was a 'commoner'.

According to the late Alfred Dodd:

"Whatever their marital relations were as she grew to maturity, the fact remains that the marriage was a childless one. How could he become a parent under such circumstances? *A child with Tudor blood in his veins would be in perpetual danger.* I am quite satisfied that the renunciation of parenthood was mutual on the part of both; and that *Alice Barnham, in many more ways than one, sacrificed herself (along with the other loyal friends) that he might complete his Divine Mission.*" (The Italics have been utilized to emphasize these important statements about the role that Alice played in St Germain's life).

It is noteworthy that St Brigid of Ireland's name is thought to have been Alice Curtayne. In a prophecy made by St Columba (St Germain), he foresaw that he, St Patrick and Brigid would be buried together in Ireland. The prophecy came to fruition in the 12th century AD and the mystery behind this prophecy is elaborated upon in the sequel to this story, *The Dove, The Rose And The Sceptre, In Search Of The Ark Of The Covenant.*

Throughout the hundreds of lives into which we have reincarnated, we have had soul-mates which are not to be confused with our twin souls for we do not always reincarnate at the same time as our twin souls. Our twin souls often choose to remain in the etheric, assisting us as our guides from the Higher Realms.

This is one reason why many people spend a lifetime searching for their twin soul, for subconsciously, we are aware that we have one. Our soul-mates are those we have also spent past lives with - husbands, wives, lovers, friends etc. Because St Germain (as Francis Bacon) upon his first meeting with Queen Marguerite, recognised her from a previous lifetime, and immediately felt closely drawn to her and was instantly in love with her, Marguerite would have been his soul-mate from a previous past-life and she may have been with him in many past-lives.

It may have been Marguerite who reincarnated during the 18th century as Marie Antoinette of the Austrian royal family of Habsburgs who, like the Medici family, were another family who rendered assistance to St Germain.

According to information given to me by St Germain, Queen Marie Antoinette in a previous life had been a queen and a responsible one, which fits the role of Queen Marguerite. However, Marie Antoinette was destined to play the role of an irresponsible Queen, for certain events had to occur in that era in order to bring down the monarchy and restore a new and fairer system, for the ordinary people were very poor and thousands were starving. Successive kings of France, including the 'Sun King' who built the beautiful but extravagant Palace of Versailles, contributed to the penury of the people which led to the establishment of certain secret societies being formed in order to bring about reform.

MASTERS DISCUSSED IN THIS CHAPTER
Francis Bacon - St Germain
The Lady Portia - St Germain's twin soul

NOTES AND RECOMMENDED READING

Alfred Dodd, *Francis Bacon's Personal Life Story* (Rider & Co., U.K. 1986)
Azena Ramanda & Claire Heartsong, *St Germain Twin Souls & Soulmates* (Triad Publishers, Qld. Australia, 1994)
Peter Dawkins, *The Great Vision*, (Francis Bacon Research Trust, Warwick, U.K.)
Peter Dawkins, *Arcadia*, (Francis Bacon Research Trust, Warwick, U.K.).
Peter Dawkins, *Dedication To The Light*, (Francis Bacon Research Trust, Warwick, U.K)
Dr Raymond Bernard, *The Great Secret - Count Saint Germain*, (U.S.A.).

Isabel Cooper-Oakley, *Comte De St Germain*, (Theosophical Publishing House, U.K. 1985)

Frank Kermode, John Hollander, *The Oxford Anthology of English Literature*, (Oxford University, U.K., 1973).

Emile Legouis, *A History of English Literature, The Middle Ages and the Renaissance*, (J.M. Dent & Sons, London, U.K. 1945).

Boris Ford, *The Age Of Shakespeare*, (Penguin Books, U.K., 1955).

Peter Alexander, *Shakespeare, Tragedies And Poems*, (Collins, London, U.K., 1958).

Ernest Rhys, *The Shepherd's Calendar And Other Poems by Edmund Spenser*, (J.M. Dent & Sons Ltd., U.K. 1932)

The Sonnets, William Shakespeare, (Leopard Books, London, 1988).

Arnold Toynbee, *A Study of History*, (Oxford University Press, U.K. 1934)

F.J. Dennett, *Europe, A History*, (Linehan & Shrimpton, Melbourne, Australia, 1961)

Robert Munro, *Journeys Out Of The Body*, (Souvenir Press, U.S.A., 1972)

Elizabeth Jenkins, *Elizabeth And Leicester*, (Victor Gollanz Ltd, U.K. 1961)

Christopher Haig, *Elizabeth I*, (Longman, U.K.)

CHAPTER 41

Francis Bacon
'Interpreter of the Law' & Author

> *"But tell us" (said the ape), "we do you pray,*
> *Who now in court doth bear the greatest sway,*
> *That, if such good fortune do to us befall,*
> *We make seek favour of the best of all?*
> *"Marry," (said he) "the highest now in grace..."*
> *"In hope to find there happier success,*
> *So well they shifted, that the ape anon*
> *Himself had clothed like a gentleman,*
> *And the sly fox, as like to be his groom,*
> *That to the court in seemly sort they come;*
> *Where the fond ape, himself uprearing high*
> *Upon his tiptoes, stalketh stately by*
> *As if he were some great magnifico,*
> *And boldly doth amongst the boldest go;*
> *And his man Reynold [fox], with fine counterfeasance,*
> *Supports his credit and his countenance...*
> *Thus did the ape at first him credit gain,*
> *Which afterwards he wisely did maintain*
> *With gallant show, and daily more augment*
> *Through his fine feats and courtly complement..."*
> ('Mother Hubbard's Tale' - Spenser/Francis Bacon)

Francis Bacon, in his early childhood was acclaimed as a child prodigy and at the age of twelve, he went to Trinity College, Cambridge University. At the age of fourteen years, he left Cambridge in 1575, fluent in the classics, Latin and Greek and in the modern languages, French, Italian and Spanish.

We have learned that when Francis was fifteen years old, he tragically received the knowledge of his true Tudor parentage and was banished from the Court by his mother, Elizabeth, to the royal Court of France where he fell in love with Queen

Marguerite. According to his biographer, Alfred Dodd, Francis had spent three years on the Continent where he became imbued with the spirit of the French Renaissance, inspired by the French poets, the 'Pleiades', and it was during this period of time that he wrote his famous work, *The Chemical Marriage* which has been discussed in an earlier chapter. Alfred Dodd referring to this work wrote, "and the startling fact emerges that the very first pamphlet laid it down that the Rosicrucians had as their goal *'The Reformation of the Whole Wide World,'* which we know today (*what the world did not know then*), was the ideal of the boy Francis, conceived by him when at University."

"We see his early dream of reformation of the world slowly crystallizing into a definite pattern. He had a number of disciples. He was going to be the founder of a secret system which both the Church and the State would destroy if it were known. He was to be a teacher of ethics. His system was to be primarily on the lines of Drama, the Mysteries. He would follow the Ancients, but he had something better to produce. He would utilize his secret princely office to further his plans and win adherents. He would Tudorize or Baconize England as Ronsard had Ronsardized France. He would create a flexible English language so that Englishmen could speak in their own tongue their most subtle thoughts without recourse to Latin."

"He would educate the common people by Stage Plays, putting before them parables in dramatic form that had as their goal the triumph of Virtue, the dethronement of Vice. He would create a reading public by the issue of cheap translations in English and staging quarrels between pamphleteers. He would teach his countrymen the history of their own times, and make them into proud patriots with the music of the great deeds done by their forebears. He would act as bell-ringer to the sciences and philosophers, calling them together to labour for man's common good, socially and politically. He would lead two lives - an open one and a secret one. He would spread Light openly where his thoughts and actions would not bring him into conflict with authority. He would lay and plan secretly and write anonymously so that his ideas might be rooted and grounded, and so widespread that they could not be destroyed. He would try to forget his bitter love-trial by hard work. He would save himself by Labour and Hope."

The Earl of Leicester's Bigamous Marriage

Two years later, in 1578, Francis' real father Robert Dudley, Earl of Leicester, 'bigamously' married Lettice, the adoptive mother of Francis' brother, Robert Devereux. Lettice's husband, Walter Devereux, 1ˢᵗ Earl of Essex had been sent to Ireland in 1576, where he died of dysentery. The marriage between Robert Dudley and Lettice took place in secret on the 21st September, at Wanstead House, when Lettice was pregnant with a child to Leicester.

Although they tried to keep the marriage a secret, one of Dudley's enemies, an associate of Robert Cecil, leaked the news to the Queen. This knowledge was to so enrage the jealousy of Elizabeth, that she banished them both from Court. Apart from the fact that Elizabeth still loved Robert, another factor which embittered her was that Lettice, the Countess of Essex, was the daughter of Sir Francis Knollys and Catherine Carey who was a cousin of the Queen.

Francis Bacon - Destitute

Then, in 1579, Francis' adoptive father, Sir Nicholas Bacon, died and Francis had experienced a premonition of the event. The news was naturally another devastating blow to Francis. It would appear that there had been some agreement reached between Elizabeth and Sir Nicholas that in the event of his demise, Francis' expenses would be taken care of by his mother, for in his Will, Sir Nicholas only provided for his own family. Francis was now destitute!

According to Alfred Dodd: "At eighteen years of age this extraordinary genius with whom Fate had so early begun to play such fantastic tricks, girds up his loins and faces the world alone. He has no money, no lands, no income, no one on whom he can legitimately depend for assistance even for ordinary necessities. He never seems to have approached in any way the Earl of Leicester, his real father. Francis regarded him suspiciously as the real cause of his trouble. He disliked his character and held him apparently at arm's length. But he had a staunch friend in Lady Bacon, and no one could have been blessed with a better comrade and foster-brother than Anthony [Bacon]. And their home was still his home."

"Imagine the feelings that swept over him as he crossed the threshold of York House for the first time after his three years' Continental travel; and his thoughts as he waited night after night for some message from the Queen...the message that would announce his recognition...*the message that never came.*"

"Think of the irony of the situation. He had returned from the gaieties of Paris, from the idealism of the Pleiade, from the light love and laughter of Marguerite's presence, from the Court of Navarre where he was treated with deferential honour by all, and regarded as an equal of the noblest lords...to find himself a real stranger to the old home in which he had been bred as a child and an outcast from the kingly inheritance to which he was justly entitled by blood. Sir Nicholas's death and his lack of monetary allowance had created a crisis in his affairs. He could no longer go to the Court, even if he had the 'open door', to feel that all eyes were looking at him, thinking of his birth-secret, whispering and wondering what would ultimately befall him. Later he was to cry out to the Queen in his agony of mind:

'I see you withdraw your favour from me, and now I have lost many friends for your sake: I shall lose you, too. You have put me like one of those that the Frenchman call *Enfans perdu... (lost children)*; so have *you put me into matters of envy without Place or without Strength.*' (*Francis Bacon to Queen Elizabeth, 'Apologia').*"

The Courtship of Elizabeth 1st

In June, 1579, Francis Bacon entered Gray's Inn to study Law, following in the footsteps of his adoptive father, Sir Nicholas Bacon, the Queen's Lord Keeper of the Seal and accordingly, it was upon the Queen's insistence that he pursue a career in Law.

It was in this same year, that another major drama erupted.

According to Peter Dawkins in his book titled *Arcadia*:

"During August 1579 a certain matter exploded like a time-bomb in Leicester's household, which affected many people connected with him. In January Jean de Simier, the close friend of and Master of the Wardrobe to the Duc d'Anjou, had been sent over to England by the Duc in order to 'court' the Queen on his behalf and to prepare his own visit to England. Elizabeth had renewed her pretended courtship of this younger brother of the French king in the summer of 1578, for political advantages, and was still 'playing the game'."

(For clarification purposes, Francois of Valois 1554-1584 whose mother was Catherine de Medici and his father Henry II of France was their youngest son and he received the duchy of Alencon in 1566, hence he was originally known as the Duke of Alencon, and he later became the Duke of Anjou. His older brother Francois II married Mary Queen of Scots in 1558 and ruled as King of France from 1559 to his death in 1560).

"Simier was well liked by the ladies at the English Court, and he began to make such an impression upon the Queen that Leicester became jealous and then extremely anxious that perhaps a royal marriage might become a reality if his own secret and bigamous marriage to Lettice became known. If this happened, Leicester would inevitably lose all his power and status with the Queen that he still enjoyed. He might even be ruined. As a result Leicester became intolerant of and exceedingly rude to Simier, doing his utmost to ruin the courtship; and it was this very reaction which brought about his own undoing."

"In April discussions were begun seriously on arranging for Anjou to visit the Queen in England, plus tentative negotiations for marriage terms. These discussions with the Queen and her councillors took place at Leicester's home at Wanstead. Subsequently Elizabeth signed the necessary passport for Anjou to enter the country later that summer. Leicester's reaction was to retreat to his own house and retire to bed in a sulk, feigning illness."

"Whilst the Earl of Leicester was absent from the Court (which was then at Greenwich) in this great sulk, an assassination attempt was made on Simier. Rightfully or wrongfully, Simier believed that Leicester was behind this attempt on his life, and so he counter-attacked. Early in July he had discovered Leicester's secret."

"So, what Simier did was to go straight to the Queen and tell her about Leicester's marriage to Lettice, giving the Queen sufficient evidence that it had taken place. The eruption was colossal! Elizabeth was deeply hurt, both in her heart and in her pride. In a burst of hysteria and fury, she ordered Leicester to be sent to the Tower. This severe and rather unwise action was somewhat mollified by the counsel of the Queen's friend and Lord Chamberlain, the Earl of Sussex, who pleaded that such a course might do her and the country irreparable damage. Leicester was instead banished from her presence and required to place himself under house-arrest in the Tower Mireflore."

"After a few days Elizabeth relented somewhat, and Leicester, although still banished from the Queen's presence, was allowed to retire to his home at Wanstead. As for Lettice, she was banished from Court for evermore, and the whole of Leicester's household lived for a while under a heavy cloud."

"This action of Leicester, in marrying bigamously and the new marriage becoming publicly known (whilst his prior marriage to the Queen remained a well kept secret), deeply affected the future of Francis and his blood-brother, Robert (Devereux)."

"It effectively placed the Queen in a moral dilemma and political straitjacket, for from that moment on any choice still left to declare her natural-born sons as her rightful heirs, was seemingly removed from her. Although she had seen to it that the law of the land had been adjusted to allow her to declare any natural-born child of hers (whether born in wedlock or not) heir to the throne, yet her inner conditioning coupled with the outer image being built of her as a Virgin Queen probably made this choice a nightmare for her."

"To the end of her life she kept her secret, unable to find the strength to declare the truth openly and so choosing instead to maintain the image of an unmarried, virgin maid. No wonder Francis referred to his mother as 'the alone Queen', and no wonder he and Robert bewailed their fate, never being quite sure of their royal mother's intentions towards them and never being able to build their lives on a firm social and political footing during her reign."

"This is possibly why Francis, as *Immerito*, named Leicester as the causer of his care and pain."

"The Catholic League made their move to attack Robert Dudley, Lord Leicester. This attack was made by use of the pen rather than the sword, playing upon Leicester's notable weaknesses - his arrogance, his infidelity, his obvious love of wealth and power, and his association or even culpability in murder and other crimes, coupled with the fact that Leicester was an exceedingly unpopular man at large and that most people suspected his responsibility for the death of his first wife (Amy), and were quite willing to believe further or even worse things of him. Truths and half-truths, of an intimate nature, were cleverly built up into a concerted and libellous attack on Leicester, in a small book entitled *The Copy of a Letter written by a Master of Arts of Cambridge to his friend in London, concerning some talk passed of late between two worshipful and grave men about the present state, and some proceedings of the Earl of Leicester and his friends in England.*"

"Anjou's (Francois of Valois') visit duly took place from the 17th to 29th August, 1579. The Queen attended him with gaiety and fervour, appearing enchanted with this lively and fascinating French prince; so much so that when Anjou left England a marriage between him and the Queen did indeed seem possible."

"But it was not a popular match with a large section of the English government and people. Leicester, Sir Philip Sidney, Sir Francis Walsingham and their families and friends, and indeed the majority of parliament, the mass of the clergy and the Protestant population of England who had not forgotten St Bartholomew's Eve, [when the persecution of the Huguenots - Protestants had taken place] the loss of Calais and the treachery of the Houses of Guise and Valois, were very much against such a marriage taking place. Many preached openly about the marriage."

"As to the royal marriage, the Queen's Council, although mostly hostile to the proposals, refused to advise the Queen one way or another, wishing to displease neither the Queen nor the country. Elizabeth was not amused by this lack of positive recommendation one way or the other, and for several weeks she stormed at them for not giving her definite support of the marriage - for without such support it would have been far too dangerous for her to proceed further. Eventually, in November of that year, she sent a quorum of her councillors (excluding Leicester) to talk marriage terms with Simier; but she made Simier agree, on Anjou's behalf, to a moratorium of two months in the marriage treaty, so that during that time she could try to win popular support for the match. But by then, in effect, she had already decided to proceed no further, or at least to procrastinate. Not until 1582 did she revive her affair with her 'Frog' (as she called Anjou), and then only because the Catholic powers had again become more menacing."

I have previously mentioned that the poem *Mother Hubbard's Tale*, attributed to Edmund Spenser, would have been written by Francis under Spenser's name. Edmund Spenser attended Cambridge University in 1576, the year after Francis Bacon had left Cambridge, and he obtained a place in Robert Dudley's household. Spenser later went to Ireland in 1580 and lived there until 1598. He died in 1599. In the introduction to the book titled *The Shepherd's Calendar And Other Poems by Edmund Spenser*, the author Ernest Rhys wrote that the 'fox' of the parable is intended for Burghley (Cecil, the enemy of Francis Bacon), while the 'ape' represents the joint persons of **Alencon** and **Simier** when the former was pushing his suit in person for the hand of Queen Elizabeth... "indeed, the satire was dangerously spoken."

Who else, but Francis Bacon, would have had such strong feelings about the whole affair, as to have written *those* feelings into a poem of satire, subtle, but 'visible' to those to whom it was attributed? It is a *very* clever poem, like all of Francis' works. Also remembering, that Francis, in his own writings (without using a pseudonym), had written of Cecil as a 'fox often seen in court...' Remembering also, that back in his days as St Columba, St Germain had purposely written under the pseudonym of *Taliesin* so as not to be caught out by the Church of Rome. The author/poet, Robert Graves stated in his book titled *The White Goddess* as follows:

"The author was a paganistic cleric with Irish connections. All the strange poems in the *Book of Taliesin* read like nonsense, only because the texts have been deliberately confused, doubtless as a precaution against them being denounced as heretical by some church officer."

One of the main reasons that Francis may have resented Alencon is because Francis probably perceived how close his mother, Elizabeth, came to marrying him. Alencon was the brother of Marguerite of Valois, the lady whom Francis had loved so deeply, deeply enough to have written those beautiful sonnets. His mother Elizabeth had prevented him from marrying Marguerite; however, she appeared quite willing to marry into this same family herself.

Continuing on with comments by Peter Dawkins:

"Before she knew of Leicester's secret marriage with Lettice, Elizabeth probably never intended to marry Francois, Duc d'Anjou, but only to play him along for the sake of politics; and she was probably advised in this way. But it would seem that the discovery of her husband's bigamous marriage very nearly threw her into the arms of Anjou out of spite, or despair, or both. The situation was clearly dangerous, and could have led to a bloody and horrendous civil war if the marriage with Anjou had taken place. If that had occurred, the English Renaissance would never have happened, for, as Francis so rightly said: 'the arts flourish only in times of peace'."

In 1581-2, Francis travelled again, to France, Spain, Italy, Germany and the Netherlands, to gather information for the Queen on the politics, religion, culture, and law of those countries.

Francis Bacon - Lawyer 'Interpreter of the Law'

Francis became a barrister in June 1583, a Bencher of Gray's Inn in 1586 and a Reader in 1587, but never built up his own legal practice, being engrossed instead with his literary output and philosophical projects, as well as being employed upon giving special services to the Queen and her Ministers of State.

It was in 1588, that the Queen made Francis her Counsel Extraordinary, the first such appointment ever made. This gave Francis a unique position with personal access to the Queen at all times, and brought him 'within the bar' with the sergeants and judges at law - rather like a modern day version of the Sanhedrin where he had once been Annas the Elder High Priest, the 'judge', the Essenes' *Teacher of Righteousness*, their *Interpreter of the Law*.

In this capacity, Francis acted as a special adviser to the Queen and her Privy Councillors on religious, political and legal matters, and as an examiner in court of prisoners and their testimonies, on the Councillors' behalf. He also acted for them as a government propagandist and, in 1589 he wrote the *Advertisement* about the Church of England, being a statement of English religious and foreign policy. His work was to protect the Queen and her realm.

However, since it was a personal service to the Queen and her realm, Francis had no means of accumulating fees in payment of his services, which meant that, since the Queen was notorious for not paying her servants, and he had scant means of his own, Francis was often in a difficult pecuniary position.

At the same time, Francis began to gather scholars, writers and poets to him, to assist him in his literary projects. His main base was at Gray's Inn where, from 1587, he had the use of the whole building with chambers next to the library. He also had the use of Twickenham Lodge as a country retreat, with gardens reaching down to the River Thames, opposite Richmond Palace, where he often went to write in peace.

From 1587, he appears to have begun to write the early Shakespeare plays, drama being recognised by him, as of major importance in his grand cultural and philosophical scheme.

Francis angers the Queen again

In 1593, Francis, who had been a Member of Parliament since 1581, stood up in Parliament against the Queen and Lord Burghley (William Cecil), in order to protect the constitutional right of the House of Commons to set the level of taxes and subsidies to be granted to the Queen and her government. According to Peter Dawkins, "In this, the Crown was in effect trying to destroy the foundation of the English democracy, and was prevented from doing so only by the perspicacity, courage and eloquence of Francis Bacon." (In a previous life, as Apollonius of Tyana, when St Germain was brought before Nero in court, he also gave an eloquent speech).

Obviously, the relationship between Elizabeth and Francis had mellowed a little over the years, but this episode brought another rift between them.

According to Peter Dawkins:

"The Queen was so angry with Francis that he was in royal disgrace for the next three years, which affected his credit with money-lenders considerably. He was forced into taking up law as a barrister in the more normal sense in order to earn a living, and pleaded four cases at the King's Bench and the Exchequer Chamber during 1594. These cases concerned fundamental issues in respect of inheritance and conveyance of land. Despite his 'disgrace', however, he was commissioned by the Queen to write the official report on the Lopez conspiracy to poison the Queen, a plot that had been uncovered by the intelligence network run by Anthony Bacon. Roderigo Lopez was a Portuguese and the Queen's physician, who was tried and convicted of being in the pay of Spain to murder the Queen."

"In 1595, the Queen made Francis Bacon her Queen's Counsel Learned in the Law, with a special commission to examine, with other law officers, prisoners involved in cases affecting the safety of the Queen and her realm. In 1596 and 1597, he appeared before the Privy Councillors in the Star Chamber both as Crown Counsel and as an examiner of the prisoners, in precisely the same role as played by Portia in *The Merchant of Venice*. (St Germain obviously utilized the name of Portia, because the Lady Portia is his twin soul). At one stage Francis was arrested for debt a fortnight before his bond was due by a spiteful usurer, the goldsmith Mr Simpson of Lombard Street. These experiences Francis built into his new play, *The Merchant of Venice* which he wrote at that time (1596-8)." (Those readers familiar with *The Merchant of Venice* will recall the money-lender known as 'Shylock').

As the Queen's son, Francis totally relied upon her for financial assistance and according to Peter Dawkins, "it was not until 1595 that the Queen provided Francis with anything substantial for his living, and she and Lord Burghley (Cecil) constantly refused to give Francis a paid position in the State, despite his immense genius and talent. But in 1595, she indirectly allowed Francis the lease of Twickenham Park, and made him one of her counsel learned in the law. Francis' main financial support during the next sixteen years seems to have come from his foster-brother, Anthony, and from his foster-mother, Lady Anne, and from various friends who supported his work in one way or another."

It was in 1597 that Francis published the first edition of his *Essays*, treatises outlining various matters, in particular a study of emotions (of which he had certainly had a great deal of experience), which he incorporated into the Shakespearian plays. Their final printed form, enlarged in number to fifty-eight, was published in 1625. The Shakespeare Folio was published in 1623, together with Bacon's great philosophical tome, *De Augmentis Scientiarum*; the Folio contained eighteen new plays, four of which had been registered before, but the other fourteen being previously unheard of.

Peter Dawkins so aptly wrote: "His (Francis Bacon's) life was an extraordinary one, not just in the great works that he accomplished but also in the smaller details. The difficulties and tragedies that he encountered and had to surmount would make anyone weep - and yet clearly there was a lot of joy and laughter."

"It is said that compassion is developed from a knowledge of suffering, and joy is experienced as a result of sorrow. Nothing could be truer in Bacon's case. He was someone who was very human - tragically so - yet also a great artist, who walked the valley of death and gave as a result wonderful gifts to humanity."

"His life and genius fit the quality, depth and details of the Shakespearian plays; Will Shakespere's [Shakespere is the way the actor spelt his name], do not."

It has been elsewhere mentioned that in January, 1999, it was announced that BBC listeners chose William Shakespeare as Britain's greatest personality of the past one thousand years. At last St Germain (Francis Bacon) is achieving the recognition he so richly deserves and hopefully, it will not be too much longer before St Germain will be truly recognised world-wide as THE WRITER OF THE SHAKESPEARIAN PLAYS! For the time is nigh.

MASTERS DISCUSSED IN THIS CHAPTER

Annas the Elder High Priest, (the Essenes' Teacher of Righteousness & Interpreter of the Law) - St Germain

Merlin (Taliesin) - St Germain

Francis Bacon (Shakespeare) - St Germain

NOTES AND RECOMMENDED READING

Elizabeth Jenkins, *Elizabeth And Leicester*, (Victor Gollanz Ltd, U.K. 1961)

Christopher Haig, *Elizabeth I*, (Longman, U.K.)

Alfred Dodd, *Francis Bacon's Personal Life-Story*, (Rider & Co., U.K., 1986)

Peter Dawkins, *Arcadia*, (Francis Bacon Research Trust, U.K., 1988)

Peter Dawkins, *The Virgin Ideal*, (Francis Bacon Research Trust, U.K.)

Peter Dawkins, *Dedication To The Light*, (Francis Bacon Research Trust, U.K., 1984)

Peter Dawkins, *The Great Vision*, (Francis Bacon Research Trust, U.K., 1985)

Francis Bacon (compiled by Peter Dawkins), *Faithful Sayings and Ancient Wisdom*, (Francis Bacon Research Trust).

Peter Dawkins, *Francis Bacon Herald of the New Age*, (Francis Bacon Research Trust, U.K., 1997)

Dr Raymond Bernard, *The Great Secret, Count Saint Germain*, (U.S.A.)

Azena Ramanda and Claire Heartsong, *St Germain Twin Souls & Soulmates*, (Triad Publishers, Queensland, Australia, 1994)

Isabel Oakley-Cooper, *The Comte De St Germain*, (Theosophical Publishing House, U.S.A., 1985)

Boris Ford, *The Age Of Shakespeare*, (Penguin Books, U.K., 1955).

Peter Alexander, *Shakespeare, Tragedies And Poems*, (Collins, London, U.K., 1958).

The Sonnets, William Shakespeare, (Leopard, U.K., 1988).

Frank Kermode, John Hollander, *The Oxford Anthology of English Literature*, (Oxford University, U.K., 1973).

Ernest Rhys, *The Shepherd's Calendar And Other Poems by Edmund Spenser*, (J.M. Dent & Sons Ltd., U.K. 1932)

CHAPTER 42

𝕿𝖍𝖊 𝕯𝖔𝖜𝖓𝖋𝖆𝖑𝖑 𝖔𝖋 𝕽𝖔𝖇𝖊𝖗𝖙, 𝕷𝖔𝖗𝖉 𝕰𝖘𝖘𝖊𝖝

"The Three Conns, the descendants of Ruadh
Of the race of Conall of great power,
It is from the paternal stock of that man,
The magnates of that stock shall derive their worth,
"The Defender who will break down his enemy,
The expert man of the race of Conn;
The successful hero, the subduer of the Galls,
This will be Hugh (Aed) the undaunted,
He shall be remarkable for his energy and wisdom,
Hugh will lead a body of troops from the north,
He, the King of Clan of Conaill of the well-tempered swords;
They will march to Dublin to force tribute,
From a young lady of the Galls of bright shields"
(St Columba/St Germain 521 -597 AD)

"I am sure, I never in anything in my life dealt with him [Lord Essex] in like
earnestness by speech, by writing, and by all the means I could devise....I did as plainly
see his overthrow, chained as it were by Destiny to that Journey, as it is possible for any
man to ground a judgement on future contingents". (*Apologia*).
(Francis Bacon - St Germain)

In this chapter, we learn of how Robert Cecil, the enemy of both Francis and
his brother, Robert, Earl of Essex, in cohorts with certain others of the 'Cecil' camp,
laid a trap for Robert. Firstly however, it is of interest to know something of the
difference in character of the Queen's young princes for the differences between
them help to explain Robert's willfulness and why he failed to listen to his brother,
Francis' warnings about journeying to Ireland.

Describing the two Tudor sons of Elizabeth, the late Alfred Dodd wrote in
his book titled *Francis Bacon's Personal Life-Story* that the two brothers, Francis

and Robert, were very different.

"Robert was a true Tudor, hot, impulsive, headstrong, full of the thought that he had a better right to the Throne as a true-born child of a morganatic marriage than anyone else. He was resentful lest anyone else should usurp his place in the Queen's affections and so jeopardize his secret birthright. This is the secret tangle behind the open life of Elizabeth's Court."

"All the evidence shows that the two men were bound to each other by no ordinary ties of friendship and that their joint fortunes were one, Francis hoping that Robert would be named to the Succession so that he, Francis, could carry out boldly - without interference - wide-sweeping schemes of reform, social, scientific etc., Robert hoping that with the advice of his elder brother, England would forge ahead in the comity of nations. They were both idealists in their own particular way, Essex being of a narrower type than Francis Bacon. One was insular and national; the other broad-based and universal. The Earl sought to rule over the fair province of England. His brother had already taken 'All Knowledge to be his Province' over which to reign."

"Francis was a dreamer of dreams and such men were dangerous in the eyes of the Cecils...Cecil knew that if once these two men held the reigns of power, he and his friends would be lost, probably their privileges of case as bureaucrats destroyed and all they stood for as 'Gentlemen by birth, education and property' swept away."

"The Cecils (Lord Burleigh and his son Robert Cecil) knew, moreover, the Queen's secret, and there is no doubt that Robert communicated the fact...to his followers, for, later this was blurted out in open Court by Coke - then related to the Cecils by his second marriage - when he spoke to Francis Bacon. The immediate object of the Cecil clan was to sow dissension between the Queen and her two sons....to drive a wedge between them...there is indeed, strong reason to believe that at a comparatively early date, Sir Robert Cecil had made up his mind that James of Scotland was to succeed Elizabeth and was pledged to further his interests."

It was unfortunate that Elizabeth totally trusted Lord Burghley, Robert Cecil's father, who was also the legal guardian of Francis. Robert Cecil's time was devoted to feeding the Queen's mind with vicious and malicious lies about her own two children, Francis and Robert, and Cecil often had his own spies watching Francis and trying to keep track of his activities. Cecil certainly did his best to prove that Francis was the writer of the Shakespearian plays and he certainly sowed the seeds of suspicion in the mind of Elizabeth.

As her secretary, Cecil was very well placed to be able to manipulate Elizabeth and the contents of the flow of information that reached her. The late Alfred Dodd summed up the character of Robert Cecil as follows:

"He was a small, shrewd man of the world...without a dash of generosity in his nature. So long as he lived there was no hope of Francis Bacon rising in the world. Cecil and his father kept him down, for they were jealous of his idealism in social and political affairs of State."

Troubled Times in Ireland

By an act Parliament in 1541, King Henry VIII, Elizabeth's father, was made sovereign of all the inhabitants of Ireland. There were repeated campaigns made by the Earl of Sussex against the Irish chieftain Shane O'Neill which were firmly rejected and so by the 1550's and the 1560's the Earl of Sussex's efforts ended in failure.

Others were sent to Ireland and the targeted family seemed to be the O'Neills (who were the original Ui Neill's, once High Celtic Kings of Tara who were known as the people of Dalriata).

Every English viceroy who was sent to Ulster had presumed that despite the political and social problems, a solution could be reached that would be satisfactory to both the native lords and the Crown of England.

In the 1560's Shane O'Neill had brought over a number of mercenaries from the Scottish Dalriada with whom he had consolidated links with by negotiating a permanent alliance with the Earl of Argyll. It was these Scots who altered the character of Ulster's politics, many of whom had settled in the Glens of Antrim. They were the descendants of the original Irish Dalriata who had preceded St Columba, Prince of the U'Neill (O'Neill) family, to Scotland in the 500's AD when Columba's ancestor, Fergus Mor mac Erc (who may have been Sir Galahad) settled in Argyll.

In 1585, Hugh O'Neill who was considered to be the Queen's protégé was affirmed as the Earl of Tyrone. He had campaigned with Essex (Lord Devereux) and often lent military aid to the Lord Deputy of the day. However, O'Neill was to become a threat because it is generally considered that he wanted power in Ulster and the whole of Ireland and thus he regarded as vital, the English support that he was being given at that particular time.

The reason for him wishing to establish himself as a 'king of Ireland' seems quite obvious. Undoubtedly, he wished Ireland to once again come under the rule of the original Ui Neill (O'Neill) family and for Ireland to be free and no longer subordinate to England. No doubt Elizabeth had taken Hugh O'Neill under her wing hoping this subterfuge would succeed and he would no longer become a threat by attempting to claim Ireland a free country, no longer ruled by Queen Elizabeth. According to the *Prophecies of Saint Columba* (St Germain) mentioned at the beginning of this chapter, 'the young lady of the Galls of bright shields' was Queen Elizabeth and Hugh was the one who was to lead his troops from the north, against hers.

Historically, the reasons why Hugh O'Neill of Tyrone turned against the queen are said to be 'veiled in mystery' and there are very few Irish documents that shed light on the struggle from the Irish point of view. Skirmishes ensued between rival factions and in 1592, Hugh the Earl of Tyrone was without rival in mid-Ulster and was inaugurated as 'The O'Neill', later to become known as the 'Great O'Neill'. It is considered that if Hugh O'Neill had remained a servant of the Queen, Tyrone could have wielded great authority in Ulster; however, for reasons of his own, he felt he could exercise greater power if he became Gaelic king of the province.

According to information contained in Peter Dawkins' work *Arcadia*, Walter Devereux, 1st Earl of Essex (foster father of Francis's blood brother, Robert, Lord Essex) was sent to Ireland in August, 1576 but unfortunately, soon after his arrival there, he became ill with dysentery and died in September, 1576. (It was not long after this that Robert Dudley, Earl of Leicester, the real father of Francis and his brother Robert, Lord Essex, 'bigamously' married Devereux's widow, Lettice).

The following year, in July and September, 1577, Francis Bacon was given orders by his adoptive father, Nicholas Bacon to go to France on a dangerous mission, in the capacity as a 'secret agent'. From letters and documents that are preserved today, it seems evident that Francis also ventured into Spain where he discovered that Philip II was making preparations to invade England and from there Francis made his way to Portugal, returning to England whilst his safety could still be guaranteed.

After Francis's visit to Spain in the capacity of a 'spy' on behalf of his country, he was then sent to Ireland on a similar mission on behalf of Lord Walsingham and the Queen. Francis and his brother Robert, 1st Earl of Essex, worked closely with Anthony Bacon and Sir Nicholas Bacon who was a prominent member of the Freemasonic Society and also in the 'Intelligence' service, as was Sir John Dee. Sir John Dee, (Kuthumi) considered that it was imperative for England to have its network of Intelligence' agents scattered across Europe and Ireland in order to protect the throne of England, lest it be taken over by some other country, i.e. the French or the Spanish.

Under the guidance of Sir John Dee, Sir Francis Drake successfully defeated the Spanish Armada and saved Britain from becoming a part of Spain and the Roman Catholic religion.

Robert, Lord Essex, Sent to Ireland

The English had tried many times to invade Ireland. When Francis's brother, Robert, Lord Essex, was sent there in 1599 to revive English rule, he seems to have done everything except that which had been requested of him.

The 'Cecil' camp had waited a long time to shame Robert in the eyes of his mother, and his sojourn in Ireland brought them the perfect opportunity.

According to information contained in Alfred Dodd's book *Francis Bacon's Personal Life Story*, "When Essex was persuaded to take the Irish command he was already in the toils of his enemies, who cared little about the reduction of Ireland and the waste of English lives in comparison with the object of ruining the Earl and securing power for themselves. Essex's genuine unwillingness to accept the command is proved by a published letter (lst Jan, 1599) from the Earl to his intimate friend, Southampton, who vehemently dissuades him from going. He is aware of all the dangers of absence from Court and the designs of his enemies, but there is no help for it; *'into Ireland I go'.*"

"Yet on the eve of his fatal voyage to Ireland, Essex rode to Gray's Inn Square for the last time to see his brother Francis, to ask his opinion, and, perhaps to crave his blessing on the venture."

"Francis Bacon told him that Ireland had been the grave of many good Englishmen and that she would never be conquered by the sword; she would only be won by the plough, drainage of bogs, new roads, new towns."

"He told Robert that his enterprise would fail if he relied on purely war-like measures and that his chief object should be to inaugurate peaceful and active co-operation between the Protestant settler and the native population with the help of Parliamentary subsidies. He warned him of the difficulty of the work that would confront him in many ways and that he was leaving the Queen in the hands of his enemies. Writing years afterwards, a report of the conversation, Francis said to him:

'It would be ill for her, ill for him, ill for the State. I am sure, I never in anything in my life dealt with him in like earnestness by speech, by writing, and by all the means I could devise....I did as plainly see his overthrow, chained as it were by Destiny to that Journey, as it is possible for any man to ground a judgement on future contingents'. (*Apologia*)."

"Once more Francis Bacon had the mortification of seeing Robert (his brother) standing on the brink of a military precipice into which (as it subsequently transpired) all his hopes and Essex's ambitions were destined to crash into nothingness."

"His conversations and warning letter fell on deaf ears; Essex had gradually fallen under the evil influence of Sir Christopher Blount, who had married his foster-mother, the Countess of Essex. He was a worthless man and made the Countess as vile as himself. But the bold, coarse, dashing ways of this bravo appealed to the martial ardour of this giddy 'step-son' of thirty. The Earl got Blount a command in the army, a seat in the House of Commons, and put him in offices of trust near his own person. He drew nearer to Blount in mind and with his (Blount's) worthless fire-eating associates. Worse than all he listened to Blount's evil counsel."

Robert considered himself to be a great military leader, having been in command when the British fleet attacked and captured Cadiz in June 1596 for which Robert felt he never received due recognition or the spoils thereof.

"Hugh will lead a body of troops from the north,
He, the King of Clan of Conaill [O'Neill] of the well-tempered swords;
They will march to Dublin to force tribute
From a young lady [Elizabeth 1st] of the Galls of bright shields"
(St Columba/ St Germain - 6th century AD)

Thus, caught up in a situation that he was damned if he did and damned if he did not, Robert, Earl of Essex who was also Lord Deputy of Ireland, went to Ireland in April, 1599 (three years after the capture of Cadiz). Storms had delayed Essex and he had to face 20,000 Irish who were armed, plus the further prospect of the Irish being given Spanish aid.

Upon his arrival, Essex was met by Hugh O'Neill, the Earl of Tyrone who had marched down from the North with his 20,000 soldiers.

Even though Essex had with him the greatest English army yet seen in Ireland, he did not keep his pledge to meet Tyrone on the battlefield. When Essex and Hugh O'Neill of Tyrone, confronted each other at Ardee, instead of fighting, a curious conversation was held between them, whereby, both Essex and Tyrone, rode their horses into the middle of a beautiful crystal clear stream where salmon were jumping over the small rapids. As the sun-light beamed down through the trees lighting both men in a golden aura, they talked in great seriousness for over an hour. No-one was able to hear their conversation in order to report what was actually discussed.

The result of the meeting was that Robert, Earl of Essex, and Hugh O'Neill entered upon a six week truce and the Ulster Irish retired having made no concessions whatsoever. This unusually peaceful meeting baffled and mystified Elizabeth and her courtiers.

Perhaps at the last meeting that Robert had with his brother, Francis, at Grey's Inn before his journey to Ireland, Francis suggested to Robert to make peace as best he could. We need to take into consideration that in his earlier life as St Columba (St Germain), he had predicted the outcome of the meeting with Hugh O'Neill, and above all, St Germain would have wanted peace for his beloved Ireland.

After the meeting with Hugh O'Neill, Robert, Lord Essex had not made war as the Queen had directed him to. It would seem that Robert and O'Neill made some sort of pact and Robert marched his tired and hungry army back to Dublin where he made plans to return to England and his mother, the Queen. (The prophecy of St Columba - St Germain referred to this invasion of Elizabeth Tudor against Hugh of the race of Conall who were the O'Neills and the warning that Francis Bacon had given Robert before he left for Ireland, would have been a similar one for St Germain would have known the outcome).

Robert, Lord Essex was replaced as Lord Deputy of Ireland by Lord Mountjoy.

The truce between England and Ireland was extended and although O'Neill wanted to maintain it, the English were preparing to renew the fight led by Mountjoy in January, 1600. O'Neill was forced into battle against Mountjoy, even though he would have preferred to keep the peace of the truce and O'Neill told his people that unless they were successful it would be 'farewell Ulster and all the north'.

For some unaccountable reason, O'Neill withdrew his troops on the 13th October from the area where Mountjoy was invading. It is not clear why O'Neill made this decision, although it is thought that he never ceased to hope that the English would make peaceful terms. For whatever reasons O'Neill had in abandoning the strong defensive position that he held, his retreat was considered to be the gravest strategic error made by the Ulster Irish since the commencement of the war which was over a period of nine years and became known historically as the 'Nine Years War'.

Lord Mountjoy had his troops destroy the ancient coronation site, especially the Stone Chair (not the original 'Stone of Destiny'), on which the O'Neills had stood when they were crowned at Tullahogue. Elizabeth regretted this abomination that had been carried out, for just as Mountjoy was preparing to finally capture O'Neill, the Queen cancelled her previous instructions and instructed him to offer O'Neill a pardon.

Lord Mountjoy was just as eager for this agreement for he knew, although O'Neill did not, that Queen Elizabeth I, had died just six days earlier and Mountjoy, the Lord Deputy, was uncertain as to whether the new heir to the throne, James I (James 6th of Scot, House of Stuart) would support him in the same way that the Queen had done. The nine years of war had been a very expensive venture for the Crown and the conquest of Ireland had risen to costs of over two million pounds. The events leading up to the Queen's demise are explained in the following chapter.

Unfortunately for Ireland, the Tudor conquest of Ireland was brought to a successful conclusion on the 30th March, 1603 at which time the most powerful magnate in Ireland, Hugh O'Neill, the Earl of Tyrone, submitted to Lord Mountjoy (Charles Blount) who had defeated Tyrone's main army. Sir Garret Moore offered the pardon to Hugh O'Neill, the Earl of Tyrone and it was eagerly accepted. The terms were exceptionally lenient, better than Tyrone had dared to hope for but the condition was that he renounce the title of being 'The O'Neill' whereby he could still retain most of his lordship of his traditional territory.

The Treaty collapsed and Ulster came under the reign of the King James Ist, Stuart King of England. Generous royal pardons were given to some of the Gaelic lords by King James. O'Neill, the Earl of Tyrone went into exile and died in Rome in July 1616 thus ending a thousand years of Gaelic order in Ulster, mainly by the family of the Ui Neill - O'Neills.

In achieving what no-one else had succeeded in doing, Lord Mountjoy was congratulated in a letter sent to him from Robert Cecil in 1603. Robert Cecil, whose father was Lord Burghley, had been determined to establish the Stuart dynasty upon the throne of England, which rather serves to prove that Lord Mountjoy was in league with the 'Cecil's.

In 'Retrospect'...

Alfred Dodd in his book titled *Francis Bacon's Person Life-Story*, quotes Strickland as saying: "The policy pursued by Essex was of a pacific character. He loved the excitement of battle when in the cause of Freedom, or when the proud Spaniard threatened England with invasion; but, as the Governor of Ireland, his noble nature inclined him to the blessed work of mercy and conciliation. He ventured to disobey the bloody orders he had received from the short-sighted politicians...."

"If the generous and chivalrous Essex had been allowed to work out his own plans he would probably have healed all wounds, and proved the regenerator of Ireland; but, surrounded as he was by spies, thwarted by his deadly foes in Cabinet, and, finally rendered an object of suspicion to the most jealous of Sovereigns, he only accelerated his own doom...

"The Queen wrote stern and reproachful letters to him. He presumed to justify himself for all he had done and all he had left undone...The Queen was infuriated, and was of course, encouraged by her Ministers to refuse everything..."

"Tyrone's conditions were no more than justice and sound policy ought to have induced the Sovereign to grant. Elizabeth regarded it as treason, on the part of Essex, even to listen to them....The fiery and impetuous Earl was infuriated, in his turn, at the reports that were conveyed to him, of the practices against him in the English Cabinet."

"He was accused of aiming at making himself King of Ireland, with the assistance of Tyrone; nay, even of aspiring to the Crown of England, and that he was plotting to bring over a wild Irish army to dethrone the Queen. Elizabeth's health suffered in consequence of the ferment in which her spirits were kept, and the agonizing conflict between love and hatred....but the treasons of Essex existed only in the malignant representations of Sir Robert Cecil, and Cobham."

According to Sean O Faolain in his book titled *The Great O'Neill*, the process of bringing the Gaelic kingdom to the rank of a feudal state, the entry of yet another of the last remaining pieces of a world older than Christianity into the modern system was not a simple process.

"If it were so then Ireland would almost be one of those happy lands without a history...the process was a labyrinthine perplexity. That perplexity arose chiefly from the fact that in England's decision to make Ireland her first real colony, two civilizations became interlocked that were in spirit utterly divergent."

The invasion of the Ireland by the Tudors became known as the 'Plantation of Ulster' and such an occurrence was contained within the Biblical prophecies.

MASTERS DISCUSSED IN THIS CHAPTER
St Columba/Merlin - St Germain
Francis Bacon - St Germain
Sir John Dee - Kuthumi

NOTES AND RECOMMENDED READING

Sean O Faolain, *The Great O'Neill*, (Mercier Press Ltd., Cork, Ireland, 1997)
Arnold J. Toynbee, *A Study of History*, (Oxford University Press, U.K., 1934)
Alfred Dodd, *Francis Bacon's Personal Life-Story*, (Rider & Co., U.K., 1986)
Barry Cunliffe, *The Celtic World*, (Bodley Head, U.K., 1979)
Jonathan Bardon, *A History of Ulster*, (Blackstaff Press, U.K., 1992)
Peter Dawkins, *The Virgin Ideal*, (Francis Bacon Research Trust, U.K.)
Peter Dawkins, *Dedication To The Light*, (Francis Bacon Research Trust, U.K., 1984)
Peter Dawkins, *The Great Vision*, (Francis Bacon Research Trust, U.K., 1985)
Peter Bander, *The Prophecies of St Malachy and St Columbkille*, (Colin Smythe Ltd., U.K. 1969)

CHAPTER 43

The Fate of Robert, Lord Essex & Elizabeth's Tragic Loss

"The Moving Finger writes; and having writ
Moves on: nor all thy Piety or Wit
Shall lure it back to cancel half a Line,
Nor all thy Tears wash out a Word of it."
(Rubaiyat of Omar Khayyam - Kuthumi)

Upon reaching England from Ireland, Robert, Earl of Essex, went straightaway to Elizabeth's Court and there he was taken into custody by the Lord Keeper at York House. At first, permission was refused for him to even see his wife who had just given birth to a child.

Whilst being kept as a prisoner of the Lord Keeper, Robert's health began to fade quickly. The Queen went to visit him but she was told by his enemies that he was shamming the illness. However, the Queen was soon able to observe that he was seriously ill and she sent her own physicians to attend to him.

According to Alfred Dodd:

"Essex was at death's door. Little hope was entertained of his recovery. He received the sacrament. Too weak to move, he could only be lifted by the sheets. He was in this condition when Lady Essex was allowed to see her husband for the first time. (Robert, the brother of Francis Bacon, had married Frances Walsingham who was the widow of Sir Philip Sidney. Robert and Frances had one son and two daughters who would have been the grandchildren of Queen Elizabeth). The following day the Queen was alarmed at Essex's condition and said she *'had only intended to humble him'*. According to Strickland, "It was noted that *her eyes were full of tears...and the Queen commanded that Essex be removed to the Lord Keeper's own chamber. But Essex did not die. He gradually recovered. And the Queen was once more persuaded that Essex had been feigning illness to enlist her sympathy."

It could be said that Essex rallied because at last his mother had shown him some love and caring, but alas, this was not to last because upon his recovery, Essex was sent before the council of Judges. According to Alfred Dodd, "at times, many wept to see him in such misery. It is said that he defended himself very mildly and discreetly, admitting errors of judgement. He implored the Lords to intercede for him with the Queen. His request was rejected."

Someone who further fanned the flames was Edward Coke, who was related to Robert Cecil through marriage and like Cecil, he was a sworn enemy of both Francis and Robert. This may have been the same Mr Coke who informed Mother Dowe about the Queen's requirement of a petticoat to hide her delicate 'condition'.

Francis Bacon forced to Prosecute his Brother

From the book titled *Francis Bacon Versus Lord Macaulay* by E.D. Johnson, we learn of the fact that Francis had no choice but to take his part as one of the lawyers for the prosecution against his own brother, Essex, based on treason to the Queen.

"When Bacon was told that like Yelverton, Coke and Fleming, he **must** bear his part in those proceedings, he wrote to the Queen, 'That if she would be pleased to spare him from that service, he would esteem it one of her greatest favours, adding that *he knew his duty*, and if she imposed the task upon him, *no obligation to particular persons should supplant or weaken his devotion to her and to her service.*'

"The moment the Queen refused it, Bacon's oath to the crown forced him to carry out his duties as an officer of the crown. Yelverton opened the charge, and he was followed by Coke, and then Bacon closed the case in an eloquent and memorable speech."

Dr Raymond Bernard wrote in his work titled *The Great Secret - Count Saint Germain* that "the tragic significance of the celebrated case of treason brought by the crown against the Earl of Essex becomes more understandable when we realise Elizabeth forced Francis Bacon to prosecute his own brother, her son. Bacon never would have consented to do this had he not been given the most solemn assurance that Essex would be pardoned in the end."

"He did not like the job of having to prosecute Essex, but he did so because he believed his mother, the Queen, would refuse to sign the death warrant, for his brother. But he misjudged. She did. His brother was executed by the order of his mother! This perfidy Bacon added to his list of injuries, the record of which he incorporated in his secret cipher story, hidden in his Shakespearian writings."

It is important to remember, however, that Francis at all times, upheld the honour of the Queen, although there were many times he felt unloved by his own mother, and at the age of fifteen years when he first discovered that he was her son, he surely would have looked for some sign of her maternal feelings towards him, just like any normal child would do when they finally discover who their real parents are. His own father, Robert, Lord Leicester, was later reputedly poisoned and suspicion fell upon the Queen at which time, although once again deeply hurt, Francis sprang to her defence.

The moment the Queen refused the request of Francis not to partake in the prosecution of his brother, Francis' oath to the crown forced him to carry out his duties as an Officer of the Crown. According to E.D. Johnson, "failure to do so would have meant that he would have been taken to prison and eventually the chopping block. Francis as one of the Queen's Counsel was called to his duty by the Crown. He owed allegiance to his country and to the Queen. He was as much the Queen's officer, armed with her commission, bound to obey her commands, as her Captain of the Guard."

Francis Bacon clearly spoke as the advocate of Essex, rather than that of the Queen's and although he was forced into a position where he had to charge Essex, he was careful to free him from the charges of disloyalty to the Queen and thus to the Crown. E.D. Johnson wrote:

"There is no doubt whatever that Bacon's speech at that time was instrumental in saving Essex from the block. Essex was released, but had not learned his lesson, and very shortly afterwards ventured on a criminal enterprise which rendered him liable to the highest penalties of the Law."

Francis in his speech appealed to Essex saying, "Oh my Lord, strive with yourself and strip off all excuses, the persons whom you aimed at, if you rightly understand, are your best friends. All that you have said or can say, in answer to these matters, are but shadows. It would be your best course to confess and not to justify." In a further speech Francis states, "My Lord, I spent more hours to make you a good subject than upon any man in the world besides."

"Essex had been deserted by all his former friends with one exception only and that was Francis Bacon who went out of his way to try and persuade the Queen to show mercy. He pestered her continually on the subject; he lavished all his wit and eloquence on this ungrateful course. In a note to Essex's former friend, Lord Henry Howard, Francis wrote, 'I have been much bound to him, (for after all, they were brothers). I have spent more time and thought about his well-being than I ever did about mine own.'"

"On one occasion, Bacon said to the Queen, "In the case of my Lord Essex, your princely word is, that you mean to reform his mind, not to ruin his fortune. Have you not drawn the tumour? Is it not time for the cure? 'The Queen replied: 'Speak to your business, speak for yourself, for the Earl, not a word'."

Francis Bacon incurs his Mother's wrath yet again!

In another letter addressed to Robert, Lord Essex, from Francis, Francis explains to him the necessity of him having to carry out his duty upon the expressed wishes of the Queen.

According to Alfred Dodd, the Queen wrote: 'An unruly Horse must be abated of its provender, that he may be the more easily and better managed.' "In short, she was going to show the world that Elizabeth and not Essex was the Ruler of England. Francis Bacon's explanation to the Queen was ingenious:

'How your Majesty construes,' he said, 'as if Duty and Desire could stand together! Iron clings to the loadstone from its nature. A vine creeps to the pole that it may twine. You must distinguish my Lord's desire to do your Service, is as to his perfection that which *he thinks himself to be born for*, whereas his desire to obtain this thing from you is but for a sustentation.'"

"The Queen was so annoyed at Francis Bacon's persistence in championing the Earl's cause that she began to look coldly upon him when he came into her presence, until at last, he said to her he could see that: 'In the integrity of his heart, he had incurred great peril for pleading the cause of the Earl to her and that his own Fall was decreed. She answered: **'My Grace is Sufficient to you'.**"

According to E.D. Johnson, "Francis Bacon saw that if he did not plead against Essex, all his hopes of advancement might, without any benefit to Essex, be destroyed and if he did plead against him, he should be exposed to oblique and misrepresentation. Essex was clearly guilty of treason and was bound to be convicted, it did not matter if Bacon took any part in his trial or not, but if he had refused to do so, the consequences would have been disastrous to Bacon's future."

And, Bacon was not the only lawyer. There was Edward Coke and Yelverton, the Attorney-General, who were enemies of both Francis and Robert. Francis did his utmost to save Robert, and all the while, behind the conspiracy were other members of the 'Cecil' camp, waiting to place a Stuart upon the throne of England. Robert Cecil could be compared to 'Judas' - what a strange quirk of fate if Cecil was a reincarnation of Judas!

E. D. Johnson further comments: "The reader must remember that Francis Bacon when a youth of fifteen conceived his magnificent idea of educating the world by the publication of books on every conceivable subject. The reason for all Bacon's actions lay in his deep laid plan for the universal reformation of the whole world through science and religion. The chief objects of his life were - the cause of reformed religion, the cause of his Queen and country, and of the human race through all its generations - and he was determined that nothing should prevent him from carrying out those aims. If his life were to be cut short before he could carry out his schemes, then all the work which he had done and which he intended to do for the Advancement of Learning and the benefit of the human race, would be lost forever."

Robert, Lord Essex's Fate is Sealed

"The Moving Finger writes; and having writ
Moves on: nor all thy Piety or Wit
Shall lure it back to cancel half a Line,
Nor all thy Tears wash out a Word of it."
(Rubaiyat of Omar Khayyam - Kuthumi)

Sadly, all attempts to save Lord Essex, the younger brother of Francis, failed and he was executed on the 23rd February, 1601, for treason. Alfred Dodd wrote that Lord Essex was beheaded on Tower Green, and that persons not of Royal Blood were executed on Tower Hill which is further proof that the Queen recognised Robert as her Royal son.

According to Alfred, "She (the Queen) had given Robert a ring with the intimation 'that if ever he forfeited her favour, if he sent it back to her, the sight of it would ensure her forgiveness'. Francis knew that Essex had only to return the ring as a symbol of distress and all would be well. He knew, too, that Essex had sent it. Up to the day of the Queen's death, he believed she had received it, and forsworn herself by trampling under foot the mute symbol of mercy."

"But the Queen never received the ring. The Warrant for Essex's execution was presented for signature the day following the trial. She waved it away. She was waiting for the ring. The Warrant was presented the next day. She would not sign. All through the following day, the twenty-third, she waited, delaying her signature until the evening. Then, in a surge of temper that Essex should be too stiff-necked and proud to ask for mercy, she yielded the importunities of Cecil, and signed the Warrant. No sooner had it been dispatched to the Tower than she sent a Messenger saying the execution must be postponed."

The ring never arrived and the Queen's pride and dignity were at stake. That evening she sent word to let the execution proceed.

According to Alfred Dodd, "But Essex had sent the ring by the hands of a youth to Lady Scrope, to take to the Queen. Unfortunately, he took it to her sister, Lady Nottingham, the wife of the Earl's enemy. She kept the Queen's ring and maintained silence for two years...until she was on her death-bed. The ring haunted her. She could not die. She sent for the Queen and confessed what she had done. So overcome with emotion and rage was Elizabeth that she seized the dying woman and shook her in a rage of mental agony, flinging her back in bed with terrible expletives, finishing with the sentence, 'God may forgive you but I never can'. Her heart that had been breaking for two years was now utterly broken. The poor Queen, she was haunted by her thoughts; Robert had sent her the ring. He had expected to be pardoned and she had doomed him in her false pride. Nothing could bring him back again."

Elizabeth's health deteriorated rapidly after the beheading of her youngest son in 1601. One can only imagine the feelings of remorse that must have plagued her. After the Queen discovered the truth about the ring, she went back to her Palace to die.

And so Elizabeth at the age of seventy years of age, died on March 24th, 1603. She was a lonely old woman whose pride had deprived her of the happiness to which she was entitled i.e.

(a)   the happiness of recognising Robert Dudley as her rightful husband, and

(b)   the right to proudly recognise her two sons as legal heirs to the Tudor Throne of England.

Elizabeth kept all Dudley's letters, and the last one he sent to her before he died, she had written upon it "His last letter."

From information contained in Peter Dawkins' book titled *Dedication To The Light* we learn the following important information:

"Elizabeth could, at any time after 1571, have named any child of hers, however begotten, as her successor. At her express wish the Act of Succession was altered in 1571, so that -

(a)   the Queen was given the power to name her Successor, and

(b)   it became a penal offence to speak of any other Successor to the Crown other than the natural issue of the body of the Queen."

The original reference to the Queen's 'lawful issue' was deliberately altered to 'the Queen's issue', leaving the way open for any child of hers, born in or out of wedlock, who was 'Heir of her Natural body', to become heir to the Throne of England."

"The historian Camden, a personal friend of Francis Bacon, recorded his remarks on this alteration in the Act of Succession:

'I remember, being then a young man, hearing it said openly by people, that this was done by the contrivance of Leicester (Robert Dudley), with a design to impose, hereafter, some base son of his own upon the Nation as the Queen's Offspring'."

"But Elizabeth never chose to exercise her freedom of choice in naming Francis as her eldest living son and heir to the Throne of England. Indeed, she actively opposed it for the rest of her life, causing difficulty and distress to Francis, always fearful lest her son should use his exceptional intelligence and command of other people's friendship to depose her 'whilst still living' - a fear fanned by the evil insinuations and lies of Francis's principal enemy, the hunchback Robert Cecil, and compounded when Leicester discovered and informed the Queen that their son not only was the author of the play *Hamlet* but also trained the actors to perform it."

"The Queen would not believe Francis's explanations, but was led to see in that play, an intent to stir up the people against her - which she also believed about a later play, *Richard III*, leading directly to the necessity to employ someone as a 'mask' to the authorship of the 'Shakespeare 'plays. At Elizabeth's death she exclaimed, when pressed by her Privy Council to name her successor by the right given her in the 1571 Act of Succession (a right applying to her own natural children rather than to anyone else), that she would have no 'rascal's son' succeed her - a pointed reference to the son of herself and her deceased husband...and that the Council were instead to carry out Robert Cecil's plan and send to Scotland and invite James VI of Scotland to sit on the English Throne; thus even in her moment of death deliberately passing over the rights of her royal son."

"The interesting fact is that the succession of James VI, son of Mary, Queen of Scots, and great-grandson of Margaret Tudor, eldest sister of Henry VIII, to the Throne of England was not 'disputable' but 'clear', ...Francis said that the right of succession was not clear prior to Queen Elizabeth's final refusal, at the moment of her death, to exercise her right under the Act of Succession to proclaim her eldest and still surviving son. When she categorically rejected the 'rascal's son' - her son - in favour of her royal Stewart relation, and Francis accepted this decision (he had little option but to do so), the succession was at last made 'clear'."

"Elizabeth enjoyed her admired status and cult worship as a 'Virgin Queen', seemingly pure, unwed and 'undefiled' in terms of the orthodox Church teachings, like the Virgin Mary was supposed to be, to such an extent that she could not bear to think of her 'mask of fame' being torn to shreds, either in life or death, by publicly declaring that (a) she was not a virgin in the accepted sense, (b) she had borne two sons by the Earl of Leicester, and had killed one of them.... with that one revelation, many dark spectres would have come tumbling out of the cupboard to tarnish her name and reputation - and the thought of that was just too much for her vanity."

The 'Virgin' Queen

"Oh God, thou has set to rule us a woman, who nature
hath formed to be in subjection unto man, and whom thou
by thine holy apostle commandest to keep silence and not
to speak in congregation. Ah Lord! To take away the empire
from man and give it to a woman, seemeth to be an evident
token of thine anger towards us Englishmen!
(Thomas Becon)

These verses typify what the majority of Englishmen felt about Elizabeth when she became Queen of England. To step into the shoes of her powerful deceased father, Henry VIII was a daunting task. And, the result was that throughout the successive years, she needed to prove to herself and England, that she would be a very capable ruler and a 'Virgin Queen'.

According to the late Alfred Dodd:

"It is a notable fact that her body was not embalmed as was usual for Kings and Queens:

'No male touch laid aside her drapery when she was dead to carry out the dissection and embalming that preceded a royal funeral in those times. The duty of preparing for burial fell to her ladies, and if one of them was over-curious we have no record of her discovery. (*Ibid*, Piers Compton, p.194).'"

"In other words, the loyalty of her ladies, allowed Elizabeth to maintain the secret of her motherhood inviolate and to continue through the ages to pose as THE VIRGIN QUEEN."

"In the north aisle of Henry VIII's Chapel in Westminster Abbey lies the recumbent marble effigy of Elizabeth on her tomb...On her delicate hand is the famous ring 'that was stayed by malice from saving a man's life and the provable breaking of a woman's heart'. (Compton). No mere Lover would have attained the ascendancy that Robert gained - but by his own stubbiness lost - over such a Queen. None but an arrogant, vain Royal Mother, who had never reared a child would have treated him as she treated him. (Parker Woodward)."

"Cut upon the wall over the doorway of the Beauchamp Tower, at the foot of the stairs, are TWO WORDS which record Essex's imprisonment and death at the Tower. Few have heeded them, fewer have understood them. They were placed there by someone in authority, and with the connivance, necessarily so, of the Tower authorities, in order to perpetuate the Memory and to provide a CLUE to the real IDENTITY of the unhappy son of Queen Elizabeth Tudor...pronounced TIDIR. The words reveal the true name of the man who walked from the cell in which he was once confined to the scaffold in the Courtyard below:

ROBERT TIDIR:

(*Welsh for Robert Tudor*)

"And the man who was responsible for this mute but ever-living memorial was his brother...Francis Bacon. Who else could it have been? Who else had the right to perpetuate the Queen's Secret in so striking and mysterious a manner but Francis, the Last of the Tudors!"

MASTERS DISCUSSED IN THIS CHAPTER

Francis Bacon - St Germain

NOTES AND RECOMMENDED READING

Alfred Dodd, *Francis Bacon's Personal Life-Story*, (Rider & Co., U.K., 1986)

Christopher Haig, *Elizabeth I*, (Longman, U.K.)

Kendra Baker, *The Persecution of Francis Bacon, The Story Of A Great Wrong*, (Stanley Hunt U.K)

E.D. Johnson, *Francis Bacon versus Lord Macaulay*, (George Lapworth & Co., U.K., 1949)

Dr Raymond Bernard, *The Great Secret, Count Saint Germain*, (U.S.A.)

Peter Dawkins, *Arcadia*, (Francis Bacon Research Trust, U.K., 1988)

Peter Dawkins, *The Virgin Ideal*, (Francis Bacon Research Trust, U.K.)

Peter Dawkins, *Dedication To The Light*, (Francis Bacon Research Trust, U.K., 1984)

Peter Dawkins, *The Great Vision*, (Francis Bacon Research Trust, U.K., 1985)

Francis Bacon, *Faithful Sayings and Ancient Wisdom*, (Francis Bacon Research Trust).

Peter Dawkins, *Francis Bacon Herald of the New Age*, (Francis Bacon Research Trust, U.K., 1997)

Edward Fitzgerald, *The Rubaiyat of Omar Khayyam*, (Collins, U.K., 1974)

CHAPTER 44

𝕿𝖍𝖊 𝕱𝖎𝖓𝖆𝖑 𝕪𝖊𝖆𝖗𝖘 𝖔𝖋 𝕱𝖗𝖆𝖓𝖈𝖎𝖘 𝕭𝖆𝖈𝖔𝖓

"I have been teacher to all Intelligences,
I am able to instruct the whole Universe.
I shall be until the day of Judgement on the face of the earth.
Is it not the wonder of this world that I cannot be discovered?"
(Taliesin/Merlin - St Germain)

"I never saw traces in him of a vindictive mind, whatever injury was done to him [Francis
Bacon], nor ever heard him utter a word to any man's disadvantage"
(Tobie Matthew)

Life in the Elizabethan era and that of James I of England was rather like
Alice in Wonderland wherein the queen was always demanding 'off with their
heads'. The Tower of London where the heads literally rolled on a regular basis
from the 'chopping blocks', was an ominous place, feared by all, and Francis too,
for a time, was imprisoned there.

Francis Bacon always walked a tight-rope, never knowing who was scheming
against him personally and so after the death of Elizabeth in 1603, Francis as Lord
Chancellor, endeavoured to stay on particularly good terms with King, James I
who was fully aware that Francis was legally entitled to have become the Tudor
King of England. Francis therefore, went to great lengths to make King James feel
at ease, re-assuring him that he would never challenge James' right to the Throne
of England, for Francis knew that should he ever do so, his life would be in jeopardy.

According to the late Alfred Dodd, when James became King of England,
"Francis Bacon said to Robert Cecil, Secretary of State: 'My ambition will now rest
upon my pen', a covert intimation that he was not an aspirant to the Throne."

Also in the year 1603, "Francis Bacon wrote to Sir John Davies, when asking
a favour: 'So **Be** kind to CONCEALED POETS', thus intimating that he was a
concealed poet."

It will be recalled that mention has been made in earlier chapters that ZEBEDEE, the 'father of James the Just and John the Beloved' who was Joseph - St Germain, was obviously a code-name inserted by Francis, i.e. ZE for ZION/SION, BE for BACON, and DEE for Sir John Dee - Kuthumi who assisted Francis in the translation of the King James Authorized Version of the Bible.

Francis' long time enemy and cousin, Robert Cecil, the Earl of Salisbury died in 1612, and according to Alfred Dodd, "perfidious to the last, he tried, when dying to poison James against Francis by whispering venomous suggestions that as a Tudor born, Francis had designs on the Crown. Cecil died in 1612, and a burst of gladness broke over the Court and country at the news."

Upon the demise of Robert Cecil, Bacon is quoted as saying that for the duration of Cecil's life in which he held so much power, Francis felt as if he had been 'a hawk tied to another's fist, that might sometimes bait and proffer, but could never fly'.

As Lord Chancellor, Francis tried to impress upon Parliament, the importance of fair government, which is one of the reasons for his *New Atlantis* which was philosophic in its content of the founding of a 'golden civilization'.

Francis Bacon was Attorney General from 27th October, 1613 to 7th March 1617, when he became Lord Keeper of the Great Seal. When Francis was promoted to Attorney General in 1613, he had to contend with another enemy, one who had been amongst the prosecutors of Lord Essex. This was Lord Coke, who was Chief Justice of the Common Pleas and he thwarted Francis to the best of his ability, resisting Francis's aims at creating a fair and just Parliament over which James I presided.

From information contained in Peter Dawkins' book titled *Francis Bacon Herald of the New Age*, we learn the following:

"It is perhaps not generally known that Francis Bacon, who had been a regular member of Parliament since the age of twenty and who had always worked to protect the rights of the ordinary citizen, was granted in April 1614, when having been re-elected as a Member of Parliament by three separate constituencies whilst at the same time being Attorney General for James I, the unique privilege of being a member of both the House of Lords and the House of Commons. It was recorded by the House of Commons that 'this tribute paid to personal merit and public service must not be drawn into a precedent dangerous to their franchise and the case shall stand alone'." (It is of interest that the title of Lord Chancellor was not bestowed again until 13th January, 1657, when Charles II conferred the title on his great supporter Edward Hyde, Earl of Clarendon).

Some 'Masks' of Francis Bacon

It has been emphasized throughout this story that dedicated scholars who have studied the works of Francis Bacon, state that the most utilized 'masked' name under which Francis wrote was that of 'Shakespeare' - the 'Spearer of the Truth' and it has elsewhere been mentioned that the real Shakespeare spelt his name without an 'a' (Shakespere) and that although he was an actor, he was uneducated, illiterate, and not particularly of noble character. Even his Last Will and Testament was signed with a cross and his daughter was also illiterate.

Two other important names used by Francis, were Edmund Spenser (as discussed in a previous chapter), and John Lyly. According to Peter Dawkins of the Francis Bacon Research Trust, in his book titled *Arcadia*, the real John Lyly had been imprisoned for debt in 1584 and was a man with little education whose fortunes had rapidly declined so it seems more than likely that Francis may have helped John Lyly out financially in gratitude for being able to use his name or that he simply invented the name for his own purposes.

Throughout the many plays attributed to Shakespeare, were philosophic ideas which demonstrated that their author was thoroughly familiar with certain doctrines and tenets peculiar to the Freemasons which stamped the creator of the plays as being one of the Illuminati of the ages. And who but one deeply versed in the legends of Parzival and the Holy Grail, could have conceived *A Midsummer Night's Dream*?

Francis Bacon knew the true secret of Masonic origin and this he concealed the knowledge of, by using ciphers and cryptograms. By reintroducing the lost 'Wisdom' (whom he called Pallas Athena), the risk factor of it falling into the wrong hands that would use it for the wrong purposes, meant that 'concealment' was still necessary and thus it became incorporated into poems and plays for those in the 'know' to decipher. There were times that Francis Bacon actually wrote and published under his own name, and one of these was the great work aptly named *New Atlantis* alluding to the continuation of his Utopian dream of founding a 'Golden' civilization.

According to the late Alfred Dodd, Plays attributed to having been written by Francis Bacon were performed at Gray's Inn and they included:

1583: The Birth of Merlin;
1588: The Misfortunes of Arthur;
1591: The Lord Mayor's Pageant, 29th October;
1592: A Conference of Pleasure;
1594-5: The Order of the Helmet or the Prince of Purpool;
1595: The Device of the Indian Prince.
In 1589, *The Arte of English Poesie* was published.

According to Edward D. Johnson, in 1590, Francis published *The Faire Queene* under Spenser's name. *The Faerie Queene,* in which Arthur is a knight in the dazzling court of the Faerie Queene, was modelled on Elizabeth, in which she was portrayed as 'Gloriana' - 'a most royal queen and empress'.

Francis also printed anonymously *The Tragedy of Tambourline* and an Elegy on the death of his old friend, Sir Francis Walsingham, in the name of 'Watson'. Under Watson's name he also translated a number of Italian Madrigals, which were set to music by William Bird, the Court Musician.

1591: Francis published a drama titled *Endimion* anonymously; *Complaintes* and *Daphnaida* in Spenser's name. In the name of Nashe, Francis wrote the preface to *Astrophel and Stella*, a book of verse by Sir Philip Sidney. He published the Play *King John* anonymously.

1592: Francis published anonymously a drama *Midas*; and *The Tears of Fancie or Love Disdained* in Watson's name - a series of sonnets. He published *Venus and Adonis* in the name of William Shakespeare.

1593: Christopher Marlowe (Kit) was killed in a brawl and Francis then printed various works with Marlowe's name as author. Francis also printed *William Longbeard and Philis*, a set of Sonnets put out in Lodge's name. He published *Gallathea* anonymously and *Aminte Gandea* in the name of Watson.

Alfred Dodd wrote that "Nashe, Lyly, Greene, as well as Peele and Marlowe, were all 'Masks' more or less for Francis Bacon's anonymous writings. We can thus well understand why Gabriel Harvey in *Pierce's Supererogation* said that: *'Nashe', 'Lyly', and 'Greene' were three faces in one hood...'*"

Another major work that Francis wrote in his latter years was the history of Henry VII who was England's first Tudor monarch and with whom he felt empathy. It is considered that this work was one of the best pieces of historical writing in English., thought to have been written whilst he spent a brief period imprisoned in the Tower of London as a result of being falsely accused by the 'enemy camp' of 'bribery'.

It is noteworthy that in first part of the play titled *King Henry the Fourth*, the word 'Francis' appears 33 times upon one page. Similarly, Francis Bacon used cryptics in many lines of his plays wherein title words in succession would contain the letters of his name. In some of his plays he would repeatedly use the word 'hog' which was another allusion to the word 'Bacon'.

According to Alfred Dodd, in the year 1609, Francis Bacon wrote "*Considerations Touching the Plantation in Ireland, The Wisdom of the Ancients*, and he reprinted *The Passionate Pilgrim* and *Sonnet to Sundry Notes of Musicke*, with the third edition in 1613."

During his time as a lawyer, he wrote *"Antony and Cleopatra, Pericles, A Winter's Tale, Cymbeline, Macbeth, Lear, Troilus and Cressida* and possibly a first draft of *The Tempest.* Some of the Rosicrucian manifestoes which we know were circulating in England and the Continent in 1610 and were openly published anonymously in 1614, especially one, *The Fama Fraternitatis."*

"In 1611, he prepared a Folio of edition of the 'Spenser Poems' in which *The Shepherd's Calendar* was *for the first time* included as a Spenser poem. The five quarto editions of *The Shepherd's Calendar* had all appeared anonymously. The 1611 Spenser Folio had neither preface nor editor's name. Spenser had died in January, 1599, so it was quite safe to attach Spenser's name to the poems."

"In 1609, we also have evidence that the six parts of *The Great Instauration* were not (and never had been) neglected, for he writes a letter to his young friend Tobie Matthew in which it is mentioned."

The above-mentioned works by Francis Bacon are only a small example and to discuss the rest would take an entire book - books would be more like it. Both the late Alfred Dodd and Peter Dawkins of the Francis Bacon Research Trust have done their work admirably in this field.

Francis Bacon's Retreat

It was on the 10th May, 1606, nine years after the death of Marguerite, that Francis Bacon married Alice Barnham, his twin soul, otherwise known as the Lady Portia who assisted him in every way possible with all he was destined to achieve.

There were times when he longed for peace and tranquility which he often sought at York House where Francis is said to have been born. In all things, Francis was a perfectionist who always extracted the maximum results from himself. With his exceptional artistic abilities, he had created the York House as a haven to which he would return from time to time, away from the harrowing trials of Parliament, away from the 'Maddening Crowd'.

The house had beautiful gardens which he had designed that went all the way down to the river's edge. He loved the scent of flowers, especially Damask Roses and orange blossoms which he would collect and dry the petals in order to make pot-pourri which would be used in the rooms of his house so that they always had the heavenly scent of flowers.

Also amongst his incredible list of talents, Francis had a wonderful sense of colour and this was displayed in the decor of his home which included many large stained-glass windows with glorious colours which were enhanced as the sun's rays shone through them. In these pleasant surroundings of his latter days here, Francis devoted his time to his philosophic and scientific writings whilst at the same time his writings on Freemasonry were of great importance to him.

In 1621, a scandal erupted, another conspiracy against Francis Bacon, for it suited the purposes of the enemies of Francis, and one of the main instigators (although there were others) was Lord Buckingham who wished to lease Francis's home, York House.

Francis was brought before the court on charges of corruption. When Francis was imprisoned in the Tower of London, Buckingham achieved his ambition, took over the lease of Francis's favourite home and Francis was released on June 4th. He was later cleared of all the charges, but the 'mud' stuck and has continued to do so down through the centuries - thanks to myopic , biased authors of past-century history books.

According to Peter Dawkins, Francis Bacon's "fall from office of Lord Chancellor, on charges of corruption, has, in the minds of the world at large, tainted his name and memory, and thus his work. Yet Bacon was innocent of corruption, and his impeachment for supposedly taking bribes was the result of a carefully planned conspiracy by others intent upon his downfall. James I, who became entangled in this web of conspiracy, commanded his Lord Chancellor to offer no defence to the charges of taking bribes and to sign the 'confession' presented to him. When examined in depth it can readily be seen that, in any true court of law, such charges would never have stood up, but that is precisely why Bacon was allowed neither a proper trial nor to offer any defence in the House of Lords."

History regards Francis Bacon as the greatest Lord Chancellor that England has ever had, and when Francis was sixty years old, he was raised a step in the peerage to become Baron Verulam, Viscount St Albans. Just to remind the readers, it is interesting to note that in the third century AD, St Germain had incarnated as 'Albanus', born into a Roman noble family in the town of Verulam in England. He was the first Christian martyr in England when he was beheaded in the 3rd century AD, for harbouring a monk who was being persecuted. St Germain is recorded as having been very active in founding Freemasonry and was later proclaimed a saint - St Alban. (The Latin word 'Veru' as in Verulam, means a 'javelin/lance/spear').

Francis Bacon - the Teacher

"I have been teacher to all Intelligences,
I am able to instruct the whole Universe"
(Taliesin/Merlin - St Germain)
"Everyman, I will go with thee, and be thy guide,
In thy most need to go by thy side."
(Edmund Spenser/ Francis Bacon)

From an excerpt of the Lady Portia's story in the book titled *St Germain Twin Souls & Soulmates* channelled by Claire Heartsong we are informed as follows:

"In the laboratories this one (Francis) secreted himself away with a few others who had a knowingness or a remembering of the roles that they had played in previous eras upon the land. In these secret places there were scores and scores and scores of books. There were vessels that contained elements, herbs and metals of many kinds. For hours and days these ones would secret themselves away and look upon the ancient tablets which had survived and which had been carried by a Brotherhood through the ages, for it was time to bring forth a grand alchemy; not just to produce gold to be worn upon the body, to bejewel the tables and the high ones in their courts, but to bring forth an understanding of the gold within the human soul, to transfigure and transmute the body, to bring forth the elixir of everlasting life and to bring forth a teaching and an awareness that would go forth upon the land and exemplify unto all who had ears to hear, how they might do this for themselves so they may be free."

According to the writer Manly P. Hall, Sir Francis Bacon wrote into the Shakespearian plays the secret teachings of the Fraternity of the Freemason - 'for those who had the eyes to see and ears to hear'.

Peter Dawkins of the Francis Bacon Research Trust acknowledges in his book titled *Francis Bacon Herald of the New Age*:

"In Francis Bacon's Natural History, *Sylva Sylvarum* (meaning 'Wood or Woods' or 'Pan of Pans', for the Arcadian Pan was called Sylva or Sylvanus, the Lord of Matter, author and director of the dances of the gods, and author and disposer of the regular motion of the universe. With his seven-reeded pipe, Pan orders everything harmoniously. Pan was known as the minister and companion of Bacchus [Dionysus], the god of tragic art and protector of theatres), Francis Bacon deliberately printed the particulars in a seemingly haphazard way, yet concealing a secret order that would reveal much if discovered. This fact is stated openly in the foreword, yet (as far as I know) few have ever penetrated this secret or even tried to. But it is certainly worth the attempt, since, as explained in the book's foreword, Francis Bacon's intention was to 'write such a Natural History as may be fundamental to the erecting and building of a true Philosophy, for the illumination of the Understanding, the extracting of axioms, and the producing of many noble works and effects'."

"Bacon's hide-and-seek' method has never been properly understood by the majority of historians and scholars, who usually say simply that Bacon never finished his writings, and look no deeper. Yet, in letters between him and his friend, Tobie Matthew, it is quite clear, for instance, that the whole *Novum Organnum* (Part 2 of *The Great Instauration*) had been complete for many years; but when it was published part was deliberately withheld from the public eye - that is to say, the 'missing' information is transmitted in ways that conceal it from those not ready for it, or who have not yet developed the eye to see and the ear to hear."

"Because Philosophy embraces not only Natural Philosophy but also Human and Divine Philosophy, which are involved with human behaviour and mankind's capacity to receive the Light of God, in order to perceive and understand the whole of Bacon's method requires a corresponding development of morality and spirituality, as well as of intuition, reason and perception. However, Bacon does not leave us to flounder about in the shallows of human knowledge. He devised and set in motion many different ways of developing and training our humanity and divinity, and of encouraging the high Laws or Forms of God to be revealed to us - most of them based upon age-old methods and traditions of teaching which he encouraged, utilised and transformed where necessary (e.g. Freemasonry and Rosicrucianism, and the Treasure Trail."

"As all three aspects of philosophy become developed in us, so we become more capable of receiving the Divine Light of inspiration, teaching us inwardly just as Bacon was taught. Like all true Cabbalists, Bacon's scheme is devised so as to avoid the problems of cult and hero worship; and, rather than allowing himself to be set up as a king or god by others, he leads us by the hand straight to the One and Only God, Truth, whence we can receive the Higher Teachings direct."

"That particular joy of discovering what Bacon has hidden is that it gives a training in the art of discovery - for the very means by which the concealed information may be found is actual method that Bacon is teaching, and once known it can be applied to life itself. He is indeed a most practical teacher! It is this practicality which is Francis Bacon's hallmark. Right from the start he was propelled into his life's work by his disgust and despair at the preponderance of intellectuals who were barren of any good works, and who actually misled the world into erroneous beliefs and superstitions; and he sorrowed at the resulting lack of concern and practical help given to alleviating the poverty, sickness, ignorance and generally miserable estate of the mass of humanity."

"Because of this game of 'hide-and-seek', not only has the world tended to misjudge Bacon's method and grand scheme, but they have also tended to misjudge Bacon himself, his character and history. His name and reputation have been libelled all too frequently, and often by those that one would have hoped would have known better."

"The various comments recorded by a great number of people who knew Francis Bacon infer much more about this extraordinary soul, and it is these comments which all help to signpost the treasure trail or game of 'hide-and-seek'. For instance, in a collection of thirty-two elegies published upon Bacon's supposed death in 1626, are given some almost blatant hints about Francis Bacon, naming him as 'Apollo', the leader of our choir'; 'a muse more rare than the nine Muses', 'the Daystar of the Muses', 'the tenth Muse and glory of the choir', 'the brilliant light-bearer'."

"Pallas Athena, the personification of the Holy Intelligence and goddess of wisdom, is known in tradition as the Tenth Muse, and Apollo, the god of Light, is her spouse. Both inhabit Parnassus, the Mount of Inspiration and Poetry where lies the oracle of Delphi. This is the same imagery as is directly associated with the Rosicrucian literature, where the Invisible Brethren and their leader are likened to Apollo and the Choir of Muses, inhabiting Mount Parnassus. Furthermore, the declared objectives of the Rosicrucian manifestos, which were to bring about a world-wide reformation of the arts and sciences, and a restoration of the original *Gnosis* or Wisdom Knowledge given by God to mankind, were identical with those of Francis Bacon's Great Instauration. This is a hint, but there are further levels of evidence and sign-posting to be found: it is not difficult to discover them."

"The elegies, for instance, describe Francis Bacon as being not just an outstanding philosopher but a supreme poet, howbeit secret, 'the prince of orators and the precious gem of concealed literature', and the author of the Comedies and Tragedies which were masked by another. They describe him as Quirinus (i.e. Spearshaker); as another Orpheus, the great poet-musician and founder of the Orphic initiatory teachings and 'Mysteries' of Divine Love (of which Plato and Pythagoras were initiates); as a Prometheus, who stole the fire of divine truth from heaven in order to bring it to the earth; as a 'Rose' author who filled the world with his writings; as another Apollo who restored the honour of Minerva (Athena) and dispelled the clouds that hid her."

"*Pallas Athena* literally means 'Shaker of the spear'. Apollo, Pallas Athena, St Michael, Britannia, St George - all are known traditionally as 'shakers of the spear of Light against the dragon of ignorance'. The Rosicrucian Brethren were all symbolised by St George, the Rose (or Red) Cross Knight, and thus were all 'spear shakers'; but Francis Bacon was their chief, his genius being equated with both Apollo and Pallas Athena. It is not by chance that Shakespeare is traditionally said to have been born and died on St George Day."

Peter Dawkins further comments:

"It has been a quirk of modern criticism to label Francis Bacon as non-religious or even atheist, yet both his writings and those who knew him well proclaim him as one of the world's most religious men. As his own personal chaplain and confessor, Dr William Rawley, stated:

'He was deeply religious, for he was conversant with God and able to render a reason for the hope that was in him.'"

"Most people assume, incorrectly, that Francis Bacon was a dry, cold intellectual, howbeit a great one, and that his knowledge was from books and personal observations and enquiry into natural things. Yet his contemporaries record that not only was he warm-hearted but also he could rarely pass by a jest, combining merry wit with silent gravity. Furthermore, he was in fact, as some have well realised, not only a philosopher but also one of the world's great mystics. Bacon himself confesses that most of his knowledge he gained from divine inspiration and illumination - i.e. from what he refers to as 'Divinity' and 'Faith', rather than from 'Philosophy', and emphasizes that Philosophy, although immensely important, should be sub-servient to Divinity."

Francis Bacon and Shakespeare

Dr Raymond Bernard wrote in his work titled *The Great Secret - Count Saint Germain* that "Bacon tried to teach the common people that kings were nothing more than men, made from the same clay and ruled by the same passions, that heaven did not ordain them nor protect them; and that a king has no right to hold his throne any longer than he behaves himself. Was this not a revolutionary idea to put forth in that day?"

"These Plays (written under the mask of Shakespeare), had the hidden purpose of educating the English people and preparing them for the day when Charles I was brought to trial and the scaffold. These 'Histories of English Kings' led to the Revolution and to constitutional government in place of monarchy and despotism and led to the birth of a new democratic age, which was ushered in by Bacon's Freemasonic Society. It is clear that the Plays were written by a humanitarian and political reformer and not simply by a poet."

"Bacon wrote the plays when he was in dire financial circumstances as a poor lawyer. It was customary for impecunious lawyers in that age to earn money by writing for the stage. While quite young, Bacon assisted in getting up a play for his law school, at Gray's Inn, if he did not write the greater part of it. It was called 'The Comedy of Errors', which then appeared at Gray's Inn for the first time, and was acted by Shakespere's company. Bacon and Shakespere then met each other, since they were both on the board of Gray's Inn at the same time, one as a writer of the play which the other directed."

"After this meeting with Shakespere, Bacon decided to use him as a mask for other plays he wrote, which permitted him to freely express his revolutionary ideas without endangering his social and political aspirations by so doing; and at the same time, it enabled him to keep out of poverty. Hence his cooperation with the actor Shakespere, in this manner, had everything in its favour."

"That Shakespere could not have written the Shakespearian plays is indicated by the fact that the appearance of the Plays antedated his coming to London, which is believed to have occurred in 1587. Yet that high authority, Richard Simpson, in his 'School of Shakespeare' showed that the Shakespeare plays started to appear in 1585! In other words, while Shakespere was still living in Stratford in the year his twins were born, plays under the name of Shakespeare started appearing in London. Are we to believe that in that 'bookless neighbourhood', the butcher's apprentice between whippings, deer-stealing and beer-guzzling, was writing plays for the stage? That would indeed be a miracle! Bacon himself, never revealed the secret of his authorship of the Shakespeare plays except in the cipher story hidden in the plays themselves..."

"A most interesting piece of direct evidence of the Baconian authorship of the Shakespeare plays is the Shakespeare monument in Westminster Abbey which had been erected by Pope. The statue is graced with the head of Francis Bacon, the stockings are engraved with the Tudor Rose and a Crown, the lace work on the ruffs of the sleeve is an exact repetition of the ruff worn by Queen Elizabeth. The fingers of the statue point to the Queen at the side. The place of honour in front is given to a beautiful youth - a crowned Prince - young Francis Bacon as in the Hilliard Miniature (found in Queen Elizabeth's prayer book). On the left side is the figure of the Queen's second son, the Earl of Essex, and the Queen's husband, the Earl of Leicester."

"Commenting on this monument, Alfred Dodd, the greatest modern authority on the Shakespeare-Bacon controversy, said: 'Think you that the Abbey authorities would have allowed this apparently meaningless foolery if they had not known to whom the Shakespeare Monument was actually being erected - to Lord St Alban, a Prince of the House of Tudor? Not likely....The High Dignitaries know the truth as a State Secret. And it is known today in the highest quarters'."

It is of interest to note that the renowned Rosicrucian and Freemasonic writer, Manly P. Hall, wrote that there is little doubt in the minds of impartial investigators that Lord Bacon was the legitimate son of Queen Elizabeth and Robert Dudley, Earl of Leicester.

The close friends of Francis Bacon - St Germain, full well knew both his secrets - that he was a royal Prince and that he was the author of the Shakespeare plays which were full of Freemasonic Teachings. A 'Mason' is a 'builder' and Francis - St Germain, was the greatest 'builder' - 'constructor' of the Sacred Mysteries handed down from the ancient days of Atlantis.

Dr Raymond Bernard writes: "No-one has yet suggested that a part at least of this 'mystery' was due to the fact that William Shakespeare was a Freemason, the centre of a Ring of Rosicrosse Masons and that he purposely seems to have lived his life as though his motto was 'By the MIND alone shall I be seen'. And in the Sonnets he writes along the same vein when he says:

'Forget me - Let my name be buried where my body is,
And live no more to shame, nor me, nor you;
For I am shamed....You in me can nothing worthy prove.'
(Sonnet 149)

One of Francis' numerous friends, Tobie Matthew wrote of him:
"I never yet saw traces in him of a vindictive mind, whatever injury was done to him, nor ever heard him utter a word to any man's disadvantage"...and further added how much he admired the greatness and nobleness of Francis Bacon's character.

From *Francis Bacon Herald of the New Age* by Peter Dawkins we learn of comments made by Pierre Amboise in his work *Histoire Naturelle* who wrote:
'Innocence oppressed found always in his (Bacon's) protection a sure refuge, and the position of the great gave them no vantage ground before the Chancellor when suing for justice. All these good qualities made him the darling of the people and prized by the great ones of the State....Never was there a man who so loved equity, or so enthusiastically worked for the public good as he; so that I may aver that he would have been much better suited to a Republic than to a Monarchy, where frequently the convenience of the Prince is more thought of than that of his people.'"

Towards the end of his life in England, Francis had endured many tribulations and at times, felt bewilderment. His close friend Sir Walter Raleigh was executed on trumped up charges of treason and piracy, but the real reason was because Sir Walter Raleigh was one of the 'Initiates' into the Arcana Mysteries and was considered as 'dangerous' because of his transcendental knowledge.

Dr Raymond Bernard in his work titled *The Great Secret - Count Saint Germain*, makes the following statement: "For Raleigh was not executed because of his depredations against the King of Spain, but because he was a member of Bacon's secret society, which played such an important role in the overthrow of monarchy and its replacement by a republican system of government, which Bacon hoped to realise across the Atlantic through the colonization of America in which Raleigh played such an important role. Every effort was made to torture Raleigh into naming his associates in his secret order, of which Bacon was the head, but he bravely died without speaking."

With one of his closest friends, namely Sir Walter Raleigh having gone the way of the 'chopping block', no-wonder Francis felt it was time to leave England and start a new life on the Continent. It is rather curious that Francis' brother Lord Essex had one son (who was born whilst Robert was imprisoned) and two daughters. They were the Queen's grandchildren. Therefore, surely today, there must be descendants of the Tudor line in existence?

MASTERS DISCUSSED IN THIS CHAPTER
Apollo - St Germain
Orpheus - St Germain
Plato - St Germain
St Alban of Verulam
Francis Bacon - St Germain
Pythagoras - Kuthumi
St George - Kuthumi
Sir John Dee - Kuthumi

NOTES AND RECOMMENDED READING

Peter Dawkins, *Francis Bacon Herald of the New Age*, (Francis Bacon Research Trust, Warwick, U.K., 1997)
Alfred Dodd, *Francis Bacon's Personal Life-Story*, (Rider & Co., U.K., 1986)
Kendra Baker, *The Persecution of Francis Bacon, The Story Of A Great Wrong*, (Stanley Hunt, U.K).
Kendra Baker, *Pope And Bacon: The Meaning of the 'Meanest' - A New Light On An Old Belief* (U.K. January 1937).
E.D. Johnson, *Francis Bacon Versus Lord Macaulay* (1949)
Martin Pares, *A Pioneer*, (Francis Bacon Research Trust, Warwick U.K., 1959).
Robert Graves, *The White Goddess*, (Faber & Faber, U.K., 1961)
Dr Raymond Bernard, A.B., M.A., Ph.D. *The Great Secret Count Saint Germain*, (U.S.A.)
Manly P Hall, *An Encyclopedic Outline Of Masonic, Hermetic, Qabbalistic And Rosicrucian Philosophy*, (Philosophical Research Society, U.S.A, 1988)
Azena Ramanda & Claire Heartsong, *St Germain Twin Souls & Soulmates*, (Triad Publishers, Queensland, Australia, 1994)
Boris Ford, *The Age of Shakespeare*, (Pelican Books, U.K., 1955)
Spenser, *The Shepherd's Calendar*, (Edited by Ernest Rhys, J.M. Dent & Sons, U.K., 1932)
Shakespeare, *Tragedies & Poems*, (edited by Peter Alexander, Collins, U.K., 1965)

CHAPTER 45

Exit Francis Bacon, Enter the Comte de St Germain

"Full many a glorious morning I have seen,
Flatter the mountain tops with sovereign eye,
Kissing with golden face the meadows green,
Gliding the pale streams with heavenly alchemy"
Sonnet Number 33 of Shakespeare (Francis Bacon - St Germain)

"Towards the close of each century,
there will be an outpouring of spirituality
during which time some one or more persons
have appeared in the world as advisers
at a critical time in history."
(Madame Helena Blavatsky)

And so the time finally arrived for Francis Bacon to fake his death and move on to fulfil his other commitments in founding Freemasonry and the Order of the Rose Cross throughout Europe and America; to spread 'heavenly alchemy' throughout as many places in the world as could be reached.

Francis Bacon reputedly died on Easter Sunday, 1626, 'Resurrection' Day, of a common cold at the age of sixty-six years. Two clues are given here, firstly, 'Resurrection Day' indicated that he would rise again and secondly, sixty-six is twice 33 - the favourite cipher code of Francis Bacon, thus indicating two lives, as in the leaving off of one life and the beginning of another. He was buried in St Michael's Church, St Albans.

The famous Theosophical and Masonic writer Manly Hall, who carried out exhaustive research, declared that Francis feigned his death and went to Germany. When the tomb of Francis was opened nearly one hundred years later, nothing was found - no coffin, no bones, no documents, nothing at all! And, there was no record of his burial in the registers of St Michael's Church.

Readers now will probably be wondering whatever happened to Francis' wife Alice? In the final chapter of the late Alfred Dodd's book titled *Francis Bacon's Personal Life Story* we learn the following:

"Another important and interesting mystery, as yet unsolved, respecting Francis Bacon's relationship with his wife Alice, is also brought into the limelight by one of the items of his Will. Says Spedding:

'His wife, with whom he had lived for twenty years without any reproach that we know of on either side, *gave him some grave offence. The nature of it is not known*; for he never specified it himself, and Dr Rawley in his biography makes no mention of any domestic difference, but speaks of their married life in terms which almost exclude the supposition of any. But that she had in some way incurred his serious displeasure, *is a fact not to be disputed*, being recorded in his Will, as a reason for revoking dispositions previously made in her favour.'

In his original Will, Francis left most of his Estate and valuables to Alice but in a codicil some years later these were omitted which caused people to speculate that there had been a falling out between Alice and him.

Alice and Francis had been married for twenty years during which time she gave him all the love, trust and support that he needed during those trying times when he must have sometimes felt as if 'fate' had turned against him. But then, on the other hand, he knew his destiny.

However, just 'knowing' one's destiny, does not necessarily mean that the trodden 'path' will be easy, even if one is a Master participating amongst humanity as a whole. Enemies are enemies and all his life, Francis was continually side-stepping and trying to outwit them. It is the opinion of the author that Francis and Alice came to an agreement. She would have been adequately taken care of and he would still have had access to money which would have been sent to a safe place in France so that he would not arrive destitute on the European scene. For after all, the great plan was to enable him to continue to write his Freemasonic works and have them published, plus continue to found Lodges throughout Europe and America.

In order to do this, Francis would have had need of finance without having to call upon his trusted friends in Europe. Alice re-married not long after the supposed death of Francis; however this might also have been pre-arranged for after all, it must be taken into consideration that she was only about thirty-four years old at that time, having been fourteen years old when Francis and she were married. Francis would have known that his time in Europe would be exceptionally busy, and that on future occasions when he would visit Britain, it would be under the disguise of the Comte de St Germain. Therefore, the likelihood is that Francis wanted his 'Alice' to be well taken care of for she was still in the prime of her life and he would have wanted the best for her. A suitable re-marriage would have ensured this.

Alfred Dodd writes:

"His plan did not hurt Lady Alice at all. The codicil did not leave her penniless as is the usual inference. Her marriage portion and gifts actually left her a wealthy woman. She had one thousand pounds a year, a large quantity of goods and chattels, and she lived rent free at Gorhambury. Her 'marriage' would be a 'sort of proof' that he was verifiably dead, though no one close to him was near when he 'died'. His wife's estate was protected by confirmation of marriage settlements, etc., specifically mentioned in the codicil."

'I go the same way as the Ancients,' said Francis Bacon, 'but I have something better to offer than the Morality Dramas of the Greeks and the Mystery Ceremonials of the Egyptians.' "So he gave the world the morality tales of 'Shakespeare' and the 'Thirty-Three' Rituals of the Free and Accepted." "Here is the summing up of Francis Bacon's finest biographer, Hepworth Dixon:

'The obligations of the world to Francis Bacon are of a kind that cannot be overlooked. Every man who rides in a train, who sends a telegram, who follows a steam plough, who sits in an easy chair, who crosses the Channel or the Atlantics, who eats a good dinner, who enjoys a beautiful garden, or undergoes a painless surgical operation, *OWES HIM SOMETHING.*'

'To him the patriot, the statesman, the law reformer, the scientific jurist, the historian, the collector of anecdotes, the lover of good wit, of humorous wisdom and of noble writing, also *OWES HIM SOMETHING.*'

'It is hard, indeed, to say which man amongst us is not the easier in circumstances, the brighter in intellect, the purer in morals, the worthier in conduct, through the Teachings and the Sufferings of Francis Bacon. The principles of his philosophy are of universal application...the true method of observing Nature is as easy in Rio and Peking as in Paris or London; while the results of an Inductive Method of Pursuing Truth are not more precious in the Palace, the workshop, on the farm and in the mine'."

Daniel Boorstin in his book titled *The Discoverers* comments: "Official documents of the English government in London were written in French until English became an official language when Shakespeare wrote his plays and the miracle of Elizabethan literature unfolded."

According to the late Alfred Dodd in his book titled *Francis Bacon's Personal Life Story*:

"The Authorized Version of 1611 will forever stand as a memorial of that one solitary victory in which destiny decreed that Francis Bacon should play an immortal part as its secret editor."

Enter the Comte de St Germain

Once on the Continent, Francis Bacon changed his appearance and he assumed the name of the Comte St Germain, the title which King Louis XIV of France bestowed upon him and gave him apartments at the Palace of Versailles and he was later allotted apartments at the Chambord Chateau on the River Loire in France.

Accordingly, he was given the support and protection of Gian Gastone of the Medici family and the Ragoczy family at which point of time, he became known as Prince Ragoczy. It was discussed in the first chapter of this story, that St Germain is sometimes referred to as the 'Master R' meaning, the Master Ragoczy but the name also alludes to the fact that he is *The Master of the Mystical Rose*.

As the Comte de St Germain, there was now plenty of work to accomplish, to bring to fruition, for strategically he was needed firstly in Europe and later, in the New World - America.

St Germain was regarded as the 'wonder-man of Europe' and one of the greatest philosophers who ever lived. Many records still exist today, confirming his brilliance and innumerable talents. St Germain was an expert in many languages which included English, French, Italian, Spanish, Portuguese, Chinese, Greek, Latin, Arabic, Spanish and Sanskrit, to name just a few.

He was also a wonderful artist, poet, alchemist, scholar, statesman, Rosicrucian, Freemason and a writer who had the incredible ability to be able to write fluently with both hands. St Germain also had the most wonderful singing voice and the ladies just adored listening to him. He was an exceptional musician and composer and he was very skilled at playing the violin. As a master alchemist he was said to be able to turn base metals into gold and small gem- stones such as diamonds, into larger flawless ones.

Upon the European scene, St Germain was known as a 'man of mystery' for no-one really seemed to know from whence he originally came. Of course, rumours abounded and there was a great deal of gossip in the European courts which he frequented during that time. Only the truly enlightened intimates of his really knew the truth.

St Germain was known to tell fascinating stories of how he had met with King Solomon [El Morya] and the Queen of Sheba and he kept the courts of Europe amused with many wonderful anecdotes of his previous lives.

Another of his abilities was that of being able to appear and disappear at will. One of the earliest records we have of this gift was when he was Apollonius of Tyana in the first century AD. During his time as St Germain it was recorded that he had been seen at the Court of Versailles, whereas, others would report that he was seen and spoken to in another country, simultaneously...no wonder he kept the tongues wagging!

He was a most elusive man, almost like the Scarlet Pimpernel. In tracing the Comte de St Germain's footsteps, it becomes obvious as to just how elusive he really was. Whenever he appeared in different parts of Europe, he had a different title.

At some stage, he visited Malta and it has been alleged that he was the last Grand Master of the Knights of Malta. He was always working behind the scenes and was known as a mystic, a most mysterious man who had the appearance and manners of nobility - he was Queen Elizabeth's son after all, although this knowledge was known by only a few of his special acquaintances.

Among the influential families that he mixed with apart from the Medici family, were the Austrian Hapsburg family, Catherine II of Russia , King Louis and Marie Antoinette of France and the Prince of Wales, to mention just a few.

Count Cagliostro

Throughout this period of time St Germain received a great deal of help and support from such people as Count Cagliostro whose real name was Giuseppe (Joseph) Balsamo, born in Sicily in 1743. It was St Germain who personally taught and initiated Cagliostro into the 'Great Mysteries' and inaugurated him as a Freemason.

Much has been written about Cagliostro and he was often maligned because of his political activities. His motives were either not known, or completely misunderstood. The Church of Rome was highly suspicious of any of the movements of the Freemasons and one of the men whom they targeted was Cagliostro for they later imprisoned him on 'trumped' up charges. On a previous occasion, he had been framed for a 'missing necklace', further details of which will be discussed under the heading of Marie Antoinette.

When Cagliostro was a young man, he travelled to Asia as a disciple of an Armenian mystic whose name was Althotas. Althotas claimed that he possessed the Philosopher's Stone which was capable of transforming base metals into gold. In his youth he went to Malta where he was initiated into the Order of the Knights of Malta and where he studied alchemy and the Kabbala. It was here that he changed his name to Cagliostro and travelled to the courts of England and Europe.

St Germain - Alchemist and Secret Agent

St Germain was known as an alchemist who was very generous with his gifts of jewellery. His wealth and his wisdom endeared him to King Louis of France who used the Comte's diplomatic abilities to his advantage and St Germain became a secret agent of the French Royal Family. He became involved in many political intrigues; his aim was to establish peace on the continent but unfortunately, there were many powerful families who wished to control most of Europe. Also there were religious upheavals taking place at the time.

As the saying goes 'politics and religion never mix' and such was the general feeling in Europe at that time. St Germain was instrumental in supporting Catherine II of Russia who in turn placed the Masonic lodges in Russia under her own protection.

On his numerous visits abroad, Sir Joseph Banks (Kuthumi) often carried important dispatches. One of these visits was to Catherine the Great of Russia. According to author Charles Lyte in his book titled *Sir Joseph Banks*, when Sir Joseph Banks visited the Empress Catherine II of Russia, "it was in fact to be a diplomatic exercise of the greatest importance. For many years Britain had enjoyed a special trading relationship with Russia, and although the trade balance was weighted heavily in favour of Russia, it was worth the cost in that it assured a steady supply of strategic supplies such as iron and steel, hemp, sailcloth, pitch, tar and timber as well as keeping the Baltic seaways open to British shipping. But in the 1700's relationships between Britain and Russia became intensely strained particularly during the era of Russia's confrontations with Poland and Turkey."

St Germain presides over troubles in Europe

In 1740, Marie Antoinette's mother, Marie Theresa, upon the decease of her father Charles VI, inherited the throne of Austria. Frederick II of Prussia then gathered his army and marched on the outlying Austrian province of Silesia, taking it by force. Maria Theresa astonished the world with her energy, courage and organizing power and she was able to hold in check all her enemies with the exception of Frederick. It has been mentioned in previous chapters that Marie Theresa of the Hapsburg family, had a close alliance with and was given the support of St Germain. By 1748, she had built up enough coalition power to destroy Frederick.

Then in 1756, Frederick made a treaty with England and an alliance between Austria, Russia and France took place. Also in the same year, the Treaty of Westminster was signed between Britain and Prussia and on May 1st, the Treaty of Versailles between France and Austria, was signed. The armies of France, Austria and Russia were put in motion against Frederick, and Sweden joined in from the north to close the ring. Thus began the Seven Years' War. Throughout this time, St Germain travelled to and fro to each country on diplomatic missions. He had been seen visiting the Hague in July 1756, returning in mid-October of the same year and was also seen at Versailles in 1756.

Information contained is Isabel Cooper-Oakley's book titled *The Comte De St Germain* informs us that "in 1760 Saint Germain was sent by Louis XV to the Hague on a political mission and then in April, 1760 according to an article which appeared in *The London Chronicle* of June 3rd, 1760, we have a long account of a 'mysterious foreigner' who had just arrived on England's shores. It is also said by one writer than Saint Germain was well received at Court, and many papers of the period mention him as a 'person of note' to whom marked attention was paid."

"In the British Museum there are pieces of music composed by the Comte de Saint Germain on both his visits; they are dated 1745 and 1760. It was said everywhere, by enemies as well as by friends, that he was a splendid violinist; he 'played like an orchestra'."

In May and June 1760, whilst Count St Germain was in England, he attended a performance of an opera he had composed, *L'Inconstanza Delusa* (Delusive Constancy). He was on good terms with Frederick, Prince of Wales and attended many musical evenings at private homes of Freemasons.

During this same year, there were a series of dispatches known as the 'Michell Papers' which involved St Germain. (Mitchell was the English Envoy in Prussia). Part of one of the letters is quoted in the book titled *The Comte De St Germain* by Isabel Cooper-Oakley. It tells of how St Germain was on particularly good terms with Madame Pompadour and that the King and all the Court and Nation desired peace with England. A reply letter on behalf of King George II of England was sent:

"Sir, I have the pleasure to acquaint you that His Majesty entirely approves your conduct in the conversation you had with Count St Germain, of which you give an account in your secret letter of the 14th (March, 1760)....his Majesty does not think it unlikely that Count St Germain may really have been authorized (perhaps even with the knowledge of His Most Christian Majesty) by some Persons of weight in the Councils of France to talk as he has done, and no matter what the channel is if a desirable end can be obtained by it."

"It was reported in the *London Chronicle* (June 3rd, 1760) a long account of Saint Germain's arrival in England, speaking of him in favourable terms. Peace appears more difficult to arrange than war, and the personal desires of the French Ministers blocked the way of this mission. Difficult indeed must have been the undertaking for the Comte de St Germain, thankless the work; at every turn he met opposition, and could not count on support."

The Czarina Elizabeth of Russia, died in 1762 and Peter III who succeeded her, was one of Frederick III of Poland's great admirers - he was profoundly unpopular in Russia and a revolution evolved, the result of which, he was deposed.

At this point of time, Catherine II became the ruler of Russia.

In 1763, a letter was written by the Graf Karl Cobenzl to Prince Kaunitz, the Prime Minister describing the Comte de St Germain; excerpts are given as follows:

"I found him the most singular man that I ever saw in my life. I do not yet precisely know his birth; I believe, however, that he is the son of a clandestine union in a powerful and illustrious family. Possessing great wealth, he lives in the greatest simplicity; he knows everything, and shows an uprightness, a goodness of soul, worthy of admiration. Among a number of his accomplishments, he made, under my own eyes, some experiments, of which the most important were the transmutation of iron into a metal as beautiful as gold, and at least as good as all goldsmiths' work; the dyeing and preparation of skins, carried to a perfection which surpassed all the moroccos in the world, and the most perfect tanning; the dyeing of silks, carried to a perfection hitherto unknown; the dyeing of woolens; the dyeing of wood in the most brilliant colours; the composition of colours for painting, ultra-marine is as perfect as is made from lapis lazuli; and finally, removing the smell from painting oils, and making the best oil of Provence from the oils of Navette, of Colsat..."

According to Isabel Cooper-Oakley:

"M. De St Germain was at Leghorn (in 1770) when the Russian fleet was there; he wore a Russian uniform, and was called Graf Saltikoff by the Graf Alexis Orloff. (It was during this time that he supplied the Russian fleet with a special Tea which he had invented to preserve the health of the troops under the severe heat). 'All his abilities, especially his extraordinary kindness,' says Heer van Sypesteyn, 'yes, even magnanimity, which formed his essential characteristics, had made him so respected and so beloved, that when in 1770, after the fall of the Duc de Choiseul, his arch enemy, he again appeared in Paris, it was only with the greatest expressions of sorrow that the Parisians allowed him to depart.....M. de St Germain came to the Hague after the death of Louis XV (May 10th, 1774)'."

"Saint Germain was in many respects a remarkable man, and wherever he was personally known he left a favourable impression behind, and the remembrance of many good and sometimes of many noble deeds. Many a poor father of a family, many a charitable institution, was helped by him in secret...not one bad, nor one dishonourable action was ever known of him, and so he inspired sympathy everywhere, not least in Holland. Thus clearly stands out the character of one who by some is called a 'messenger' from that spiritual Hierarchy by whom the world's evolution is guided."

Because of the secret missions that St Germain was carrying out, it was often necessary for him to disappear from public life and the best way to do this was by faking his death. According to Isabel Cooper-Oakley, even as St Germain, he faked his death. The date in a church register showed that he died on February 27th, 1784. However, he was next seen in February the following year, 1785 with his friend Count Cagliostro at a congress meeting at Wilhelmsbad, Germany. After this sighting of St Germain, he was reportedly seen in many places, so it is no wonder that he established the reputation of being the 'Wonder man of Europe'!

It was during the 18th century, that St Germain became a close friend of the Prince of Wales. He had once again strategically set himself up in a situation so that he could be instrumental as an adviser in sorting out the political difficulties of that time. If fate had turned out differently during the 16th century AD, St Germain would have been the Prince of Wales!

Marquis de Mirabeau (1693 - 1774 AD)

Another famous person of that era, who would have come into contact with St Germain and was most probably under his instructions, was the brilliant Francois Quesnay (1694-1774). From Daniel Boorstin's book titled *The Discoverers*, we learn that Quesnay was King Louis XV's consulting physician "who had been installed at Versailles under the patronage of Madame de Pompadour...at sixty, Quesnay had begun writing about economics, on which he had already become the King's pundit. Quesnay's *Tableau Economique* (1778), aiming to accomplish for social forces what Newton had done for physical forces, invented a whole vocabulary for the new science."

"Quesnay introduced the notion of economic classes, each with its own flow of products and receipts; he proposed the idea of economic equilibrium, and planted ideas about capital, savings, and investment, which would flower into a vast literature of economic analysis in the following centuries. His *Tableau Economique* was first printed in a small edition on the King's private press, but when Madame de Pompadour warned him of the King's certain displeasure with such flighty notions, he let the work reach the larger public under the name of the Marquis de Mirabeau."

"Quesnay's disciples, first known simply as *les economistes,* became famous as the Physiocrats, offering the first modern model for economics. Their leading ideas were quite simple. The wealth of a society consisted not in its store of gold and silver but in its total stock of commodities, and the best way to increase that stock was to allow the free flow of products in the market without monopolies or tax restrictions. These pioneer economists were appalled by the poverty of the French peasants in stark contrast to the luxury of the nobles, the tax-farmers and other monopolists. 'Poor peasants, poor kingdom', they proclaimed, 'poor kingdom, poor king'."

"Their remedy for the nation's ills focussed on the plight of the peasants. Improve the techniques of agriculture, remove all blocks to the flow of goods, abolish all existing taxes and all the tax-farmers, and instead establish a single tax on the product of the soil to be collected by honest government officers."

If Louis XIV had only listened to Quesnay, he might have prevented much misery for France and saved his great great grandson, Louis XVI from the guillotine.

MASTERS DISCUSSED IN THIS CHAPTER

Apollonius of Tyana (1st century AD) - St Germain
Francis Bacon (16th century AD) (Shakespeare - St Germain)

NOTES AND RECOMMENDED READING

Isabel Cooper-Oakley, _Comte De St Germain_, (Theosophical Publishing House, U.S.A., 1985)

Alfred Dodd, _Francis Bacon's Personal Life Story_, (Rider & Co., U.K., 1986)

Dr Raymond Bernard, _The Great Secret Count Saint Germain_, (U.S.A.)

Daniel Boorstin, _The Discoverers, A History of Man's Search To Know His World And Himself_, (Random House, U.K. 1983)

Peter Dawkins, _Francis Bacon Herald of the New Age_ (Francis Bacon Research Trust, Warwick, U.K., 1997)

F.J. Dennett, _Europe A History_, (Linehan & Shrimpton Pty Ltd., Melbourne, Vic. Australia, 1961)

Rosemary Ellen Guiley, _Encyclopedia of Mystical & Paranormal Experience_ (Grange Books, London, U.K. 1991)

Arnold J. Toynbee, _A Study of History_, (Oxford University Press, U.K., 1934)

J.J. Cosgrove & J.K. Kreiss, _Two Centuries_, (Whitcombe & Tombs Pty Ltd., Australia 1969)

C.W. Leadbeater, _The Hidden Life In Freemasonry_, (Theosophical Publishing House, U.K., 1975)

Francis Hitching, _World Atlas Of Mysteries_, (Pan Books, U.K., 1978)

Charles Lyte, _Sir Joseph Banks_, (David & Charles, U.S.A., 1980)

Madame Helena Blavatsky, _The Secret Doctrine_, (Theosophical Publishing House, U.S.A, 1966)

CHAPTER 46

The French Revolution

"Some years will come to pass by in a deceitful calm,
then from all parts of the kingdom will spring up men
greedy for vengeance, for power, and for money;
they will overthrow all in their way.....
Civil war will burst out with all its horrors;
it will bring in its train murder, pillage, exile.
Then it will be regretted that I was not listened to."
(St Germain)

As prophets, both St Germain and his friend the Comte Cagliostro had foreseen the beginning French Revolution. St Germain did his utmost to warn King Louis and Marie-Antoinette, but to no avail, the consequence of which resulted in the historical storming of the Bastille in 1789.

The Revolution was inevitable; the people demanded a fairer system of government, one that would not drain the people through heavy taxes. The peasants of that time lived in extremely poor conditions whilst the nobles and royalty, lived above their means. It was a time in history, when there was a great deal of corruptness and greed. Dictatorial monarchies ruled most of Europe surrounded by the nobles of the aristocracy. There was no fair distribution of wealth; it was from one extreme to the other and people were starving.

Because of his position as a diplomat and adviser to King Louis, St Germain had many enemies in the Court of Versailles. They were powerful men, who were greedy and suspicious of the Comte's activities. Many suspected him of being a sorcerer who could conjure up incredible wealth by manifesting gold and beautiful gem stones. They did not understand St Germain's ability of being the 'Grand Alchemist'. Notwithstanding this however, they still wished to acquire his knowledge and wealth. As a result of this he was always being spied upon, however, because of his clairvoyant abilities, he knew just who his enemies were and what they were plotting.

Only the truly enlightened intimates of St Germain's circle knew the truth about his royal background, that he was the son of Elizabeth I of England. Those who were not envious or jealous of him agreed that he was of 'noble' birth, a very gentle man with exquisite manners and they accepted that he was a 'man of mystery' and were always glad to make his acquaintance.

In the years prior to the Revolution, St Germain had been a good friend of King Louis XV and had been one of his diplomatic advisers, as he had also been to King Louis XIV. His career as a diplomat was not confined to the French Court, for he was a great friend of many of the other royal and noble families of Europe. Letters and documents exist which relate of his travels and the people whom he visited; however, as he was most elusive, it was difficult to fill in some of the gaps when there were years that no mention was made of him.

One of St Germain's enemies was the Prime Minister, Monsieur de Maurepas and one of the prophecies of St Germain was that de Maurepas would wreak havoc on the Kingdom of France, after which time, Napoleon Bonaparte would become emperor of France. St Germain explained to Madame d'Adhemar, a close friend of Queen Marie Antoinette that he would not stay in Paris for long because he knew from his prophetic powers, that he would be arrested upon the orders of de Maurepas.

As discussed in a previous chapter, St Germain had always been on exceptionally good terms with the Austrian Hapsburg family, to which Marie Antoinette belonged. Throughout the childhood of Marie Antoinette, until the time that she married Louis XVI in 1770, St Germain had watched protectively over the young Queen.

It was most unfortunate that the King was so influenced by St Germain's enemy, Monsieur de Maurepas. However, with the assistance of friends such as Count Cagliostro, St Germain continued his undercover surveillance.

Although the warnings were given several years prior to the commencement of the downfall of the House of Bourbon, when all concerned failed to take notice, there was very little that St Germain could do, except watch and observe as the stage was set.

There were many times throughout St Germain's life that he had feelings of futility and disappointment. He felt disheartened when people failed to heed his advice which led to their untimely end. When given advice, people either choose to listen or disregard it and then their fate is sealed.

Although the Masters choose to reincarnate at a certain time in history when some major event is to take place in order that they may advise and be of assistance, they cannot force anyone to obey, for the Creator gave us the gift of 'free will'. In the evolution of the world, there are many catastrophes that could have been prevented, numerous wars would not have taken place and many lives would have been saved, if only those who were warned had listened. Although something is predictable, that does not mean that history cannot be changed.

The Masters are able to warn people, and this includes the 21st century when we are on a similar self-destructing pattern as Atlantis aeons ago. However, if no-one listens, then fate plays out its cards. History continually repeats itself and time does not change this because humanity chooses to ignore the lessons of the past. It has been said that 'we learn from history that we do not learn from history'.

King Louis XIV (1638 - 1715 AD)

The Sun King (Grandfather of Louis XVI) of the Palace of Versailles, Louis XIV was born in 1638 at Saint-Germain in Paris. His father was Louis XIII and his Habsburg mother, was Anna of Austria.

Louis' grandmother was Marie de Medici and his grandfather was Henry IV. Marie was the daughter of Francesco de Medici, grand duke of Tuscany. Marie married Henry IV (1589-1610) in 1600 and their son was Louis XIII who married Anna of Austria.

Henry IV's first wife was Margaret of Valois, the daughter of the notorious Catherine de Medici and Henry II. Margaret, the reader will recall, was the beautiful 'Marguerite', Queen of France, whom Francis Bacon - St Germain loved dearly to whom he dedicated his fabulous Sonnets. The fact that Louis XIV's great great grandson, Louis XVI was to marry Queen Marie Antoinette, (who according to St Germain was an incarnation of Margaret of Valois), would not have been coincidental.

(Margaret de Medici, St Germain's 'Margurerite' of Valois who married Henry IV, had an older brother Francois II of France who married Mary Queen of Scots in 1558. Francois became King of France after the assassination of his brother, Henry III. He died of an ear infection in 1560, and Mary Queen of Scots, returned to Scotland where in 1565, she married her cousin, Henry Stewart, Lord Darnley. They became the parents of James 6th of Scotland, who became King James 1st of England).

(Marguerite's younger brother who was also called Francois [1554-1584] was known as the Duke of Alencon and the Duke of Anjou. It was this Francois who courted Elizabeth I, mother of Francis Bacon - St Germain).

The kind things that could be said of Louis XIV, the 'Sun King', were that he was very gracious, dignified (which some were to call 'arrogant') and charming. History mainly remembers Louis for the construction of his enormous palace, the palace of Versailles which became known as the 'Sun Palace'.

For political reasons, Louis had married Marie Therese who was the daughter of King Philip IV of Spain. Louis XIV was known for his notorious affairs and when Queen Marie Therese died in 1683, Louis secretly married the governess of his children, Madame Francoise Scarron.

One of his more notorious mistresses was Marquise de Montespan, who was considered to be a sinister woman who dabbled in 'witchcraft', practicing the 'black arts' in order to keep the King infatuated with her. In fairness to Louis, Madame de Montespan may well have been the driving force that urged him on a path of arrogance and greed. There is the old saying 'behind every good man is a good woman' - but this was a complete reversal!

Louis' children by Marie Therese loathed Madame de Montespan who bore him eight children whom he recognized as legitimate, probably because she forced him to. It was an unfortunate relationship because of the power she yielded over the King. Madame de Montespan was feared by everyone who came into contact with her and her greed knew no bounds.

It was the vanity of King Louis XIV, probably prompted by Madame de Montespan, which helped to bankrupt France, long before his great grandson Louis XV was to inherit the throne. History records that the building of the Palace of Versailles was to satisfy the arrogance of the King who totally disregarded the cost in money. The Palace took fifty years to complete and more than thirty thousand workmen were employed, many of who were forced into labour and never paid wages. Their living conditions were so bad that hundreds died from epidemics. However, despite the turbulent years that the palace has undergone, and the many rulers who have lived there, it still stands today as a glorious monument to the past.

The Palace is enormous, very imposing and surrounded by beautifully landscaped gardens with fountains. Just inside the entrance of the palace before the great marble staircase that leads up to the famous Hall of Mirrors, there is the beautiful small chapel in which the royalty of France were wed. After leaving the chapel, tourists are directed to climb the marble stair case. It is easy to imagine the elegant, jewelled adorned ladies of those times, sweeping graciously down the stairs in their beautiful ball gowns.

One of the unusual features about the bedrooms was that they all led from one to the other, with no privacy or toilets. The main passage faces out towards the enormous gardens below which seemed to extend as far as the horizon. On our visit there, our Guide informed us that there were secret passages behind the walls with secret entrances to the bedrooms for those who wished to carry out a clandestine affair and obviously these passages were frequently used by the Sun King himself.

On our visit there, The Hall of Mirrors was our favourite place with all its beautiful chandeliers reflected in the hundreds of mirrors. The sheer cost that would have been involved in the decor of this room alone, was beyond comprehension. It was also a wonderful experience to have visited the Palace that

St Germain had frequented which was later to become the Palace of Napoleon, after the French Revolution.

As a consequence of the extravagance by the Sun King, his future descendants were to inherit the enormous upkeep of this fabulous palace. This surely was the beginning of the downfall of the Kingdom of France. The descendants of the workers, who had died in the building of Versailles, would have known of the hardship and poverty which their ancestors had to endure at the expense of the folly of the King and so through at least two generations onwards, the resentment would have been brewing.

Toward the end of his long reign, he lost both his son and grandson. Louis died on the 1st September, 1715 and was succeeded by his great great grandson, Louis XVI.

Queen Marie Antoinette
(1755-1793)

Marie Antoinette was the daughter of Marie Theresa who founded the Hapsburg Lorraine Houses - the Imperial House of Austria and Hungary and her father was the Holy Roman Emperor, Charles VI. From previous chapters we have learnt that St Germain had a close association with the Hapsburg family and some of the secret records had been hidden by the Habsburgs in their courts.

According to St Germain, she had been a queen (Queen Marguerite) in a previous life, one in which she had been a noble and responsible Queen; however, by reincarnating as Queen Marie Antoinette, she had 'chosen' to 'play' the part of an irresponsible Queen in order to bring about the downfall of the monarchy to make way for a fairer system of government. This was quite a common theme throughout the history of the world when certain events were destined to occur in order for reform to be established. It was not unusual for kings and queens to reincarnate as future kings and queens, and confirmation of this is that Henry II, Plantagent is said to have later reincarnated as Henry VIII, Tudor King of England. The ancient Kings of Egypt also incarnated over and over again as pharaohs.

In Alfred Dodd's book titled *Francis Bacon's Personal Life Story*, he relates how after she was divorced from King Henry IV of France (whose second wife was Marie de Medici), Margurerite retired into semi-private life in a mansion near the River Seine, facing the Louvre Palace. This same palace which today is Paris' famous art gallery which displays the *Mona Lisa* by Leonardo da Vinci, became one of the palaces of Marie Antoinette. I wonder if Marguerite knew then, as she spent her last years gazing across at the Palace, that she would one day be Queen of that Palace.

To illustrate further that Marguerite was a 'noble and responsible Queen', I refer to information given by Alfred Dodd relating to her retirement years in Paris.

"Marguerite seems to have spent much of her time in serious reflection and devotion. She spent large sums in founding and endowing hospitals, convents, churches and colleges. An estimate of her gifts mounted to 120,000 livres a year without counting her private alms. Richelieu said, 'She preferred to give to an undeserving person than to fail to give to one who was deserving'."

From her early youth, St Germain watched over and protected Marie Antoinette. It must have sometimes been rather an emotional time for him, knowing that she had once been his beloved 'Marguerite'.

(It is noteworthy that Marie Antoinette's ancestors were the Merovingian's and it will be remembered that it was mentioned in an earlier chapter that the Merovingians' capital was the French town of Avallon, which was part of the kingdom of Aquitaine. They were a Germanic people who were also known as the Franks and they claimed their lineage of descent from Noah. They are thought to have derived ultimately from Troy or Arcadia. One of the most sacred Merovingian symbols was the 'bee'. King Childeric I was the most famous and influential of all Merovingian rulers and his tomb contained about three hundred miniature bees made of solid gold, which were entrusted to Leopold Wilhelm von Habsburg of Austria).

In her early teenage years, Marie Antoinette wed the teenage King Louis XVI, bringing together two great royal houses. The young King Louis adored Marie Antoinette, however, because of their youth it was several years before their marriage was consummated. Her husband lavished presents upon her and she gradually became spoilt. In Marie's youth, her mother Queen Therese had been very strict upon her and in her wisdom, continued to pay visits to her daughter when Marie became the Queen of France, warning her of her extravagances and of the political intrigues which surrounded her and her husband; however, the warnings like those of St Germain, fell upon deaf ears.

It is known that St Germain gave assistance to three Bourbon Kings, Louis XIV - the Sun King, Louis XV and Louis XVI.

King Louis XVI and Queen Marie Antoinette

Louis XVI was born at the Palace of Versailles in 1754. In defence of Louis XVI, it could be said that he was born into luxury and that he neither knew nor could imagine any other way of life. The same could be said for his bride. He ascended the throne when he was twenty years old.

Marie Antoinette was considered to be quite thoughtless and a great lover of pleasure. History records her great extravagances and seeming indifference to the poverty of her people. This is not an accurate description of Marie Antoinette. When Louis married Marie Antoinette, it was not only a marriage that aligned two great houses, but one that was a love match. Louis was only sixteen years old, one year older than Marie who was only fifteen years old at the time, a very young age to become a Queen. They were just children in the beginning, surrounded by courtiers, spies and officials. The Court of Versailles was no different from any other court of those times and there are letters and diaries mentioning conversations with Marie Antoinette in which she writes of how fearful she was at times, and that she felt that there were very few people in whom she could place her trust. One of these was the Comte de Germain and the other was Madame d'Adhemar.

Someone, whom Marie greatly feared, was Cardinal Duc de Rohan who had been the French ambassador at the court of her mother, Marie Therese, when Marie was still a young girl. He was later to join the Court of King Louis and he was anti-Hapsburg. He became involved in the scandal of the 'Necklace of Misfortune', which served as the catalyst in bringing about the downfall of Marie Antoinette, as we shall shortly see.

When the English settlers in North America revolted against Britain, Louis decided he would take the opportunity to take revenge upon the English for his lost Canadian colonies and he granted permission to the Marquis La Fayette and other French lords to help the Americans fight for their independence. In 1778, he declared war on the English and sent an army to America. The Treaty of Versailles in 1783 recognized the independence of the United States of America.

One year later, in 1784, St Germain is recorded as having approached Madame d' Adhemar, Queen Antoinette's close friend, and warned her that the reign of Louis XVI would be a fatal one. St Germain pleaded with her to do what she could to persuade Marie Antoinette to listen.

He explained to Madame d'Adhemar that there was no ill-will towards the royal family or the nobility, but that a new plan of government was to come into existence and that there was still time to warn the nobility and as stated previously, St Germain even predicted the rise of power of Napoleon Bonaparte which would occur after the Revolution.

The following day, the Queen gave an audience to St Germain and he patiently foretold all the events that would happen, if she and the King failed to take action. In the book *Comte De St Germain* by Isabel Cooper-Oakley, the conversations between St Germain and Marie Antoinette are mentioned for they were recorded in a diary by her friend Madame d'Adhemar who was present at the meeting.

St Germain warned Marie Antoinette that *"some years yet will pass by in a deceitful calm; then from all parts of the kingdom will spring up men greedy for vengeance, for power and for money; they will overthrow all in their way"*. He then continued to tell her that a civil war would be the end result bringing a train of murder, pillage and exile. St Germain warned her that one of his own enemy's, Monsieur de Maurepas, (who was the Prime Minister of France) whom the Queen trusted, would be one of the men behind her downfall.

The Queen told St Germain that she trusted his advice because she knew he had been an intimate friend of her father-in-law, Louis XV, who had relied so much upon the Comte's diplomatic abilities. However, she could not be convinced that the Monsieur de Maurepas was her enemy, nevertheless, she conceded to speak to her husband the King.

After the meeting, the St Germain confided in Madame d'Adhemar that he already knew in advance, the outcome of the meeting that Marie Antoinette would have with the prime minister and the King. St Germain told her that de Maurepas would draw up a warrant of arrest against him and would issue orders of execution, and furthermore, that he knew if he did not leave France, he would end up in the Bastille!

Madame d'Adhemar in jest replied, "What would it matter to you? You would get out through the key-hole."

St Germain replied, **"I prefer not to need recourse to a miracle, farewell Madame."**

The prediction came true for upon hearing that St Germain was in Paris, Monsieur de Maurepas gave orders to have him arrested. It was in this same year of 1784, that St Germain faked his death as St Germain so that he could continue to work anonymously.

The Necklace of Misfortune

Back in the year 1772, Madame du Barry who was the mistress of Louis XV, was determined that Louis should purchase a diamond necklace for her, one that would be the most expensive in the world, one that she obviously felt would give her the prestige that she was lacking! The court jeweller designed and made the necklace which by today's values would probably have fetched around $6 million dollars. Before the jeweller received payment for the necklace, King Louis XV, developed smallpox and died. The jeweller tried to interest the new heir to the throne, Louis XVI and his Queen Marie Antoinette into buying the necklace, however, Marie was not in the slightest bit tempted, for she considered it to be ostentatious.

Cardinal de Rohan, who had been the French ambassador at the court of her mother, Marie Therese, when Marie was still a young girl and whom Marie loathed and distrusted, had a notorious reputation with women and she continued to thwart his ego. As Cardinal of the Roman Catholic Church, as well as a courtier, he amassed a fortune in bribes, much of which was spent upon his mistresses.

Hoping to win her affection, de Rohan was tricked by a certain Countess de Lamotte, into buying the necklace for Marie Antoinette. The Countess was to secretly deliver the necklace to the Queen but the Countess had contrived with her husband to have him take it to London where the stones were broken up and sold to several of London's best known jewellers.

It was to be several months before Cardinal de Rohan realized that Marie Antoinette had never been the recipient of the necklace. Marie Antoinette was extremely angry and loathed the Cardinal even more. Somehow, the Countess de Lamotte, who by now was extremely wealthy, managed to have St Germain's friend, Count Cagliostro and his wife Lorenza, jailed for stealing the necklace and charged with fraud.

In his defence, Marie Antoinette demanded that the case go before Parliament and eventually Count Cagliostro and his wife were cleared. The Countess de Lamotte was found guilty and thrown into prison although somehow, she mysteriously escaped. The revolutionaries considered her to be the innocent victim who had been 'framed' and so it is thought that they aided her escape to England.

The case became known as 'The Queen's Necklace Affair', and the word 'affair' was ambiguous. This unfortunate necklace was to bring misfortune on several people. The citizens of France blamed Marie Antoinette and believed that she really was having an 'affair' with Cardinal de Rohan. The 'mud' had stuck and could not be removed. The whole incident served to escalate the onset of the Revolution by the anger felt by the people. They really believed that the necklace was given by the Cardinal, to Marie.

Count Cagliostro, who was always held in suspicion because of his undercover work with St Germain, was never thought to be entirely innocent either for there were certain people (enemies in the Court) who kept on fuelling the rumours.

The Final Days

In May 1789, St Germain advised his friend the King, to establish a constitutional monarchy in order to replace the old royal system that had been used for centuries and was no longer working. However, the King and Queen were quite distracted at the time for their elder son, the Dauphin who was only seven years old, was gravely ill and he died a month later on the 4th June. With the months of worrying about their son's health and his untimely death, very little attention was paid by either parent, to the political climate of the time.

The resentment amongst the people built up to a fever pitch and when the peasants were on the way to the palace, there is a legend that tells of how a guard rushed to the King to inform him. The guard said to the King "Sire, the peasants are revolting!" and the King replied, "Oh, I know they are revolting!" This statement of the King, if true, typified the lack of feeling that he held for his people. However, it should be taken into consideration that both the King and Queen were in mourning for their lost child and probably could not concentrate on the more serious problem of the impending Revolution.

The Storming of the Bastille and the Palace of Versailles

By the 14th of July, 1789, the people stormed the Bastille and then three weeks later on the 4th August; the National Assembly abolished all feudal rights and the privileges of the aristocracy. Pressure was placed upon Louis by the members of the nobility who were thoroughly alarmed at the way things were set in motion, for they had so much to lose. Louis gathered some forces together hoping to attempt a coup but word of this reached the ears of the peasants and a large mob marched from Paris to Versailles on the 6th October. They raided the Palace of Versailles and took Louis and Marie Antoinette as prisoners to their Tuileries royal palace in Paris. The French Revolution ended in 1789.

Two years later, in June 1791, by then thoroughly frustrated with their confinement, Louis and Antoinette carried out the plans of their escape. They left in a large coach and headed for the freedom they hoped to attain. However, a warrant was issued for their arrest and they were soon captured and imprisoned. There was a trial that lasted for several weeks but the facts were stacked against them and as history records, they both met their death at the Palace de la Concorde, on the guillotine.

In 1793, Louis was condemned to death and his kinsman, the Duke of Orleans, was one of those responsible for voting the death penalty and the following day, Louis was taken to the guillotine. (The guillotine was named after its inventor Doctor Guillotin).

One of the charges that were trumped up in court against Marie Antoinette, was the 'Queen's Necklace Affair' and her persecutors refused to believe her innocence. This was one of the main charges that they used to blemish her reputation, making her out to be extremely extravagant and ruthless. How sad, that a mistress of her husband's grandfather (Louis XV), Madame du Barry, by now long gone, who through her own greed, could cause so much misfortune in a future generation.

As a result of the false charges that were brought against the Queen, Marie Antoinette went to the guillotine on 16th October, 1793. In her final hours, St

Germain comforted her till the end. For the second time in his life, St Germain had lost his beloved 'Marguerite'.

Louis XVII

The Missing Heir to the throne and the Bourbon Inheritance

The young son, of Marie Antoinette, was Louis XVII (who was about ten years old at the time of her death), had been placed in the care of a couple and it was rumoured that he died in 1795, two years after the death of his mother. However, other rumours stated that a substitution of another child had taken place and that the future Dauphin had escaped. If this was the case, then it is indeed highly probable that St Germain was behind the plan. It stands to reason that he would do his utmost to protect Marie Antoinette's son and in her final hours, she may have influenced him to do so.

Over the years there were many pretenders claiming to be the Dauphin and descendants are still making claims to the Bourbon royal wealth. Because of the persistent rumours, the body was exhumed in 1846 and the two doctors who carried out the examination, claimed that the body was that of a sixteen year old.

In 1894, the body was again re-examined and the same confirmation was made, that it was that of a sixteen to eighteen year old. In 1833, a claimant to the throne appeared whose name was Karl Wilhelm Naundorff and he seemed to have strong evidence to support his claim. However, his sister Marie Therese refused to see him in order to identify him, for she gave full support to her uncle Charles who had proclaimed himself as Louis the King of France. The whole story is very similar to that of the missing child of the Czar of Russia, the Grand Duchess, Anastasia who survived but would not be recognised by her family, the Romanovs.

Rulers of France after the death of King Louis XVI

Napoleon Bonaparte I, Italian by birth, was born in 1769 at Ajaccio on the island of Corsica. He was crowned Emperor of France in 1804 in the Cathedral of Notre-Dame-de-Paris. His excellent statesmanship, coupled with his great military victories, won him the support of all Frenchmen except the royalists who wanted to restore the Bourbon monarchy.

Napoleon's fleet was defeated in the Battle of Trafalgar in 1805 by the English Admiral, Lord Horatio Nelson. Napoleon undoubtedly had his part to play in history; however, he made the mistake of becoming too power hungry and was finally defeated by the English at the famous Battle of Waterloo on June 15th, 1815.

He surrendered to the British and was exiled for life to St Helena.

According to the authors J.J. Cosgrove and J.K. Kreiss in their book titled *Two Centuries*:

"Napoleon Bonaparte, one of the greatest men who ever lived, failed in the end because, like many another great man, he attempted to do too much. He did not have sufficient men to hold his extensive Empire of Europe in subjection."

"As we contemplate his fall, and, in particular, his gravest errors, we may distinguish three destroying weaknesses in his character: as a 'man without a country', and Italian ruling France, he could not understand that nationalism could be so ardent that it would impel ordinary men and women to burn their homes and barns to prevent their falling into enemy hands; as an agnostic, he could not understand why his treatment of the Pope should have raised intense religious fervour against him; and as a man of almost tireless mental and physical energy, he could not understand that the strength of most men is strictly limited. [In 1809, Napoleon annexed the Papal States because Pope Pius VII refused to enforce the Continental System. Pious VII then excommunicated Napoleon who retaliated by imprisoning him at Fontainebleau]."

Louis XVIII, (the uncle of the Dauphin prince mentioned under the previous heading), then became King of France and he reigned until his death in 1824. However, he did not have the power to rule as his ancestors had for the French Revolution had achieved its aim with the establishment of a fairer system of government.

Upon Louis's death, Charles X became the next King but he made the mistake of attempting to return to the old system wherein he ruled by divine right. History records him as being a true example of the Bourbons who 'had learnt nothing and forgotten nothing'. His coronation took place at Rheims in 1825 and it was to be the last coronation of a King of France. Charles made the fatal mistake of illegally dissolving the elected Chamber of Deputies and this was a fine example of his arrogance and ignorance. By this act, he was totally ignoring the history of the previous years and the reasons why the new government had been established.

On the 28th July, 1830, a revolt broke out and once again Paris was under siege. Charles and his elder son were forced to abdicate, thus ended the reign of the Bourbon kings of France during which time St Germain had been in the diplomatic service on behalf of three of them.

NOTES AND RECOMMENDED READING

Isabel Cooper-Oakley, *Comte De St Germain*, (Theosophical Publishing House, U.S.A., 1985)

Dr Raymond Bernard, *The Great Secret Count Saint Germain*, (Penn. U.S.A.)

F.J. Dennett, *Europe, A History*, (Linehan & Shrimpton, Melbourne, Australia, 1960)

Arnold J. Toynbee, *A Study Of History*, (Oxford University Press, London, 1934)

J.J. Cosgrove and J.K. Kreiss, *Two Centuries*, (Whitcombe & Tombs Pty Ltd., Australia, 1969)

Francis Hitching, *World Atlas Of Mysteries*, (Pan Books, U.K., 1978)

CHRONLOGY OF EVENTS

We may divide Bacon's (St Germain's) long life into the following chronological periods taken from information contained in Isabel Cooper-Oakley's book titled *The Comte De St Germain*, Francis Hitching's book titled *The World Atlas of Mysteries*, and Dr Raymond Bernard's work titled *The Great Secret, Count Saint Germain*.

1561-1626?	Life of Francis Bacon.
1603:	Death of Queen Elizabeth 1st, Tudor, mother of Francis Bacon
1603:	James the 6th of Scotland becomes James the 1st of Britain.
1626:	Francis Bacon faked his death and went to the Continent. He is thought to have initially stayed with Elizabeth ex-Queen of Bohemia who was the daughter of James I (Stuart) of England (James 6th of Scotland).
1642:	Civil war broke out between the Puritan Parliament of Britain and the followers of King Charles I.
1644:	Oliver Cromwell led the Parliamentary forces (the 'Roundheads') to victory at the Battle of Marston Moor. Charles I fled to Paris.
1646:	Charles 1st surrendered himself to the Scots. Was taken to trial in England and publicly beheaded.
1649:	Oliver Cromwell led a bloody campaign in Ireland. Even today, the saga is still deeply imbedded in the memories of the Irish.
1650:	A meeting was held in the Dutch town of Breda between Scots and Irish commissioners, not long after Oliver Cromwell had led the ruthless campaign in Ireland and Scotland. The meeting was reputedly attended by Charles II (Stuart) who was residing at Breda. St Germain was also reputedly in attendance.
1658:	A sigh of relief was felt all over Britain and Ireland when the news of the death of Oliver Cromwell was released.
1670:	Francis Bacon travelled western across Europe and appeared as the famous *Polish Rider* who delivered a series of discourses to Abbe Monfaucon de Villars. The work was titled *Comte de Gabalis* which first appeared anonymously and which was subsequently reprinted in 1715, 1742 and later in 1910, which edition had a picture of the *Polish Rider* on the frontispiece, represented as being the unknown author who came from the direction of Germany.
1676-1735:	St Germain was 'reputedly' born into the Ragoczy family of Transylvania in 1676 as Franz (Francis) II.
1685:	Death of Charles II Stuart King of England. He was succeeded by his brother James VII.

1687:	It is well documented that St Germain appeared in Venice using the pseudonym of Signor Gualdi, in 1687. He was described as being a middle-aged man. Prince Francis Ragoczy (born 1676) would only have been 11 years old then.
1688:	Prince William of Orange and his wife Mary nee Stuart, invited to England where they were duly crowned in February, 1689. When James learned of their arrival he fled in exile to France.
1694:	Francis Ragoczy II (born 1676) married Princess Charlotte-Amalie (born 1678) von Hesse-Rheinfels who was the daughter Karl Hesse born 1649, and his second wife, Countess Leiningen-Westerberg.
1694:	St Germain, using the title of Prince Ragoczy, had a meeting in Germany with Prince William of Orange (King of England).
1701:	The composer, Rameau met St Germain who accordingly looked about 50 years old.
1710:	The Countess von Georgy had seen and spoken to St Germain in Venice and said that he looked to be about 45 to 50 years of age at that time. He also visited Holland. In the following years he made appearances using the titles of:

1. the Marquis de Montferrat,
2. Comte Bellamarre in Venice,
3. Chevalier Schoening at Pisa in Italy,
4. Chevalier Weldon at Milan and Leipzig,
5. Comte Soltikoff at Genoa and Leghorn,
6. Prince Ragoczy in Dresden.

1735:	St Germain visited the Hague in Holland.
1735:	Death of Prince Ragoczy, Francis II.
1737-1742:	St Germain visited Persia where the East India Company had a trading post. He spent time at the Court of the Shah of Persia.
1742:	St Germain visited Holland. Visited Versailles and King Louis XV.
1742:	Book published bearing the name of *Comte de Gabalis* - a mask for St Germain.
1743:	St Germain famed at the Court of Louis XV. He appeared to be about 40 to 45 years of age. The composer Rameau was surprised to find St Germain looking the same age as he had in 1701.
1743:	Birth of Sir Joseph Banks - incarnation of the Master Kuthumi.
1744-1745:	St Germain visited London and the Prince of Wales (George). Spent two years in London, during which time he composed music, operas and violin pieces.
1745:	Charles Edward Stuart, known as the 'Young Pretender' marched from Edinburgh to fight King George's army. St Germain was

sighted in Scotland in the company of the Provost of Edinburgh. This was during the Jacobean Revolution, at which time St Germain was suspected of being a French spy and was arrested because the English were suspicious of anyone who was French, owing to the fact that the French had aided Charles. St Germain was questioned and soon released.

According to correspondence between two Englishmen at that time, St Germain had been in Edinburgh for two years.

1748: St Germain visited Holland. He paid at least two visits to India.

1749: King Louis XV of France employed St Germain on diplomatic missions.

1755: St Germain spent time with General Clive of the East India Company.

1757: St Germain spent time in Paris with Louis XV who gave him rooms at the Royal Chateau of Chambord and allotted him a laboratory where St Germain taught students the study of Alchemy (chemistry and physics). St Germain was seen again by the Countess von Georgy then in her seventies who was astonished to find him looking as youthful as their first encounter in 1710. When she questioned him about his age, he said "Madame I am very old". She replied that he must be nearly 100 years old and St Germain replied "That is not impossible".

1760: Visited Holland.

1760-1762: St Germain went upon a mysterious mission to England as an envoy, followed by a temporary retirement to Holland to continue his work. He had a meeting at the Hague with William Bentinck whose father, Hans William Bentinck (Lord Portland) a general with the army in Flanders, had sailed with William of Orange on his voyage to England when he had been elected King of England.

1762: St Germain visited St Petersburg during the reign of Peter III.

1763: St Germain spent a year in Berlin and received a visit from the Princess Amalie.

1765: St Germain spent time in Venice under the name of Marquis d'Aymar during which time he made a variety of experiments with flax, which he was bleaching to look like Italian silk. His factory employed a hundred workers.

1769: St Germain visited the island of Corsica where Napoleon lived.

1770: St Germain visited Leghorn when the Russian fleet was there; he wore a Russian uniform and used the name, Graf Soltikoff/ Saltikoff.

1770:	After the fall from grace of his arch enemy Duke de Choiseul, St Germain again appeared in Paris.
1770:	St Germain met with the American, Benjamin Franklin in Paris.
1770:	Marie Antoinette of the Hapsburg family of Austria married King Louis XVI of the House of Bourbon, France. It will be recalled that St Germain 'hid' documents at the court of the Hapsburgs.
1770:	Sir Joseph Banks (Kuthumi) sailed with Captain Cook on the *Endeavour* and discovered New Zealand and Tahiti in 1768, and Australia in 1770. Sir Joseph Banks was the founder of the colonization schemes for Australia and New Zealand.
c.1770-1774:	St Germain visited Australia.
1773:	St Germain spent time in Mantua.
1774:	After the death of Louis XV on May 10th, 1774, St Germain visited the Hague, Holland and then left for Schwalbach.
1775:	St Germain visited the United States of America where he was known as the 'Professor'. Together with George Washington and Benjamin Franklin, St Germain was a member of the committee selected by the Continental Congress to create a design for the American Flag.
1776:	On the 4th July, this 'mysterious' stranger, the 'professor' suddenly appeared in the Independence Hall and delivered a stirring message to all who were gathered there. The signing of the Declaration for Independence for America took place. St Germain was the 'invisible hand' behind the scenes who was responsible for the design of the Great Seal of America.
1777:	St Germain appeared in Leipzig as Prince Ragoczy, sometimes known as Graf Tzarolgy (the latter is an anagram for Ragotzy - Ragoczy). If St Germain (Francis Bacon) was actually re-born in 1676, as Prince Francis Ragoczy II, then by 1777 he would have been 101 years old. However, the real Prince Francis Ragoczy II had died in 1735.
1778:	Sir Joseph Banks (Kuthumi) was knighted by his good friend King George III in honour of his services. He was elected president of the Royal Society of London, founded by Sir Francis Bacon - the Society was an off-shoot of the Rosicrucian Society. Sir Joseph Banks was president of the Royal Society for 50 years and no president had ever reigned that long before. Sir Joseph Banks served on the Privy Council and became an honorary member of 40 societies, including the Imperial Academy of Sciences in St Petersburg, Russia. He mixed with and advised heads of state, kings

	and queens of Europe, and the American Philosophical Society of Philadelphia.
1778:	Czar Peter I of Russia founded a Secret Circle of Freemasons with the assistance of St Germain.
c.1779:	St Germain visited Hamburg, then visited Prince Karl of Hesse and stayed with him.
1784:	Back in Paris, St Germain fruitlessly warned Marie Antoinette of a 'gigantic conspiracy' which would overthrow the order of things. St Germain faked his death on the 27th February, 1784 in Germany - after which time there followed many appearances of him amongst the various groups of Freemasons throughout Europe.
1785:	St Germain attended a Masonic conference in Wilhelmsbad, Germany.
1788:	St Germain was again active in France, giving ominous warnings to the nobility on the eve of the Revolution. St Germain was seen and recognised in Venice.
1789:	St Germain departed for Sweden to try to prevent ill befalling King Gustavus III and before his departure informed his friend Madame d'Adhemar (who thought he still looked about 45 years old) that he would see her five more times. Each visit did eventuate.
1790:	After the storming of the Bastille, Marie Antoinette received an anonymous note from St Germain, asking her for her own safety, to distance herself from certain members of the aristocracy and informing her that he would continue to communicate with her. When she failed to take notice, another note arrived in which St Germain informed her that he has done everything within his power to warn her and the King, but that alas, they had scorned his advice and now it was too late. St Germain added to the note that he would continue to watch over her, but that there was little left that he could do to save her from her enemies. Marie Antoinette, in her diaries, regretted not taking his earlier advice.
1813:	The Countess D'Adhemar was paid a visit by St Germain in January of this year.
1820:	Death of Sir Joseph Banks (incarnation of Kuthumi).
1822:	St Germain embarked upon a journey to India and Tibet and it is thought that he remained there for many years. Madame Helena Blavatsky (1831-1891), studied with the Masters in Tibet, including El Morya and Kuthumi in the 1880's. Her major work, *Isis Unveiled* was the result of their teachings.

1925: According to information contained in *The Great Secret Count Saint Germain* by Dr Raymond Bernard, A.B., M.A., PhD, St Germain made a reappearance in the West and was seen at a Masonic convention in France and, in 1933, St Germain sent a letter to the head of a Co-Masonic Society in San Jose, Costa Rica.

PART FIVE

CHAPTER 47

The Navigators & the Colonization of America As Part of the Divine Plan

"Roll on, thou deep and dark blue Ocean-roll!
Ten thousand fleets sweep over thee in vain...
The wrecks are all thy deed, nor doth remain...
He sinks into thy depths with bubbling groan,
Without a grave, unknell'd, uncoffin'd, and unknown."
(The Ocean, by Lord Byron)

"The colonization and development of the British Empire is in furtherance of the Divine
purpose. I still think that this was no accident, but part of the great purpose of the
Infinite, that we should have carried these responsibilities as we have."
(Lord Bennett, - a former Canadian Prime Minister)

"Rarely it comes, and unforeseen,
In the life of a man, a community, a nation,
The moment that knits up struggling diversity
In one, the changing transverse lights
Focussed to a pin-point's burning intensity
Rarely and unforeseen.
But in the minute is the timeless and absolute
Fulfillment of centuries and civilisations."
(The 'Jervis Bay' by Michael Thwaites)

"So, the years passed and the grandeur that was England captured the minds and the
adventuresome spirit of an awakening race. Ships set sail and conquered distant lands
and marriages were taking place to wed the courts of many nations and to begin a union
which was so heartfelt by this one whom I Loved." (Excerpt by the Lady Portia,
channelled by Claire Heartsong in the book titled *St Germain Twin Souls & Soulmates*).

As new countries were discovered as part of the 'Divine' plan, communication between other parts of the world was established. There were many during this era that brought the birth of science and technology and contributed to the sharing of plant life specie, animal and bird life, with other countries.

Some of the well known names are Marco Polo and his discovery of China, Christopher Columbus (St Germain) who discovered America, and Captain James Cook, accompanied by Sir Joseph Banks, who discovered Australia and New Zealand.

As ships set sail and conquered distant lands, marriages were taking place to wed the courts of many nations. Under the guidance of St Germain, the Freemasons were active, particularly in the shipping business. Many of those who were active in the East India Company were members of the Royal Society which had been founded by St Germain in his incarnation as Francis Bacon.

Sir John Dee, (Kuthumi) a Grand Master of the Order of the Rose Cross who had played such a major role in navigation during the Elizabethan Renaissance, reincarnated in the 18th century as Sir Joseph Banks, into a life where he would participate in a grand way in the continuity of this Order, which was so closely affiliated with the Order of the Freemasons and that of the Royal Society.

Between the 18th and 19th centuries, navigation and technology became more sophisticated as countries shared their ideas and discoveries which also resulted in competition on the 'high seas' to discover the most land as quickly as possible and with the settlement of Australia, many shipping lines were instrumental in transporting emigrants and live-stock to Australia, returning to England with our own produce.

On the list of lands to be discovered, Australia was almost the last 'port of call'. With the colonization of Australia came people of many lands, firstly the settlers and convicts from Britain whom the British termed 'the undesirables' and when the convict days were over, the Gold Rush was in full swing, resulting in Australia becoming a wealthy asset to Great Britain. It is important to remember that the convicts were transported to Australia for having committed very minor misdemeanors, such as stealing a piece of bread or fruit.

When Francis Bacon and Sir John Dee (Kuthumi) in the Elizabethan time of the mid 1500's were instrumental in founding many Freemasonic lodges in England and Europe, their great plan was to colonize the 'New Atlantis' - America. During his era as Francis Bacon, St Germain had secretly laid the groundwork for the establishment of the United States of America to be based on a utopian society which was to become a Golden Civilization.

After the colonization of America, Australia, New Zealand and Hawaii were next on the list. The founding of the East India Company was also of great importance. It was to become the most powerful company the world has ever known.

However, before entering into the story of just how these great plans eventuated, it is necessary to give some background of the navigators who were instrumental in making these plans possible.

The Navigators

The major development in Western Asia was the rise of the Ottoman Turks. The Ottoman Empire began as a minor Islamic principality in modern western Turkey, but soon its control extended over most of Asia Minor and the Balkans. The Byzantine capital, Constantinople, eventually fell to the Ottomans in 1453 AD and was renamed Istanbul.

Ottoman rule closed Middle Eastern ports to Europeans, thus blocking long-distance trade routes to the East. This was one factor behind the European quest for new sea routes to the east via the southern tip of Africa and west across the Atlantic.

The drawing together of diverse cultures gathered pace at the very end of the 15th century AD with the voyages of the Portuguese navigators Bartholomew Dias and Vasco da Gama in their voyages to the tip of Africa and the Indian Ocean. Further discoveries were made when Christopher Columbus (St Germain) made his first voyage to the Caribbean.

In just over eighty years, from 1440 to 1520 AD, European explorers had established sea routes that embraced the whole world within a vast trading system thus laying the foundations of the modern world. Many Masters reincarnated into these eras, this time as navigators, many of whom were Freemasons.

Freemasons/Knights Templar

The Freemasons, once known as the Knights Templar, were an extremely wealthy and powerful organization, involved in owning many shipping companies, having established ship- building companies and subsequent trading companies in ports of countries that their navigators had discovered, on their behalf.

Ever since the early days of the Crusades and the Knights Templar, the Knights held very strategic ports all around the Mediterranean and in particular, Malta. During the 14th century, the Order of the Knights Templar was reformed, taking the name of the Knights of Christ, which survived until the late 16th century. Its members included several famous navigators and explorers, such as Christopher Columbus and his father-in-law. Christopher Columbus inherited the charts and maps from his father-in-law which contributed to making his voyage to the New World, America, a success. Other important maps and documents came into the hands of Christopher Columbus, such as those which had belonged to Marco Polo.

Marco Polo (1254? - 1324)
Italian navigator

Kublai Khan was the ruler of the greatest empire in the Middle Ages. In the 13th century (1200's) there occurred a 'golden age' of expansion of geographical knowledge. This was one of the significant phases of new contacts between Western Europe and the Far East and it was thanks to the 'travellers' of this period who contributed much to the accumulation of geographical data related to distance, that frequently unknown areas stimulated further interest in geographical exploration.

This was further assisted by the numerous accounts of their travels and maps which had been carefully documented for posterity. In the 13th century the East was ruled by the Mongols who occupied a vast territory which stretched from the coasts of China to the eastern borders of Europe.

The date of Marco's birth and death are thought to have been 1254-1324, but what is known is that he was born into a family who were the leading 'merchants of Venice' at the time. Marco Polo's father, Niccolo, and his uncle Maffeo, travelled across land to far-off China where they were very well received by Kublai Khan and after spending some time there, the Khan appointed Marco's father and his small party, as his ambassadors. Upon their return journey to Italy in 1269, they were given a letter from the Khan to the Pope.

In 1271, Marco joined his father and uncle on a trading expedition to China and reached Peking in 1275 by way of land, visiting such places as Syria, Mesopotamia, Persia, Turkistan and across the Gobi Desert until they reached the summer resident of Kublai Khan at Shangtu. Kublai Khan's court was regarded as the political centre of the Eastern world and he ruled over an empire that was greater in territory and inhabitants that any other ruler of his time.

Marco became the favourite of Kublai Khan. He entered the Chinese civil service and later ruled the city of Yangchow for a period of three years. The Marco family spent many years living in China under the patronage of the great 'Khan' and when they were finally ready to return to Italy, the Khan gave them a sacred 'golden stone' which was to guarantee them safe conduct through his extensive lands.

As a favour to the Khan, Marco and his father and uncle had agreed to escort the Mongolian princess to the court of the Khan of Persia.

Before his death in 1292, the Khan gave them ancient sea maps which enabled them to this time return to Venice by sea and not by land. These ancient maps were to become of significant importance to Christopher Columbus (1451-1506) (St Germain) and because of the 'destined' great achievements of Marco and the great influence he had upon the Great Kublai Khan, he would have been one of the Masters of the Great White Brotherhood. When they reached the Khan of Persia, the princess was delivered safety and they spent some time there before returning to Venice in about 1295.

Within one year of their return, the Polo's were taken prisoner whilst fighting for Venice against the Genoans in 1296. Whilst imprisoned, Marco dictated his memoirs which included the visits that he had made to China, Persia, Japan, Sumatra and East Africa. His 'work' became very popular and was one of the best known travel accounts of the medieval period; in fact, it became the main source of European knowledge of China until the 19th century - a remarkable achievement!

To place events in a perspective of time, the Knights Templar were active during this era until Jacques de Molay (who was possibly the Master Kuthumi, the last Grand Master of the Knights Templar) was burned at the stake in France in the year 1314. Marco Polo died ten years later in the year 1324. St Germain had incarnated as Roger Bacon 1214? - 1294.

It was not by 'co-incidence' that an early printed edition of Marco's work came into the possession of Christopher Columbus (1451-1506), in the 15th century. This great work of Marco, which Christopher Columbus had utilised, is now preserved in the Bibliotheca Columbina in Seville, Spain.

Description of sailing vessels: The vessels used by the early navigators of this period in the 1400's were three-masted caravels, with stout hulls and a combination of square sails. These allowed the vessels to make progress in a wide range of wind conditions and made them highly maneuverable.

Products of trade: High prices were fetched in European markets on such commodities as silk from China which was one of the main products that Marco Polo had been the first to bring back with him to Venice. Silks were very popular among the ladies of the English and European courts. Other products in high demand were spices from East Asia. During this time, the ports of the Mediterranean were blocked by the expansion of the Ottoman Empire which had forced the European merchants to seek alternative routes.

The exploration of the West African coast in the 1430's and in 1498 by the Portuguese, also opened up more trade routes and thus new products when they sailed round the Cape of Good Hope and sailed east to the Indian Ocean. Some navigators are thought to have reached the top of Australia and left maps for future navigators.

John Cabot (1450 - 1498)
Italian Navigator

"Roll on, thou deep and dark blue Ocean-roll!
Ten thousand fleets sweep over thee in vain...
The wrecks are all thy deed, nor doth remain...
He sinks into thy depths with bubbling groan,
Without a grave, unknell'd, uncoffin'd, and unknown."
(The Ocean, by Lord Byron)

John Cabot was born in Genoa, one year before Christopher Columbus (St Germain) and two years before Leonardo da Vinci (Kuthumi). John and Christopher Columbus trained as seamen in Genoa before establishing themselves in different countries. John was to settle in Bristol in England, in about 1485 and as we have already seen, Christopher spent a great deal of time in Spain.

There is not a great deal known about the life of John Cabot whose son Sebastian also became a famous navigator but it is interesting to note that the Royal family in 1996, held a 'belated' ceremony of recognition of his achievements. John Cabot did spend some time in Venice in the early 1470's where he became a citizen of Venice.

A contemporary of his, later wrote that Cabot had reported having travelled as far as Mecca and been engaged in the spice trade. Upon learning that spices originated in the Far East, he had conceived a plan to reach Asia by sailing westward across the North Atlantic. There are documents in the archives of Valencia, Spain, that reveal that he had been there on his travels.

John had a theory that Asia could be reached by sailing westwards, a theory which appealed to several wealthy merchants of England who were members of the Freemasons and who agreed to give him the financial support for his voyages.

In the year 1493, reports reached Bristol, England, that John's childhood friend Christopher Columbus, had made the westward passage to Asia guided by the maps left to him by Marco Polo.

There is evidence that a Venetian calling himself Johan Caboto visited Barcelona in Spain in 1492-1493. It is generally considered that this was the John Cabot of which this story is concerned and that being in Spain at that time, he would have undoubtedly been aware of the triumphal return to Spain by his friend, Christopher Columbus.

John and his supporters began to make plans to take a more direct crossing to the Orient and the expedition was authorized on March 5th, 1496 by Henry VII King of England (father of Henry VIII and grandfather of Elizabeth I, thus great-grandfather of Francis Bacon - St Germain).

John Cabot sailed from Bristol on May 2nd 1497 on a ship called the

'*Matthew*' which headed generally North-west. He proceeded to Dursey Head, Ireland and then sailed westwards. After a rough voyage, on June 24th, they landed on Cape Breton Island, Nova Scotia, Labrador, Maine and New Foundland. Even though they were forced to turn back due to lack of supplies, the voyage was reported as being successful according to a letter from an English merchant named John Day, written to an Admiral considered to be Christopher Columbus.

Cabot formerly claimed the land for Henry VII of England and returned to Bristol in early August during which time he had an interview with King Henry on the 10th August. Although the King had given him a pension, John Cabot felt the need of more sea adventures and was not content to be retired.

By May 1498, he planned a second expedition which he hoped would bring him to Cipangu (Japan) and so with a fleet of five ships, he left Bristol via Ireland again. Unfortunately, they struck bad weather in the Irish Sea and one of the ships soon put into Ireland in distress but the fate of Cabot and the other four ships, remains a mystery. Thus, it was left to his son Sebastian to complete the plans of his father.

Sebastian Cabot (1476? - 1557)
Italian/English navigator

Sebastian Cabot is thought to have been born in Venice in 1476, during the time his father John, had become a citizen of Venice, however, the family later settled in Bristol, U.K. Sebastian was an experienced navigator and cartographer, having accompanied his father John, on his voyages. Sebastian has been credited with a voyage in search of the North-west Passage, where it is believed that he reached the coast of the present day Labrador in 1508 and cruised northwards as far as Hudson Bay, which at that time was not named until Henry Hudson later journeyed there, using maps left to him by Sebastian.

Impressed by his skills as a cartographer, Henry VIII of England engaged Sebastian to prepare maps of south-western France in preparation for an invasion by Henry and Ferdinand V King of Spain.

Ferdinand V was Henry's father-in-law when Henry married his first wife, Catherine of Aragon, the daughter of Queen Isabella. (Catherine of Aragon was the mother of Mary Tudor who was succeeded by Elizabeth I). It is of historical interest to note that Isabella and Ferdinand instituted the Spanish Inquisition in 1478 which was under royal rather than ecclesiastical control and between them they engineered the expulsion of Jews from Spain in 1492.

Whilst abroad in 1512, Sebastian entered the services of Spain and after Ferdinand died, Cabot was retained by Charles, King of Spain who later became

Charles V, Holy Roman Emperor. In 1518, Sebastian was promoted to the ranks of pilot major, chief pilot of Spain and he was generally considered to be a successor of Ferdinand Magellan.

In 1525, Sebastian received command of an expedition of exploration to the Pacific Ocean and in 1526 he reached the coast of what is now known as Brazil. *His last year of service in Spain was in 1544 whereby he had completed an engraved map of the world. This was of significant importance and a very relevant aid to future exploration.*

Sebastian returned to England and through the influence of friends and admirers in English court circles, he received a pension from King Edward 6th of England. *In 1551, Sebastian initiated the founding of the Muscovy Company of merchant adventurers which was an English trading company made up of Freemasons. He was to become governor of the company which financed an expedition to the North-West passage - a sea route from Europe to Asia whereby they engaged in trade with Asia and Russia.*

One of Sebastian's navigators, Richard Chancellor (died 1556), reached the Russian port of Archangel by way of the White Sea, laying the foundations for commercial relations between England and Russia.

The inspiration behind these navigational explorations was Sir John Dee (1527-1608), (Kuthumi). The precise date of the death of Sebastian is not known but it is believed to have been in 1557 at which time his pension payment was stopped.

Christopher Columbus (The 'Dove') (1451-1506)
St Germain

Christopher Columbus has been discussed throughout our story where it has been relevant to make mention of him, and now we learn a little more concerning his activities.

He was born in the sea port of Genoa, Italy in 1451 and was 'destined' to be a famous navigator and explorer. He was born one year after John Cabot who trained as a seaman with him in Genoa. In earlier chapters, it was mentioned that Christopher's voyages of discovery were sponsored by Leonardo da Vinci (Kuthumi), Lorenzo de Medici of Florence and King Ferdinand and Queen Isabella of Spain.

Christopher's brother, Bartholomew, was a cartographer; Christopher's father-in-law had in his possession ancient maps, plus the documents of Marco Polo, so with maps and sponsorship, Christopher Columbus set out to discover the world.

In the story of Noah, St Germain's symbol of peace was the 'Dove' and when he reincarnated as Christopher Columbus, his first name meant the 'Light

Bearer' and his surname, Columbus was Latin for the 'Dove', just like in a previous incarnation as St Columba, his name also meant the 'Dove' as did the island of 'Iona' upon which he had founded his famous Celtic monastery.

When St Germain reincarnated as Roger Bacon (1214-1294), (whose life has been briefly discussed in previous chapters), he was an English monk, philosopher, alchemist and scientist years ahead of medieval thinkers, who had written many prophecies for which his fellow monks regarded him as an 'heretic'. Sadly because of this, he was imprisoned for fourteen years and it is thought that he died in 1294, shortly after his release. During this time, he had foreseen hot air balloons, flying machines, machine-driven cars and ships. He wrote three major books for Pope Clement I, namely Opus Majus, Opus Minor and Opus Tertium.

However, his major prophecy was that he would one day return at a future time, to discover the 'New Atlantis' - America. Upon returning as Christopher Columbus, St Germain is recorded as having stated that he was just returning to fulfil the prophecy that he had made when he was Roger Bacon.

When Christopher was a widower, he journeyed to Spain in 1486 with an introduction to Queen Isabella, Queen of Castile and her husband King Ferdinand. The race was on between the European countries to find new land and thus wealth from trade. Under the instructions of Queen Isabella and her husband King Ferdinand, Christopher set sail on his ship the *Santa Maria* (Saint Mary) in the year 1492. He tried to reach East Asia by sailing west across the Atlantic but instead encountered the Caribbean islands, thus discovering America and thus fulfilling his prophecy.

After his life as Christopher Columbus, his next incarnation was as Francis Bacon, at which time St Germain wrote a work titled *The New Atlantis*, published in 1627, after the foundation of the English colonies in America, in which he projected a vision of an era of Utopia, a Golden Age and America was to be the Golden Civilization. What actually became the impetus, instigating the founding of America at an earlier time than had been planned, was the threat of the Spanish who had already started to colonize North and South America, having failed to conquer England.

During the time when the Spanish Armada invaded Britain, Francis Bacon was well aware that the Armada had carried not only troops on board, but also many agents of the Spanish Inquisition. Sir John Dee had been instrumental in setting up his own agents by the code name of OO7. In 1583, Lord Walsingham and Francis had agents everywhere, both home and abroad, pursuing the intentions of Philip II of Spain.

One plot which they discovered was to be an invasion of England via the coast of Scotland, with full Papal and Spanish backing. The plot involved the Spanish Ambassador in England, whose name was Mendoza. Their plan was to install Mary

Queen of Scots as Queen of England, thus bringing England under the rule of a Roman Catholic Queen.

It was fortunate for England that Sir John Dee, Lord Walsingham, Sir Francis Bacon and the rest of their intimate circle, were able to discover the plot and from that time onwards, an even closer surveillance was kept on Mary and her 'circle'

The Spanish Armada had been defeated by England's Sir Francis Drake in 1588 and King Philip II of Spain and Portugal died in 1598. During the early 17th century (1600's) Spain was a country with a navy of great strength which as a consequence, made her a dominant power and a successful rival of Portugal in the world of trade. Spain was fiercely Roman Catholic and had resisted all the reforms that had swept through Europe and England in the 16th century.

By decree from the Church of Rome, the extra-European world had been divided between Spain and Portugal. The whole area of the Indian Ocean had been considered to be the preserve of Portugal and Spain.

From information contained in the book titled *The Discoverers* by Daniel J. Boorstin, we learn that as early as 1504, when Prince Henry the Navigator and his successors did everything in their power to establish and preserve a monopoly over commerce with their newly discovered coasts of Africa, they would not let out the word about where the places were and how to reach them. "When King Manuel developed his plans for a pepper monopoly in 1504, he ordered that all navigating information be kept secret. 'It is impossible to get a chart of a voyage', an Italian agent complained, 'because the King has decreed the death penalty for anyone sending one abroad'."

"This policy was not easy to enforce, since the Portuguese kings had to rely on foreigners like Vespucci to do their work of discovery. In 1481 the Portuguese Cortes petitioned King John II to exclude foreigners, especially Genoese and Florentines, from settling in the country, because they habitually stole the royal 'secrets as to Africa and the islands'. Yet a few years later, the young Genoese, Christopher Columbus, went on his voyage to help the Portuguese build their fort at Sao Jorge da Mina on the Guinea coast. Still, the Portuguese conspiracy of silence was effective - at least for a while. Until the middle of the 16th century other countries seeking information about the Portuguese seafaring commerce to Asia had to rely on scraps gathered from ancient writers, casual overland travellers, occasional turncoat sailors, and spies. It was despite this policy that maps of Asia leaked out to the rest of Europe."

"The Spanish, trying to enforce a similar policy, kept their official charts in a locked box.....but all these precautions were not enough. The Venetian-born Sebastian Cabot (1476? -1557), while serving as a pilot-major to Emperor Charles V, tried to sell 'The Secret of the Strait' both to Venice and England."

By 1550 Spain had already colonized most of the Caribbean, Mexico,

California and South America. Due to the discoveries of New Foundland by John Cabot and his son Sebastian Cabot, and Henry Hudson, the English were able to colonize Newfoundland, whilst the French were busy colonizing Canada.

We learn from information contained in Peter Dawkins' book *Arcadia* the following   :

During 1583 plans were made to form a company to carry out the colonisation of 'Atlantis', as America was termed by the Dee circle. The plan was concocted between Dr John Dee and two of his circle - Adrian Gilbert and John Davis. Dee was a primary influence on the Elizabethan explorers and navigators, and his *Mathematical Preface* ....and his *General and Rae Memorials pertayning to the Perfect Art of Navigation* were the greatest of all encouragements to the development in England of mathematics, navigation and hydrography. Dee was probably the major guiding spirit behind the Elizabethan expansion - the great voyages of discovery and the colonisation in the New Worlds. He had been one of the principal advisers in the early English attempts to find a north-eastern passage to Cathay, and in the searches for a north-western passage to Cathay, and in the searches for a north-western route to the Orient. He was almost certainly involved in Sir Francis Drake's epic voyage around the world....his stories and records of the journey no doubt being eagerly assimilated by Francis and Anthony Bacon."

"In September, 1580, on the return of Drake, Dee had entered into a witnessed agreement with Sir Humphrey Gilbert that granted Dee the rights to all newly discovered territory north of the 50th parallel (i.e. the majority of what is now known as Canada); but, after reaching Newfoundland, the voyage failed when both the flagship (the *Delight*) and a sister ship (the *Squirrel*) sank, and Gilbert was drowned."

"The 1583 plans were a continuation of the 1580 agreement and voyage. One of the hopes behind the voyages of this kind was to find a direct way to the East and to the Oriental wisdom, and from this to begin to establish a *concordia mundi* and a universal faith that transcended the man-made limitations of sectarian religion... in which England (or Britain) was seen as playing a critical role. Freemasonry was probably the form envisaged that this universal faith might take. This plan formed an integral part of the Baconian *opus mundi*, and which Francis Bacon treats of (or hints at) in his *New Atlantis*."

"The 1583 expedition was not wholly successful and was somewhat tragic. The five small ships of the expedition reached Newfoundland, which were 'the first of our nation that carried people to erect a habitation in those northerly countries of America', and formally took possession of the harbour of St Johns and of the land 200 leagues in every direction. In this manner Newfoundland became the first and oldest dominion of the English Crown overseas. But Gilbert then sailed south from Newfoundland in order to explore the mainland coast, and in doing so lost the ship that carried the majority of the stores and equipment for colonisation, plus one hundred men. The expedition had no choice but to turn back, with Gilbert determined to return the following spring. But his own ship, including himself, was lost in a storm. However, what Gilbert and his explorers had accomplished was to form an impulse and a stepping-stone to the whole process of North American colonisation by Englishmen."

When James VI of Scotland, became James I of England, due to the influence of Sir Francis Bacon who was by then the Chancellor of England, the Virginia Company was set up in 1606 - being named after Elizabeth (the Virgin Queen).

The members were mostly made up of aristocrats and Freemasons who were furthering the cause of the Church of England, which was otherwise the Celtic Church under the Royal patronage of the Stuart King, James I of England. By colonizing what they could of what remained of America, the Freemasons whose original order had been the Knights Templar, Guardians of the Grail, were protecting it from the stronghold of the Church of Rome. Some of the first people to colonize America were members of the Bacon family and their friends who were members of the Order of the Rose Cross and by the 1650's the Masonic influence had spread to many of the colonies.

Henry Hudson (d. 1611)
English Navigator

The place and date of Henry's birth are unknown, as are the facts of his early life. He had the reputation of being a very skilled navigator and he made four famous great voyages of discovery. In 1607 Henry was chosen by the English Muscovy Company which had been established by Sebastian Cabot, to lead an expedition in search of the North-East Passage to China. In this particular voyage, Hudson reached Greenland and returned via a previously unexplored section of the coast of Spitsbergen. The result of this voyage was significant because it opened up very profitable whale fisheries in this area from which England benefited.

In 1609, the Amsterdam branch of the Dutch East India Company contracted Hudson to search for the North-East Passage and they reached New Foundland in July and finally anchored off New Jersey. Their ship the *Half Moon* proceeded to explore the river which is now named after him 'Hudson River'.

Upon his return to England, Hudson wished to return to Amsterdam but the English government refused him permission to continue in the service of the Dutch. The following year, the Dutch East India Company began its operations in what today is known as the Hudson River Valley. Hudson began his fourth and last voyage in April 1610 when he was contracted to a group of London merchants, some of whom were Freemasons.

This time he reached Greenland and explored the great inland body of water now known as Hudson Bay. On the return trip, the ship *Discovery* encountered icebergs and incredibly cold conditions which resulted in the crew being rebellious. They seized Hudson, his son John and several others and set them to drift without any provisions.

Sadly, nothing was ever heard of Henry Hudson and his companions again, although the *Discovery* finally reached England, but only a handful of men had survived. However, it is thanks to Henry Hudson that so many important discoveries were made which were to be to the advantage of England and future navigators.

Sir John Dee's (Kuthumi's) Influence upon the Navigators

As we have seen in previous chapters, from information contained in Peter Dawkins' book *Arcadia*, Sir John Dee (1527-1608) was known as a Renaissance 'Magus' who was totally knowledgeable in geography, navigation, mathematics, numerology, mechanics, astrology, alchemy (chemistry), Greek, Hebrew, Cabbala, Hermeticism, and astronomy. The Renaissance period was from 1440 to 1620 and corresponded to the zodiacal period of Virgo in the cycle of the Piscean Age which meant that the Elizabethan period in history would be very important.

Sir John Dee was highly skilled in the art of cartography and had written many articles on the subject of navigation. It was not by accident that many ancient maps had come into his hands for it had all been planned by the Masters, long ago and through many incarnations, particularly as navigators and explorers, and the plans were coming to fruition. It was as if they had a giant jig saw puzzle of the world which was being fitted together piece by piece. Now, with the help of many others working with Francis, the time had come to colonize the new 'Atlantis'.

It was Sir John Dee who had also been instrumental in the voyage of Sir Francis Drake's voyage around the world who returned to England in 1580. The navigational skills of Sir Walter Raleigh and Sir Francis Drake, were reminiscent of their ancestors, the Phoenicians, who were the Arcadians - the 'Bear' race, 'the Guardians of the Covenant' who navigated by the star constellation of Ursa - the 'Bear'.

Sir John Dee wrote *Mathematical Preface to Memorials pertaining to the Arte of Navigation* which was of great encouragement to navigators of the Elizabethan period. It is considered that Dee was the major guiding spirit behind the Elizabethan expansion leading to the discovery and colonisation of new worlds. Sir John Dee had been one of the principal advisers in the early attempts by the English, to reach the North-Eastern Passage to Cathay. These navigational maps would have come into his hands via Christopher Columbus (1451-1506) and Marco

Polo (1254?-1324).

Dee was also assisted by the famous cartographer Gerhardus Mercator (1512-1594) who helped him with knowledge of map-making. Mercator had within his possession, maps which showed the land of *Terra Australis*. The maps which were in his possession were thought to be a legacy from the Portuguese navigator Ferdinand Magellan's (1480-1521) voyages of discovery. Although it is generally considered by most modern day scholars, that there were earlier explorers to our coast of Australia, the maps made by Magellan were to be of significant importance.

Magellan set sail in 1519 under the instruction of the Emperor Charles V on a voyage around the world which lasted until 1521 when he met his untimely death. One of the maps depicted in an atlas made in 1570, showed a coastline which was stated as having been discovered by Magellan in 1520 which was identified as *Terra Australis* which was later to become known as Australia. A map dated 1550 which came into the possession of the British Museum in 1861, showed an island, thought to be one of the Abrolhos Group, off the coast of Western Australia. Thus, although there was knowledge and maps available for English navigators to come out and explore and colonize our country, it was put 'on hold' during the 1500's because it was planned to open up the *New Atlantis* and colonize America first.

According to Peter Dawkins in his book titled Arcadia, the epic voyage of Sir Francis Drake (1540?-1596) around the world in 1577, was instigated by Sir John Dee and backed by Sir Francis Walsingham, Robert Dudley - Earl of Leicester, and several others. When Sir Francis Drake returned to England in September 1580, an agreement was drawn up and signed that granted Dee the rights to any of the newly discovered lands. This agreement was to lay the foundations of colonization.

As Peter Dawkins comments in his book *Arcadia*, "Sir John Dee's influence upon the whole course of Elizabethan civilization was immense."

The Founding of the East India Company

In 1599, Queen Elizabeth I held at a meeting at Hampton Court with some of the London merchants, to discuss a plan to establish direct trade with the east. The charter was signed by 'Elizabeth' to the Honourable East India Company. In 1601, a fleet of five small ships were filled with cargo and sent on a voyage to trade their cargo. "On each, overhead flew the red-and-white flag of St George [Kuthumi] and England."

Whilst the fleet was away, Elizabeth died and upon their return, James I was King of England. Other voyages were undertaken and the East India Company became very profitable. From the book titled *A Maritime History of Australia* by

John Bach, we learn the following pertinent information:

"For the first three decades the most significant restriction was that created by the East India Company's monopoly of all British trade between the Cape of Good Hope and the Straits of Magellan, an area that included all the commerce of India, China, the East Indian archipelago and, of course, Australia. The monopoly, increasingly resented though it was by a large number of influential people in Britain, effectively prohibited all British ships not belonging to the company, nor enjoying special concessions granted by the company, from trading with any port within its prescribed limits."

"In practice a select group of private merchants resident in India and acceptable to the company were permitted to trade with ports in India and in the adjacent seas since the company's own ships were fully employed in conducting the trans-oceanic trade from the East to Britain. It was therefore legal for these 'country' ships to trade between the new settlements in Australia and Indian ports, but the trade from Australia to Canton, the main Chinese market, and to Britain, was reserved for company ships. Since the company did not choose to trade with the small settlement, that latter's market was restricted to India; any trade with Canton, the natural market for some of the earliest exports, or with Britain had to go through an Indian port for the trans-shipment."

The Dutch East India Company had been founded in 1602 (one year before the death of Elizabeth I) and was a powerful military and naval organization which considered the English company a potentially dangerous usurper into its trade. The London East India Company, aware of the friction between Holland and themselves, kept up its pressure in the Far East whilst at the same time, looking for new routes which would lead them to new ports in which they could trade.

From the book titled *The East India Company* by Brian Gardener:
"The rivalry between Dutch and English in the 'Spice Islands' archipelago had become intense and clashes had become almost inevitable with each voyage. The Dutch were extremely jealous of their new acquisitions, for which they had fought bitterly with the Portuguese. Although English ships were often able to hold their own, the Company was being defeated in its efforts to establish itself in this region - more highly prized than India - by sheer weight of numbers. The Dutch East India Company, an amalgamation of interests, was much richer and more powerful than its London counterpart. At length the Dutch settled the matter by a simple expedient; they massacred most of the Englishmen at the East India Company's main depot."

"The new trade with Europe had now moved beyond Java and Sumatra to the Moluccas (now all part of Indonesia). The most important British depot in the East Indies was at Ambon, which was also the capital of Dutch interests in the Moluccas. A treaty had been signed between the Dutch and the English, in 1619, on a live-and-let-live basis; the British were to be allowed one-third of the trade, and would contribute the same proportion to the cost of the forts, which were, however, to be manned by the Dutch; the treaty had solved nothing."

"In India, meanwhile, the Dutch and the English had worked together a little better. For a while they had been allies against the Portuguese: the English warring at sea and the Dutch on land. In the Arabian Gulf, the East India Company strengthened its interests by means of a treaty with Persia, a naval victory, and the capture of the important Portuguese bastion of Hormuz after a ten-week's siege. But soon the Dutch and English were at loggerheads in India, full of suspicions and accusations. In the mid-century, the Dutch took Ceylon from the Portuguese by force. The East India Company's wide interests stretched - by the standards of those days - over enormous distances, and financially it was often in extreme difficulty. The expense of its operations was frequently greater than its income and it was often in debt. But a new generation of directors was as ambitious as the founders. They persisted in increasing the operations, except in the East Indies."

"In 1640, the Company built the trading post of Fort St George - around the walls of which grew an increasing settlement - to become one day known as the great city of Madras. It was the first land to be held by the British in India. By 1670 the post had developed to about 300 English, with some 3,000 Portuguese living under their protection."

"By 1700 the English in India had taken the place of the Portuguese. The East India Company, beset with difficulties in its East Indies, Persian, and even China trade, was to make India the centre of its operations. But something even more immediately important for the English had happened. The *Compagnie des Indes Orientales* had been founded in 1664. The French had been late on the scene. There was not much yet to indicate that they would be even more dangerous rivals than the Dutch had been."

The important event to affect the East India Company was America gaining her Independence from Britain after which time, it was deemed necessary to find Terra Australis (Australia) and colonize her. (This will be discussed in greater detail in the following chapter).

America gains her Independence from Britain

"Listen, my children and you will hear
Of the midnight ride of Paul Revere
On the eighteenth of April, in Seventy-five;
Hardly a man is now alive
Who remembers that famous day and year.

He said to his friend, "If the British march
By land or sea from town to-night,
Hang a lantern aloft in the belfry arch
Of the North Church tower as a signal light, -
One, if by land, or two, if by sea..."
(Paul Revere's Ride by Henry Wadsworth Longfellow)

Paul Revere was an American patriot at the time of the struggle for independence. He was one of the leaders of the Boston 'tea-party'. He is remembered for his famous ride from Charlestown to Lexington on 18-19th April, 1775, to give warning of the approach of the British troops. The engagement that followed was the beginning of the War of American Independence.

Benjamin Franklin, writer, philosopher and scientist, was initially a Quaker but joined the Order of the Freemasons in 1731 and he was eventually to become the Grand Master of St John's Lodge. A man of numerous talents, Franklin, as a scientist, was able to harvest electricity and he is credited with having invented lightening rods, the same type that are still in use today. Franklin was a close friend of St Germain and in the first chapter, Dr Bernard was quoted, mentioning Francis Bacon's philosophy on prophesied inventions..."it has guided the thunderbolt innocuously from heaven to earth; it has lighted up the night with the splendour of the day ['electricity']..." St Germain prophesied the invention of electricity when he had been Roger Bacon in the 12th century AD. Therefore, it seems highly probable that St Germain advised Franklin on this scientific project that has so benefited man-kind.

At the time of the American Revolution, Benjamin Franklin was to become most influential in its instigation. He travelled to Paris seeking support for the American colonists and he was a guest of King Louis XVI and Queen Marie Antoinette. Benjamin Franklin was very popular amongst the French nobility; they held him in very high esteem. During his time in Paris in 1770 he met up with St Germain. It had been the dream of Francis Bacon/St Germain to found America as an independent country, with religious and political freedom that would become like a beacon of hope of which other countries might follow the example. From Paris, Benjamin Franklin then visited England.

By 1772, arguments about the taxes being levied on the American colonies by the British had been simmering for years. The British government considered that they could gain extra money to prop up the East India Company, by extorting money from the American colonies by way of taxes. The taxes were levied due to the British government attempting to save the East India Company from bankruptcy.

Events finally came to a head with the passing of the Tea Act. A group of Boston citizens disguised as Indians, raided the East India Company's ships in the city harbour, and threw their cargo overboard. From that time onwards, history has recorded it as the 'Boston Tea Party'. Those who instigated the revolt were Freemasons who belonged to the Saint Andrew's Lodge in the city of Boston. As a consequence, war broke out between the British and its American colony.

The American War of Independence created many problems for England and in particular they were faced with the enormous headache of where they could next send their 'undesirables'.

Another famous American who was a high-ranking Freemason was George Washington and among fifty-six American rebels who signed the Declaration of Independence, there were only six who were not members of the Order of the Freemasons. Working behind the scenes during this time, was St Germain.

During St Germain's absence from the European scene, no-one knew of his whereabouts; he was visiting the United States of America to impinge upon them the necessity to found a peaceful, harmonious society within their country.

An important event occurred in the year 1775, which involved St Germain and Benjamin Franklin. It involved the plans for the design of the American flag which were discussed by Benjamin Franklin at a dinner at a home of one of the members of the Freemasons when the arrival of an unusual visitor, was announced. He was described as having the appearance of an elderly professor and when he entered into conversation with the guests around the table, it became very evident that he was extremely well read, could speak many languages, and knew all the historical events that had happened in the last century.

This mysterious 'professor' carried with him a large oak chest which contained many ancient manuscripts and rare books. It was reported that it became obvious to all in attendance, that the 'Professor' and Benjamin Franklin knew each other very well. This mysterious person was the Comte de St Germain, a 'Master' of disguises or 'guises'.

Dr Raymond Bernard in his work titled *The Great Secret Count Saint Germain* writes:

"The flag unfurled at Cambridge, Mass. in 1775, which the 'Professor' designed, symbolized the union of the colonies; it was called the Grand Union Flag, and its design was as follows: In the blue field of the upper-left-hand corner was the white diagonal cross of St Andrews [the 'Saltire' also appears in the Irish *Book of Kells* written by St Columba when he was the Merlin of the 6th century AD]. Imposed on this was the Red (Rose) Cross, which was given the name of St George [Kuthumi]. The thirteen stripes, seven of red and six of white, alternating in the flag, represented the thirteen colonies."

To the early members of the American Congress, in the time of George Washington, St Germain was known as 'The Invisible Hand' shaping the affairs and guiding its destiny. Following his dream of establishing a New Atlantis, St

Germain was instrumental in designing the Great Seal of America and the signing of the Declaration of Independence took place on the 4th of July, 1776.

The first design was drawn by a French artist named Eugene du Simtiere who was commissioned by the committee. Each member had his own ideas for the design of the Seal which originally incorporated the Tudor Rose of England, the thistle of Scotland, the Celtic harp of Ireland, the Fleur de Lys of France, the Eagle of Germany and the Lion of Holland. However, agreement by the committee, could not be reached and a new one was designed which became acceptable, still designed in occult symbolism. The same Seal is still used today.

As the years progressed, the dream of a Golden Civilization, with the right to freedom of speech, religion and politics, began to fade. Heartless, greedy landowners imported Negroes from Africa, to become their slaves.

The Civil War began, from which emerged the Klu Klux Klan and the colour of people's skin defined whether or not they would be persecuted.

St Germain looked on in despair. All the hopes and dreams quickly dissipated.

The discovery of new continents, ones that had once been a part of Lemuria, were the next hope of founding a peaceful civilization that would set an example to the world, ones that would not participate in civil wars, ones that would not be prejudice about the colour of people's skins - ones whose hearts would be big enough to take in people from many nations.

These countries were to be Australia, and New Zealand, which according to St Germain were once part of Lemuria and although America is still a special place, watched over by the Masters of the Great White Brotherhood, for it had once been part of Atlantis, the new countries were also to take their place in the importance of the scheme of things.

MASTERS DISCUSSED IN THIS CHAPTER

Noah - St Germain

St Columba - St Germain (521 - 597 AD)

Roger Bacon - St Germain (1214? - 1294)

Christopher Columbus - St Germain (1451 -1506)

Francis Bacon - St Germain (1561 - ?)

St George - Kuthumi

Leonardo da Vinci - Kuthumi (1452 -1519)

Sir John Dee - Kuthumi (1527 -1608)

NOTES AND RECOMMENDED READING

Isabel Cooper-Oakley, *Comte De St Germain*, (Theosophical Publishing House, U.S.A., 1985)

Dr Raymond Bernard, *The Great Secret, Count Saint Germain*, (U.S.A.)

John Bach, *A Maritime History of Australia*, (Nelson, Melbourne, Australia, 1976)

Brian Gardner, *The East India Company*, (Rupert Hart Davis, London, U.K., 1971)

Arnold J. Toynbee, *A Study Of History*, (Oxford University Press, U.K., 1934)

F.J. Dennett, *Europe, - A History*, (Linehan & Shrimpton, Melbourne, Australia, 1960)

Daniel J. Boorstin, *The Discoverers*, (Random House, U.S.A., 1983)

Francis Hitching, *The World Atlas Of Mysteries*, (Pan Books, U.K., 1978)

W.M. Smyth, *Poems Of Spirit And Action*, (Butler & Tanner, London U.K. 1957)

CHAPTER 48

Sir Joseph Banks, the Royal Society, & the Destined Time for Australian Exploration

"For nearly 50 years Banks was a dominant figure of natural science in a time celebrated as the age of reason, an era when intellectual ferment, artistic and literary expression, and political and religious experimentation blossomed and science became an international language that crossed all borders. No one nurtured the bloom of knowledge longer, more faithfully, or more effectively than Joseph Banks. Companion to Captain James Cook on H.M.S. Endeavour, he enlarged the Western world's knowledge of existing plant species by nearly 25 per cent. Beyond that, he was the father of the Commonwealth of Australia, confidant of kings and gardeners, a statesman of biological commerce who enhanced Great Britain's economic power, and was the longest serving president in the history of the Royal Society of London, perhaps the most prestigious body of scientists in the world."

"Few men were as famous in his time or more important to the history of the natural sciences. Few saw more of the world; few did more to change it. And few enjoyed life quite so much as Banks, sitting at the centre of the web."

(T. H. Watkins, *National Geographic Magazine*, November, 1996).

After America received its independence from Britain, it was decided that the time had come to discover, explore and colonize Australia for after the Boston Tea Party episode, Britain needed a new trading post and somewhere to send their convicts as America would no longer accept them. The Dutch East India Company had been founded in 1602 mainly because of the trouble that many countries were having with regards to trade negotiations being made difficult owing to the fact that Spain held the monopoly. There was a great deal of bitterness at that time for not only were the Protestants being persecuted but the Spaniards had forbidden the Dutch to trade with Spain, the result of which the East India Company was formed.

Originally, the route that the Dutch and Portuguese took was via the Cape of Good Hope, then sailing northwards to Madagascar, the Seychelles, and south to Batavia (now Jakarta). Then in 1611, a quicker passage was found by utilizing the prevailing winds east of Cape Town, South Africa, and then using the trade winds to take them northwards before turning. This route managed to cut down the time of the voyages and was adopted by the Dutch East India Company in about 1616.

It is currently accepted by scholars that there were earlier explorers to our shores, before the Dutch, Spanish, Portuguese and English. The Chinese are thought to have visited our shores in the 1420's AD. There is evidence that our land mass was documented firstly among Greek cartographers, nearly 2,000 years ago and although Australia then was just a 'theory', it at least had a name - *Terra Australis Incognita* - the *'Unknown Southern Land'*. It was not until Marco Polo related the stories of his voyages to China in the 13th century (1200's) that any interest was generated to learn more about the rest of the world, the interest of which began to eventuate faintly in Europe.

This was a period of time in history that was one of rivallry between many countries, each competing to be the first to discover new lands with financial backing being given by the kings and queens of their respective countries.

Captain James Cook (1728 - 1779)
Explorer of Australia, Tahiti and New Zealand

James Cook, son of a Scottish farm labourer, was born on October 27th, 1728 in Yorkshire and went to sea as an apprentice at the age of eighteen, then joined the Royal Navy in 1755. Since Cabot's 1497 voyage, the idea of a north-west passage round the top of America had fascinated those in commerce and trade.

Within two years, Cook was appointed his own vessel to chart the St Lawrence River in Canada. He commanded a schooner surveying the coast of Newfoundland, spending the winters in England perfecting his charts. It was in Newfoundland that he observed an eclipse of the sun in 1766 and he volunteered his calculations to the Royal Society of London.

At the request of the Royal Society of London, (an offshoot of the Rosicrucians, which Francis Bacon/St Germain had founded), the Lords Commissioners of the Admiralty, impressed with Cook's qualifications and experience, deemed him worthy to be given the command of the *HMS Endeavour*, a replica of which was recently built in the town of Fremantle, Western Australia and has since been making successful voyages around the coast of Australia and to England. The *Endeavour* was originally a collier named *The Earl of Pembroke*. (During the era of Francis Bacon, the Earl of Pembroke belonged to the close circle of Sir John Dee and was married to Mary Sidney, sister of the famous Philip Sidney and they were great supporters of Francis Bacon).

On the front page of the *London Gazette* dated August, 19th, 1768, there appeared a notice about Cook:

'Secret Voyage
Lieutenant Cook awaits fair winds
Search for unknown continent south of the equator'

"Much secrecy surrounds the preparation for the departure from England of HIS MAJESTY'S Bark, Endeavour. Endeavour, under its Commander Lt. James Cook, is awaiting fair winds to begin its long Voyage to the Pacific Ocean island of Tahiti to observe, for the Royal Society, the Transit of the planet Venus across the face of the Sun."

"In view of extensive preparations being undertaken, your correspondent asks whether this Scientific study is the only reason for the Voyage of the Endeavour?"

"We have received Certain Information to the contrary, but this is denied by the Lords of the Admiralty and by Lt. Cook himself. The information we have acquired is that Lt. Cook a gentleman of great experience and ability in surveying, is in receipt of additional sealed Orders which are not to be opened until he leaves Tahiti after the conclusion of the Scientific observations. We have reason to believe these Orders are for a Voyage of Discovery, and will carry Endeavour to lands far distant in the South Pacific, and even to that vast Continent which is said to be quite as big as Europe and Asia together, and which is now marked on the maps as Terra Australis Nondum Cognita."

"Such orders would no doubt contain instructions to Lt. Cook to take for HIS MAJESTY possession of such uninhabited Countries as may be found, and to set up proper marks as first Discoverers and Possessors."

"Discussions have long been pursued by men of Knowledge concerning the existence of this mysterious Continent. Some men say there must be an equivalent amount of land in the distant Southern Hemisphere to counteract the weight of the land in the Northern Hemisphere and thus balance the Earth."

"It is no secret that the noted hydrographer, Alexander Dalrymple, who was originally the Royal Society's choice for the Commander of the Endeavour, before the Lords of the Admiralty insisted on Lt Cook, has given to Mr Joseph Banks a secret document he discovered while on expedition in Madras."

"This is believed to contain the statement of Capt Louis Vaez de Torres that he sailed between two great land masses in the far South more than one Century and a half since. Further evidence is that the Endeavour will carry among her stores, every chart, book and scrap of evidence relative to the Pacific Ocean - and, your correspondent presumes, to Terra Australis. If your correspondent is correct in surmising the ultimate destination of the Endeavour, the task will indeed be one of great endurance, but it could solve a puzzle that has been debated since men first started making maps."

The Royal Society was made up of scientists and astronomers who hoped that this observation of the planet Venus would greatly improve future navigational techniques. When Cook reached Tahiti in 1769, he followed the transit of Venus across the sun. After leaving Tahiti, he chartered the coast of New Zealand and then sailed towards Australia where the *Endeavour* ran aground in 1770 on the Great Barrier Reef, Queensland. Fortunately, the crew managed to free the ship before it was broken to pieces on the sharp coral reef.

Whilst James Cook was busy exploring the South Pacific and claiming Australia for Great Britain in 1770, William Dampier, at that time also employed by the Royal Navy, had sighted the north-west coast of Australia, which was then called *New Holland*. He returned to Australia in January 1699, as commander of the *Roebuck* and anchored at Shark Bay. The Royal Society was behind the scenes in urging the Royal Navy to send out explorers to both coasts of Australia, anxious to claim the whole of Australia for Great Britain, in order to prevent the Dutch, French or Spanish achieving this aim first.

When Cook discovered the east coast of Australia, he claimed it for Britain and upon his famous voyage of discovery he was accompanied by a brilliant young man named Joseph Banks who was to become the most famous botanist of all time.

Sir Joseph Banks (1743 - 1820) (Kuthumi) and the Royal Society

Joseph Banks, an incarnation of the Master Kuthumi, who had been the Magus Sir John Dee in the 16th century AD, was born into a wealthy family in Lincoln, England. It was no mere coincidence that he was born in Lincoln, for in an earlier incarnation as St Hugh of Avalon, Kuthumi became the Bishop of Lincoln, whose story has been discussed in an earlier chapter.

From the early days of his youth he was blessed with good looks, charm, and a brilliant mind. As a child, Joseph loved to wander through the countryside, woods and streams that surrounded the family's estate in Lincolnshire. He had a tremendous love of nature and when he was sent to Eton, he studied Botany and began his first collection of plants, the love of which eventually led Joseph to developing London's famous Royal Kew Gardens under the patronage of his good friend, King George III.

Joseph Banks was the most prominent English patron of natural history. He was the 'Father of the Commonwealth' who with Captain Cook was instrumental in discovering Australia. Joseph was also was behind the colonizing schemes for Australia, as he had been behind the colonizing schemes in his previous life as Sir John Dee.

By the age of twenty years, he was six feet tall and incredibly handsome. Needless to say, the pleasure of his company was much sort after. By the age of thirty-five years, Banks was very successful and a well-known figure. He became President of the Royal Society in 1788 and had been a Fellow of the Society since 1766.

An article upon the subject of Sir Joseph Banks which appeared in the *National Geographic* magazine in November, 1996, written by T.H. Watkins described him as follows:

"For nearly 50 years Banks was a dominant figure of natural science in a time celebrated as the age of reason, an era when intellectual ferment, artistic and literary expression, and political and religious experimentation blossomed and science became an international language that crossed all borders."

"No one nurtured the bloom of knowledge longer, more faithfully, or more effectively than Joseph Banks. Companion to Captain James Cook on H.M.S. *Endeavour*, he enlarged the Western world's knowledge of existing plant species by nearly 25 per cent. Beyond that, he was the father of the Commonwealth of Australia, confidant of kings and gardeners, a statesman of biological commerce who enhanced Great Britain's economic power, and was the longest serving president in the history of the Royal Society of London, perhaps the most prestigious body of scientists in the world. *Few men were as famous in his time or more important to the history of the natural sciences. Few saw more of the world; few did more to change it. And few enjoyed life quite so much as Banks, sitting at the centre of the web.*"

The Royal Society had been founded by St Germain and was an off-shoot of the Order of the Rose Cross and the Freemasons. Its intention was to have a profound influence upon the world of science, inventions, naturalists etc. and many famous people became members including Sir Isaac Newton (1642-1727) who was a prominent member of the Order of the Rose Cross who would have often had meetings with St Germain. St Germain spent time in London in 1745 with the Prince of Wales and was active in the Royal Society.

From the book titled *The Discoverers* by Daniel J. Boorstin we learn the following pertinent information:

"Sir Joseph Banks founded what became known as the select Linnean Society of London in 1788 to preserve the library, herbarium, and manuscripts which Linneaus had left his son, and which upon his son's death had been bought for them by an English botanist. (Carolus Linneaus, 1707-1778, who was born in Sweden, was a botanist and one of Banks' Royal Society colleagues. In July 1858, the Linnean Society published observations made by Darwin twenty years earlier on his round-the-world voyage on the *Beagle*)."

"In retrospect it is easy to forget that the Royal Society was a company of pioneers. When science was still securely tied to religion, novelty had the stigma of heterodoxy. In the early years the defence of the Royal Society was less a catalogue of its useful work than an effort to prove that the work of the society was really innocent. When Bishop Sprat published his copious *History of the Royal Society* (1667), he devoted a third of the book to prove 'that the promoting of Experiments, according to this idea, cannot injure the Virtue, or Wisdom of Men's minds, or their former Arts, and Mechanical Practices; or their established ways of life: Yet the perfect innocence of this design, has not been able to free it from the Cavill of the Idle, and the Malicious; nor from the jealousies of the particular Professions, and Ranks of Men'. John Glanville (1636-1680) wrote 'this great ferment of useful and generous knowledge, makes a bank of all useful knowledge, and makes possible the mutual assistance that the practical and theoretical part of physics affords each other...*the Royal Society...has done more than philosophy of a notional way since Aristotle [Kuthumi] opened shop'*."

"The intention of the Royal Society, Bishop Sprat explained, was 'not the Artifice of Words, but a bare knowledge of things'. At that moment in British history, the voluble Puritans, despite their professed aim at a 'plain style' had given eloquence a bad name. To many their lengthy florid sermons and their parliamentary bombast seemed fuel for civil disorder. Their 'superfluity of talking' had led Bishop Sprat and other respectable Fellows to declare 'that eloquence to be banished out of all civil Societies, as a thing fatal to Peace and good Manners'. To reform ways of speaking would refresh ways of thinking."

"The Royal Society, hoping to accomplish this, therefore 'extracted from all their members, a close, naked, natural way of speaking; positive expressions; clear senses; a native easiness: bringing all things as near the Mathematical plainness, as they can: and preferring the language of Artisans, Countrymen, and Merchants, before that, of Wits, or Scholars'. The 'Universal Temper' of the British, Sprat boasted - 'our climate, the air, the influence of heaven, the composition of the English blood; as well as the embraces of the Ocean' - all tended 'to render our Country, a Land of Experimental Knowledge'. The travels of Marco Polo, the voyages of Columbus and Magellan, were experiences to be recounted, and enjoyed in the reading and hearing. In the new world of 'Experimental Knowledge' this was not good enough. To be an experiment and experience had to be repeatable."

From the book titled *Sir Joseph Banks* by Charles Lyte:

"Banks was not without his enemies, especially when he was appointed President of the Royal Society. On top of all his other activities there was not a new learned society mooted to which Banks was not asked to lend his name. He helped to found the Linnean Society, the first specialist scientific society in Britain. The Horticultural Society, now the Royal Horticultural Society, famous throughout the world for its annual Chelsea Flower Show, benefited from his zeal and from a number of learned papers by him."

"The list of societies to which he gave support seems endless: the Society of Arts, the Engineer's Society, the Dilettanti Society, the Society of Antiquaries and the Society for the Improvement of Naval Architectural and many others. Such tireless work brought its rewards. In 1781 Banks became a Baronet and in 1795 he received the Red Ribbon of Knight of the Order of Bath. As he was given the Order by George III, the King murmured: 'I have many years wished to do this'."

According to the article printed in the *National Geographic* magazine (November, 1996), by T.H. Watkins, by the time he was twenty-nine years old, "Banks was perhaps the most famous young man in England. His was an incredibly busy and prominent life. It was the Cook Expedition that had given Banks his fame, but it would be his work with the Royal Society that would absorb the rest of his life and mark his most enduring contributions to science....he became an honorary member of no fewer than 40 societies, from the Imperial Academy of Sciences in St Petersburg, Russia, to the American Philosophical Society of Philadelphia. There was no denying the power that centred in his London house at 32 Soho Square (long since torn down), a kind of scientific crossroads where a constant stream of the learned and the connected came and went with Banks' blessings for more than four decades."

"Scholars from all over the world were welcome to sift through the specimens in his herbarium and the books in his ever growing library, which ultimately would include nearly 8,000 titles. In any week, visitors might include government officials from Whitehall, emissaries from foreign courts, and members of an expanding international network of natural scientists."

It is noteworthy that in 1775 the Royal Society had been asked to assist in the development of an efficient lightning conductor which had been invented by Benjamin Franklin. During this era, St Germain was in England and he had a great deal to do with the American Freemason Benjamin Franklin.

The Dutch explorers en route to the Spice Islands seem to have accidentally discovered various parts of Australia. The Dutch East India Company had forbidden the exploration of *New Holland* because at the time, they had more trade than they could deal with. Although this was vigorously denied by the Dutch, a certain document came into the hands of Sir Joseph Banks in 1770 when he was turning over the old archives at Batavia. (To place this event in a perspective of time, in the same year that Joseph Banks made this discovery, Queen Marie Antoinette and Louis XVI were married).

One of Sir Joseph Banks' close friends was Lord Sandwich (who was the inventor of what we call a 'sandwich'). Lord Sandwich not only belonged to the Royal Society but also the Admiralty and he gave assistance to Sir Joseph in gaining a passage aboard the *Endeavour* for the Admiralty were very careful as to who were chosen for their naval expeditions.

According to *The London Gazette* (August 16th, 1768):

"The Ship's Company has been chosen most carefully. It includes Lt. Zachary Hicks, First Lieutenant, who is an experienced seaman; [Zachary Hicks was the first to sight land and was duly commemorated, having Point Hicks named after him before the *Endeavour* left the shores of Australia], Lt. John Gore who has survived already two circumnavigations of the World...and the Royal Society has appointed its own representative body of Scientists and Naturalists led by the brilliant botanist, Mr Banks. Mr Banks is also paying his own expenses, and also the expenses of his assistants and servants. His second-in-command is Dr Daniel Solander, a knowledgeable student of natural history. Mr Alexander Buchan and Mr Sidney Parkinson have been engaged to sketch views and plants."

Sir Joseph Banks was the first person to introduce the Spanish Merino sheep into Britain - the fine wool was essential in the production of fine cloth. He confided in his close friend King George III of his idea to cross-breed Merinos with native breeds so that the British wool would become finer and there would no longer be the need to import wool from Spain. However, they were not as successful in Britain as had been anticipated. Thanks to Sir Joseph Banks, when Captain John Macarthur sailed to Australia, he brought Spanish Merino here and they did indeed prosper and wool became one of Australia's major industries, one by which Australia could export exceptional fine quality.

Then in 1851, upon the discovery of gold, the Colonial trade increased dramatically as did a steady stream of Irish, Scotch and English emigrants, migrating to Australia to make their fortune. The amount of sailing ships to Australia also increased and new companies, owned by Freemasons, were established.

According to information contained in the book titled *Sir Joseph Banks* by author Charles Lyte, all Banks' journeys were "devoted to collecting and observation. As he made his way steadily across Wales, Banks studied ruins, ancient carvings, fossils; he studied the local agriculture and watched men fishing from coracles; he examined the inscriptions on gravestones and tramped around castles. His journal is peppered with minute detail, local history, carefully recorded legends and scientific observation. Nothing seem to miss his eye; iron works, wagon building, gun-making, they were all worthy of study. Everywhere he went curiosities and oddities were produced for his inspection....he was laden with biological and geological specimens, fossils, flint arrowheads, ancient coins."

From further information contained in the above-mentioned book, we find that "in the 18th century, the Highlands and Islands were remote and relatively visited and for a man of Banks' inquisitive character they held an inevitable fascination." (In 1772, Banks chartered a ship called the *Sir Lawrence* for four months eventually arriving at the Scottish Isles).

"Their first stop was the Isle of Islay. During the days that followed, they explored Jura and Oronsay." (These were all places where St Columba had visited and founded Celtic monastic settlements). "On the 11th August, they continued their voyage through the islands with Banks becoming lyrical at the sight of Morven, the wooded 'land of heroes'. He wrote '*I could not even sail past it without a touch of enthusiasm, sweet affection of the mind which can gather pleasure from the empty elements and realise the substantial pleasure which three-fourths of mankind are ignorant of. I lamented the busy bustle of the ship and had I dared to venture the censure of my companions, would certainly have brought her to anchor. To read ten pages of Isian under the shade of those woods would have been a luxury above the reach of kings*'.

They then journeyed on to Staffa and "from Staffa they made their way to *Iona* for the ruins of St Columba's great religious house. Later on the afternoon of the 14th August, the party set off for St Columba's house which they found a total ruin only inhabited by crows and jackdaws. But at the 'Chapel of Oran, a fellow saint, they paid their respects."

It will be remembered that St Columba was an incarnation of St Germain and it therefore stands to reason that Sir Joseph Banks felt drawn to the Island of Iona, for back in the 6th century AD, Kuthumi, as King Aedan (Arthur) had been crowned by St Columba (Merlin) upon the famous Stone of Destiny and he, like Columba, had been buried on the island.

Letter of Sir Joseph Banks, 1801

In 1801, Sir Joseph Banks was elected as a foreign member of the French Institute National. Charles Lyte quotes a letter written by Banks to the French people concerned, part of which is quoted below:

'*To be the first elected to be an Associate of the first Literacy Society in the world surpassed my most ambitious hope, and I cannot be too grateful toward a Society which has conferred upon me this honour, and toward a nation of which it is the literary representative. A nation which during the most frightful convulsions of the late most terrible revolution, never ceased to possess my esteem; being always persuaded, and even during the most disastrous periods, that it contained many good citizens who would infallibly get the upper hand, and who would re-establish in the heart of their countrymen, the empire of virtue, of justice, and of honour.*' It is not unreasonable to suppose that during this visit to France, Joseph Banks would have met up with the Comte de St Germain.

Sir Joseph Banks visit to the Lost City of Petra in 1806

We learn from information taken from the book titled *Petra* by Iain Browning that in the year 1806 (fourteen years before the death of Joseph Banks) John L. Burkhardt of Switzerland, journeyed to London in order to contact Sir Joseph Banks for it was John's desire to discover the lost city of Petra. The author writes:

"John seems to have hit it off very well with Sir Joseph for he was soon volunteering to carry out exploration for the Association (for Promoting the Discovery of the Interior Parts of Africa). The offer was accepted."

John then spent time in London and "at Cambridge attending lectures on chemistry, astronomy and medicine and in taking a 'crash course' in Arabic." He disguised himself as an Arab and spent several years searching for Petra until he finally discovered it and he discovered the lost tomb of Aaron." (It will be remembered that Aaron had been an incarnation of St Germain).

"Knowledge of Burckhardt's discovery of Petra had spread before the publication of his Journals, for in May 1818 two commanders of the Royal Navy, the Hon. C. L. Irby and *Mr. J. Mangles, spent some days sightseeing in the ancient city...accompanied by Mr Banks.*" From a local historical point of view, it is noteworthy that Mr J. Mangles was Captain James Mangles, Royal Navy, who was a cousin of Sir James Stirling's wife, Ellen (nee Mangles). Sir James Stirling has been mentioned in previous chapters of this story with the emphasis being placed upon the importance of him being the founder of the colony of Perth, Western Australia.

According to Malcolm Uren in his book titled *Land Looking West*, Captain James Mangles travelled a great deal and wrote much of his travels. *He was a Fellow of the Royal Society and was particularly interested in botany.* Thus we learn that not only did Captain Mangles accompany Sir Joseph Banks to the lost tomb of Aaron, and the lost city of Petra, but he also belonged to the Royal Society, and, what he also shared in common with Sir Joseph was his great love of botany.

Western Australia is famous for its beautiful native flower which we call the 'Kangaroo Paw', however, many may not realise that its proper botanical name is *Anigozanthos Mangelsii*, named after Captain James Mangles' eldest brother George, who was also a very prominent botanist who would also have been well acquainted with Sir Joseph Banks.

Also noteworthy is that *"Lady Stirling's eldest brother Ross Donnelly Mangles was one of the highest officials in the Honourable East India Company's service,* and upon his retirement he became a director and Chairman of the company, a member of the Council of India, a Member of Parliament for Guildford in the House of Commons from 1841 to 1856. His eldest son, Ross Mangles, also went to India, became a judge and was one of the three civilians to receive the Victoria

Cross during the Indian Mutiny."

The biographer of Sir Joseph Banks, Charles Lyte, commented that "Part of his (Banks') success, at least, he owed to the two women in his life - his wife Dorothea and his sister, Sarah Sophia. The two women worked tirelessly in his interest. They shared the same house in, it would seem, an atmosphere of peace and tranquility. But what they both had in common was a selfless devotion to Banks and his career."

"Banks survived his sister by two years, dying on the 19th June, 1820, and was buried in Heston parish churchyard. At his request his grave was not marked with either a stone or tablet. He left no heir to carry on his work."

Update on Kuthumi's lives:

1. Kuthumi had once been the First Master of the Grail, St Joseph of Arimathea, otherwise known as St John Joseph the Beloved, the brother of Jesus, to whom Jesus had handed over the responsibility of the Grail. He established the first Christian Church whose emblem was the *Rose and the Cross.*

2. In the 4th century, Kuthumi had been St George whose emblem was the *Rose-Red Cross.* Upon his grave, the *Rose of Sharon* was planted.

3. In the 6th century AD Kuthumi had been King Aedan mac Gabran who was the King Arthur of this story who was crowned by Merlin, (St Germain).

4. In the 9th century AD, it appears that Kuthumi was John of Ireland (Johannes Eriugena, died 877 AD) who became the greatest Philosopher of his time, responsible for the Carolingian Renaissance, whose like was not seen again in Western Christendom until the Italian Renaissance. He was appointed by King Charles I of France as the main teacher and head Philosopher of the Royal Court School in France. Charles I of France was none other than Charlemagne the Great, an incarnation of St Germain.

5. In the 11th century, Kuthumi reincarnated as the famous Mathematician/ Philosopher, Astrologer, Omar Khayyam who became the main teacher at the Royal Court of the Shah of Persia and who was also engaged to design and make stained glass, by means of 'alchemy' for the Carthusian and Cistercian cathedrals of Europe. He undertook a journey to the Crusades. Upon his grave, the *Rose of Sharon* was planted.

6. In the 12th century, Kuthumi reincarnated as Hugh of Castle Avalon, later to become known as St Hugh of Lincoln. His father and brothers were members of the Knights Templar. Upon the side of St Hugh's tomb in Lincoln Cathedral is a shield with a *Rose- Red Cross* with a white background. The cross is in the form of a saltire.

7. In the 14th century, (1314), the last Grand Master of the Knights Templar was burned at the stake. His name was Jacques of Molay who in all probability, was an incarnation of Kuthumi, who having once been John Joseph (of Arimathea), the First Master of the Grail, and Master of the Rose, became the last Grand Master of the Knights Templar whose emblem was the *Rose-Red Cross.*

8. During the Italian Renaissance period, Kuthumi reincarnated as Leonardo da Vinci (the 'Lion of Vinci'), who became the *Grandmaster of the Priory of Sion,* which was affiliated with the *Order of the Rose Cross and the Order* of the Freemasons.

9. As Sir John Dee, the Magus of the Elizabethan Renaissance, Kuthumi was a Grand Master of the *Order of the Rose Cross* and established an *Order of Sion* at his own home. He also established an enormous library of ancient books and manuscripts and people came from all over the world to study them. Sir John Dee was also the chief exponent of Navigation whose collection of navigational charts, just like his library, was enormous.

10. Sir Joseph Banks was born in Lincoln, where he had once lived in his incarnation as St Hugh. Like Sir John Dee, Sir Joseph Banks established an enormous library and people came from all over the world to study there. *Banks was the greatest botanist the world has ever known.* Sir Joseph Banks founded the Royal Botanical Kew Gardens. He travelled the world collecting hundreds of thousands of specimens for the Royal *Botanical Gardens.* He enlarged the Western world's knowledge of existing plant species by nearly 25 per cent.

    In an earlier incarnation as the Pharaoh Tutmoses III (1504 -1450 BC), Kuthumi had been a Teacher of the Secret School of the Great White Brotherhood. He built a new temple in Karnak, Thebes, which was named the 'Festival Hall' and was decorated like and *was called, the 'Botanical Garden'* with the walls covered in flora and fauna.

11. According to an ancient prophecy, *an Obelisk* once erected in Egypt upon the instructions of Tutmoses was destined to be re-erected in the country where the Eagle spreads its wings and *the Obelisk* now stands in Central Park, New York, America. (The Eagle became the emblem of the Great Seal of the United States of America, designed by St Germain and it will be remembered that the 'Eagle' is the symbol of St John the Beloved).

12. In an earlier paragraph in this chapter, it was mentioned that Daniel Boorstin commented in his book titled *The Discoverers* that the Royal Society has done more than philosophy of a notional way since Aristotle opened shop. (It will be remembered that Kuthumi had once been Aristotle). Sir Joseph Banks reigned as President of the Royal Society (an off-shoot of the *Order*

of the Rose Cross) for 50 years, the longest reigning president in history whose influence upon the whole world was immense. Apart from St Germain, no-one else in the world at that time, achieved so much!

MASTERS DISCUSSED IN THIS CHAPTER

St Columba - St Germain

Merlin - St Germain

Aristotle - Kuthumi

Tutmoses III - Kuthumi

Joseph of Arimathea (alias John the Beloved), First Master of the Grail and Master of the Rose (1st century AD) - Kuthumi

St George - (3rd century AD) - Kuthumi

King Aedan mac Gabran (Arthur) - (6th century AD) - Kuthumi

John of Ireland (9th century AD) - Kuthumi

Omar Khayyam (11th century AD)

St Hugh of Avalon and Lincoln (12th century AD) - Kuthumi

Sir Joseph Banks (18th century AD) - Kuthumi

NOTES AND RECOMMENDED READING

Daniel J. Boorstin, *The Discoverers*, (Random House, U.S.A., 1983)

Iain Browning, *Petra*, (Chatto & Windus, London, U.K., 1973)

National Geographic Magazine, (November, 1996)

London Gazette, August 19th, 1768

Brian Gardener, *The East India Company*, (Rupert Hart-Davis, London, U.K., 1971)

John Bach, *A Maritime History of Australia*, (Nelson, Australia, 1976)

Basil Lubbock, *The Colonial Clippers*, (Brown, Ferguson Ltd., Glasgow, 1955)

Charles Lyte, *Sir Joseph Banks*, (David & Charles, U.S.A., 1980)

Malcolm J. Uren, *Land Looking West*, (Oxford University Press, U.K., 1948)

Arnold J. Toynbee, *A Study Of History*, (Oxford University Press, U.K., 1934)

Isabel Cooper-Oakley, *Comte De St Germain*, (Theosophical Publishing House, U.S.A., 1985)

Dr Raymond Bernard, *The Great Secret, Count Saint Germain*, (Mass. U.S.A., 1960)

CHAPTER 49

Sir James Stirling & The Early Sailing Ships To Australia

*"But for Stirling's energetic action, it is possible
that Western Australia would not have become a British colony,
and if that had been so, the political integrity of the colony,
which in itself is a very remarkable achievement,
would not have been attained....hence his importance
As one of the founders of the political structure of
Australia as we know it today."*
(Sir Ernest Scott)

"Captain Sir James Stirling was one of the creators of what is now the territory of the Commonwealth of Australia, but because his place in the line of succession came long after the drama of Lieutenant James Cook's original discovery of the continent, and its first settlement under Governor Phillip, Stirling's important part in Australian history has been very much under-estimated and in many cases entirely overlooked."
"His most enduring service to the British Empire was the carrying out of his personal plan to claim for England the western coast of Australia. In so doing, he added to the British Empire an area of almost a million square miles."
(*Land Looking West* by Malcolm Uren)

James Stirling was born on the 28th January, 1791, the eighth child of Andrew and Anne Stirling at Drumpellier House at Lanarkshire, Scotland. His parents were both first cousins and it has been mentioned in previous chapters that they were descendants of Prince David of Scotland and his brother King William the Lion (St Germain) of Stirling Castle. The family had produced many notable Freemasons and had a great naval background. Their great great grandfather, John Stirling, became famous as the Lord Provost of Glasgow during the troubled times of Charles II and another of their famous ancestors, Walter Stirling of Stirlingshire, assisted

Mary Queen of Scots, the mother of James I (Stuart) of England.

From the book titled *Admiral James Stirling* by G.S. Stirling we learn the following information: "Though the family had been party to the full score of Scotland's often bloody and turbulent history, from Bannockburn to Flodden, from Halidon Hill and Culloden moor, by the 18th century, its fortunes had declined with the loss of lands and wealth and the speculation of the tobacco trade, and in what was regarded as the enlightened benevolence of that age - as was the case of Admiral Stirling's great uncle, Walter Stirling who was to found Scotland's first public library by donating his fortune and his mansion house to the city of Glasgow, which is known to this day, as the Stirling Library."

"Admiral Stirling's naval career was to span the Napoleonic wars, the wars of South American Independence, the Crimea and China."

At the age of twelve years, James entered the Royal Navy as a 'first class volunteer' and had his first real taste of warfare in action against the French and Spanish fleets off Cape Finisterre. Not all the enemy fleets were destroyed until Lord Nelson's famous victory at Trafalgar, three months later.

In 1808, James was posted to the *Warspite* under the command of Captain Blackwood who had been a witness to Nelson's Will and was with him in the *Victory* at the time of his death. Under Blackwood's command, the *Warspite* saw service in the North Sea, the English Channel and the Mediterranean. Twenty years later, James Stirling named the Blackwood River in the south of Western Australia, in honour of Captain Blackwood, whose families were from County Down, Northern Ireland and of whom many were knights and members of the Freemasons.

It was in 1812, that James Stirling received command of his first ship, the *Moselle* with eighteen guns and then took command of the *Brazen* with twenty-eight guns. It was an opportune appointment for at that particular time the United States of America declared war, the 'War of 1812' on England. James' instructions were to harry the American ports in the Gulf of Mexico. He admirably carried out this task and within four months, had completely destroyed the enemy's fortifications at the mouth of the Mississippi River. However, the task was not an easy one. He had to fight the forces of nature as well as the land and sea forces of the enemy and in one of the hurricanes which lash this coastline, the *Brazen* was badly damaged. Repairs were made by using suitable trees from the forests to replace the lost masts.

Stirling's achievements were noticed by the Royal Admiralty and in 1813, James was sent to protect the settlers and the British shipping at Hudson's Bay. In this too, he was successful and in the winter of the same year, he was sent across the Atlantic Ocean to the coast of Holland and then to the West Indies.

In his book titled *Spanish Colonial Influence on Sir James Stirling*, A.C. Staples wrote the following pertinent information:

"His experience in Western Australia lasted only 12 years. Because we have given him an honourable place among our founding fathers, we excuse our ignorance of his earlier Royal Naval career of 14 years chiefly in the Caribbean Sea along the north coast of America and of his subsequent Royal Navy career of 23 years, until his retirement as Admiral, Commander-in-Chief of the Royal Navy and China and the Eastern Seas."

"Two classes of documents written in 1817 provide illuminating information on the activities of the young naval officer, James Stirling, in the Caribbean Sea. One consists of Spanish correspondence referred to by Salvador de Madariaga, biographer of Simon Bolivar, which reveals Stirling as a British diplomatic agent on a mission to the leadership of the Venezuelan colonists in revolt. Based on that material, the historian provides a detailed account of the rebellion at the period of Stirling's assignment in the West Indies. The other class of documents is found in archives of the British Admiralty and the Foreign Office."

"As early as 1817, the Foreign Office was considering the advisability of recognising the independence of the South American colonies....Stirling was sent back to Bolivar....to ask for written assurances that a colonial government actually existed. From his description of the ancient colonial system operated by Spain for three hundred years, it is clear that Stirling was highly critical of its general features, and was certain that 'nothing liberal was to be looked for' from Spain. He deplored the actions of the 'chiefs' or 'leaders'. The 'plantation' type of production seemed to a part of the 'ancient' system."

"These documents reveal something of Stirling's diplomatic activities as a member of Rear Admiral Harvey's staff in the Caribbean during the first 4 months of 1817. For 6 years Stirling had been on active service in the Caribbean Sea, between the two great colonial areas of the past three centuries, Latin Central and South America, and British North America. The latter had rebelled successfully against Britain about 10 years before Stirling's birth."

"As a young naval officer he had watched at close quarters the bloody war which the South American colonists fought against their mother-country. Though independence was achieved in the 1820's, the legacy of the devastation still lies heavily upon South America almost two centuries later. We may assume that Stirling's chief objections to the Spanish 'ancient colonial system', lay, to stress his words, 'in the rigour with which it is enforced'; 'in the exactions of the officers'; and 'in the restoration of the Inquisition'. (The colonial community was dominated by 'chiefs', 'leaders', with characteristics we might describe as medieval, reminiscent of Spain before the days of Columbus)."

When he was twenty-seven years old, Captain James Stirling married Ellen Mangles who was the daughter of James Mangles, J.P. of Woodbridge near Guildford, Surrey. He was High Sheriff of Surrey and a director of the *Honourable East India*

Company, and who in 1831, became a Member of Parliament for Guildford. (When James founded the colony of Western Australia, he and Ellen settled on a property on the Swan River which they named Woodbridge and the surrounding district, 'Guildford' was named in remembrance of their home in England. This home in Western Australia has been preserved and is opened to the public). (Of local interest is that the bay around which the town of Rockingham, just south of the Port of Fremantle, is named Mangles Bay).

The Mangles, like the Stirling family, had played a very important role in history. Apart from their interest in the East India Company, it was briefly mentioned elsewhere that Ellen Mangles' (Lady Stirling's) eldest brother, Ross Donnelly Mangles, was *one of the highest officials in the officials in the Honourable East India Company's service and on his retirement he became a director and Chairman of the company, a member of the Council of India.* His son Ross, also went to India, became a judge and was one of three civilians to receive the Victoria Cross during the Indian Mutiny. Also mentioned was the fact that Lady Stirling's (Ellen Mangle's) cousin, *Captain James Mangles of the Royal Navy, was a famous botanist in his own right, a Fellow of the Royal Society who in the year 1818 had accompanied Sir Joseph Banks to the lost city of Petra and the lost tomb of Aaron (St Germain)* which was the same year that Sir Joseph visited the Island of Iona and St Columba's (St Germain's) tomb.

According to A.C. Staples in his book titled *Spanish Colonial Influence On Sir James Stirling*, "internationally, in 1818 Britain had been brought face to face with the Quintuple Alliance of that year, consisting of Russia, Austria, Prussia, France and Britain in the European Congress System of continental powers all opposed to vital British policies, and all supporting the Spanish efforts to recover control of her South American colonies. The British Parliamentary government, viewed as 'revolutionary' by the European monarchs, was controlled by the more commercially-minded Tories under Lord Liverpool and Lord Castlereagh as Foreign Secretary. Ship-owners and overseas traders were strongly represented in Parliament and as the only supplies of ships and sailors; they exercised a dominating influence over the Royal Navy."

"While the government was bound by treaty obligations to the European congress which urged the Spanish to send troops to South America to suppress the colonial rebellion, the strong Parliamentary support for South American colonial independence forced Castlereagh into passive resistance to any positive action against the colonists. The problem was not resolved until 1824 when Canning acted in concert with the United States of America which had proclaimed its Monroe Doctrine warning European powers to keep out of American affairs. *During that period, we cannot suppose that Stirling dropped all interest in colonial affairs. We know that he travelled Europe both before and after his marriage to Ellen Mangles in 1823. His alliance with the Mangles shipping empire assured his interest in ships and trade, in the affairs of the East India Company of which Donnelly Mangles became a director."*

In 1825, Captain Stirling was given the command of the HMS *Success* and in 1826, he sailed her from Portsmouth to Sydney, Australia, with orders to confer with Governor Darling of New South Wales. Malcolm Uren comments: "Why Stirling should have been sought out at Woodbridge, his home in Surrey, and given command of a new ship and sent on an unusual mission to the other side of the world, is not clear. True, he had experience of foreign stations and had shown initiative and resource as well as courage, but even these were not the most outstanding qualifications that might be sought in a naval commander required to determine matters of policy on colonization - and on colonization in a very distant part of the world which Stirling had never previously visited. But whatever the reason for his appointment to *Success*, the occasion was a momentous one for him."

It stands to reason that the main person, who would have been behind the choosing of Captain Stirling, would have been St Germain. Kuthumi in his incarnation as Sir Joseph Banks had done his part in being instrumental in founding and colonizing the rest of Australia. When he died in 1820, someone else whose ancestors had a long history of belonging to the Order of the Freemasons and who had also devoted their lives to the Celtic cause throughout the earlier centuries, was deemed worthy. Sir Joseph Banks had died five years before Captain Stirling was chosen for his important mission, and there could be little doubt that his prowess and activities on behalf of his country, Great Britain, had been under close surveillance for quite some time. It was not mere coincidence that the Stirling family was genetically related to William the Lion of Scots (St Germain) of Stirling Castle, Scotland, nor that he named Perth, after Perth in Scotland, which is close to Stirling. Nor was it coincidence that Stirling's wife's family, the Mangles, were so highly appointed in their connections with the East India Company - the greatest trading company that the world has ever known.

Continuing with Malcolm Uren's comments:

"In fact, a study of Stirling's subsequent career strongly suggests that when he set out for the southern seas, he determined to be much more than a successful commander; it is even possible that at that stage his mind became aflame with the prospects of colonization and he determined to seek out and settle some spot in the little known Southern Hemisphere."

The timing of this voyage was perfect for rumours abounded of the threat of occupation of the western coast of Australia by the French and if it wasn't for the amazing abilities and determination of James Stirling, Western Australia could quite easily have become a separate country from the rest of Australia...a French, Dutch or even American country, as will be seen in future paragraphs.

A.C. Staples writes: "The Foreign Office was also worried lest France might lay claim; were the Dutch or the Portuguese at all concerned? Who better than Stirling, while travelling in Europe, to make discreet soundings in Portugal and Holland? If so, there could be a file of 'agent' Stirling's reports somewhere in the relevant Office."

"In March 1826, a dispatch was sent off to Governor Darling instructing him to examine King George's Sound in New Holland and to warn off any French visitors in sight. A month later in April, 1826, Stirling received his order to embark on the *Success*. It is not at all unreasonable to suppose that Stirling left the Thames with verbal instructions to return, if possible, with a description of that south-western part of New Holland."

It was the decision of the Home Government to set up settlement on the south-western coast of Australia. In 1826, Governor Darling of Sydney, issued instructions for Major Lockyer to accompany a garrison to what became known as King George Sound on the south-west tip of Western Australia and they landed on the site which became known as Albany. The town of Albany was named in honour of the Duke of York who was also the Duke of Albany. He was the brother and heir to King George IV and Commander-in-Chief of the British Army.

In 1833, Sir Richard Spencer was appointed as Governor at King George Sound and he was the man who launched the town of Albany and accomplished so much for the development of the South-West for which he has received little recognition.

From the book titled *Western Australia's Tempestuous History* by John Nairn, we learn that what is generally not known is that "Sir Richard Spencer was the Royal Navy's 'Scarlet Pimpernel', an athlete and proficient swordsman who played a leading role in the capture of at least eight warships and nine Spanish galleons. Spencer was born in 1779, the son of a London merchant and at 14 was serving as midshipman in the *Arethusa*. He led the boarding party which took the famous French ship *Guillaume Tell*, and, promoted to the rank of Lieutenant for his courage and leadership, navigated the crippled and battered prize-of-war much of the way from Sicily to Minorca. Even as Lieutenant, he was in constant communication with Lord Nelson, who assigned him to diplomatic and under-cover work on land, as well as on sea."

"Spencer intercepted vital enemy dispatches sent from Napoleon Bonaparte to General Regnier, commander of the French Navy, and in 1804, [two years before Sir Joseph Banks journeyed to the lost city of Petra] he led the chase on the remnants of the French Navy, finally capturing five warships. (In 1833, William IV conferred the Hanoverian Guelphic Order of Knighthood upon Spencer)."

Sir Richard Spencer would have come into contact with both the Comte de

St Germain and Sir Joseph Banks who also carried secret dispatches on behalf of Britain. St Germain was very active in Europe during this period of time, travelling back and forth.

Another famous person who was associated with Captain Sir James Stirling was Sir George Cockburn who was a Junior Lord of the Admiralty in 1841 and in 1846 was the First Sea Lord. He was given the important task after the battle of Waterloo, of carrying Napoleon to St Helena aboard the HMS *Northumberland.* (Cockburn Sound, just south of the port of Fremantle in Western Australia, is named after him).

Although Albany was established, Captain Stirling realised that a more suitable site was needed for settlement. Stirling persuaded Governor Darling that a French expedition was already acting suspiciously in Australian waters and he felt it necessary to examine the west coast of Australia to see whether it provided a suitable site for a garrison or for another settlement to open trade with the East Indies.

Sir James Stirling is credited with having been the one to suggest the exploration and colonization of the Swan River settlement and having convinced Governor Darling in Sydney of the wisdom of this expedition, he sailed on the *Success* in January, 1827 and arrived at the mouth of the Swan River (so named because of the unique black swans which inhabited it), in March.

With a small party, including a botanist and an artist, Stirling explored the upper regions of the Swan River. The beautiful blue-mauve hills in the distance, he named the 'Darling Ranges' in honour of Governor Darling of New South Wales. During the explorations of the Swan River, Stirling and his small party landed on the shore, not far from where the old land-mark called the Swan Brewery stands today. Captain Stirling took a party of explorers to the highest point in the area, which he named after Eliza, the wife of Governor Darling and it is now known as Mt Eliza situated in the picturesque King's Park from which can be viewed panoramic views of the hills and the Swan River. Here, he surveyed the area from this high position in order to ascertain whether the area was worthy of settlement.

James originally named the Swan River Settlement, 'Hesperia' - denoting a 'Land looking West' towards the setting of the sun and in whose night sky *Hesperus,* the Evening Star, often hung low and brilliant. However, approval for this name was not granted and he then named it Perth after the Argyll area in Scotland. A small island off the coast of Albany in King George Sound, on the south-west tip of the West Australian coast, was named *Michaelmas Island* due to its discovery on the 29th September, 1791, which happened to be the celebration day held in honour of the Archangel Michael. Another town that we have named with a Celtic connection to Scotland is *Esperance* which is east of *Albany.* The family motto of William Wallace's family, was *'Esperance'* -'Hope'

Before final approval was given to establish a colony at 'Perth', the East India Company had to be consulted and Captain Stirling also had to report his findings to Governor Darling in Sydney for the Secretary for the Colonies, Mr Huskisson, had written to Governor Darling stating that it was inexpedient and expensive to occupy the western part of Australia unless the East India Company intended to do something with the Swan River. A portion of the letter which James sent to Governor Darling is as follows:

"Referring to winds - these two streams of wind offer great facilities to navigation on those shores for it is evident that vessels whatever may be their destination, may always be assured of fair winds and a speedy voyage across the Indian Ocean. Another advantage in navigation peculiar to the neighbourhood of the Swan River is its position with respect to Europe, Cape of Good Hope, Isle of France, the Peninsula of India and the Malay Islands. Vessels bound from those places to Swan River would reach it in 3 weeks less than they could reach Port Jackson and vessels bound from Swan River to those places would reach them in 6 weeks less time than from Port Jackson, in fact the Eastern ports of New Holland (Australia) including Van Diemen's Land (Tasmania), are cut off from all convenient communications with the Indian Seas to the Eastward during the greatest portion of the year, for Merchant Vessels cannot beat up against the strong westerly winds and lee currents which prevail on the southern coast of New Holland in all seasons except January and February."

"The third advantage peculiar to that position arises from its being very little out of the track of ships bound to China through the Eastern Passages, they generally make the outward passage light of laden in consequence of the great difficulty of making up a cargo for the Chinese market, but if there was a Settlement at Swan River, its supplies from England might be brought out in these ships at a cheap rate and they might there find some articles, suitable to the wants of the Chinese such as oil, and ship timber, besides obtaining for themselves the refreshments rendered necessary by such long voyages."

"As a Naval and Military station, the neighbourhood of Swan River is of the highest importance. Finally Sir, at a time when we have a French vessel of war in these seas, with objects not clearly understood and when we hear of an American vessel of war being also in this neighbourhood, seeking a place of settlement, it becomes important to prevent them from occupying a position of value, particularly as you were pleased to state that his Majesty's Government is desirous of not being anticipated in such views by any foreign power."

"From all these statements, it appears that agriculture and commercial emigrants, the Indian Company and their servants, the Naval and Military forces of His Majesty and the protection of His Majesty's possessions formed or forming in the seas, would all be benefited by the establishment of a Colony in the position pointed out. In proportion the possession of that country would be valuable to Great Britain, so would its occupation by any Foreign power be injurious and ruinous."

"The Dutch and French have already visited these shores, the latter might obtain millions of slaves among the Malay Islands and in any future war might pour out swarms of privateers upon some of the most important channels of our trade in its neighbourhood and in the possession of that country, they would find more than a full compensation for the loss of St Domingo."

In order to further plead his case, Sir James Stirling returned to London. Malcolm Uren in his book titled *Land Looking West* writes: "Again contemporary events favoured Stirling. His return to England almost coincided with the replacement of Mr Huskisson by Sir George Murray as Secretary for the Colonies and Sir George Murray was both a fellow Scot and a friend of the Stirling family. But for all that Stirling had to fight and win his battles on its merits. All that Sir George Murray can be said to have done, beyond what his predecessors had done, was to turn a sympathetic ear and listen to Stirling's arguments. That was enough for Stirling. At the moment he was content to be merely heard."

From the book titled *Admiral James Stirling* by G.S. Stirling we are informed as follows;

"On returning to England in 1828, Stirling set about canvassing support for the founding of his colony which was to become for him almost an obsession. He spent months visiting politicians at Westminster and then merchants in the City of London, in the hope that if the colonial ministry refused to help him, it might agree to a settlement that would be founded and financial settlers themselves under the protection of the government. After almost a year of official indifference and at times, even ridicule, he eventually managed to persuade the newly appointed secretary for the colonies, Sir George Murray, (an old family friend from Scotland), to accept his proposal for what was to become *Australia's only non penal colony.*"

From June to December 1829, beginning with the arrival of the *Parmelia*, more than 1,800 Settlers were landed upon the shores of Western Australia. Captain James Stirling was promoted from Lieutenant Governor to Governor of the colony. As the years went by, James was dismayed with the conditions that the early settlers had to endure and he wrote many letters of complaint to Earl Gray in England. However, given the conditions that he found himself in, and the general lack of support from England, he set out to accomplish the best he could under the circumstances.

Sir James had been insistent that there be no convicts sent to Western Australia. It was to be a free-colony. The reasons for this were because during his earlier naval career fighting on behalf of Britain off the southern coasts of America, on many occasions, Sir James witnessed the harsh treatment given to slaves and it left a deep impression in his mind. (Unfortunately, after Captain Stirling retired as Governor of the Colony and returned to England to carry out further duties for the Royal Navy, the Colony did become a penal colony. Saddened by this, Captain

Stirling never again returned to visit the Colony he had founded).

Sir George Murray appointed Captain Stirling as Lieutenant Governor and granted him the sum of one thousand pounds for the founding of the colony. Because of his loathing of the treatment of slaves, Stirling did his utmost to befriend the Aboriginals and learnt to speak their language. He was eventually to face his own personal tragedy. G.S. Stirling in his book titled *Admiral Sir James Stirling* wrote the following:

"One of the colony's soldiers had been killed by an Aboriginal and Thomas Peel, the Colony's principle landowner, and cousin of the Prime Minister, demanded a punitive expedition be sent against the tribe responsible for the soldier's death." (The Murray River, south of Perth in Western Australia named after Sir George Murray was discovered by Captain Stirling and his team of explorers. It covered a huge area and the land was claimed by a large investor of the City of London, namely Mr Thomas Peel). It can therefore be seen, that Thomas Peel carried a great deal of power and influence in many quarters.

"Stirling argued passionately against such an expedition but his opinion was opposed by a majority of settlers, who now perceived the Aborigines as a growing menace, and by Peel who threatened to refer the matter to the Colonial authority as it involved the murder of a soldier of the Crown."

From information contained in the book titled *Western Australia's Tempestuous History* by John Nairn we learn the following pertinent information:

"On April 24th, 1834, George Shenton's mill (the Old Mill at South Perth) was raided by Murray River tribesmen...they stole 8 sacks of flour and other irreplaceable articles. Records from the W. A. Historical Society reveal that the local natives were annoyed with the Murray River tribesmen for the 'trespassing' on Swan River territory. The raiders had also stolen flour which could well have been taken by the Swan River natives. So, as a reprisal, local native trackers speedily identified several of the raiders, by footprints left in spilt flour. Their identifications led to four Murray River tribesmen being flogged and gaoled for a month. Two Aborigines were wounded while the arrests were being made, and the whole tribe - numbering about 75 - lusted for revenge. Revenge was also plotted against big, burly Thomas Peel."

Whilst all this trouble was brewing, Sir James Stirling was still in London, seeking more funds and support for the struggling Swan River colony, to which the Crown had appointed only the minimal of funds.

From author John Nairn we learn that: "When Governor Stirling returned to the settlement from London in August that year, he was hailed by a barrage of complaints...and a priority demand was protection against theft and violence by Murray River Aborigines."

It was said of Sir James Stirling by E.W. Landor who wrote *The Bushman or*

Life in a New Country who was a resident of the Swan River Colony, that "except the waiter at a commercial inn, no man has so much upon his hands, or so many faults to answer for, as the Governor of the Colony...he is expected to do something and not a little for all who are in trouble...it is amongst his duties to console, to cheer, to advise, to redress, to remedy, and above all, to enrich."

Thus, upon his return from London, with all the pressure placed upon him, Captain Stirling had no choice but to concede to the wishes of the colonists. In fairness to Captain Stirling who had befriended and learnt the language of the Aboriginals, he was away when all the trouble started and it was obviously a rival territorial tribal skirmish of one tribe versus another.

Unfortunately also, his meeting with officials in London to secure more funds for the Colony had fallen on deaf ears.

From information taken from an old document in the Stirling Library in Western Australia, we learn that "the British government was not at all pleased to have a truant governor on its doorstep and he was lucky to escape censure for leaving his post without permission. He was saved mainly by his obvious sincerity on behalf of a group of settlers who had long since ceased to welcome new shiploads of either capitalists or workmen."

"For nearly two years, Stirling doggedly explained to officials and politicians in London the necessitous circumstances of the colonists, but to no avail. He returned to the colony more than ever apprehensive about its future. The British officials eagerly seized on the failure of the grandiose land settlement scheme of Thomas Peel which they misguidedly identified with the whole colony, and whose failure they wrongly and maliciously attributed to faults in government policy rather than to the calibre of its promoter or to the deficiencies of nature. Stirling gave Thomas Peel no priority in the choice of his land and he was not responsible for Peel's financial difficulties."

Thus, under all the pressure, Stirling returned to the Swan River Settlement from England, to find other troubles had erupted concerned with Thomas Peel. It was a most unfortunate situation for both the Aboriginals and the settlers, which led to a battle at Pinjarra, on the Murray River in which people on both sides were killed and some were taken prisoners. There is no denying that it was a most unfortunate situation for the Aboriginals but the events that followed certainly saddened Sir James and within three years, he handed in his resignation as Governor of the Colony.

John Nairn writes: "Later, Stirling received commendations from the settlers for his compassion and understanding when he released the prisoners, with a message to be relayed to the remnants of their tribe that further misconduct could only result in harsher reprisals."

One of his concerns was for the welfare of the aborigines and he founded an institution at Mt Eliza for the betterment of native welfare. By October 1837, after eight years of struggling with the slow progress of the colony, James forwarded his resignation to the Colonial Secretary, Lord Glenelg. Much of the slow progress was attributed to the lack of finance and lack of sympathetic understanding shown by the British Government who had increased the land prices from one shilling and sixpence an acre to five shillings per acre. This caused a financial struggle amongst the early settlers and disappointed by this lack of co-operation, Governor James Stirling, having done his best, decided to resign and return to England.

A.C. Staples writes: "By 1839, Stirling and his young government officials had guided the quite minute settlement through an Indian Ocean trade depression which followed the bankruptcy, between 1830 -1834, of all the large Calcutta commercial houses. Then the colony enjoyed an increasing flow of emigration to Australian shores when in 1839, the Papineau Rebellions upset the development of Canada."

Malcolm Uren in his book titled *Land Looking West* wrote: "In these days it is easy to overlook the variety of parts played by a colonial governor over 100 years ago, especially by a governor such as Stirling. A man who had to sympathize as well as to organize, to encourage as well as to direct, to sit in judgement on petty, personal squabbles - for there was no other court of appeal nearer than England, and to attempt to solve all problems connected with the infant struggles of the new settlement. Stirling had to listen at the same time to all the wildest optimism and most dispirited pessimism of the colony."

"Stirling's last official function was a ball held on the 20th December, 1837. Almost everybody was invited and there was dancing till dawn during which time the sad farewells were said. In a diary by George Moore, *'Contrary to what is usual the Governor has become more and more popular every day, and we cling to him with the greatest tenacity in proportion as the time approaches his departure'.*"

"These sentiments culminated on the last day of the year, Stirling's very last day of office, by the presentation to him of an address by the people. This address told him of their sorrow at his going and their hopes for his future. It must have touched him deeply, for there had been moments in those 10 years when he saw little thanks and small gratitude for the efforts he had made on their behalf. To be fair to him, it must also be conjectured that with the passing of time, he saw the mistakes he had made, or some of them and realised the right of human nature to assert itself in criticism and condemnation as well as in thanks and applause."

Malcolm Uren wrote: "His most enduring service to the British Empire was the carrying out of his personal plan to claim for England the western coast of Australia. In so doing, he added to the British Empire an area of almost a million square miles."

The people of the colony showed their appreciation by presenting him with a cup in 1833 upon which was inscribed:

"Presented to Captain James Stirling, R.N., first Governor of Western Australia, by the relatives and friends of the settlers of the Swan River in testimony of their admiration of the wisdom, decision, and kindness uniformly displayed by him and of their gratitude for his strenuous exertions with the Colonial Department for the benefit of the settlement."

Thus having founded the Swan River Colony, and served as Governor for ten years, the time had come for Sir James to further his naval career and so in 1837, James and his wife Ellen (nee Mangles), returned to Britain. By then he was forty-eight years old and was appointed by the Royal Navy to command the *Indus* on the Mediterranean Station where he remained until 1844. After another three years ashore he was appointed to the *Howe*, which he commanded in the Mediterranean for three years until 1850 when he was knighted by the King of Greece for his service in the Mediterranean, with the insignia of Knight Commander of the Order of the Redeemer.

On returning to England, *James Stirling was knighted and became a member of the Royal Society.* In 1862, he attained the rank of Admiral and undertook many voyages on behalf of the Royal Navy, serving in the West Indies where he fought against the French and the Spaniards.

Discovery of Gold
And
The Early Sailing Ships to Australia

Gold was discovered in Australia in 1851 and the Colonial trade began to look promising as gold-fever drew a steady stream of emigrants. According to Basil Lubbock in his book titled *The Colonial Clippers*, the first ship to land Australian gold in the British Isles was called the *Phoenician*, arriving in Plymouth on the 3rd February, 1852, after a passage of 83 days from Sydney, which was considered to be a record run. Her cargo was valued at eighty one thousand pounds. "Between the years of 1852 -1857, when the rush to find gold was at its height, 100,000 Englishmen, 60,000 Irish, 50,000 Scots, 4,000 Welsh, 8,000 Germans, 1,500 French, 3,000 Americans and no less than 25,000 Chinese - not to speak of the other nationalities of the world, all of whom were represented - landed on the shores of Australia."

The discovery of gold set up keen competition to produce larger and faster ships as well as better accommodation. Basil Lubbock writes in his book titled *The Colonial Clippers* "the Colonial trade became one of the most important in the entire world's Mercantile Marine. And when the gold fever drew a stream of English, Scotch and Irish peasants to Australia, men, women and children, most of whom had never seen a ship before, embarked, and who were as helpless and shiftless as babes aboard, it was seen that something must be done to improve the conditions of the emigrant ships. The discovery of alluvial gold in Australia was mainly brought about by the great Californian strike of 1849. That strike upset the theories of geologists and set every man on the world's frontiers searching for the elusive metal."

"With the arrival in England of larger and larger consignments of gold, there was a rush to taking shipping to the Antipodes that both the Emigration Commissioners and the ship-owners found themselves unable to put sufficient tonnage on the berth to carry the clamouring hosts of adventurers. Liverpool ship-owners began hiring or buying American Transatlantic packets and clippers."

The British owned trading companies, mostly owned by Freemasons, were prospering, and eventually the idea of convict founded colonies was abolished. The people were free at last to choose where they wished to establish themselves. On 30th September, 1865, the *Vimiera*, owned by the shipping line *Devitt & Moore*, the only time that this shipping line ever carried convicts, sailed from Portland, England, to Fremantle, Western Australia. The passage took eighty three days and every convict was landed in good health, which was quite an achievement for a convict ship.

By 1868, convicts ceased to be shipped to Australia. The race was on to build the best clipper ships for trade between Britain and Australia and this company played a major part in Australian shipping, numbering among some of its more famous ships, the tea and wool clipper, *Cutty Sark*, the *Hesperus*, (which became a training ship for mid seamen), the *Sobraon, La Hogue, Harbinger, St George, Duke of Athole, Tamar, Rodney, Torrens, Dunbar Castle, Queen of the Thames, South Australian, St Vincent, Pekina, Hawkesbury, Derwent, City of Adelaide, Illawarra, Macquarie, Collingwood, Port Jackson* and the *Medway*. (As far back as 1836, *Devitt & Moore* loaded ships bound for Australia).

According to Basil Lubbock in his book titled *The Colonial Clippers*, the company's ships were amongst the pioneers in the passenger and wool trade of Adelaide in South Australia. One of the first larger type sailing vessels to be built was the *La Hogue*. Her outstanding feature was her figure-head. This was a very large shield emblazoned with the St Andrew's cross. The *La Hogue* whose wool trade was with Sydney, was so popular with the Australians that they would wait weeks and often months on purpose to sail in her.

The *Collingwood* carried out wool trade with Melbourne and had the distinction of being on the 'Ship's Roll of Honour in the Great War', being sunk by a German submarine in 1917 after forty-five year's of service.

Authors who have written about the early sailing shipping companies comment that the Company of *Devitt & Moore* contributed greatly to Australian shipping lines with the vast improvements in accommodation on board and faster passages to Australia, so much so, that passengers were quite content to be placed on a waiting-list until there was room available for them.

Although the sailing ships are now long forgotten, the Company was most notable for founding the Pangbourne Nautical College in England, which trained seaman for the navy which is still in existence today.

Because of the foresightedness of Sir Joseph Banks, of introducing wheat, and merino sheep into Australia, Australia's wool industry flourished as did our sales of wheat. Basil Lubbock wrote: "These were the days when great races home from Australia took place - not only did ship race against ship, but it was the aim and object of every skipper to get his ship home in time for the first wool sales in London. And in the wool trade, unlike the custom in the tea trade, the fastest ships were loaded last - the pride of place - that of being the last ship to leave an Australasian port for the London wool sales being reserved for that which was considered the fastest ship in the trade.

In the eighties, when the tea trade was entirely in the hands of the steamers, this pride of place in Sydney was always kept for the famous clipper *Cutty Sark*, no other ship, either wood or iron built, being able to rival her passages both out and home in the wool trade."

The *Devitt & Moore* sailing ship, the *Sobraon* who made her first voyage to Australia in 1866, was the biggest and most stately ship on the England-Australia run with a service record second to none. There was no Suez Canal in *Sobraon's* day so she took the long way round the Cape to England once each year. When she returned to London she was loaded with wheat and wool - her fastest trip was sixty-eight days and it was said of her that she was never passed by any other sailing ship either on or off wind. On her homeward voyage she called at Cape Town, and then St Helena for three days to enable her passengers to see the island and climb the six hundred and sixty-nine steps to Napoleon's tomb.

Thus, with numerous emigrants happily and voluntarily coming out to Australia to 'try their luck', very early in our young history, we became a nation of mixed races and once settlement by convicts was abolished, Australians came to realise how fortunate they were when compared with the rest of the world's history because we were never to become a war-faring nation. Australia is a blessed country, a young country when compared to British and European civilization.

According to St Germain in the book *Earth's Birth Changes*, Australia is the Heart Seal of the world, the younger sister of America and as such has her special purpose in the future of the world. St Germain also told of how Lemuria at one time was situated alongside Australia and New Zealand. When the land of Lemuria submerged beneath the sea forever, there was a shifting of plates and the continents of America and Lemuria came together. Also according to St Germain, America and Australia were born very close to the same point in history and that they will help the rest of the Earth in future times, in the understanding of harmony and co-operation, as will our neighbour, New Zealand.

MASTERS DISCUSSED IN THIS CHAPTER

St Germain

Sir Joseph Banks - Kuthumi

NOTES AND RECOMMENDED READING

Malcolm J. Uren, *Land Looking West*, (Oxford University Press, U.K., 1947)

J.S. Stirling, *Admiral James Stirling*, (W.A. Stirling Library/Museum)

John Nairn, *Western Australia's Tempestuous History*, (North Stirling Press, W.A. 1976)

A.C. Staples, *Spanish Colonial Influence on Sir James Stirling*, (W.A. Stirling Library/Museum)

Captain A.G. Course, *Painted Ports, The Story of the Ships of Devitt and Moore*, (Hollis & Carter, London, 1961)

V.G. Fall, *The Sea And The Forest*, (University of Western Australia Press, 1972)

Brian Gardner, *The East India Company*, (Rupert Hart-Davis, London, U.K., 1971)

Basil Lubbock, *The Colonial Clippers*, (Brown & Ferguson Ltd., Glasgow, 1948)

John Bach, *A Maritime History of Australia*, (Nelson, Melbourne, Australia, 1976)

CHAPTER 50

The Legacy

"I have been Teacher to all intelligences,
I am able to instruct the whole universe,
I shall be until the day of judgement,
Upon the face of the Earth"
(Taliesin/Merlin - St Germain)

"....and from her ashes spring,
New Heaven and Earth, wherein the just shall dwell,
And, after all their tribulations long,
See golden days, fruitful of golden deeds,
With joy and love triumphing, and fair 'truth'."
(Milton - Excerpt from Paradise Lost)

"Oh my Beloved, fill the Cup that clears
TODAY of past Regrets and future Fears -
Tomorrow? Why, Tomorrow I may be
Myself with Yesterday's Seven Thousand Years"
(Omar Khayyam - Excerpt from Rubaiyat)

In this final chapter, it is necessary to repeat the phrase used in a previous chapter in order to place emphasis upon the fact that "we learn from history that we do *not* learn from history"!

Throughout this story, examples of how the Masters of the Great White Brotherhood have always guided and watched over Earth and humanity's destination have been given and the purpose of writing this story has been to demonstrate this fact. In the first chapter and elsewhere throughout this story, it has been emphasized that the 'White Brotherhood' is not meant in any racial sense as a descriptive word; for it is important to understand that the Masters come from *all* nationalities of men and women.

In a world that is full of uncertainly we make take heart that all is not doom and gloom, for we are continually being watched over by the *Masters of the Mystical Rose* and we may rest assured that we have a choice of what we wish the future of our world to be. Whether people are able to accept 'reincarnation' or that there is a 'Higher Intelligence' and a 'Divine Blueprint' for humanity matters not as long as we remember to have 'faith' and 'love'.

What is important is the fact that we can choose to change the world in which we live into one of beauty, joy, and peace, which has always been the loving aim and desire of the Masters who are the 'Guardians' of this planet Earth. An apt old adage is that 'aptitude alters altitude'; in other words, we are capable of choosing to 'rise above' the judgemental attitudes of colour, race and creed, so prevalent in today's society.

The modern day Prophet, the late Edgar Cayce told of how the Creator/God gave us 'free will' on this planet. He also told of how the Atlantean influence is still as headstrong as ever it was. According to Edgar Cayce, "this influence applies particularly to those soul-groups who chose *not* to reincarnate at a steady rate of progress. In other words, with each reincarnation, they choose not to change their Karmic pattern for the better. The Law of Karma states that 'we reap what we sow'."

"At their zenith, the Atlanteans commanded the powers of ESP (extra sensory perception) and telepathy, harnessed electricity, mastered the mechanical propulsion of air and sea vessels, established short wave communications, induced longevity, and performed advanced surgery, using as their source of energy, the Tuaoi Crystal Stone, their own forerunner to the laser ray. It was the misuse of this same source of energy which destroyed them."

Elsewhere in our story, the Egyptian 'Eye' in the centre of the triangle-shaped capstone which makes up part of the design of the American Great Seal, designed by St Germain, was briefly mentioned. There have been various theories expounded which say that the Tuaoi Crystal Stone is the missing cap-stone of the Pyramids in Egypt which will be replaced when the time is ripe - a time when all the secrets of the Universe contained within the Hall of Records which are reputed to be hidden in the Pyramids, will be revealed.

According to Edgar Cayce, an archaeological discovery of profound significance will be found early in the second millennium and it will be to do with the Great Pyramid and the Sphinx at Gizeh. Gizeh traces its origins back to before the Great Flood of Noah's time. Cayce related that a king by the name of Arart moved his tribe into the Nile valley and Arart's spiritual leader was a priest by the name of Ra Ta, who was a previous incarnation of Edgar Cayce.

'Pyramid' means 'fire in the middle' or a focus of cosmic energy. ('Pyra means 'fire' and 'pryo' means middle). It is believed that the Tuaoi Crystal Stone which the Atlanteans misused was capable of holding the harmonic resonance of Earth in its orbit. Another name for it was the Lodestone which was originally the apex of the Great Pyramid. Its function was to create fusion between Earth and the Cosmos and it was capable of capturing and storing information received from the Cosmos.

Dr Paul Brunton in his book titled *A Search In Secret Egypt* described his experience of spending a night of solitude and darkness inside one of the pyramids. The author came into contact with many strange forces and he supports the theory that the pyramids and the Sphinx were created by emigrant colonists from Atlantis who had command of the elemental spirits and were capable of working many miracles. On the night that he spent 'alone' inside the Great Pyramid, two ancient High Priests, tall and dressed in white robes, appeared to him in etherical form.

"There was light a-glimmer all around them, which in a most uncanny way, lit up the part of the room. Was I functioning in some *fourth dimension*, aware and awake in some far-off epoch of the past? Had my sense of time regressed to the early days of Egypt? No; that could not be, for I perceived quickly that these two could see me and even now were about to address me. Their tall figures bent forward; the lips of one spirit seemed to move, his face close to mine, his eyes flashing spiritual fire, and his voice sounding in my ear."

Then, Dr Paul Brunton telepathically received an important message from the ancient Egyptian High Priest.

"Know, my son that in this ancient fane (temple) lies the lost record of the early races of man and of the Covenant which they made with their Creator through the first of His great prophets."

"Know, too, that chosen men were brought here of old to be shown this Covenant that they might return to their fellows and keep the great secret alive. Take back with thee the warning that when men forsake their Creator, and look on their fellows with hate, as with the princes of Atlantis in whose time this Pyramid was built, they are destroyed by the weight of their own iniquity, even as the people of Atlantis were destroyed."

Edgar Cayce prophesied of the return of both types of Atlanteans in vast numbers. He warned that for every advance in science and emancipation, the *Sons of the One God* (the ones who worked for the 'Light') might bring with them the *Sons of Man* (who worked for the 'Dark') as in corruption, greed, abuse, dominance, power and 'control'. This is a typical example of the battle of 'Light' versus the 'Dark'; and whose Karma has not yet been resolved throughout their numerous reincarnations since the days of Atlantis. This is the Battle of Armageddon; the battle of good versus evil forces within man's own consciousness.

Continuing with the information relayed to Dr Paul Brunton by the ancient Egyptian priest in spirit form: "It was not the Creator who sank Atlantis, but the selfishness, the cruelty, the spiritual blindness of the people who dwelt on those doomed islands. The Creator loves all; but the lives of men are governed by invisible laws which He has set over them. Take back this warning, then: 'it matters not whether thou discoverest the door or not. Find but the secret passage within the mind that will lead thee to the hidden chamber within thine own soul, and thou shalt have found something worthy indeed'."

'Dark' versus 'Light'

As stated, Edgar Cayce referred to the pure ones (the Light Bearers) of Atlantis as the *Sons of God*, however, the others who meddled with the laws of Nature, striving to attain fantastic power and at the same time abusing it, he called the *Sons of Man*.

According to Cayce, when the abusive ones meddled with the laws of 'Nature', "they became hopelessly entangled in the procreative processes, and onto earth came an anguished hybrid, neither human nor animal - a half-man, half-beast - unable to conform to or escape from the laws of animal evolution. And there crept into those pollutions; or rather, the Sons of Man polluted themselves with those mixtures. This brought contempt, hatred, bloodshed, and those impulses which build for self-desire, without respect for another's freedom. They reduced the backward hybrid souls, or mutants, to slavery, subjecting them to every degradation and abuse."

Although Cayce wrote of these things in the 1940's, he prophesied that the Atlanteans, the ones who had abused their powers so long ago, were still continuing to reincarnate. During Cayce's era, there was no such thing as 'cloning' or any of the other somewhat horrific scientific experiments that are taking place today - all of which are interfering with 'Nature' itself.

As discussed in the first chapter of our story, Cayce stated uncompromisingly that "Atlanteans souls are extremists (the abusive ones), who know no middle ground. Atlanteans of every genre were to be found *amongst the leaders of all the nations* involved in the two World Wars. As a rough standard of comparison, we can set Roosevelt and Sir Winston Churchill at one end of the scale and Hitler and Stalin at the other."

He further stated that: "The advances which civilization has made from barbarism to practicable democracy leave the impenitent type of Atlantean unmoved. When he reaches a psychotic level, he then stuffs himself with LSD, or climbs into a school bell tower and shoots those around him."

"At a cannier level of self-preservation, he is the person who scoffs, who is the cynic that undermines his society. You will find him behind the corrupt politician, the rabble rouser, the ones who are racists, those who do not give heed to the sick and infirm, those who follow the path of the 'get rich quick scheme', and those who are reducing the popular cultures to semi-literate trash."

Amazingly, Cayce predicted all of the above over fifty years ago and no one in the world today, taking into consideration all the events that have happened recently, could deny the accuracy of his predictions.

The New Age

It is of interest to note that in February, 1999, it was announced in *The West Australian* newspaper based upon an article written by Mike Peacock in London that: "The world got weirder last year as the approaching millennium fuelled a global surge of interest in the paranormal, according to a journal of strange and unexplained phenomena. The Fortean Times said 1998 was a bumper year for reports of *reincarnation,* prophecies, apparitions and UFO encounters. '1998 was by far the strangest year since our records began', said Joe McNally, associate editor of the journal."

"The Fortean Times Weirdness Index, measuring the number of stories printed in the journal, rose 4.1 per cent from 1997. But with the new century fast approaching, the experts expect the weird count to climb further."

What is today termed 'New Age' is an awareness of a different kind of spirituality which is sweeping the world, ably assisted by access to today's modern technology - computers and websites. As has been established throughout this story, it really is not 'new', it's just that the time is now ripe for its re-emergence. There is a global 'awakening' occurring and it is 'Divinely' timed. The 'Light' workers, spoken of by Edgar Cayce are aware of their individual roles to work towards global peace and love for all mankind, no matter what colour, race, or creed. In Revelation written by the Master Kuthumi in his incarnation as John the Beloved Disciple, we are informed in Chapter Four of the 144,000 children of every tongue and of every nation who incarnate throughout the planet to assist in lifting human consciousness. The number is merely symbolic for by utilizing the Pythagorean system (of Kuthumi) it adds up to nine and according to J.C. Cooper in the book titled *An Illustrated Encyclopaedia of Traditional Symbols*:

NINE - composed of the all-powerful 3 x 3, it is completion, fulfilment; attainment...it is an 'incorruptible' number.

Commenting about the New Age in his book titled *The New Age Emerging*, the author J.L. Simmons, Ph.D., wrote:

"Are there special circumstances that increase the likelihood of psychic experiences teaching full consciousness? At first glance, such occurrences might seem random and haphazard. However, a closer inspection of cases reveals something of a pattern - circumstances where they are more likely to arise. It seems there must be some sort of *triggering* to override a person's physical-plane immersion and clickety-click-click logical thought processes."

"Interestingly, there are two extremes of experience in which paranormal happenings are most likely to burst through into awareness: extreme stress conditions on the one hand, and extreme lightheartedness on the other. There are no doubt other factors which increase the chances of psychic phenomena reaching awareness. An obvious one is the social climate within a family or network in which there is some conscious experience of, and belief in, things spiritual, and where they are not just dismissed as imagination. Growing up in a family or running around with people who freely talk about spiritual experiences and ideas provides a more nurturant atmosphere for having ideas and experiences oneself. Being raised in a region or culture where these things are accepted is also supportive of such personal experiences and explorations."

"The most reliable factor for increasing anyone's awareness of psychic incidences and influences is through achieving a higher level of consciousness."

"Psychic events are always occurring. It is our *awareness* of them that fluctuates. When a person is deeply focused and actively immersed in the physical plane, the larger spiritual realms seem quite unreal and mostly irrelevant. The pull of physical activities, involvements, and problems can be very strong, even all consuming, as we call attest. I've seen even professional psychics and mystics get utterly bogged down in the business side of their occupations."

"The 'bridges' between physical life and spirituality, between the physical and spiritual planes, seem to be tricky and tenuous ones for most people. People, are having 'minor' psychic experiences all the time, but these usually go unrecognized or are shrugged off or explained away. In our mainstream society, some physiological or psychological explanation is commonly given for the valid hunch, or even the vivid dream, or the uncanny recognition of a person or place."

"...when spiritual occurrences are condemned as rubbish by some Establishment preacher or scientist, there is a wide-spread backlash of 'well, there's *something* to all these things', followed by a story about some unexplainable experience. And so it goes."

In his book titled *A Search In Secret Egypt,* Dr Paul Brunton wrote:

"We are beginning to discover that the ancients' knowledge of the powers and properties of the human kind was in some directions superior to ours. The apparition of immaterial forces has startled our agnostic age. Our best scientists and foremost thinkers are joining the ranks of those who believe there is a psychic basis to life. What they think to-day, the masses will think to-morrow."

Three Great Truths

"Hear me, my brother, he said. "There are three truths which are absolute, and which cannot be lost, but yet may remain silent for lack of speech."

"The Soul of man is immortal, and its future is the future of a thing whose growth and splendour has no limit."

"The principle which gives life dwells in us and without us, is undying and eternally beneficent, is not heard nor seen, or smelt, but is perceived by the man who desires perception."

"Each man is his own absolute lawgiver, the dispenser of glory or gloom to himself; the decreer of his life, his reward, his punishment."

"These truths, which are as great as is life itself, are as simple as the simplest mind of man. Feed the hungry with them."

('Three Great Truths', from the Idyll Of The White Lotus extracted from Dr Douglas Baker's book titled 'The Jewel in the Lotus')

The English author, Dr Douglas Baker, B.A., M.R.C.S., L.R.C.P.,.F.Z.S., made the following comments in his book titled *The Jewel in the Lotus*: "I began the study of Medicine at the late age of thirty-four, by which time I had been able to integrate a stable personality, otherwise I would never have been able to survive what soon became the common knowledge of my medical school, that Baker 'hears voices of what he calls the Masters' and even writes about them in his journal AQUARIUS."

For those who have experienced the paranormal, they know their experiences to be real. According to Dr Baker:

"The number of people who have experienced altered states of awareness, to say nothing of outright mystical experience, is so large and the weight of the evidence for psychic phenomena so vast, that, as Professor H.J. Eysenck, psychology chairman at the University of London pointed out, one would otherwise have to postulate a gigantic worldwide conspiracy involving dozens of universities and hundreds of scientists."

Commenting upon his own individual experiences and contact with the Masters, Dr Baker wrote: "No one ever then, or subsequently, called me a schizophrenic, even though I have always described and paid tribute to the influences upon me of a vast inner world inhabited by Beings and intelligences as high above my own as mine is above an animal. Together these Masters form an inner government of the world, and the teachings They give out are to the initiated few in the form of the 'Mysteries'."

"Those inner worlds have always been...they influenced the minds of men like Socrates, Pythagoras, Plato and Aesculapius in Greece and before that in Egypt,

Persia, and China. Later, after the Dark Ages, the 'Mysteries' reached Europe and were spread unobtrusively by many esoteric groups such as 'The Illuminati', the Knights Templar, the Rosicrucians etc."

"In the last hundred years, a new outpouring of the perennial Wisdom reached the West through the offices of Madame Blavatsky [founder of the Theosophical Society]. Her inspirers were Masters of the Himalayas, and in an unbroken stream They continued to 'speak' through Annie Bessant, Alice Bailey, C.W. Leadbeater, Rudolf Steiner and others. They continued the true tradition of classical Ancient Wisdom given out in all ages by enlightened Beings."

Annie Bessant (1847-1933) became the second President of the Theosophical Society (1907-1933) and was described as a 'Diamond Soul', for she had many brilliant facets to her character. She was an outstanding orator of her time, a champion of human freedom, educationist, philanthropist and author of more than three hundred books. She also guided thousands of men and women all over the world in their spiritual quest. According to information contained within her book titled *The Ancient Wisdom*:

"A whole volume might easily be filled with the similarities between the religions of the world. All these similarities point to a single source, and that is the Brotherhood of the White Lodge, the Hierarchy Adepts who watch over and guide the evolution of humanity, and who have preserved these truths unimpaired; from time to time, as necessity arose, reasserting them in the ears of men. From other worlds, from earlier humanities, They came to help our globe, evolved by a process comparable to that now going on with our ourselves, and that will be more intelligible when we have completed our present study than it may now appear and they have afforded this help, reinforced by the flower of our own humanity, from the earliest times until today. Still They teach eager pupils, showing the path and guiding the disciple's steps; still They may be reached by all who seek Them, bearing in their hands the sacrificial fuel of love, of devotion, of unselfish longing to know in order to serve; still They carry out the ancient discipline, still unveil the ancient Mysteries. The two pillars of Their Lodge gateway are Love and Wisdom, and through its strait portal can only pass those from whose shoulders has fallen the burden of desire and selfishness."

Dr Barker informs us as follows: "I grew up with a great admiration for D.H. Lawrence and have never found any reason for not sharing his attitude on the subject of Ancient Wisdom:

'I honestly think that the great pagan world of which Egypt and Greece were the last living terms...had a vast and perhaps perfect science in terms of life...I believe that this great science...was universal, established all over the then-existing globe. I believe it was esoteric, invested in a large priesthood. Just as mathematics and mechanics and physics are defined and expounded in the same way in the universities of China or Bolivia, or London or Moscow, today, so, it seems to me, in the great world previous to ours, a great science and cosmology were taught esoterically in all countries of the globe - Asia, Polynesia, America, Atlantis and Europe...This is simple theosophy'."

Edgar Cayce spoke of the New Age era and that it had already begun in his own time. He prophesied on a number of occasions that by the year 1998, many earth changes and social changes would be gradual but then become more pronounced. He said: "In 1998 we may find a great deal of activities as have been wrought by the gradual changes that are coming about. These are at the periods when the cycle of the solar activity, or the years are related to the sun's passage through the various spheres of activity, become paramount, or tantamount to the change between the Piscean and the Aquarian Age. This is a gradual, not a cataclysmic activity in the experience of the earth in this period. There will be less wars, peace will eventually come to the world and man will learn more and more how to benefit from scientific discoveries still awaiting discovery."

In another reading, Cayce stated that when world peace came into being "individually, know that right, justice, mercy, patience - as was represented by Him, the Prince of Peace, is that basis upon which the new world order *must* eventually be established before there *is* peace. Then, innately, mentally, and manifestedly in self, prepare self for co-operative measures in all phases of human relations in this direction. The New Age is coming about both because of and in spite of, mankind! God doesn't need man, man needs God. But man can, by his own free will, *delay* or *hasten fulfilment of God's plan*. And so may you, as seekers for divine guidance, be uplifted and thus may you hasten the day when war will be no more."

Back in 1941, Cayce predicted the very day that the Second World War would end. Cayce died in January, 1945 and on September 2nd, 1945, the Japanese formally surrendered and World War II ended.

Cayce also discussed the principles upon which world peace would be built: "For with those changes will be wrought, Americanism - the ism - with the universal thought that is expressed and manifested in the brotherhood of man into group thought, as expressed in the (Free) Masonic Order - will be the eventual rule in the settlement of the affairs of the world. Not that the world is to become a Masonic Order, but that the principles which are embraced in same will be the basis upon which the new order of peace is to be established." The founder of Freemasonry was St Germain.

'The Teacher of Righteousness'

In Matthew 5:6 we are clearly told: *Blessed are they which do hunger and thirst after righteousness: for they shall be filled.*

And in verse 9 we are given the message about 'peace': *Blessed are the peacemakers: for they shall be called the children of God.*

Throughout this story, the Teacher of Righteousness has been discussed and that within the Dead Sea Scrolls, there is information pertaining to two men who will appear in the 'Last Days' (of the Piscean era). The first is the Teacher of Righteousness who will have the task of revealing 'all the Mysteries of the Scripture'. He is the Teacher of Wisdom ('Sophia/Athena'), who is spoken of as the 'Star', *who will gather around him the faithful, the spiritual* and reveal to them the real Truth behind the scriptures. It will be remembered that St Germain writing under the pseudonym of Taliesin in the 6th Century, when he was St Columba and Merlin, gave us clues as to who he was:

"I have been teacher to all intelligences,

I am able to instruct the whole universe,

I shall be until the day of judgement

On the face of the earth."

It will also be recalled that according to John Allegro, the Teacher of Righteousness of the Qumran Community had access to the Sacred Mysteries which is mentioned in the commentary of the prophet Habakkuk:

"to whom God made known all the secrets of the words of His servants, the prophets."

"The Teacher had the responsibility of passing on these secrets to his followers and in another Qumran commentary, is referred to as 'the Mediator of Knowledge' and that he is probably the author of the hymn who styles himself as 'Mediator of Knowledge in the wonderful Mysteries'."

We are further informed in the Essenes' *Manual of Discipline*:

"He will purge by his Truth all the deeds of Men, to give to the upright insight into the knowledge of the Most High and into the Wisdom of the sons of Heaven, to give the perfect way of understanding. Thus, the Spirit of Truth enlightens man to 'an understanding and insight and mighty wisdom which believe in the works of God'."

Francis Bacon's (St Germain's) motto was *Bene visit qui bene latuit* meaning 'one lives best by the hidden life' - for in those days, for fear of persecution, his places of teaching had to be kept hidden, i.e. the Order of the Rose Cross lodges, the Freemasonic lodges, and the Royal Society which was a veil for similar teachings where philosophy, science and alchemy were taught.

In one of his works, *Magna Instauratio* (the Great Reconstruction), he wrote:

"I am labouring to lay the foundation not of any sect or doctrine, but of utility and power - knowledge is power, not mere argument or ornament."

The *'Teacher of Righteousness'* is St Germain and he is teaching us the 'Truth' if we care to open our minds and seek it for we all have a role to play in the overall plan of humanity's destiny. Through developing the 'spiritual' part of us, we develop individual wholeness (or Holiness if you will), whence comes illumination. In other words, we receive true enlightenment and we come to understand that we are all part of the whole universe - we are not separate.

We have seen how St Germain was the Master who founded hundreds of Freemasonic and Order of the Rose Cross lodges in England and Europe and how he was the Master behind the plans for the United States of America to become a free country. We have seen how he was the one who designed the Great Seal of the United States which portrays the great eagle (symbol of John the Beloved who wrote the Book of Revelation). Francis Bacon was honoured in 1910 by Newfoundland on a commemorative stamp which stated "The Guiding Spirit in Colonization Schemes". We have also seen how Sir Joseph Banks - Kuthumi, was the guiding spirit for the colonization of Australia.

The second person of important significance mentioned in the Dead Sea Scrolls is the Sceptre, a king from the lineage of the House of David (Kuthumi) who will lead his people to victory.

By referring back to the Dead Sea Scrolls and the prophecies of the expected Messiah, there is a reference to the New Age. According to Peter Lemesurier in his book titled *The Armageddon Script*, the Essenes believed that when wars were finished, *"there would be everlasting peace and prosperity under the benevolent rule of a king of the line of David, or even the reborn David himself."*

We are assured by the Arthurian legends that Arthur (Kuthumi) will return.

Peter Lemesurier wrote that "if one thing was clear to the 'Teacher' and his successors, it was that the New Age would not dawn until the promised Messiah (meaning 'the anointed one') had appeared to inaugurate it."

"The Qumran Messiah ben Aaron, the 'Interpreter of the Law', in true Essene fashion, would be the superior partner. The appearance of the Messiah or Messiahs was quite a separate matter from the expected semi-miraculous Divine intervention which would finally establish the New Age itself." (As we have learned in previous chapters, Aaron was an incarnation of St Germain).

Concerning the dawning of the New Age, Edgar Cayce wrote:

"Will ye have part of it, or will ye let it pass by and merely by a hanger-on?"

The late Isabel Cooper-Oakley wrote in the final chapter of her book titled *The Comte De St Germain*: "His [St Germain's] work was to lead a portion of the eighteenth century humanity to that same goal which now, at the end of the nineteenth century, again stands clear before the eyes of some Theosophists. From his message many turned away in scorn, and from the present leaders the blind ones will to-day turn away also in scorn. But the few whose eyes are opening to the glad light of a spiritual knowledge look back to him who bore the burden in the last century with gratitude profound."

There can be little doubt left in the mind of the reader, of the great contributions that the Masters have made, and that we are always guided and watched over. Will we choose to follow the teachings of the Ancient Masters and in particular, the Teacher - St Germain? If we are able to accept that the codes in the Bible exist and that they were placed there by a Higher Intelligence, to be deciphered for the benefit of our future, then, with our power of 'freedom of choice', we are able to change the prophecies for the betterment of civilization. The Age of Aquarius is upon us. St Germain is known etherically (in the 5th dimension) as the Lord of our Civilization for our present world epoch.

According to Peter Dawkins:

"His Baconian incarnation was prophesied beforehand by Paracelsus as being a major event for the world; it was heralded as such by the Rosicrucian fraternity at the time and afterwards; and it was marked by certain extraordinary planetary conjunctions and star signs in the heavens."

Peter Dawkins writes in his book titled *Francis Bacon - Herald of the New Age*: "When the philosopher Elias Ashmole was 'accepted' into the Warrington Lodge of Freemasons in 1648, a Brother Frederick Nicolai was recorded as saying that:

'The object of the meeting at Warrington, so far from being masonic, was simply for the purpose of carrying out a philosophical idea which had been promulgated by Lord Bacon in his New Atlantis of the model of a perfect Society, instituted for the secret purpose of interpreting Nature and of producing new Arts and marvellous inventions for the benefit of mankind, under the name of Solomon's House or the College of the Six Days' Work, which in plain language was intended to be an ideal Society for the study of Natural Philosophy...'"

"The persons present, including Ashmole, are said by Nicolai to have been Rosicrucians. He further reveals that:

'These men erected, in their Lodge, two great Pillars, which they called the Pillars of Hermes, in front of Solomon's House, and they used a chequered pavement, a ladder of seven staves or rounds, and many other secret symbols. And as they held their subsequent meetings in Mason's Hall, London, they adopted the tools of working masons'. 'This', Nicolai says conclusively, 'was the origin of Symbolical Masonry.'"

"The Twin Pillars are the 'Ancient Landmarks' of Freemasonry. Freemason means 'Builder of Love'. Free is derived from the Sanskrit priya meaning 'love'. The word 'Free' is used to described a Master of Love in both Eastern and Western

Philosophies. It is noteworthy that the main text of *The Tempest* begins with the word 'Master' [unspoken] and ends with the word 'Free' [spoken]. The relationship between Rosicrucianism and Freemasonry can be explained perhaps by a biblical description of these pillars:

"And there stood upon the pillars as it were Roses." (See I Kings, vii, 14-22). 'Roses' is sometimes translated as 'lilies' or simply as 'flowers'), i.e. Through the labour of love of the true Free-Mason, the Rose of Beauty is grown, crowning all endeavours with the fragrance of joy."

Ben Jonson wrote of Francis Bacon:

"Triumph, my *Britaine*, thou has one to showe,
To whom all Scenes of *Europe* homage owe,
He was not of an age, but for all time!
And all the *Muses* still were in their prime,
When like *Apollo* he came forth to warm
Our ears, or like a *Mercury* charme!"

THE HOLY GRAIL

It is important to stress that we are *all* Noah's descendants and that in his reincarnation as St Germain, at which time he became the Master Teacher for the New Age of Aquarius, (Jesus having been the previous Master of the Rose during the Age of Pisces), his *legacy* to us was to search for the 'Truth' hidden in the ancient Teachings which he endeavoured to combine within his great literary philosophical output of his Baconian works and those of the Shakespearian plays. The symbolic importance of the Stone of Destiny has been emphasized throughout this story and in particular, its custodians, the Guardians of the Holy Grail. The Holy Grail is a universal symbol, capable of the widest application possible. Although written about in 'mystical' terms, it has kept its 'mystique' alive for over a thousand years, since the time that it was first put in writing.

Mary, the Mother, was a living Grail, the vessel who gave birth to the Grail family and whose supreme symbol is the *Rose* - the 'Rose of the World' and it is also the symbol of her son Jesus. Her other son of prominence was John Joseph, the Beloved who as Joseph of Arimathea, became the 'Guardian of the Grail', and of the ancient Grail Teachings of the sacred Arcana preserved by Noah (St Germain) from the ancient days of Atlantis. He too was a *Master of the Rose* as has frequently been demonstrated throughout this story.

In simplistic terms, the goal for each of us is our own Holy Grail, that of seeking the 'Truth', thereby gaining wisdom, strength, courage and inner peace. It is working on the Inner Being which is our whole being, body and mind aiming at the 'Mastery of Life', which we are capable of mastering through knowledge and observation.

When we understand that knowledge and apply it with love and compassion felt through the 'heart' - our centre of feeling, it is only then that the end result is Wisdom - Sophia! It is purely a matter of spiritual development through personal effort which consciously has the ability to transform humanity as a whole. This is exactly what the Ascended Masters (Masters of the Great White Brotherhood, also known as Avatars) who reside in the 'invisible' dimensions, have achieved through their numerous incarnations. Their legacy to us is to encourage all of us to take this profound path of 'spiritual' enlightenment. The Grail experience could be described as the equivalent of mystical illumination.

In a programme on the Discovery Channel on cable television, it was disclosed that many scientists have discovered at least twelve dimensions and many cited cases of people who have experienced time-warped dimensions and become invisible.

Others have walked through walls, by unknowingly changing their energy vibration. It was disclosed on the programme that as far back as 1943, a United States Navy carrier was seen to simply disappear into thin air. It suddenly appeared in a harbour hundreds of miles away. Many witnessed this event, including those sailors on board, but the Navy has never acknowledged that it ever happened, although they are reputed to have been working on the 'invisibility' techniques for aeons. At the Munroe Institute in America, numerous studies have been undertaken and they have invented a machine which allows people to have out-of-body experiences.

Dr Paul Brunton wrote: "We have begun - and perhaps rightly - as complete sceptics; we shall end as complete believers: such is my positive prediction. We shall rescue belief in the soul from the cold air of modern doubt. The first great message of the ancient Mysteries - *'There is no death'*, although always susceptible of personal experiential proof by a mere few, is destined to be broadcast to the whole world."

According to Dr Paul Brunton:

"The idea of survival does not necessarily imply that we shall all scramble out of our coffins at some uncertain future date. To confuse ourselves with the fleshly houses wherein we reside is hardly creditable to our intelligence. The word resurrection has so often carried a false, purely material connotation, both in the medieval European and the uninitiated Egyptian mind, that we have to rediscover the laws that govern the secret constitution of man. The best minds among the ancients - the initiates of the Mysteries - were well versed in those laws, but, whereas their lips were sealed and their truths kept in the gloom of the temple crypts, no such inhibition is expressly laid upon us to-day."

"The Mystery which hath been hidden from ages and generations, (as one of Christ's Apostles declared), would be revealed to the unprivileged masses and the common folk. But what the antique institutions communicated to the elect few by a difficult process would be communicated to all the people by the simple power of faith. Jesus had too much love in his heart to provide for a few alone, he wanted to save the many."

"He showed them a way which required nothing more than sufficient faith in his words; he offered them no mysterious occult process of initiation. Yet it was a way which could give those who accepted it as a great certitude of immortality as could the Mysteries. For the Open Path of Jesus taught humility and invoked the help of a higher Power, a Power ever ready to confer complete certitude merely by bestowing Its presence upon the hearts of those who allowed Its entry. He proffered in return the amplest of rewards - the conscious presence of the Father."

"In that presence, as he knew, all doubts would melt away and man himself would grasp the truth of immortality without having to undergo the experience of entrancement. Man would know this because the Father's Mind would have suffused his own intellect, and in that ineffable suffusion simple faith would be transformed into divine intuition."

Venus - the Goddess of 'Wisdom'

"I Jesus have sent mine angel to testify unto you these things in the churches. I am the root and the offspring of David, and the bright and morning star." (Revelation 22:16)

The 'morning star' is Venus. From excerpts taken from the book titled *The Rise Of The Morning Star*, by Vincent Selleck, we learn the following pertinent information:

"Venus, the planet and goddess is the most esoteric, magical and mystical influence upon our lives. She inspires all art, music and magic. Venus, apart from the sun and moon, is the only planet which is bright enough to cast a shadow. As she weaves a path between sun and earth, her alignments create a pentagram against the stars. She guards the passage way between light and dark. As the morning star, she precedes the dawn. As the evening star, she shines first at sunset."

"The secret nature of the planet Venus is evident in many spiritual and esoteric cultures. In South American legends of the Aztecs and Mayan, Quetzalcoatl is the representation of Venus as the smoking mirror or evening star, and her counterpart is Tezcatlipoca, the morning star. Numerous goddesses are attributed to Venus, including Ishtar, Astarte, Aphrodite and Isis. In Egypt, Venus was called Muth, meaning 'mother of all living'. Even Jesus is likened with Venus in Revelations 22:16."

"Venus is the source of the holy spirit. She represents the innate feminine aspect of God through matter which is created in the universe. The Hebraic Cabbala calls this holy spirit the 'Shekinah' or bride of God. As a higher aspect of the divine feminine, she represents 'SOPHIA', the spark of the pure mind. The lower aspect of the feminine is represented by the moon. This aspect educates the soul about the light which shines in the heart of darkness or of light. She is connected with the fall of Lucifer: 'being visible in the sky at sunset, Venus was called Vesper, and as it rose before the sun, it was called the false light, the star of the morning, or Lucifer, which means the Light Bearer."

"Madame Blavatsky also exposes that in early Christian favour, Lucifer was enjoyed: 'Venus', or Lucifer - also Shukra and Ushanas, the planet, is the light bearer to our earth, in both the physical and mythical sense. The Christians knew it well in early times, since one of the earliest Popes of Rome is known by his pontiff name as Lucifer'. Madame Blavatsky also sees the connection between the spirit and Venus in her *Secret Doctrine* Vol. IV page 110... 'Venus (the Holy Spirit), Sophia the spirit of Wisdom, Love and Truth, and Lucifer as Christ, the 'bright and morning star'."

"She (Venus) is also shown in the tarot card as the Empress, and bearing the glyph of the planet Venus upon her throne which is set amid a luxuriant garden representing nature, her realm. The orb she holds above her head is the new earth. We also see in the Taro that each card is associated to a pathway on the Tree of Life (Cabbala), the mystical symbol representing the creative power of heaven and earth, and the pathway of revelation within humanity. The Cabbala was pre-evident in the Hebraic scrolls within the cultures of Mesopotamian and northern Africa as a symbol of cosmic alignment."

"In the gnostic myth *Sophia* descends into the waters below the firmament in the form of a Dove. It is not the male deity who is the creator, but the feminine spirit, Sophia, Shekinah, or Elohim. The early translators of the Bible have designated spirit as male, possibly due to patriarchal influences. However, as S.L. MacGregor Mathers points out in his book *The Kabbalah Unveiled*, the word *Ruach*, spirit, is feminine, as appears from the following passage... *Acath Elohim Chiim*; 'One is *She* the spirit the Elohim of Life'."

The 'Line of Promise' and Eternal Hope

Author Simon Peter Fuller in his book titled *Rising Out Of Chaos* informs us as follows:

"The line of promise given to the House of Israel but inherited only by Manasseh and Ephraim (the sons of Joseph of the 'coat of many colours' story in the Bible), was that one would be 'a great nation and company of nations', while the other would be 'a great people'. The British nation evolved into a Commonwealth of nations plus the United States of America, and interestingly each was founded exactly at the predicted end of each cycle of punishment originally imposed on Manasseh and Ephraim: the USA in 1787-9 through a ratified Constitution and the United Kingdom in 1800 with Ireland's official joining of the Union, and the Union Jack becoming the national flag of the UK. This technically makes the USA Britain's elder brother - by just a few years!"

"The prophecy also foretold that 'the elder would serve the younger'; **a clear indication that the Christ consciousness emanating from Britain will liberate America from the stranglehold of Christian fundamentalism currently permeating every level of that nation."**

"Finally there is the comforting prophecy by Isaiah in 54; 17, 'No weapon that is formed against thee shall prosper.'"

"Britain and the USA now, have to set a peaceful example to the rest of the world, and there is no further place for weaponry in either 'protected' land."

As Victor Hugo so aptly once said: "Truth is the first casualty of war."

'No one will think that a fool is honourable or say that a scoundrel is honest. A fool speaks foolishly and thinks up evil things to do. What he does and what he says are an insult to the LORD, and he never feeds the hungry or gives thirsty people anything to drink. A stupid person is evil and does evil things; he plots to ruin the poor with lies and to prevent them getting their rights. But an honourable person acts honestly and stands firm for what is right.' (Excerpts taken from Isaiah 32, Good News Bible).

'All of you that plot to destroy others will be destroyed by your own plots'. (Isaiah 50:11)

Let us look at some additional prophecies of Isaiah regarding our future.

'Some day there will be a king who rules with integrity, and national leaders who govern with justice. Each of them will be like a shelter from the wind and a place to hide from storms. They will be like streams flowing in a desert, like the shadow of a giant rock in a barren land. Their eyes and ears will be open to the needs of the people. They will not be impatient any longer, but they will act with understanding and will say what they mean.

'Once again you will see a king ruling in splendour over a land that stretches in all directions. Your old fears of foreign tax-collectors and spies will be only a memory. You will no longer speak a language that you can't understand. The Lord himself will be our king; he will rule over us and protect us. No one who lives in our land will ever again complain of being ill, and all sins will be forgiven.' (Isaiah **33**)

'The desert will rejoice, and flowers will bloom in the wilderness. The desert will sing and shout for joy; it will be as beautiful as the Lebanon mountains and as

fertile as the fields of Carmel and Sharon. Everyone will see the Lord's splendour, see his greatness and power.'
(Isaiah 35)

'The Lord says, 'I am making a new earth and new heavens. The events of the past will be completely forgotten. Be glad and rejoice for ever in what I create. The new Jerusalem I make will be full of joy, and her people will be happy. I myself will be filled with joy because of Jerusalem and her people. There will be no weeping there, no calling for help. Babies will no longer die in infancy, and all people will live out their life span. Those who live to be a hundred will be considered young. Like trees, my people will live long lives. They will fully enjoy the things that they have worked for. The work they will do will be successful, and their children will not meet with disaster. I will bless them and their descendants for all time to come. Even before they finish praying to me, I will answer their prayers. Oh Zion my sacred hill, there will be nothing harmful or evil.' (Verses selected from Isaiah 65).

King of Kings, and Lord of Lords

'Listen to me, you that know what is right,
who have my teaching fixed in your hearts.
Do not be afraid when people taunt and insult you...'
(Isaiah 51)

In the introduction to this story of *The Masters of the Mystical Rose*, mention was made of the message given to me from the Ancient Masters (the Great White Brotherhood) and the *Master of the Rose*. As to all the answers to the questions posed by me in the Introduction, they did not come immediately, and nor do I have them all now, but what has occurred upon the journey of 'discovery' and 'knowledge' - St Germain's game of 'hide and seek', is that searching for the 'Truth' has been a most joyous path to follow, one that is readily available to all who are able to have enough faith that there is a Divine Blueprint.

The purpose of writing this story has been to demonstrate this fact by using many examples of certain periods in history when the Masters reincarnated to assist our civilization and to show us that we are not 'alone'.

In the beginning, I had no idea of who the 'Ancient' Masters were, or of how they would teach me, and what it was that they required of me. However, as the years went by, I received from St Germain and Kuthumi, a great deal of information which they wanted me to research in order to write this story, a story that took four years to complete, and, at the completion, another book written by Peter Dawkins arrived, titled *The Mystery of the Master*.

Peter writes: To talk about the past lives or incarnations of any soul is a route bestrewn with perils, and without some kind of direct evidence such information is by its very nature rather subjective. *Yet there are guides to this, including information given by the Masters themselves when they wish something to be known or a line of enquiry to be followed."*

"Besides direct teachings, another guideline to follow is the type of work performed, and the way in which it is carried out, by various people in successive times throughout history. With an initiate or master soul it is often possible to recognise the particular life-thread running through successive incarnations, stamped by the character, spiritual purpose and other idiosyncrasies of that soul. Also, the character of a strongly developed soul such as a Master will often be visible in the various faces and personalities of that soul's successive incarnations. There is a pattern to everything and to everyone."

"With all the Masters a continuity of consciousness from one life-time to another is fairly common, so that they themselves know in relative detail who they have been in previous lives; but that in itself is no definite proof to others...it requires a well-established teaching system with well-trained disciples to operate efficiently. In the Western world this is not quite the case, and other factors have to be taken into consideration and other means invented. The Age of Aquarius is an age of mind; but the acquisition of highly developed thoughts and mental capabilities will be fruitless without a corresponding development of the heart, so that love and wisdom can increasingly warm and illumine the mind, and keep it free from harshness and illusion."

"A method and programme for the training of the mind in such a way that it might always be inspired and illumined by heart-love, and free enough of erroneous thoughts of 'idols of the mind' so as to be able to see the truth clearly, was established by the Master whom this book is about, in his vitally important incarnation as Francis Bacon. It could be said that the Aquarian Age is to do with SEEING, with each and every soul becoming able to soar to the heights like an eagle and perceive clearly the light of truth. Such ability is associated with St John the Beloved [Kuthumi], whilst the purification of the mind and heart which is necessary in order to have clarity of perception is associated with John the Baptist [El Morya].... Not for nothing is it said that the Age of Aquarius is the Age of John."

Alice Bailey wrote in her book titled *The Externalisation of the Hierarchy*:

'The ending of the present evil situation is, therefore, a co-operative measure and here, in this connection, we have the appearance of the Lord of Civilisation who voices and engineers upon the physical plane the fiat of the Lord of Liberation and of the Rider from the secret place. He aids and makes possible, owing to his control, the precipitating upon the Earth and in the arena of combat, of the power generated by the Lords of Liberation, expressed by the coming One and focused through him as the hierarchical representative. The work of the Master R has always been recognised as of a peculiar nature and is concerned with the problems of civilisation, just as the work of the Christ. The Master of all Masters is concerned with the spiritual development of humanity, and the work of the Manu is occupied with the science of divine government, with politics and law'."

(In Peter Dawkins' book titled *The Mystery of the Master*, he explains the meaning of Christ. "...it has been forgotten that the name *Christ* is derived from the Greek word *Christos* [Latin *Christus*], which itself is derived from the Egyptian word *Kheru*, meaning 'The Word'. *Kh* in Egyptian became C in Greek and *Ch* in Latin).

"The Rider on the White Horse, who will come forth from a secret place - the place of the heart - is the One described by St John (the Beloved) from his vision on the Isle of Patmos:

'And now I saw heaven open, and a white horse appear; its rider was called Faithful and True; he is a judge ['Interpreter'] with integrity, a warrior for justice. His eyes were flames of fire, and his head was crowned with many coronets; the name written on him was known only to himself, his cloak was soaked in blood. He is known by the name The Word of God. Behind him, dressed in linen of dazzling white, rode the armies of heaven on white horses. From his mouth came a sharp sword to strike the pagan [i.e. ungodly or unloving ones] with; he is the one who will rule them with an iron sceptre, and tread out the wine of Almighty God's fierce anger. On his cloak and on his thigh there was a name written: KING OF KINGS, AND LORD OF LORDS'. (Revelation 19:11-21, The Jerusalem Bible)."

"This being is known in Europe as Christian Rose Cross, the Rider of the Heavens, who dwells in and issues out from the Heart of God, accompanied by his great army of the Rose-Cross knights, the Masters and Adepts of the world. He is 'the Coming One', who wields the solar and cosmic powers of transmutation and liberation bestowed on him by the Lords of Liberation. The destruction spoken about is of all that is evil or unhelpful, leaving behind only the good, the beautiful and the true, thereby creating a Paradise on Earth."

The symbol of the Rider on the White Horse refers to:

"...an emerging revelation of the consciousness of Deity as revealed through some Great Divine Expression, through some manifesting Son of God. The point to bear in mind is that this Rider on the white horse is no extra-planetary Entity or Life, but is essentially One like unto ourselves - human and animal combined as are we all, but fused with divinity and inspired from on high, informed by some cosmic and divine Principle, as Christ was informed with the Love of God and carried the revelation of love to man. The Rider is one of our humanity who has reached a pre-destined goal and who - for very love and understanding of man - has remained for ages in the secret place of revelation (as it is esoterically called), waiting until his hour comes around again and he can then issue forth to lead his people to triumphant victory."

"This coming One is on the Path of a world Saviour just as the more potent Lives, the Lords of Liberation, are on the Path of world Service. They issue forth via that highest spiritual centre wherein the Will of God is held in solution or custody, for gradual release or revelation as humanity can arrive at the needed point of understanding response and receptivity."

"Though They can be reached relatively easily, it must be through the massed intent of the many focussed minds. The Rider on the white horse can be reached by the individual aspirant if he can raise his consciousness adequately high. This Rider comes forth (from the centre wherein the Love of God is held for distribution) as the human centre (which we call humanity) becomes attuned to true love and can identify itself with all men, responding freely and without any inhibition to divine Love - which is wisdom, understanding, and effective, skilful activity." (Alice Bailey, *The Externalisation of the Hierarchy*).

According to Peter Dawkins in his book titled *The Mystery of the Master*:

"He himself, through his own attunement...will be able to channel the energy of the Lords of Liberation into humanity and the world at large, including all kingdoms and nature.

We have, therefore:

1. The Lords of Liberation, reached by the advanced spiritual thinkers of the world whose minds are rightly focused.
2. The Rider on the white horse or from the secret place, reached by those whose hearts are rightly touched.
3. The Lord of Civilisation, the Master R, reached by all who, with the first two groups, can stand with 'massed intent'."

"Conditions will consequently be brought about and energies will be set in motion which will end the rule of evil and bring war to an end through the victory of the Forces of Light, recognised and aided by Humanity."

Peter comments: regarding the above quotation of Alice Bailey:

"I have used them [words channelled to Alice Bailey by the Master known as Djwhal Khul] because they help to enlighten some of the more obscure aspects of symbolism used by the Master R, who is himself deliberately veiled - but only so as we can have the joy of discovery. As Prince Rakoczi (also Ragoczy) or the Comte de St Germain, he completed the fourth degree (of Resurrection) and entered the fifth degree (of Ascension) as a Master. Since then he has risen to and completed the sixth degree (of Unification), that of a *Chohan* and has now entered the seventh degree (of Enthronement) as a *Mahachohan*, where he acts as the Lord of Civilisation for our world."

"Thus I understand the epithet of 'R' refers not just to Rakoczi, but also to something much greater and more profound: the title 'Master R' signifies 'MASTER OF THE ROSE'."

On a final note, I leave the readers with a message from the other important *Master of the Mystical Rose*, Kuthumi, who in his incarnation as John the Beloved Disciple was a son of St Germain. Kuthumi is the Guardian of the Holy Grail who in his incarnation as Lao Tzu, founder of the Taoist Religion, wrote the following pertinent verses:

"A leader is best when people barely know that he exists,
Not so good when people obey and acclaim,
Worst when they despise him,
Fail to honour people,
They fail to honour you;
But of a good leader, who talks little,
When his work is done, his aim fulfilled,
They will all say,
'We did this ourselves.'"

MASTERS DISCUSSED IN THIS CHAPTER

Noah - St Germain
Aaron - St Germain
The Essenes' Teacher of Righteousness (Joseph) - St Germain
Francis Bacon - St Germain
Shakespeare - St Germain
King David - Kuthumi
Lao Tze - Kuthumi
John Joseph the Beloved Disciple (alias Joseph of Arimathea) - Kuthumi
King Arthur (Aedan mac Gabran) - Kuthumi
Omar Khayyam - Kuthumi
Madame Helena Blavatsky
Edgar Cayce - Modern Day Prophet

NOTES AND RECOMMENDED READING

Peter Dawkins, *Francis Bacon, Herald of the New Age,* (Francis Bacon Research Trust, Roses Farmhouse, Epwell Road, Upper Tysoe, Warwick CV 35 OTN, United Kingdom)
Peter Dawkins, *The Great Vision,* (Francis Bacon Research Trust, U.K.)
Peter Dawkins, *Arcadia,* (Francis Bacon Research Trust, U.K)
Peter Dawkins, *Dedication To The Light,* (Francis Bacon Research Trust, U.K)
Peter Dawkins, *The Virgin Ideal,* (Francis Bacon Research Trust, U.K.)
Peter Dawkins, *The Mystery Of The Master,* (Francis Bacon Research Trust, U.K)
Dr Douglas Baker, BA. MR.C.S. L.R.C.P.F.Z.S., *The Jewel In The Lotus,* (Douglas Baker, U.K. 1975)

Dr Paul Brunton, *In Search of Ancient Egypt*, (Samuel Weiser, Inc., U.S.A., 1979)

Simon Peter Fuller, *Rising Out Of Chaos, The New Heaven & The New Earth*, (Kima Global, South Africa, 1994)

Mary Carter, *Edgar Cayce, Modern Day Prophet*, (Bonanza Books, U.S.A., 1970)

Dr Raymond Bernard, A.B. M.A., Ph.D., *The Great Secret Count Saint Germain*, (U.S.A.)

Isabel Oakley Cooper, *Comte de St Germain, The Secret of Kings*, (Theosophical Publishing House, U.K. 1985)

Annie Bessant, *Ancient Wisdom*, (Theosophical Publishing House, U.S.A., 1992)

Madame Helena Blavatsky, *The Secret Doctrine*, (Theosophical Publishing House, U.S.A., 1966)

Madame Helena Blavatsky, *Isis Unveiled* (Volumes 1 & 2), (Theosophical Publishing House, U.S.A 1972)

(Available through Adyar Bookshop, Sydney, N.S.W., and Australia)

J.L. Simmons, *The Emerging New Age*, (Bear & Co. Santa Fe, New Mexico, 1989)

Vincent Selleck, *The Rise Of The Morning Star*, (1990)

Michael Taylor, *Master R, Lord of Our Civilisation*, (The Rawley Trust, Christchurch, NZ., 1997)

C.W. Leadbeater, *The Hidden Life In Freemasonry*, (Theosophical Publishing House, U.K., 1975)

Manly P. Hall, *An Encyclopedic Outline of Masonic, Hermetic, Qabbalistic and Rosicrucian Philosophy*, (Philosophical Research Society Inc., U.S.A., 1998)

Rosemary Ellen Guiley, *Encyclopedia Of Mystical & Paranormal Experience*, (Grange Books U.S.A., 1991)

Emile Legouis, *A Study of English Literature, The Middle Ages And The Renaissance*, (J.M. Dent & Sons, U.K., 1945)

Daniel J. Boorstin, *The Discoverers, A History of Man's Search To Know His World And Himself*, (Random House, U.K., 1983)

W.S. Cerve, *Lemuria, The Lost Continent Of The Pacific*, (Rosicrucian Library, AMORC, U.S.A., 1959)

John Allegro, *The Dead Sea Scrolls*, (Penguin Books, U.K. 1964)

Charles W. Hedrick & Robert Hodgson Jnr., *Nag Hammadi, Gnosticism And Early Christianity*, (Hendrickson Publishers, U.S.A, 1986)

Spencer Lewis, *Rosicrucian Questions And Answers*, (AMORC., U.S.A, 1977)

Robert Graves, *The White Goddess*, (Faber & Faber, U.K., 1961)

Michael Baigent, Richard Leigh & Henry Lincoln, *The Holy Blood And The Holy Grail*, (Arrow Books, U.K., 1996)

Michael Baigent, Richard Leigh & Henry Lincoln, *The Messianic Legacy*, (Arrow Books, U.K. 1996)

Michael Baigent & Richard Leigh, *The Temple And The Lodge*, (Corgi Books, U.K. 1996)

Christopher Knight & Robert Lomas, *The Hiram Key*, (Century, U.K. 1996)

Christopher Knight & Robert Lomas, *The Second Messiah*, (Century, U.K. 1997)

Robert J. Scrutton, *The Message Of The Masters*, (Jersey Neville Spearman U.K., 1982)

Zachary F. Lansdowne, *Rules For Spiritual Initiation*, (Samuel Weiser Inc., U.S.A, 1990)

White Eagle, *Morning Light On The Spiritual Path*, (The White Eagle Publishing Trust, U.K., 1957)

White Eagle, *The Way Of The Sun*, (The White Eagle Publishing Trust, U.K., 1982)

Grace Cooke, *The Jewel In The Lotus*, (White Eagle Publishing Trust, U.K., 1973)

Joseph J. Weed, *Wisdom Of The Mystic Masters*, (Parker Publishing Co., U.S.A., 1968)

Dr Hiroshi Motoyama, *Karma & Reincarnation*, (Piatkus Publishers, London, U.K., 1992)

Maggie Hamilton, *Home Coming, Rediscovering Our Sacred Selves*, (Penguin Books Australia Ltd., 2002)

POST SCRIPT

The sequel to this story is titled *The Dove The Rose And The Sceptre - In Search of the Ark of the Covenant*. Within this story, significant clues are divulged as to where in my belief, the Ark of the Covenant is hidden.

In circa 586 BC, the Prophet Jeremiah, mentioned in the Bible, took the Stone of Destiny and the Ark of the Covenant from Jerusalem to a mystical 'land far away', to the 'Blessed Isles', prior to the Invasion of Jerusalem by the Babylonian King, Nebuchadnezzar. What Jeremiah achieved, was in accordance with the Biblical prophecies. Two hundred and thirty years after this event, St Germain incarnated as Alexander the Great (356-323 BC) - he died at the age of 33 years, although his burial place has so far remained undiscovered.

According to the information taken as an excerpt from the book titled *Blue Apples* by William Henry, sent to me by a reader of the above-mentioned book *The Dove The Rose And The Sceptre - In Search of the Ark of the Covenant*, Alexander the Great would 'summon the power of the Green Man. He believed in the tales of this wandering god, who the Greeks called Dionysus." (It was discussed in this story of the Masters of the Mystical Rose that Dionysus had once been an incarnation of St Germain - Dionysus was also known as Bacchus. Michelangelo's Renaissance statue of Bacchus depicts him as a youth crowned with vine-leaves and grapes).

William Henry further informs us that according to legend, Alexander the Great was carried by the 'spirit' of the Green Man to the top of a *Mount* in a distant land, and there he discovered *two large Pillars measuring 60 feet in height.* Alexander also saw a *"Golden Rod -* the key Secret of *all* mysteries - *the branches of a vine with a cluster of grapes at the top."* ('Grapes' signify 'wisdom' and also represent the wine of life). In *The Dove The Rose And The Sceptre - In Search of the Ark of the Covenant*, mention of Aaron's (St Germain's) *Rod, the two Pillars of Moses* and their connection to the Ark of the Covenant is discussed.

'Branches of a vine' is also very relevant, because it concerns the vine of the Royal House of David, and thus the Royal Family of the Holy Grail who settled in this mystical land to which Jeremiah referred as the 'Isles Afar Off'.

As St Columba, St Germain would begin his prayers with psalm 45 which in the Good News Bible, is referred to as a Royal Wedding Song. It concerns the marriage of a princess who was the great grand daughter of the Prophet Jeremiah, who accompanied him upon his journey from Jerusalem with the Stone of Destiny and the Ark of the Covenant, to the 'Isles Afar Off'. In Biblical terminology, this princess was *'a tender twig' - a branch of the vine* of the Royal House of Judah/David. By utilizing the Pythagorean method, Psalm 45 = 4 + 5 = 9.

Targum Onkelos **33**:12 (Aramaic Version of the Bible): *"The beloved of the Lord shall dwell safely by him: the shield shall be over him all the days, and the Shekinah (Ark of the Covenant) will dwell in his land."* (Excerpt from *Life Understood* by F.L. Rawson, 1920).

Pythagorean method: **33** + 12 = 45 and 4 + 5 = 9.

Throughout his numerous incarnations, St Germain was in charge of the Ark of the Covenant and its 'Mysteries' - the 'Arkana/Arcana' and in one of his incarnations, he was buried in close proximity to the Ark of the Covenant's location. This location is 54 degrees north and once again utilizing the Pythagorean method, 5 + 4 = 9 which is also the sum total of story in the Bible of The Royal Wedding Song of the princess. The Princess was buried beneath a *Mount* in which the Ark of the Covenant was concealed and the *Mount* measures 60 feet.

In St Germain's incarnation as St Alban, he founded Freemasonry and is said to have died in the year 303 AD, whereas the actual date was 209 AD; the date of 303 AD was alluding to his connection with Freemasonry. In number ciphers, 0 is not counted.

Apart from its location being 54 degrees North, the main key of the location of the Ark of the Covenant lies in the measurement of 60 feet, of which I have now found three references (i.e. two in ancient Celtic literature and the reference of Alexander the Great - St Germain). To find two references of 60 feet being specified would be rather amazing, but to find three would be far beyond the laws of 'probability'. And, 60 feet consists of two of the number 3, which when placed side by side, gives us the number of Freemasonry and the cipher code of St Germain, 33. Thirty three comprises of twin capital letters of the letter 'T' which in turn correspond to the *Twin Pillars of Moses*, concealed within the Ark of the Covenant.

CHRONOLOGY

circa 30,000 BC:
Estimated time of the colonization of Asia and Australia by the inhabitants of Lemuria.

The original people of Australia, our Aborigines, have recorded their ancient history in the legend of the *Dreamtime* and the *Rainbow Serpent*. Lemuria was considered to be a very large continent which included Australia, New Zealand and Hawaii. Many of the mountain peaks of the thousands of islands in the Pacific Ocean are remnants of the submerged continent. The next civilization after Lemuria was Atlantis.

The story of the lost city of Atlantis was first recorded by Plato (St Germain) (circa 429-347 BC).

Noah - St Germain
At the time of the Great Flood, the result of which was the sinking of Atlantis, St Germain was Noah, who in the Biblical tradition is featured in the story of the Dove and the Ark. The 'Dove' was symbolical of 'peace' and the 'Ark' was symbolical of the Arcana Teachings he always preserved through each incarnation. As Noah, St Germain was the progenitor of the Arkadians (Arcadians) whose dream was to found a new and glorious Golden Civilization after the decline and fall of Atlantis. Prior to the Great Flood, Noah was a High Priest in the Temple of Atlantis and knowing that they needed to protect the Sacred Teachings of the Arcana (Arkana), he and the other High Priests who were considered to be trustworthy, fled to Egypt. According to Peter Dawkins of the Francis Bacon Research Trust, the name of Noah represents IOA, the Word of Wisdom. The dove is His holy spirit, who bears the Word to Earth, (i.e. into incarnation). The actual Hebrew word for Dove is *Iona* (or *Jonah*) and denotes the Holy Spirit, bearer of the Word of God, from which the name 'John' is derived, as also the Hebraic *Jihovah*. *Jihovah* was written in Ancient Hebrew with only the consonants *JHVH*, which were said to be a representation of the sacred Name, not the Name itself. The vowel sounds were hidden and considered a priestly secret, with only the 'Elect of Israel' knowing how to correctly pronounce the sacred Name. 'The Lord' is a title of *Jihovah* which eventually became Jehovah.

circa 1900 BC: Abraham
Abraham arrived in Palestine. His son was Isaac. Isaac's son was Jacob whom the Lord re-named 'Israel'. According to the antiquarian Stukeley, who was a member of the Druids, Abraham was the 'Father of all Druids'.

Jacob's Vision and the Stone Pillow (Stone of Destiny)

Jacob, who was later re-named 'Israel' by the Lord, had a vision when he laid his head upon his stone pillow, whereby the Lord told him that his descendants would begin a lineage which would be known as the House of David. Jacob had twelve sons who became the ancestors of the twelve tribes of Israel. The descendants were known as the Israelites, named after 'Israel/Jacob'. The most prominent of these sons was Joseph, who became the adviser to the King of Egypt. According to legend, the Stone Pillow, also known as the *Stone of Destiny*, was later taken to the Royal palace of Tara, in Ireland, where from that time onwards, all the High Celtic Kings stood upon it when they were crowned. In all probability, Jacob/Israel was an incarnation of St Germain. His descendants formed the 12 Tribes of 'Israel' - hence they were the Israelites.

circa 1504 BC- 1447 BC: Pharaoh Tutmoses III - Kuthumi

Kuthumi was the Pharaoh Tutmoses III whose great great grandson, was the famous Pharaoh Akhnaton (Amenhotep IV, 1378-1350 BC), an incarnation of El Morya. Tutmoses III and Akhnaton were the original founders of the Rose-Cross (the Rosicrucians). The Essenes belonged to the Order of the Rose Cross (Rosicrucians). Tutmoses III was a military expert, one of the greatest foreign conquerors in Egyptian history.

He also established a Temple which he called the 'Botanical Garden'. In a later incarnation as Sir Joseph Banks, Kuthumi toured the world collecting hundreds and thousands of botanical species. He was the greatest botanist the world has ever known and he established the Botanical Gardens at Kew, near London. It was also during this time that he reigned as Grand Master of the Royal Society (which was an off-shoot of the Order of the Rose Cross) for fifty years.

An obelisk, once erected in Egypt upon the instructions of Tutmoses III, was destined to eventually be re-erected in the country where the Eagle spreads its wings and the Obelisk now stands in Central Park, New York, United States of America.

1378-1350 BC: Pharaoh Akhnaton (Amenhotep IV) - El Morya

Akhnaton was the famous great great grandson of Tutmoses III (Kuthumi). He became the ruler of Egypt in 1367 BC at the tender age of eleven years. During the course of his reign, he changed his name from Amenhotep to Akhnaton. He was born at the Royal Palace of Thebes in 1378 BC, and his mother Queen Tia, was of Arian birth. Akhnaton married the beautiful Queen Nefertiti.

According to the Rosicrucian authority, the late Spencer Lewis, Akhnaton was the Pharaoh who assisted Moses [early incarnation of the Master Jesus] and his brother Aaron [St Germain] to lead the Chosen tribe (the Essenes) out of Egypt.

Akhnaton was the first to introduce the symbol of the Rose and the Cross and taught that there was only one Deity, not many gods as the Egyptians then believed. After some time, the Egyptian priests of the Temples rejected Akhnaton's beliefs and reverted back to worshipping many gods. The temples became corrupted and Akhnaton sought the assistance of the wise man known as Hermes Trismegistus. Together, they invented hieroglyphics and thus managed to hide the secret Arkana (Arcana) teachings which had been handed down from the days of Noah (St Germain).

circa 1378-1350 BC: Aaron - St Germain and Moses
St Germain reincarnated as Aaron, the brother of Moses and Miriam. Moses was an earlier incarnation of the Master whom we know as Jesus. During this period, Moses and Aaron led the 'Children of Israel' out of Egypt. Moses gave the sacred tablets/stones of the Covenant to Aaron for safekeeping. Moses was initiated by the Pharaoh Akhnaton, (El Morya), in the Great Pyramid of Egypt. Moses was the son of a Princess, Akhnaton's sister and she raised him in the palace. By royal birth, he was a Tut-moses.
Akhnaton assisted the 'Chosen Tribe' in their Exile out of Egypt. It is of interest to note that Sir Joseph Banks (Kuthumi) paid a visit to tomb of Aaron when the lost city of Petra was discovered in the 18th century AD.

circa 1050 BC: Prophet Samuel - St Germain
Samuel the Prophet was an incarnation of St Germain who anointed David as King of the Israelites. Amongst David's many wives was Bathsheba (another name for Elizabeth is Eli Sheba meaning *'Consecrated to God'*). Their son was to become the wise King Solomon who was an incarnation of the Master El Morya. Samuel was the Zadok High priest mentioned in the Bible and he was given the responsibility of the Ark of the Covenant which he had also been responsible for in his life as Aaron.

circa 1010 - circa 970 BC: King David - Kuthumi, House of David commences
Kuthumi was King David, whom the Prophet Samuel (St Germain) anointed. David married Bathsheba and their son was King Solomon (El Morya). Prior to his demise, King David made Solomon promise to build the Temple in which to house the Ark of the Covenant, which had been protected by Samuel (St Germain). Solomon carried out his promise and the Temple became known as the Temple of Jerusalem (Zion/Sion). This was the same Temple which the 9 Knights Templar tunnelled into during the 11th century AD, when Sir Hugh de Payen (possibly an incarnation of St Germain) was the First Grand Master of the Knights Templar.

circa 970 - 913 BC: King Solomon - El Morya and the 'Queen of Sheba'

King Solomon was the son of King David (Kuthumi) and Bathsheba. In his early youth, Solomon journeyed to Egypt where he was initiated into the Great White Brotherhood. (According to the Rosicrucian authority, the late Spencer Lewis, Solomon was in Egypt in 999 BC). He spent some time in Egypt as tutor to the Pharaoh Shishak's son. According to the Bible, Solomon married Shishak's daughter, a princess, and returned with her to Jerusalem.

According to the Bible, the Queen of Sheba paid Solomon a visit and was much impressed by his 'wisdom'. It is possible that the Queen of Sheba was Queen Hatshepsut. The similarities between the Biblical story of journeys of the Queen of Sheba and those of Queen Hatshepsut, which are historically recorded in Egyptian records, appear to be too much for mere 'co-incidence'.

circa 530 BC: Pythagoras - Kuthumi - 'Father of Mathematics'

Pythagoras was the famous Greek Philosopher, known as the 'Father of Mathematics'. He entered the *Illuminati* (The Great White Brotherhood) and studied in the Temples in Egypt. Pythagoras encouraged women to become members and he and his wife Theano, established 'Mystery Schools' in Crotona, Italy. He was a Druid and travelled to Marseilles in Gaul (France) where he was received with a warm welcome. Pythagoras encouraged suitable candidates to search for the 'Truth' behind the Ancient Mysteries. Pythagoras was a gifted prophet with 'second sight' and he was also able to communicate with animals and birds. In a future incarnation as St Hugh of Avalon/Lincoln, he was to retain the same wonderful abilities and his favourite pet who watched over him, was a beautiful white swan which became his symbol.

469-399 BC: Socrates - Greek Philosopher

Socrates was born in Athens, Greece and was an earlier incarnation of the Master we know as Jesus. The basis of his teaching was that 'Virtue is knowledge' and the cardinal virtues that he taught were wisdom, temperance, courage and justice. Some of his teachings were not acceptable to the local hierarchy and he was executed. Plato (St Germain) is said to have witnessed the execution of Socrates. The theme of what happened to Socrates is very similar to that of Jesus.

circa 429-347 BC: Plato - St Germain - Greek Philosopher

Plato was born in Athens and many of his works have survived through to the present day. From the word 'Plato', the School of Platonism and the word 'platonic' was derived. In the 15th century AD, during the Italian Renaissance, St Germain incarnated as Christopher Columbus, during which time Kuthumi incarnated as

Leonardo da Vinci. They were both members of the Platonic Academy founded by Cosimo de Medici in Florence. During this era, Leonardo da Vinci became the Grand Master (Helmsman) of the Order of Sion (Jerusalem).

Plato dedicated his life to the discovery of the 'Truth' and he founded the Academy in Athens in 387 BC which became Europe's first University. Those who knew St Germain in his incarnation as Sir Francis Bacon equated him with Plato.

384-322 BC: Aristotle - Kuthumi - Greek Philosopher

Aristotle was the famous Greek Philosopher who became a tutor to Alexander the Great (St Germain). Aristotle later established the Lyceum in Athens where students came from far and wide to study the Greater Mysteries. In his incarnation as Leonardo da Vinci, during the Italian Renaissance, Kuthumi had been the Grand Master (Helmsman) of the Order of Sion (Jerusalem). He also financially assisted Christopher Columbus (St Germain) for his voyages.

When Kuthumi incarnated into the 16th century as Sir John Dee, Elizabeth I's Astrologer, he acquired the habit of buying books and manuscripts from home and abroad and set up a magnificent library at his home. He also established the Order of Sion at his home which also drew many important visitors from abroad. As Aristotle, Kuthumi wrote of the existence of *terra Australis incognita*, 'the unknown southern land'. In his incarnation as Sir John Dee, Kuthumi was known as the Master of Mathematics and Navigation who collected numerous maps of the world and he was also considered to be the Master behind the exploration of the world during the Elizabethan Renaissance. It was he who encouraged Sir Francis Drake's voyage around the world.

In a later incarnation in the 18th century AD, the Master Kuthumi was Sir Joseph Banks who accompanied Captain James Cook on the *H.M.S. Endeavour* at which time they discovered *terra Australis incognita* - the 'unknown southern land' - 'Australia'. As Sir Joseph Banks, Kuthumi reigned as Grand Master of the Royal Society for fifty years, no-one had ever before or ever since held the position for such a great length of time. The Royal Society was an offshoot of the Order of the Rose Cross affiliated with the Order of the Freemasons.

356-323 BC: Alexander the Great - St Germain

St Germain was Alexander the Great who established Greek Rule in Palestine in 333 BC. He also founded the City of Alexander and established a wonderful library. His tutor was Aristotle (Kuthumi), but it is more likely that Kuthumi was assisting the young Alexander who had such a great destiny. It was Alexander's dream to unite the West and this he achieved in his incarnation as Charlemagne the Great who became King Charles I of France when Pope Stephen III crowned him in 800 AD. Alexander died one year after Aristotle.

1st CENTURY AD: St John the Beloved Disciple (Theophilus) - Kuthumi

After his mission was completed as the elderly Magi, (Magus, meaning 'wise man') Baltazar, Kuthumi made his next appearance as John the Beloved, otherwise known as the mysterious 'Joseph of Arimathea'. John's second name was 'Joseph', obviously named after his father, Joseph - St Germain.

John the Beloved wrote the Book of John and the Book of Revelation whilst in exile upon the island of Patmos in 70 AD. He was one of the Four Evangelists whose symbol is the Eagle which appears on the Great Seal of the United States of America.

In his incarnation as the Pharaoh Tutmoses III, Kuthumi had prophesied that his Obelisk would one day be re-erected in the country where the Eagle spreads its wings and the Obelisk now stands in Central Park, New York, United States of America.

1st Century AD: St John the Baptist - El Morya

El Morya had once been the Pharaoh Akhnaton (Amenhotep IV), great great grandson of Tutmoses III (Kuthumi). El Morya was also once the prophet Elijah and in the era of Jesus, he incarnated as his cousin, John the Baptist whose parents were a High Priest and Priestess of the Essenes, namely Zachariah and Elizabeth, respectively. John Baptist was the one expected by the Essenes as a forerunner to the Messiah. He was born some months before Jesus. The initiations which he carried out by immersing people in water eventually became known as 'Baptism'. These same initiations he had introduced in his era in Egypt, as Pharaoh Akhnaton.

BC-AD: St Joseph - St Germain

St Germain was the husband of Mary (who reputedly was the Lady Master known as 'Portia').

He was the father of the Family of the Holy Grail of the Essenes, namely, Jesus, John the Beloved (Disciple), James the Just (Disciple), Simon (Eleazar/Lazarus) the 'Magus' (Disciple), Matthew the (Disciple and the Evangelist), and Judas Iscariot (the 'traitor' who betrayed Jesus); Martha and Mary Magdalene. The parents of Mary (wife of Joseph) were St Anna and St Joachim, both first cousins who were from royal lineage.

Joseph was the one known as 'Annas the Elder High Priest' of the Temple of the Sanhedrin and he died about 15 AD at which point of time he was replaced by his son Eleazar (Simon/Lazarus), the 'Magus' also known as 'Zelotes' - the Zealot freedom fighter of the Essenes.

According to the late Spencer Lewis, the Essenes were the 'Rosicrucians of Palestine'. The Essenes lineage was that of Zadok/Levi and the royal House of David (Kuthumi), King of Judah.

Joseph was also called 'Zebedee', the 'Fisherman' whose sons were the 'fishers' for 'initiates' into the 'Greater Mysteries'. 'Zebedee' was a code name. 'Ze for Zion/ Sion (Jerusalem), 'be' for Bacon and 'dee' for Sir John Dee (Kuthumi) - both men were responsible in the 16th century AD for the translation of the Bible which became known as the King James Authorized Version of the Bible and it is the Bible given to the Freemasons upon entering into Freemasonry.

It is recorded in ancient texts that Jesus and John the Baptist undertook initiations in the Temples of the Great White Brotherhood in the Great Pyramid in Egypt.

1st century AD: Apollonius of Tyana - St Germain

Apollonius was born during the reign of Nero. He spent a great deal of time in Rome. This was during the era of the persecutions of the Christians by Nero. Apollonius was a philosopher, whose reputation was that of a wonderful Holy man who travelled through many countries including India, and he was an Essene and therefore he belonged to the Order of the Rose Cross. He had the gift of prophecy and it is recorded that he could disappear and materialize in distant places. These incredible powers would be utilized in his incarnation as the Comte de St Germain in the 16th century, for he was known as the 'Wonder Man of Europe', the man who never died.

Joseph of Arimathea's (alias John the Beloved's) daughter, Anna (named after her grandmother St Anna), married Bran the Blessed King otherwise known as Cymbeline and Cunobelinus. Their son, Caradoc (whom the Romans called Caractacus), married the Emperor Claudius' daughter, Venus Julia and for a time they lived at the palace in Rome which became known as 'The Home of the Apostles', where Apollonius (St Germain) would have been a frequent visitor.

From Anna's ancient royal lineage combined with the ancient lineage of Bran the Blessed, came the descendants who were to be called 'Tudor' - the royal house into which St Germain incarnated as Sir Francis Bacon in the 16th century AD.

d. 209 AD: St Alban (St Albanus) - St Germain

St Germain reincarnated as St Albanus (Alban), the first Christian martyr in Britain to be beheaded following his persecution by the Roman Emperor Septimus Severus (who reigned from 193-211 AD). According to the Theosophical writer, C.W. Leadbeater, St Germain was born into a noble Roman family in the town of Verulam in England. It was during this time that as St Albanus, St Germain introduced Freemasonry into Britain. St Germain was to use the name of Verulam in a later incarnation as Sir Francis Bacon when King James I (Stuart) of England bestowed the title of Viscount Baron Verulam upon him.

St Alban's cult was extended all over Briton and areas of Gaul (France) under the influence of St Germanus, whom St Germain incarnated as after his life as St Alban.

St Albans was the site of the first battle of the *War of the Roses* on the 22nd May 1455. In St Germain's incarnation as Sir Francis Bacon in the 16th century, his family home was Gorhambury near St Albans, where his adoptive father, Sir Nicholas Bacon, founded a Platonic Academy.

280-304 AD: St George - Kuthumi

St George of Lydda, an incarnation of Kuthumi, was one of the most famous of the early martyrs. He defended the Christians and as a result, was executed by the Romans. His close friend was Constantine the Great who gave instructions for the Rose of Sharon which was the emblem of St George's family, to be planted on St George's tomb.

Constantine the Great used the 'Red' or 'Rose' Cross to commemorate his friend George, whom Constantine made 'the Champion Knight of Christendom'; under Constantine, the Rose Cross became the public symbol of Christianity everywhere. (The Crucifix was adopted by the Church of Rome towards the end of the 7th century). With the association of St George's name with the flag, Britain adopted the name and the saint as its own during Richard I's time, the name 'St George's Cross' being an alternative or substitute for the 'Red Cross' or 'Rose Cross'.

342-420 AD: St Jerome (Hieronymous)

Known as St Jerome in England, his correct name was St Eusebius Sophronius Hieronymous who was born near Dalmatia. He became a monk and was very well educated in Rome. He spent much of his time travelling to such places as Gaul. He was particularly well versed in the Greek and Hebrew languages and became the secretary to the Pope and translated the Bible, beginning with the Gospels. The new translation became known as the Vulgate version. During his time in Rome, as secretary to the Pope, St Jerome discovered some of the lost documents of the Essenes and translated them. He later journeyed to Bethlehem in 385 AD where he spent the rest of his life writing and teaching. The significance of this life was both the translating of the Bible and his translating of the Gospels of the Essenes, which later came into the hands of Edmond Bordeaux Szekely. The original manuscripts were in Aramaic, and stored in the secret archives of the Vatican. Others that were in old Slavonic were in the Royal Archives of the Habsburgs who maintained strong ties with St Germain. St Jerome was obviously one of the Masters of the Great White Brotherhood.

circa 378 AD- d. 446 AD: St Germanus of Auxerre - St Germain

After being martyred as St Albanus, St Germain's next known incarnation was that of Bishop of Auxerre, Gaul (France). St Germanus whose name means *Germain* was the teacher of Ireland's St Patrick (Kuthumi).

St Germanus fought battles on English soil on their behalf against the warring Picts of the North, and he would appear to have been the 'Ambrosius Aurelianus' of the Merlin/Arthurian legends by Geoffrey of Monmouth. He was a 'Prince of the Sanctuary' and also a Pendragon, meaning 'Head military leader'. St Germanus twice visited the tomb of St Alban and it is thought that he had hidden documents there from his past life which he wished to retrieve. This was a common practice of St Germain.

circa 400: St Brigid of Ireland (possibly The Lady Portia - Twin Soul of St Germain)

Born into a royal family in Ireland, Brigid otherwise known as 'Mary of the Gauls', worked with St Patrick (Kuthumi). Her real name is purported to have been Alice Curtayne and her father was a High King of Ireland whose name was Dubtach. The Church of Rome Christianized her into St Bride. Brigid had the reputation of being able to perform miracles and she was a healer. It seems highly probable that Brigid (Alice/Mary) was an incarnation of the Lady Portia - St Germain's twin soul, who had been Mary, the Mother of the Grail Family. It is also noteworthy, that St Germain in his incarnation as Sir Francis Bacon married his twin-soul, the Lady Portia, whose name was Alice. Brigid is buried with St Columba (St Germain) and St Patrick (Kuthumi) in Northern Ireland. This was a prophecy made by St Columba which came to fruition i.e. that one day the three saints would be buried together. It is a curious fact that the prophecy was fulfilled during the 12th century AD, by Sir John de Courcy, a Norman Knight in the service of King Henry II, Plantagent King of England. During that era, St Germain had incarnated as William the Lion of Scots and Kuthumi had incarnated as St Hugh of Avalon/Lincoln.

circa 386-461 AD: St Patrick of Ireland - Kuthumi

St Patrick was born in Nemthur (later to be called Dumbarton), Scotland of Roman/ Gallo parents from Amorica (Gaul). His mother was Conchessa reputed to have been a sister of St Martin of Tours, and his father was Calpornius a magistrate under the Roman government. Patrick was captured in his youth and taken as a slave to Ireland where he initiated St Columba's (St Germain's) great grandfather, Conall Crimthan at the royal Palace of the Kings of Ulster, the O'Neill's (Ui Neill family) at Tara. Patrick eventually escaped from Ireland and journeyed to Amorica, Gaul. He was then tutored by St Germanus (St Germain) at Auxerre and instructed to return to Ireland to teach and found hundreds of monasteries.

In his incarnation as St Patrick of Ireland, Kuthumi introduced the Cross within the Circle, which symbolically is known as *Rose of the Wind*. In Europe the energy Ley lines were given a French name which translates into *Roses of the Wind*.

Both he and St Brigid (Alice Curtayne/Mary of the Gaels) prophesied that in the following century, the 'Dove of the North' would be born. The prophecy came to fruition, for St Germain incarnated as St Columba whose name means 'the Dove' and he was born in the North of Ireland.

circa 500-570 AD: St Gildas

Gildas was a Roman-British historian and was born at Strathclyde in Scotland. His famous work was titled *De Excidio et Conquestu Britanniae*, 'Concerning the Ruin and Conquest of Britain'. In it, warning lessons are drawn from the history of Britain under the Romans. Gildas visited Ireland and is reputed to have had a considerable influence on the development of the Celtic Church. He lived in the same era as St Columba (St Germain) who was the Merlin of that era. Gildas is also reputed to have been a friend of King Arthur (Aedan mac Gabran) who was Kuthumi. St Gildas would have been one of the Masters of the Great White Brotherhood.

521-597 AD: Merlin - St Germain

St Germain reincarnated in the 6th century AD, as *Merlin*, the famous Archdruid, Prophet, Bard, author/poet who 'initiated' and anointed *Arthur*, as King of the Celts upon the *Stone of Destiny* ('Jacob's Pillow'), on the island of Iona, otherwise known as the *Island of the Druids* and *Island of the Masons*. In an effort to control the many disputes amongst the rival clans, Merlin accompanied King Arthur into battle. Some of these skirmishes are written about in the poems of the Bard *Taliesin* which was a pseudonym St Germain utilized to prevent being detected by the powerful Church of Rome, who at that time, was making its presence strongly felt in Britain and was doing its utmost to penetrate Ireland. As the *Merlin* (meaning 'wise man') of that era, he was also the 'Prince of the Sanctuary' and at times was a Pendragon meaning 'Head military leader.'

688-741 AD: Charles Martel - St Germain

Born the illegitimate son of Pepin of Herstal, Charles ruled as Mayor of the Palace in the capacity of protector of the Merovingian King, Theuderic IV. The Merovingians are reputed to have been of Judaic descent, deriving from the royal line of David (Kuthumi).

Charles Martel saved Carcassonne near Rennes-le-Chateau in France from an invasion by the Arabs in a battle that took place at Poitiers. His main determination was to weld the Franks together and in a series of campaigns, he defeated his adversaries and distributed lands and positions amongst men upon whom he could totally rely. The problem of security in the Mediterranean world changed dramatically, and the danger spot had shifted from the West to the East. After this victory, Charles earned his nickname of 'Martel' - the 'Hammer'. He confiscated lands held by the Church of Rome and appointed his own bishops.

According to Frankish custom, Charles Martel divided his power between his two sons, Carloman and Pepin III (known as 'the Short') but in 747 AD, Carloman resigned to become a monk and Pepin III became the sole ruler.

The last of the Merovingian kings, Dagobert I, died in 639 AD and between 639 AD and 751 AD the Merovingian dynasty still ruled over the Kingdom of the Franks (French). In the 7th century AD, the kingdom was divided into three parts, Neustria, Austrasia and Burgundy. Charles Martel was the Mayor of the Palace of Austrasia, Neustria, and Burgundy from circa 714 to 741 AD (and he ruled on behalf of the Merovingian king, Theuderic IV).

Charles Martel was the *founder of the Carolingian Empire* and he is reputed to have been an incarnation of St Germain.

768-814 AD: Charlemagne the Great (742-814 AD) - St Germain

Pepin III, died in 768 AD, leaving his two sons Charles and Carloman. Charles ruled over the Carolingians until his death in 814 AD. He is better known as Charlemagne the Great and he was the most important of all the Frankish kings. He considered it his duty to not only protect his subjects but to educate them. Charlemagne surrounded himself with learned men and established a school of learning at his palace where the arts could be cultivated.

In the year 800 AD, Pope Stephen III crowned Charles (Charlemagne) the Great as Emperor of the West. According to his biographer, Einhard, the Pope's action took him by surprise. By being crowned Emperor of the West, Charlemagne was invested with full temporal authority over the Christians and had the corresponding duty of protecting them. He could therefore be classed as a 'Defender of the Faith'. Like Alexander the Great (St Germain), his plan was to unite the Western world and in his life as Charlemagne the Great, St Germain succeeded.

Charles (Charlemagne) was Charles I, King of France (the Franks).

Died 877 AD: Johannes (John) Eriugena (of Ireland) - Kuthumi (Philosopher)

As mentioned under the previous heading, Charles I of France who was crowned by Pope Stephen in 800 AD was an incarnation of St Germain.

All evidence points to John Eriugena, as having been an incarnation of Kuthumi. John was born in Ireland and travelled to Gaul (France) *where he was appointed by King Charles I (Charlemagne/St Germain) as Head Philosopher of the Royal Court.* He was the greatest philosopher for his time, responsible for the Carolingian Renaissance, the like of which was not seen again until the Italian Renaissance when Kuthumi incarnated as Leonardo da Vinci. In 1225, Pope Honorius ordered the works of Eriugena to be burnt.

Circa 900-circa 960 AD: Theophilus Bogomil - Kuthumi

The name of the Cathars is thought to have originated from the Greek 'Katharos' which means 'pure'. The Cathars called themselves 'good Christians' or 'friends of God'; the locals called them 'Parfaits' meaning 'good men' and the Slav word for them was 'Bogo-mil'. The country in which the religion of the Cathars had been established the longest was Bulgaria, where one known as Bogomil preached in circa 950 AD. It is thought that his real name was Greek and that it was 'Theophilus'. In Kuthumi's incarnation as John the Beloved (alias Joseph of Arimathea), he was also known as 'Theophilus', the philosopher teacher of 'Gnostic' wisdom (a 'lover of Sophia') who was an Annas High Priest of the Sanhedrin in the Temple of Jerusalem. John the Beloved/Joseph of Arimathea became the First Master of the Grail.

The Cathars followed the teachings of John the Beloved and they were sometimes referred to as 'Johannites'. Bogomilism did not disappear from the Balkans until the Turkish conquest which started in 1463 and ended in 1481.

Died 1123 AD: Omar Khayyam - Kuthumi (Persian Philosopher)

The Persian poet-philosopher (a 'lover of Sophia' - Wisdom) was considered to be the greatest mathematician and astrologer of his time who was appointed as the Royal Astrologer to the Shah of Persia. Having once been Pythagoras, it stands to reason that Omar would have been brilliant at mathematics. In his incarnation in the 15th century as Leonardo da Vinci, he was also brilliant at mathematics because he was an engineer (amongst his other numerous talents). As Sir John Dee, the Magus, and Royal Astrologer of the Tudor Queen Elizabeth I's court, he was also brilliant at mathematics.

Omar was born during the era of the Crusades and made a pilgrimage to Jerusalem. No doubt, whilst he was there he would have met up with Hugh de Payen, the First Grand Master of the Knights Templar. After the death of Omar in 1123 AD, the Rose of Sharon was planted upon his grave, as it had been after his demise as St George, whose emblem was the Rose-Cross.

1070-1136 AD: Sir Hugh de Payen - St Germain? First Grand Master of the Knights Templar:

Hugh was born into a noble family in the Burgundy area of France, an area that was originally ruled over by the Merovingians and the Carolingians whose first King of France, Charles I (Charlemagne the Great), had been an incarnation of St Germain. As Charlemagne, St Germain had been the founder of the Carolingian Empire.

Hugh de Payen entered into the service of the Count of Champagne and in 1118, under the patronage of St Bernard of Clairvaux, Hugh was the first to establish the Order of the Knights Templar which originally consisted of nine Knights who called themselves the Knights Templar (after the Temple of Jerusalem), and they also called themselves the Order of the Poor Knights of Christ. For nine years they lived near the Temple of Jerusalem (Zion/Sion) and accordingly spent that time tunnelling beneath in order to gather its treasures and place them in a secret place where they would be safe. Some say that this was in the Cathar region of Rennes-le-Chateau and others say that the treasures are buried beneath the Rosslyn Chapel in Scotland.

In 1101, Hugh de Payen married Katherine St Clair. Upon the marriage of Hugh to Katherine St Clair, her family donated Blancradock as part of the dowry. The St Clair family in a later century donated the land at Rosslyn to the Knights Templar where the building of the famous Freemasonic chapel commenced in1446. The founder of the Chapel was Sir William St Clair, and although the Chapel was never completed, it took 40 years to build.

1090-1153 AD: St Bernard of Clairvaux

St Bernard founded the Cistercian movement at Citeaux which is how it obtained its name. His uncle was the Count of Champagne. In 1112, he founded another abbey at Clairvaux. He was the patron of the Knights Templar and preached the Second Crusade in 1146. His teachings were those of the Celtic Church and he would have been a Master of the Great White Brotherhood. In 1128, the grandfather of King William of Scots (St Germain), King David, had met the First Grand Master of the Knights Templar, Hugh de Payen (possibly St Germain), and granted land in Scotland to the Order of the Cistercians which had become integrated with the Celtic Church.

St Bernard was a close friend of St Malachy of Ireland who wrote the prophecies of the Popes and the eventual downfall of Rome. Malachy died in the arms of St Bernard when he was visiting France, and St Bernard wrote his biography.

1118-1170 AD: Thomas Becket, Archbishop of Canterbury - El Morya

El Morya is reputed to have incarnated as Thomas a Becket, who was Chancellor of England from 1154 to 1162 AD, and archbishop of Canterbury from 1162 until he was murdered in his own cathedral in 1170 AD. He was a very close friend of Henry I, Plantagenet King of England, until they had a falling out and through a misunderstanding, some of Henry's knights thinking that Henry wanted to rid himself of Thomas, then killed Thomas. Shortly after his death, miracles occurred at his tomb and it became a place of pilgrimage. Chaucer's *Canterbury Tales* is a tribute to Thomas.

The year 1118 was the time when Hugh de Payen, the First Grand Master of the Knights Templar and his nine knights, began their excavation of the ruined Temple of Jerusalem.

1140-1200 AD: St Hugh of Avalon & Lincoln - Kuthumi

Hugh of Lincoln was born into a noble French family at Castle Avalon in the Burgundy area of France. This area was originally occupied by the Merovingians and then the Carolingians. His father and two brothers were Knights Templar who fought in the Crusades. Hugh could have become a member of the Knights Templar but chose instead, to become a monk belonging to the Order of the Carthusians. It is possible that they were linked to the 'Cathars' for the name is almost identical. The Cathars were known by religion to be *Johannites* following the teachings of John the Beloved. Earlier in the 10th Century AD, Kuthumi had been Bogomil/ Theophilus who preached the religion of the Cathars.

Hugh spent the first forty years in France. His first position was as a bishop at the church of St Maximin where Mary Magdalene was buried. Kuthumi as Joseph of Arimathea (John Joseph the Beloved Disciple), had accompanied Mary to Gaul (France) in 37 AD, four years after the crucifixion.

Hugh was eventually brought to England by the Plantagenet King, Henry II of England, whose son was Richard the Lion Heart. Hugh became the prior of the first Charterhouse in England, in Witham, Somerset. Somerset means 'the Summerland', the name originated from the ancient land of Sumer. It was in Glastonbury in Somerset that Joseph of Arimathea founded the first Celtic Church in Britain.

Hugh was adviser to three Plantagenet kings of England and also a great friend of King William the Lion of Scots (St Germain). Hugh was appointed as Bishop of Lincoln by Henry II and Hugh built the beautiful cathedral on the hill of Lincoln where it stands today as a fine memorial to his memory. During his incarnation as Hugh of Lincoln, Kuthumi played a tremendously important role in history which has generally gone unrecognized. He had a great affinity with animals and birds and his favourite pet who watched over him was a white swan which became his emblem.

1143-1214 AD: William the Lion, King of Scots - St Germain

King William was born at Stirling Castle, Scotland and was the grandson of King David of Scotland. He was also an ancestor of Captain Sir James Stirling who founded the colony of Perth, Western Australia.

William was the great grandson of Malcolm Canmor (Canmore) whose lineage could be traced back to Fergus Mor mac Erc who first brought the *Stone of Destiny* to Scotland (then called Albany) from the Royal Palace of Tara in Ireland. William's great grandmother was St Margaret who first introduced the cult of St Andrew to Scotland - their emblem being the 'Saltire' (X). They were also descendants of the same family as St Columba and King Aedan mac Gabran (King Arthur) who was Kuthumi.

William was to subdue the areas of Caithness. Sutherland in the late 12th century and the Scandinavian Western Isles were added to Scotland by the *Treaty of Perth* in 1266. It was the desire of William to have the Church of Scotland declared independent of the Church of Rome. This was denied him by Pope Clement. William dedicated the Church of Arbroath to St Thomas a Becket (El Morya). Like his grandfather, King David of Scots, William continued to support the Order of the Cistercians (founded by St Bernard of Clairvaux) who were linked with the Order of the Knights Templar. If he had been the original Grand Master of the Knights Templar, Hugh de Payen, this would make sense. When his close friend, St Hugh of Lincoln (Kuthumi) died in 1200 AD, William helped to carry his coffin.

1146-1220 AD: **Gerald of Wales** (Giraldus Cambrensis)
Gerald was an historical chronicler born into a noble family in Wales. His mother was Angharad, daughter of Gerald of Windsor and the Welsh Princess Nesta (Nest). His father was Gerald de Barri, Lord of Manorbier. Gerald studied in Paris and then travelled extensively, sometimes in the company of Baldwin, archbishop of Canterbury who became a member of the Knights Templar and who died at Acre during the Crusades. Gerald's family lineage through his grandmother Nesta could be traced back to St Columba and Fergus Mor mac Erc who first brought the *Stone of Destiny* from Ireland to Scotland. Gerald was a very close friend of St Hugh of Lincoln (Kuthumi) and wrote his biography. He would have been a member of the Masters of the Great White Brotherhood and may have, in a past life, been one of the Disciples, possibly the one known as John Mark (a cousin of Jesus and his brothers and sisters) who was the Master known as Djwhal Khul. Kuthumi, in his incarnation as John the Beloved, worked closely with his cousin, John Mark.

1209-1229 AD: **Persecution of the Cathars**
The Cathars otherwise known as the Albigensians and Bogomils, were savagely persecuted when in 1209, Pope Innocent III preached the Albigensian Crusade (1209-29) in the Languedoc area in which the Cathars resided. The crusade failed to stamp out those whom the Church of Rome labelled the 'heretics' and this led to the setting up of the Inquisition whose cruelty by torture almost completely eradicated what was known as Catharism, by the 14th century. The same fate was dealt out by the Catholic Church to the Knights Templar in the 14th century.

1244 -1314 AD: **Jacques de Molay** - Last Grand Master of the Knights Templar - Kuthumi?
According to the authors of *The Hiram Key*, Christopher Knight and Robert Lomas: "In our trawl through post Jewish-war literature, we came across a wide-spread belief, known as 'Bereshit Rabbati', that the power of prophecy would return to

Israel in 1210 AD...in 1244, just thirty-four years after the power of the prophecy was to return to Israel, an infant was born into a family of minor nobles in eastern France; his name was Jacques de Molay. The young knight had a clear sense of mission and he joined the Knights Templar at the earliest age possible - twenty-one. He did well and developed a reputation for organisation underpinned by rigorous discipline and rose to be the Master of the Temple in England before being made Grand Marshal with responsibility for military leadership of the Order. Few people can have been surprised when Jacques de Molay was elected as Grand Master of the Knights Templar in 1292, the highest office." (During this era, St Germain had incarnated as Roger Bacon, a Grand Master of the Order of the Rose Cross in England and he no doubt had close contact with Jacques de Molay).

Jacques of Molay distinguished himself in defending Palestine against the Syrians and when the Templars were driven from the Holy Land to Cyprus in 1291. On Friday 13th October, 1307, ('Black Friday'), he was arrested by Philip IV of France, tortured for seven years and burned at the stake in Paris in 1314. Christopher Knight and Robert Lomas have asserted that the *Shroud of Turin* was actually the one in which Jacques' body was laid after he was tortured in the same manner as Jesus, with a crown of thorns placed on his head. It would appear that the authors are correct because recent carbon-dating places it in the same-time frame as Jacques de Molay and it is said to be about six or seven hundred years old, and not two thousand years old.

Kuthumi as John the Beloved (alias Joseph of Arimathea) had once been the First Guardian of the Grail; the Knights Templar protected the Holy Grail (and the teachings of the 'Arcana) and it stands to reason that Kuthumi was therefore Last Grand Master of the Knights Templar.

1214?-1294 AD: Roger Bacon - St Germain (Philosopher, Prophet, and Scientist)

Roger Bacon was a philosopher, a prophet, essayist and scientist who graduated from Oxford University. He predicted flying machines for the future, electricity, ships that would be run by engines, hot air balloons and the future discovery of America. He was considered to be a heretic and was imprisoned in France, dying not long after his release. It was during this same era that Jacques of Molay was the last Grand Master of the Knights Templar. Roger Bacon was a Grand Master of the Order of the Rose Cross in England.

1451-1506 AD: Christopher Columbus - St Germain

St Germain incarnated as Christopher Columbus (the 'Dove) to fulfill the prophecy that he had made during his incarnation as Roger Bacon - that he would discover America. Christopher was married to the daughter of a former Grand Master of the *Knights of Christ*, an offshoot of the Knights Templar. He was a member of this

Order that studied the writings of Dante, a Grand Master of the Rosicrucians. Christopher was given financial backing for his voyages by Lorenzo de Medici, and also by his friend, Leonardo da Vinci (Kuthumi).

1452-1519 AD: Leonardo da Vinci - 'The Lion of Vinci' - Kuthumi

Leonardo da Vinci was born one year after Christopher Columbus. A man of incredible talents he is remembered as one of the greatest artists of all times. Leonardo was also a marvellous inventor, sculptor and engineer. Both he and his friend, Christopher Columbus (St Germain) were given the patronage of Lorenzo de Medici (Lorenzo the Magnificent), and were frequent visitors to the Platonic Academy which had been founded by Lorenzo's grandfather, Cosimo de Medici. Leonardo invented the first mechanical theatre curtain which was used for a play staged in Florence, and in his next incarnation as Sir John Dee during the Elizabethan Renaissance, he produced a similar invention.

The Renaissance period into which Leonardo was born, was a time of resurgence in the teachings of Plato (St Germain), Pythagoras (Kuthumi), and Dante Alighieri (Grand Master of the Rosicrucians 1265-1321 AD).

Leonardo became the Grand Master (Helmsman) of the Order of Sion (Jerusalem). In his next incarnation when he returned as Sir John Dee, the Elizabethan Magus, Kuthumi founded the Order of Sion at his home and continued the work of Sir Thomas More (El Morya) who had founded a Platonic Academy.

1478-1535 AD: Sir Thomas More - El Morya

Sir Thomas More is reputed to have been an incarnation of El Morya. He was raised in the household of John Moreton, Archbishop of Canterbury. The archbishop recognised in the young child, his excellent potential and predicted that he would become a great man. He sent young Thomas to be educated at Oxford University where he became one of the most accomplished classical scholars of his generation in Latin and Greek. According to information contained in Peter Dawkins' book titled *Dedication to the Light*: "Sir Thomas More was right at the centre of affairs and acknowledged as England's leading exponent, writer and philosopher of the 'New Learning' who received a constant stream of visitors from both home and abroad who visited More's Platonic Academy of Learning." Sir Thomas was executed when he greatly displeased Henry VIII by failing to attend the coronation of Anne Boleyn who became the mother of Elizabeth I. Sir Thomas More's unfortunate story is told in the movie *A Man For All Seasons*.

In an earlier incarnation El Morya is reputed to have been St Thomas a Becket, Archbishop of Canterbury and Henry VIII is reputed to have once been King Henry II, Plantagenet. It would appear that history repeated itself, for Becket was murdered in his own Cathedral of Canterbury by knights of Henry II who had fallen out with Becket.

1527-1608 AD: Sir John Dee - the Magus of the Elizabethan Renaissance - Kuthumi

Sir John Dee was an incarnation of Kuthumi, and was known as the Magus of the Elizabethan Renaissance. He was also a Grand Master of the Order of the Rose Cross (Rosicrucians). In a much earlier incarnation, Kuthumi had been the Pharaoh Tutmoses III, a member of the Great White Brotherhood who introduced the Teachings of the Rose Cross. As John the Beloved Disciple, he built the first Christian Church at Antioch, known as the Christine Church whose symbol was the Rose and the Cross. John the Beloved was also Joseph of Arimathea who built the first Christian/Celtic Church in Britain, at Glastonbury.

There were many Masters who incarnated during the Elizabethan period for it was a time when a great deal of change was taking place. Among the many things that Sir John Dee was famous for was the invention of a mechanical device for use in a play performed at Trinity College. This was an invention that he had achieved in his previous life as Leonardo da Vinci. Like Pythagoras (Kuthumi), Sir John was brilliant in mathematics, astrology and he was also brilliant at writing, poetry and navigation. In his incarnation as John the Beloved Disciple, Kuthumi had written the Book of John and the Book of Revelation when exiled to the island of Patmos. In his incarnation as Sir John Dee, Kuthumi assisted Sir Francis Bacon (St Germain) in the translation of the Bible into English which became known as the King James Version of the Bible. (Sir John Dee was a Master of ciphers and codes and was known as the original 007).

Sir John Dee was Queen Elizabeth I's Royal Astrologer and her tutor during her early childhood.

In a previous life as the famous poet/philosopher/mathematician, Omar Khayyam (d.1123 AD) Kuthumi had been appointed as the Royal Astrologer to the Shah of Persia. (During that era, St Germain was possibly the First Grand Master of the Knights Templar - Hugh de Payen who married Katherine St Clair of Roslin, Scotland).

In Kuthumi's life as John Eriugena (died 877 AD) of Ireland, he was appointed by the French King Charles I (Charlemagne - an incarnation of St Germain), as the Head Philosopher of the Royal Court School, in France. During that incarnation, he was the greatest philosopher of his time, responsible for the Carolingian Renaissance. St Germain, as Charles Martel (688-741) was the founder of the Carolingian Empire.

Sir John Dee was the person responsible for Sir Francis Drake's exploratory voyage of sailing around the world, and is credited with being the man behind the colonizing schemes during the Elizabethan Renaissance.

1743-1820: Sir Joseph Banks - Kuthumi

Sir Joseph Banks, an incarnation of Kuthumi, was born in Lincoln in 1743, the same place where he had died as St Hugh of Lincoln, in 1200 AD. As a young man, Joseph studied botany, science, navigation and astronomy. He sailed on the *Endeavour* with Captain James Cook on their voyage to discover *Terra Australis* as it was then known. In a much earlier incarnation as the philosopher, Aristotle, Kuthumi had expressed the opinion that there existed south of the Equator, areas of land at least equal to those above it and it was referred to as *Terra Australis.*

Sir Joseph Banks was also privy to ancient maps handed down from the time when he had been Sir John Dee, the man behind the colonizing schemes during the Elizabethan Renaissance. As Sir Joseph Banks, he is credited with having been the man behind the colonization of Australia.

Joseph Banks' talents were incredible. He commenced the most ambitious botanizing expeditions ever launched, collecting and documenting hundreds and thousands of plants from all over the world. He then established the famous Kew Gardens in London, which he dedicated to his close friend King George III.

In 1778, Joseph was elected as president of the Royal Society of London, which was founded by Sir Francis Bacon (St Germain) and was an off-shoot of the Rosicrucian Society (Order of the Rose Cross). The position of president was once held by Sir Isaac Newton, a famous Rosicrucian (1624-1727).

Sir Joseph Banks' contributions to the world during the 18th century outshone any other person. He was president of the Royal Society for fifty years and thus a prominent Freemason. He served on the Privy Council and became an honorary member of forty societies, including the Imperial Academy of Services in St Petersburg, Russia. He mixed with, and advised heads of state, kings and queens of Europe, and the American Philosophical Society of Philadelphia.

In 1778, the year that Sir Joseph Banks became president of the Royal Society, Czar Peter of Russia, founded a Secret Circle of Freemasons with the assistance of St Germain.

Sir Joseph Banks accompanied by Captain Mangles of the Royal Navy (a brother of Ellen Mangles who married Captain Sir James Stirling who founded the colony of Perth, Western Australia) undertook a journey to the newly discovered lost city of Petra and the tomb of Aaron (St Germain).

He later hired a boat and visited many Scottish islands, including Iona (Avalon) where in an earlier life, Merlin (St Germain) had crowned Kuthumi as Aedan mac Gabran (King 'Arthur') upon the sacred Stone of Destiny.

Sir Joseph Banks was knighted by King George III in honour of his years of service and he died aged seventy-seven years in 1820, and was buried at Lincoln.

1561-1626? Sir Francis Bacon - St Germain

After his incarnation as Christopher Columbus, St Germain incarnated as Sir Francis Bacon, born a prince into the royal House of Tudor. His mother was Elizabeth I and his father was Robert Dudley. After Francis' secret birth, he was handed over for adoption to the Queen's lady-in-waiting, Lady Anne Bacon and he was raised by her and Sir Nicholas Bacon as their own son.

As Francis Bacon, he wrote numerous famous works including his *New Atlantis*. However, for political reasons and for his own safety, he also chose to write under many pseudonyms, one of which was *Shakespeare - the 'Shaker of the spear - truth'.*

Francis Bacon faked his death on Easter Sunday 1616 and then appeared on the European scene, using the title of the Comte de St Germain, one of the numerous masks/titles that he utilized. A well-known one was the Prince Ragoczy. St Germain was the Master 'R' - *Master of the Mystical Rose.*